Hello, Gorgeous

Books by William J. Mann

Wisecracker: The Life and Times of William Haines

Behind the Screen: How Gays and Lesbians Shaped Hollywood

Edge of Midnight: The Life of John Schlesinger

Kate: The Woman Who Was Hepburn

How to Be a Movie Star: Elizabeth Taylor in Hollywood

Hello, Gorgeous: Becoming Barbra Streisand

Hello, Gorgeous

BECOMING
BARBRA
STREISAND

William J. Mann

Houghton Mifflin Harcourt · BOSTON · NEW YORK · 2012

ISBN 978-0-547-36892-4

Book design by Brian Moore

Printed in the United States of America

Contents

For H.B.K.L.

Hello, Gorgeous

Why Streisand Now

Just five years after arriving in Manhattan as a seventeen-year-old kid without money or connections, Barbra Streisand was the top-selling female recording artist in America and the star of one of Broadway's biggest hits. Twenty-two years old, her face graced the covers of *Time* and *Life*. That was only the beginning of a career that has marched its band and beat its drum now for half a century, but everything Streisand has accomplished in that time can be traced right back to this first half decade of her professional life.

The young Barbra was like nothing the world of entertainment had ever seen. So fresh, so fearless, so unself-conscious — so bursting with desire — that today, even the lady herself seems to cower when confronted with the memory of that young upstart. If Streisand has ever been afraid of anything, I suspect that it's been the burden of living up to that sexy, vulnerable, sensational younger self who gate-crashed her way to fame during the turbulent 1960s, defying old definitions of talent, beauty, and success by harnessing an extraordinary confluence of talent, hard work, and shrewd salesmanship. In these all-important formative years, Streisand first learned how to dazzle, how to connect, and how to get what she wanted.

It was also during these years that she learned — in that less comfortable and far less controllable world offstage — how to love, be loved, and lose love. These were the years that the budding Brooklyn teenager born Barbara Streisand would become both a personality and a person, a time when she got her first inkling of how much the artistic affirmation she craved — and the fame that came with it — would cost.

This book charts Barbra's climb from her earliest days in Manhattan to her first major triumph, the Broadway musical *Funny Girl.* After that, her chronicle becomes a very different kind of story: a Cinderella tale after she's secured prince and palace. (Or at least the palace; princes, for Barbra, weren't so easy to come by.) My goal has been to understand this early, groundbreaking Streisand, the artist and the woman who, out of need and lack of nurture, transformed herself into a superstar the world loved or loathed, an ambivalence that seemed to mirror the feelings in her own head and heart. I've attempted to zoom in as closely as possible on this complicated young woman — not the constructed myth or icon — in order to document how this unlikely kid from Brooklyn turned herself, in just five years' time, into the biggest star on the planet.

Much of it, of course, was due to her astonishing talent, and to a voice that pianist Glenn Gould called "one of the natural wonders of the age." Streisand came out of a time when talent still mattered, when the pursuit of greatness, not infamy, was rewarded — a world very different from ours, where Snooki and the Kardashians and drunken "real housewives" grab the lion's share of media attention. Still, for all her gifts, Streisand wasn't above merchandizing her fame, and during these first five years, she learned to do so expertly. She would cultivate an eccentric personality to go along with the mellifluous voice, knowing it would be the combination of the two that would keep audiences and interviewers coming back for more.

Yet Streisand's vaunted ambition remains very different from the lust for notoriety that drives so many of today's celebrities. Barbra's determination to reach the big time was never simply an engine to accumulate fans or headlines or even dollars. From the start, she made it clear that she did not wish "to be a star having to sign autographs or being recognized and all that." Instead, there were much more human reasons. Barbra wanted to make it big so she could demonstrate she had talent and appeal to a father who had never known her, a mother who hadn't seemed to care, and a world that had thought she was too different to succeed. No surprise, then, that being acknowledged as good would never be enough; Barbra had to be great. And as for paying her dues, she showed little patience: "It was right to the top," she declared early on, "or nowhere at all."

Of course, Streisand's rise has been told before. To say something new and valuable, to put her career into fresh perspective, I have tried to re-create the vanished world of her beginnings. Given my subject's refusal to speak with biographers, I knew I would need to uncover new, authoritative source materials on my own. Happily, I discovered that there were, in fact, several never-before-used collections that provided exactly the kind of detailed inside information I needed — material that, as I discovered, did not always jibe with the established canon of Streisand's early years.

I can't say that I was surprised by this — the written historical record often serves as an important corrective to the faulty human memory — but I was nonetheless struck by how many oft-told tales and assumptions about Streisand's career turned out to be false. The personal papers of Jerome Robbins, for example, revealed that, contrary to what has always been written, Ray Stark wasn't opposed to Barbra's casting in *Funny Girl;* rather, he was her most ardent champion right from the start. Claims made by Garson Kanin that he'd had to persuade Stark to hire Streisand were latter-day self-embellishments (something Kanin was very good at). The Robbins papers clearly show that Barbra was on the project months before Kanin came on board. Likewise, the papers of Bob Fosse finally flesh out that director's rather shadowy involvement with the show. Streisand buffs might want to read my notes thoroughly, as I present evidence that debunks many of the famous myths about her career, such as the story of her being fired from a nightclub in Winnipeg.

Also documented here for the first time is the prodigious amount of backstage maneuvering and public-relations chicanery that propelled Streisand forward. Her ticket to the top was indisputably her voice, but her great good fortune was to choose a crackerjack team of managers, agents, and publicists who made sure that her voice got heard. This able corps of lieutenants, operating largely unseen and unsung, was led, almost from the start, by Marty Erlichman, second only to the lady herself in engineering her brilliant career. Erlichman understood that, contrary to conventional wisdom, Streisand's very difference — her unusual looks, her Jewishness, her offbeat manner — could assist her rise, not hinder it. He was able to argue that she was so uniquely talented that her huge fame was simply fated; all they had needed to do to make Barbra a star was wait "for her talent to speak for itself." As such, her celebrity wasn't "artificially created," Erlichman insisted, but something that simply "had to happen." Such a platitude, of course, obscures all the press releases, publicity gimmicks, and backstage deals that Erlichman and his efficient band of foot soldiers waged on their client's behalf, especially during these crucial first five years.

Yet to acknowledge such clandestine efforts would have been to undercut the image of a singularly talented star to whom the world had flocked instinctively and unbidden. Now, thanks to publicists and advocates finally sharing their accounts, another story emerges, and it is every bit as fascinating and compelling as the myths that have long been spun. Here is the chronicle of a girl — so green, so raw, such a diamond in the rough — carried along on a wave of masterful salesmanship to the attention of such influential figures in the world of theater and music as Arthur Laurents, Jule Styne, Harold Arlen, and Sammy Cahn, who then adopted her, anointed her, and presented her to the world. With such an entrance, Streisand's acclaim was instant and overwhelming.

None of that diminishes Barbra's talent or star quality. If she hadn't been as sensational as her handlers said she was, she would have crashed and burned like so many before her had done. Nor, significantly, should it minimize Streisand's own role in making it all happen. Styne said she "carried her own spotlight." Certainly no one knew better than Barbra what worked best for her, and she had little time for false modesty. In fact, Streisand's very narcissism — a trait that has created a vocal minority of detractors — proved a key ingredient of her success, perhaps as essential as her ample talent and capable assistants. Greatness cannot be achieved, after all, without a corresponding belief in one's own greatness. That single-minded egoism left some people resentful, however, and others simply perplexed. Rosie O'Donnell, a fervent Streisand devotee, once pressed Barbra on whether she, too, had had idols in her youth. There was a long pause, in which Streisand seemed to struggle with the very concept. "I don't think so," she said at last. Of course not: It had always been just her.

For all of Streisand's self-confidence, there was also the corresponding self-doubt. "That goes so deep," she admitted — right back to those days in Brooklyn when her mother withheld praise and the girls at Erasmus Hall High School turned up their considerably smaller noses at her. As much as she'd been determined to make it, when success came, it still seemed strange to her. Seeing her name in lights was hard to accept. "Barbra Streisand doesn't sound like a star," she told a reporter in 1963.

Since that time, she has made "Barbra Streisand" synonymous with stardom, becoming the bar by which others measure their success. But fifty years earlier, she'd had her own hurdles. There had been Jewish stars before her — Lauren Bacall, Joan Collins, Piper Laurie, Judy Holliday — but none who seemed to announce it quite as forcefully as Streisand did when she walked into a room or onto a stage. There had been stars who had looked different, stars who hadn't fit conventional expectations of beauty or glamour, but none who had insisted they were beautiful — leading-lady material — as Streisand did. She was fortunate to emerge at a time when the old order was breaking down: Diahann Carroll and Chita Rivera were challenging the white-bread glamour handbook of Audrey Hepburn and Doris Day, and people such as Bill Cosby, Woody Allen, Lenny Bruce, Dick Gregory, and Joan Rivers were introducing new voices into the American conversation.

Streisand's times were, therefore, right for her — but she was also right for her times. Though the critics started out calling her ugly and strange, within five years she had transformed not only their opinion of her, but also their very concepts of beauty and talent.

That was a lot to accomplish for a young woman barely out of her teens, especially one who had to be great and not merely good. Early on, Streisand learned she could only achieve her goals by taking charge herself; her first album, engineered and orchestrated by others, wasn't nearly as masterful as her second, on which she exerted more control. That word "control," however, had "negative implications," she argued; Streisand preferred to say that she took "artistic responsibility." Yet sometimes in her quest for the best, she seemed to overshoot and expect perfection, especially from herself. Part of the reason she didn't have pierced ears, she explained to Oprah Winfrey, was because "each ear is a different length, so how could you possibly put a hole in exactly the same place on different ears?"

But she has always worn this insistence on precision as a badge of pride. "I really don't like being called a 'perfectionist' as if it's a crime," she has said. Certainly Arthur Laurents and Jerome Robbins, her earliest examples of auteurship, had been no shrinking violets when it came to taking control over their work. "What is so offensive about a woman doing the same thing?" Streisand has asked. Even her detractors concede she has a point on that score.

Perhaps this accounts for Streisand's recent prominence on the scene. Suddenly she's everywhere: giving concerts, celebrated on *Glee,* collecting awards, invoked in pop-rap songs, top-lining a movie for the first time in sixteen years. I suspect that our renewed fondness, even adoration, of Streisand is evidence of a nostalgia for a time when striving for excellence was at least as important as making a buck, and when originality was prized over focus-grouped packaging.

In the early 1960s, Streisand reset the cultural parameters when she walked onstage in *Funny Girl* and said "Hello, gorgeous" to herself in the mirror — a slender, unusual girl who wouldn't compromise on appearance, performance, or integrity. Fifty years later, she still matters, and for all the same reasons.

All scenes and events described herein are based on primary sources: interviews, letters, production records, journals, and contemporary news and weather reports. Nothing has been created simply for dramatic sake. Anything within quotation marks comes from interviews or other sources; dialogue is used only when it originates directly from these sources. Attitudes, motivations, and feelings attributed to Streisand or others always come from descriptions given in interviews. Full citations are found in the notes.

CHAPTER ONE

Winter 1960

1.

For sixty-five cents you could get a piece of fish, a heaping helping of French fries, a tub of coleslaw, and some tartar sauce at the smoky little diner on Broadway just south of Times Square. But since they only had ninety-three cents and some pocket lint between them, they decided to order one meal and split it, throwing in an additional dime apiece for a couple of glasses of birch beer.

It hadn't escaped Barbara's attention — few things ever did — that today, February 5, was her father's birthday. He would have been fifty-two if he hadn't died when she was fifteen months old, and quite possibly, instead of eating greasy fried fish with her friend Carl, she'd have spent this unseasonably warm winter day wandering through the city discussing Chekhov with the man she had come to idolize, a devotee of the Russian playwright, as well as of Shaw and Shakespeare. It was, after all, Chekhov's centennial, and as serious students of the theater, both Barbara and Emanuel Streisand would have been well aware of that fact. She and her father might even have taken in *Three Sisters* that night at the Fourth Street Theater in the East Village — a production Barbara had been dying to see, but for which she'd been unable to afford a ticket.

Looking up at Carl over their French fries with a sudden, surprising passion, Barbara insisted that everything would have been very different if her father had lived. Certainly she wouldn't have had to spend her nights at the Lunt-Fontanne, ushering giddy housewives from New Jersey to their seats to see Mary Martin warble her way through *The Sound of Music,* hiding her face "so nobody would remember" her after she became famous.

Barbara Joan Streisand was seventeen years old. She had been living in Manhattan now for almost exactly a year, and she was getting impatient with the pace of her acting career. So far her résumé consisted of summer stock and one play in somebody's attic. But she wasn't anywhere near to giving up. Her grandmother had called her "*farbrent*" — Yiddish for "on fire" — because even as a child Barbara had never been able to accept "no" for an answer. Growing up in Brooklyn in near poverty, she'd existed in a world of her own imagination of "what life should be like." She was driven by "a need to be great," she said, a need that burned in her like the passion of a "preacher" and necessitated getting out of Brooklyn as soon as she could. And so it was that, in January 1959, just weeks after graduating (six months early) from Erasmus Hall High School, Barbara had hopped on the subway and, several stops later, emerged into her new life amid the lights of Times Square. Manhattan, she believed, was "where people really lived."

With the childlike enthusiasm that could, in an instant, melt her usual steely resolve, Barbara looked over at Carl with her wide blue eyes, telling him about her father, the intellectual, the man of culture. Her hands in frenetic motion, her outrageously long fingernails drawing considerable attention, she insisted that her father would have understood her. She missed him "in her bones." All her life, she'd felt she was "missing something," and she had to fill up the empty place he had left.

But, asked about her mother, Barbara fell silent. Crumpling her napkin and tossing it onto her plate, she slid out of the booth, plopped her share of coins onto the table, and trudged out of the restaurant. Carl had to gulp down the last of his birch beer before hurrying after her. Barbara was already out the door and striding down the sidewalk, the fringe of her antique lace shawl swinging as she walked.

Carl Esser knew very little about this strange urchin he'd met just a few weeks before in a Theatre Studio workshop, except that she fascinated him. Sex and romance had nothing to do with the attraction, at least not for him. At twenty-four, Carl was seven years Barbara's senior, and besides, the small girl who was already half a block ahead of him wasn't exactly what most people would call pretty. A layer of heavy pancake makeup covered an angry blush of teenage acne. Her eyes, no matter how cornflower blue, had a tendency to look crossed. Most of all, she had a nose that was likened by some in their acting class to an anteater's snout — behind Barbara's back, of course. But her breasts were full, her waist was small, and her hips were nicely rounded, making for an odd and rather contradictory package.

Carl knew — everyone in their acting class knew — how intensely Barbara wanted to be great. She wanted to be Duse, she said, though she'd never seen Duse act, only read about her in books on theater in her acting teacher's library. That didn't matter. Duse had been a great artist, perhaps the greatest, and that's what Barbara wanted. There were others in the class who claimed they wanted to be great, but what they really wanted was fame and applause. That wasn't what fired Barbara up. She didn't sit around idolizing movie stars or the latest Broadway sensation du jour. She wanted to be remembered for being great, for making art.

Taxicabs bleated their horns as Barbara and Carl crossed Times Square. Policemen blew high-pitched whistles as tiny brand-new Ford Falcons scooted past sleek Chevrolet Impalas with their sweeping tail fins. Steam from the Seventh Avenue subway rose through the grates like fog from an underground river. On every block hung the fragrance of roasting chestnuts, while tourists in fur coats gaped up at the news ticker on the New York Times Building, its 14,800 bulbs spelling out the latest in the U.S.-Soviet space race.

Barbara and Carl headed west on Forty-eighth Street. At Barbara's apartment, number 339, the friends bid each other good-bye, and if Barbara was hoping there might be a kiss, she didn't wait for it. It was clear that Carl, like all the others, wasn't interested in her that way. If anyone had asked, she would've insisted it didn't matter. With all her big dreams, she would've said that she didn't have time for romance.

That day, or one very much like it, Barbara walked up the stairs to her apartment to the smell of boiled chicken. On the stove bubbled a pot of her mother's chicken soup. Barbara's roommate, Marilyn, told her that her mother had just walked in, dropped off the soup, and left. No message, no note. But the chicken soup, as always, was welcome because that fried fish and coleslaw would last only so long.

2.

Striding into her acting class, Barbara was boiling with all the ferocity of her mother's soup. *Who* did this Susskind guy think he was?

Word around the Theatre Studio had been that the producer David Susskind was always looking for new talent. It might be only for television, not the stage, but Susskind's production of *Lullaby* for Channel 13's *Play of the Week* had recently won approving notices for Eli Wallach and Anne Jackson, and next up was *The Devil and Daniel Webster* for *NBC Sunday Showcase.* The guy was making something worthwhile out of the boob tube. And since Susskind had been an agent, Barbara no doubt figured stopping by his office on Columbus Circle couldn't hurt, to drop off some headshots if nothing else.

But rarely had she encountered such rudeness. Carl, who'd gotten an earful on the way to class, was trying to calm her down, but Barbara was on a roll. Susskind had agreed to see her, but then Barbara had sat in his office for hours to no avail. Finally she'd stormed out, and the storm had yet to subside. People such as Susskind, she raged, were refusing to let new talent emerge, almost as if they had a "duty to squelch" it. That was the problem with this business, Barbara carped. Whenever she tried to sign up with agents, she was told they only represented people who were working. But you couldn't get work without an agent! Talk about double binds! Barbara took it all very personally.

The others in her class looked on with a mixture of amusement and weariness. To them, Barbara was that nutty kid who was always stumbling in late eating yogurt and wearing "a coat of some immense plaid," as one of them described. When she spoke, Barbara reminded some people of a Jules Feiffer cartoon from the *Village Voice* — cynical, ironic, sometimes angry, and always quintessentially New York. When asked why she talked so much, often to the point where other students closed their eyes in exhaustion, she was apt to blame it on her tinnitus, a condition that had plagued her since she was eight. "I never hear the silence," she said. Neither, her classmates might have replied, did they.

The Theatre Studio was located at 353 West Forty-eighth Street, just a few doors from Barbara's apartment, precisely the reason she'd chosen to live there. The school was one of about a hundred such institutions in a twenty-block radius of Times Square. In the previous decade acting schools had proliferated in New York. With the elite "big three" — the American Academy of Dramatic Arts, the American Theatre Wing, and the Neighborhood Playhouse — only being able to accommodate about six hundred aspiring actors, newer schools quickly formed to fill the need. Celebrated coaches like Herbert Berghof and Stella Adler established their own ateliers. The Theatre Studio was part of this same tradition, having been founded in 1952 by Curt Conway, a member of the groundbreaking Group Theatre and a major proponent of Method acting. In addition to the classrooms on Forty-eighth Street, Conway had acquired the Cecilwood Playhouse in Fishkill, New York, for summer productions, and a weekly radio program on station WEVD where his students interpreted new and classical work. The school offered three levels of courses, from fundamental to advanced acting, and special workshops conducted by

some of the greats Conway had worked with, including Joseph Anthony, Howard Da Silva, Paddy Chayefsky, and Harold Clurman.

Not that Barbara, a neophyte, had gotten to study with any of them.
Her primary teacher was Allan Miller, a young up-and-comer who'd
studied under Lee Strasberg and Uta Hagen and who was best known
for playing the second lead (behind Warren Beatty) in a summer tour
of *A Hatful of Rain*. Under Miller's tutelage, Barbara was beginning to
blossom. Finally she was in an environment where people believed in
her potential as much as she did. Any student with enough "appetite,"
Miller believed, could be trained to act. With such a philosophy, it
was no surprise that Barbara responded well to Miller's instruction.
"We all have deep, secret feelings," he told his students — and that was
certainly true enough of Barbara. With enough craft and discipline,
Miller said, she could use those feelings to hone and express her acting talent.

Barbara had enrolled at the Theatre Studio when she was not quite
sixteen, younger than most people who were admitted. Her only real
acting experience came from a summer internship with the Malden
Bridge Playhouse in upstate New York between her sophomore and
junior years, where she'd gotten to act in *Picnic* and won a nice review in the local newspaper. Her acceptance into the Theatre Studio
had come about only through the intercession of Miller's wife, Anita,
whom Barbara had met at the Cherry Lane Theatre in Greenwich
Village, where she'd secured herself yet another internship. As soon
as Barbara had realized that her new friend's husband taught at the
Theatre Studio, she'd bombarded her with questions, coming across
to Anita "like someone who had been starved." Impressed by her passion, Anita had prevailed upon her husband to accept Barbara into
his class. Instead of paying tuition ($180 for a fifteen-week course),
Barbara babysat the Millers' two young sons. It wasn't unheard of for
students to barter their tuition in this way; another young hopeful, an
enterprising kid from California named Dustin Hoffman, swept the
floors and emptied the trash at night. Barbara told her mother she'd
received a "scholarship."

Although she took classes with other teachers, it was Allan Miller who became Barbara's mentor. Handsome, intelligent, passionate, Miller offered Barbara a glimpse of what her life might have been like if her father had still been around. In the days before she got her apartment, Barbara would sometimes sleep on the Millers' couch instead of schlepping back to Brooklyn. She'd fall asleep with books about theater, art, or literature resting on her chest. These were the kind of treatises she believed her father would have kept around the house: Socrates, Euripides, French farces, and Russian literature. *Anna Karenina* "changed her life," she said. During this same period Barbara also heard her first classical music: Respighi's *Pines of Rome* and Stravinsky's *The Rite of Spring*. "Can you imagine what that's like?" she asked, looking back. "To hear that music for the first time?"

At the Millers' house, Barbara soaked up more culture than she "ever did in high school." She viewed the Millers' life with a sort of wonder. They were happy; their kids were happy; they were smart and curious and engaged with the world. It was as if she were peering through a looking glass into another world.

During Barbara's first semester at the Theatre Studio, she took Miller's Fundamentals course, which met twice weekly and included an hour of body training and seventy-five minutes of voice and speech instruction. "Acting is the only art in which the actor is both the piano and the pianist," Miller wrote. Her teacher found Barbara "very awkward, emotionally and physically, in her expression of herself," so in the beginning he insisted she perform her scenes in class using sounds instead of words.

Gradually, Barbara shed some of her awkwardness and developed some effective techniques, though she seemed, to some at least, to be surprisingly ungrateful to those who helped her. To her, it was as if her new skills were her accomplishments and hers alone. One teacher, Eli Rill, thought Barbara eschewed "the political niceties . . . the brown-nosing" that most students practiced. There was no "thank you very much," Rill said — no card, no phone call, even after he took a chance on her and cast her in a production he was directing. Rill didn't mind, though he found Barbara's behavior different enough to comment on it.

Barbara then advanced to Miller's Intermediate Acting class. Here a "sensory approach" was taught to perfect "concentration, relaxation, and emotion." Barbara was fascinated by this forceful man who taught her how to breathe, how to move, how to delve deeply into a whole range of emotions. She was a girl who knew very little about men. She'd never known her father, and her mother's second husband, a crass used-car salesman who'd barely ever spoken to her, had been gone by the time she was thirteen. Her brother, Sheldon, seven years older than she was, had left when Barbara was ten to study at the Pratt Institute. By the time Barbara moved out of the apartment, the household consisted of her, her mother, and her younger sister, Rosalind, who was now an overweight child of nine.

Her encounters with the opposite sex had been fleeting — though intense enough to leave her extremely curious. The longest lasting one had been her fling with her fellow student Roy Scott the previous year. Roy was Barbara's brother's age, twenty-four, a grown man — even if he still poured ketchup on his macaroni and drank cheap wine. She had spent many late nights at Roy's place, the two of them talking about acting, the theater, and life. Barbara thought Roy was the best-looking guy in Miller's class, and she couldn't fathom why he paid so much attention to a girl like her.

That such a brash, outspoken girl harbored such self-doubt surprised many people. When she wasn't striving to become the great Method actor who could believe herself to be anything, including beautiful, Barbara would inevitably remember the "real ugly kid" she'd been in Brooklyn, "the kind who looks ridiculous with a ribbon in her hair," as she described herself. When someone avoided her eyes, she felt certain they "couldn't bear to look" at her. But Roy assured her that all this was nonsense. She was "very pretty and attractive." It may have been the first time Barbara had ever heard those words.

Barbara's mother, however, hadn't been pleased with the relationship. Barbara rarely spoke of her mother; her roommate, Marilyn, only knew she existed from the chicken soup she'd drop off at the apartment. To her daughter's friends, Diana Streisand Kind seemed "somebody far removed from Barbara, somebody she preferred not to even think about." But she would be heard. "My daughter's too young to be involved with your son," Diana told Roy's mother after tracking her down through the school. Barbara's mother was adamant about such things. Even holding hands was frowned upon in Barbara's household. "You'll get a disease," Diana warned. Thereafter, Roy kept his distance.

The breakup with Roy hadn't helped Barbara's confidence or her faith in her own appeal. But Allan Miller identified a raw sexuality in her work in class. Acting out a scene from *The Rose Tattoo*, Barbara was embarrassed to play the seductress, so Miller advised her to find a way to convey the girl's desire without thinking about sex. What followed astonished him. Barbara pretended she was blind, and as she spoke, she touched her partner's face. At one point, she stood on his feet; at another, she jumped on his back. Miller thought it was "the sexiest scene" he'd ever witnessed in his life.

Yet toward men, Barbara seemed skeptical and wary. She was content to bask in the lectures of her intense, impassioned teacher and to pal around with platonic friends such as Carl Esser, heedless of the game of musical beds being played by other Theatre Studio students. Those who watched Barbara as she sauntered in and out of class wearing her fringed jackets and oversized boots, projecting that fragile pretense of superiority so peculiar to misfit teenagers, had the sense that she was somehow frozen in midbloom.

3.

The flyer tacked to the wall contained only the barest of details, but Allan Miller suggested that his students give it a read.

Barbara, Carl, and the others gathered around. A group called the Actors Co-op was holding auditions for a play called *The Insect*

Comedy, written by the Czech playwrights Josef and Karel Čapek and set to be staged at a little playhouse on East Seventy-fourth Street. The director was a man named Vasek Simek, who, according to word around the Theatre Studio, was "a big deal," a Czech who'd once worked for Radio Free Europe. *The Insect Comedy,* therefore, would be a "very significant play."

Both she and Carl decided to audition. This, Barbara hoped, could be her big break. True, she had a rather sparse résumé, but challenge was what Barbara thrived on. She'd gotten herself to Manhattan to make something of herself, and to show her mother and everyone back in Brooklyn that they just hadn't known how special she was. When Barbara was nine, a gang of girls had formed a circle around her, making fun of her until she cried. Although Barbara wasn't crying anymore, she still tried to understand what she had done to elicit such cruelty. What exactly did she "vibrate," she wondered, that brought out such hostility from people, even in her acting class?

One friend thought part of the answer was that people were threatened by her. Barbara had a way, this friend said, of "letting you know that she thought she was better than you were, and that she'd be a big success and you wouldn't." Barbara wasn't being hostile, or even necessarily conscious of the attitude she was projecting. But the impression came through nonetheless. Her sense of superiority masked her self-doubt; Barbara had to believe that she was special since no one else did. Whether that specialness was good or just different, she had yet to fully discover. But she knew one thing clearly: She was not like anyone else.

Her tinnitus, for example, was evidence of "supersonic hearing," Barbara believed, an ability that enabled her to hear sounds beyond the range of normal people. It frightened her; she wore scarves "to try to cut out the noise." And it wasn't just sounds. She experienced colors in a way no one else did. When she'd look at a white wall, she'd see textures. Her sensory perception seemed "an overemphasizing on the processes of being alive," she thought. In some very real sense, Barbara existed outside the realm of ordinary people. Of course a girl with such extrasensory powers was going to have certain advantages over mere mortals. She felt as if she were "chosen," that only she could "see the truth." A girl like that was either going to go crazy or succeed beyond anyone's imagination — except, of course, hers.

To Carl, Barbara insisted that if she got a part in *The Insect Comedy*, it could catapult her to the kind of success she'd always dreamed about. The show was bound to inflame her ambition. It would be her first real play in New York, because *Driftwood*, the little thing she'd done the previous year in the attic of its playwright's fifth-floor walkup on East Forty-ninth Street, didn't count, at least not in her mind. She needed a part that would get her noticed. She'd already wasted too much time in the trenches, she believed. For Barbara, there was no patience for the chorus line. For her, it was "right to the top," she insisted, "or nowhere at all."

So all her laserlike focus was brought to bear on winning a part in *The Insect Comedy*.

4.

Never had Barbara known a friend quite like Terry.

It was Terry to whom she turned for help in her quest. For her *Insect Comedy* audition, she needed an especially impressive outfit, and Terry had a way of finding things. Not long ago, he had given her a scarf of sheer silk netting, over which Barbara had gushed, "Where did you *ever* find it?" Terry had replied mysteriously that it just "turned up" somewhere, and when Barbara asked him what she owed him for it, he shrugged and said, "Never mind about that."

Terry Leong was an absolute doll. Barely taller than Barbara's five-five, he was twenty-one, finely boned, soft-spoken, and, according to one friend, as "delicately attenuated as a Chinese rod puppet carved of linden wood." Terry's father had been born in China, his mother in Boston, and the young man lived with them on Chrystie Street in Chinatown, though he was hankering to move uptown. Weekdays Terry toiled for McGregor-Doniger, the men's sportswear company, designing golf shirts at their offices in the Tishman Building at 666 Fifth Avenue. Golf was far from Terry's passion, however; he wasn't happy with his job at all. He had studied at the Fashion Institute of Technology, and what he really wanted to do was design for the theater — which was why he jumped at the chance when his friend Marilyn Fried asked him to help her roommate Barbara put together outfits for Theatre Studio shows.

Barbara protested; she had no money. She was barely making her rent with the pittance she took home from ushering at the Lunt-Fontanne. But Terry told her not to worry about that. Where he was taking her, he explained, you could get treasures for pennies.

As they emerged from the Fifty-ninth Street subway, Terry explained to Barbara all about the thrift shops that lined Third Avenue. Here was the source of his fabulous finds. The rich people of the Upper East Side, he explained, were forever tossing out such treasures as original Lalique jewelry and Pauline Trigère jackets. They just boxed them up and sent them over to the little boutiques on Third Avenue that sold used goods to benefit charity. An alert shopper could snatch up these precious items for a fraction of their original prices. Terry was astonished that so few people had caught on to this, but he was loath to let the secret out. Then every fashion acolyte from Jersey and the boroughs would be arriving via bridge and tunnel to plunder all this bounty.

Barbara and Terry headed into Stuart's, just south of Sixty-second Street. In the window, tall white ceramic obelisks of uncertain function stood beside a cluster of delicate porcelain tulips. Inside, one wall was covered in panels of gold, emerald, and tangerine felt — an attention to color that was carried throughout the shop, where all the accessories were arranged by hue. This way, the discerning shopper could ensure instantly that her earrings complemented her belt. Barbara was enchanted.

From Stuart's, it was onward to other places such as Lots for Little, at Seventy-seventh Street, which benefited Catholic missionaries, and Bargains Unlimited, at Eighty-second Street, where proceeds went to

Bellevue Hospital. On one of their shopping ventures, either this one or one very much like it, Terry discovered a Fabiani dress hanging on the rack and breathlessly insisted Barbara get it. When she admitted, a little shamefacedly, that she didn't know who all these designers were, Terry sat her down and patiently explained that she needed to learn such things. If Barbara was going to stand out among all the other hopefuls looking for parts, she needed to develop her own particular style, Terry declared. Barbara latched on to his advice with conviction.

She was a fast learner. Even if she didn't know the names of designers, Barbara had an instinctive understanding of what worked for her. She could pick up a skirt and know, without even trying it on, whether the color and the fit would suit her. Terry had been right to take her under his wing. He might need to help her decide which choker was best, but it was Barbara who knew, in her gut, that a choker would be the perfect finishing touch for the outfit they were putting together.

That day, strolling in and out of the boutiques on Third Avenue, Barbara was a happy girl, laughing and joking, trying on funny sunglasses and hats. The determination that frequently kept her face tight, hard, and unsmiling was missing. To see Barbara and Terry together, giggling, rummaging through a table of beaded blouses from the 1900s, was to spy something very special between them. They were like a brother and sister with "secrets, and codes, and a language of shared experience," as one observer described it. And yet there was never a thought of romance.

Surely, at some point, Barbara must have wondered why. It was obvious that Terry, like no other man in her life, found her beautiful, even exquisite. He rhapsodized about her swan neck and long, graceful fingers. He adored the way fabric draped over her lithe, elegant, slender body. Yet standing next to him never produced the kind of charge she felt when standing that close to another man. It wasn't because Terry was Chinese. Barbara had worked in a Chinese restaurant in Brooklyn where she'd become close with the family who ran the place. Muriel Choy, the proprietor, had been like a surrogate mother, teaching her "about love and life and sex." So Barbara never had hang-ups about race. At Erasmus Hall, she'd even dated a black boy — nothing serious, mostly just hanging out and talking, but she'd liked him in the way a girl likes a boy. Not so with Terry. This was different.

Eventually Terry told Barbara that he was gay. She accepted the news with nonchalance. This was why she loved Manhattan, after all. Here was every kind of person, coming and going. She was glad she'd been born in Brooklyn, she said, because it gave her a certain character. But she was also very glad she no longer lived there. "You know, once you cross the bridge, everything changes," she'd say — and for the better, she believed.

5.

The best thing about Cis's house was the refrigerator. It was always full. And since Barbara was always hungry, the combination worked out perfectly.

On this day, Barbara arrived at her friend's stately townhouse on West Seventy-eighth Street near Riverside Drive with some big news. She'd won the part of a butterfly named Clythia in *The Insect Comedy.* The strange little play had been produced on Broadway in 1948 starring José Ferrer. It was a piece about human survival as seen through the lives of "double-dealing, marauding" insects. While she was also playing a few other small parts, Barbara believed it would be Clythia, with her fragile, flirtatious hold on life, that would get her noticed. After all, Rita Gam, who'd played Clythia in 1948, went on to a long acting career on stage and screen — not to mention serving as a bridesmaid at the wedding of Princess Grace.

No doubt Cis encouraged Barbara in this latest endeavor. Cis always encouraged her. Cis Corman — born Eleanor Cohen — was sixteen years Barbara's senior. All of Barbara's friends were older than she was, but Cis, at thirty-three, was one of the oldest. Cis was also married, to a psychiatrist, Harvey H. Corman, and they had four children, the eldest of whom was only a few years younger than Barbara.

Cis, far too creative and intelligent to be content with just playing mother and wife, had signed up for classes at the Theatre Studio and had encountered the young waif from Brooklyn soon thereafter. Yet she'd found nothing even "remotely adolescent" about Barbara. She'd been deeply impressed that the teenager already knew her own mind so well. Ten people might tell Barbara they didn't like the dress she was wearing, but she stuck to her guns and insisted that she did. After Barbara played Cis's lady-in-waiting in a Theatre Studio production of Christopher Fry's *The Lady's Not for Burning,* the unlikely friendship took off.

The Cormans were now Barbara's proxy family. It wasn't just that their refrigerator was full of food. They also had "roots," as Cis put it. Barbara believed that her father would have felt equally at home in the Cormans' house as she did. Both Cis and Harvey were people who valued ideas and learning. Harvey was proud of the fact that he'd been one of the first to teach at the Albert Einstein College of Medicine, the new graduate school of Yeshiva University, located in the Bronx. His brother Sidney, known as Cid, was a highly esteemed poet who had founded the influential poetry magazine *Origin* and was currently teaching literature in Japan.

Most friends of Barbara's knew that discussions of her family, especially her mother, were off limits. But here, in the safe, book-lined cocoon of Cis's house, Barbara could open up. Sitting on Cis's comfortable couch, Barbara may well have thought about how, growing up, she had lacked such a piece of furniture in her own living room. For that matter, she had lacked a living room.

After Barbara's father died, Diana Streisand, overwhelmed with debt, had taken her children and moved into her parents' small apartment in Williamsburg. For the next eight years, Barbara's grandparents' living room was her bedroom. Barbara and her mother shared a bed while her brother slept on a rollaway cot next to them. To Barbara, an actual living-room couch was "an amazing thing" — a symbol of real life, normal life, a life she knew very little about.

Except for the time she spent with the Cormans, who were simpatico with her in so many ways. For starters, the Cormans were Jews, but not very religious, the same as Barbara. On Harvey's daily walks to his office, he was often asked by the rabbi of a small synagogue at Seventy-third Street if he'd help form a minyan, the quorum of ten males needed for prayers, but Harvey always politely declined. Likewise, Barbara's mother rarely lit candles or kept kosher. Although Barbara believed in God — as a young girl, she'd tried earnestly to argue one friend out of her atheism — she didn't take her religion all that seriously. "I am deeply Jewish," she'd say, "but in a place where I don't even know where it is." She had attended yeshiva on her grandparents' insistence and had learned to read Hebrew, even though she didn't understand a word of what she was saying. What stayed in her memory most was one teacher's insistence that good Jewish children should never utter the word "Christmas." To a girl as rebellious as Barbara, that was too good to resist. "Christmas, Christmas, Christmas," she had chanted as soon as the teacher left the room. When nothing bad happened to her, she figured she knew better than her teachers.

Barbara made jokes about a lot of things. But if anybody made a dent in that armor of sarcasm and indifference, it was Cis Corman. To others Barbara might remain tight-lipped about her childhood: "I don't remember it. I was born at six. Came out, a full set of teeth." But Cis knew that Barbara remembered her childhood all too well. Every step she took, every word she uttered, reflected the facts of Barbara's short life, and all of it could ultimately be traced back to that day in August 1943 when Emanuel Streisand — scholar, poet, professor — had died of respiratory failure brought on by a morphine injection intended to alleviate an epileptic seizure.

It was a source of both pride and comfort for Barbara that she inherited her father's ambition and intellectual curiosity. Emanuel had received his bachelor's and master's degrees in English and education from City College in upper Manhattan, and at the time of his death, he had been working on his doctorate. He'd taught elementary and junior high school English, then got a job tutoring juvenile of-

fenders at a Brooklyn trade school. During the summers, he counseled kids at upstate camps. He was a good, decent man who wanted
to make a difference in the world while also making something of
himself. A pedestrian existence in Brooklyn would never have been
enough for Emanuel Streisand, Barbara was certain. All of their lives
would have been different if only her father had lived. It was clear she
was her father's child. Her mother had simply borne her.

And while Barbara hadn't gone on to college like her father, she
could have. She'd done well in school, even though she'd hated it. She
would lie on the floor on Sunday nights, watching *What's My Line?*,
and feel it was her "last chance of freedom before going to school
the next day." Still, she'd graduated with a ninety-four average. When
her guidance counselors saw her grades they called her mother in to
ask, "Why isn't this kid going to college?" But if they had bothered to
pay attention, they would have known the answer. Barbara's senior
book reports had all been on Stanislavski and acting. She had only
one ambition, and that was to go to Manhattan and act. Her mother
had finally given in to her demands, allowing her to accelerate her
classes and graduate early so she could, as Diana explained to Barbara's teachers, obtain "further experience in the city."

Barbara had never fit into the routine of school. She'd been a loner
at Erasmus Hall, and even when the girls stopped ganging up on her,
she still kept largely to herself. She was an odd duck who, to alleviate boredom one day, dyed her hair platinum blond. Sometimes she
wore purple lipstick to boot. She fit into no clique. The other smart
kids shunned her because she looked like a beatnik while the "actual
beatniks" avoided her because she had "brains."

Barbara's mother despaired over such antics. Diana simply didn't
understand her. What her sophisticated father had seen in her pedestrian mother Barbara could not understand. Her mother wanted her
to be just another cog in the wheel. She told Barbara she should be a
school secretary, just like she was. "You'll get paid vacations and summers off," she argued. "It's a steady job."

If Allan Miller had filled some of the emotional space left by her father, then Cis Corman stepped in where Barbara's mother had never ventured. Never had her mother said, "You're smart, you're pretty, you're anything, you can do what you want." To outsiders, it might seem as if Barbara's mother coddled her: "Don't go out in the rain, don't do this, you'll get a cold, don't do that." But when Barbara did come down with a cold, she felt as if her mother's response was always, "I told you so. Now you take care of it." Emotionally, Barbara believed, her mother had left her at the same time her father had. Barbara felt that her mother had gone into shock after her father's death, a shock that had now lasted seventeen years.

Affection wasn't forthcoming from her grandparents either. Barbara's maternal grandfather, with whom she lived during the first years of her life, was a strict taskmaster who resented the intrusion of his daughter's family into his household. Her paternal grandmother, blaming Emanuel's widow for not taking good care of him, would actually look the other way when she saw Barbara on the street, dressed all in black and wearing purple lipstick. From nearly every adult in Barbara's early life had come the same message. She wasn't any good. She did not matter.

Instinctive actress that she was, Barbara had learned to play up the melodrama of it all, probably even to Cis. If she wasn't going to give people real emotional details, she seemed only too glad to provide some sentimental theatrics. Much hay would be made over a hot-water bottle Barbara had used as a doll, supposedly the only doll she ever owned. She'd swear its warm "rubber tummy" felt more real than any doll bought from a store. Many times she told the story of her babysitter, a kindly lady from downstairs named Tobey Borokow, knitting a pink sweater for the hot-water-bottle doll.

Barbara liked to foster an image of herself as a sort of street kid, and, in fact, for much of her childhood she was on the street, singing on stoops with other girls from the neighborhood while people looked down from their tenements. Unlike the other kids, however, Barbara was never called in for meals. Instead, she came and went as she pleased, often eating from pots her mother left simmering on the stove — which was why the Cormans' dining-room table, with actual meals being shared around it, fascinated her. When Barbara was a little older, she started smoking. Nightly she'd litter the rooftop of her building with the butts of her Pall Malls. Her mother didn't object. In fact, at ten, Barbara taught her mother how to smoke.

If that seemed rather lenient for the usually strict Diana, it was almost certainly because she, like her daughter, needed a break from the man downstairs, her new husband, who had come into their lives when Barbara was eight — the same year, not coincidentally, that her tinnitus began. Louis Kind was a coarse man, nothing like the image Barbara carried around of her noble father. Kind, already divorced and the father of three, moved with his new family into a cramped apartment on Newkirk Avenue, where he could usually be found hunkered down in front of the television set watching pro wrestling with a beer and a bag of pretzels. Her mother warned her that Kind was "allergic to kids," and no doubt especially to "obnoxious" ones, as Barbara admitted she could be. With her flair for melodrama, she'd tell of slithering on her belly under the TV instead of walking in front of it and risk getting yelled at by her stepfather.

Yet no melodramatic tricks were needed to elicit sympathy for the worst of Kind's behavior. More than once he had called Barbara ugly to her face. He was truly cruel enough to call an adolescent girl ugly. And though friends insisted that Barbara's mother had tried to shield her from her stepfather's foul moods, Barbara could never remember her mother defending her.

For the teenager, such hell seemed as if it would go on forever. "I tried to imagine my future, like other kids," Barbara said, "but I couldn't, it just stopped. There was a big blank screen, no husband, no children, nothing. I decided that meant I was going to die. I would think, 'That's too bad, because I really could have done things.'"

To Cis, she could admit such fears. There was no one else she trusted enough to share such private thoughts. Cis was what Barbara's mother could have been. Both Cis and Diana were daughters of working-class Russian Jews. Cis's father had sold hardware in Boston; Barbara's grandfather had labored as a tailor in Brooklyn. The Cormans might have been financially well-off by the time Barbara met them, but Cis knew what it was like to struggle. The critical difference between her and Barbara's mother was that Cis had always tempered her struggle with an appreciation for style, knowledge, and talent. Like Muriel Choy before her, Cis Corman made Barbara feel valuable in a way her own mother seemed incapable of doing.

Louis Kind was gone by the time Barbara was thirteen, but his stink remained. Barbara found she could no longer stand being in that small apartment with her mother and her meager view of the world, or with the little girl who had been born of her mother's union with Kind. Pudgy Rosalind had a round, pretty face and was the apple of her mother's eye. Rather than watch her mother dote over this angelic little child, who seemed so different from her, Barbara spent even more time away from home, living for herself and only herself—"kind of a wild child," she'd tell people.

Yet she believed all that wildness—the fact that she'd never had parents who taught her the "rules" of proper behavior—had helped her. She never learned that "you weren't supposed to do certain things or say certain things." Convictions were meant to be acted upon: "You feel it, you make it happen," she said. "Imagination and belief manifest reality."

This was her current mantra. Several months earlier, she'd found—either at the Cormans' or in Allan Miller's library—George Bernard Shaw's *The Quintessence of Ibsenism*. Surely it was a work her father must have known and studied; surely he must have been as struck as Barbara was by the words "Thought transcends matter." The idea that she could make things happen simply by believing in them was staggering. By the time Barbara was seventeen, she had become convinced she could manifest greatness for herself simply by believing in it strongly enough.

And so there came into her mind the idea to make one last try with her mother. Maybe it was suggested by Cis, sitting in her living room, talking about *The Insect Comedy* and human survival and Shaw and

Ibsen. Or maybe it was an idea entirely of Barbara's own formation, a conviction that, if she believed strongly enough, even her mother might come around to seeing her talent and her worth.

Back at her little flat on Forty-eighth Street, Barbara picked up the telephone, called her mother, and invited her to come watch her act.

6.

The first thing one noticed walking into the Brooklyn apartment of Diana Rosen Streisand Kind was the smell. Even when nothing was cooking on the stove, the place reeked of kale. Diana used kale to make soup, which she then ladled into Tupperware containers and lugged into the city to drop off at Barbara's apartment. She did this twice a week. And no, she didn't expect a thank-you for her efforts because none had ever been forthcoming from that girl in the entire seventeen years of her life.

The idea of watching Barbara perform in some little playlet did not thrill Diana, but she agreed to go. Otherwise, no doubt, Barbara would say that Diana never showed her any support or encouragement. So she pulled on her coat, locked the door to apartment 4-G, and headed down to the subway at the corner of Nostrand Avenue.

Diana knew how unhappy Barbara had been growing up. She knew that her daughter thought she didn't understand her. But Diana did understand "in her own way," as at least one of her friends believed. Barbara's mother hadn't been very happy in her own life either. For most of the last two decades, she was found in either one of two places: at her typewriter at work trying to earn a living to support her family, or at the stove in her apartment cooking soup or potato pancakes to feed her family. "If I close my eyes and picture Diana," said one friend, "she's always standing at that old, rusty stove."

Depositing her fifteen-cent token, Diana pushed through the turnstile and waited on the platform for the train. She was a small woman, not unpretty, even at fifty-two, though the years and the struggle had left their marks on her face. Her eyes always seemed tired and the corners of her mouth tended to droop down. Bundled in her coat, standing by herself, she drew no particular attention from the others who gathered on the platform. They didn't know she'd once had dreams not dissimilar to her daughter's, that the little girl who had been born Ida Rosen in the East New York section of Brooklyn had adopted the name Diana because it sounded more glamorous, or that she'd once been accepted to sing with the Metropolitan Opera Chorus — when she was Barbara's age, in fact. For a couple of heady weeks, Diana, who'd been told for years she had a beautiful voice, imagined herself singing arias at the Met. But her father, a cantor at their Orthodox synagogue, objected to how late she got home, so that was the end of that.

Instead of singing at the Met, Diana had married Emanuel Streisand, whom she'd met at the home of one of her friends and who had impressed her with his love poems and grand ambitions. She'd enjoyed being Manny's wife and had never really gotten over his death. She knew Barbara hadn't either, though she never spoke of him to her. It was too difficult. In Diana's memory there was etched the image of Barbara at the age of one, pulling herself up in her crib to look out the window. "Watch for your father," Diana would say, and when Manny came through the door, he'd lift the tiny girl in his arms. But then came the day when Manny no longer came home. For several nights, Barbara still hoisted herself up to look out the window. Diana never said a word to her about what had happened. After all, Barbara was just a baby.

The train arrived with a loud grinding of metal against metal. Diana stepped inside and took her seat as the subway started to move again. Six years earlier, Diana had taken this same route with Barbara, then eleven years old. The fare was only ten cents then, and tokens weren't in use yet so you had to use a real dime. Hearing Barbara sing with some of the neighborhood girls on the tenement stoops, Diana had come to believe that her daughter might have inherited her musical talents so she'd taken the child into Manhattan for an audition for MGM Records. She'd dressed Barbara in a pretty blue dress with a white collar and cuffs, and instructed her to warble "Have You Heard?" for the record-company executives. But the little girl wasn't offered a contract, only a spot in their training program. When Diana heard "No pay," she said, "No child," and hustled Barbara back home to Brooklyn.

Two years later there was another trip into the city. Barbara was now thirteen. She'd told her mother about the Nola Recording Studio, where anyone could go in and make a record on real vinyl disks. With memories of her own childhood dreams, Diana had agreed to give it a whirl. It was with considerable excitement that both mother and daughter practiced what they were going to sing. Diana arranged for a pianist to meet them at the studios, housed inside Steinway Hall on West Fifty-seventh Street. Barbara sang "Zing! Went the Strings of My Heart" and "You'll Never Know," revealing a surprisingly strong voice for a girl so young, though the child in her could still be heard, especially when she struggled to reach the high note at the end of the phrase "how much I care." Diana's voice was more polished. She'd chosen "One Kiss" from the operetta *The New Moon*. With Barbara watching from behind the glass, Diana stood at the microphone and sang with all the feeling she could muster: "One kiss, one man to save it for . . ."

It had been a rare interlude of happiness and lightheartedness for Diana and her elder daughter. But the "one man" they headed back home to in Brooklyn that night was hardly the Galahad that Diana sang about in "One Kiss." In the beginning, Lou Kind had been charming, bringing Diana little gifts. But when she'd found herself pregnant with his child, Kind had balked at marrying her. He had just left one wife; he didn't want another. Diana's father forced her to leave the house when he discovered she was pregnant. So she'd found the place on Newkirk Avenue for herself, Sheldon, Barbara, and the upcoming baby. Finally, just two weeks before Rosalind was born, Kind gave in and married Diana.

For the next five years she was miserable, probably even more miserable than her daughter. Kind slept with other women, "scandalously flaunting" his affairs with them in front of her, Diana later told a judge. He mocked her. He shouted at her. He used "vile, obscene, and scurrilous language." He stayed out all night. And he hit her.

Kind countered that Diana had used the same sort of language with him and that she refused to cook for him when he came home from work. He worked two jobs, he charged, because of Diana's "ever increasing demands for money."

But he wasn't working two jobs, or even one, when he finally left the house some five months after Diana's trip to the Nola Recording Studio. When Diana sued him for child-support payments for six-year-old Rosalind, he told the judge he was too sick to work. The judge called him a "pathological liar" and ordered him to pay Diana thirty-seven dollars a month. It wasn't much, and Diana didn't always get it.

So the mother who often seemed to be the bane of Barbara's existence had her own heartaches. Friends who knew her well insisted that Diana wasn't really opposed to her daughter's dreams of being an actress. She had signed the form allowing her to graduate early, hadn't she? And she'd allowed Barbara — at the tender age of fifteen — to apprentice one hundred and sixty miles away in Malden Bridge. A year later Diana had even permitted Barbara — at sixteen! — to move *on her own* into Manhattan in order to pursue her dreams. How could Barbara say her mother didn't support her? That was something Diana simply couldn't comprehend. *Of course* she supported her. She took this long subway ride twice a week to bring her chicken soup!

What worried Diana most about Barbara living in Manhattan was that she'd get sick. Barbara, to her mother's mind, was not a strong girl. When Barbara was five, Diana had to send her to a health camp because she was so anemic. She also suffered from asthma whenever she spent too much time in the fresh air. Now, making matters worse, Diana feared that Barbara's acting school was working her way too hard. How that Allan Miller could expect so much from a teenaged girl Diana could never understand. If anemics didn't eat right, they could get very, very sick — maybe even die. That's why Diana had insisted Barbara attend Hebrew health camps. She knew the girl hated them, but it was the best thing for her — just as breaking up her entanglement with that older boy, Roy Scott, had also been for her own good. It was very hurtful that Barbara never trusted that Diana knew best.

Rosalind did, however. Rosalind was a far more obedient, pliable, and cooperative child than Barbara was, eating whatever Diana put in front of her. So what if Rozzie was a little plump? It was better than having Barbara's skinny arms.

Diana was aware that she spent more time with her younger daughter than she ever did with her older one and that it might appear to some that she played favorites. But she was hoping to do for Rozzie what she "had failed to do with Barbara — be more involved in her life." But the truth was that Barbara had never wanted advice, Diana felt, only approval. Barbara scared her a little, Diana acknowledged, because she was "so smart [and] had an answer for most things." And for the few questions Barbara *did* ask, Diana "never knew how to answer."

Diana admitted that she wasn't all that affectionate. Anyone who knew her knew how stiff she could be when they hugged her hello or good-bye. She wasn't a kissy type and never claimed to be. Who had time for sentiment when they were struggling to make ends meet and raise three kids all by themselves? And no, she didn't gush all over Barbara's wild dreams about becoming a big Broadway star. How could she do that and then sit back and watch her fail? Why would she encourage her daughter's hopes for something that simply was never going to happen? Where was the love in that? Better to protect Barbara from the kind of disappointment that she, Diana, had felt — the disappointment that life inevitably handed to people like them. Diana had no patience for criticisms that she didn't hug Barbara enough or that she didn't jump up and down supporting her dreams. She brought her chicken soup. Twice a week. What more could she do?

At last the train reached Times Square, and Diana got off. The sun was setting, striping the corridors of the theater district with long purple shadows as she made her way across town to watch her daughter playact on the stage.

7.

Inside the Theatre Studio, the students were busy preparing for their show. On hand that evening to lend support to Barbara were Terry, Carl, and Barbara's roommate, Marilyn. Even Allan Miller was aware that tonight's little presentation was Barbara's big moment to convince her mother that she was on the right course. Not an easy task, Miller knew. Mrs. Kind had once called him and accused him of putting her daughter into "white slavery."

Setting up the room to perform the little playlet, Barbara was certainly aware that the real drama tonight was between her mother and herself. She could be acutely self-reflective at times. She knew very well that she'd sought an acting career to fill up an empty place inside of her, to get the attention she had "missed as a child." In downtown Brooklyn she had spent "a lot of time and money in the penny arcades," snapping pictures of herself in the little photo booths, experimenting with different colored mascara on her eyes, trying out "all kinds of different hairstyles and sexy poses." Living in this colorful world of her imagination, Barbara could be as pretty as she wanted to be. And so, as an actress, Barbara would never be content with the heroine's less attractive, wisecracking best friend. She was going to be the lead, the *star*. "Is it crazy for me to want to play the love scenes?" she asked. "Is love only for blue-eyed blondes?"

Those in her class knew her dream parts. She wanted to play Camille and Juliet. She could "bring so many facets" to Juliet, she believed. So far, her favorite part had been Medea, which she had performed soon after her arrival at the Theatre Studio. In her head she carried one of the lines from that play: "I have this hole in the middle of myself." The line actually read: "Why . . . this open wound in the middle of myself?" Either way, its resonance in Barbara's life was understandable.

Looking up, she saw her mother enter the room wearing her old cloth coat. Diana took her seat, and the little presentation began. Barbara was no doubt anxious. Diana sat watching, her hands folded in her lap.

Just what scene Barbara enacted for her mother's benefit that night has gone unrecorded. But whatever part she played, she no doubt gave it everything she had. This night had been a long time in coming — at least since Barbara's fourteenth birthday, when she had seen *The Diary of Anne Frank* at the Cort Theatre on West Forty-eighth Street, just a couple of blocks from where she now lived and went to classes. Watching Susan Strasberg enact the role of Anne, Barbara had been filled with envy. "I can do that," she told herself, and she also told her mother the same thing when she returned home that night to Brooklyn. But Strasberg had the kind of connections Barbara did not: she was the daughter of Lee Strasberg, director of the Actors Studio, the most prestigious acting school in the country.

For Barbara, the Actors Studio was her own personal mecca. The Theatre Studio was fine as far as it went, but Strasberg was king. On the subway, Barbara had written impassioned letters to the great acting teacher, begging him to see her. Once, angry and resentful that only people with connections seemed to be admitted to the Actors Studio, she'd scrawled to Strasberg, "I hear you're a starfucker."

Wisely, she never mailed any of the letters — because there did come a day when she finally got a chance to show Strasberg what she could do. Almost a year earlier, Anita Miller had asked Barbara to be her audition partner at the Actors Studio (Allan was a member). That had given Barbara the "in" she needed, and soon afterward, she secured a spot in a three-month course at the studio. The letter telling her she'd been accepted became a "prized possession." But disillusionment quickly set in. The course had "so many people," Barbara discovered, that the chance of any one-on-one time with Strasberg was minimal to nonexistent. There was also little connection with her fellow students, who seemed like alien creatures to her. They loved "struggling" during class, Barbara observed, but when they put on "a regular face . . . they would freeze up." She had crashed the gate, but she still wasn't one of them.

Even worse, when she'd gotten up to perform a selection from the Richard Nash drama *The Young and Fair,* her nerves had taken over, and she'd cried all the way through her rendition. No surprise, she was not invited to join the Actors Studio after that.

Might it have been a scene from *The Young and Fair* that she performed that night with her mother looking on? Or maybe it was Medea. Whatever it was, at the end of it, everyone applauded, including Diana. Marilyn thought Barbara was "very proud of it." But Diana said little. Outside on Forty-eighth Street, she agreed to accompany Barbara and Marilyn back to their apartment. Terry trooped along as well.

Climbing the several flights of stairs, no one said a word. The old building had settled, and the steps weren't always even. The walls were cracked, and the fragrance of mold and dust was everywhere. Inside the flat, the three younger people sat on the bed while Barbara's mother stood and lectured them on eating right. Finally Diana said she'd seen nothing tonight to convince her that Barbara had what it took to be a success as an actress. She didn't want Barbara's heart broken, her hopes dashed. "And look at you," Diana said. "Your arms are still too skinny."

Soon after that, she left.

Barbara seemed unfazed. To her friends, she expressed no anger or hostility toward her mother. Instead, when she and Marilyn sat imagining what their lives would be like after they became successful, Barbara said that the first thing she'd do was buy her mother a mink coat.

CHAPTER TWO

Spring 1960

1.

For Barbara, telling a director he was wrong was a radical new idea and possibly a dangerous one at that. But that's exactly what Barré was doing, and it was with wide eyes and open mouth that she stood behind him watching.

From the auditorium Vasek Simek was shouting, "Did you never see moths?" His arms were flailing and his bushy eyebrows were moving across his forehead like caterpillars. "Flap, flap, flap! They keep moving!" Except, in his Czech accent, it came out, "Dey keep movink!" It was all Barbara could do to keep from laughing.

But Barré wasn't amused. "The girls can burst into little flurries of flap-flap-flaps," he argued. "But we have to figure out exactly when. It can't be all the time."

For Barbara, Barré Dennen was a revelation. He had joined the cast late. He was a friend of Carl Esser's from UCLA, where he'd known Simek on campus. And unlike the rest of the cast, Barré wasn't intimidated by their director's temper tantrums. Since rehearsals had begun in April, Vasek had used his association with the Actors Studio to lord over his cast, parading around the Jan Hus Playhouse like some cut-rate Stanislavski. But when finally confronted by Barré Dennen, he spilled his coffee all over himself, swore, and stalked off in a huff. That was probably the last they'd see of him for the day.

Barbara tapped Barré on the shoulder. She wanted to know if he really thought what he'd just done was a good idea. Did he want to keep them there all night? She explained that when Vasek got upset, it often took him hours to get over it. *The Insect Comedy* was opening in less than a week. Getting Vasek riled up was not helpful.

Barré just shrugged. Taking advantage of their volatile director's absence, he sat on the edge of the stage and motioned for Barbara to sit beside him. She complied. He lit up a cigarette and asked if she wanted one. She demurred; she'd given up smoking for the time being. The late-afternoon sun was filling up the hall. From the open windows came the heavily accented voices of Czech women on the street below. Barré looked over at Barbara with dark, soulful eyes. Yes, he told her, he did think confronting Vasek was a good idea. It was never worth staying quiet if it meant the difference between being mediocre and being good. And was he wrong to feel she wanted to be good?

"More than good," she replied quickly.

He smiled. The discussion was over.

Barbara liked this guy. They'd been hanging out a lot together since he'd joined the cast. Something very different was crackling between her and Barré than what she felt for Terry. With Terry, Barbara whispered and giggled; with Barré, she found herself holding eye contact for a few seconds longer than necessary, which made her cheeks flush as she finally looked away. The attraction between them was obvious to Terry, and to anyone else who saw them together. A few inches taller than Barbara, Barré had jet-black hair and a smile that was both sweet and sly. He could be flip and funny, smart and ironic, but he could also be sensitive.

He was a rich kid—a "Beverly Hills brat," in his own words. A theatrical life had been foretold when his mother had bestowed upon him at birth an *accent aigu* even though his name was pronounced

"Barry." His father had come to Southern California as if he were the hero in a Horatio Alger tale, fleeing a hardscrabble life in Chicago to make a fortune selling venetian blinds in the land of sunshine and palm trees. Barré grew up in a luxurious modern glass house in Coldwater Canyon, with a pool and a yard and housekeepers and gardeners. When Barré announced he wanted to be an actor, his father hadn't tried to talk him out of it, but happily enrolled him in UCLA's theater department. After graduation, he had generously paid for Barré's move to New York. Since that time, Barré had understudied the role of Bub in the revival of *Leave It to Jane* at the Sheridan Square Playhouse and landed a rather exquisite apartment in a brand-new building on Ninth Street in Greenwich Village, all paid for by Dad. Friends predicted that golden boy Barré Dennen was on his way to big things.

He was twenty-two. Barbara had just turned eighteen. Their first time out together, sharing a baked potato with sour cream and chives at a midtown diner, she'd drilled him like an investigative journalist. What was it like to have a live-in maid? What did his pool look like? What kinds of cars did his parents drive? What kinds of furs did his mother own? Barré found her questions captivating. There'd been no one like her in California.

As the rest of their class chattered about Francis Gary Powers, the American pilot who had crash-landed in Russia and was being called a spy, Barbara and Barré spent the time talking about acting. The sun was setting; the rehearsal was done. Given Vasek's intransigence, it was only at times like these, after they had disbanded for the night, that Barbara could get any real advice about her craft.

The auditorium was emptying as Barbara stood facing Barré, arms akimbo. She wanted the truth. He was a theater-school graduate, after all, so his opinion mattered. She wanted to know if she'd gotten to the heart of her character — a sexy little butterfly who makes violent love, desperate to stay alive. "Be honest," she insisted.

Barré smiled. He asked her if she'd ever seen Mae West. Barbara didn't understand why he was asking the question, but she told him she thought she had, in some old movie, late at night. Barré suggested that maybe her butterfly was a little too esoteric, that it might benefit from "a little Mae West." Barbara was surprised. *That* was his suggestion? Mae West? Nothing about going deep down inside and feeling what a butterfly might feel when it's winter and she knows she's got to mate because she's about to die? Barré nodded. "Try a little Mae West," he said. "Can you do Mae West?"

Barbara tried, but couldn't quite get the right Westian inflection, so Barré demonstrated for her. "Oh, you," he intoned, one hand on his hip, the other pushing at an imaginary bouffant. "You shameless creature, you."

Good mimic that she was, Barbara quickly got the hang of it. "Oh," she purred. "You great, strong, handsome thing."

"That's it," he told her. "Play it like that!"

They both dissolved in laughter.

Method acting indeed.

2.

The Insect Comedy came and went, three performances, May 8, 9, and 10, with barely a notice from anyone. So much for Vasek's eminent reputation. So much for Barbara's going straight to the top. One German-language newspaper had, however, called her "*ausgezeich-net*" — excellent — so Barbara hung on to that, thankful she'd come up with that Mae West business to set herself apart. That had been clever on her part. But now she needed a job. She had rent to pay.

The ushering at the Lunt-Fontanne had ended when she'd signed up for *The Insect Comedy.* For Barbara, jobs never seemed to last longer than a few months. Her first job in Manhattan had been as a clerk at a business firm. There she'd driven her bosses crazy by stumbling in late nearly every morning, groggy from late-night, after-class critiques she and the others held over pancakes and syrup at some Times Square eatery. Yet what really grated on her employers' nerves was Barbara's tendency to hum as she sashayed around the office filing papers and answering telephones. "Stop humming around here!" one of them barked at her. "What do you think you're in, a show?"

She wasn't in a show then, but she was hoping she would be now. *The Sound of Music* was preparing for a fall tour. Florence Henderson, a perky chanteuse who'd made a splash on Broadway in producer David Merrick's *Fanny* a few years back, was likely to take over Mary Martin's part. The other roles hadn't yet been cast, so Barbara had set her sights on Liesl, the pretty eldest daughter who sings "Sixteen Going on Seventeen." She had no worries about her singing voice. When she was a kid trilling on the stoops of her neighborhood, she knew the reason people didn't chase her away was because they liked her voice. At Erasmus Hall, she'd sung in the Chorale Club, even if she was frustrated that she never got a solo — strictly ensemble work was never for Barbara since it precluded a chance for her to shine on her own. But anyone who'd ever heard her recording of "You'll Never Know" agreed that she could sing.

Still, trying out for *The Sound of Music* was a lark. Liesl wasn't Juliet or Medea. The show was hardly Barbara's idea of great theater. This time there were no grand hopes tucked between the pages of her audition script. Heading into the audition, she knew this was just about getting a job. But warbling "Sixteen Going on Seventeen" would be better than filing papers in an office.

Greeting her at the audition was Eddie Blum, a bluff, hearty fellow who'd been casting director for Rodgers and Hammerstein for the last couple of years, overseeing *Flower Drum Song* before taking on *The Sound of Music*. At the piano was Peter Daniels, an Englishman with piercing blue eyes that looked out from behind a pair of thick glasses. No doubt both were surprised by the young gamine who'd wandered into the studio to sing for them. Barbara stood there chewing gum, as obviously Jewish as a girl could be, trying out for the part of Liesl von Trapp, that flower of young Aryan maidenhood. Blum was amused — and impressed — by Barbara's chutzpah in thinking she could convincingly play the stepdaughter of Florence Henderson.

She asked Daniels if he could accompany her on "Allegheny Moon,"

Patti Page's hit from a few years back. Daniels began tickling the ivories. "Allegheny moon," Barbara sang. "Your silver beams can lead the way to golden dreams . . . So shine, shine, shine . . ."

Blum was transfixed.

"What Eddie Blum saw," said one friend, "was this brave little *meydele* with a big schnozzle and acne on her face singing her heart out for the part and not seeing any reason why she shouldn't. She was a teenage girl. Liesl was a teenage girl. Why *shouldn't* a Jewish girl come in and try out for Liesl? And that's what charmed Eddie Blum."

3.

Barré was pleasantly surprised. The kid could really sing.

They were at his apartment at 69 West Ninth Street. The windows were closed tightly to seal off noise from the traffic below. Carl Esser was tuning his guitar and Barbara was practicing a few bars of the song she was about to sing. Barré listened approvingly as he screwed microphones onto stands and plugged cables into the jacks of his Ampex stereo tape recorder. No longer would Barbara have to wait weeks or pay big bucks to have a record made of her singing. Barré possessed the latest technology right here in his apartment to give her a tape this very afternoon.

She had called, asking for a favor. Eddie Blum had thought she was terrific, and although he didn't give her the job on the spot, he'd asked for a tape of her singing, presumably so he could convince some higher-ups — maybe Rodgers and Hammerstein themselves — that she was perfect for Liesl.

Listening as she practiced Sammy Cahn's "Day by Day," Barré was impressed not only with the quality of Barbara's voice but with the determination and focus she brought to the job at hand. She was "on fire with commitment to get it right," he thought. Should she sit or stand? Where should she position herself so the tape recorder could best pick up her voice? Was Carl's guitar tuned correctly?

Barré supposed it was Barbara's preoccupation with making the tape that led her to barely react when he shared his own big news. Just days before, he'd been signed by Joseph Papp and the New York Shakespeare Festival, which put on free plays during the summer at the Belvedere Lake Theatre in Central Park. First up was *Henry V,* and Barré had landed the small but potentially scene-grabbing part of a French soldier. He'd told Barbara all about it when she and Carl first arrived, and her response was to say "great" and then ask whether she should use the microphone or not when making her tape.

She had arrived, as usual, lugging her crumpled paper shopping bags. Feathers and sequined clothes tumbled over the top of one bag; another seemed ready to burst from her collection of buttons and scraps of cloth. A third bag held costume jewelry and shoes. Barbara told anyone who asked that she never knew when she might be called upon to whip up a costume. But a fourth bag was a relatively new addition to Barbara's luggage. Barré noticed that she was now toting around crackers, fruit, and bottles of juice. He was aware she was leading a rather nomadic existence at the moment, having been forced to give up her apartment due to a lack of funds. She was staying at various places, including her brother's office on West Forty-fifth Street, and sometimes housesitting for friends Barré had never met who lived on West Fifty-fourth Street. He knew better than to offer any sympathy or express any concern about her living situation. Barbara would have just brushed him off by insisting she was fine.

She was looking at Barré now, waiting for his signal to start. Checking the connections on the tape recorder one more time, he nodded.

Carl played a few chords on his guitar, then Barbara began to sing. "Day by day, I'm falling more in love with you, and day by day, my love seems to grow . . ."

Barré watched and listened. She was good. No doubt about that. Very good. He wondered why Barbara had never told him that she could sing. Certainly she knew about his love of music. Visits to his apartment meant listening to Edith Piaf or Shirley Horn or Billie Holiday on Barré's record player. But never had Barbara told Barré that she could sing herself. He found it very odd. Certainly Barbara was never shy when it came to announcing or demonstrating her talents.

When she was done singing, Barré switched off the tape recorder. He told her he'd make a copy since he was certain she'd never get the tape back after she gave it to Blum. Barbara thanked him. He added that she had a beautiful voice. Again, she thanked him, and their eyes, as usual, held a little longer than absolutely necessary.

Barré wasn't surprised that Barbara hung around after Carl packed up his guitar and left. She sat beside Barré on the couch, their shoulders touching. Barré told her she needed to do something with her voice. It was a gift he hadn't known about. Her ability to sing opened up a whole new range of options for her. But beyond trying out for the part of Liesl, Barbara seemed ambivalent about the idea. Barré kept on pressing her. Down the block, he said, there was a nightclub called the Lion. He went there sometimes. The Lion held talent contests on Tuesday nights. She should enter. She could win fifty bucks. She could certainly use some cash at the moment, couldn't she?

Barbara said she'd consider it. But nothing, she said, could get in the way of her becoming an actress.

Barré countered that singing was really just another form of acting. An Edith Piaf record was playing on the stereo, and Barré told Barbara to listen carefully to the way Piaf told a story with her songs. This particular song was about a depressed man who turned on the gas before he got into bed. From the record player, Piaf hissed like an open gas jet: "You were so sure, so sure, sooo sssssssure . . ." Barbara leaned forward, "sitting stone still," Barré observed, listening. When the record was done, she said it was "really something."

They sat there on the couch, quiet for a moment, still shoulder to shoulder. Every time they'd been in each other's company, the buzz between them had grown stronger, though neither of them had spoken of it or made a move. Barbara was unlike any girl Barré had ever known. Not that there had been all that many — in fact, he'd only slept with two girls in his life. But one of them, about a year ago, on a night of a power outage, had gotten pregnant. Somewhere out there Barré had a three-month-old son he'd never seen. So he was understandably cautious about moving too fast. He didn't want a repeat of what had happened on the night of the blackout.

But, if he was honest with himself—which, these days, he was struggling more and more to be—he knew that his careful approach with Barbara was even more complicated than that. The girls he'd been with—slept with or simply dated—had all been diversions from the real feelings he'd always done his best to hide. The club he told Barbara about, the Lion, was a gay club, and Barré didn't patronize it just for the talent contests. He went because he felt he belonged there. Not that there had been all that many men in his life either. But Barré was a percipient young man. He was twenty-two. He'd had these feelings since adolescence. He knew they weren't going away.

But he might be able to contain them. And Barbara excited him like no girl had ever done. He found her "adorable, sweet, funny, tender." She had beautiful eyes and a beautiful body, though her skin troubled him a bit because the smell of Clearasil repelled him when he got too close. But she was neat and clean, almost compulsively so—surprising for a girl who practically lived out of a shopping bag. If an article of clothing came back from the dry cleaners not cleaned to her specifications, Barbara would be irate. She made sure she always looked put together, from her hat down to her shoes, even if, to some, her wardrobe seemed eccentric. But Barbara had her own particular style, a trait Barré very much admired.

As he'd learned these past few weeks, she was a girl of very definite likes and dislikes. She loved gardenias, she told him. They had a smell that no perfumer could ever replicate, which made her like them even more. She loved Cokes, and ice-cream cones, and French fries that tasted of bacon. She also adored chantilly lace, avocados, gingerbread, and lavender roses, as well as "the feel of fur blankets and the smell of Italian cooking." But while she loved "the color of wine," she didn't care for "the taste of it," she said, and among her greatest dislikes were eggs, arriving early to appointments, crowded streets, dirty ashtrays, and "opportunistic people." That last one would make Barré laugh when he heard it because he felt she — he — all of them — were just waiting to pounce on the very first opportunity that came their way.

He was impressed by how much Barbara knew about literature. She could speak at length about Chekhov and Shakespeare and Euripides, thanks to her time with the Cormans and the Millers. But about music she was largely ignorant, except for some classical works and pop singer Joni James. She knew nothing of the great vocalists — Piaf, Holiday, Judy Garland, Peggy Lee. Still, she'd learned quickly after Barré started playing their records. Barbara admired Piaf, but it was Holiday she loved, sinking down into the cushions of Barré's couch, closing her eyes as she soaked up Billie's blues. She had a similar response in museums, Barré noticed. Barbara might know little about art, but she was drawn instinctively to the very best as they walked past — Monets at the Met, Picassos at MoMA.

But for all her flair, Barbara could be terribly shy, too, especially in gatherings of Barré's UCLA friends. When these slightly older college graduates came by, Barbara seemed to shut down, to become physically smaller than she was. Carole Gister, one of Barré's closest friends, had perceived the slender girl sitting off to the side as "a perfectly nice quiet child who'd seemed to have run away from home with a mattress on her head." Barbara would explain that her shyness was "unconventional." She might be strong and assertive in most areas of her life, but upon first meeting people, she didn't always "like them straight away." She was "a little more wary," she said. Barré's friends would have agreed with her assessment.

Once, trying to engage Barbara, some of those friends had begun asking about her acting ambitions. Someone came up with the idea that she could work as a hand model, and everyone enthusiastically agreed since Barbara had "these fabulous hands with long, delicate fingers," Gister observed. But Barbara, not surprisingly, wasn't interested. She would have had to cut her nails, for one thing.

Sitting next to her on the couch now, Barré suddenly reached over and kissed her. At least that would be how he remembered that day, insisting that, in addition to kissing her, he played records for her all afternoon: Billie Holiday's "Strange Fruit," Ruth Etting's "Ten Cents a Dance," Lee Wiley's "Baby's Awake Now," and comedy vocals from Bea Lillie and Mae Barnes. Whether every single one of those records spun on his turntable that day or not, they certainly did so in the days that followed. There was also some Helen Morgan, Ethel Waters, Libby Holman, and Marion Harris. And also more kisses. Eventually Barré took a cloth and tenderly wiped the Clearasil from Barbara's face.

But one thing was certain about that day Barbara recorded her tape for Eddie Blum in Barré's apartment. When she left, she still had not asked anything about Barré's part in *Henry V.* He wasn't offended. He understood how "desperate she was to make it," how "hungry she was for attention and success." Barbara's ambition, Barré felt, "had become a kind of living, breathing ache inside her that blotted out everything else."

4.

Cis and Harvey Corman were eating dinner when Barbara wandered in. They weren't expecting her. They looked up with some surprise as she approached the table.

"Ya know," she said. "I'm going to enter a contest for singing."

"Why would you do that?" Cis asked. "You don't know how to sing."

"Yeah, I do."

This they didn't know. "Well, sing for us," Cis said.

"I'm too embarrassed," Barbara replied.

They encouraged her, saying that she had no reason to be embarrassed around them. So Barbara decided she'd sit on the table and face the wall. Setting down their forks, Cis and Harvey gave her their full attention. Barbara began to sing.

"When a bee lies sleepin' in the palm of your hand . . ."

It was the Harold Arlen song "A Sleepin' Bee," originated by Diahann Carroll in the musical *House of Flowers.* Truman Capote had contributed to the lyrics, and June Christy had covered it a couple of years earlier. Barré had taught it to Barbara over several painstaking days in his apartment. The Cormans listened raptly.

Barbara finished with "A sleepin' bee done told me I will walk with my feet off the ground when my one true love I has found."

Slowly she turned around, anxious to see how her friends had responded. Cis and Harvey were "drenched in tears," as Cis would admit. None of them would ever forget the moment.

5.

The King Arthur Room was a small, intimate space tucked within the spacious if low-ceilinged Roundtable on East Fiftieth Street. Formerly the Versailles, the venue was the New York home of the Dukes of Dixieland, and it was here that Barré brought Barbara on this special night. With his father's Diners Club card, he'd splurged on a dinner of steak and mashed potatoes. Yet no matter how tasty the London broil, it was for what came after dinner that Barré had brought Barbara to the Roundtable.

That tonight was a celebration at all was a relief. Barbara had won the contest at the Lion! Barré had been worried that the two numbers she'd felt comfortable enough singing — "A Sleepin' Bee" and "When Sunny Gets Blue" — were both ballads, and he knew the crowd at the Lion tended to go for more up-tempo show tunes. But there'd been no time to practice anything new, so they'd gone with what they had. Terry had dressed Barbara in a feathered boudoir jacket and layered skirt, all in shades of lavender — appropriate, given the venue. But then, on the way to the club, she'd gotten the jitters, and Barré had had to talk her through them by reminding her that a good actress could play any part, even a nightclub singer.

The place had been packed. The talent shows, held Tuesdays at eleven PM, were very popular. Given that Barbara's competitors that night were a couple of typical comics, Barré figured she had the thing aced—until he'd looked up to see a striking young woman stride into the club, all legs and self-confidence. She was Dawn Hampton, a jazz singer and dancer who was tight with Burke McHugh, the club's manager. She was also part of a family of musicians well-known in the world of jazz, and she had performed at the Apollo Theater and Carnegie Hall. McHugh thought Hampton "sang like there was no tomorrow." With her expressive eyes, spirited laugh, and gorgeous legs, Dawn Hampton was everything Barbara was not: experienced, polished, and lovely. Plus she had connections. Barré's heart had sunk.

Hampton had indeed been spectacular when she got up on stage, bringing down the house with her hot jazz. But Barré had noticed a very different alchemy when Barbara took the microphone. Maybe the gay men in attendance had been rooting for the homely girl over the pretty one, the underdog over the luminary. Whatever their motivation, the audience had responded to her intimately. Their usual raucous bar behavior had been stilled. There'd been something about the simplicity of it all, this small girl in purple feathers, standing beside a piano, singing an uncomplicated song about a sleeping bee. Dawn Hampton was a polished pro. Barbara was a tenderfoot, though she made it all seem so terribly easy. The lyrics that came from her lips were "liquid and languorous," Barré thought, and even when she'd decided to improvise a bit, taking the mike and walking among the tables—plunging herself into darkness when the spotlight couldn't find her—she hadn't lost the audience. She'd kept right on singing. Even tripping over a patron's chair on her way back to the stage hadn't stopped her from ending with the big finish she'd practiced in Barré's apartment. The room had exploded into cheers for her, and she won the contest.

Cheers meant something for a girl like Barbara. Dawn Hampton had heard them many times before—at Carnegie Hall, no less. The comics and pianists at the Lion had also basked regularly in the hoots and whistles of the crowd. But for Barbara, this was something very new. She'd taken her bows for *Picnic* and *Driftwood* and *The Insect Comedy*—but she'd been part of ensembles then, and the audiences had been cheering for everyone, not just her. That night at the Lion, however, the cheers had been solely for her, and they went on and on. Suddenly the invisible girl from Brooklyn was being seen by everyone in the room. What's more, they liked what they saw.

The Lion expected her to appear again, on Saturday night, and sing on a bill with three other acts. Barbara was leery about being roped into a gig that might keep her from auditioning for roles in the theater. She told friends that she only agreed to the Lion's request because they promised dinner—a line that quickly became a running joke among Barré's friends, that Barbara could be had for a baked potato. But Barré had convinced her that a gig at the Lion would be great exposure for her, as both a singer and an actress. And he pointed out that they had nearly a week this time to prepare a really strong repertoire.

That was why they'd come to the Roundtable. In between rehearsals for *Henry V* in Central Park, Barré had been playing his records nearly nonstop for Barbara, seeing if anything from Ethel Waters or Ruth Etting might tickle her fancy. He instructed her to listen to the way they all told stories with their songs. As an actress, she could do that, too. "A Sleepin' Bee" could be a three-act play, Barré suggested, told first by a young girl, then by a grown woman, then finally by an old lady looking back. Barbara responded well to the technique. But she insisted she couldn't "learn from a record," and Barré agreed. So he'd brought her here to the Roundtable so she could watch and listen to someone on whom she might model her act.

By this point, Mabel Mercer was an old crust of a chanteuse, sitting like a dowager queen on a throne before her audience, her voice croaky and tattered from decades of singing in smoky rooms like this one. Barbara watched closely as Mercer came out onto the stage wearing a brocade gown. A soft pink light picked her out in the dark mahogany room. At sixty, she looked much older. Her cinnamon skin had turned to leather. With perfect posture Mercer sat down in her chair, barely moving at all as she started to sing. The most she did was occasionally lift a shaky hand toward the audience.

Mercer began her first song, and Barbara wasn't impressed. "She can't sing," she whispered to Barré.

Barré understood that Mercer was "an acquired taste, like certain ripe cheeses." So he tried explaining to Barbara that the old pro was a "song stylist" and that she should concentrate on her phrasing, not her voice.

Barbara complied. She listened to Mercer rasp her way through a couple of ballads, a storyteller as much as a singer. "I can do this," she whispered to Barré at last. It was the same conviction that made her sure that she could play Liesl or Hamlet or Juliet — the belief that she could do anything if just given the chance.

Mercer ended with Bart Howard's "Would You Believe It?" Looking out over the audience with half-lidded eyes, she suddenly snapped her fingers, just once, as she was finishing the song. Barré had never seen Mabel Mercer snap her fingers before, and he was overjoyed, leading the applause with enthusiasm.

Barbara was less enthusiastic. But Barré had seen how she'd observed the old pro, taking note of the way Mercer had turned her head, the way she'd sung her songs with beginnings, middles, and ends. It was exactly the way Barré had been coaching Barbara to do. He hoped she'd picked up enough bits and pieces to make into her own.

Barbara, however, when she was asked, insisted that watching other performers taught her absolutely nothing — except "what not to do."

6.

The first time they'd tried to make love Barré had stopped midway through because he didn't have protection. He'd made that mistake before, and he told Barbara they should plan their first time carefully. They should pick a night, he said, and he'd buy some rubbers, and she'd bring some baby oil. Barbara complained that this didn't feel very spontaneous, but she went out and bought the baby oil.

Now, watching Barré lather his face in the bathroom mirror, wrapped only in a towel, she told him she'd never seen a man shave before. Sheldon had been out of the house by the time she was paying attention, and she'd certainly never looked at Lou Kind for any longer than she absolutely had to. That Barré's beard was so heavy intrigued her. Barbara found it "very masculine," she said, so much so that she couldn't resist lifting a corner of Barré's towel and purring like Mae West, "Whaddya got under there, big boy?"

Barré had told her that he was bisexual. While other girls might have been taken aback by such an admission from a boyfriend, Barbara had seemed to view it as a challenge. In the last few weeks she'd become increasingly sexually aggressive, quite a step for a girl whose mother had done her best to instill in her a fear of sex. "You don't screw anybody until you get married," Barbara remembered her mother saying, or words to that effect. And Barbara was hearing such admonitions from her mother more frequently these days. Her lack of funds had forced her into the once-unimaginable scenario of retreating back to Brooklyn several nights a week.

Making love to Barré was the logical next step, and a little bisexuality shouldn't prove to be an obstacle. They were always flirting, throwing around Mae West double entendres that they had picked up from late-night movie viewings. And so Barbara kissed the back of Barré's neck and played with the towel around his waist. "What's the matter with your animal?" she cooed, using their favorite West line. But Barré once again begged off, arguing he'd be late for rehearsals. Barbara wanted to know when they'd finally make love. He promised her soon.

He kept that promise. On a night after Barbara had wowed them yet again at the Lion and agreed to defend her title once more the following Tuesday, Barré took out a canister of marijuana, rolled a couple of joints, and taught Barbara how to smoke. Soon they were both high, and naked, and making love. Nothing the matter with the animal now.

Barré believed that he was Barbara's first lover. She told him he was, and that she was giving herself to him. Holding her in his arms, he felt her tremulous vulnerability. During daylight hours she might believe fervently that she could do anything and be anyone. But at night — naked in Barré's arms — the little voice that insisted she wasn't good enough, or beautiful enough, was as real as anything else. In these more vulnerable moments, Barbara needed reassurance, and Barré did his best to give it to her. Lying there with Barbara in his arms, he felt the enormous weight of the trust she had placed in him, and he hoped he would never hurt her.

Of course, she wasn't entirely vulnerable. With sensuous strokes of her long fingernails, Barbara caressed Barré's back, a sensation both relaxing and arousing, but occasionally painful, too. Barré realized that Barbara's nails — by now three inches long, forcing her to use a pencil eraser to dial a phone — would forever "prohibit a certain degree of intimacy" between them, or between Barbara and anyone else. Never could she fully touch another human being with her hands. And if her nails symbolized her own reluctance to get too familiar, they were also ever-present reminders that if anyone trespassed too closely, she could, and would, fight back.

7.

Burke McHugh ran the Lion like his own little Vegas showplace. It didn't matter that the club was just a cubbyhole in a brownstone on West Ninth Street near Sixth Avenue, the kind of place that never saw its shows listed in the calendar section of the *Times*. McHugh still populated his stage with people he considered stars, such as Dawn Hampton, whose hot jazz regularly burned up the back room. The Streisand kid — the one who'd been winning his contests for the last few weeks — also had potential. She was back again tonight, handing her music to pianist Pat McElligott, telling him that she'd added a couple of new numbers. If she won again tonight, McHugh had decided, he'd have to retire her from the contest so somebody else could have a chance. He regretted having to put an end to Barbara's run, however, since the little waif had been good for business. Word had gotten around that she was special. "Talented in a way nobody else is," patrons were saying. And what showman didn't love discovering someone like that?

She was a sharp cookie, that Streisand. After winning her second contest, she'd told McHugh that she wanted three pictures of herself, not just one, on the sign promoting the Saturday night show. She wasn't beautiful, but she had a look, McHugh thought. He would know. With his classic all-American handsomeness, he'd been one of the nation's top male models. For several years he'd been the man shaving his face in the Gillette razor television commercials. He'd also managed his own modeling agency, where he'd learned that beautiful people weren't always the best salespeople. "Perfect" models didn't have the same appeal, McHugh believed, as those who looked "real," who were "believable," and thus "saleable."

Barbara was as real as they got, and the Lion's regulars had taken to her. She'd been hired to work the coat-check room during the week. The offbeat characters who patronized the club all adored her. Barbara had quickly figured out that the clientele was largely gay, but had nonetheless been surprised to learn just *how* gay. That first Saturday she'd performed, Cis had come to cheer her on, and Barbara had pointed out that they were the only women in the house, as if Cis couldn't have seen that herself.

For tonight's competition, Barbara was adding "Why Try to Change Me Now?" and "Long Ago (and Far Away)," both Sinatra standards, to her set. She and Barré had been practicing them all week, giving the songs as many unusual touches as possible. It was Barbara's offbeat personality as much as her gorgeous voice that drew other performers to the Lion to check her out. Popular stage and television actor Orson Bean was brought by some friends one night, and he'd thought she was "simply fabulous." Paul Dooley, who'd recently made a splash in *Fallout,* a revue at the Renata Theater on Bleecker Street, was another who'd heard about this "crazy girl with the beautiful voice" and came by the Lion to see for himself. Dooley was struck by the fact that Barbara "had the poise of a forty-year-old saloon singer" when she was only eighteen years old. Of her audience she seemed to demand, "Look at me!" — and, indeed, Dooley found that he couldn't look away. "Young people don't usually have that kind of confidence," he said. "They don't usually trust their talent."

Yet Barbara was so unusual that not everyone responded to her in the same way. While Bean and Dooley saw her as fabulous and confident, Walter Clemons, who played piano for Mabel Mercer and, like the others, had slipped in to see what all the fuss was about, perceived her as "terribly nervous." In Clemons's view, Barbara was "hostile" to her audience, with none of Mercer's legendary generosity. Her eccentric syntax seemed to him "convoluted and interior," leaving him confused as to what she was talking about. All he could feel coming from her was the "terrible resentment of an ugly girl."

But Clemons was in the minority. That night Barbara won the contest once again, and Burke McHugh made much hoopla over the fact that he was retiring her as the Lion's "undefeated champion," which, of course, only prompted more hoots and hollers and whistles from the crowd. Barbara would perform one more week as the winner, then it had to be someone else's turn.

Standing off to the side, Barré noticed the look in Barbara's eyes. He'd seen it every time she'd been declared the winner, the champion, the best. Her face would come alive as if she'd been "plugged into the wall," an "electric" look generated by the power of the applause. Barbara had been so hungry for attention, so desperate for praise and affirmation, Barré thought — and "now she was getting it." And the look in her eyes told him that she believed "she could *go on* getting it for the rest of her life."

8.

In the cab on the way over to one of her final performances at the Lion, Barbara told Terry Leong that she was changing her name. He was surprised. He didn't think she'd ever do such a thing.

Not her last name, Barbara told him. Her first.

Terry had always known his friend wanted to be unique. But he also knew that she didn't want some made-up stage name such as Joanie Sands, which some people had been suggesting, "because that was too false." The name Barbara had never thrilled her — in fact, she said that she "hated" it — but ditching it entirely seemed too drastic, an indication that she was "losing touch with reality." So she told Terry that she had come up with a different idea.

When they got to the club, she strode over to Burke McHugh and instructed him to change the spelling of her name on her posters. "I wanna take an 'a' out of Barbara," she said. An "a," he repeated, not understanding. "Yeah," she said. "The second one." From now on, she insisted, her name would be spelled B-A-R-B-R-A.

There were millions of Barbaras out there, she reasoned. But by dropping one little vowel, she would become "the only Barbra in the world."

CHAPTER THREE

Summer 1960

1.

It was time to get serious again. That's what Barbra was telling her new friend Bob Schulenberg as they strolled through Times Square. She was pointing up at the marquees — Anne Bancroft in *The Miracle Worker* at the Playhouse Theatre and Chita Rivera and Dick Van Dyke in *Bye Bye Birdie* at the Martin Beck — and wishing her name was up in those lights. This was where she wanted to be, not in some little club on the first floor of a brownstone in the Village.

Bob seemed to understand her like no one else did. He was so different from Barré, who in his push for Barbra to sing seemed to have forgotten that what she really wanted to do was act. In fact, Barré had seemed to forget her entirely of late. He'd been spending most of his time up in Central Park, where *Henry V* had opened on June 29. Barbra felt his absence keenly, especially since most nights she had to trek back to Brooklyn and stay with her mother if she wanted a roof over her head. She had never been very good at playing second fiddle, even to William Shakespeare.

That summer day, she was lonely and feeling not a little bit insecure, her friends believed. Here she had given herself to a man she thought truly loved her, and now suddenly he was gone for long stretches at a time. Her fears weren't difficult to understand. The knowledge of Barré's bisexuality "was always there in the back of her mind," said one friend. When he wasn't with her, Barbra wondered, where was he?

One friend also believed that a certain amount of professional jealousy had bubbled to the surface. When the *Times* review came out the day after *Henry V* opened, Barré had been ecstatic to see he'd gotten a mention. Critic Arthur Gelb had felt that Barré's scene was "as funny as Shakespeare intended." Getting his name in the *New York Times* was thrilling — and even the omission of the *accent aigu* hadn't dampened his excitement. Of course Barbra was happy for him. But it wasn't long after this that she resolved "to once again get serious about her own acting career," her friend observed.

And no one seemed to encourage her as much as Bob did. He was an old friend of Barré's whom Barbra had met late one night just after he'd arrived in New York from Los Angeles. Bob was staying with Barré until he could find a place of his own. He was a good-looking young man who, when Barbra first met him, was wearing a conservative suit and glasses. But when he'd looked at Barbra's outfit, he'd revealed a rather eclectic interest in fashion. "Are those authentic T-strap shoes?" he had asked with excitement.

Barbra had smiled and told him that they were indeed. Bob adored the shoes, as well as Barbra's knee-length velvet skirt of mulberry violet and her pink nylons. "Who knew there were pink nylons!" Bob exclaimed. Heading over to the Pam Pam, an all-night diner on Sixth Avenue and Eighth Street, the three of them had talked until nearly dawn about clothes, theater, and ambition. Bob was an artist; his tattered sketchbook was rarely out of his hands. He'd come to New York to be an illustrator, though in the interim he was paying his bills by working for the advertising agency Ellington & Co. at their Fifth Avenue offices. Like Terry, Bob was an artist stuck, for the moment anyway, in a nine-to-five job.

Yet it was precisely that nine-to-five schedule that allowed Bob to spend more time with Barbra lately than Barré was. And now that Bob had found his own apartment on Gay Street, Barbra found it easier to store her clothes at his place than at Barré's, since she never knew when Barré would be home. The sequined skirts sparkling next to Bob's tweed jackets had led more than one of his friends to inquire jokingly if he'd become a transvestite since moving to New York. "No, just the friend of a girl who's going to be a big star," he would reply. Barbra, of course, was enchanted.

2.

A measure of relief washed over Barbra. She'd been asked by Curt Conway to take over the part of Hortense the French maid in *The Boy Friend,* slated for the following month at the Cecilwood Playhouse, the Theatre Studio's summer theater in Fishkill, New York. To be chosen to perform at the Cecilwood was quite an honor. Although all Theatre Studio members were eligible, no student was "promised participation as a condition of his training." Barbra was ecstatic that her teachers seemed finally to be recognizing her talent and hard work.

But before she did anything else, she had to see Barré in *Henry V.* For weeks she'd been saying that she would and now it was Saturday, July 16, closing night. Although Shakespeare Festival productions were free, Barré had arranged for Barbra and Bob to be given special house seats up close to the stage. He desperately wanted Barbra to see his "first real moment of triumph on stage." Scoping out the sight lines, Barré had assured himself that his ladylove would be able to view him perfectly.

For the occasion, Bob was giving Barbra a whole new look. At her temporary house-sitting digs on West Fifty-fourth Street, Bob painstakingly glued false eyelashes to Barbra's lids, extending them around to the sides of her face the way Claudette Colbert and Katharine Hepburn had popularized in the 1930s. From studying photographs of movie stars, Bob knew it wasn't the length of a woman's eyelashes that made them beautiful, but the thickness. So he cut a second pair of lashes very short and glued them just above the first pair, providing the fullness Barbra's eyes needed to really pop out.

This wasn't the first time Bob had experimented with different looks for Barbra. When they went out on the town, he sometimes glued sequins to her eyelids, a trick he'd learned designing Ice Capades shows at UCLA. Another time, while having herring for dinner, they'd both admired the fluorescent skin of the fish and wondered if it might work better than the sequins. So they tried cutting it up with the idea of gluing it to Barbra's eyes, but the skin stunk so much that they soaked it in perfume overnight. In the morning all the color was gone. They stuck with the sequins.

Another night, on a whim, Bob had told Barbra to pick out everything she had in red. Out came a knit dress, a belt, shoes, and a cloche hat. Sitting Barbra down in front of a mirror, Bob applied her makeup in similar shades of red. Not just her lips and cheeks, but also her eyelids, which "made it seem as if red was her natural color," Bob said. The whole look was finished off with a classic black trench coat.

Of course, such glamour needed to be shared, Bob declared. Even though it was close to midnight, they ambled over to the all-night Brasserie in the Seagram Building on Park Avenue. Along the way, people stopped and stared at the woman in red with the gorgeous legs, long neck, and tiny waist. At the brightly lit Brasserie, the usual clientele of artists and sophisticates cast their eyes in Barbra's direction as she sauntered in, dramatically flung her coat over a chair, and ordered choucroute garnie — sauerkraut with sausages and potatoes. A man came by the table and told her he'd loved her at the Lion. He asked her to sign his napkin. Barbra was thrilled. Bob, she felt, was turning her into a star.

At long last people were seeing her as she'd always believed she should be seen. Bob was bringing out an inner beauty that even Barbra hadn't suspected was there. When Bob had first turned her around in her chair to face the mirror, she'd found herself liking what she saw reflected there. No Method acting was required, no exercise in self-persuasion. She honestly saw how beautiful she could be, and the sensation was intoxicating.

In the last couple of weeks, Barbra and Bob had grown very close. Barbra sensed her new friend had something more in common with Barré than just their years together at UCLA. Bob eventually admitted that he, too, was gay to Barbra, though, like Barré, he wasn't fully open about it yet; telling friends back in L.A. that he lived on Gay Street in Greenwich Village was never easy for him. As she did with Barré, Barbra accepted the information placidly, though she rarely brought it up.

Bob found that, free of the kind of sexual tension that existed between Barbra and Barré, he could take real pleasure in shaping his protégée, who was making remarkable progress. Not so long ago, he wouldn't have risked taking Barbra to the Brasserie. When he'd first met her, she didn't have what he called "restaurant smarts." The napkin never went into her lap, for example; instead, Barbra would clumsily set her plate on top of it. If a vegetable was unrecognizable, she'd pick it up and dangle it across the table between her long fingernails to ask Bob what it was. Horrified, Bob realized that Barbra's mother had never taught her the fine points of etiquette that had been so meticulously imparted to him. But instead of embarrassing Barbra by alerting her to her mistakes, he just made sure that she saw everything he did, from putting his napkin in his lap to keeping his elbows off the table. It was difficult, Barbra admitted, training herself "to keep one hand" in her lap. But eventually, to Bob's great admiration, she caught on.

This night their outing was supposed to be very simple. No restaurants, no nightclubs, no particular etiquette. Just a trip to Central Park to see Barré's show. Still, Bob wanted Barbra to look striking. He dressed her in a black turtleneck and black Danskin tights under a black cardigan. He applied her makeup in shades of ash and gray. It took time to get her look just right. Bob would step back and look at his creation, who would sometimes turn to catch glimpses of herself in the mirror. "Patience," he'd tell her, and Barbra would giggle in anticipation. She was never happier than when a man was fussing over her. A little more blush, Bob decided, then another layer of mascara.

Meanwhile, the hands on the clock behind them continued to turn. Neither of them noticed the time, or at least neither of them commented on it.

Uptown in Central Park, however, Barré did notice the time. It surprised him how much it mattered that Barbra see him in this play. Maybe it was because of all the time he'd spent preparing her for the Lion, and he wanted some acknowledgment, some support, in return. Barbra always seemed so indifferent to Barré's own work, his own goals. As showtime neared, he kept peeking out to see if she and Bob were there yet. As the curtain went up, their seats were still empty.

It was a warm evening. Temperatures had reached eighty degrees that day, with humidity near seventy percent. People sat on the grass that surrounded the stage fanning themselves with their programs. The sun was dropping lower in the sky, turning the waters of Belvedere Lake pink. By the time Barré made his entrance in the second act, long blue shadows had stretched across the park. Taking "a quick gander" out at the audience, he could see through the dusky night that the house seats he'd reserved for Barbra and Bob were filled. Barbra must be there watching him, Barré thought. He felt that he played his scene better than ever that night and that the applause went on even longer than usual.

But when the play was finished and the footlights went out, he realized he didn't recognize the two people in the house seats. Barbra and Bob must have been too late, Barré realized, and their seats had been given away. Scanning the crowd, he spotted his errant friends hurrying toward the stage, "fighting their way upstream against the exiting crowd" as if they had just arrived.

As Barbra neared him, Barré asked her, "You just got here?"

"Uh, yeah," she admitted.

Bob stepped up, blaming their lateness on the subway and on how long it had taken him to get Barbra's clothes and makeup just right. "But she looks great, though, Barré," he said. "Don't you think?"

Yes, Barré thought to himself, she did look great. And looking great, he realized, had meant more to her than making it to his show on time. This show was the first thing he had done in New York "that had made any kind of a dent," he kept repeating to himself, "and she couldn't be bothered to come."

Unable to speak, he stood there "chewing on his fury." Meanwhile Bob kept up a running commentary in Barbra's ear about all the people who were admiring her. "There's a handsome man across the way staring at you," he whispered. "And another one over there. Look away. Look bored."

And Barbra, sweltering in her black turtleneck, did just that.

3.

Not long after, a contrite little girl knocked at Barré's door.

She didn't apologize — Barbra rarely said she was sorry — but she was clearly wrestling with guilt. Barré let her in. She seemed scared, unsure of herself. The insecurities she usually kept so well hidden were suddenly bubbling up into view. She seemed to need to talk. So Barré let her ramble.

She felt *farblunget,* she said. "All mixed up." The owner of the Lion, Ernie Sgroi, had persuaded his father, the proprietor of the Bon Soir, one of the most important nightclubs in the Village, to give her an audition. But did Barbra really want to keep singing for a living? Would it take away from learning her part for *The Boy Friend,* which required a French accent? Pacing around Barré's apartment, Barbra was confused, indecisive, and a little bit teary — a far cry from the poised creature in black who'd swaggered across the grass of Central Park just a few days earlier.

But it wasn't just her career that left her feeling *farblunget,* Barré sensed. Barbra's head was filled with thoughts, she said, and her tinnitus was ringing in her ears. She'd taken Barré's absence during the last few weeks of *Henry V* very personally. He knew that, but he couldn't decide whether Barbra's state of mind reflected the genuine feelings she had for him or just the narcissism he'd come to recognize in her,

Others, however, were inclined to be more sympathetic. Bob had come to believe that Barbra was "very much in love with Barré." Another friend thought Barbra's guilt over missing Barré's show had made her realize "how much she cared about him and how much she didn't want to lose him." After all, Barré was Barbra's first lover, which was a powerful connection for an inexperienced eighteen-year-old girl. She had come back to Barré now with as much humility and contrition as she could muster — never much in Barbra's case — but the fact that she was there at all spoke volumes.

She also needed him. She had the Bon Soir audition to prepare for.

Barré took her in his arms. He blamed Bob for "seducing" her into missing the show. Barbra had been "carried away" by her new friend, Barré believed, spellbound by the way Bob could transform her from an ugly duckling into a swan. So, sitting her down on the couch, he reassured her that he was still committed to helping her in any way he could. That seemed to make her relax, and for the rest of the afternoon they snuggled on the couch, practicing the French accent she was going to need for *The Boy Friend.*

But something else was bothering her. It may have been that day, or one very much like it, that Barbra announced she wanted to have her nose fixed. Having had a taste of what being beautiful felt like, she seemed hungry for more. All she would need to do, Barbra believed, was "change the tilt . . . and take off a little bit." The bump in the center of her nose, she said, would be left intact because Bob had told her if she changed too much of her nose, she'd have to change her chin, too. Besides, she "loved her bump," she said. Her nose was her father's nose. When she thought about changing it, she felt disloyal.

Barré told her that she shouldn't change a thing, that she was perfect as she was. No doubt that's what she wanted to hear. It's what Bob had told her too, but no doubt she really wanted to hear it from Barré.

Cuddling next to him on the couch, she wanted very much for their relationship to work out. By the middle part of the summer of 1960, all of their friends knew that Barbra had fallen deeply in love with Barré. And not a few of them wondered if that was really such a good thing.

4.

Walking back from lunch with his sister, Sheldon Streisand told Barbra to walk a few feet behind him. He was joking, but the runs in the backs of her stockings did embarrass him. Never one to take jokes at her expense very kindly, Barbra bristled. "They're not ripped in front and I don't see them in back, so they don't bother me," she told her brother, and walked on ahead of him defiantly.

For a girl who was usually so fastidious about her appearance, the runs in her stockings bespoke just how strapped for cash she was that summer. The money from the Lion was over, and *The Boy Friend* was still weeks away. Sheldon had come to her rescue, securing her a job at the ad agency he worked for, Ben Sackheim, Inc. But Barbra could take only so much of his help. When Sheldon offered to buy her a new pair of stockings, Barbra adamantly refused. She was already in debt to her brother enough as it was, and being in debt to Shelly was too close to being in debt to her mother.

With a halfhearted gait, Barbra trooped back up the steps of the Plaza Hotel at Central Park and Fifth Avenue, where Sackheim had its offices. Stepping into the elevator, Barbra was well aware that Shelly shared their mother's concerns that she'd never make good. To a coworker, he called his sister "uncontrollable." The two siblings, so far apart in age, had little in common. They probably exchanged few words as they rode the elevator back up to the twenty-first floor. There, Shelly went one way, heading back to his office, where he worked as an art director, and Barbra went the other way, trudging glumly to the front desk. She'd been put in charge of the switchboard for two weeks, replacing the regular operator who was out on vacation. To alleviate the boredom, Barbra often answered the phone using different accents, usually French, practicing for *The Boy Friend* — a way, she said, to keep her "acting alive."

It may have been that day, or one very similar (they all blurred together for Barbra anyway), that Shelly suddenly reappeared over her shoulder and told her there was a problem. Barbra, it seemed, was keeping callers on the line so long, rattling on in all her "made-up foreign languages," that Sackheim employees couldn't get calls in or out. And if the problem wasn't her practicing accents, it was her penchant to gab with Bob, who was always amused by Barbra's inept mastery of the switchboard. Never entirely sure which person's extension was which, Barbra would be gabbing away with Bob when she'd suddenly announce that one of her lights was flashing. Bob would eavesdrop as she'd say, "Good afternoon, Ben Sackheim agency" and then connect the caller as best she could — a process she often got wrong, plugging people together who hadn't called each other. Many times Bob listened in as Sackheim employees ordered lunch from a nearby deli, covering his mouth to muffle his laughter as the deli's return call got routed to a person who insisted that, no, *absolutely no,* he had *not* ordered herring for lunch. Dissolving in laughter at his office fourteen blocks downtown, Bob couldn't help but imagine Barbra playing the tangled-up switchboard scene from *Auntie Mame.*

5.

They had become regular events, these little concerts in Barré's apartment. Barré would arrange and orchestrate Barbra's numbers, and Bob would do her makeup. Carole Gister sat among the usual UCLA clique in the living room, waiting for the show to begin. Barbra was on a stool in the kitchen, where Bob was touching up her lipstick. Carole understood these concerts were dry runs for Barbra's upcoming gig at the Bon Soir. The shy little runaway had certainly blossomed, Carole thought.

At her audition, Barbra had wowed Ernie Sgroi Sr. The Bon Soir was the closest the Village came to a posh supper club, the "Greenwich Village version of uptown Blue Angel," according to *Variety*. The *New York World-Telegram* called the venue "one of the lead funspots" in the Village, a "yock-laden place" given the number of comedy acts that alternated with the torch singers and jazz artists. Every night patrons would line up down the block from the Bon Soir's front door. Downstairs in the club's dark interior, regular joes rubbed shoulders with celebrities. Frequent headliner Kaye Ballard never knew who she might spot sitting in her audience. Sometimes it was Gregory Peck, other times it was Marlene Dietrich. Shows at the Bon Soir generated a real buzz, with patrons often returning two or three nights in a row.

For her audition, Barbra had brought along Barré, Bob, and Burke McHugh to provide support. Not surprisingly, she'd sung "A Sleepin' Bee," since all the arrangements had already been worked out. It was the first time Bob had ever heard Barbra sing. He was so impressed, so moved, that when they all decamped afterward to the Pam Pam for French fries and coleslaw, he'd been unable to speak.

Sgroi had been equally impressed, but he'd wanted to make sure this ambitious little tyro could actually work an audience. So he'd told Barbra to come back that night, where he'd slip her in as a "surprise guest" on the bill. In between numbers by comedian Larry Storch and the jazz trio the Three Flames, Barbra came out on stage to sing "A Sleepin' Bee" as well as one other song, a new orchestration that she and Barré had worked out. It was a strange, whimsical choice, and it was this song that she came out of the kitchen singing at her little concert in Barré's apartment. Carole Gister and the rest of the UCLA contingent were stunned. The song on Barbra's lips was "Who's Afraid of the Big Bad Wolf?" from the Disney cartoon *The Three Little Pigs*.

It had started as a joke. One day while rehearsing for the Bon Soir audition, Barbra had said she "wanted to do something completely wrong" and out of place for the "sophisticated, posh little nightclub." Sophistication "annoyed" her, she told Barré. She felt like going in there and singing "a nursery rhyme or something."

A bell went off in Barré's head. He knew part of the reason Sgroi

Jr. had recommended Barbra to his father was her irreverent style. So he located the sheet music for "Who's Afraid of the Big Bad Wolf?" in an old record shop, brought it home, and was stunned by how "double-entendre" the lyrics were. Barbra would sing them just as they were written, he decided, but with a little of her own razzmatazz.

That razzmatazz was evident from the moment she stepped onto the stage the night of her surprise tryout at the Bon Soir. As soon as the spotlight was on her, Barbra removed the gum she'd been chewing and stuck it on the microphone. It was something she often did during practice, and both Barré and Bob had suggested she keep it in the act. As they predicted, the audience howled with laughter. Barbra would tell people she'd forgotten the gum was in her mouth, but that, too, was part of the act, part of the saucy, impertinent stage persona they were developing. So when she capped her set with her sexy rendition of "Big Bad Wolf," the cheers went through the roof. "Kid, you are going to be a very great star," headliner Larry Storch told Barbra. Right on the spot, Sgroi hired her for a two-week run starting September 9 at $108 a week.

For the crowd in Barré's apartment, "Big Bad Wolf" went over just as well. Barbra bounded throughout the living room, looking into the faces of each person present, trilling lots of tra-la-las and rolling her r's. "Forrrr the big bad, very big, very bad wolf, they did not give three figs!" Her voice was full and rich and utterly confident. But after she was finished and her friends all applauded, she covered her face with her hands and blushed a deep scarlet.

She was uncomfortable with their acclaim. Singing just came too damn easy. "It just seems the right sounds come out of me in the right way," she said. Barré thought singing came so effortlessly for her that Barbra "didn't consider it valuable." At the end of the night, as people filed out of the apartment praising her voice as a "gift from God," Barbra's attitude in response was "Well, yeah, but that's not what's important." Her voice wasn't anything that she had worked on or studied for. To become an actress, she'd worked very, very hard, harder than she'd ever worked for anything else. But when she sang, Barré said, it was as if she were "on automatic pilot."

He remained convinced her voice was her ticket to the top, however, and he tried to persuade her of the same. She wanted to be successful, didn't she? She wanted to find a way to beat all those agents who wouldn't take her on at their own game, didn't she? She wanted the whole world to know who she was, didn't she?

Barré pulled her close to him on the couch and kissed her forehead. "When you make your first record, promise you'll let me produce it." She nodded against his chest. "Promise?" he asked again, lifting her chin so he could look her in the eyes.

She returned his smile. "Cross my heart," she said.

6.

Transistor radios all over the city were blaring the summer's number one hit "Itsy Bitsy Teeny Weeny Yellow Polka Dot Bikini" as Barbra lugged the last of her stuff out of Fifty-fourth Street and downtown to Barré's via the hot and sweaty subway. Likely this was one of the times she dreamed about a future as a successful actress being "chauffeured around" the city. But for now, Barbra hauled her bags herself across the stifling subway platform then up the grimy steps to Sheridan Square.

By now, the concierge of Barré's building knew her; the guy who ran the elevator greeted her by name. Since returning to Manhattan from her two-week run in *The Boy Friend*, Barbra had been living with Barré. His friends now officially considered them a couple. The only person who didn't know they were together was Barbra's mother, who thought Barbra was living with a girlfriend. But Cis was pleased to see Barbra looking and acting so happy for a change, even if, as was Barbra's custom, she kept most of her friends separate from each other. Barré had met Cis only once, briefly at the Lion, despite Barbra's describing her as her "best friend."

The Boy Friend had enjoyed a good run. Audiences had applauded heartily for Barbra as Hortense, even if one of the other members of the company had quipped that if Hortense's accent was French, it was "French from the moon." Hortense had one number in the show, "Nicer in Nice," which everyone agreed Barbra sang humorously and energetically. But in her spare time she could be heard out back practicing "A Sleepin' Bee." She'd come to understand that the Bon Soir gig was vitally important. Barré might pontificate about her voice being her ticket to fame, but Barbra saw other reasons to anticipate her appearance at the Bon Soir. She knew that some of the city's most influential columnists were likely to be in the audience. A blurb from one of them would be extremely helpful in getting casting directors to take her seriously for parts on Broadway.

She'd had fun playing Hortense — she was an actress, after all, and needed to act — but Barbra was glad to be back in the city, gladder still to be back with Barré, hunkered down in their intimate little practice sessions. Barbra loved Barré's apartment, loved calling it home even more. Even if she could have decorated it herself, she wouldn't have changed a thing. The place evoked a nostalgia for past decades, especially the Gay Nineties and the Roaring Twenties. Theatrical posters hung on the walls; a ventriloquist's dummy was propped in a corner. Bookshelves were crammed full with old volumes and record albums, ornamented with fans and feathers. In the evenings, Tiffany lamps cast a soft amber glow over everything. Sitting cross-legged on the slipcovered Victorian couch, happily ensconced among Art Nouveau and Art Deco, Barbra seemed more at home here than she ever had anywhere else.

The summer was rapidly drawing to a close. More sunshine than people filled the Village streets, the usual throngs having decamped to Jones Beach or Fire Island for the long Labor Day weekend. But for Barbra and Barré, there was no such holiday. Less than a week stretched between them and Barbra's opening at the Bon Soir. As they settled down in their living room for some last-minute polishing, they both hoped Barbra hadn't forgotten too much during her two-week sojourn in Fishkill. Setting the needle down on the phonograph, Barré began singing the words to a song they'd been practicing almost nonstop since Barbra had returned, "Lover, Come Back to Me." It was a Sigmund Romberg ballad from the operetta *The New Moon,* the same show from which Diana had chosen "One Kiss" when she and Barbra had made their records at the Nola Recording Studio. The words to "Lover, Come Back to Me" were simple, but one line had continually given Barbra trouble, leaving her tongue-tied: "When I remember every little thing you used to do . . ."

Maybe it was the idea of remembering things that tripped her up. Barbra rarely looked back and kept her eyes securely on the future. Whatever it was, the line always stopped her cold, and she developed what Barré called a "psychological block." She insisted that she wanted to scrap the song from the act, but Barré argued it was too good to cut. They'd given it a faster beat, and when she got going on it, Barbra could drive the song "like a freight train," Barré told her.

So he'd suggested that she not worry so much about the words. When she started to sing, he advised, she should think about his wet socks hanging in the bathroom, one of his habits that had driven her crazy since moving in. Smiling, Barbra agreed to give the technique a try. Now, as she sang along with Barré, she nailed it. They both let out whoops of triumph when they were finished.

Up went the needle and another disk dropped onto the turntable. This time it was "Nobody's Heart" from the Rodgers and Hart musical *By Jupiter.* In the show, the song was sung by the tomboyish Amazon warrior Antiope, a misfit in the world of men: "Nobody's heart belongs to me, heigh ho, who cares?" The emotion behind the words, Barré believed, came from the misery of lyricist Lorenz Hart's own unhappy existence as a repressed gay man. Barré suggested that Barbra perform it very personally in order to make people believe she was singing about herself: "Nobody's arms belong to me, no arms feel strong to me." The irony was that for the first time in her life, Barbra felt loved by a man. But she understood all too well what loneliness felt like — and she'd benefit if waves of sympathy came at her from the audience, Barré argued. The misfit girl who wants to be loved had always been a successful character on stage and in movies.

Any pathos in Barbra's stage presence, however, needed to be quickly offset by an even stronger sense of resilience and grit, and the next record that dropped onto Barré's phonograph offered the necessary balance. By now Barbra had become very familiar with the Bronx-accented voice of Helen Kane, a popular singer of the Roaring Twenties and the inspiration for the cartoon character Betty Boop. As soon as she recognized Kane's music, Barbra wrapped one of Barré's feathered boas around her shoulders and started to sing along with the record: "I wanna be kissed by you, just you, and nobody else but you, I wanna be kissed by you, alone . . . boop boop a doop!"

But as he listened to her sing it, Barré nixed the song. It might have made a fun little addition to Barbra's act, he said, but it was "too well-known to be surprising" and would probably just sound "camp and precious" if Barbra sang it at the Bon Soir. So they settled on a less familiar Kane tune, "I Want to Be Bad." Rehearsing the song that Labor Day weekend, Barbra was the perfect reincarnation of Kane, a mix of sex and silliness with an overlay of New York character: "If it's naughty to rouge your lips, shake your shoulders and shake your hips, let a lady confess, 'I want to be bad!'" When she finished singing, Barbra took her bows to her enthusiastic audience of one.

But the most important lady that Barré kept playing for Barbra that weekend was one who had no song in the Bon Soir lineup. From the phonograph came the creaky voice of Gertrude Lawrence, the eccentric musical-comedy star of the 1920s and 1930s, singing the songs of Cole Porter. When Barbra had first heard Lawrence, her reaction had been similar to her opinion of Mabel Mercer: "She can't sing." But as he had done the night at the Roundtable, Barré told her to listen to Lawrence's voice "through the squeaks and the faulty pitch." What they were working on was style and presence. Gertrude Lawrence was the "quintessence of vulnerability," Barré explained, who, despite her less-than-mellifluent voice and rather plain appearance, made "every man in the audience think she was singing only to him." Barbra asked how she was able to do that. "It's called acting," Barré told her.

During that summer of 1960, Barbra came to understand that when she sang a song, she was as much an actress as a singer. "If I can identify as an actress to the lyric and sail on the melody," she realized, "it will be me." The actual singing came easy. But the emotional backstory that went into the song required all the skills she'd been sharpening for the past two years at the Theatre Studio. So "Lover, Come Back to Me" became a miniature play about a woman who wanted to hang on to the love of her life, "Nobody's Heart" the story of a homely girl who's never known love, and "I Want to Be Bad" the chronicle of a girl finally set loose on her own to live her life as she pleased. All of them were aspects of herself, and Barré told her to make sure her audience saw that.

No doubt somewhere in that cluttered apartment there was a clip of the August 21 edition of *Flatbush Life,* a Brooklyn newspaper that her mother had saved for her. Cranking out press releases for *The Boy Friend,* the Theatre Studio had made sure one of them reached the city desk of Barbra's hometown paper. The photo of herself that looked up at Barbra was one she had come to despise — with her rather pretentious dangling earrings and her hair piled up on her head. But the headline compensated for any disdain for the photo: FLATBUSH ACTRESS HEADS FOR STARDOM. The article, probably lifted verbatim from the press release, noted her work on stage in *The Insect Comedy* and *The Boy Friend,* as well as her upcoming appearance at the Bon Soir. If Barbra needed any affirmation — and occasionally, despite her fervent belief in herself, she did — there it was, spelled out in black and white. Barbra Streisand was "headed for stardom."

Barré and Barbra had taken a break from their rehearsals and were sharing a BLT when the intercom buzzed. It was Bob, and Barré told him to come up. When Bob entered the apartment, he saw Barbra nibbling on the sandwich while Barré still held it in his hands. On the phonograph floated the strains of Ralph Vaughan Williams's elegant piece for violin and orchestra, *The Lark Ascending*. Walking into this happy little love nest, Bob was unprepared for what he was about to discover. "Hey, Bob," Barbra purred. "Guess what?"

"What?" he asked.

"Barré and I are talking about getting married."

Bob was stunned. Barré and Barbra as a married couple was a concept he had a hard time "getting his head around." Carole Gister, when she heard the news a short time later, had a similar reaction. For all his claims of bisexuality, Barré was essentially attracted to men, and both Bob and Carole knew it. They thought Barbra did as well. "They're going to have to work very, very hard to make a marriage between them succeed," Bob thought to himself.

Yet he dared not articulate such misgivings to the dreamy-eyed lovebirds who sat shoulder to shoulder on the couch, eating from both ends of a BLT, the hypnotic sound of the violin from *The Lark Ascending* wafting through the living room.

7.

A bit of a heat wave had settled over the city on the night of Friday, September 9. Temperatures that day had reached the high eighties and hadn't dropped much since the sun had set. Summer wasn't quite ready to release its grip on the city. Yet there was a sense that things were about to change. At that very moment, Hurricane Donna was lashing the Florida Keys, on target to swipe the entire eastern seaboard in the next few days. She'd bring torrential rain, massive flooding, and powerful gusts.

But Hurricane Donna wasn't the only thing about to hit New York.

With careful steps in her white buckled shoes, Barbra headed out of her apartment and onto Sixth Avenue, Barré and Bob in tow. For her debut at the Bon Soir, she wore a long black dress under a Persian vest of silk brocade that Terry had found for her in a boutique on Ninth Avenue. Female nightclub performers were expected to wear evening gowns, she'd been told, but both Barré and Bob had felt that

Barbra needed to dress to make a statement, to assert the quirky individuality that had set her apart at the Lion. So she buttoned herself into the vest and slipped into the 1920s-era shoes with the big buckles. Her eyes were ringed with Bob's signature two rows of false eyelashes, and her cheeks and lips were painted in homage to Helen Kane and other ladies of the period.

The decade they'd just completed, all three agreed, had been dull and boring. "The twenties and thirties were where the real excitement was," Bob insisted, and they hoped the sixties might have a little of those earlier decades' style and polish. With Barbra's closet full of vintage clothing and shoes, Bob's assortment of old fashion magazines, and Barré's collection of classic recordings, they'd been able to evoke the glamour of the past while making it all seem fresh and new. Barbra had slipped into the persona of a saucy Roaring Twenties chanteuse as easily as she had that vintage black dress. As Barré lugged his heavy Ampex tape recorder behind her, the onetime misfit from Brooklyn strode confidently through the streets of Greenwich Village, looking as if she'd just stepped out of the pages of *Harper's Bazaar,* circa 1925.

The Village was teeming with eccentric, creative types like Barbra who dressed in fashions that, to the rest of the world, seemed outré, but here along these crooked and narrow streets were deemed trendsetting and cutting-edge. The Village was in the midst of a cultural renaissance, or so claimed the *New York Times,* "once again throbbing with talent" in a way not seen since the post–World War I era of the Provincetown Players. "Box offices are busy," columnist Dorothy Kilgallen noted as the season got underway. "Taxis are spinning around Manhattan full of people pleasure bent."

Many of those taxis were heading to the Village, where this new phenomenon called "off-off-Broadway" was coalescing. No longer was theater the sole province of Midtown. Now it could be found "tucked behind a façade of food and drink," one critic remarked, a popular alternative due to "the felicitous marriage of the muse and booze." And while clubs like the Bon Soir had been around for a long time, with some insisting they were past their primes, the new energy flowing into the Village signaled a "rebirth," a sense of "florescence" that Barré believed was centered in the supper clubs. To Barré, it all seemed a replay of the glory days of André Charlot's revues of forty years earlier, when Beatrice Lillie, Gertrude Lawrence, or Jessie Matthews sang the songs of Noël Coward.

What was more, the young performers dancing and singing in revues across Village stages were exceptionally talented, people such as Beatrice Arthur, Charles Nelson Reilly, and Dody Goodman. One could wander through Village cabarets and catch a young actor named George Segal playing tunes from the 1920s on a banjo, or a sarcastic comedian named Joan Rivers (who'd played with Barbra in that attic production of *Driftwood*) kvetching about men, or an amiable Englishman named Dudley Moore playing the piano downstairs at the Duplex. All of them were in this together, Barré believed, and any one of them had as good a chance as any other of becoming a star in the fertile proving ground of the Village.

Rounding the corner onto Eighth Street, Barbra and her boys found themselves in front of the Bon Soir. Down the thirty-one steep steps they went, Barbra slowly and deliberately in her high heels. It seemed as if they were descending into a pit of darkness, for the only light flickering below came from a single shaded bulb over the cash register. The walls of the Bon Soir were painted jet black. People in the club moved as if they were shadows.

Terry was there to greet her, throwing his arms around her and finding her "a bundle of anxious energy." She had reason to be anxious. Entertainers in nightclubs faced challenges unthinkable elsewhere. "Customers who jam the darkened, smoky rooms to eat and drink up their $3 to $7 minimums," the *Times* observed, "have a tendency to grow sulky if their funny bones are not tickled or their heartstrings tweaked at the rate of at least once every twenty seconds." When the pace lagged, hecklers took up the slack.

At the Bon Soir, Barbra had awfully big shoes to fill. Here in this small, dark club — a "refreshing blend of Greenwich Village bohemianism and East Side smartness and sophistication," one critic thought — some of the most exciting acts of the last decade had made their marks, many of them the "far-out females" for which the Bon Soir was famous. The cheeky ladies who played the club broke all the rules. The boisterous Mae Barnes, whose records Barré had played for Barbra, had become a sensation at the Bon Soir after dancing in all-black revues in Harlem. The brash-talking Sylvia Syms, who'd polished her bluesy style under Billie Holiday, had blown the roof off the joint a few years earlier, and Felicia Sanders, who made "Fly Me to the Moon" a standard well before Sinatra, regularly had patrons lined up out to the curb. The Bon Soir was a particularly good space for female performers, singer-actress Kaye Ballard thought, because of its small, intimate shape, but also because of "all the gay guys" who regularly patronized the club.

Ballard's shtick — lying on the piano and delivering her monologue as if the audience were up on the ceiling — had earned her a place in the club's hall of fame, but her record as the Bon Soir's biggest money-maker had been overtaken by the current headliner, Phyllis Diller, a crazy-haired housewife from San Francisco. Dorothy Kilgallen called Diller "the funniest woman in the world . . . a flax white blonde who comes out on the stage in a vaguely outrageous costume that might be chic on someone else, points a cigarette holder at the audience, and talks. When she talks, the audience screams. It's as simple as that." For all her wild hair and makeup, Diller was known as a clotheshorse, always wearing the latest designers — sometimes topped with a necklace of maraschino cherries that she'd eat, one by one, on stage. All this was done while taking potshots at her husband, whom she called Fang, and, most of all, herself. "Isn't my fur stole pitiful?" she'd ask the audience. "How unsuccessful can a girl look? People think I'm wearing anchovies. The worst of it is, I trapped these under my own sink." Then she'd let loose with her trademark fingernails-on-the-blackboard laugh — a gimmick that had originated from nerves, but which had stayed in the act after Diller noticed the laughs the laugh got.

When Barbra and her friends arrived, only a few customers were milling about the place. Sgroi emerged from the back office to greet her. Taking her by the arm, he escorted her to the women's dressing room. Diller frequently grumbled that the room was the size of a peapod and that she and her fellow performers were forced to change clothes "butt to butt." From a single window, a rusty old air conditioner dripped water into a bucket. Clothes hung from hooks on the wall since there wasn't room for a closet or shelves. When Barbra walked in, Diller was sitting on a stool threading her maraschino cherries. Sgroi introduced them, and Diller told Barbra she liked her unusual shoes. "They cost me thirty-five cents," Barbra replied. That was the extent of their conversation. Diller found the kid standoffish and deemed her way too young to be singing in a club.

Around eleven, the place started filling up and the band began to play. The Three Flames was a wisecracking piano, bass, and guitar trio who integrated the jive of the Harlem streets into their act. The Bon Soir was that rare place where blacks and whites mixed without tension and without rank, where three black guys from Harlem could share a stage with a white housewife from San Francisco and a Jewish girl from Brooklyn. On many nights a touch of class was provided by Norene Tate, a stately, silver-haired pianist who'd also played the Lion. The emcee was Jimmie Daniels, a Texan who'd sung in Parisian boîtes before the war. Always impeccably dressed and unfailingly polite, Daniels was famous for never uttering a bad word about anyone, a far cry from the often raucous acts he introduced. In the 1930s, he'd run an eponymous club in Harlem and was rumored to have been one of Cole Porter's lovers.

Around midnight, the Three Flames gave way to the comics Tony and Eddie, whose act consisted mostly of mime and sight gags, using wigs, false teeth, and prop weapons. In one bit, Tony played a patient and Eddie a doctor, with the recording of a coloratura soprano giving voice to Tony's pain each time he got a shot.

If Barbra had ventured to peer out from the dressing room, she would have discerned waiters weaving in and out among the tables carrying tiny flashlights in order to spot who needed refills. This produced a flickering, bouncing light that made the room seem, in the words of *New York Times* reviewer Arthur Gelb, "a-twinkle with glow worms." Gelb wasn't the only major newspaperman sipping vino and smoking cigarettes in the audience. Dorothy Kilgallen, one of the widest-read syndicated theater columnists, was out there, too. If the news made Barbra anxious, she could take heart that the Bon Soir's pianist that night was Peter Daniels, the same friendly Englishman she'd met back when she'd auditioned for Eddie Blum several months earlier and who'd helpfully rehearsed with her at his apartment on Riverside Drive in the days leading up to this night.

Finally, it was Barbra's turn to go on. Jimmie Daniels stood in the middle of the stage and introduced her as "a girl with a magical set of pipes." Suddenly the bright white spotlight swung across the stage and caught Barbra, already seated on her stool and staring directly out into the audience. It was her moment, and she was ready for it. The applause she received was respectful, though hardly the enthusiastic greeting bestowed upon the more familiar Tony and Eddie. Hoping to fill in the spaces, Barré and Bob leaped to their feet, cheering as loudly as they could, nudging friends to do the same.

Once the applause died down and Barbra was sure all eyes were on her, she slowly and deliberately removed the gum from her mouth and stuck it on the microphone. It was by now a well-practiced bit of shtick that won the hoped-for snickers. Still, the audience, including those hard-to-please columnists, didn't know quite what to make of the small girl in the spotlight with the queer shoes and absurdly long fingernails. She seemed both frightened and confident, her quivery smile revealing as much pluck as it did apprehension.

Barbra took a deep breath. Giving a nod to Peter Daniels, she launched into the first song of her set, Fats Waller's "Keepin' Out of Mischief Now." The little love ditty became a "sexy, playful, naughty" flirtation with the audience, just as she and Barré had worked out. The applause at the end was heartier this time, and sailing on a burst of adrenaline, Barbra segued into the song that had started it all for her. "When a bee lies sleepin' in the palm of your hand . . ." The audience was riveted. Cries of "Gorgeous!" were heard when she finished the song.

Barré was sitting on the edge of his seat, mouthing the words to each song along with Barbra while his Ampex tape recorder, off to the side, captured the music for posterity. Bob sat sketching Barbra as she sang, preserving the night in his own way with pen and ink. When Peter Daniels's piano introduction indicated it was time for "I Want to Be Bad," Barbra stood from her stool so she could move her body seductively to the words. The audience hooted and whistled. "She's killing them," Barré whispered. "They love her!" Three songs in, Barbra had them eating out of her hands — those lovely, exquisite hands that Bob watched in a sort of awe that night as they moved through the air with all the grace and precision of an orchestra conductor.

At the beginning of her fourth number, Barbra closed her eyes. For the sad ballad "When Sunny Gets Blue," Barré had told her to think about a classmate of hers back at Erasmus Hall who'd been even more of a misfit than she was. Picked on, lonely, the girl had elicited sympathy from Barbra, who would smile at her in the corridors. Barré had told Barbra to think of that girl when she sang the song, and so, drawing on all of her acting ability, Barbra stood on the stage, emotions exposed. This tender number was immediately followed by her bouncy rendition of "Lover, Come Back to Me," with the line Barbra had once found so difficult now flying "like a bullet," Barré thought. All those weeks of practice, of picturing his socks in the bathroom, had paid off.

Then came "Nobody's Heart," the perfect penultimate song for Barbra's set. As she and Barré had planned, the audience seemed to feel that she was singing about herself. How could they not? There she was in front of them, so small, so unusual, seeming so desperate for their approval, coming more alive with each round of applause. The lyrics seemed to fill in all the autobiography that had been missing from Jimmie Daniels's scanty introduction of her. She was a girl who'd been "sad at times, and disinclined to play, but it's not bad at times, to go your own sweet way." That's what people took away from hearing her. When, at the finish of the song, she dropped her chin onto her chest, the audience was on its feet, shouting "Brava! Brava!"

The spotlight swung back to Jimmie Daniels. "Miss Barbra Streisand!" he announced. As expected, the cries of "Encore!" began. With a smile and a wave of his hand, Daniels surrendered the stage again to Barbra. Back into view she charged, all five feet five inches of her, a hundred and fifteen pounds of determination, singing "Who's Afraid of the Big Bad Wolf?" She was suddenly transformed into a ringleader of merriment, letting her instinct take over in ways that even Barré hadn't expected. With "semioperatic swoops and shrieks," she bounded across the stage warbling the words that many people in the audience remembered from their childhoods. They laughed, clapped, and nodded their heads along to the familiar but utterly unexpected tune. Singing about the third pig, Barbra put her hands on her hips and spontaneously invoked Mae West: "Nix on tricks, I will build my house of bricks!" The audience roared its approval.

Barré was overwhelmed. He'd coached Barbra to think about Jean-Paul Sartre's play *The Flies,* which he called "an homage to madness," during her rendition of "Big Bad Wolf," but this was beyond anything they'd rehearsed. It was anarchic brilliance cooked up on the spot, one observer said, "almost like the Marx Brothers, if Groucho had been able to sing." To each pig she had bequeathed a different voice, and when the brick house stands firm and the wolf gets roasted in the fireplace, she let out a "triumphant roar." At the end of the song, Barbra fled the stage laughing hysterically, as if she were "being chased by the Furies," Barré thought. The audience, in his words, went "nuts."

Bob's reaction was quieter. He sat in a kind of stunned silence, remembering the time he'd seen Edith Piaf at the Biltmore Theatre in Los Angeles. No elaborate orchestration had supported the great French chanteuse. Piaf had relied only on the force of her voice and personality. Bob had wondered then why America had no Piaf of its own, why the best his country had seemed able to produce was Patti Page singing "(How Much Is) That Doggie in the Window?" Watching Barbra that night, alone on the stage working her magic without any props, without any major orchestration, Bob thought solemnly to himself, "This could be our Piaf."

Friends, of course, might be expected to imagine such heights for each other, but Bob wasn't alone in his response. Terry was once again in tears hearing Barbra sing. Carole Gister, also in the audience, was "blown away" by the fact that each of Barbra's songs had seemed like "a self-contained play." In her dressing room, Phyllis Diller had been drawn by the sound of Barbra's voice, and despite having been unimpressed with the kid in person, found herself getting goose bumps listening to her sing. It wasn't often that Diller had to take the stage with an audience still buzzing over the warm-up act.

Part of what the audience had responded to was Barbra's obvious awareness of, and proficiency with, the traditions of the stage. It hadn't just been West she'd invoked up there. She'd displayed the raw power of Piaf and sung her songs in the storytelling style of Mabel Mercer and connected with her audience as personally as had Gertrude Lawrence. She'd flirted like Helen Kane, belted like Mae Barnes, and smoldered like Ruth Etting. Yet the audience wasn't applauding any of those venerable ladies. Barbra was no imitator. When Mercer sang, she barely moved a muscle on stage, but Barbra had used her hands to dazzling effect. Lawrence's cadences had often induced cringes, but Barbra's euphonious voice had soared through the room mesmerizing her audience. The spontaneous combustion that had left Barré stunned and Bob speechless was the result of an inexplicable alchemy that had taken all of those influences, shaken them together, and conjured something entirely new. Something that called herself Barbra Streisand.

CHAPTER FOUR

Fall 1960

1.

Diana would have come earlier, she insisted to friends, but Hurricane Donna — "one of the biggest hurricanes ever to hit New York" meteorologists had called it — had prevented her from making the trip in from Brooklyn. The fact that the storm had been over for several days now, with sunshine and mild temperatures returning to the city, was not pointed out to Diana by her friends. They were just glad that she was finally heading into Manhattan, accompanied by Sheldon, to see Barbra sing at the Bon Soir.

Word had spread fast — even out to Brooklyn — that Barbra was a hit. Diana was aware of the reviews, even if she hadn't read them all. The *New York World-Telegram* had declared Barbra "the find of the year," praising her "range and power," her "natural gift for musical comedy," and her ability to handle "with aplomb the most meaningful of ballads." But it was Dorothy Kilgallen's syndicated column that had the most tongues wagging in Brooklyn. "The pros are talking about a rising new star on the local scene," Kilgallen wrote. "Eighteen-year-old Barbra Streisand never had a singing lesson in her life, doesn't know how to walk, dress, or take a bow, but she projects well enough to bring the house down." Diana's circle of friends were dazzled that somebody as well-known as Kilgallen — a panelist on the TV game show *What's My Line?* in addition to her newspaper duties — had even acknowledged such a neophyte.

Most people overlooked the mild criticism of Barbra's unpolished presentation that was imbedded in Kilgallen's review, but Diana had keyed right into it. At least one of her friends suspected that, as she waited in line with Sheldon outside the Bon Soir, she was probably fretting over the fact that Kilgallen — always so elegant in her cocktail dresses and pearls on television — had declared to the world that Barbra didn't know "how to walk, dress, or take a bow."

Yet the fact remained that this teenage tyro had somehow managed to seduce everybody else who queued up outside the club that night waiting to see her. Barré had been extremely percipient. Barbra's audiences had conflated her lyrics with her life, no matter how manufactured that might have been, and taken her utterly into their hearts. As one reviewer observed, on stage Barbra displayed "a dynamic passion that tells the listener that this plain Jane is holding up a vocal mirror to her own life."

For most people, this presumption of autobiography, along with the sheer force of Barbra's personality, had been enough to smooth over the rough edges Kilgallen had identified. Critic Frank Judge thought Barbra might sometimes wander off pitch, but her audience was "too trapped by her bewitching theatrical interpretation of the song to notice." And if they did notice, like Kilgallen, they seemed not to care.

What finally won people over, however, was Barbra's own steadfast belief in herself, a quality that seemed to radiate from her the moment she stepped onto the stage. "Barbra believed she was beautiful," said Kaye Ballard, who'd snuck in one night to watch her. "She was thoroughly convinced of the fact. Me, when I started, I thought I was so ugly that I had to do comedy and *then* sing. Barbra knew right off she could do ballads."

At nine thirty, the doors of the Bon Soir opened. Diana and Sheldon made their way down the steep steps and found seats at one of the small tables crowded in front of the stage. It was unlikely that Barbra was even in the house yet. She was probably still out running around somewhere — running herself down and getting herself sick, her mother likely worried. Diana still fretted over her daughter, although she no longer schlepped into Manhattan with any regularity. She hadn't even seen Barbra's latest apartment or met her latest roommate. But whenever Barbra came home, Diana still made sure to load her up with groceries she could take back with her on the subway.

Shortly after ten, the Three Flames started to play. Diana and Sheldon watched as the comics came out and did their thing. Finally, close to midnight, Jimmie Daniels introduced Barbra. The spotlight found her and the slight teenaged girl burst into "Keepin' Out of Mischief Now." Diana shuddered. What was her daughter *wearing*?

To Barbra, it was a chic white-lace Victorian combing jacket, and her shoes the scarlet satin T-straps Bob had so admired. But to Diana she looked as if she had come out onto the stage wearing a nightgown and slippers.

Still, as Barbra continued to sing, Diana's distaste gradually faded. As her daughter skated gracefully from song to song, trading the campy lyrics of "I Want to Be Bad" for the touching sentiments of "When Sunny Gets Blue," Diana began to mellow. She watched Barbra closely. That was her daughter up there, receiving all that applause between each number. And Diana couldn't deny that Barbra deserved it.

Maternal pride, however, was no doubt mixed with another, less noble emotion. Later, when Diana returned to Brooklyn and told her friends about Barbra's performance, she seemed "just the trifle bit jealous," one friend said. Sitting there in the Bon Soir audience, was Diana imagining what it might have been like if she had gotten the chance to sing with the Metropolitan Opera Chorus all those years earlier, instead of being ordered to quit by her overbearing father?

During the break between the two shows, Barbra came out to see her mother. Barré stood in the wings, watching the interaction.

"What did you think, Mama?" Barbra asked.

"You were good," Diana told her.

You were good. For a second, Barbra seemed frozen. It seemed as if she had never heard such a sentiment from her mother before. She looked as if she might cry.

"Now, look, your clothes," Diana continued, shaking her head in horror. "You should let the world see you sing in your nightgown?"

"But you thought I was good?" Barbra asked.

Diana looked at her. For a moment there was something like compassion, or at least a truce, between the two women. "Yes," Diana said. "I thought you were good."

If anyone was hoping there might be an embrace, however, they were disappointed.

"Sometimes the voice was a little thin," Diana added, never knowing when to leave well enough alone. "Maybe you should see a vocal coach."

Back in Brooklyn, Diana bragged to her friends that Barbra had "all the big critics falling down on their knees in front of her." But never would she let her daughter know how proud she was of her. "It would just give her a swelled head," Diana insisted to friends. She still hoped Barbra would settle down with a steady job, grabbing what little security she could from a world that would crush her ambitions and break her heart, much as it had her own.

2.

It was supposed to be a day of fun, a break from performing, as Barbra and Barré rode a tandem bicycle downtown and then took the ferry to Staten Island. But something had gone wrong between them.

From the moment it was clear that Barbra was a hit at the Bon Soir, their lives had become, in Barré's words, "a series of manic ups and crashing downs." They veered between "hysterical fits of uncontrollable laughter to the black pit of . . . misunderstandings . . . arguments and screaming." Barré blamed it on "the bubble" they lived in, "a circumscribed universe . . . in which nothing else existed except what we were doing together: the creation of 'Barbra.'"

Pygmalion had grown resentful of his Galatea.

Friends noted that while Barbra was suddenly the sensation of Greenwich Village, Barré's success in *Henry V* just a couple of months earlier seemed utterly forgotten, and no new jobs were beckoning on the horizon. Barré might not have minded so much if Barbra had seemed genuinely thankful for all he'd done for her, but he took her growing distance from him as a lack of gratitude and an indifference to his place in her life. Try as he might, he "couldn't seem to let go" of the memory of how she'd missed his Central Park performance. It was always there, burning away, popping up in unexpected moments.

They stood looking out over the water as the sun dropped lower in the sky. Barbra was quiet. It wasn't just Barbra's usual self-absorption that was the issue. There was more going through her eighteen-year-old mind than Barré seemed to understand. Finally, looking across the blue water at the gray and copper skyline of Brooklyn, she shared a little of how she was feeling.

Too much good was happening to her, she said. And whenever that happened, she explained, whenever God saw her happy, he swooped down and — "boom!" — took it all away. Barré told her that was nonsense, but Barbra explained that was how she'd been brought up to think. "Whenever anything good happened," she told him, "my mother would dry-spit through her fingers." And she demonstrated the gesture for him as they stood on the pier.

Boarding the ferry, Barbra's contemplative mood only deepened. Sitting beside Barré on a wooden bench in the empty passenger room, the grinding of the ferry's motors serving as unpleasant background music, she dared to articulate at least one of her fears.

"So," she asked quietly, "what are we gonna do about sex?"

Barré was taken aback. "What do you mean, what are we gonna do about sex?"

"We ain't having any," Barbra said plainly.

It had been nearly two months since they'd last been intimate. Barré tried making excuses. They were both so busy, he said, so focused on her performance, that they simply didn't have the time or energy. But Barbra was smarter than that. She fell silent again as a cold wind blew off the East River. Barré put his arms around her to keep her warm.

She knew Barré's story, of course, but she blamed herself at least partly for the failings in their relationship—at least Barré thought she did. Barbra's belief in her own beauty and talent, so powerful and convincing on the stage, always seemed to dim in private moments such as these. She lamented that she'd never learned "feminine wiles." Growing up ignorant of the opposite sex, she'd never mastered the art of "manipulating men"—her own words—and she envied those women who had. For all her street smarts and stage presence, Barbra still felt she didn't know how to "sidle up" to a man or "sweet-talk" him. It was something she'd have to learn. But that day on the ferry, she was no doubt just waiting for God to move in and—boom!—take Barré away.

Once they arrived on Staten Island, the sun set completely. They turned around and rode the ferry back through the steely darkness, Barbra resting her head on Barré's shoulder. Neither of them spoke a word on the way home.

3.

The two of them together produced more noise than Grand Central Station during rush hour.

A flurry of silk scarves trailed behind Barbra and Phyllis Diller as they made their way across Union Square, their voices ricocheting through the park like competing bursts of gunfire. Pigeons took flight as the two women hurried toward the statue of George Washington on his horse, Phyllis's cackle rising up into the trees, where the leaves were just beginning to fade to yellow. That autumn day, the two friends, twenty-five years apart in age, "talked, talked, talked about everything under the sun," Phyllis said—money, managers, men, marriage. Everything except politics, as Phyllis learned when she asked Barbra what she thought about the recent presidential debate between Vice President Richard Nixon and Senator John F. Kennedy. On that subject alone, Barbra had no opinion to offer — because "the only politics she was interested in were the politics of how to get a job," Phyllis quickly realized.

On that score, Barbra was apparently learning fast. So successful had she been at the Bon Soir that Ernie Sgroi had just extended her run into November. At first, Barbra admitted to Phyllis, she wasn't sure if she should accept; nightclub singing drained her of the energy she needed to look for acting jobs. Phyllis told her opportunity could happen anywhere; after all, Phyllis had just finished playing Texas Guinan in a cameo for the upcoming movie *Splendor in the Grass* with Natalie Wood and Warren Beatty. And she'd gotten that job because of her nightclub work.

As they crossed Fourteenth Street, Phyllis told Barbra she should consider herself lucky that the club had renewed her contract. She shouldn't expect to coast by on luck and her fresh face and sound for much longer. Barbra's habit of showing up at the very last minute before she was set to go on was eventually going to work against her with the management, Phyllis warned. On a night not long before, Phyllis had waited anxiously for Barbra to arrive, while a grumbling, muttering Sgroi smoldered in his office. Finally Barbra had come skidding in with the explanation that she'd been at a movie and had to "wait to see all the credits." The applause that had followed her performance that night had momentarily assuaged Sgroi's pique, but Phyllis cautioned her young friend that it would come roaring back if she kept pulling stunts like that.

Barbra was never good at hearing criticism about herself. She'd go silent when Barré was sharp with her, turn a deaf ear to Bob or Terry, and had never put much stock in what her mother had to say. But for some reason, she didn't get defensive when Phyllis counseled her. Like Allan Miller, Phyllis was an older figure Barbra respected, someone who possessed qualities that she wanted for herself: knowledge, experience, expertise. So she was inclined to listen when Phyllis spoke.

The older woman, who had daughters not so far from Barbra's age, was another of those mother figures she was drawn to who showed her the kind of interest and regard that Diana never had.

That was because Phyllis understood what the kid was up against. Barbra was "just starting out . . . and when you're that young, everybody around you thinks they're an expert." Barré was always telling her how to sing, Bob how to dress. One of the Three Flames' girlfriends routinely camped in the dressing room to advise Barbra on fixing her nose and styling her hair. The first time the woman had started in on her, Barbra had looked up to catch a sympathetic glance from Phyllis. In that moment, the two of them had "bonded," Phyllis said.

It had been inevitable. "We're two of a kind," Phyllis told Barbra, "just two slightly unusual girls trying to make it in showbiz." With their offbeat looks, Phyllis figured she and Barbra "faced exactly the same kind of pressures." And so Phyllis had taken the teenager under her Chanel-draped wing.

They made their way into S. Klein's department store. Klein's sold clothes, dishware, toys, and furniture, and even offered a full-service pet department. At the moment, the store was pushing a sale on RCA color televisions "just in time for the World Series." Color television was something Barbra could scarcely imagine, but Phyllis hadn't brought her to the store to look at TVs. She hurried her across the polished wood floor toward Klein's "Fashion Annex."

The day before, Sgroi had approached Phyllis with a problem concerning Barbra that, in his opinion, was even more serious than her tardiness. "The little black lady in charge of the restroom," Sgroi told Phyllis, "overheard some of the ladies complaining about Barbra's outfits." The eavesdropping attendant had promptly rushed the tidbit to Sgroi, who came to Phyllis pleading, "Would you take Barbra out and get her some clothes she can wear on stage?" If the buzz about her sloppy appearance continued, Sgroi worried, it could stall her career — and hurt his ticket sales.

Phyllis took great umbrage at the suggestion that Barbra was "sloppy"; in fact, the teenager was fastidiously put together, Phyllis believed. It was just that she dressed in her own idiosyncratic style. Phyllis, in fact, thought Barbra "looked good in anything." She was "a real beauty," Phyllis thought, with "beautiful lips, sexy legs, all the right curves, those beautiful hands with those long nails." She told Sgroi he was a "crazy Charlie" for wanting Barbra to change her style.

But Sgroi was insistent. He flattered Phyllis by calling her "terribly chic," pointing to her wardrobe full of Chanels and Trigères. Sgroi pleaded with Phyllis to give Barbra a makeover. Predictably, the manager didn't offer to pay for it. But wanting to help out her young friend, Phyllis agreed to take Barbra shopping.

And so they embarked on a frustrating day of traipsing from boutique to boutique, trying on dozens of dresses. For Barbra, it was a world very different from the thrift shops she was used to. She despised department stores as a rule. They were "too dear," she said, and the salespeople "so unpleasant and haughty." Besides, they wouldn't bargain. It wasn't surprising that nothing caught Barbra's fancy on her outing with Phyllis. "None of this stuff is me," she said.

So it was on to Klein's. But it seemed that this, too, was a lost cause. Then Phyllis spotted the store's "Designer Room," which contained "original designs created by America's foremost 'name' fashion houses" — and all at S. Klein bargain prices between $39.99 and $150. Here, Phyllis hoped, was their answer. Slipping Barbra into what she called "the dress of the year" — a black knee-length Chanel she'd seen in *Vogue* and *Harper's Bazaar* — Phyllis stood back to admire her friend. Barbra looked gorgeous, Phyllis declared — sophisticated and all grown-up. Reluctantly, Barbra agreed to the dress, and Phyllis hurried to pay the cashier. It was getting late, and they had a show to do that night.

A few hours later, at the Bon Soir, Phyllis observed the dress hanging forlornly from a hook in the dressing room while Barbra buttoned up her usual antique thrift-shop garb. "I'll wear the dress tomorrow night," Barbra said. "I already had this all laid out. I'll wear the dress tomorrow. Or maybe on the weekend."

Phyllis just smiled. Nobody, she realized, told this kid what to do.

4.

At a little candlelit Italian eatery on Cornelia Street, the waiter asked them if they wanted a bottle of wine with dinner.

"I don't think so," Bob said. "She's performing in a couple of hours."

But Barbra insisted it was fine. She'd enjoy a little drink. There was talk up in Albany of raising the state drinking age from eighteen to twenty-one, so she might as well get it while she could. Besides, a night out with Bob allowed her to forget, for a little while anyway, the tensions with Barré and the stresses of the Bon Soir.

Sipping her wine, laughing as she twirled her spaghetti around on her fork, Barbra began to lament the "drudgery" of having to sing every night. She missed the old days when she and Bob — or Barré or Terry or Cis or any of her friends from the Theatre Studio — could just wander around the city, unrestricted by time. Now she had to be at the club every night by nine o'clock — though she often pushed it as late as she could, to nine thirty or even ten. Looking over at Bob and slurring her words ever so slightly, she told him she could not *wait* for this gig to be over. Then she surprised him by ordering another bottle of wine.

By the time they were rushing up Sixth Avenue in order not to be late to the club, Barbra was tipsy. Bob watched uneasily from her dressing room as she headed out onto the stage when Jimmie Daniels called her name. "Keepin' out of mischief now," Barbra sang. "I really am in love and how . . ."

She seemed okay, and Bob breathed a sigh of relief. But it wasn't long before he began to notice a couple of missed lyrics. Anxiously he stood and peered out at Barbra from the wings. She wasn't messy or slurry, but she wasn't the disciplined creature she usually was out there. Her timing was off, just by a fraction, but it was enough to cede control of the show to her audience. When people began singing along with her and clapping their hands to the beat, Bob knew she had lost them. They were having fun, but this audience would not leave the club enthralled as their predecessors had, telling their friends that they just *had* to get down to the Village to see this girl. Tonight Barbra had not been extraordinary. Bob felt she had "broken the illusion."

Afterward, he told her plainly, "We shouldn't have had the wine. That was a bad show, Barbra."

She reacted angrily. "They come to see me. Whatever I do, that's what they get."

But Bob could tell she was troubled. He hadn't needed to tell her it was a bad show. She'd known it, even if she wouldn't admit it.

Barbra stewed. She kept insisting she'd been fine, that Bob was overreacting, that the audience had been pleased, that it was her show and she could do it any way she wanted to. This damn singing business was taking away her life! But for all her defensive blather, never again did Bob see her take a drink before a show.

5.

Heading into the dressing room, Phyllis noticed that the black Chanel dress, which had been hanging on its hook for days, was now wrapped in paper and placed in a box.

She turned to see Barbra hovering nearby, unusually timid.

"Phyllis," the girl asked, "would you mind very much if I took that dress back and bought fabric instead and used it to make a dress that I design myself?"

Phyllis looked at her. How sweet the kid was for worrying that she might hurt her feelings — or maybe, Phyllis thought, Barbra was just worried she'd "blow a gasket," since Phyllis had paid for the damn thing. No matter what motivated Barbra's timidity, Phyllis just smiled at her.

"Of course, baby," she said. "In fact, that's exactly what you *should* do."

Barbra beamed.

Phyllis had no idea if the kid would make it in showbiz. It was a tough racket, after all. But even more than talent, which she had in spades, Barbra had something else, Phyllis thought. She had the courage to be herself — which would either boost her to the top or keep her forever on the bottom. Watching the kid head back to Klein's, the dress tucked under her arm, Phyllis figured if she had to bet, she'd lay odds with the former.

6.

Tonight Barbra was on fire.

"Every note was perfect," said the man who was sitting in the front row looking up at her, impressed and surprised by this ungainly neophyte. "Every move she made, every gesture, every lift of her eyebrows was on target."

The man's name was Ted Rozar. His broad-shouldered, six-foot-plus frame was barely contained in the small chair on the Bon Soir floor. An entertainment manager by occupation, Rozar had come down to the Village that night to see his client, comedian Paul Dooley, who'd taken over from the departing Tony and Eddie. Dooley was performing material written by another of Rozar's clients, David Panich. At Rozar's side was a third client, Orson Bean, who had told him before the show began that this Streisand kid was a "knockout." But Rozar hadn't expected to be as impressed as he was.

It was an exciting period all around. Just ten days before, John F. Kennedy had been elected president. The air vibrated with newness, change, and youth. Maybe some of that came through in Barbra's performance that night. Yet what lifted her up most was the review she had long been waiting for, which had just been published days earlier.

"A startlingly young, stylish and vibrant-voiced gamine named Barbra Streisand is one of the pleasures of a club called the Bon Soir,"

Arthur Gelb had written in the *New York Times*. "[Patrons] seem to enjoy the way she sidles up to a microphone and gargles love songs into it in Spanish, French and broken English."

Gelb was the same reviewer who had given Barré a mention that summer. And now Barbra had gotten her own name in the *Times*, with considerably more ink than Barré had received.

What's more, Gelb hadn't just liked her voice and her banter (lately she'd been throwing out a few phrases in other languages, including Yiddish). He'd also called her "stylish." Barbra took great satisfaction from that. So much for those bluenoses in the ladies' room who'd made disparaging remarks about her clothes.

Ted Rozar thought she was perfect. Everything about her — "her voice, her look, her way with the audience" — was "superb." Leaning over to Bean during the applause, he whispered that Barbra was a cross between Eydie Gormé and Lily Pons. He said he wanted to represent her.

So, after the show was over, Bean took Rozar backstage.

"Barbra Streisand!" Rozar called out in his big, booming, deep-throated voice. She couldn't have avoided him even if she'd wanted to. Rozar's giant frame towered over her and he took her face into his large hands. She looked up at him with wide eyes.

"Barbra Streisand," he repeated. "I love you."

And with great dramatic flair, he kissed her on the cheek.

"My name is Ted Rozar. Do you know who I am?"

She said she did. Orson Bean had already filled her in.

"Do you have a manager?" Rozar asked.

Barbra replied that she did not. Her voice was small, wavering, unsure of this giant who still held her in his grip.

"I'd like to manage you," Rozar said. He explained that he'd been an agent at MCA before going into management at Bean's request. He was building "an impressive roster," he told her, and wanted to add her to it.

"Will you hang on a minute?" Barbra asked, slipping out from Rozar's grip and scrambling into the Bon Soir's kitchen to call Barré.

When she got him on the phone, she told him he had to come over. Right away.

Barré was there in less than ten minutes. Taking one look at Rozar, he thought he was "the whitest white man" he'd ever seen. Rozar had long blond hair that was combed straight back from his forehead and a "blazingly white smile" that made Barré think he might have to shield his eyes. Indeed, Rozar distinguished himself in a field predominated by Jews by calling himself "the only Gentile in the business." Wary of him for some reason, Barré nonetheless suggested they head over to the Pam Pam to talk.

As they slid into a leatherette booth, Rozar was already pitching. "I think we can make great music together," he was telling Barbra.

Barbra stared over at him. She wanted to *act,* she said, not just sing. "Absolutely," Rozar said. "You should do it all."

The coffee and pastries were on him, he said, which won him some points in Barbra's favor. In fact, he told her, all of her meals would be on him when they were together. He'd only let her pick up the tab, he said, when she hit it big. Then, he said, "you can take me to dinner."

Barbra listened as Rozar promised to promote her for not just club dates and record deals but theater and television as well. She'd need an agent, and he could help her find one. Barré looked over and saw Barbra's mind whirling. She seemed on the verge of saying yes and signing with Rozar right then and there, but suddenly she backed off. She had to get back to the club for her second show, she announced. She told Rozar she'd have to think about it for a while. He gave her his card. "Please, please, call me," he implored.

Barbra said she'd give his offer some consideration.

Out on the street, when they were alone, Barré asked Barbra what she thought.

It was clear she was enticed by the promises Rozar had made. Theater. Television. That meant acting, she said, not just singing. But there was something about the manager's blond all-American good looks that had left her uneasy. Could he really understand her? Did he really, honestly *get* her? "He's such a goy," she said at last to Barré, and they started to laugh. They laughed all the way back to the club, walking arm in arm.

It was a rare moment of levity and connection between them these days, and both of them made sure to relish it.

7.

Less than a week later, on November 23, Barbra signed with Ted Rozar. They agreed on a three-year contract, with Rozar taking ten percent if she made less than $350 a week, and twenty percent if she earned more. With his assistance, she had just signed with an agent as well, Irvin Arthur of the Associated Booking Corporation, who'd briefly run the RSVP nightclub and kept Mabel Mercer employed. Associated Booking had represented Billie Holiday until her death in 1959 and currently helmed the careers of Louis Armstrong, Dave Brubeck, and about "ninety percent of jazz's top stars."

And this — *this* — was where they booked her.

From the little raised stage in the dining room of this "family" hotel somewhere deep in the fir forests of the Catskill Mountains, Barbra did her best to win over her audience, an assemblage of senior citizens who looked and sounded an awful lot like her grandparents, aunts, and uncles. They were far more interested in discussing the lackluster menu offerings and the pinochle games they'd played that afternoon than listening to the little girl who'd gotten up to sing. Barbra trilled the first strains of "A Sleepin' Bee," but the audience kept right on talking. Rozar, who sat with his wife and Barré at a table near the back, finally stood and asked people to quiet down, waving his long arms and big hands. But it did no good. People just looked at him, perhaps wondering why this blond *meshuggeneh* goy was making so much noise.

Driving back to New York after the show, Rozar told Barbra that she shouldn't be discouraged. Lady Luck was an unpredictable dame. When he was eighteen years old, he told her, fighting in the Korean War, he'd parachuted from an airplane and broke his back, spending nine months in a Stryker Frame as his spinal cord healed. That turned out to be "the luckiest thing that ever happened" to him, he said, because it allowed him to count his blessings. He could still see, hear, feel, think — and that deep belief in himself had allowed him to walk again. "It's all in the attitude," he said, puffing on his cigarette.

No doubt Barbra felt that her new manager wasn't telling her anything she didn't already know. She'd been carrying plenty of attitude ever since she was twelve years old. But attitude was nothing without instinct, and her gut was telling her she was off to a bad start with Rozar. Barbra did not want to make a career singing in clubs and resorts. She thought she had made that clear. Nearly all of her acting-school classmates were practicing the craft they'd spent years — and buckets of blood, sweat, and tears — honing at the Theatre Studio. Carl Esser had just opened in *Whisper to Me* off-Broadway after spending the summer touring with Hans Conried in *Not in the Book*. Even Barbra's old boyfriend, Roy Scott, was currently in rehearsals for *Montserrat,* a revival of Lillian Hellman's adaptation of Emmanuel Roblès' play. Everybody was acting, it seemed.

Everybody except Barbra.

8.

Barbra sat very still, chin in the air, eyes looking upward. Determined to get out of the advertising game and make his living as an artist, Bob needed a sample portrait for his portfolio, and Barbra, he insisted, with her swan's neck and aquiline nose, was an ideal model. The flattery won her over, and she'd agreed to sit for him. After all, there wasn't much else going on for her these days. Since the disaster in the Catskills, not a single job offer had come her way. Calling Irvin Arthur every day had produced the same answer: "Sorry, nothing." So she spent her days perched up on a stool, striking a pose like a queen, while Bob drew her with his charcoal pencil. But as much as she enjoyed playing artist's model, Barbra's mind was a million miles away.

Or, to be more accurate, three thousand miles away. Not long after they'd returned from the mountains, Barré had flown to Los Angeles to visit his family for the week of Hanukkah. Even before he left, Barbra had started missing him. She'd bought him a book of French art to read on the plane and had slipped little notes into it every ten or fifteen pages. On one note she'd written that she knew it was tough living with her, but she promised that when Barré returned—and here he had to flip the note over to continue reading—it would get even worse! Barré had laughed reading it, just as he was sure she had intended him to do.

But it was her last note, slipped into the final pages of the book, that had contained as much vulnerability as Barbra ever let herself reveal—offstage, that is. In that last note, she wrote that she would miss Barré and that she hoped he knew she was with him in spirit. It was signed with "a small bundle of love."

Bob asked her to lift her chin a bit more.

Barbra complied. It was a very specific look that Bob was going for in his sketch. He wanted it to evoke the kind of drawings René Bouché did for *Vogue,* languid renderings of the rich and famous, people like Lady Astor and Elsa Maxwell and the Duchess of Windsor. For the sitting, he'd helped Barbra select a gorgeous Geoffrey Beene dress, one of those finds she'd snatched up at a thrift shop. As usual, he'd done her makeup, exaggerating her eyes with the now-standard double set of false eyelashes.

But something had been troubling Bob about Barbra's look, and it took this sketch to figure it out. Until then, she'd been wearing "very elaborate teenage hairstyles," usually with bangs and hairpieces and sometimes a ponytail. Bob arranged her hair simply, without any of the hairpieces, and instantly an entire new persona emerged.

For the first time, Bob thought, Barbra exuded a kind of "legitimate, mainstream beauty," sophisticated and mature. The Victorian combing jackets and Roaring Twenties buckle shoes, while stylish, had been more like costumes. Now, looking over at her, Bob thought she seemed to conjure Audrey Hepburn, gamine yet elegant, youthful yet sophisticated, delicate yet durable.

Out of the corner of her eye, Barbra managed a few peeks at herself in the mirror as she sat there on her stool. Bob thought she liked what she saw, discovering parts of herself she hadn't known were there. Without the romantic complication that existed with Barré, Barbra's friendship with Bob could be a safe haven from whatever else might be troubling her, and she seemed to confide in him things she revealed to no one else. One time they gabbed for a solid nine hours on the telephone, then, realizing they both had a hankering for ice cream, met up for a cone and talked some more. Bob had observed that Barbra didn't have a "tight group of friends" with whom she could take refuge and comfort. She still kept her friends distinctly separate and saw them one-on-one. Bob had never met Cis or Harvey Corman, for example, and while he'd met Terry Leong, he never socialized with him and Barbra.

Sometimes he wondered if the Barbra he knew was the same Barbra they knew. Did she share different parts of herself with different people? How many Barbras were there? Looking at her that day, as she sat on her stool appearing so comfortable in her newly created, cosmopolitan persona while secretly longing for a man who seemed increasingly unavailable, it would have been fair for Bob to wonder.

9.

Barré was coming home, and Barbra was beside herself with anticipation.

It had to be today, she reasoned. She'd mixed up the dates, expecting him the day before, and when he hadn't shown, she figured she'd been a day off. Barré had told her that he'd be gone for a week. Hanukkah was over by now. So it must be today.

She and Bob had prepared quite the welcome-home feast. The table was loaded with lox and bagels, cream cheese, olives, and smoked fish, all of Barré's favorites. The apartment was decorated with candles and flowers. When Barré hadn't shown at what Barbra was certain was his appointed time of return, she'd become worried. Maybe there'd been an accident, she said to Bob. A plane crash. She called the airline and was told that the flight from Los Angeles had touched down safely earlier that day. She couldn't phone Barré's parents' house to inquire if he was still there; Barré, like Barbra, hadn't told his family that he was living with anyone. Barbra was stymied.

Outside, it was snowing again. A blast of cold rain had rid the city of much of the snow and grime that had pocked its streets for the past week, but now another storm was blowing across the island of Manhattan. Temperatures were dropping close to zero. The weatherman said a bitter cold wave was expected to stick around straight through Christmas, which was almost upon them. Barbra worried some more.

Finally, close to midnight, she accepted the fact that Barré wasn't coming home this night either. It must be tomorrow, she told Bob. How could she have mixed the dates up so badly?

They ate some of the bagels and lox, fearful they'd spoil, and stuffed the rest of the food into the refrigerator. The next day, they took it all out once more and laid it on the table. The wait was on again. Barbra relit the candles, freshened the flowers. She and Bob sat in the living room on the slipcovered couch, under the fans and the feathers and the theatrical posters, beside the ventriloquist's dummy and the cabinets filled with Barré's collection of old record albums. All afternoon and into the evening they sat there, trying to make light conversation, trying to laugh about silly, inconsequential things, but Bob noticed how often Barbra's eyes flickered over to the door, how every sound in the hallway made her jump.

No Barré that night either.

Once again, they ate some of the food and refrigerated the rest. For nearly a week, they repeated the process, until there was no food left and all the flowers had wilted.

And still Barré did not come home.

10.

Barré finally returned to New York more than a week late. He walked into the apartment to find Barbra on the telephone. She didn't look up or say hello. "As cold as salted ice," he described her when she finally hung up, and it had remained that way between them for these past few days. Barbra was "fed up" with him, Barré realized, and he was fast becoming "just as fed up with her."

Barré knew that he had been wrong to stay so long in California without calling Barbra to explain. Sitting in his parents' living room, he had watched the weather reports of the cold wave barreling down over the Northeast. "What are you hurrying back there for?" his father had asked. "You got anything to go back to?"

Barré had told his father no.

Part of his behavior, he admitted, was an attempt "to stick it" to Barbra. After all, he'd spent the last nine months completely in her service. Everything they did—everything they talked about—was somehow related to her career, her ambition, her life. It was never about him, Barré felt. That was why he told his father he had nothing to go back to in New York. But surely his reluctance to return to the apartment he shared with his girlfriend also had something to do with Barbra's question: "What are we gonna do about sex?" It hung over Barré's head like the sword of Damocles.

Now he was back. And Barbra was having her revenge.

It was New Year's Eve. She'd left him alone in their apartment without telling him where she was going or when she'd be back. Turnabout was fair play after all.

As the hands of the clock drew ever closer to midnight, Barré sat in the apartment stewing. Yes, Bob had given him the details of how Barbra had waited for him, night after night, constantly hoping he'd walk through the door. But hadn't that been exactly the way Barré waited for her the night of his show in Central Park?

Finally he decided that he was not going to sit at home by himself on New Year's Eve.

Fifteen miles southwest, Barbra was feeling exactly the same way. She had sought out a girlfriend, one of those acquaintances she kept separate from Barré and Bob, and together they'd taken the ferry over to Staten Island. Barbra's companion had suggested they ring in the new year at a club called the Townhouse. Finding the manager, Barbra offered to sing a few songs if he paid her fifty dollars. Without any work over the last month, she was strapped for cash, and she'd learned that this voice of hers could be merchandized. The manager had no idea about her Bon Soir success, but since he was short an act, he agreed, and Barbra climbed up on stage.

The crowd liked her, but a few of them didn't much care for her friend, who was black. So, while Barbra was singing, the manager made a "cutting gesture" across his throat — "eight bars and off." Taking the cash, Barbra and her friend beat it out of there, no doubt glad to leave such a racist place behind.

It was in such a mood that Barbra returned to the apartment.

She walked in to find Barré having sex with a man, a light-skinned black man she didn't recognize. In that moment, the shocking truth of their nine months together suddenly came crashing down on her — a truth she had known, of course, but had done her best to block out of her mind.

When Barbra had fallen in love with Barré, she had just turned eighteen. He was her first love. She was young, innocent, and inexperienced. She had given Barré her body. When asked later if she remembered much about the night she'd lost her virginity, she'd say, "A lot, yeah." That was because she'd given Barré more than just her body; she'd given him her heart. She thought he had changed, that *she* had changed him. She had even allowed herself to imagine a future with him, going so far as to speak of marriage. Now her illusions were shattering around her like glass. The image of Barré and his lover seared itself into her brain. She would live with it, she'd admit, for the rest of her life.

CHAPTER FIVE

Winter–Spring 1961

1.

Sometimes the best way to heal a broken heart is to get out of town.

The streets of Detroit were a lot wider than those in New York, and Barbra missed the subway. But it was good to be away.

She almost hadn't made it. Hurrying with Bob to Penn Station, she had insisted she needed to stop at the drugstore first. Bob warned her that she risked missing her train if she did so. What could she possibly need at the drugstore?

"Toothpaste," she answered.

"Barbra," Bob told her, trying to be patient, "they have toothpaste in Detroit."

Now she was six hundred miles from New York, the farthest she'd ever been from home. She'd arrived in the Motor City alone, without knowing a soul. Irvin Arthur had finally landed her a gig, and the owners of the Caucus Club, a swanky supper club in Detroit's bustling downtown, had hired her sight unseen on the agency's recommendation. They'd arranged for her to stay at the high-rise, Venetian-styled Henrose Hotel on Cadillac Square. It was almost as if Barbra were a real star.

Yet her audiences at the Caucus Club these past several nights hadn't exactly been standing room only. The buzz from the Bon Soir hadn't traveled quite as far as Detroit, and the Caucus Club's lack of newspaper advertisements hadn't helped either. So now Barbra was undertaking something she'd never done before in her short career: a media blitz. To drum up some business for this unknown out-of-towner, the club's publicist, Ross Chapman, had booked Barbra on the Jack Harris radio show, which aired mornings on WJR at nine thirty. They'd taken a cab over to the studio together. Taking a deep breath to calm herself — in a few minutes, not just a few dozen people would be listening to her but a few *thousand* — Barbra headed inside the station.

Chapman had already given Harris a heads-up on what to expect. Barbra was "different," Chapman had warned him, and indeed, as the young woman walked into the studio, Harris had to agree. Barbra was wearing a bulky antique coat and, as often happened when she was nervous, was twitching noticeably. Not quite knowing what to make of this unusual-looking kid, Harris asked her, on the air, "How'd you get into the singing business, for goodness' sake?"

"Well," Barbra replied, her voice trembling, "I had no money . . ."

From behind her, laughter rose from the technicians and others in the studio.

" . . . and I entered a talent contest at a little . . ." Barbra hesitated. She couldn't exactly describe the Lion honestly for what it was. "A little joint," she finished.

It was the first time Barbra had been asked to tell her story in her own words. When Harris queried if she hadn't then gone on to perform at one of the bigger New York clubs, she seemed to find her footing by reiterating the talking point that Rozar had been pushing these past few weeks. She told Harris that, yes, indeed, from there she went on to the Bon Soir "for eleven weeks, my first professional engagement." No matter how she looked, eleven weeks at a New York club for an untrained singer was very impressive.

It already seemed like a long time ago. Soon after the new year,

Barbra had moved out of Barré's and into a hotel; she couldn't go on living in Barré's apartment with "all the cold-shouldering" they gave to each other, not to mention the heartbreak she carried around with her but didn't dare articulate. Thankfully a pal from the Theatre Studio, Elaine Sobel, invited her to move in with her temporarily at her place on East Thirty-fourth Street, near Second Avenue. In no time, Barbra had stuffed all her clothes and belongings back into a half dozen shopping bags and lugged them right over.

But even twenty-nine blocks was still too close to Barré, so it was with tremendous relief in early February that she learned Irvin Arthur had secured the Detroit assignment. The Caucus Club would pay her $125 a week, which was seventeen dollars more than she'd made at the Bon Soir. Barbra was pleased.

Yet from the moment she arrived in Detroit, it would have been difficult to miss the posters announcing the touring company of *The Sound of Music,* starring Florence Henderson, which opened at the Grand Riviera Theater the same week Barbra opened at the Caucus Club. Barbra, it seemed, had been destined for Detroit. If she'd won the role of Liesl, she would've arrived in the city this very same week, though under very different circumstances. She wouldn't have arrived alone, for one thing. She would have been happily ensconced within a company of fellow actors as she found her way through a city that was so very different from New York.

But while she fervently wished she was acting on a stage instead of singing in a club, at least she'd been impressed by the venue that had hired her. The Caucus Club was run by two brothers, Les and Sam Gruber, who also owned what was considered by many to be Detroit's finest restaurant, the London Chop House, directly across the street. The Chopper, as it was called, was a favorite spot for the barons of the city's auto industry, for whom special red phones were brought over to the tables so they might continue doing business as they ate their lunch or dinner. The Caucus, however, was a different animal altogether. It was a private men's club — a discriminatory policy Barbra surely found antiquated — though the entertainment in the back room, where she performed, was open to everyone.

Barbra's bohemian style didn't fit with the Grubers' regimented precision. The first day Barbra showed up, Les Gruber had looked at her bulky black turtleneck and black slacks and snapped, "Go back to your hotel and put on a dress." For Ross Chapman, "weird" was the only way to describe Barbra's appearance. The club's pianist, Matt Michaels, was more specific: He thought she looked like "a hippie." If Barbra's "thrift-shop couture" had encountered some criticism even in anything-goes Greenwich Village, it sure wasn't going to work in buttoned-down Detroit.

Even worse from the management's point of view was the fact that Barbra arrived knowing only a handful of songs. Under her arm she carried "a big stack of dog-eared music" — the songs she'd practiced with Barré and arranged with Peter Daniels. With only a few additions, she'd stuck to basically the same set for her entire run at the Bon Soir. But the Caucus Club was a very different kind of engagement, as she quickly discovered. A flushed Matt Michaels walked up to Chapman after running over material with Barbra. "My God, Ross," he said. "That broad only knows four songs."

She knew more than four, but Michaels's point was taken. Barbra was to do four spots a night at the Caucus Club; Chapman estimated she'd need at least eleven numbers. No one had expected her to arrive with such a limited repertoire. For her part, Barbra had naïvely assumed that she could just keep coasting along on what she knew. After all, she hadn't had Barré's help these past few months in expanding her song list.

For the first few nights, they determined, they could get by with "A Sleepin' Bee" and the rest. But in a very short amount of time, Chapman insisted, Barbra would need to add seven or eight numbers to her act. Could she do it? Looking him straight in the eye, Barbra replied, "I'm a fast learner." And so she and Michaels got down to work.

Matt Michaels, however, was no Peter Daniels, enchanted with the quirky young imp standing in front of his piano. To Michaels, Barbra looked like a witch — "All she needed was a broomstick" — and acted like one too. At twenty-eight, Michaels was a veteran musician highly regarded in Detroit, and he didn't take kindly to Barbra refusing his suggestions on how to arrange a piece or insisting he play the piano precisely the way she told him. Practicing in the ballroom of a nearby hotel, Michaels told Barbra that if she actually knew how to read music, he might take her demands more seriously. But when he offered to teach her, he discovered she had no interest in learning; he thought she was afraid to try. A "tough lady," Michaels told people when they asked about her. Throughout their time together, although he found it a "pleasure to accompany her," he never grew "particularly enamored of her."

It wasn't the first time Barbra's single-minded, unflappable dedication to her own way of doing things had come across as rude or self-absorbed. But there was a method, she believed, to her madness. While it was true that she couldn't read music, those eleven weeks at the Bon Soir — and probably that fiasco in the Catskills as well — had taught her what worked for her and what did not. On one of her first nights at the Caucus, Barbra had stunned Michaels by telling a talkative audience to "shut up." If she had to sing old ditties for a living, and not play Juliet, then she'd at least do it her way.

Working with her in that hotel ballroom, Michaels saw very clearly Barbra's intense desire "to be a star." Patrons had begun to comment on the delicacy of her hand movements on stage, an innate characteristic that had served her so well at the Bon Soir. But it was no longer spontaneous, Michaels discerned. He watched as Barbra stood "in front of a mirror four and five hours a day perfecting her gestures." Everything about herself needed to be fine-tuned, Barbra believed. Yet for all her drive and determination, Michaels doubted Barbra would succeed in the end. She just carried too much "belligerence" around with her, he thought.

Of course, that belligerence had always been Barbra's shield, a lesson absorbed from Diana. It was an attitude that enabled her to deflect criticism and refuse to take no for an answer. It also allowed her to ignore hecklers, which won Gruber's grudging admiration one night after he witnessed some patrons razzing her.

So the decision was made to get Barbra out talking to the newspapers and radio stations. Ross Chapman asked her to tell him a few salient facts about herself so he "could do a squib on her to hand out." To Chapman's frustration, Barbra had brought no publicity material with her from New York, not even any photographs. Chapman declared they needed to build her up, make her interesting, get people talking.

So she told him she was from Turkey, and Chapman dutifully wrote it down. If it seemed an odd lie, it wasn't really. Calling herself Turkish, one friend surmised, hinted at some embarrassment Barbra may have felt about "her appearance . . . [about] how Jewish she looked to everyone the moment she walked into the room." Such a thought, of course, was never raised with Barbra — her friend didn't dare — but the idea lingered, and there may have been something to it. Barbra would admit that when she told people she "came from Brooklyn," she assumed they got a certain "image" of her: "She must be *that* kind of performer," she assumed they thought, though she didn't explain just what "that" kind of performer was. Being Turkish, however, could explain away so much — the name, the nose — and it could turn being just a plain outsider into being an exotic one.

Chapman asked what other interesting nuggets she could tell him about herself. She said she'd taken belly dancing lessons once. That got written down too. He asked about previous work. Barbra likely enthused over the Theatre Studio and *The Insect Comedy* and *The Boy Friend*, but Chapman wasn't much interested in any of the acting credentials, undoubtedly to Barbra's chagrin. But he seems to have paid attention to her meeting with Eddie Blum and wrote that part down.

In the resulting press release that was cranked out on Chapman's mimeograph machine, the success Barbra had enjoyed in New York was hyperbolized with adjectives such as "phenomenal," "unprecedented," and "groundbreaking" — standard publicist jargon. It was effective enough to get a few bites from various outlets, and that was how Barbra, nervous and fidgety, found herself sitting with Jack Harris in front of a microphone, speaking haltingly to perhaps twenty thousand listeners in metropolitan Detroit.

But what wasn't halting was her rendition of "Right as the Rain," one of the songs she'd banged out with Matt Michaels over the last few days. When Harris turned the mike over to her and asked her to sing, the kid with the strange clothes and crossed eyes let loose with a voice that left everyone in the studio impressed. "Right as the rain," she sang, "that falls from above, so real, so right as our love . . ."

And out there in radioland, thousands listened and took note.

2.

By day Fred Tew was a PR guy for Chrysler, but at night he got to do what he loved best. Arriving at the Caucus Club, he was known by everyone. The Grubers clapped him on the back as a waiter brought over his regular drink. Being the Detroit point man for the entertainment trade paper *Variety* had its perks. Tew got to see every important new act or show that came through the city. So when he got a call from Ross Chapman telling him that the new kid at the Caucus was worth checking out, Tew was there. It was March 2. Barbra had been doing her show for about a week.

And in that week's time, a lot had changed. The media campaign had paid off. Many of those filing into the Caucus that night had heard Barbra on Harris's show, or on another radio program, *Guest House*, which also aired on WJR, at seven o'clock in the evening. Her little press junket had also included some print interviews with local newspapers. Once again, Barbra had made sure to point out that she was on her way to being an actress and that singing was just a temporary diversion. With such an attitude, it was easy to become even more cavalier with the facts. Everyone had bought the idea that she'd been born in Turkey. Now, to a *Detroit News* reporter, Barbra fibbed further that her name had always been spelled with just two a's. To a *Windsor Star* scribe, covering the Caucus for the Ontario city across the river, she created an imaginary happy family for herself: two parents living in Brooklyn and a ten-year-old sister who showed "great possibilities as a singer."

Much of what else was written about her in the local press also played a little loose with factual history, appearing to be largely lifted verbatim from Ross Chapman's press release. Detroit readers learned how Eddie Blum, "casting director for Rodgers and Hammerstein," had seen "such potential in the slender brunette with the sultry, dark eyes," and how Barbra's dramatic "success story" could be considered "as exciting as the Lana Turner soda-fountain legend." Old legends, after all, had a way of being recycled into new ones.

Taking his seat in the back room, Fred Tew waited for the show to begin. While *Variety* was hardly loved among showbiz types — its reviewers were notoriously tough, and Tew was no exception — it was certainly respected, being read by everyone in the business who mattered. A good review in *Variety* didn't stay local; it was read in New York and Los Angeles and everywhere in between. The same thing was true, of course, for a bad review.

Around Tew, the room was filling up. Whether the star attraction was there or not, however, was anyone's guess. What had become apparent, even in one week's time, was that Barbra's steely resolve to succeed was paired with an incongruent, distracted unprofessionalism. Just as she had at the Bon Soir, she was frequently late; at least once in the last week she'd taken the stage a full hour after she was scheduled — at eleven instead of ten. She explained that she couldn't get a cab, an excuse the Grubers wouldn't abide; walking from her hotel to Congress Street, where the club was located, took about five minutes. Yes, it had snowed a couple of days that week, but temperatures had averaged in the low forties. There had been no need for her to try to hail a cab.

One night, a bass player, who'd come in to work for free as a favor to the Grubers, grew irate as he waited for her. "I'm comin' in to play for nothing," he said when Barbra finally arrived, "and the least you can do is be on time." Barbra began to cry.

But her tears had no effect on her behavior. One young man, a local actor and a regular at the Caucus Club who'd gotten to know Barbra soon after she arrived in Detroit, thought her heart was "simply not into" singing for a living, and so she "dillydallied and went window shopping and wrote letters back to New York" before finally "realizing what time it was and making a mad dash" for the Caucus. No matter how hard she had worked to get ready for the gig, and she'd worked very hard; no matter how much she gave to her audience when she was onstage, and she gave her all; underneath, she wasn't "all that happy about the singing thing," her friend thought, "and that showed up as unprofessionalism."

Maybe knowing that Fred Tew from *Variety* was in the audience that night caused Barbra to be on time. Certainly the reviewer made no comment about her being late. When she came out on stage, Barbra received a hearty welcome. Tew found her "striking rather than beautiful, with a classic profile" emphasized by the "elevated hairdo" Bob had created for her before she left New York. Unlike so many others, including the Caucus Club proprietors, Tew had no problem with Barbra's wardrobe; he thought she dressed "simply but effectively."

But it was her voice that he came for, not her look. As her first number, Barbra had chosen the Gershwins' "Lorelei," from the 1933 musical *Pardon My English.* As Matt Michaels played the sassy opening few bars, Barbra began to sing. "Back in the days of knights and armor, there once lived a lovely charmer..." With gusto she got into the part of the sea siren who lured sailors to their death with her beauty. No doubt Tew's eyes grew a little wider as Barbra complemented the lyrics with "plenty of body action to capture interest," as he wrote in his review. Translated from "reviewerese," that meant she was "slinking her sexy little body all across the stage," said Barbra's actor friend, who was sitting only seats away. With utter confidence Barbra sang, "I'm treacherous, yeah, I just can't hold myself in check, I'm lecherous, yeah, I wanna bite my initials on a sailor's neck." Her facial expressions, Tew thought in his typically understated fashion, were "uninhibited and unusual" — which, according to Barbra's friend, meant that she was "mugging and flirting all over the place." In "Lorelei," she had found a great choice for an opening. The audience was hooting and whistling by the time she sang the last note.

It helped that she had made a number of friends in the last week, many of whom came back night after night to see her. Sitting with her after the show, taking day trips to the Institute of Arts, these folks wouldn't have recognized the tardy or "belligerent" girl described by Matt Michaels or others at the club. These people, like the actor friend who sat up front nearly every night, were bohemians, artists, and merrymakers — the "sociable downtown gang" as one writer called them — who responded to Barbra's offbeat charm. Bernie Moray, a furniture salesman, and Dick Sloan, a movie exhibitor, were self-described "bachelors about town" who took a liking to the young singer and invited her to join them for dinner one night at the London Chop House. When Les Gruber spotted her at their table, he pulled her aside for a lecture on his policy against fraternizing with clients in his restaurant. But that didn't deter the friendship. Moray and Sloan might have been a decade older than Barbra, but they loved her style, even offering "critiques" of her outfits. They found her naïveté absolutely endearing. "Do you know, Bernie," Barbra once remarked in wonder, "they change the sheets on my bed [at the hotel] every night!"

It was that more innocent Barbra who took over after the applause died down for "Lorelei." Softly she began to sing, "When a bee lies sleepin' in the palm of your hand . . ." Once again, her audience marveled at how easily Barbra could move from vixen to vulnerable. In moments such as these, when she sang numbers that seemed to expose the tender girl inside, it became possible to believe that her so-called belligerence might be explained by reasons other than self-absorption and ambition. The girl up on the stage — being critiqued and reviewed by *Variety* — had yet to turn nineteen. Her voice, however, demanded that she be accorded the respect of a much older performer, and she was being judged against people such as Judy Garland and Patti Page, not Annette Funicello, who was exactly Barbra's age and still being treated like a Mouseketeer. Just six months into her career, Barbra was already playing for adult stakes. And it could be daunting.

For all his frustration with her tardiness, Les Gruber found himself increasingly sympathetic to the pressures Barbra faced. In the privacy of his office, he encountered not just the demanding Barbra but the depressed Barbra as well, a teenager who wasn't sure that she was good, who was afraid she was disappointing him, and who was self-conscious about her looks, even if she pretended not to be. Gruber tried boosting her up as best he could. "You're great," he told her. "You're going to be great. It takes time." Obviously her talent had already trumped her tardiness, for Gruber had just given Barbra a new contract, extending her run through April and raising her salary to $150 a week.

But there was likely more to the "depression" Gruber witnessed than any of them knew. While Barbra was running around Detroit talking to radio stations and newspaper reporters, Barré's twenty-third birthday had come and gone. Barbra was a girl who missed nothing; she certainly knew what day it was. She was also someone who had the power to just "turn off people" who had hurt her, she said. So she made no call to Barré, sent no card. Back in New York, however, her friends were certain she was thinking about him.

For her third number that night Barbra sang "When the Sun Comes Out," but it was her fourth, "Cry Me a River" — the last before the audience's applause brought her back for an encore — that seemed to reveal what was really going on in her heart during that cold winter spent alone in Detroit. Vocally, it was her best, Fred Tew thought. That wasn't surprising, given how much feeling must have gone into the words.

"Now you say you're sorry, for being so untrue . . ."

When Bob heard her sing the song back in New York, it was obvious to him that she was singing about Barré. "All the anger and heartache, it was right there," he said. Often in the past, Barbra's songs had implied autobiography, sometimes calculatingly so. This time there was no need for calculation. The emotion was real.

"Come on and cry me a river, cry me a river . . ."

Deep breath.

"I cried a river over you."

The crowd at the Caucus Club was on its feet as Barbra headed backstage in tears.

3.

Bob had very specific instructions, relayed to him in an urgent telephone call from Detroit just a few days earlier. Barbra had ordered a pair of shoes — a very expensive pair of shoes — and Bob was to pick them up at Madame Daunou's salon on East Fifty-seventh Street and deliver them this afternoon to Studio 6B in the RCA Building. Barbra, it seemed, was coming home. And she needed the shoes for a very important gig.

She was going to be on *The Jack Paar Show.*

National television. Millions of people were going to see her. Except for Ed Sullivan, Paar was the biggest star-maker on TV. It had all happened rather suddenly — and quite serendipitously. Paar himself was on vacation; Orson Bean was scheduled to guest host. Ted Rozar pressed one client to help another, and so Bean had suggested to the NBC brass that Barbra, wunderkind of the Bon Soir, might appear on the show that coming Wednesday, April 5. Phyllis Diller was also slated to be a guest, so it would be perfect casting all around. NBC agreed, no doubt having read Fred Tew's *Variety* review, which had extolled Barbra's "natural talent." The network would pay her $320 to sing two songs, as well as cover all transportation costs from Detroit. It would be Barbra's first time on an airplane.

In the days leading up to the show, she'd been in a whirlwind, planning what she should sing and what she would wear. The first was not difficult: she knew "A Sleepin' Bee" front and backward, and she'd been practicing Harold Arlen's "When the Sun Comes Out" with Matt

Michaels, which would give her set some up-tempo balance. But her sartorial choices weren't quite as easy. She needed to wear something really striking for all those millions of television viewers, she told Bernie Moray, and as singular as her wardrobe might be, she felt there was nothing in her suitcase that quite did the trick. So she asked Moray if she might pilfer some upholstery fabric — burgundy damask, to be exact — from the furniture store where he worked. When he agreed, presenting her with several yards, Barbra set about designing a dress with the help of a local seamstress. For Barbra's second number, Moray persuaded a female friend of his to loan Barbra a simple black dress — a frock not unlike the one Phyllis had bought for her at S. Klein's and Barbra had returned to the store unworn.

There was also the matter of her shoes. To Barbra's way of thinking, it didn't matter that they'd barely be seen on the air. This was national television, after all, so she was going to splurge. She recalled a pair of shoes she'd spotted at Madame Daunou's salon back in New York — an establishment patronized by Babe Paley, Betsy Bloomingdale, and the new First Lady, Jackie Kennedy. Emboldened suddenly to think of herself in their company, Barbra rang the sixty-four-year-old Mina Daunou, a Parisian fashion doyenne, and ordered the shoes. But there was a slight complication, she explained. The shoes would clash with her burgundy dress, a problem since the show was broadcast in color. In passable French, Barbra asked the salon if it was possible to have the shoes dyed to match the dress. *Oui, madame,* she was told. The shoes and the dye would cost her sixty-five dollars — a fortune, but Barbra blithely agreed. A friend, Monsieur Robert Schulenberg, would be by to pick up the shoes, she told the salon.

On a crisp, sunny spring day, Bob performed his errand as instructed, collecting the shoes at Madame Daunou's and hurrying them over to the NBC studios. Barbra wasn't quite there yet, so he left the shoes in her dressing room and then passed the hours until showtime at the counter of a drugstore in Rockefeller Center.

Barbra, meantime, was being whisked into the city from the airport by an NBC driver. Flushed from the thrill of her first flight, she was escorted like a real celebrity up the elevator to the sixth floor where, in her dressing room, she found not only the shoes but a gorgeous bouquet of flowers from Bernie Moray and Dick Sloan. Astutely, her Detroit pals had suspected no one else would send her flowers: Bob couldn't have afforded to do so and her mother was simply not the type. Besides, when Barbra had called home, Diana had told her that Shelly's wife had just gone into the hospital to have a baby — Diana's first grandchild. So it wasn't clear that anyone in Barbra's family would even be watching the show, which would be taped for broadcast later that night at 11:15.

No doubt Barbra wondered if Barré would be watching. Bob hadn't told him, but the information was out there, although it may have been easy to miss. Barbra, feeling creative, had given her name as "Strysand" to the NBC publicists, and so it was as "Barbara [misspelled] Strysand [not misspelled]" that her name was printed in newspaper television listings throughout the country. But at the *New York Times*, the typesetter left off a few crucial letters, which ensured that potential television viewers throughout the New York metro region — who would have included Barré, Barbra's paternal grandparents, and all those snooty kids back in Brooklyn — would read only that a "Barbara Strys," whoever that was, was appearing that night on the Paar show.

The booking wasn't a guarantee of success — hundreds of unknowns had made appearances on the show over the years and hadn't gone on to bigger things — but Barbra understood she now had a better chance at realizing her dream than the thousands who never got a shot on national TV. It was extraordinary, really; a little more than six months ago, she had been wandering the streets, traipsing through auditions and being stood up by David Susskind. Now she was on the Paar show.

She waited backstage — "a nervous wreck," according to Bean — as the show opened. Hugh Downs called Bean onstage to deliver his monologue. Currently headlining at the Blue Angel uptown, Bean had a quick, dry sense of humor, displaying an easy rapport with the audience as he sat at the desk smoking cigarette after cigarette. His first guest was the erudite author and playwright Gore Vidal, whose novel *Messiah* was being issued in paperback the following week. Phyllis came on next, having just completed another run at the Bon Soir, and ran through her frantic comedy shtick. Then came veteran character actor Albert Dekker, perhaps best known for *Dr. Cyclops,* the 1940 horror film. Finally, nearly an hour into the show, Bean looked into the camera to introduce Barbra.

"This girl was a young girl I saw down at a nightclub called the Bon Soir when she was there a couple of months ago," Bean said. "She's never been, to the best of my knowledge, on network television before. She has the most charming manner and the most charming voice. She's flown in from Detroit to be with us for the night. She's working out there at a club called the Caucus Club . . . Her name is Barbra Streisand . . . Welcome her." Placing his cigarette back between his lips, Bean led the applause, and the camera switched over to the stage.

To Bob, sketching her in the audience, Barbra looked tiny. And she was — slight and slender in her burgundy dress that, except to the handful of viewers with color sets, looked gray on the screen, and her upswept hairdo, the one Bob had created to make her seem more sophisticated, but that actually made her look like a kid trying to play an adult, which wasn't really so far from the truth. Barbra sang "A Sleepin' Bee" with all the feeling she'd given it in her nightclub appearances, and with all the delicate hand gestures she'd perfected over the last several months, the ones Matt Michaels had observed her practicing so earnestly in the mirror.

The applause that followed the number was prodigious, but Barbra barely had time to hear it. She was rushing back to her dressing room to change into her second-act outfit while the technicians in the booth slipped in a commercial and Orson Bean lit another cigarette, convinced that Barbra's transformation from a terrified kid into a silvery songstress could only be "a gift from God."

After the break, Barbra was back in her slinky black dress with its

Barbara Joan Streisand, age three and age seven. By the time she was seven, she already possessed what she called "an uncontrollable itch" to make it out of Brooklyn and into the big world beyond.

Collection of Stuart Lippner

Barbara with friends outside their Brooklyn tenements. Unlike her playmates, Barbara was never called in for regular meals. She lived, she insisted, like a "wild child."

Collection of Stuart Lippner

Barbara with her sister, Rosalind, known as Rozzie. The younger girl was the apple of their mother's eye, leaving Barbara often feeling left out. *Collection of Stuart Lippner*

The teenaged Barbara was self-conscious about her looks, but others pointed out that her curves were in all the right places.

Collection of Stuart Lippner

The seventeen-year-old acting student, ambitious and sometimes overly serious. Despite shyness and self-doubt, she was averse to taking no for an answer. *Collection of Stuart Lippner*

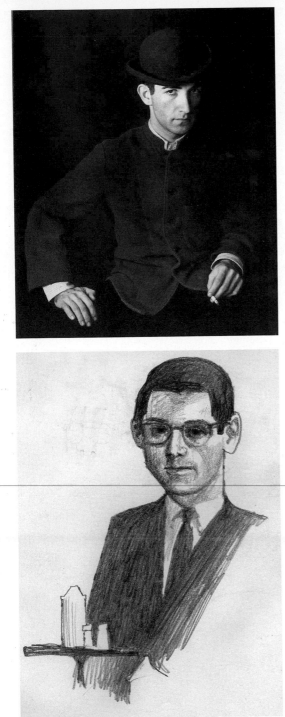

Barbara fell hard for the charismatic Barré Dennen, who shaped her early performances and style, and started her off on the road to fame. He also broke her heart. *Courtesy of Bob Stone*

Artist Bob Schulenberg helped design Barbra's look—clothes, makeup, hair—and his sketchbook was perennially in hand as he sat in the audience during her performances. He also sketched a self-portrait of himself around the time of *Another Evening with Harry Stoones.*

Courtesy of Bob Schulenberg

In 1962, on an interview with a journalist set up by her enterprising publicist, Don Softness, Barbra is in full kook mode. *New York Daily News Archive / Getty Images*

Barbra was a smash hit as Miss Marmelstein in *I Can Get It for You Wholesale,* which opened on March 22, 1962. The critics didn't like the show as much as they liked her, however. *© George Silk / Getty Images*

Barbra and her *Wholesale* costar Elliott Gould on the way to the Tonys, April 29, 1962. She didn't get the award, but she did get Gould.

Collection of Stuart Lippner

Herbert Jacoby and Max Gordon audition a hopeful at the Blue Angel on the same stage where Barbra would perform. Note the quilted walls. *New York Daily News Archive / Getty Images*

At first, radio and television microphones unnerved her, but eventually Barbra faced them with confidence. *Collection of Stuart Lippner*

STEREO
CS 8807

STEREO
"360 SOUND"

The Barbra Streisand Album

Cry Me a River
My Honey's Loving Arms
I'll Tell the Man in the Street
A Taste of Honey
Who's Afraid of the Big Bad Wolf
Soon It's Gonna Rain
Happy Days Are Here Again
Keepin' Out of Mischief Now
Much More
Come to the Supermarket (In Old Peking)
A Sleepin' Bee
Arranged and Conducted by Peter Matz

Columbia chief Goddard Lieberson at first thought Barbra "too special for records." But he was surprised and pleased to see how, after a slow start, *The Barbra Streisand Album* shot up the charts. Barbra chose the name herself, after rejecting the company's suggestion: *Sweet and Saucy Streisand.* © *Getty Images*

Three of the men responsible for launching Barbra Streisand into superstardom. David Merrick (left) did so reluctantly, but even he admitted that her talent was remarkable. Jerome Robbins (below) initially wanted to hold out for Anne Bancroft for the part of Fanny Brice in *Funny Girl*, but he eventually became one of Barbra's biggest boosters. But more important to Barbra's success was Ray Stark (right, with John Huston), who believed from the beginning that nobody but Barbra should play Fanny Brice. Even as he conferred with Huston in Mexico over *The Night of the Iguana*, his mind was on *Funny Girl* back in New York.

Merrick: © Arnold Newman / Getty Images; Robbins: © Bettmann / CORBIS; Stark and Huston: © Gjon Mili / Getty Images

Barbra famously broke protocol to ask for President Kennedy's signature after singing for him at the White House Correspondents' dinner on May 24, 1963. She's flanked here by two of the most influential men to guide her career: her indefatigable manager Marty Erlichman and arranger-accompanist Peter Daniels. *National Archives / Newsmakers / Getty Images*

"If I'd known the place was going to be so crowded, I'd have had my nose fixed," Barbra said on opening night at Hollywood's Cocoanut Grove, August 21, 1963, instantly winning over the jaded movie-star crowd. Afterward, Natalie Wood, barely glimpsed here, told Barbra she was gorgeous. Barbra designed both of the outfits she wore at the Cocoanut Grove.

Barbra on stage: © 1978 Chester Maydole/mptvimages.com; close-up of Barbra: © Nat Dallinger/Globe Photos/ZUMA

After pretending to be married for six months, Barbra and Elliott finally tied the knot in Carson City, Nevada, on September 13, 1963. Their honeymoon was spent at the Beverly Hills Hotel, though Barbra was also working on various television shows. Photographer Bob Willoughby told the newlyweds to get in the pool and have fun.

Both images: © 1978 Bob Willoughby/ mptvimages.com

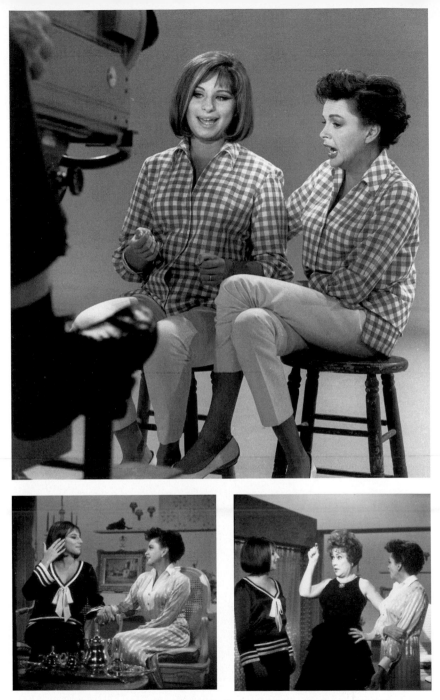

An iconic collaboration: Barbra Streisand, Judy Garland, and "surprise" guest Ethel Merman.

Barbra and Judy: © *Nat Dallinger / Globe Photos / ZUMA; Barbra, Ethel, and Judy: Estate of Roddy McDowall*

By the time *Funny Girl* opened on Broadway on March 26, 1964, it was less about Fanny Brice than it was about Barbra Streisand. Sydney Chaplin and Kay Medford watch as Barbra is lifted to superstardom. *Photofest*

thin shoulder straps, suddenly looking a couple of years older than she had before the commercial. There was nothing kiddish about that perfect figure. Bean told his audience, "I want you to hear another song by this delightful young lady, Barbra Streisand, who is an actress, as I told you before." He hadn't, actually, but no doubt that little addition to her bio had been urged by Barbra from backstage. For tonight, however, she was a singer, and she poured everything she had into "When the Sun Comes Out." The song was far more lively than her first number, and when she got to the last note she gave it a little added oomph — "Then you'll know the one I love walked in, when the sun comes . . . ow-oot!" She bowed, showing a flash of cleavage, and mouthed, "Yes!" She had nailed it, and she knew it.

The camera followed her as she walked over to join the group of guests and caught the triumphant grins she and Phyllis exchanged. Shaking hands with Gore Vidal, Barbra sat to his left, crossing her shapely legs. For a split second, she looked down at her new shoes. Hovering over all of them was a cloud of tobacco smoke. Orson Bean was on what seemed to be his twentieth cigarette, Phyllis was brandishing her trademark long cigarette holder, and Albert Dekker was puffing contentedly on a cigar.

"This is your first television show, isn't it?" Bean asked her.

"This is so exciting, I just can't tell you," Barbra gushed, but the emotion that came from her lips seemed manufactured. She was nervous and excited, no doubt. But she was also acting, because that's what actresses do when they are on a stage. "All these people," she said grandly. "And lights. And people. Oh!"

"You were sensational," said Phyllis, who was sitting on her other side. She took her hand.

"My hands are so cold," Barbra said.

"Warm up her hands there, Gore," Bean joked to Vidal, who took Barbra's free hand for a moment, then, seeming to think better of it, let it go.

"I'll give you my gloves," Phyllis offered, getting a laugh from the audience as Barbra protested. Bean told her she should take the gloves because otherwise she'd catch cold. "And you'll never play again," Phyllis joshed.

Barbra took the gloves.

"I got some beautiful flowers from my friends," she suddenly blurted out, looking around. "Where do I thank them?" She spotted the light on the camera and directed her eyes there. "Thank you, Bernie and Dick and everybody!"

She'd been coached to look at Bean or the other guests when she spoke, but she went her own way instead, sitting on the edge of her seat and looking into the camera or at the studio audience. Bean had tried leading her along with a host's usual questions, but it was Barbra, all smiles and big hand gestures, who was running this show, her backstage nervousness evaporating now that she was front and center.

"I'm clothed by the Robinson Furniture Company of Detroit tonight," she volunteered.

"You're clothed by a furniture company?" Bean asked.

"Isn't everybody?" Barbra asked, in what had to have been a rehearsed response.

"Such a beautiful chair you have on tonight," Bean said, getting a big laugh.

"I'm the original Castro Convertible, moveable parts," Barbra said. If she'd been hoping for a bigger laugh, she had to settle for merely a titter.

Bean pointed out the obvious: that it was her *first* dress of the night that had been made of upholstery material, not the one she was wearing. Phyllis arched an eyebrow in Barbra's direction and concurred. "*That* one is sprayed on," she quipped.

Barbra played her response perfectly. First came a big smile, then a double take, then a kind of vaudevillian mock offense. "You're all heart, Phyllis," she joked.

"You're right," Phyllis replied. "That's why I'm shaped this way." This got a huge laugh from the audience, and the old pro tilted her head toward Barbra. "Thanks for feeding me the lines, sweetie. You give me one more laugh and you're through."

But Phyllis quickly added, lest anyone think that there was any real competition between them, "I love Barbra. This is one of the great singing talents in the world."

After the show, Phyllis and her husband, Sherwood — the "Fang" of her stand-up act — treated Barbra and Bob to a late dinner at the Brasserie. Barbra was giddy. She took considerable pleasure from the fact that, on national television, she had been treated like a sex symbol, with no caveats about her looks being "different" or "unusual." She'd been sexy, plain and simple. And she'd been good, too: both songs had come across exactly as she'd hoped. Bob and Phyllis and Phyllis's husband all lifted their glasses to her. Barbra was a hit, they said, and she could expect big things from now on.

When she called home later that night, she learned that her mother had watched the show after all, but most of the conversation centered around Sheldon's new daughter, Erica. The next morning Barbra boarded a plane to head back to her pals in Detroit, who showed far more excitement about her television debut.

4.

The first — and as far as Barbra could see, the only — "big thing" to come out of the Paar show appearance was a gig in St. Louis at a place called the Crystal Palace. It wasn't exactly the superstardom Barbra was hoping for, but it had come, unexpectedly, with a few enjoyable perks — not the least of which was a young man named Tommy. Sitting opposite him, Barbra listened as he strummed a few chords on his guitar and made eyes at her. Not a bad way to mark her nineteenth birthday. Not bad at all.

After a final week and a half at the Caucus Club — during which the Grubers had given her a bonus for the great publicity they'd gotten when Orson Bean mentioned the name of the club on national television — Barbra had boarded the train to St. Louis, some five hundred and fifty miles southwest of Detroit. The Crystal Palace was a very different kind of venue than the chic Caucus Club. Phyllis had worked there the previous December, so she'd likely given Barbra the lowdown.

The owner, Jay Landesman, was a St. Louis–born Greenwich Village beatnik who'd founded the literary quarterly *Neurotica* in 1948, publishing Allen Ginsberg, Jack Kerouac, and Carl Solomon. Norman Mailer said that Landesman and his wife, Fran, "could be accused of starting it all," meaning the whole "beat" culture. Now Landesman was bringing the avant-garde, the offbeat, the new, and the different to America's heartland. He'd opened the Crystal Palace in 1958, spurring a movement of restaurants and cabarets into St. Louis's bustling Gaslight Square. The club's "hep audience" sat in a semicircle around an apron stage.

When Irvin Arthur had pitched the idea of a revue starring three acts from the Paar show, Landesman had quickly signed on. In addition to Barbra, there was Marc London, a young comic whom *Variety* called "as relaxed as an old shoe" and who'd made a name for himself with his humorous take on the daily news, and the Smothers Brothers — Tommy and Dick — a guitar-and-bass duo who "lampooned folk singers to a fare-thee-well," *Variety* opined, "satire with a capital S." The Smothers Brothers had been on the Paar show on February 20. Grouping the three acts under a single banner, "Caught in the Act," Landesman publicized the revue as the first in a series "to showcase rising new talent." The Smothers Brothers were billed first, and though Barbra came next, newspaper ads persisted in spelling her name "Barbara."

Between the four performers a close bond was formed; in letters back to Bob, Barbra called them "her family on the road." But the most intimate connection was with Tommy. Four months after her breakup with Barré, Barbra's heartbreak was finally healing — at least enough to respond when a man flirted with her. And to her great surprise, she had flirted back. Finally, it seemed, she was learning a little of those "feminine wiles."

Twenty-four-year-old Tom Smothers was the comic to his brother Dick's straight man, often playing dim or naïve, when, in fact, he was as sharp as a tack, politically astute, and savvy in business. The brothers, who hailed from the Los Angeles area, had cut an album, *The Smothers Brothers at the Purple Onion,* due to be released the next month by Mercury Records. Blond and soft-spoken, about as goyish as one could get, Tom came from a North Carolina family that dated back to the Confederacy. He was very attentive to Barbra. Jay Landesman, who had an eagle eye, felt certain the two of them were sleeping together.

On this night, Barbra's birthday, "Caught in the Act" was staged twice, first at eight thirty and then at ten, as it was every weeknight (there were three shows on weekends). Barbra was in good spirits. The spelling of her name had finally been fixed in the ads, and their audiences had been picking up after a rather slow start. On the night the revue had opened, April 17, they'd been up against the telecast of the Academy Awards. That meant they'd played to a number of empty seats, since it seemed the entire world was tuning in to watch Elizabeth Taylor — at death's door from pneumonia just weeks before — accept the Best Actress prize for *Butterfield 8.* In the following days, some people had stayed home out of anxiety over the Kennedy administration's attempted intervention in Cuba — a failed enterprise the newspapers called the "Bay of Pigs invasion." But as hostilities died down, people started filing into the Crystal Palace looking for some diversion from world affairs. Soon the word on the street was that "Caught in the Act" was "a zippy revue, full of fun."

The fun proved infectious. Working alongside three comedians, Barbra endeavored to keep up the pace, slipping in more and more of "their sort of patter between her numbers," Landesman noticed. Barbra had always included a few quick, humorous asides in her act, but now her rap was turning into rambling stories about the benefits of eating nuts or the hazards of sitting too close to a television. And she was amping up the Jewish shtick considerably. "Such *toomel,*" she'd giggle, using the Yiddish word for noisy chaos, when the audience would applaud her after a number. "You like my *schmatta?*" she'd ask, gesturing to her outfit. She told friends she was playing a character;

she was an actress, after all, and it came naturally. But Landesman worried that the patter might distract from the mood of her songs, many of which were tender ballads. "But I get so bored doing the same thing every night," Barbra replied, when he asked her to tone it down a bit. Landesman gave in and allowed her to continue.

People began to comment on Barbra's speaking voice, which could be soft and wispy, compared to her singing voice, which seemed to grow bolder, stronger, and more confident every time she performed. Certainly that night, on her birthday, Barbra had every reason to feel confident about herself and her career. Singing "Soon It's Gonna Rain" from the off-Broadway musical *The Fantasticks,* she had the audience shouting for an encore. The *Variety* review that appeared a few days later declared that Barbra had an "inimitable, sultry way with a ballad . . . She shapes as a comer."

Yes indeed, reason for confidence. Three cities in a row had now gotten behind her. Three major cities, where she had brought people to their feet, cheering and hooting for more. But perhaps what was even more important to her that spring was a quieter, more personal breakthrough. She had discovered that there were other fish in the sea than Barré Dennen, and some of them might even find her attractive. Tommy Smothers's attentions had come at exactly the right moment. Barbra came to understand the power she could have when she zeroed in on someone and turned on the full seductive force of her personality.

5.

Coming home to New York after eight weeks in Detroit and three in St. Louis should have been a happy occasion. But it wasn't.

Rain fell as Barbra made her way from Elaine Sobel's apartment in Murray Hill to Greenwich Village. She'd been back in the city for less than forty-eight hours and here she was, schlepping right back to where she'd started, to the Bon Soir to commence another four-week singing engagement. Arthur had completed all the arrangements for the gig while she was in St. Louis, ensuring no disruption in Barbra's income, for which she was undeniably grateful. He'd even gotten her salary raised to $175 a week. But where were the acting jobs? Before she'd left Detroit, Barbra had interrupted the radio host Jack Harris when he'd observed on air that she'd "switched to singing" from acting. "I'm going back to acting!" she'd insisted.

Indeed, this time around, the Bon Soir seemed rather sordid, Barbra told friends. Making her living as a singer struck her as "wrong." Deep down, she thought, singing in a nightclub was "a floozy job."

Her companion in the tiny, cramped dressing room this time was Renée Taylor, a big, blowsy, twenty-eight-year-old powerhouse whose broad, blatant comedy, heavily accented with Jewish shtick, was familiar to television audiences through regular appearances on the Jack Paar and Perry Como shows. It was Taylor who was the headliner this night, so it was magnanimous of her to lend Barbra a pair of stockings, since the younger performer had discovered a run in hers at the last moment. Barbra trooped out onto the stage and sang her songs, then yanked her stockings off and tossed them to Taylor backstage, who promised to slip them back to her in time for the second show.

This was definitely not the kind of career Barbra had dreamed about. During the break between shows, she stood by the coffee urn in the Bon Soir's steamy kitchen, the aromas of garlic and grease hanging in the air. Waiters rushed past her, carrying trays of the club's latest delicacy, a three-layer pastry that *Variety* decreed had "only intermittent nutritional value." How could she be a serious artist in a place like this? Was this what she had labored so hard for at the Theatre Studio? Was this why she had dug so deep into her heart and soul during Allan Miller's acting classes?

During the day, in the privacy of her room, whether she was in Detroit, St. Louis, or New York, Barbra had endeavored to keep her dreams alive by acting out scenes from Shakespeare and Chekhov. And even though she carried that passion and determination with her into the clubs, striving to use her acting skills every time she sang, invoking Shakespeare to interpret Gershwin, Barbra still couldn't shake off the feeling that she was "bastardizing her art." Hadn't Rozar promised her work in the theater?

She'd begun having second thoughts about her big blond manager. For one thing, his roving eye, quick to follow any pretty girl who walked into the room, irritated her to no end. Barbra was never one to tolerate a gaze that wandered too far from her own direction. And wouldn't it be nice, she added in her rants to her pals, if she had a manager who actually *traveled* with her, as other performers did? Then she wouldn't have to make her way on the road all by herself.

Before the show that night, she'd exchanged a few sharp words with Rozar. She was annoyed that he expected her to reimburse him for phone calls and postage. Whatever happened to him never expecting a woman to pay for anything? That was just the way things were done, Rozar tried explaining, but he knew Barbra's pique was about more than just money. He understood that she was irritated by the fact that he spent, in her opinion, "too much time" with his other clients and even with his family. He'd come to recognize in Barbra the same self-absorption that had so exasperated Barré, the furious narcissism that blazed within her, fueled by that old pipeline of insecurities. Barbra wanted a manager "who would pay all his own expenses and expect nothing from her," Rozar now realized, "who would travel with her wherever she went, who would be there to hold her hand, fight her battles, tell her she was wonderful, and be her slave."

In between shows that night, they didn't speak. Rozar sat with his wife in the audience. Barbra stood by herself beside the coffee urn in the Bon Soir kitchen. That was when she looked up to see a stocky, bespectacled man approaching her. He told her his name was Marty Erlichman.

6.

Marty had been looking forward to seeing his old pal, actor and comedian Phil Leeds, perform that night at the Bon Soir. Phil was sharing a bill that included Renée Taylor and her comedy partner, Frank Baxter; and some girl singer Marty had never heard of. On a night as raw and rainy as this, Marty probably wouldn't have come out except to show his support to Phil. Bluff and often brusque, Marty nonetheless had a sentimental side.

Yet the performer who impressed him the most that evening was that unknown girl singer. Barbra sang five songs that gave Marty "chills through all of them." The rest of his table, all "industry people," hadn't been as impressed. Instead of the usual up-tempo number, Barbra had opened with a ballad, no doubt trying to alleviate the boredom she felt doing the same thing every night. One of the agents at Marty's table shook his head and called that a mistake. Barbra, he said, had "a lot to learn."

Marty wasn't so sure. He had a feeling this kid knew exactly what she was doing. As an entertainment manager, he had an eye for talent in the rough. Not long before, he'd spotted a group of Irish singers who called themselves the Clancy Brothers and pegged them, despite their lack of experience and polish, as potential stars. When he noticed one of the Clancys wearing a white Aran sweater sent over from Ireland by his mother, Marty had decided that the whole group should wear them. It gave them a look. And so the sweaters had become their trademark, launching a bit of a national fad when Marty succeeded in booking the Clancys on *The Ed Sullivan Show* just a couple of months previous. That appearance had led to a five-year, $100,000 recording contract with Columbia Records, with none other than Pete Seeger on backup banjo. The Clancy Brothers were suddenly riding high — and along with them, their manager.

Marty shared not a few characteristics with that girl singer he so admired. He'd been born in Brooklyn, about two and a half miles from where Barbra grew up, though Martin Lee Erlichman was thirteen years older than Barbra Joan Streisand. But like her, Marty was also the grandchild of Russian Jewish immigrants and had dreamed of making a name for himself in the world of showbiz from a very young age. His father, Jack, short for Jacob, managed a confectionery;

his grandfather Joseph had worked in an ice-cream factory in Manhattan. But vending candy and sweets was not going to be Marty's fate. As a young man he got a job as a time-log clerk at CBS radio. In the summer of 1959, he produced "Jazz on the Hudson," a series of four-hour cruises that left Pier 80 at the foot of West Forty-second Street every Friday night, regaling passengers with the sounds of Morgana King, Donald Byrd, Sam Most, Pepper Adams, the Horace Silver Quintet, and others.

With a business partner, Lenny Rosenfeld, Marty broke into the personal-management field when he signed his first client, Josh White, the blues singer-songwriter. With White now working primarily on English television, Marty was primarily concentrating on the Clancy Brothers. But he was still looking for "the big one" — the client who could put him up there with George Scheck, the powerful manager of Connie Francis, or maybe even Colonel Tom Parker, who had guided Elvis Presley to the top.

Marty certainly wouldn't have pegged Barbra as being his ticket to the big time, but he was clearly impressed. Her vulnerability and the poignant sense of autobiography that resonated in her songs had been strikingly apparent. To Marty, Barbra had "what Chaplin had." Moviegoers always rooted for the little tramp against anyone who tried to beat him down. It was the same, Marty felt, with Barbra. To him, Barbra was "the girl the guys never look at twice," and when she sang of the pathos of that — of "being like an invisible woman" — the audience rose up and wanted "to protect her." This was definitely a marketable act, Marty told himself, and so, during the intermission, he excused himself from his table and went to look for this girl named Barbra Streisand.

He found her beside the coffee urn in the kitchen.

Without any niceties or small talk, he bluntly told her that she was terrific and asked if she had representation. Barbra liked Marty's direct manner, so much like her own. But she had to reply that she already had a manager. Marty pulled his card from his pocket and handed it to her. She should call him, he said, if her situation ever changed. Before he had a chance to leave, Barbra asked Marty if he thought she ought to fix her nose or change her name. Marty told her she shouldn't change a thing.

Barbra made sure to keep Marty Erlichman's card.

7.

Ted Rozar had seen the little transaction between Barbra and Marty. He'd spotted Erlichman in the audience and knew who he was, and he'd watched with interest Marty's hasty beeline backstage between shows.

"He wants her," Rozar told his wife as they headed out of the club. "I could see it in his eyes."

Once inside a cab, Rozar laughed. "Well, if he wants her, let him try to get her," he said. "He'll see what she wants. And if he can give it to her, then he can have her."

8.

It was time for a little makeover, Barbra felt, and it came, as always, courtesy of good old Bob.

She sat on her usual stool in Bob's apartment on Gay Street as her pal walked in circles slowly around her, stroking his chin, as if she were a half-finished piece of sculpture and he was considering where to wield his chisel next. They laughed, often and easily. But Bob was quite serious in believing Barbra's appearance was critical in taking her to the next level of her professional career. She was definitely on the move. She'd just been booked for a second appearance on the Paar show, and the Bon Soir had, once again, extended her run by a couple of weeks. Bob thought it was time she left behind anything too girlish, anything too "Greenwich Village beatnik," and homed in on something entirely new and surprising.

For all Barbra's flirtation with the idea of a new manager, she was grateful that Rozar had landed her a repeat appearance on the Paar show, again with the able assistance of Orson Bean, who was once more in the guest host's chair. So she was up for whatever Bob had in mind for her. A new wardrobe or hairdo. Anything to make her stand out on television.

Bob got down to work. A dress was shortened; a pair of long gloves was tried on. It was Bob's desire that Barbra stop conversation when she made an appearance. She had to be "queen of the room," he said. Terry Leong's thrift-shop creations had been interesting, Bob thought, but "they were costumes, not clothes." That look had worked very well to get her noticed, Bob believed, but it was entirely "too theatrical" to take Barbra to the next level of her public success. Now, Bob urged her, she needed to think "sophistication . . . poise . . . Park Avenue cocktail party."

He was careful not to dictate to her, to never say anything as crass as "tone it down." Barbra was far too headstrong to simply follow orders. So instead he brought out stacks of magazines, pointing to celebrities and models whose looks seemed right for Barbra. She studied them carefully, especially Audrey Hepburn in costume for the soon-to-be-released *Breakfast at Tiffany's*. Bob said this was the kind of "severity" and "extreme chic" he thought she should go for. Barbra nodded, warming to the idea. Who would have thought that she'd ever be like Audrey Hepburn?

He hauled out a book that had made a great impression on him. It was *The White Goddess* by Robert Graves, which posited the concept of a female deity at the center of much of Western culture. From Graves's essay, Bob took the idea that men had a primal need to worship women, dating back to pre-Christian goddess religions. The "remnant of the divine goddess," Bob believed, could still be found in certain cultural prototypes: Garbo, Dietrich, Monroe, even the new First Lady, Jacqueline Kennedy. He explained to Barbra that the public's veneration of these women was "tapping into something very subconscious, very deep." He wanted the same for Barbra. He saw her potential to be as irresistible, as spellbinding, as *divine* as any of those other legendary ladies.

If they could cultivate that, Bob told Barbra, if — through the combination of talent, clothes, hairstyle, makeup, and attitude — they could bring out the "white goddess" within, then there would be no stopping her.

Barbra told him to get to work.

9.

Diana Kind was hopping mad. How dare that man say such a thing about a daughter of hers?

Only a short time ago, on May 22, she'd watched Barbra on the Paar show. It had been Barbra's second appearance on national television, and Diana had allowed ten-year-old Rozzie to stay up to watch. How excited Rozzie had been to see her sister on TV. Diana had found it amusing how the little girl was so interested in and impressed with Barbra's career.

Diana had to admit that Barbra looked good. A little classier and more stylish than in the past. Somebody must be helping her pick out nicer clothes, Diana thought. She was pleased about that, though, of course, she wouldn't tell Barbra she was pleased; if she did, that stubborn kid would probably decide she was doing something wrong if her mother liked what she was wearing and go back to her old ways.

Diana thought Barbra had sounded good, too, when she'd sung a couple of songs on the show. Of course, Diana wouldn't tell her that either, because to do so would just encourage her in this crazy show-business dream she had, and Diana would never, ever do that. But she'd told her friends that Barbra "sang very well on the Paar show." And she'd enjoyed watching her kid make conversation with Orson Bean and the other guests, Henny Youngman and that funny "Professor," Irwin Corey.

But tonight the Paar show hadn't been nearly as enjoyable. There, on the same set where Barbra had sat not so long ago, Barbra was derided, not applauded, and Diana was furious.

Jack Paar was back in the host's chair, and he must have seen the show while he was on vacation, because he mentioned "that Barbra Streisand" who'd been a guest and made a joke at her expense. A joke that implied Barbra was ugly. That was how Diana described it to friends, and she was "so angry she could have spit."

It was true that Diana rarely complimented her daughter. But, as one friend understood it, "she thought Barbra had her own beauty, her own style, and that she was certainly not ugly." And here Barbra was, looking better than ever, Diana thought, and that boor, Jack Paar, was making a joke at her expense. And on national television where all Diana's friends could hear it!

Diana snapped off the set. Taking a piece of paper from her desk, she began to write. "Dear Mr. Paar, I am Barbra Streisand's mother," she scrawled — or words to that effect. "How would you feel if I said something unkind about *your* daughter on national television?" She called him "incredibly rude." Then she put the letter in an envelope and mailed it off to NBC.

Typically, she had couched her letter from her own perspective: She hadn't asked how Paar's *daughter* would have felt, after all. But that didn't mean her own embarrassment had obliterated any concern for Barbra's feelings. She told her friends that she wouldn't tell her daughter about any of this. If Barbra hadn't heard what Paar had said about her, then it was best to keep it that way, Diana believed.

As far as her friends knew, Diana never got a response from Paar. Nor, they thought, did Barbra ever know how her mother had tried, in her own small, imperfect way, to do right by her.

CHAPTER SIX

Summer 1961

1.

That early summer day, trooping up to the WNEW television studios in the former DuMont Tele-Centre on East Sixty-seventh Street, Barbra looked like a goddess, just as Bob had intended.

She was a young woman transformed. Her eyes appeared Egyptian — making her look like Isis, perhaps, or at least like the photos of Elizabeth Taylor coming off the set of *Cleopatra*. Her hair was styled in a long, fashionable inverted bob; no more ponytails, Bob had decreed. On her forefinger she wore a silver ring — all the rage at the time, not to mention a symbol of Jewish marriage — and for a blouse she'd chosen a ruffled middy, the kind Jackie Kennedy had popularized when she was pregnant. Some people thought Barbra looked a little pregnant herself with all those ruffles at her waist. But those were people who simply didn't understand style.

It was the eyes, however, that really got her noticed, that caused the studio technicians to stop what they were doing and look twice at her. Bob had always emphasized Barbra's eyes when doing her makeup, but now he'd come up with something entirely new. With a tiny watercolor brush, he had extended the shape of her eyes outward with a long stripe of black eyeliner. Then, before applying her false eye-lashes, he drew a thin, almost imperceptible white highlight along the rim of her eyelid to lighten the heaviness of the dark lashes. To teach her how to do it herself, Bob made up one side of Barbra's face and then had her do the other. But without Bob's help, she could never seem to glue the eyelashes on herself. Too often her fingers got stuck to the lid of one eye, leaving Barbra screaming, "I'm going blind!"

So when she didn't have Bob to help her, she would forego the false eyelashes and go out with only the white lines above her eyelids and the long black lines extending around to the sides of her face. In so doing, Bob thought, Barbra had inadvertently created "a stylistic signature" for herself. Had she been able to apply the eyelashes on her own, the result would have seemed more natural; but without the lashes, the lines around her eyes became more apparent — and, by default, a statement. If Barbra and Bob had been going for the ex-otic — the "white goddess" look — they had succeeded in ways they hadn't even imagined.

As it turned out, their timing was perfect. The television show Barbra was taping, *PM East,* was a new talkfest produced by WBC Productions, a subsidiary of Westinghouse, and syndicated to various stations throughout the country. Paired with a second half, *PM West,* taped in San Francisco, the show was intended to give Jack Paar a run for his money. The New York hosts were Mike Wallace, the hard-driving interviewer from the old *Night Beat* series, and Joyce Davidson, formerly of the Canadian Broadcasting Company, and the theme for the segment Barbra was taping today was "glamour." Among the other guests were model Suzy Parker, *Life* magazine photographer Milton Greene, and agent Candy Jones, herself frequently on the annual best-dressed lists. Barbra might have been hired to sing a couple of songs, but if the conversation was going to be about glamour, there was no way she was going to be left out. She made sure she showed up ready to take on the best of them.

Yet just how she had nailed this particular job, she wasn't telling. When Ted Rozar found out she'd been booked on the show, he was mystified. He hadn't had anything to do with it. Apparently, a *PM East* staffer had heard Barbra sing at the Bon Soir and had arranged for an audition. But, Rozar wondered, who had arranged her contract? It wasn't Irvin Arthur; Associated Booking only handled club dates. So who was it? Rozar had his suspicions. A week or so before Barbra turned up at the station, Marty Erlichman's clients, the Clancy Brothers, had also taped an appearance on *PM East*. Had Erlichman, already working with the show's staff, made a call, talked to some people, helped Barbra out? Was this a way of wooing her? Barbra didn't say.

But no doubt she was happy to take the job. Since its debut on June 12, *PM East* had lured a diverse roster of guests up to Sixty-seventh Street. Retired Admiral Chester W. Nimitz, war correspondent William Shirer, film director Otto Preminger, and comedian Jonathan Winters had all appeared during the show's kickoff week. An episode focusing on rock and roll with Paul Anka was in the can. Another show looked at the issue of violence, featuring pacifist Jim Peck and psychiatrist Fredric Wertham.

Parading into the studio Barbra wore her ambition like a debutante might flaunt a mink stole. And for the first time in her career, she ran headfirst into another personality with an ego as big as her own. Mike Wallace was aggressive, grouchy, suspicious by nature, and eager to prove himself with *PM East* after a series of ratings disappointments. Paul Dooley, who'd been a guest on the show, thought the host "didn't know anything about variety or singing," so he came across as tough when, in fact, he was just defensive. Wallace was determined, against all odds, to vanquish Jack Paar and claim late-night supremacy.

Dooley thought Wallace had "a certain kind of ego that bumps into other performers' egos" — a perfect description for what happened with Barbra. When the young singer with the extravagant eye makeup walked in, Wallace took one look at her and decided he didn't like her. True, during her audition, the host had thought her voice was "magnificent," and he'd agreed with his producers that the kid could be a real asset to the show. But Wallace had also homed right in on what he called Barbra's "self-absorption." Of course he did. Narcissists tend to recognize each other. Wallace thought Barbra had "the demeanor of a diva," and expected the "world [to] revolve around her" — even though, in his opinion, she'd yet to prove she deserved such treatment.

It's not surprising, then, that he tried to pull Barbra down a peg. When the cameras began to roll, Wallace began his introduction. "New York is just full of unusual and interesting girls who are starting out in show business, but few of them have the style as early as this young lady." He was reading a prepared script, of course; Barbra's "style" was not something Wallace admired. Unimpressed with Bob's "white goddess" attempts, the newsman thought Barbra looked "more like the studio mail girl than a singer." Suddenly going off script, he asked for a close-up of Barbra's hand. It was a show about glamour, after all, and Barbra seemed to be trying to make a statement. "Isn't this really an affectation?" Wallace asked. "Come on now, this ring on the forefinger? And these nails that are a little bit short of two inches long each? What's that all about?"

Barbra, probably prepped by the producers, didn't let Wallace knock her off stride. "Well, see, I was very poor," she said, "so I wanted to grow them really long so I could get ten dollars a nail from Revlon." She laughed, barely concealing her annoyance at Wallace's question. "I happen to like long nails!"

"And the ring on the forefinger?" Wallace pressed.

"Well, I could tell you the ring . . . would be too big, which it is for this finger," Barbra said, indicating the traditional ring finger. "But I like it on this finger! So did King Louis XIV!"

According to the show's publicist, Don Softness, Barbra had displayed a similar sassiness during her audition, and the producers, delighted, had told her to "play up the kookiness" on the air. Barbra didn't disappoint. When Wallace asked what she was going to sing first, she replied, "The Kinsey Report," which got a big laugh from the technicians in the studio. (She actually sang "A Sleepin' Bee.") When he asked what she wanted to be "when she grew up," Barbra quipped,

"A fireman," before adding, grandly, that what she really wanted to do was "direct opera."

"Do you know anything about directing operas?" Wallace asked.

"I don't know anything about opera really," Barbra replied, "except that it's a magnificent medium to express things theatrically and vocally, if you have the vocal equipment. It could be a very exciting theatrical experience. The kind of plots you could — "

"They're telling us from the control room — " Wallace interrupted.

"That's awful," Barbra said, peeved at being cut off.

" — that they understand the answer and they'd like another song."

As Barbra headed over to the stage to sing, Wallace asked his viewers to decide whether she looked more like the regal actress Judith Anderson, best known for playing Medea on Broadway and Mrs. Danvers in Hitchcock's *Rebecca,* or Fanny Brice, the Ziegfeld Follies comic best known for playing Baby Snooks on the radio.

The orchestra began playing and Barbra sang "Lover, Come Back to Me" with all the power she'd given it at the Bon Soir. In the control booth, the contrast between Barbra's two personae — the quirky kid and the soulful woman — was received with great appreciation by the show's producers. Even before Barbra had finished singing, they had decided to have her back whenever her schedule permitted.

2.

In the late afternoon of the first Sunday in July, Barbra arrived at the Village Vanguard, one of the oldest clubs in the Village, located in a cellar at 178 Seventh Avenue South. Here Eartha Kitt, Harry Belafonte, Blossom Dearie, and Sonny Rollins had all made names for themselves, but the biggest star currently associated with the club was trumpeter Miles Davis. Davis's band was setting up the day Barbra walked in. The Shirley Horn Trio was also on the bill.

Barbra had come to the Vanguard at the behest of an old friend from acting school, Rick Edelstein, who worked as a waiter at the club. In the past, Edelstein had sometimes sneaked Barbra into the club so she could catch the last show. Primarily a jazz club, the Vanguard had recently headlined Gerry Mulligan, Ahmad Jamal, Nina Simone, and the edgy comedian Lenny Bruce. Any of these shows Barbra might have seen. Edelstein served her ginger ale, because he understood that Barbra "didn't drink"; perhaps the memory of that one bottle of wine too many with Bob had lingered. After the show, Barbra and Rick would head over to the Pam Pam, split a baked potato, and talk until three AM.

This afternoon, however, Barbra had come for more than just the show. During the Sunday matinees, which began at four thirty, the Vanguard occasionally allowed a few surprise acts, who hoped a warm reception from the afternoon audience might get them invited back as an official part of the bill some evening. In the extremely competitive nightclub business, such opportunities were rare, but the Vanguard's easygoing owner, Max Gordon, was known to have "an eye for promising newcomers and the ability to help them blossom." When Edelstein suggested that Barbra perform a few numbers that afternoon, Gordon agreed; he'd heard her sing before, probably at the Bon Soir, and thought she was "great." He even asked Miles Davis to play backup for her, but the jazz great refused, saying he didn't play "behind no girl singer."

Yet, if singing in a club made her feel like a floozy, why was Barbra even there? Why had she curled her hair, drawn those elaborate lines around her eyes, picked out a fashionable dress, slipped into some antique shoes, and trooped over that afternoon to the Village Vanguard? She didn't even really need the money, at least not at that particular moment. She'd just been paid for *PM East,* and there was a looming gig in Winnipeg, Manitoba. Irvin Arthur would surely get her more nightclub jobs if she needed them. So why put herself through all of this?

The answer, perhaps, came from the most recent man in her life.

His name was Stanley Beck, and he had told Barbra that her problem was simple: She didn't like herself very much. Stanley had known

Barbra long enough to speak with some degree of authority. He'd first met her at the Malden Bridge Playhouse when Barbra was fifteen and he was twenty-one. Though he'd found her attractive, Stanley had kept a respectable distance from the underage girl. It was not until one night in the late spring of 1961 that they'd reconnected. Barbra and her roommate, Elaine, had gone to see *The Balcony*, the Jean Genet play being directed by José Quintero at the Circle in the Square Theatre. Stanley had recently taken over the part of the executioner, and Barbra had recognized him. After the show, they met up, and during the past few weeks had been seeing quite a bit of each other.

Barbra, according to friends, had initially been smitten. Shortly before meeting Stanley, she'd lamented to Elaine, "Will I ever get a guy? Do you think anyone could ever love this face?" The affair with Tommy Smothers may have given Barbra a boost, but for someone with self-doubts that ran as deep as hers, it was going to take much more than that to convince her of her own allure. So when Stanley returned her interest, she was elated.

Stanley had picked up on her insecurities. He'd told Barbra plainly that the reason "she was attracted to guys who paid no attention to her" was because it confirmed her own deep-seated belief that "she was nothing." That might explain, some friends thought, why she kept trudging into nightclubs, craving the approval of the managers and the applause of their patrons.

Standing in the Vanguard now, waiting for Rick Edelstein to corral a musician to play backup for her, Barbra was as alone as she'd ever been in her life. Nearly seven months after the breakup with Barré, her renditions of "Cry Me a River" had lost none of their intensity. Even Stanley's muscular frame couldn't compete with the memory of Barré. At first, Barbra had been attracted enough to Stanley to buy a diaphragm in case she ever gave in and had sex with him. But as time went on, she told Elaine that she "could take him or leave him." Stanley wasn't the devoted, nurturing mentor Barré had been. He was also perhaps just a bit too honest. He spoke with a directness that Barbra wasn't used to, and he articulated a truth that went to the core of her being. To no one's great surprise, shortly before her audition at the Vanguard, Barbra had stopped seeing Stanley Beck.

Up on the stage, Edelstein was motioning to Barbra that the musician was ready. Barbra stepped up and sang three numbers. The audience, as expected, cheered and whistled. Watching from the back of the room, Max Gordon's wife, Lorraine, felt as if there was nothing Barbra "couldn't do with her voice — she had such control, top to bottom." But her husband didn't offer Barbra a job that day. The Vanguard was a jazz club, and Barbra was no Nina Simone. This day, the affirmation she sought so desperately would not be forthcoming.

At least not from the club managers. As Barbra was leaving, an older woman from the audience stopped her. "You are fantastic," she said. "Don't ever change."

Barbra looked at her matter-of-factly. "Of course I'll change," she said. "Life changes people."

Indeed, she was counting on change. She didn't want to stay the same, singing in clubs, bastardizing her art, begging for jobs. That lady was *crazy*. Barbra was *impatient* for change. Bring it on, she might well have said. The sooner the better.

3.

Homesickness can get pretty acute seventeen hundred miles away.

Everything seemed so different in Canada. At the nightclub, men wore short-sleeved shirts with no ties. No matter that the temperatures had reached ninety degrees Fahrenheit that week, Barbra found the practice peculiar, especially since the Town 'n' Country, the three-story theater-restaurant where she was playing, seemed more like a palace than a club. "Beautiful," she proclaimed. "Very posh." Yet the club's management wasn't even springing for her accommodations. For her two-week stint in Winnipeg, from July 3 to 15, Barbra had to pay her own way at the local YWCA. True, she was being paid better than she had ever been before — $350 Canadian a week, about the same in American dollars — but that was quickly whittled down when she figured in travel, food, and lodging. She'd made a few friends, who had taken her out horseback riding, which she'd enjoyed. But mostly she spent her days alone in her room, talking with Elaine on the phone or writing letters to Bob.

Worst of all, however, were the audiences, to whom she played three shows nightly, finding them both dull and noisy. On this night, it was the latter. People kept on talking as she tried to sing. It was like being in the Catskills all over again. With her tinnitus probably clanging in her ears, as it usually did in loud, stressful situations, Barbra stopped singing and abruptly walked off the stage.

The club's manager, Auby Galpern, wasn't pleased. He liked Barbra, even if he'd been distinctly unimpressed with her sartorial choices. He'd also been befuddled by her singing style. For a rendition of "Come to the Supermarket in Old Peking," one of Cole Porter's less well-known and more outlandish compositions, Barbra pounded on a bongo drum, flung her hair around, and swayed her torso. Reviewers took note. "Miss Streisand is the type of singer you'd expect to find in the Blue Angel or San Francisco's hungry i," Gene Telpner wrote in the *Winnipeg Free Press*. "That's why Winnipeggers may find her rather strange." Telpner repeated the fiction, still part of Barbra's official publicity, that she'd been born in Turkey. He thought it gave her a "semi-Oriental look."

Still, in the end, the review had been positive. Barbra's act, Telpner concluded, "was really worth hearing." That was what had saved her in Galpern's view, at least so far. Barbra might be different from the acts he usually headlined at the Towers, the Town 'n' Country's performing space, but she was good. Very good. The boys in the band had declared she was "terrific," and Galpern knew his musicians were his best judges of talent.

But walking off the stage as Barbra had done — that was unacceptable. Galpern and his young singer exchanged some heated words over the incident. No doubt, there were some tears. Phoning Elaine, Barbra said she might have just been fired.

But she wasn't. Galpern forgave her, and she went on the next night. The gig would turn out just fine. In the beginning, she may have had Winnipeggers asking, "What's she doing?" But "after they knew who I was," she said, "they listened to me."

4.

Back in New York, Elaine was very excited to watch her roommate on *PM East*. It was Wednesday, July 12, and Barbra's episode was finally set to air. With Elaine was her boyfriend, the young actor Dustin Hoffman, who remembered Barbra from the Theatre Studio. Since those days, Hoffman had done some impressive off-Broadway work and had just appeared on *Naked City*, the television police drama.

Elaine told Hoffman that he had to hear Barbra sing. But the young man tried to demur. "I've seen her act," he said, remembering some rather stilted Theatre Studio student productions. "She's not that great."

But Elaine insisted. So it was with some reluctance that Hoffman stood in front of the television set, watching as a grid of lights flashed across the screen and came together to spell out *PM East*. Host Mike Wallace conversed with his guest models — the "beauties of New York," the ads had called them — and then finally introduced Barbra. To Hoffman, his old schoolmate seemed to be "really laying on the New York thing, the accent." Finally, Barbra headed over to the stage and sat on a stool to sing.

"When a bee lies sleepin' in the palm of your hand . . ."

Hoffman had to sit down. He "couldn't believe" the beauty of Barbra's voice. This little girl, this offbeat character who'd skulked around acting school with acne on her face and clothes smelling of mothballs, had opened her mouth and "this blessing," as Hoffman described it, had come out. He was surprised by how emotional he got.

All across the country, many others were feeling exactly the same way.

5.

Barbra was fed up. She'd thought of Detroit almost as a second home, but here were the Grubers, having hired her yet again to sing at the Caucus Club, refusing her request that meals be included in her contract. On a tour that had been one long hassle, this was the last straw. Furious, Barbra rang Irvin Arthur, but he couldn't help; she wasn't even able to get Ted Rozar on the phone. So she dug out Marty Erlichman's card and placed a call to New York. When she learned that he was in San Francisco, Barbra tracked him down there.

Finally getting Marty on the line, Barbra asked if he still wanted to manage her. He replied that he did. So she told him about the stalemate she'd reached with the Grubers. Marty listened. And then he did something Barbra couldn't have predicted.

He got on a plane and flew to Detroit.

Now, cloistered with the club owners in their office, Marty leveled with them. Barbra was distraught, and he was certain they didn't want a distraught singer. He pointed out that they were paying her just $150 a week, the same as her last appearance at their club, while she'd made more than $300 in Winnipeg. Even her last gig in New York had brought her $175. The Grubers agreed to match the $175, but Marty knew that wouldn't satisfy Barbra. She was holding out for the meals for the principle of the thing. So Marty told the brothers, in confidence, that he'd pay them an additional $25 if they threw in dinners for Barbra. The Grubers' jaws nearly hit their desks. "Let us get this straight," one of them said. "You flew here at your own expense so you could pay us twenty-five dollars and you're not even her manager?"

Although the Grubers might not have thought so, Marty Erlichman was a shrewd operator. He knew his investment of $25 had just raised Barbra's American asking price from $175 to $200. Her next employer would have to top that.

Yet Marty's shrewdness went beyond dollars. Barbra's new manager — although he couldn't quite call himself that yet, given the contract still in place with Rozar — had no intention of keeping his deal with the Gruber brothers a secret. Right from the start, it was meant to leak, and already Marty knew exactly how he'd sell it. "You must really believe this girl is going to be a star," he'd quote the Grubers as saying, to which Marty replied he "sure as hell did." It was a great anecdote with which to sell a new client.

There was no question that Marty truly believed in Barbra's potential — he wouldn't have taken her on if he hadn't — but managing the Clancy Brothers had taught him a valuable lesson. You didn't let the public decide if an act was important or worthy. You told them so ahead of time. The Clancys had been sold as groundbreaking musicians who had single-handedly jump-started America's love affair with Irish music, and that was exactly how the public had bought them. Therefore, a similar angle was needed to merchandise Marty's latest client. For Barbra, it wasn't national identity that he figured he could sell. Rather it was sheer, raw, once-in-a-generation talent.

So Marty let the word get out that Barbra wasn't paying him any commissions, that he was helping her simply because he thought she was so amazingly gifted. In doing so, he was building the narrative he wanted associated with her. Of course, Marty's spin also had a more immediate, practical application. It prevented Ted Rozar from claiming that Barbra had violated her exclusive contract with him by paying someone else.

For Barbra, a switch in managers couldn't have happened fast enough. Marty was far easier to relate to than Rozar ever was. He was a fellow Jew from Brooklyn, but he also had a reassuring manner about him; Rozar had often made her feel uneasy. With Rozar, Barbra had to take care of so many little details herself; Marty promised he'd oversee everything from contracts to cab rides. He was there to listen to her as she kvetched in Detroit; in the past, Barbra had had to kvetch alone. Rozar had always been flirting with other girls, but Marty only had eyes for Barbra. Rozar had declared that what Barbra wanted in a manager was a "slave." Marty wasn't quite that, but he made sure Barbra felt as if she were his top — his only — priority. Nothing less would have sufficed.

And he told the world that she paid him not one dime.

In many ways, Marty was the strong, indulgent, protective father Barbra had always dreamed of having. His thirteen years of seniority — there had been only a few with Rozar — made all the difference. With his thick accent and frank way of speaking, Marty might not have been as erudite as Barbra expected her father would have been, but she could have a conversation with him about Chekhov or Mozart or Billie Holiday, and that was important to her. Most of all, Marty was the kind of direct and forthright advocate she'd longed for all her life — the kind of father who might have stood up for her at school or provided a counterbalance to her mother's lack of encouragement. The white-knight rescue Marty had performed for Barbra in Detroit seemed to suggest that he could be as devoted to her as Barré had once been for those few short, wonderful months. And devotion was what Barbra wanted. Needed.

Rozar would have to be dealt with when they got back to New York. But for now, Barbra settled in for a happy month at the Caucus Club, enjoying all the Rocqueburgers and corned beef she could possibly eat.

6.

Given the stresses she faced on her return to New York, it was no wonder that Barbra took solace from what might have seemed an unlikely source: Zen Buddhism.

Sitting in quiet meditation, the sounds of the city quickly receded from her consciousness. For a little while, Barbra was able to push from her mind the stressful fact that she had nowhere to live. Sharing Elaine's apartment was never meant to be permanent, and now Barbra found herself traipsing from friend to friend, sometimes staying with Bob, sometimes with Peter Daniels, sometimes crashing at Sheldon's office. She'd taken to carrying a cheap fold-up cot under her arm because she never knew when she might stumble across a good place to spend the night.

But during her Zen meditations, Barbra could forget all of her troubles, which included a recent, and nasty, break with Rozar. Associated Booking had advanced her $700 to "buy him off," though Rozar insisted that it was money she owed him for commissions. Barbra had shown up at his office with what he called a "big goon" at her side. As she handed her former manager the money and gathered her belongings, Barbra refused to look Rozar in the eye so he was forced to talk to the back of her head. He told her he felt "disappointed" and "somewhat betrayed." But when Barbra and the goon left — just who he was Rozar didn't know, and Barbra didn't say — there was "no apology, no explanation, not even a good-bye." Rozar was deeply hurt. He felt he had done right by Barbra, negotiating her salary up, connecting her with nightclub owners. But he knew he'd never be the "hand-holder" that she wanted.

Lost in her meditations, Barbra could forget about such unpleasant moments. Zen was a handy tool to have. At the moment, the practice was rather fashionable among Barbra's crowd. One friend, who got turned on to the practice at the same time, thought Barbra seemed "an expert, really so smart about Zen, really knowledgeable about going within." When she wasn't traveling, Barbra liked to hang out in the Village and talk Eastern philosophy with her pals. What Barbra sought, her friends understood, was "peace of mind."

Recently, she'd endured another scene in Irvin Arthur's office. With no gigs on the horizon, Barbra had shown up to see her agent, and she ran into Enrico Banducci, proprietor of the influential San Francisco club, the hungry i, who was on "one of his cyclical forays into New York to ferret out fresh talent." It was, of course, very likely that Barbra knew Banducci was going to be there that day and her confrontation with him had been planned. "Why don't you give me a job?" Barbra asked the club manager. She'd admit the question was "a bit" — a performance. She was acting the part of an aggressive character demanding a job. But she was also serious. Banducci took chances on unknowns. So why not take a chance on her? He ought to hire her now, Barbra declared, because later, when she was famous, she'd be too expensive for him. The iconoclastic Banducci, an expert at self-promotion himself, enjoyed her little performance. He promptly signed Barbra up for $350 a week for an unspecified future date.

Yet this kind of "begging" for jobs was one of the main reasons Barbra detested the nightclub life. She had no choice, however. She needed the money so she could get an apartment. She couldn't keep lugging that cot around forever.

That summer Barbra faced a career slump. Zen might help her attain some peace of mind, but there was another force — more practical, more tangible — that was also coming to her aid. Marty Erlichman was walking the pavement and knocking on doors on Barbra's behalf — something Rozar had never done. Marty was hopeful that he could get his new client an engagement at the uptown, upscale Blue Angel. And given his contacts at Columbia Records through the Clancy Brothers, he was optimistic about landing a record deal for her as well. But most important, at least to Barbra's mind, was that Marty had helped secure her an audition for a *play*. Not a nightclub gig, but a play. Sure, it was a revue, but *Another Evening with Harry Stoones* would require learning lines and playing parts in addition to singing songs. Barbra wouldn't just be some floozy standing next to a piano. How refreshing that would be.

And so Barbra closed her eyes and meditated some more. She could see her success, as clear as ever. Now only if the rest of the world would as well.

7.

His mother kept mispronouncing the name of his show as *Another Evening with Daniel Boone* or *Another Evening in Harry's Saloon,* but author-composer-lyricist Jeff Harris was convinced his debut production had the right stuff to be a major hit. Until now Harris had been best known for playing the homicidal maniac Jenning Carlson on the television soap opera *The Edge of Night*. But since Carlson had bled to death on a special Christmas Eve episode last year, Harris had turned his attention to his revue *Another Evening with Harry Stoones*.

Except that it wasn't really a revue; it was just set up to look like one. In fact, *Harry Stoones* was conceived for "people who hate revues" — a takeoff on all those tiresome "Evening with" shows that lately had become "epidemic" off-Broadway. No cheesy lounge singers with velvet voices here. This was going to be smart, sassy, and successful. Indeed, Harris and his collaborators were so confident that they'd agreed to a long-term lease on the Gramercy Arts Theatre at Twenty-seventh Street and Lexington Avenue.

On such youthful hubris did *Harry Stoones* run. Harris and his two producers, Harvard graduates G. Adam Jordan and Fred Mueller, were all just twenty-six years old. Their newly formed Stenod Productions had managed to raise $15,000 from twenty-five investors in the last few months. The show would consist of comedy skits divided into two acts, "The Civil War" and "The Roaring Twenties" — time periods that had absolutely nothing to do with the subject of the show. This same sort of cheekiness was also evident in the non sequitur Harris had pulled out of thin air to use as a title: No Harry Stoones ever appeared (or was even mentioned) in the script.

Problems arose with casting, which Harris felt was "absolutely impossible." In the auditorium of the Gramercy Arts, the playwright sat with Jordan, who would direct the show, growing bleary-eyed as they looked at headshot after headshot. What they needed were "down-to-earth performers," Harris said, "not the typical smiley, happy, hooray type." For days they'd been auditioning dozens of actors, but so far had only settled on a few. Diana Sands, who'd won the Outer Critics Circle Award for her portrayal of the daughter in *A Raisin in the Sun,* was their big name. The rest of the actors they'd chosen were largely newcomers: Kenny Adams had been in the ensemble of the Frank Loesser musical *Greenwillow* the previous year, while Sheila Copelan and Lou Antonio had done some television. To round out their cast,

Harris and his partners needed two more women and two more men. The hopefuls kept trotting onto the stage, and the search continued.

Looking over the pile of headshots one more time, Harris kept pausing whenever he'd spot the face of one particular girl. Her name was Barbra Streisand. She'd come in with her manager, a boxy guy named Erlichman who wore a suit with a hole in the left sleeve. The small, slender kid with the large nose and curious eyes had climbed up on the stage and belted out a couple of songs for them, and they'd all thought she was "hot, clearly talented, and very different" — precisely what they wanted in the show. But she was a singer, they believed, not an actress, and the show didn't need singers; it needed people who could act. The skits demanded perfect comedy timing; the gags couldn't be played too broad. So, with some regret, they had turned the Streisand kid down.

But her face kept coming back to Harris. It was her difference that stayed in his mind. The way she had looked, the way she had "answered funny" when they'd asked her questions. Few of the actors they'd interviewed so far had been more "down-to-earth" than she was, and no one would ever describe Barbra Streisand as "the typical smiley, happy, hooray type." She was, when they came right down to it, exactly what they were looking for. If Streisand couldn't act, Harris decided, then he'd write a few extra songs for her. So, with little more than a month before their scheduled opening date, he and his partners decided to call the kid back.

8.

On an afternoon in mid-September, Barbra walked alongside Marty as they entered the Columbia Records building at 799 Seventh Avenue, between Fiftieth and Fifty-first streets. It was an old building, seven stories tall, with peeling paint and pipes that frequently burst, hardly the place one would imagine as the home of one of the biggest record companies in the world. The first floor was rented out to shops, but the rest of the building was a beehive of constantly humming activity. The basement contained the record archive — a treasure trove dating back to the 1920s with the Paul Whiteman Orchestra and Ruth Etting that also included original Rodgers and Hammerstein cast recordings, Frank Sinatra, Rosemary Clooney, Tony Bennett, Johnnie Ray, and Leonard Bernstein. The top two floors of the building housed the recording studios. But it was to the fourth floor, entirely occupied by the offices of company president Goddard Lieberson, that Barbra and Marty were heading this day.

That Marty had managed to wrangle a meeting — a prelude to an actual audition — with the big cheese of Columbia Records was only one of his miracles that late summer of 1961. No doubt, as she rode the rickety elevator up from the ground floor, Barbra was awash in excitement, her mind filled with everything that was suddenly going on for her. Record deals were fine; "easy money" was how Barbra told friends she viewed the chance to record an album. But far more important to her was the fact that she'd gotten the part in *Another Evening with Harry Stoones,* just as Marty had predicted. Rehearsals had recently gotten underway at the Gramercy Arts. Now Barbra had the chance to prove to the world that she was so much more than just a singer.

The deal Harris had offered her, of course, had been terrible. "This is off-Broadway," he'd told Marty; there was practically no money. Barbra would be paid $37.50 a week — a huge drop from the $350 a week she'd just been promised by the hungry i. But it was a chance for her to *act,* to do the kind of work she'd been denied now for more than a year, ever since she'd closed in *The Boy Friend.* And Barbra truly believed that *Harry Stoones* was going to get attention from the critics. Advance buzz on the show was good. New cast members included Dom DeLuise, who'd done *Little Mary Sunshine* off-Broadway, and Susan Belink, a wonderful student from the Manhattan School of Music who would be singing most of the songs, for which Barbra was extremely grateful. Best of all, however, in terms of garnering critical attention, was the addition of Joe Milan, who'd assisted none other than Jerome Robbins on *Gypsy,* as the show's choreographer.

Surviving on the thirty-seven dollars that *Harry Stoones* promised to pay her, however, would have been impossible. But yet again Marty had come to Barbra's rescue. As they stepped out of the elevator and entered the reception area for Lieberson's office, Barbra could thank Marty for a good many things, and he'd been her manager for barely one month. But it was the gig he'd just gotten her, at the Blue Angel, that could prove to be the most lucrative.

Barbra had tried once before to audition at the Angel, one of the toniest nightclubs in the city, but hadn't gotten anywhere with its owner, the snobbish Herbert Jacoby. Then Marty had intervened. He'd had some success getting the Clancy Brothers onto the Angel's stage, so he knew the best strategy was to bypass Jacoby and work directly with the club's second owner, Max Gordon. While Gordon had little to do with the daily ins and outs at the Angel — concentrating instead on the Village Vanguard, where he'd heard Barbra sing not long be-fore — his opinions carried weight, even if Jacoby wished he'd keep them downtown. And while Gordon had decided Barbra wasn't right for the Vanguard, he thought she'd fit in quite well at the more eclectic Angel. So he'd pressured Jacoby to relent and give Barbra the audition she wanted. Of course, whenever Barbra was given the chance to sing, she usually won over any doubters, and Jacoby was no exception. He'd signed her to a two-week run in November with a salary in excess of three hundred a week. So, thanks to Marty, that thirty-seven dollars a week from *Stoones* could be used as pocket change — bus fare and late-night noshing at the Brasserie.

At last things were going Barbra's way. So it was with some re-newed spring in her step that she accompanied Marty into Goddard Lieberson's office. Few people ever made it this far. Lieberson was a formidable figure, keeping his record company remarkably indepen-dent from its corporate parent, CBS. His recently hired legal counsel, Walter Yetnikoff, described Columbia as Goddard's "own fiefdom," over which he ruled as a benevolent — and stylish — dictator. The man who was now shaking hands with Barbra and Marty had all his shirts custom-made in London; his tweed jackets inevitably sported leather patches on the elbows. He was the rare man who could get away with wearing pink — shirts, ties, pocket silks — without any collateral damage to his masculinity. When he wore an ascot, it seemed "appropriate," Yetnikoff said, "never pretentious." Married to the former ballerina Vera Zorina, the dark-haired, graying-at-the-temples Lieberson was the only employee CBS president William Paley and his wife, Babe, considered their social equal.

It had been Lieberson who'd overseen the introduction of the 33⅓ rpm LP record that had revolutionized the music industry in 1948. It had been Lieberson who'd convinced CBS to invest in the musical *My Fair Lady,* which had made the company a fortune. It had been Lieberson who'd launched the Record of the Month Club, which had caused profits to skyrocket. Whatever Goddard Lieberson wanted, he got; what he didn't want, no one took. It wasn't surprising that people shuddered when summoned to his office: "God would like to see you now" was how the memo read.

Standing before God, neither Barbra nor Marty cowered. They were there on a mission. Lieberson gestured for them to sit at the large round table in his office, where Marty pulled a few of Barbra's reviews from his briefcase and read them out loud. Then he set a tape recorder on the table and played some of her songs. Lieberson listened politely, not saying much. No doubt he was aware that much more than a table separated him from the two people across from him. They all might have been Jewish, but Lieberson had been born in Hanley, Staffordshire, England, not Brooklyn, New York. And while his immigrant father had been a manufacturer of rubber heels, Lieberson had attended the prestigious Eastman College of Music instead of hustling his way into show business like these two characters. At Eastman, Lieberson had written chamber music set to Elizabethan poetry. By 1939, he had composed more than a hundred works, many of which were performed by Works Progress Administration orchestras. Even after being hired by Columbia, he'd found time to write a novel and master Japanese.

With seemingly infinite patience, the erudite Lieberson now sat back in his chair and listened as the plain-talking Erlichman made his pitch. After all, the guy had brought the Clancy Brothers to Columbia; Lieberson owed him that much. But the slender, odd-looking girl sitting beside Erlichman did not impress God. Marty seemed to sense this, and so, instead of asking for an immediate decision, suggested that Lieberson keep the tapes for a while. He told him that Barbra was special. "Listen to her when the phones aren't ringing," he told Lieberson, who indulgently agreed.

Leaving the office that day, Marty may well have been filled with anxiety about getting a positive answer from Lieberson. But Barbra, friends noticed, was much more tranquil about her prospects. What held far more opportunity than a record deal, Barbra believed, was *Another Evening with Harry Stoones,* and for that she didn't need to wait for any decision from God. With a little help from Marty, she had done that herself.

CHAPTER SEVEN

Fall 1961

1.

With her hair piled up on top of her head, wearing a dark sleeveless dress and an air of entitled nonchalance, Barbra took complete charge of the taping of her second appearance on *PM East*. Disregarding the script and directing the conversation, she forced the pugnacious Mike Wallace to follow her lead. When he asked about life in Brooklyn, Wallace found himself in the rare position of being outmaneuvered by a guest who didn't want to answer the question. "In Detroit they think I come from Turkey," Barbra said. "In St. Louis they think I come from Israel. It doesn't matter where I come from." Then she launched into "Come to the Supermarket in Old Peking" with all the eccentricities that had startled her audiences in Winnipeg: "They have sunflower cakes, moonbeam cakes, gizzard cakes, lizard cakes, pickled eels, pickled snakes . . ."

It was precisely for this outsized personality that they'd brought her back. The reaction to Barbra's debut on the program had been "so enthusiastic," Wallace admitted, that they decided to make her a semi-regular guest. Watching from the booth, the show's publicist, Don Softness, marveled at the way the kid bantered easily with the hosts and then segued into musical numbers that left audiences dazzled. "She was born a star," Softness thought. Not only did Barbra have "this beautiful voice," but she had "something more than self-confidence." It was a quality of "expectation," Softness realized, of "claiming what was her due."

Of course, at that particular moment, Barbra had every reason to feel on top of her game. For one thing, she finally had a place to live. A cousin had passed on to her a sublet he'd been renting on West Eighteenth Street in Chelsea, and Barbra had redecorated with feather boas and esoteric posters. She was even considering getting her own phone for the first time in her life. Meanwhile, rehearsals for *Another Evening with Harry Stoones* were going well, with everyone convinced that it would be a hit. What was more, Marty was angling to get her an audition for an honest-to-god Broadway show, David Merrick's *What's in It for Me?* Columnist Hedda Hopper had reported that Tony Franciosa might star, and the *Times* had just announced that Arthur Laurents would direct and Sylvia Sidney would play the protagonist's mother. If Barbra got a part in the show, she'd have to bow out of *Harry Stoones*. But everyone would understand. After all, this was David Merrick, the biggest producer on Broadway!

While it may have been a long shot, Barbra told Softness and the rest of the folks at *PM East* about Merrick's show. When Mike Wallace suggested on air that being on *PM East* would help her attract the attention of big-time producers such as Merrick, Barbra just laughed and cut him down to size. "Now, let's be honest," she said. "Those people don't watch television, not the ones that do the hiring. A show like this just gets the public interested in paying the minimum to see me at places like the Bon Soir." No doubt, despite his outward amusement, Wallace seethed.

There was more sass to come. Before she went on to sing, Barbra scolded Wallace for failing to give a plug for *Stoones*, which was opening soon. "You forgot to mention the play I'm in," she said, shouting over the host to give the name of the theater and the opening date.

After all, the whole reason she appeared on *PM East* was to get publicity for herself.

Watching her, Don Softness understood her attitude and figured they could work to each other's mutual advantage. His job was to publicize *PM East,* and "an interesting guest could be used as a peg" to bring the show some notice. But at the same time, those same interesting guests would benefit by having their own profiles raised by doing publicity for the show. And Barbra, Softness thought, "was as interesting as they came."

So when Barbra was finished taping that day, Softness approached her. He asked if she'd be willing to do some publicity. Even as the question was still on Softness's lips, Barbra blurted out, "Yes!" She had a manager and an agent; a publicist was the logical next step. And Softness seemed a good man for the job. He and his brother, John, had opened the Softness Group two years earlier; their client list had been building steadily ever since. So they made an appointment to meet at Softness's office on Madison Avenue in order to "get some press material out on her." They shook hands.

The merchandizing of Barbra Streisand was about to begin.

2.

Who cared that the house wasn't even half full? The show was only in previews. There was still time for word to get out and bring in the crowds. Besides, how could Barbra be upset about anything when she'd just gotten her picture in the *New York Times*? Even if they'd spelled her name with three a's, and even if the photo wasn't all that flattering — her mouth was open midsong — it was still her, and no doubt everyone in Brooklyn (and a certain ex-boyfriend in Manhattan) had seen it.

On stage at the Gramercy Arts Theatre, Barbra had just gotten a big laugh from the small audience for telling her lover in one skit that she was pregnant. The lead-up to the punch line was a group of jocks bragging about their conquests with all the pretty girls at school while their nebbish friend listens, seemingly in envy. But it's only the nebbish who turns out to have gotten any action, for after everyone has left, the homely tagalong of the pretty girls (Barbra) comes up to him and announces, "Barry, I'm pregnant." Only Barbra would have appreciated the irony of the boy's name.

Most of her bits in *Harry Stoones* were in the first act. She played an Indian maiden, sang a goofy song called "Value" about being in love with a guy called Harold Mengert, and lampooned, in two different skits, the blues and New Jersey. So after her "I'm pregnant" line, which led off the second act, she mostly just sat backstage. But she was "just happy to be acting," one friend understood.

And that photo in the *Times*! How could she not be happy? Barbra might be listed last in the credits for the show, but it was *her* picture with which the *Times* had chosen to announce *Stoones's* opening—not Sands's, not Dom DeLuise's. No one could be quite sure how that had happened, but in addition to the official mimeographs issued from the show's publicists, newspaper editors were also receiving notices from Don Softness promoting *PM East's* latest discovery, a brilliant singer and offbeat character named Barbra Streisand. In choosing to go with a picture of the television personality, the *Times* was counting on the fact that Barbra might actually be more recognizable to its readers than the revue's other, ostensibly bigger names.

As Barbra rejoined her castmates on stage for the final curtain call, taking her bows as the meager audience got to its feet, there was a sense in the air that it was she—last on the bill, the butt of so many of the jokes—who was the fastest on the move.

3.

At Bob's little "postshow get-together" after *Harry Stoones's* opening night on Saturday, October 21, Barbra seemed less focused on the reviews than on the fact that Barré had come to see the show. The critics hadn't been kind. The reviewer who'd shown up from the *Times*, Lewis Funke, was perhaps the least simpatico with a revue that strove so earnestly to be avant-garde. Funke was a former sports reporter and, at fifty, part of another generation entirely than the kids cavorting up on stage. If Funke gave them a negative review, which everyone expected, there would likely never be another evening with Harry Stoones.

But the fear of closing didn't seem to be in the forefront of Barbra's mind. Rather, she was more interested to learn from Bob that Barré had taken notes on her performance. Instead of being offended, she was eager to see·what her former boyfriend had written. Holed up in a corner of Bob's new apartment — he'd taken a gorgeous place on Gramercy Park South just a few blocks from the theater, with sixteen-foot ceilings, a Steinway grand piano, and enormous windows that overlooked the park — Barbra pored over Barré's notes. He thought she'd been "great," beautifully "underplaying her numbers." Her voice had been terrific, he said, especially on "Value" — the Harold Mengert number — but it was her timing and her acting that had really impressed him and that was what mattered most to Barbra. Barré's opinion, Bob realized, was still "very important to her." Part of her had moved on from that heartbreak, but another part remained tethered to this man who had meant so much.

For a performer faced with the closing of her show, Barbra seemed to Bob to possess remarkable sangfroid. It wasn't just *Another Evening with Harry Stoones* that had proved to be a disappointment either. She'd also recently learned that Goddard Lieberson wouldn't be offering her a record deal. But Barbra seemed calm, collected, confident. That fall, many of her friends sensed that she was getting very close to something big. And so as one show faced the ax, Barbra seemed to roll with the punches and turned her determined eyes to another — the appropriately named *What's in It for Me?*

.

4.

The temperatures were mild on Thursday, November 16, but the skies had turned a solid slate gray, pregnant with rain, which only made

Jerome Weidman's mood all the bleaker. The novelist-playwright had just come from his doctor's office where he'd been told he needed an abdominal operation. He should have gone home and rested, but instead he took a taxi up to the St. James Theatre on Forty-fourth Street. Auditions were being held that day for the show he was scheduled to start rehearsing in five weeks, which Weidman had adapted from his 1937 novel, *I Can Get It for You Wholesale.*

It wasn't as if the auditions that day were all that important. Most of the bigger parts had already been chosen. Weidman could have, "without compunction or hesitation," left the selection of these less vital players in the very capable hands of the director, Arthur Laurents. But after writing the books for such successful shows as *Fiorello!* and *Tenderloin,* he had learned that it was "as impossible to become partially involved with a show" as it was "to partially fall in love."

Laurents was already at the theater. The director sat in the audience, watching the hopefuls on the stage. Although he'd written the books for many of Broadway's biggest hits of recent years — *The Time of the Cuckoo, Gypsy, West Side Story* — this was only his second time directing, and his first time directing someone else's material. When David Merrick had asked him to take the helm, Laurents, never one to be impressed by hype — his or anyone else's — took it in stride. Merrick, he believed, "must have been turned down by the big-name directors he went after first." He accepted the job, despite his belief that the script — the story of a scheming con man named Harry Bogen — was "flawed" and "unmarked for success," because he'd always wanted to work with Merrick. He also believed he could make something special out of that flawed script.

Sitting there that day, watching the aspiring actors troop across the stage at the St. James Theatre, Laurents felt confident he could pull it off — so long as Weidman didn't fight him too much. He considered that unlikely. Of the two, Laurents was known as the greater wordsmith, with a body of work that also included such esteemed films as *Rope, Anastasia,* and *Bonjour Tristesse.* Weidman, for his part, had never written anything to top *Wholesale,* his first novel, and his one major film had been the middlebrow melodrama *The Damned Don't Cry*, starring Joan Crawford.

If any script battles were to come, however, they lay in the future, so when Weidman arrived at the theater, he and Laurents greeted each other warmly. There were backslaps and good words also with Harold Rome, the lyricist, and Herbert Ross, the choreographer. For the moment, everything was smiles and handshakes, and the men putting on this show for David Merrick settled down into the darkened red-velvet auditorium and turned their attention to the stage.

All auditions followed a similar pattern. The applicant would trudge up to the stage and stand beneath the glare of a bare bulb while the stage manager shouted out a name. To Weidman, "the names of all unknown actors and actresses, when heard for the first time in a darkened theater at an audition," sounded like anagrams "composed of letters taken from the sides of Lithuanian Pullman cars." With such incomprehensible cacophony, the name "Barbra Streisand" reached Weidman's ears.

Barbra wore "a fur coat . . . a combination of tans, browns, yellows, and whites, all swirling around in great shapeless blotches, like a child's painting." From below the coat Weidman discerned "a couple of very shapely legs." Laurents astutely pegged the coat as "an old movie-star wrap," and Barbra was indeed intentionally hoping to evoke a bit of old-time movie-star glamour. Dressing for the audition with Bob, she'd chosen a "fabulous" caracul coat. The lamb's fur was also ornamented with a bit of fox. The coat had come from a thrift shop, but it still looked "pristine," Bob thought, "like something Dietrich would have worn."

Yet for this particular audition Barbra would play the white goddess only on the outside. When she opened the fur coat, she revealed a simple wool dress, hardly the high couture most would-be actresses wore to auditions. Her hair wasn't coiffed either, but was instead knotted in an old-maidish bun on the top of her head. Laurents got precisely the impression she wanted him to get: "Spinster incarnate," he thought to himself when he got his first good look at her.

There was a method to Barbra's madness, of course. The only role of any consequence left to cast—and the only one she was remotely qualified for—was the harried, homely secretary Miss Marmelstein. Barbra knew exactly what she was doing.

And so she performed a brilliant routine of what Laurents immediately recognized as "calculated spontaneity." First came the "elaborate shedding" of the coat, revealing her "gawky, disorganized body." Then there was a complicated bit with the sheet music, produced from a red briefcase and held comically to her waist. Extravagant whispers to the accompanist followed. Then the kid asked a stagehand for a chair. She was nervous, she claimed, and wanted to sit, but Laurents thought her nerves, while possibly real "somewhere deep down," were part of her routine. As the chair was wheeled over to the center of the stage, Barbra marched to meet it—while her sheet music, taped together, suddenly accordioned after her. Laurents shook his head in bemusement. "Funny, attention-getting, a good trick," he thought, especially since it was punctuated by a "trilling giggle of feigned surprise."

Sitting back in his seat, the director thought this Streisand kid was maybe "too much," maybe "trying too hard." She was entertaining, but he was on to her tricks. Everything she did, Laurents observed, was staged. When she sat down in the chair, she didn't just sit—"she sprawled in it, flung her legs out, took them back, wrapped her arms around them, under them, across them," all the while "elaborately chewing gum." When it came time for her to sing, she took the gum out of her mouth and—using a bit of business as old as her act itself—proceeded to stick it under the chair. (Or at least she seemed to. When Laurents checked later, there was no gum.) Laurents just rolled his eyes. "She'd better have a voice," he thought to himself.

From farther back in the theater, another set of eyes watched her, eyes belonging to a young man who could barely believe he was there at all. Six foot three, two hundred pounds, Elliott Gould had leaped from the chorus line of *Irma la Douce* right into the starring role of this production, pushing aside such established names as Tony Franciosa and Laurence Harvey, both of whom had been considered.

Gould's casting had surprised him as much as it did Broadway insiders. The twenty-three-year-old was almost a complete unknown, and it was on his untried shoulders, broad as they might be, that the entire weight of a David Merrick vehicle was now being placed. So it was with considerable fascination that Gould watched this "fantastic freak" — his words — cavort up on the stage. This Barbra Streisand might be "the weirdo of all times" — his own words again — but she seemed to have reservoirs of confidence that he envied, with none of the self-doubts that kept him awake at night.

Barbra had plenty of her own self-doubts, of course, but she kept them well hidden. What people saw was that old ferocious belief that she had to make it to the top or go nowhere at all. At this particular moment, that belief was being fueled by the adrenaline produced by the reviews for *Another Evening with Harry Stoones*. True enough that the show had closed after only one official performance, and true, too, that the stodgy Lewis Funke hadn't even mentioned Barbra in his scathing critique in the *New York Times*. "None too stimulating," he'd concluded about the show, an opinion shared by reviewers for the *New York Post* and *Herald Tribune*. But others, a little more in tune with *Harry Stoones*'s offbeat sensibility, had responded very differently, both to the show and to Barbra. Edith Oliver in *The New Yorker* had thought *Stoones* was "quick, flippant [and] sometimes bright and original," and she "particularly admired" Barbra. Martin Gottfried in *Women's Wear Daily*, who'd been one of those hooting and whistling for Barbra right from the start at the Bon Soir, had proclaimed *Harry Stoones* "gleeful" and "riotous," and observed, "Barbra Streisand has been a fine singer for some time and continues to be one." Michael Smith in the *Village Voice* had gone so far as to declare that no one in the cast, not even Sands or DeLuise, had been "quite strong enough" to play opposite Barbra. But such raves appeared days after the show had closed, too late to do any good.

Too late for the show, perhaps, but not for Barbra. By the time she strode into the St. James Theatre, it was with an air of supreme confidence. It hadn't been just her voice the critics had applauded, but her acting: *Variety* thought Barbra had shown "excellent flair for dropping a dour blackout gag." Now, with that same sort of flair, she sauntered up onto the St. James stage, playing the part of the eccentric kid, a role that had worked so well for her on *PM East,* a persona Don Softness, her shrewd new publicist, had encouraged. It was shtick that bordered on being disrespectful — the well-executed slip of her music, for example, or her demand for a chair — but it never quite crossed that line. Instead, it was funny. Different. It got the men in power to sit up and pay attention. Now all that was left for Barbra to do was sing. And that, of course, was the easy part.

The timing couldn't have been better. Barbra was set to open at the Blue Angel that night, so her voice was in top form. She was also fortunate that Peter Daniels had moved over to the Angel from the Bon Soir; he'd helped Barbra expand her repertoire. So she could have chosen to sing any number of songs for her audition. She went with the broadly comic "Value," which had been such a success for her in *Harry Stoones.* "Call me a schlemiel, call me a brain with a missing wheel . . ." Both Laurents and Weidman found the song delightful, and burst into applause when Barbra was done. When Laurents asked if she had a ballad, Barbra briskly replied that she'd sing "Have I Stayed Too Long at the Fair?" — which they all knew and approved of. Halfway through the song, as they all sat silently listening, Harold Rome leaned over his seat and whispered to Laurents, "Geez, she's really *something,* isn't she?"

She was. Laurents agreed Barbra was something special, but Miss Marmelstein was supposed to be fifty years old, and this kid would barely be twenty by the time the show opened. Still, she was good — very good — with exactly the kind of "Jewish sensibility" the show needed — which, no doubt, Barbra had been counting on. *What's in It for Me?* was a show where her Jewishness would be an asset, not a liability. Without that cultural flavor, the show lost everything, a fact Laurents understood very well. Back in 1951, Twentieth Century-Fox had turned Weidman's novel into a movie, keeping the original title, *I Can Get It for You Wholesale,* but practically nothing else. Harry Bogen was turned into Harriet Boyd in a star vehicle for the titian-haired, Irish-Swedish Susan Hayward. The film was a flop. This new version, Laurents knew, had to retain its gritty, urban, ethnic identity, and for this, Barbra Streisand fit perfectly.

Still, he also knew that she wasn't what Merrick had in mind for the part, so for the moment he just thanked her and said they might call her back. That was enough for Barbra. She hadn't been rejected out of hand; she still had a chance. She left the stage in a bubbly, effusive mood, inviting everyone to come see her at the Blue Angel. And call her, yes, please, call her! She finally had a phone number all her own, she told everyone, and she sang it out with exuberance.

Everyone laughed. It was the perfect shtick with which to end her audition. Laurents made sure to write her number down, while several rows behind him in the theater, someone else did so as well.

5.

Later that evening, leaving her sublet on West Eighteenth Street to head uptown to the Blue Angel, Barbra heard her telephone ring.

She picked up and heard a male voice.

"You said you wanted to get calls, so I called," the man said. "You were brilliant."

It was Elliott Gould. The big, gangly lead from *What's in It for Me?* Barbra thanked him, and that was the extent of their conversation. She hung up the phone and told Terry Leong what had just happened. Gould was the star of the show; maybe he made such courtesy calls to everyone who auditioned. But Terry told her that wasn't likely. The guy would be on the phone all night if that were the case.

At the audition, Barbra had barely noticed Gould. There'd been no real feeling about him one way or the other. Gould wasn't really Barbra's type, which tended toward more handsome, polished men. Gould was, instead, long-limbed and lantern-jawed, with a nose that some likened to a large dill pickle. But he had called her. He had called her and told her that she was brilliant. It left an impression.

How could it not? It made her, friends said, curious, at the very least, to see Gould again.

6.

The Blue Angel, with its long, rectangular shape and oddly quilted walls, left more than one performer struck by its resemblance to a coffin — an ironic analogy for a place known for giving birth to cabaret stars. From the Angel's tiny stage the likes of Felicia Sanders, Harry Belafonte, Eartha Kitt, and Dorothy Loudon had dazzled audiences for nearly two decades. Now in the second week of her run, Barbra stepped into the spotlight dressed in a pink gingham sleeveless dress with a sequined jumper-style bodice — hardly the image of a traditional nightclub singer, but very much the mod, stylish icon Bob had been endeavoring so hard to create — and smiled at the faces in the crowd, many of whom were familiar to her this night.

For one, there was Lorraine Gordon, whose husband, Max, had helped Barbra land the gig. Lorraine had also involved Barbra in her political cause, the antinuclear group Women Strike for Peace. Mostly oblivious to politics until this point, Barbra had been suddenly inspired by Lorraine's passion, and she had accompanied her to rallies and helped her pass out leaflets on the street condemning the U.S.-Soviet arms race.

But her primary focus, at least for the moment, remained her own career. And so it was to another table that Barbra made sure she was directing her performance that night. The team from *What's in It for Me?* had come to see her: Arthur Laurents, Jerry Weidman, and Harold Rome. The fact that Barbra was performing at the Blue Angel was a definite point in her favor for these theatrical power brokers. The crème de la crème of New York society regularly showed up at the Angel. It was, by far, Barbra's most prestigious booking yet.

Barbra was third on a bill topped by comedian Pat Harrington, Jr., best known for the comic Italian-immigrant stereotype named Guido Panzini that he played on Jack Paar's show. Also on the bill were another comedian, Barbara Heller, and the Canadian folksingers Sylvia Fricker and Ian Tyson. After the opening, *Variety* had declared Barbra the best of the bunch. In the trade paper's recent review, Harrington had been called "undisciplined" and Heller "another disappointment." But Barbra had known "her way with a song." Her routine with Peter Daniels was by now seamless. No doubt *Variety*'s endorsement had pleased Barbra very much, especially as the trade paper was required reading for Laurents and his compadres.

Yet there was something else in the review that had left her steaming. "She's very youthful," the *Variety* critic observed, "and if intent about her professional ambitions, perhaps a little corrective schnoz bob might be an element to be considered." The reviewer opined that comics such as Fanny Brice, Jimmy Durante, and Danny Thomas were one thing, but "ingénues, of good figure and advanced vocal interpretation, with many years before them," constituted something else entirely. In other words, Barbra would have to choose: Keep the nose and settle for being a comic or whittle the nose down and all those other "professional ambitions" might come true.

It was the first time any critic had so baldly disparaged her looks. Here was *Variety*, the showbiz bible, insisting that if she was truly "intent" on being successful, then she should plane down her schnoz. The review left Barbra "overcome with a new burst of insecurities," one friend discerned.

Yet for the three men sitting in her audience that night, any suggestion to change that big, glorious Jewish nose was absurd. It was Barbra's nose — along with her voice, manner, and style — that made her so right for the show. No doubt Barbra understood this, but that didn't make getting up there on that stage any less difficult, the words "corrective schnoz bob" fresh in her mind. Still, she belted her heart out on song after song, projecting as much confidence as ever. She'd learned how to do that long ago.

Barbra's performance this night was, in effect, another audition, despite the fact that she'd already traipsed back to the St. James Theatre more than once to sing, hoping something, anything, might finally convince David Merrick to give her the part of Miss Marmelstein. It was Merrick who would make the final decision, Barbra knew, but the "abominable showman," as he was called around Broadway, hadn't come to the Angel to hear her this night. Barbra could only hope that if she could fire up those who *had* come, then maybe they could persuade Merrick for her.

She had, in fact, already sold herself to Laurents, Weidman, and Rome, though she didn't know that for sure. Laurents had already concluded that Barbra "had to be in the show," and Weidman had determined she had "the X quality" that made a star. To confirm their opinions, they'd brought lyricist Stephen Sondheim, Laurents's collaborator on *Gypsy* and *West Side Story*. As Barbra sang, they all sat back and listened, soaking up the strains of "A Sleepin' Bee," "Cry Me a River," "Right as the Rain," and even "Come to the Supermarket in Old Peking."

After the show was over, Sondheim didn't quite share his colleagues' appreciation of the young singer. "Too pinched and nasal," he said of Barbra's voice. But that didn't deter Laurents, who made a beeline to see Barbra backstage and offered some tips on lighting. "Don't look down," he told her. The Blue Angel's single unmoving spotlight cast unflattering shadows, he explained. He was already thinking of how she'd look on the Broadway stage. Now if only David Merrick would see things his way.

7.

As Bob tiptoed into his kitchen, the rain was coming down outside in heavy sheets, splashing against the tall windows that overlooked the park. It was early on the morning after Thanksgiving, and Barbra was sound asleep on his couch. Quietly, Bob opened his refrigerator and began making turkey sandwiches from the leftovers he'd saved from the feast the day before. Wrapping one sandwich in wax paper, he slipped it into a paper bag, scrawling BARBRA'S LUNCH on the side.

He knew she had a big day ahead of her. And she'd had a long night, too, so he was letting her sleep for a while longer. Barbra had missed Thanksgiving dinner because she'd been performing at the Blue Angel, and it wasn't until well after midnight that she had arrived at Bob's, long after everyone else had left. He'd kept a plate aside for her, and Barbra had wolfed down the turkey, stuffing, and gravy as they gabbed into the wee hours. She'd been invigorated by her performance, but also anxious about the next day because she was scheduled to meet with Merrick at the St. James Theatre. She was hoping that he'd give her the news she'd been waiting for. It had been more than a week since she'd first auditioned for *What's in It for Me?*, and the not knowing was killing her. If she couldn't get into a show by and about Jews, she feared, then she'd never get into anything.

As audition time neared, Bob gently woke his friend. Barbra showered and washed her hair, but the only clothes she had with her were those she'd worn at the Blue Angel the night before. Still, her rather "severe" black silk dress, black nylons, and black shoes made for a good look, Bob thought, especially topped with the caracul coat. Bob handed her the lunch bag, then walked her outside and helped her hail a cab in the rain.

The show was coming together, according to press reports. Instead of Sylvia Sidney, the part of Mrs. Bogen had gone to Lillian Roth, another old-time star. Roth hadn't been on Broadway since the early 1930s, when she'd been one of the sensations in the *Earl Carroll Vanities*. A brief stint in movies had followed until alcoholism cut short her career. Her candid autobiography, *I'll Cry Tomorrow*, chronicled her addictions, brought her back to public notice, and was made into a film with Susan Hayward. Now sober, Roth made many television appearances after that, usually closing with her theme song, "When the Red, Red Robin Comes Bob, Bob, Bobbin' Along." David Merrick, recognizing that he needed a name above the title, made Roth the ostensible star of the show.

Everyone in the cast had impressive résumés. Harold Lang, Bambi Linn, and Jack Kruschen were all veterans. Even the show's love interest, Marilyn Cooper, had played small parts in *Gypsy* and *West Side*

Story, so she already had a working relationship with Laurents. Everyone was a lot more "in" than Barbra—except, she realized, the star of the show himself, that big, lumbering Elliott Gould, the guy who had called her on the phone. He was almost as green as Barbra was.

Clearly, Gould had been chosen not because of any name recognition with the ticket-buying public, but because he was *right* for the role of the enterprising, crafty—and very Jewish—Harry Bogen. Would Merrick use the same logic in selecting Barbra? Laurents had already declared that Miss Marmelstein didn't have to be a fiftyish spinster; a twentyish wallflower could serve the same purpose. But would Merrick agree?

David Merrick was one of those larger-than-life showmen, like Barnum and Belasco, who were geniuses not only at picking box-office hits but also at promoting their own legends. In his finely tailored suits, cheap toupee, and silent-movie-villain mustache, Merrick cut an easily recognizable—and just as easily parodied—figure on the Great White Way. He lived, breathed, ate, drank, and slept theater. He liked to say that he was born the night his first big show, *Fanny,* starring Florence Henderson and Ezio Pinza, opened at the Majestic Theatre on Broadway—which effectively obliterated his hardscrabble early life in St. Louis as the son of a Russian Jewish immigrant tailor. Like the girl he was considering hiring, Merrick had been an ambitious soul fleeing less-than-glamorous origins. Whenever he flew across country, he wouldn't permit his private plane to fly over St. Louis, unwilling to risk an emergency landing in his hated hometown.

At least that was the story. And there were lots of stories about Merrick. Some of them were even true. He gained his reputation as a master promoter in 1949 when his show *Clutterbuck* was struggling to find an audience. To generate publicity, Merrick's savvy publicist, Lee Solters, began phoning restaurants throughout the city and asking them to page a nonexistent "Mr. Clutterbuck." That made the columns and guaranteed the show a reprieve of a few weeks. Merrick was known for big, glossy productions: *The Matchmaker, Gypsy,*

Irma la Douce, Do Re Mi. But he had also distinguished himself with some notable succès d'estime, such as *Look Back in Anger* and *The Entertainer,* both by John Osborne, the latter of which marked one of Laurence Olivier's most acclaimed roles. At times, close to a quarter of the entire Broadway workforce was employed by Merrick.

Arthur Laurents, for his part, was quite pleased to finally be working with Merrick on *What's in It for Me?,* even if they had immediately clashed on how the sets should look. Laurents wanted subtle Brechtian blacks, whites, and grays; Merrick, not surprisingly, wanted lots of bright reds. Only after much back and forth did Laurents prevail. The director tolerated the belligerence because he believed Merrick had a "genuine . . . love and respect for the theater." Still, the producer could be Machiavellian in getting what he wanted, pitting collaborators against each other, saying one thing when he wanted another, and humiliating actors, whom he despised. To Merrick, actors were merely puppets to be used in the best interests of the production. And he liked pretty puppets. That was why he was being so pigheaded about Miss Marmelstein.

As Barbra stumbled out of the rain into the theater, she kept her coat wrapped around her, not wanting to step out onto the stage in her black silk evening dress. That would have been a bit much, even for her; it wasn't even noon yet, after all. From the assemblage of principals seated in the audience — Laurents, Weidman, Rome, Herbert Ross, and Merrick himself — it seemed obvious that a decision had been made. Barbra braced herself for what she was about to hear.

Laurents had finally been able to pin Merrick down on his choice only a few hours earlier. The producer had tried arguing that Barbra was simply "too ugly," that if they were making Miss Marmelstein younger, then why not go with some "cute girl," a suggestion Laurents argued, quite rationally, went completely against the character. But actors were "window dressing," Merrick told him. They had to be appealing enough to draw in customers. They were already saddled with an unattractive lead in Elliott Gould, he argued. Did they really want another homely face up on the stage?

Laurents said yes, in fact, they did. And so, with a long sigh, Merrick gave in. It was a small, insignificant part anyway. They had the winsome long-legged Bambi Linn and the pretty brown-eyed Marilyn Cooper to take up the slack.

As Barbra stood on the stage, Laurents gave her the news. The part, he said, was hers. She responded calmly, with a dignified equanimity, thanking them all and promising to make them proud of her. She was invited back to Merrick's office to work out the details of her contract, which Marty stepped forward to handle. She would be making only $150 a week, Barbra learned, far less than she made in clubs, but the expectation was that *What's in It for Me?* would run for months, maybe even years, so financially, Barbra would be more secure than she'd ever been in her life. If the show was a hit, that is. And after *Harry Stoones,* Barbra knew better than to count her chickens too soon.

Still, she couldn't help being elated as she stepped off the stage, still wrapped in her wet caracul coat. This was it. The dream. She was going to Broadway.

8.

The *Variety* review still bugged her. But Barbra found a way to defuse it.

On the November 27 *PM East,* she sat alongside fellow guest Mickey Rooney, the legendary child star of Metro-Goldwyn-Mayer now grown into a puckish character actor. "I can't get in the movies," she lamented.

"Why not?" Rooney asked.

"My nose."

Rather than shrink from the insult or pretend it had never happened, Barbra had decided to put it right out there on national television, ensuring that her nose would become even more discussed. The only way to make the criticism go away, she seemed to believe, was to confront it head on, bring it up to bring it down.

"What's wrong with your nose?" Rooney asked.

"It's different."

"It's a lovely nose."

Barbra giggled. That was what she was hoping he'd say. And the gallant Rooney kept the compliments coming.

"It's an adorable nose," he insisted.

"Most people don't like it," Barbra said. "It's a different commercial market."

"That's all in your mind," Rooney told her.

Barbra looked over at him. "How did you ever work — ?" She indicated Rooney's own nose, a little bulbous and splotchy from years of heavy drinking.

To his credit, Rooney didn't take offense and instead seemed to agree with her. "Look at mine!" he said. "Mine is . . . is . . . is . . ."

"It fits," Barbra said. "W. C. Fields." And then she laughed.

It was a strange little interaction. Rooney had complimented her, but in response, Barbra had insulted him. No doubt she didn't mean to be cruel, even if it had come across that way. She appeared to just want to point out that people with oversized noses could be successful.

Of course, she'd also been warned by Don Softness that Rooney was a notorious scenery chewer, so she was making sure to take control. She wasn't going to let anyone, movie legend or not, hog her spotlight.

Even when Rooney tried to change the subject away from *schnozzolas*, asking his costar if she'd dedicate a song to him, Barbra kept the imperious attitude going. "No," she replied, and laughed again. Her feistiness may actually have been a prelude to the duet she then sang with Rooney, "I Wish I Were in Love Again," a humorous riff on lovers' quarrels. After all, Barbra often got into character for a song. "The sleepless nights, the daily fights," she and Rooney harmonized, "the quick toboggan when you reach the heights, I miss the kisses and I miss the bites, I wish I were in love again!"

Whatever Barbra's motivation, the duet was successful, Softness thought. Rooney had sung the number with Judy Garland in the 1948 film *Words and Music,* and Barbra filled Garland's shoes surprisingly well, bringing exactly the right kind of winking combativeness to her rendition. She seemed to know exactly what she was doing and where she was going. She seemed on top of the world.

9.

Not long afterward, Don Softness took Barbra out to dinner. The publicist knew that his client "didn't sing unless she was paid for it," so he fully expected her to decline when Mimi, the gregarious, florid proprietor of their favorite Italian eatery on East Fifty-third Street, asked if she'd step up to the piano and give them a number. But to Softness's great surprise, Barbra agreed, accepting the scattering of applause from their fellow diners. From her bag she produced some sheet music and handed it over to the pianist. That was when Softness understood why Barbra had said yes. The song she'd sing for them was "Moon River," which she was scheduled to perform on an upcoming *PM East.* This impromptu rendition at Mimi's would give her a chance to practice.

To Softness's great delight, Barbra was proving to be a natural television performer — galvanized, she said, by the knowledge that thousands of people were viewing her. "You can't see them," she said, "but you know they're there and watching you." Such exposure inspired and emboldened her. And in the process Softness witnessed one of the most interesting public personas he'd ever seen take shape.

On the December 8 show, for example, appearing alongside Paul Dooley, singer Lillian Briggs, pianist Lee Evans, and a rising young comedian named Woody Allen, Barbra had gone off on a riff about smoked foods. There was no stopping her — not that anyone wanted to. Smoked foods caused cancer, Barbra insisted, in a voice that got more nasal every time she appeared on the show. People in Iceland got cancer at much higher rates than anyone else, she pontificated, because all they ate in Iceland were smoked foods. "Streisand's a little sick, folks," Mike Wallace deadpanned. Barbra's absurd claims needed no facts to support them, because it wasn't *what* she said, but *how* she said it. Even the phrase "smoked foods" was funny the way it rolled off her tongue.

Softness had clued into her act very quickly. Barbra was deliberately building an eccentric reputation because she knew it got her attention, and she did so "carefully and assiduously," he observed. She understood that she had to be "somewhat — but not too — outrageous." Softness thought Barbra walked that line very well because the *PM East* producers kept rebooking her for more appearances. But the publicist also knew that they could capitalize on the gimmick even further. Together they could build her into a real character, stringing together the many little quirks that already defined her.

Over the last few weeks, given all the time they spent together on publicity, they'd grown quite close. When Barbra was evicted from her apartment on Eighteenth Street — the tenant of record had returned and, appalled at how she'd redecorated the place, insisted that she leave immediately — it had been Softness to whom she'd turned for help. Loading up his car with all of Barbra's shoes and boas and cloche hats, the publicist told her he'd take her to her mother's in Brooklyn. "Anywhere but there," Barbra said. So Softness allowed her to live in his office, just down the block from Mimi's. Barbra was grateful, but also depressed to find herself a nomad again. Quite the predicament for a young woman who, in a matter of weeks, would begin rehearsals for a Broadway show — now retitled *I Can Get It for You Wholesale*, the name of the original novel.

Being thrown out of her apartment so soon after winning her first big role simply affirmed Barbra's old belief that whenever anything good happened to her, God threw down a thunderbolt of bad luck. But if anyone had the resilience to get through this, Softness believed, it was his young, determined client. He was determined to make Barbra's stay at his office as comfortable as possible. She could sleep on the couch in the main room and use the office's kitchen and full bathroom, but she had to be out by nine every morning unless it was one of those days when they were working on press releases together, which were more and more frequent of late.

As he watched her warble "Moon River" beside Mimi's piano, wearing old dungarees and no makeup, Softness realized the noisy room had fallen silent. The girl sure had something. Softness was enjoying the process of building her up. Barbra's thrift-shop habit was a great angle that her publicist knew could be used for maximum advantage. A shawl that served "double duty as a bed cover," he said, was a terrific detail. So was a hunter's bullet bag that could be publicized as "one of the most marvelous purses" Barbra owned. There was plenty of raw material like this that the publicist could fashion into a compelling public persona — if Barbra was willing.

She was. She was glad to do anything if it meant moving her closer to what she told Softness was "the epitome of achievement" — success as a "straight dramatic actress." Miss Marmelstein might be one giant step toward that goal, but she was still, bottom line, just a small-bit character who sang. Barbra made clear to her publicist that she hadn't given up her long-held dream of playing Juliet. That was all well and good, Softness replied. But before she could be Juliet, Softness told her, she had to become something else. For now, he was calling it a "kook."

10.

In San Francisco, Los Angeles, Chicago, and New York, in all of the markets across the country that carried *PM East,* television viewers on the night of December 21 tuned in to see kooky Barbra Streisand do her thing. And they bore witness to the particular satisfaction she took in having her revenge, at long last, on David Susskind.

"People like you are ruining show business because you don't let new talent emerge," she said, sitting right beside the producer two years after she hadn't even been permitted into his office. "You think it's your duty to squelch it."

The usually eloquent Susskind, there to promote his upcoming production of *Requiem for a Heavyweight,* seemed at a loss on how to respond to Barbra's accusation. He only stammered in reply. In the booth, the show's producers were beaming. Although they'd never admit it publicly, they loved Barbra's broadside against Susskind. Moments like these were what made for great television.

Indeed, the theme of the show that night was success. "The uphill grind, the knifings, the falls and the comebacks, the heartbreaks and the rewards," Don Softness had written in his press release. Barbra would lead off the show "as a young performer aspiring to glory," producer Mert Koplin intended, "and then Susskind's famous people would come in." These would include Anthony Quinn and a returning Mickey Rooney, the stars of *Requiem.* No one expected Barbra to do and say what she did, but no one stopped her either. She was on a roll. The kooky Jewish kid from Brooklyn spoke her mind to the big-shot producer, then delivered a touching rendition of "Bewitched, Bothered, and Bewildered" before wrapping it all up with a big, mod, offbeat reimagining of "Ding–Dong! The Witch Is Dead." It was fair to say there was no one else quite like Barbra Streisand on television, or anywhere else, for that matter.

"I scare you," she said, quite astutely, to Susskind. "I'm so far out, I'm in."

Or she would be soon if she and the team behind her had their way.

CHAPTER EIGHT

Winter 1962

1.

On the first day of rehearsals for *I Can Get It for You Wholesale*, stagehands were busy sweeping up the snow and slush tracked in by the cast and crew on this cold and wet day. A New Year's Day storm had left the streets a mess. Flurries continued today, January 2, with temperatures hovering around twenty-five degrees Fahrenheit. More than ever, Barbra loved her caracul-and-fox coat.

With more than a little bit of trepidation, she stepped into the Fifty-fourth Street Theatre, where rehearsals were being held, with a satchel bag slung over her shoulder. Another of David Merrick's shows, *Do Re Mi,* was presented here at night, but during the day, the stage was theirs. The cast was already sitting in a circle — most on the floor, though Lillian Roth was perched gracefully on a metal folding chair — when Barbra walked in, a burst of cold air following her from the open door.

Elliott Gould caught one glimpse of her and thought she looked like "a young Fagin," the vagabond leader of the street urchins from *Oliver Twist.* Barbra caught his glance and thought the long-limbed, curly-topped Elliott was "funny looking." Then she settled down into the circle, cross-legged, with the rest of the cast.

Walking around them was a very serious taskmaster, the likes of whom Barbra had never known before. Arthur Laurents, with *Gypsy* and *West Side Story* under his belt, was a name, a power, a force to be reckoned with. He told his cast he expected them to be "better than excellent." Anyone who wasn't up to the challenge, he said, looking each one of them in the eye, should leave immediately.

The cast went over the script. Miss Marmelstein was one of the first to appear, with a whole stretch of dialogue talking into a phone — never the easiest task for an actor — while also simultaneously carrying on a conversation with her boss, Mr. Pulvermacher. So that first read-through saw Barbra, the youngest and least experienced of them, carrying on not one but two conversations all by herself.

"Maurice Pulvermacher, Eye, En, See," she said, pretending to answer a phone in her best Jewish Brooklynese. "Gowns of distinction, street and formal."

She looked up as if speaking to her boss while the caller droned on in her ear. "What should I tell I. Magnin?"

Then into the phone: "Boston?"

Covering the mouthpiece, speaking again to her boss: "Oh, it must be Filene's."

Back into the phone: "Yes? Hello? I'm sorry. We don't know when we can ship your order. This strike — it's the shipping clerks, yes — they've tied up the whole garment center."

Here she was instructed by the stage directions to once again cover the mouthpiece and "hiss" over to Pulvermacher: "You want to talk to them?" She did as directed and then, finally, thankfully, it was someone else's turn to speak.

Laurents was pleased. He liked this kid. He liked her style, her gumption, her ambition. But most of all, he liked her voice. Liked it so much, in fact, that he'd called Goddard Lieberson, an old friend, and asked him to reconsider the record deal he'd been too quick, in

Laurents's less-than-humble opinion, to dismiss. On the strength of Laurents's recommendation, Lieberson told Marty Erlichman to bring Barbra into the Columbia studios and record a demo tape. The Columbia chief wanted to hear how she'd sound on a professionally produced album.

No such orchestrations, however, had been necessary to convince Laurents of Barbra's talent. On that first day of rehearsals, the director felt nothing but optimism — toward Barbra, the rest of his cast, and the entire show. Their budget might be small, but Laurents believed a show needed imagination more than it needed money. "A limited amount of the latter," the director said, forced "an almost unlimited supply of the former."

And while he knew the book needed work, Laurents was pleased with its "tough, cynical attitude toward society" — precisely the reason he'd accepted the assignment in the first place. *Wholesale,* he felt, was something new and radically different for Broadway, something that was infused with "a sarcastic energy, a drive, a reality almost exotic for musicals." It was the story of Harry Bogen, a pushy, ambitious, unethical garment-trade worker in Depression-era New York. For Bogen of the Bronx — much like a certain young lady from Brooklyn — it needed to be right to the top or nowhere at all. But unlike Barbra, there was nothing disarming, vulnerable, or redeeming about Bogen's ambition. He embezzles, betrays his friends, and dumps the girl who loves him to take up with a floozy from the Club Rio Rhumba. By the time of the final curtain, he's lost his friends and his job and is facing bankruptcy. Not exactly Curly and Laurey heading off on their honeymoon in that shiny little surrey with the fringe on top.

But Laurents had never been interested in stories that simply upheld the status quo. He'd subverted norms in *Rope,* upended expectations in *Home of the Brave,* and challenged the way audiences saw themselves in *West Side Story.* With *Wholesale,* there was similar potential, Laurents believed, providing he could overcome the flaws of the script. To do this, he was going to need the help of his actors, who would have to find ways to ground their performances in an "emotional reality" — never easy to do in the surreal world of musicals — but made even more difficult by Weidman's substandard book.

Still, he was confident his actors were up to the task. Laurents had chosen them well, often fighting Merrick and the moneymen for the person he felt was best. Barbra hadn't been his only battle. Laurents had also gone against Merrick's wishes in the casting of Elliott Gould, arguing the young, rangy actor looked more the part than Laurence Harvey, Merrick's original idea, or Steve Lawrence, who'd been championed by "those who threw the best theater parties." The director insisted that "the only chance" the show had "to succeed completely was for it to succeed artistically."

As he looked around at his cast that first day, Laurents felt *Wholesale* was on track to do just that. He had in his company some "exceptional singers and dancers," and every one of them, including the neophyte who was playing Miss Marmelstein, could act. With these actors, Laurents believed, "the prosaic flatness of [the script] could be given theatrical life." He could "trust his players to make his inventions work."

From the very first moment, it was clear that Laurents was in charge, that he would oversee everything. The director knew not only how they should say their lines, but where they needed to be standing when they said them, and what they should be wearing, and how the light should be hitting their faces. Barbra, whose character was only in a handful of scenes, had plenty of opportunity to sit back and observe the director at work. She understood, right from the first day of rehearsals, that they could either be good or they could be great. Without a strong director, the show might still be a hit. But Laurents wanted more than box-office success. He wanted excellence. That was why he took such authority over every last detail of the show. It was a lesson that Barbra absorbed well.

Already she shared some of Laurents's proprietary attitude. A few days earlier, she'd run into May Muth, *Wholesale*'s stage manager, at the Brasserie. "I hear you're gonna be with my show," she'd said to the Broadway veteran, whose credits dated back to 1929. And when, after the read-through was finished, she met her understudy, a young redhead named Louise Lasser, the girlfriend of rising nightclub comic Woody Allen, Barbra felt even more possessive of Miss Marmelstein. Barbra told one friend she would never give Lasser the chance to play the part "even if she was as sick as a dog."

Barbra was, at that moment, the very picture of a theater gypsy. Some nights she stayed at Don Softness's office, other nights at Peter Daniels's studio ("very spooky," Barbra called the big dark space). There were at least four other crash pads, some of which were in "very bad neighborhoods," as she told Mike Wallace on the air. Diana was once again making regular grocery visits: Softness's brother, John, often found "all this great kosher food" in his office refrigerator, like applesauce and Doxsee clam chowder.

For the next several weeks, however, most of Barbra's time would be spent at the Fifty-fourth Street Theatre. Elliott Gould, passing out celebratory cigars after their first rehearsal was over, noticed her standing off to the side and thought she seemed like "a loner." With apparently some special earnestness, he approached her with a cigar. At his solicitude, Barbra couldn't help but smile. Elliott handed her the cigar, his big, dopey grin stretching across his long face. Barbra thought he seemed "like a little kid." Although she didn't inhale when he bent down and lit the cigar for her, she was enchanted by his gesture just the same.

2.

That night, Lorraine Gordon turned on the television to watch *PM East*. The show had been taped a week or so earlier. A friend of Mike Wallace's, Gordon had inveigled her way on the program despite the host's rather chauvinistic disregard for Women Strike for Peace. She brought along Dagmar Wilson, the founder of the group. Barbra was also scheduled to be on the show, so Gordon figured she'd have a good chorus of voices espousing the antinuclear position.

It didn't quite turn out that way. Though the sparring between Barbra and Mike Wallace was entertaining to audiences, the two were growing to dislike each other more and more. The show started out well, however, with Wallace lauding Barbra's recent accomplishments. "You know it's exciting when something starts to happen in front of you," he read from the prepared script. He pointed out that in the few months since Barbra's debut on the show, she'd begun "to get into all kinds of interesting jobs." While he couldn't yet reveal anything about *I Can Get It for You Wholesale,* as Merrick hadn't officially announced the cast, Wallace did mention the Blue Angel and the fact that Barbra's run there had been extended. "So it's beginning to happen," the host said, looking over at Barbra.

"It's crazy," she replied.

"And she owes it all to Zen Buddhism," the host said with a laugh.

Barbra had known ahead of time that they would talk about Zen. With the show's producers, she'd gone over how she'd describe her meditation. She would explain how it had helped her and, as always, was willing to make her explanation amusing and eccentric. Still, Wallace's condescending tone irked her.

"Do you have to ask me like that?" she responded. "You think you're gonna ask me about Zen Buddhism and you think I'm going to tell you that I'm enlightened and all about Zen Buddhism, but that's all foolishness."

"But you wanted to talk about it," Wallace said. "So go ahead and talk."

Barbra remained silent. Wallace told her she was being impolite.

"Let me tell you something," Barbra finally said, leveling her gaze at the host. "I used to like you."

Nervous laughter in the studio.

"This is the truth," Barbra continued. "I really like what he does. A lot of people don't."

More nervous laughter.

"It's the truth," Wallace admitted.

"I like the fact that you are provoking," Barbra said. "But don't provoke *me*."

Of course, that only made Wallace want to provoke her more. Soon he was making a joke about the keys on Barbra's keychain. "So you sort of sleep all over town?" he asked. Barbra insisted he make a distinction between "sleeping around" and "sleeping around town." It got a good laugh, but the hostility was now palpable.

So it was perhaps not surprising that by the time Lorraine Gordon and Dagmar Wilson came out to discuss nuclear testing and the folly of building fallout shelters, Barbra seemed exhausted. After her comrades in the peace movement delivered impassioned calls for disarmament, Barbra was next in line for Wallace's questioning. "You're involved in this, too?" he asked, seeming to imply: Zen Buddhism, thrift shops, long fingernails, a crusade against smoked foods — and now the *peace movement*?

"Oh, yeah," Barbra said, as Gordon remembered it. "We're like a bunch of lemmings. We all follow each other and jump off the cliff."

She gave Wallace the laugh he wanted instead of taking the opportunity to endorse the politics so fervently expressed by Gordon and Wilson. Gordon was livid at what seemed like a betrayal. She gave Barbra a kick under the table.

Yet few could stay angry with Barbra for long when she started to sing. On that show, she finally had a chance to show off how she'd mastered "Moon River." Once again, the nineteen-year-old girl became ageless. "Moon River, wider than a mile," Barbra sang. When she was finished, Mike Wallace looked into the camera and said, "It's always a pleasure to listen to that girl sing." No matter how much the kid might get under his skin at other times, the admiration in Wallace's voice was real.

3.

The harmony and good feeling of the first day of rehearsal had quickly evaporated at the Fifty-fourth Street Theatre.

"No, that is *not* the way to do it!" Laurents shouted at Barbra. "Too much, too much!"

She paid him no mind and kept on singing. She was rehearsing her solo number, "Miss Marmelstein," a song that had been written for the show, then taken out, then put back in so Barbra would have more to do. As written, Miss Marmelstein was "just another piece of furniture," Weidman admitted, but Barbra's stage presence, so big, so overpowering, made that unworkable. Therefore, early in the second act, a battalion of garment execs would march across the stage, ordering Miss M to perform various tasks for them. "At the end of her tether" — or so the stage directions described — the harried, homely secretary would look out at the audience and launch into her eponymous number.

"Why is it always Miss Marmelstein?" Barbra wailed as Laurents watched from the sidelines. She lamented how nobody ever called her "baby doll, or honey dear, or sweetie pie," like they did other girls. Even her first name would be "preferable," she griped, "though it's terrible, it might be bettah, it's Yetta." The kvetching went on like this, as offstage voices kept up a running chorus of "Miss Marmelstein!" The number was intended to give the script a lift at a particular moment when it could use one. The audience needed a chance to laugh, Laurents realized, as Harry Bogen's odious schemes began to unravel.

The problem was that Barbra had no sense of restraint. She was flailing around the stage, arms flying, eyes bugging out. She used her long fingernails to great effect as she flung her hands around — but it was the mannerism of a diva, Laurents grumbled, not a secretary. "Overkill," Laurents called Barbra's interpretation of the part. "Too many twitches and collapses, giggles and gasps, too many take-ums." He didn't want to lose her uniqueness — he thought her characterization of Miss Marmelstein was "very funny, a bizarre collection of idiosyncrasies which came from instinct and were probably rehearsed at home" — but he did want to "edit, to cut out the extraneous contortions." Her performance, he realized, was coming "from the fingernails, not from inside."

Striding out onto the stage, the director gave Barbra the signal to stop the number. The pianist broke off playing, and an uneasy silence fell over the empty theater.

Barbra wasn't pleased. This back-and-forth with Laurents had been going on for a while. Not long before, they'd come to loggerheads when she'd asked to be excused from a rehearsal because she had to appear on *PM East*. Expecting permission to be granted, Barbra was already choosing what outfit to wear when Laurents had said no. Vexed, she tried finagling permission from Herbert Ross, who sent her back to Laurents. The director came to realize that Barbra felt "she was different, she was special" and that "future stars were not to be ignored." When Laurents proved intransigent, Barbra sulked.

Even worse from her perspective was the director's insistence "on blueprinting exactly how [she] should do everything." That had never been her style. She preferred "to work slowly into the part," playing it "by ear." As in her nightclub acts, Barbra found it very difficult to do "anything twice in exactly the same way." So she spoke up, arguing her point of view forcefully, a far cry from the timid little girl who'd blanched when Barré had dared to challenge Vasek Simek during *The Insect Comedy*.

But when she argued, she always did so respectfully, which Laurents appreciated. As much as she had her own, very definite opinions, she was also smart enough to recognize that, on her own, she lacked the discipline needed to shape Miss Marmelstein into a well-balanced character. That was one reason, she admitted, that she was glad she was in *Wholesale*—"to learn discipline in the theater." But discipline required concentration, and concentration required listening—one skill Laurents felt Barbra lacked. It was her "low threshold for boredom" that gave her so much trouble, Laurents believed. It was also that old unremitting narcissism. When it was her turn to perform, Laurents noted, Barbra came alive, but when she had to listen—to him or to other performers—"Miss Marmelstein went home and in her place stood Barbra Streisand, uncomfortable in a costume."

Laurents tolerated the narcissism because of Barbra's specialness. Others weren't as forgiving. Harold Rome had fought to have "Miss Marmelstein" put back into the show, arranging it specifically for Barbra. He'd also written her into several other numbers, agreeing that Barbra's enormous stage presence had to be balanced throughout the two acts. But for his efforts, Rome never got a word of thanks, a fact the composer resented. To him, the teenager was "ungrateful" and "arrogant." But Barbra figured she gave and they gave; they each "got something out of it." There was no need, therefore, for any thanks. It was the same attitude her acting teacher Eli Rill had observed: Barbra was unwilling to perform the expected niceties — the "ass-kissing," as one of Barbra's friends put it bluntly. Rill hadn't minded, but Harold Rome did. And from that moment on, the composer soured on the girl he'd once been so enthusiastic about.

There was indeed a degree of youthful hubris about Barbra. She was riding high, and even a second rejection from Goddard Lieberson (he'd told Laurents that Barbra was "too special for records") had been only a minor irritant. Music, after all, was only a means to an end. "I want to be a straight dramatic actress," she'd tell a reporter around this time. "I really can't explain it. It's almost a compulsion."

That was her underlying attitude, her core belief, as she stood face-to-face with her director, arms akimbo. It took choreographer Herbert Ross to break the impasse. Hurrying up the stairs to the stage, Ross had an idea. He was a young man, just thirty-four, but already a veteran Broadway choreographer. He'd staged *A Tree Grows in Brooklyn* and a revival of *Finian's Rainbow,* and just recently he had finished the critically praised *The Gay Life* with Barbara Cook. Ross was talented, perceptive, and diplomatic. Why not, he asked, as he wheeled Miss Marmelstein's chair across the stage on its casters, let Barbra do the number sitting down? After all, she'd auditioned that way. Laurents agreed to give it a try.

It worked — wonderfully. Miss Marmelstein could sing her humorous tale of woe while sliding across the stage in her secretary's chair, first this way, then that way, all precisely choreographed by

Ross. Barbra was pleased as well, feeling the chair had really been her idea — which, no doubt, Ross had anticipated when he'd suggested she use it.

In the wings, Elliott Gould watched it all unfold. Though he'd been enjoying a bit of a flirtation with his leading lady, Marilyn Cooper, the more Elliott observed Barbra, the more "fascinated" he became. She might have a formidable stage presence, but underneath, Elliott felt, she needed "to be protected." Barbra was "a very fragile little girl," Elliott suspected, one he found "absolutely exquisite." Although he figured Barbra didn't "commit easily," he had "a desire to make her feel secure."

And so, that afternoon or one very much like it, Elliott Gould asked Barbra Streisand out on a date.

4.

It was two o'clock in the morning in Rockefeller Center. They'd been wandering the city together all night, their cheeks cold and rosy, their conversation as meandering as their walk. Suddenly, without warning, Barbra bent down, shaped a snowball in her mittened hands, and lobbed it across at Elliott, nailing him perfectly. His competitive nature triggered, Elliott scooped up his own ammunition and retaliated, his aim proving to be as good as hers. Within moments, a full-scale snowball fight was underway, the laughter of the two combatants echoing through the empty plaza.

More than snowballs were ricocheting between them that night. Elliott was utterly smitten. To him, Barbra was a combination of Sophia Loren — love goddess — and Y. A. Tittle — the New York Giants' tenacious quarterback who'd helped the team win the Eastern Division title in December. Walking Barbra to the subway after rehearsals, Elliott had come to think of her as the "most innocent thing" he'd ever seen. But something about Barbra scared him, too. She was a beatnik and a bohemian, after all, so very different from the other girls he knew. Yet despite his fear, or maybe partially because of it, Elliott "really dug her" — and he sensed he might have been "the first person who really did."

At last overwhelming her with snowballs — he called it a "hex" — Elliott began to chase her around the skating rink. Barbra squealed with delight. Elliott's pursuit of her was "strange and wonderful," she'd admitted to one friend. His interest was plainly evident, whereas, in the past, there had always been doubts with other men. Barbra had come to feel that her pursuit of men who weren't as interested in her as she was in them reflected "a throwback" to Louis Kind, when she'd tried in vain to make her stepfather like her.

But Elliott — she'd started calling him "Elly" — was the antithesis of all that. He'd phoned her; he'd walked her to the subway; he'd asked her out. She hadn't gone after him; he'd come after her. That was significant. Now, wrestling her down in the snow, Elly looked into her blue eyes. He saw insecurity behind the bravado; Barbra's "weirdness," he realized, was merely a defense. Scooping some snow in his hands, he "very delicately" washed her face with it. Then, just as tenderly, he kissed her lips. Nothing too demonstrative, but it was perhaps the most romantic gesture any man had ever extended to her. "Like out of a movie," Barbra thought. And for once she was playing the part of the leading lady, as she'd always believed she could.

5.

Moonlight filled a cloudless sky over Philadelphia in the early morning hours of February 13. At the Bellevue-Stratford Hotel, its magnificent French Renaissance architecture resplendent in the moonlight, Barbra and the rest of the *Wholesale* company hurried down the famous marble-and-iron elliptical staircase to the Tiffany-glass ballroom, where a celebration was underway after their first-night preview performance. But the cheers and clinking of champagne flutes belied the anxiety they all — but mostly their director — felt. The morning edition of the *Philadelphia Inquirer* would soon be out, and the critics would have their say.

Arthur Laurents still worried that the book wasn't entirely right. He had hoped some clever directing and skillful acting might bridge the gaps, but after tonight's performance, he knew the problems wouldn't be solved until Weidman's script was chopped up and reassembled. The director concluded he'd been too respectful of the writer's work, and he feared the critics wouldn't forgive him for such a dereliction of duty. Many shows died in Philadelphia, he knew all too well, before they ever reached New York.

On the surface, everything had seemed to go well. Showtime at the Shubert Theatre had been at eight o'clock, and the house, to Laurents's great relief, had been full. That same week, David Merrick had opened a second show in Philly, the touring company of *Irma la Douce,* but he'd insisted that the two premieres be staggered so as not to compete with each other.

Most people in that first-night crowd had turned out to see Lillian Roth, who'd received the lion's share of preshow publicity. In the *Inquirer* just that morning, Whitney Bolton had devoted an entire column to Roth's comeback. "Just thirty years after her last appearance on Broadway," Bolton wrote, "she is destined to be back again on the street where the lights twinkle, where the only thing that counts is talent — and one's use of it." Roth's connection to a glamorous, long-vanished Broadway — she'd worked for Florenz Ziegfeld and Earl Carroll — impressed the columnists and the public.

But not Barbra. Barré and Bob and Marty had all tried to instill in her an appreciation of the old-time greats, but she never had much feeling for history. She was smart enough, and decent enough, to treat Roth with the proper respect. But there was never any adulation, never any closeness. One friend asked Barbra if she ever sat at Roth's knee and listened to her stories about Broadway's Golden Age. Barbra replied, "What, are you crazy? Why would I do that?"

She was, in fact, frustrated that the advance publicity for *Wholesale* barely mentioned her at all. A caricature of the cast in the February 11 edition of the *Inquirer* had included nearly everyone but her. The young stars being promoted with the most press releases and interviews were Elliott, of course, and Marilyn Cooper, who played Harry Bogen's girlfriend. But Harold Lang, Jack Kruschen, and Bambi Linn had also been singled out for publicity. Not a word, however, about Barbra.

Part of the publicists' reluctance to highlight their youngest cast member no doubt stemmed from Merrick's continued distaste for her, and his not-so-subtle hints to Laurents that she be replaced. Even this late in the game, it remained a possibility: Marilyn Lovell, playing the voluptuous showgirl, had been given the boot just before they'd headed to Philadelphia and was replaced by Sheree North, the one-time rival to Marilyn Monroe who Merrick thought had more sex appeal. But Barbra refused even to contemplate such a possibility. Instead, she was blithely planning how she might get herself noticed even without the help of the show's press agents. Her strategy, as it turned out, was nothing if not original.

Jerome Weidman discovered what she was up to at one rehearsal. He'd spotted her scribbling away, presumably taking notes. But when he got a closer look, he discovered that Barbra had actually been writing her bio for the show's playbill. "Born in Madagascar and reared in Rangoon," Barbra had written of herself. Encouraged by her publicists at the Softness Group, Barbra saw a golden opportunity to get herself some attention, in the same way she'd used comparable gambits in Detroit and Winnipeg. She'd written a similar bio for the *Harry Stoones* program, too, but this one would be seen by a lot more people. After all, Barbra reasoned, she was playing a Jewish secretary, so saying she was "from Brooklyn and brought up in Flatbush" would have "meant nothing." But if audiences thought she came from Madagascar . . .

That wasn't all she wrote. Miss Streisand, the bio concluded, "is not a member of the Actors Studio." With that one simple little line, Barbra had her revenge against all those pretentious up-and-comers who loved to flaunt their training at the Actors Studio — an education that Barbra had, of course, *not* been able to secure for herself. Indeed, by thumbing her nose at the "pompous and serious" tradition of program biographies, Barbra had turned a deficiency into an asset. If it seemed more like the modus operandi of the kook from *PM East* than the unassuming, by-the-book Miss Marmelstein, it didn't matter. That night it was Barbra's bio that stood out in the program more than anyone else's, and that was the point.

Barbra herself also stood out on the stage. When Miss Marmelstein had come rolling out on her chair, kvetching about her life, she had gotten the loudest, most sustained applause of the night. Barbra had to have felt good about her performance, and about the reception she had received from the audience. Certainly Laurents did. He was pleased that her performance, even if it came more from her fingernails than it did her heart, had made such a connection with the audience. But critics had been known to see things very differently from those sitting around them.

It wasn't yet light out when the first editions of the *Inquirer* made it to the Bellevue-Stratford. The ink was still moist as Laurents pulled open the paper, bypassing the news on the front page — Secretary of State Dean Rusk was trying to negotiate with the Soviets about nuclear arms — to go directly to the theater section. Under the headline GARMENT SHOP BACK ON STAGE, the review confirmed Laurents's fears. Critic Henry T. Murdock, who'd been with the *Inquirer* since 1950 and whose tastes tended more toward musicals such as *Guys and Dolls*, thought Harold Rome's score possessed "range and versatility" and that Herbert Ross had taken a "unique approach to dancing." But when it came to the book, he wrote, "our enthusiasm dwindles." *Wholesale* was supposed to be a musical comedy, Murdock argued, but he couldn't find the comedy. The "hero-heel," the critic wrote, was just not redeeming enough in the way Gene Kelly or Robert Morse had been in similar parts in *Pal Joey* and *How to Succeed in Business Without Really Trying*. The fault, Murdock wrote, could not be handed to Elliott, "who gives Harry everything the libretto demands." Rather, the flaw of the show was the script. Laurents felt as if he could have penned the review himself.

But there was one moment Murdock felt compelled to single out.

With comedy in such short supply, the critic welcomed the show's "most truly comic song": the "Miss Marmelstein" number that had roused the audience from its near torpor the night before. "Barbra Streisand," Murdock wrote, "brings down the house." Among the company it was now obvious that the show had problems — perhaps serious ones — but the one part that worked without question was Barbra.

A few days later, when a second review appeared in the *Inquirer*, the strength of her position was confirmed. Barbra was the only cast member singled out for praise. "She stops the show in its tracks," the reviewer declared, a line Merrick's publicists were quick to incorporate into all of their press releases from that point on. The acclaim kept coming. Dorothy Kilgallen, a fan of Barbra's since the first Bon Soir appearance, reported in her syndicated column — which reached far more readers than the local Philly papers — that none other than Henry Fonda had seen *Wholesale* and had "registered considerable enthusiasm for comedienne Barbra Streisand." Merrick's grumbling about her abruptly ceased.

No matter what might happen to *I Can Get It for You Wholesale*, one thing had become abundantly clear by the end of February. Barbra was going to be a hit.

6.

Elliott Gould's eyes, one reporter observed, were "as large and melancholy as a Saint Bernard's, an animal with which he shares the same shambling gait." But this night, those hangdog eyes seemed to flicker with a kind of electricity as the young man made his way up the elliptical staircase of the Bellevue-Stratford.

Arthur Laurents knew where Elliott was headed, and it made him smile. Only now was the company catching on to the fact that Harry Bogen was romancing Miss Marmelstein. Marilyn Cooper had been stung when Elliott transferred his attentions from her to Barbra. But despite his leading lady's disappointment, Laurents had encouraged the budding affair — "Godfathering the romance," he called his efforts. To the director, Elliott and Barbra seemed a "Jewish show-business Romeo and Juliet, in love with each other and ice cream." The sweet treat was indeed a point of commonality between them. Many nights Elliott would carry a box of Breyer's coffee ice cream up to Barbra's room, two spoons tucked into the front pocket of his shirt.

Sex was in the air. The newspapers were filled with dispatches from the set of *Cleopatra* in Rome about the affair between Elizabeth Taylor and Richard Burton, both married to other people. So notorious was the scandal that it bumped John Glenn's historic space flight off the first pages of many tabloids, keeping "Liz and Dick" front and center. In Philadelphia, as in most places around the planet, talk of "Le Scandale" was on everyone's lips, and the *I Can Get It for You Wholesale* company was no exception. For the freethinkers among them — which included Barbra and Elliott — the chutzpah of Taylor and Burton would have seemed remarkable, even admirable. Instead of offering denials or apologies, the celebrity pair seemed to be insisting that love — and sex — was more important than propriety.

Elliott hadn't always been such a freethinker. He'd been "scared most of [his] life," he admitted. As a kid, he'd been convinced that he possessed a strange ability — almost a "psychic power," he said — that enabled him to intuit a person's true feelings toward him. Someone might say he was smart, or talented, or handsome, but Elliott knew they were actually thinking just the opposite. For most of his twenty-three years, he had walked around with his head down avoiding making eye contact — not just from a sense of insecurity, but also from a preponderance of caution. Keeping his eyes on the floor, Elliott explained, ensured he wouldn't "trip on anything."

He became an actor, he said, so he could "communicate in a world that was alien" to him and "get beneath the roots of self-doubt." Winning the lead in a Broadway play had gone a long way toward that goal, but those roots of self-doubt ran very deep — as deep, or even deeper, than Barbra's. It was unlikely that one show — or any amount of playacting on the stage — could ever completely overrule a belief that had been instilled in him from the time he was a very young boy.

He was born Elliott Goldstein in the Bensonhurst section of Brooklyn. His father, Bernard, the son of a Russian Jewish immigrant, was a salesman in the garment industry — further reason Arthur Laurents saw such verisimilitude in Elliott's casting. Bernard was a distant, reserved man who was never demonstrative with his son; he had "too much pride" for that, Elliott believed. Indeed, the elder Goldstein sometimes seemed resentful of the little boy, telling a story of how he'd taken a very young Elliott to Ebbets Field to see the Dodgers play the Cubs. "Four home runs were hit in the game," Bernard groused. "I didn't see one of them. I was in the men's room with Elliott each time."

Part of his resentment may have stemmed from the fact that he'd never been in love with the boy's mother, the former Lucille Raver, whom he'd married on the rebound after his true love's parents had put a halt to their elopement. It was telling, no doubt, that Elliott was Bernard and Lucille's only child.

Like her husband, Lucille was the offspring of a Russian Jewish immigrant; her father had worked as a glass salesman in the Bronx. After her marriage, Lucille peddled artificial flowers throughout Bensonhurst to supplement Bernard's income as a salesman. Unlike Emanuel Streisand, Bernard Goldstein was no intellect. He seemed to have no sense of the world beyond Bensonhurst, even after he came back from the war. He worked hard to support his family, but there was never any quest for something more.

What Bernard lacked in ambition Lucille made up tenfold. From a young age she'd had stars in her eyes. Lucille wanted more than just a two-and-a-half-room apartment on Bay Parkway, but she knew her husband was never going to get it for her. They argued constantly. By the time Elliott was three years old, he instinctively understood that his mother and father didn't belong together, that they "didn't understand one another." The unhappiness of his parents' lives meant that the lessons they taught Elliott would be relentlessly pessimistic: "Be careful, don't trust anybody, you've got to save." With tension always crackling just under the surface, Elliott lived in constant fear that everything could explode at any moment. He grew up "in terror of conflict," a feeling that lasted well into adulthood.

And yet, on another level, Elliott absolutely worshipped his parents. They were his entire life. Until he was eleven, he shared a bedroom with them; the concept of privacy was completely alien to the boy. To Elliott, his parents were "Mr. and Mrs. Captain Marvel" — his heroes. "You won't ever have better friends than us," they often reminded him. Everything Elliott did, he did for them, because without them, he was lost. Lucille, especially, dominated her son's daily thoughts. She dressed him, pampered him, took him everywhere with her. Eventually she'd come to acknowledge that she might have been a bit smothering, but it was always "done out of love," she insisted. She would have cut off her arm for Elliott, Lucille declared.

But even his mother's constant doting couldn't dissuade Elliott from the belief that he was an ugly child — yet another bond shared with Barbra. Growing up, Elliott felt too big for his age. He thought he had a "fat ass." His hair was too curly, impossible to slick down — a problem because he wanted to look like Robert Wagner. More than anything Elliott wished he were Irish — a big, tough Irish brawler, the kind he saw on the streets, the kind who never let life beat them down. Despite being bar mitzvahed, Elliott maintained even less of a connection to his Jewishness than Barbra did with hers.

Where Elliott could escape was in the darkened Marlboro Theatre, where, like Barbra in a similar movie house three miles away, he imagined himself up on the silver screen. His favorite stars were Humphrey Bogart and Gary Cooper because they seemed like ordinary people, unlike so many of the others — Robert Wagner perhaps most of all — who filled the fan magazines. Elliott wondered if anyone would ever want to see real people on the screen — people like himself — and not "creations of Hollywood."

At the age of eight, he started on a path to find out. Bored and desperate to find a way out of their dead-end life, Lucille began dragging her son off the basketball courts he loved so that he could audition for music shows and talent contests — anyplace, Elliott said, that was "looking to buy a kid." Problem was, this kid couldn't sing or dance. Elliott remained "very withdrawn, very shy and inhibited." So Lucille enrolled him in Charles Lowe's School of Theatrical Arts, located on an upper floor at 1650 Broadway, where, in the summer, giant electric fans turned in the windows as little children tap-danced across the oak wood floors. "Uncle Charlie," as Lowe was known to his students, was a former vaudevillian in his late sixties with "parentheses-shaped legs" who, with his wife, a one-time silent-movie actress, taught the progeny of ambitious stage mothers how to tap, sing, and project personality.

But when Lucille first tugged Elliott up the narrow stairs to Lowe's school, her hopes for her tongue-tied son were much more modest. "Fix up his diction," she pleaded with Lowe.

"Sure," the teacher replied. "We'll give him a little drama, teach him to sing, teach him to dance."

"He'll never dance," Lucille predicted. "Just fix the diction."

But Uncle Charlie gave Elliott the works. "That meant everything," Elliott griped, looking back. "Blow-your-nose lessons, dance lessons, wipe-yourself lessons." All because of the "compulsions of a dissatisfied mother," he later came to understand. But he went along with all the singing and dancing because he couldn't imagine saying no to Lucille — because he never, ever questioned his parents.

Lowe didn't just teach. He also acted as a kind of agent, placing his students in shows on local stages and local television. "Whoever got any of the bread," Elliott said, using the slang for money, "the kids sure as hell didn't." Every once in a while, he'd be rewarded with "a pastrami sandwich or a flashlight or something," but his job was to go out there on stage and sing and dance while Lowe and his mother took home the cash.

By the time he was ten, Elliott had been transformed into a little trouper straight out of old-time vaudeville. "Mary had a little lamb," he'd warble onstage. "Some peas and mashed potatoes, an ear of corn, some buttered beets and then had sliced tomatoes." Taking a breath, he started in on the next verse. "She said she wasn't hungry, so I thought I had a break, but just to keep me company, she ordered up a steak." Eight more cringe-inducing verses followed before he would tip his straw hat to the audience's applause and run into the wings.

On television he appeared on the *Bonny Maid Versatile Varieties* program, a song-and-dance fest on WNBT. It was for this show that Uncle Charlie tried to persuade Lucille to drop the name Goldstein and bill Elliott as "Gold." Lucille deemed "Gould" a little more elegant, so it was as Elliott Gould that the boy made his television debut.

By the time he was twelve, however, Elliott was a "has-been," or at least that was how Lucille described him. He was "too old to be cute," she thought. So she got him work as a model. Elliott was a standard size eight, perfect for merchandise catalogs. For several years he dressed as a miniature grenadier and handed out pens at dry-goods conventions. And all the money he made went straight to his parents' bank account.

Barbra could barely comprehend such a childhood. In her typical way, she had grilled Elliott for all the details he could remember: the dancing classes, the elocution lessons, the backstage dramas. Most of all, she was fascinated by the idea of a mother who was so determined that her child succeed that she paid for all sorts of professional training — and by the idea of a child who really would have preferred to stay home. Here their experiences diverged sharply. Barbra had always wanted to be an achiever; Elliott had just wanted to play basketball. Their struggles with self-worth might have been similar, but Elliott, unlike Barbra, had felt no need to prove himself the best in everything he did. He was just hoping to get through it without falling down.

When Elliott was in the eighth grade, his father relocated the family to West Orange, New Jersey. But if Elliott hoped that living an hour and a half outside the city would mean an end to all that singing and dancing, he was wrong. Lucille kept accepting assignments for him, and since his schooling would undoubtedly be affected by his performing schedule, she enrolled him in the Professional Children's School at Broadway and Sixty-first Street in Manhattan. Since 1914 the school had been accommodating young performers, slipping in an education for them in between shows. Several times a week, Elliott commuted into the city and "got sick on the bus every time." He hated the school, considered his education there "lame," and said the teachers made him "feel like shit." The anxiety that he felt "when [he] didn't do well was severe." More than anything, he wished he could have an ordinary life, but he never dared to say that to his parents.

Yet there came a point when he, too, got bit by the bug of ambition. It was in May 1952, when he was thirteen, and he was booked at the Palace, the grand old theater at Broadway and Forty-seventh Street that was then featuring a bill of eight vaudeville acts plus a movie. Elliott had a short little number that he performed four times a day for two weeks straight. He would walk out onto the stage in a bellhop's uniform shouting, "Telegram for Bill Callahan!" Callahan was then a popular song-and-dance man (he'd just finished a featured part in the Johnny Mercer musical *Top Banana* at the Winter Garden Theatre) who was next up on the bill. When the orchestra leader chased after Elliott, protesting that they had a show going on, Elliott replied with a song that served as Callahan's musical introduction. The teenager always got a big hand from the audience and a wave of appreciation from the older performer.

By now Elliott had shot up to six feet, which meant he could partner with his mother in mambo contests during the summers at borscht belt resorts in the Catskills. He also entertained resort guests twice a night on weekends dressed in high-waisted dancer's pants and matching silk shirts, nervously shuffling his way through a soft-shoe rendition of the jazz standard "Crazy Rhythm." Yet as much as he detested this part of his show business career, he was old enough to quit — and he didn't. By the age of eighteen, he was auditioning for Broadway shows on his own, and he won a spot in the chorus line for the musical *Rumple*. In 1958 there was another spot in another chorus line in another musical, *Say, Darling,* composed by Jule Styne.

Though he may have been more motivated these days, Elliott

was still embarrassed by auditions. He considered it unnatural for a grown man to walk into a room, and sing and dance for other people's approval. Maybe that was part of the reason that soon there were no shows at all. Out of work at the age of twenty-one, Elliott started gambling. For a while, it got pretty bad; he found himself deep in debt. He had to pawn some of his father's jewelry, then he took jobs as a rug-cleaner salesman and an elevator operator at the Park Royal Hotel on Seventy-third Street. For another job, he wore yellow makeup and a long fake mustache to hawk a game called Confucius Say in Gimbel's department store. Then, after pushing himself to audition for David Merrick, he'd landed the gig in *Irma la Douce*, which had led to *Wholesale*.

To survive in the cutthroat world of the theater, Elliott had learned to become more of an extrovert, though it remained posturing: He still felt like turning and running away. But his mastery of dozens of dialects entertained guests at parties, and unsuspecting diner patrons were always amused when he pretended to make a meal of his napkin — a bit of an homage to Charlie Chaplin in *The Kid*. "For a repressed, inhibited, shy person," Elliott said, to discover that he "could have an effect on people by making a joke" was a major revelation. So, rather late in the game, Elliott became a joker.

And Barbra loved his jokes. After listening to her speak passionately about the Dalai Lama — a hero and a holy man to Zen Buddhists — Elliott had sent her a package of corned beef, pastrami, pickles, and coleslaw with a card signed "From the Deli Lama." It was exactly the kind of offbeat humor she enjoyed, and the kind she used herself on *PM East*. They laughed together; they understood each other's insecurities; they shared enough personal history to make communication easy. In so many ways, they seemed to be kindred souls.

But that didn't make Elliott any less nervous as he headed up the hotel stairs to meet her. This moment had been coming ever since he'd put that snow on her face in Rockefeller Center and kissed her lightly on the lips. Now the passion and energy of opening in Philadelphia had made the consummation of more than a month of flirtation inevitable.

Elliott was terrified. His mother's "ferocity," he believed, had left him "scared of women," so, at twenty-three, he was still a virgin. That was about to end. He had chosen Barbra to be his first.

Ever since the very first play was performed, there has been something seductive about the daily ritual of putting on a show. With people living and working together so intimately, romances tend to blossom. Affairs begin and end, often dramatically. And usually one member of the cast — often the star, but not always — stands out from the rest as a sort of prize to be won. Arthur Laurents thought it was ironic that, due to the spotlight shined on her by the critics, Barbra became "the most attractive member of the show." And as the acclaim for her grew, Barbra saw her desirability increase in Elliott's eyes — especially since he was painfully aware of his own shortcomings. He knew Merrick wasn't happy with him; he knew he was "terribly green" and was "trying too hard." But Barbra seemed to do what she did so effortlessly. That gave her remarkable cachet with Elliott. Marilyn Cooper — prettier and higher on the bill — could never have offered the kind of aphrodisiac Barbra provided.

The attraction went both ways. From Barbra's perspective, she had landed the star of the show and that was exciting on its own, raising her profile among the company even higher. And the fact that she had won him away from pretty Marilyn Cooper likely made the romance even sweeter for her. The initial attraction between Barbra and Elliott had been random and impulsive. But it had deepened into something that dovetailed quite nicely with their individual ambitions and their own senses of themselves.

By now, Barbra was as interested in Elliott as he was in her. Except when it came to looks. Elliott was everything Barré had been — smart, funny, devoted — but with a couple of crucial extra benefits. First, he was successful — or at least he was on the verge of being successful. Last Barbra knew, Barré was still struggling off-off-Broadway. And — no doubt the most important attribute of all — Elliott was heterosexual to his bones. "I bat from just one side of the plate myself," he said, describing his sexuality. "The right side. I'm no good on the left." After being surrounded by so many gay men over the past couple of years — all of whom loved her but could never give her what she really wanted — Barbra seemed, at least to some friends, to be absolutely relishing this sudden, surprising connection to a guy who was so unambiguously straight. Finally a guy — a real guy's guy — wanted her.

And yet Elliott was also sensitive and seemed completely unchauvinistic. Women's liberation, he said, should have nothing to do with gender, but should instead be concerned with "both men and women, with breaking tradition." No wonder that by late February 1962, Barbra was head over heels in love with him. She'd find herself talking "gibberish" around him; one night, distracted by thoughts of Elliott, she'd gone on stage with only half her face made up. She guessed this was love.

That night in Philly, they met in his room. Only they know what transpired, who kissed whom first, who undid the first button. But at one point, a bunch of the guys from the show began pounding on the door. Elliott ignored them. He was "trying to become a man," he admitted, and this was "his moment" — a moment for which he'd waited a very long time. He "wasn't about to let anyone take it away." As Barbra and Elliott remained very still, the pounding finally died down, and they returned to the business at hand. Apparently, despite his fears, Elliott did okay; Barbra, after all, had a little more experience in such things. She remembered Muriel Choy telling her that the man didn't "necessarily" always have to be on top, and so Barbra took charge. She was always good at running a show. So good, in fact, that within a very short time, Wilma Curley, a dancer in the chorus who had the room next to Elliott's, had to rap on the door and tell them to keep it down.

7.

It was cold on February 27, opening night in Boston, but New Englanders were used to that. They were lining up outside the box office of the Colonial Theatre on Boylston Street well before showtime. That meant a full house for opening night. Cast and crew, taking their places backstage, were ecstatic.

Arthur Laurents wasn't as serene, however. A big audience was good news only if the show was worthy of it. He'd made some changes to the book since Philadelphia, but whether they were enough, he wasn't sure. In fact, he suspected they weren't. But he'd been put through hell just to achieve this much. He'd wanted to make alterations only in cooperation with Weidman and Rome, but the changes the writers had come up with had been laughable in Laurents's opinion. Recognizing that the first commandment of out-of-town musicals was "survive," he did what he, as a writer himself, had once considered unthinkable: He cut, he pasted, and — "mea culpa, mea culpa" — he rewrote the book. "Poison-pen notes" from Rome started appearing under Laurents's door every night until they grew so fat they had to be left at the front desk.

His friend Stephen Sondheim understood what he was dealing with. He had seen the show in Philadelphia and thought, despite its script problems, that *Wholesale* was terrific. If Laurents could resist the pressures from Merrick to "sweeten" and "explain" the nasty central character, then *Wholesale* "ought to have enormous impact," Sondheim believed.

On a strictly financial basis, the company was looking pretty good. Attendance had been steady in Philadelphia through the very last show on February 24, and tonight's packed house boded well for the Boston run. Merrick might not be able to make back his costs during previews, one critic observed, but ticket sales had been strong enough to allow him to "approach New York with a little less nail-biting than usual."

The show was also getting good press. There had been Dorothy

Kilgallen's column singling out Barbra, and a couple of other mentions from Leonard Lyons, and a whole slew of articles profiling Lillian Roth's comeback. Weidman and Rome had appeared on *PM East,* largely due to Barbra's relationship with the show. There were also a series of syndicated articles about Elliott, which described him as a former child entertainer who had "persevered . . . despite the usual rough time in the beginning."

If Merrick had his way, however, there would be no more publicity on Elliott. Even as the company moved to Boston, settling in at the Ritz-Carlton Hotel, the producer was still pressing Laurents to fire their leading man. Merrick was furious that when Elliott danced, the first several rows of the orchestra "were sprayed with sweat" — a charge Laurents had to admit was true. To solve the problem, they'd called in Dr. Max Jacobson — known as "Dr. Feelgood" for the amphetamine injections he gave to Tennessee Williams, Eddie Fisher, and President Kennedy — but the medication not only dried up Elliott's flying perspiration but also his vocal chords. Merrick just wanted him gone. Laurents stepped in and said that if Elliott was fired, he'd quit. So far, the producer hadn't called Laurents's bluff.

Backstage, Barbra, in full makeup and costume, was already in the wings, since she was one of the first actors on the stage. The overture was playing. It was one of those rare moments of quiet contemplation right before a show. Perhaps Barbra meditated; perhaps she thought about everything that had brought her to this point. It was true that the Boston newspaper advertisements had billed Lillian Roth at the top, with Elliott and Sheree North at the bottom in special, larger print. It was true, too, that Barbra came dead last. (While Bambi Linn technically was listed after her, she was on a special line, denoting a special appearance.) So Barbra remained last billed. The least important, it would seem.

But those glowing reviews had followed her. No doubt she had taken some satisfaction in the fact that, a week earlier, it had been her stand-alone photograph — not Roth's, not North's, not even Elliott's — that had been used to promote the show in the *Boston Globe.*

Barbra had been called a "stage newcomer"; her name had even been spelled correctly. When the overture ended and the curtain went up, she bounded out with all the confidence in the world. Backstage, there was a bit of a panic when Marilyn Cooper revealed she was having trouble with her voice, but such things didn't concern Barbra. The director and the writers might be struggling over the show, but the young woman playing Miss Marmelstein wasn't worried. She knew there was only one thing that would matter in the end, and that was her.

8.

The Softness brothers looked up in surprise when Barbra came barreling into their office. She'd always been an "assertive young woman," in John Softness's view, but never more so since returning to New York from the out-of-town tryouts of *I Can Get It for You Wholesale*. Now she seemed to the Softness brothers to be a woman on a mission. She barged into the room, shuffled through stacks of papers, made a couple of phone calls, and snapped out questions at the publicists in rapid-fire, machine-gun style. "She goes through brick walls," John Softness thought in awe. Ever since Barbra had become their client, he'd observed that everything she did was fast, direct, and often aggressive. It wasn't so much energy that propelled her, Softness felt, but rather a sense of "I've gotta get the work done, get it over with, finish it." He imagined there must be "a softer, more relaxed side" to Barbra, but so far he had yet to witness it.

And he'd been spending plenty of time with her of late. The Softness Group was no longer only publicizing Barbra as part of *PM East*. Marty Erlichman had also asked them to handle Barbra's personal publicity. (They'd taken on Marty's other clients, the Clancy Brothers, as well.) The Softness brothers found a receptive audience for Barbra's publicity as theatrical insiders had been buzzing about her for weeks. But the buzz wasn't nearly as positive when it came to *Wholesale*.

The Boston critics, much to Arthur Laurents's dismay, had been even less kind to the show than the ones in Philly. Elinor Hughes in the *Boston Herald* had found it "generally entertaining" but she confirmed all of David Merrick's fears about Elliott when she said he "lacked enough style or experience to carry the difficult role of Harry Bogen." Cyrus Durgin in the *Boston Globe* was still more dismissive of the show, playing off Miss Marmelstein's song "What Are They Doing to Us Now?" when he wrote "What, indeed, are they doing to show business when such an acrid and gritty, unimaginative, literal and generally uninteresting item as this comes along under the guise of entertainment?"

After reading Durgin's review, Weidman and Rome had thumped their chests in vindication, demanding that Laurents reinstate their original script. Merrick, much to the director's chagrin, seemed to back them up. But it was a Machiavellian maneuver on the producer's part. When Laurents tendered his resignation rather than return the show to "the piece of blubber" it had been, Merrick told Weidman and Rome that he had no choice but to close the show. Faced with such a possibility, the writers capitulated and accepted Laurents's rewrite as permanent.

Yet throughout all this hullabaloo, there was one thing that everyone agreed was working: Barbra. The critics had been kind to Lillian Roth, but it was the young newcomer who had really excited them. Elinor Hughes thought Barbra displayed "a nice original sense of comedy," and while Cyrus Durgin, known to be persnickety in his reviews, called Miss Marmelstein a "stock" character, he acknowledged that Barbra "wins applause" for playing her.

As the company returned to New York, the Softness brothers knew they had a hot commodity on their hands. With Marty, they often discussed Barbra's future: what she could do, where she might go, who might give her a boost. There were so many avenues where Barbra could be marketed: the stage, television, records. That day in their office, as on so many similar days, they brainstormed for a while — Barbra and Marty and John and Don — and then one of the brothers rolled a piece of paper into their heavy black Royal typewriter and started banging out a press release.

"Barbra is striking in appearance" began one such release, which would be syndicated as a feature story. "She has a lithe and supple body, extremely expressive hands and arms, and the haughty mien and mesmeristic gaze of an Assyrian goddess." It wasn't so different from the "white goddess" image Bob had positioned her for: Barbra might play an ugly duckling on the stage, but she was hardly that in real life, or so her publicity went. It was a hard sell, but that was the course they all decided on.

Some of the publicity undertaken by the Softness Group on Barbra's behalf wasn't as flagrant as that, however. There were tidbits passed along to gossip columnists, photos dropped off on editors' desks in case they ever needed "to fill a hole on the amusements page." There were also the popular "Q-and-A" columns that ran in many newspapers and TV-listings supplements. Not long before, a "Jane Ryan" had written to one syndicated column, "Viewers Speak," asking about a girl on *PM East* "by the name of Barbara Smarzan or something." She had appeared the same night as Julie Wilson and Rose Murphy. "Could you tell me if this girl has made any records?" Miss Ryan asked.

"The young lady's name is Barbra Streisand," the answer came. "My present information is that she has not made any recordings, but I am checking further and will make mention here if I find she does have a recording credit."

Both question and answer, of course, had been penned by Barbra's publicity team. Those ubiquitous "Q-and-A" columns were in actuality patched together by publicists using them as platforms for their clients. The question from "Jane Ryan" had appeared precisely at the point when Goddard Lieberson was reconsidering whether to give Barbra a record contract. The idea, obviously, was to create the impression that the public was clamoring for this exciting newcomer.

The record deal hadn't materialized, but Don Softness kept the press releases flying out of his typewriter. He knew there was something else cooking out there that might be right up his client's alley. As the buzz about Barbra's performance in *Wholesale* grew louder in theater circles, inevitably another show in David Merrick's pipeline was mentioned. During rehearsals, assistant stage manager Robert Schear had watched Barbra intently on the stage, then walked over to Lillian Roth and asked, "Who does that girl remind you of?" Before Roth could reply, Schear told her to write the name down on a piece of paper. He did the same. When they compared notes, they saw they had both written the same name: Fanny Brice.

For some time now, Merrick had been talking with Brice's son-in-law, the producer Ray Stark, about a musical version of the late comedienne's life. In December, just after Barbra had won the part in *Wholesale*, the columnist Sam Zolotow had announced plans for the Brice show in the *New York Times*. That winter, the show was on everybody's lips — as was Barbra's resemblance to the eccentric Jewish funny lady with the large honker. Mike Wallace had already made the comparison on the air on *PM East*.

But Merrick was having none of it. "She is not going to be Fanny Brice," he told Schear when the stage manager made the suggestion. And that, apparently, was that.

The Softness Group wasn't dissuaded. Barbra might have more immediate things to concentrate on: Some future show that might or might not ever be produced was surely way down on her list of priorities in the winter of 1962. But her publicists were paid to think down the road. And while Merrick might seem, at the moment, absolutely intransigent on the idea of Barbra's casting, the Softness brothers knew there were still a few things they could do to change the Abominable Showman's mind.

9.

I Can Get It for You Wholesale opened on Thursday, March 22, at the Shubert Theatre on West Forty-fourth Street, and Barbra couldn't have been more pleased. Since then, the house had been packed every night, and the applause for her regularly reached the rafters. Not even two years after her first anxious performance at the Lion, Barbra was now walking in the footsteps of Peggy Wood, Clifton Webb, Katharine Hepburn, Alfred Lunt, and Lynn Fontanne, all of whom had trod the boards of the Shubert in decades past. On opening night, Barbra's mother, brother, and sister had been there to see her, and Diana had even offered some hearty congratulations — hearty for Diana, that is.

And so, on a night not long after the opening, everything seemed to be in perfect alignment for Barbra — except for one nagging detail. As she came off the stage from the final curtain call, the makeup still on her face, the large collar of Miss Marmelstein's dress still flapping around her neck, Barbra couldn't help but admit that Elliott simply wasn't as good in the show as he needed to be. Put another way, he wasn't as good as she was.

Most of the reviews had thought the same. At the first-night cast party at Sardi's, the entire company had waited breathlessly for the notices. First came the *New York Times,* where Howard Taubman had declared that while Elliott was "a likeable newcomer," Barbra was "the evening's find." Every review that followed, rushed into Sardi's by newspaper boys eager for tips, had been a variation on that theme. John Chapman at the *New York Daily News* griped he couldn't find one character to "give affection or admiration," then corrected himself to say there *was* one: Barbra, who played "the homely frump of secretary . . . hilariously." John McClain at the *New York Journal-American* hated most everything about the show, calling it "How to Almost Succeed in Business Without Really Being Very Honest, or Very Amusing Either, for That Matter," but he couldn't deny that Barbra, resembling "an amiable ant-eater," had "her moment in the sun."

McClain's insult, even if it came wrapped in praise, rankled. "Why are people so mean?" she asked Bob. But Barbra could console herself that while the reviews for the show were very mixed — Walter Kerr at the *Herald Tribune* called it "a good, solid show" while Robert Coleman at the *Daily Mirror* thought it was a disappointment — the acclaim for her was unanimous. Taubman said Barbra's "oafish expressions . . . loud irascible voice and . . . arpeggiated laugh" made her "a natural comedienne." Kerr called her "great."

That was the rub. In the days since the show's opening, most of the buzz had centered around Barbra, not the actual stars. The breakout player wasn't Elliott, as some had once expected; instead, it was his girlfriend, who was playing a much smaller role. To be sure, some reviews had been very kind to Elliott. The *Wall Street Journal* had called him "something of a find." But Barbra was the one the critic declared had the "first-rate gift."

The imbalance between Barbra and Elliott was something she felt quite keenly, friends observed. She felt "protective of him," said one, and "wanted him to get the same kind of accolades" she was getting. It wasn't really his fault, she believed. Elliott, after all, hadn't had the benefit of training at the Theatre Studio the way she had. So the criticism of her new beau "really bothered" Barbra, friends knew.

That night, Bob had come backstage after the show, marveling at the hustle and bustle and all the well-wishers who were flocking to Barbra's dressing room. Every corner of the space was filled with flowers. Less than a year ago, as Bob well remembered, a single bouquet — from her friends in Detroit — had celebrated her appearance on the Paar show. And less than two years ago, the tiny peapod-sized dressing room at the Bon Soir could never have accommodated all the people who were crowding in now to see her, to congratulate her, to tell her she was going to be huge. Watching his friend receive her admirers, Bob felt as if he were witnessing a fairy tale come true.

But for Barbra, there remained the niggling little problem of Elliott's performance. Laurents might have been finally satisfied to leave things the way they were, but Barbra wasn't so tranquil. She rarely was, of course, when she saw a detail out of place.

After everyone left her dressing room except for Bob, Barbra took out a piece of paper and began writing furiously. Bob asked her what she was doing. She was putting together some notes on how Elliott might improve his performance, she replied.

Bob thought that this might not be such a good idea, but he said nothing. Maybe Elliott would welcome such criticism; after all, he certainly seemed enamored enough of Barbra. Everyone had noticed his tremendous, and obvious, attraction to her. The sexual shenanigans between Barbra and Elliott made for titillating backstage gossip. In Boston, Barbra had been spied naked in the hotel corridor, locked out of Elliott's room as a joke. Now they were frequently closed off in one or the other's dressing room, only opening the door after persistent and forceful knocking.

For Barbra, it was a heady adventure. The short-lived affairs since Barré had never been this passionate, nor had her beaus been infatuated with her in the way Elliott was. That may have been because, for the first time, Barbra was realizing her own sexual power. Arthur Laurents marveled at how sexy Barbra was — or rather, how sexual. On the stage, she did something very special with Miss Marmelstein, he thought. The harassed secretary had been written as an old maid, but as Barbra played her, she became a young woman brimming over with sexual drive and desire. The face might have read spinster, but the body and the mannerisms were all siren — as alluring as the Lorelei she had sung about in her nightclub act, who'd wanted to bite her initials into a sailor's neck. It had taken Elliott's devotion to bring Barbra's sexuality out so fully.

So it was with a kind of audacious nonchalance that she handed Elliott her list of criticisms, expecting him to be grateful for her noblesse oblige. But as Bob watched the exchange, it was not gratitude he saw in Elliott's eyes when he read what Barbra had written.

It was fury.

Elliott was indeed smitten with Barbra. But his own ego had taken quite enough assaults from the critics; he didn't need Barbra weighing in, too. It was bad enough that his girlfriend, in a minor part not integral to the plot, was the one everyone was talking about, but to have her now, suddenly empowered, presume to instruct him how he might do his job better . . . well, that was just a little too close to what his mother had once done, telling him what to do and when and how to do it.

Elliott tossed the note aside and stormed off down the hallway.

Bob saw the distressed look that crossed Barbra's face, a look that only worsened as Elliott's voice echoed through the dressing rooms.

"Hey, Marilyn!" He called into Marilyn Cooper's dressing room. "You want to head out together?"

It was clear to Bob that Elliott was trying to make Barbra jealous, to get her back for her presumptuousness. He succeeded — though only Bob, having known Barbra longer than anyone else there, saw it. With carefully controlled actions and an utterly expressionless countenance, Barbra gathered her things and left the theater. Only much later did Elliott even realize that she had left.

And then he was devastated. His devotion to Barbra was greater than his wounded ego; he feared his impulsive rage had lost her. Hurrying off into the chilly March night, he barricaded himself in a telephone booth and used up a pocketful of change calling Barbra's flat. Each time she answered and he started to speak, she hung up. Finally, dejected, Elliott went back to his own place and fell into a restless sleep.

Four o'clock that morning, his bell rang.

Groggily, Elliott made his way to the intercom. It was Barbra, and he buzzed her in. When he opened his door, she stood there in the hallway looking "like a little orphan child, in her nightgown, tears streaming down her face." Putting his long arms around her, Elliott brought her inside. Their first fight was over. It had lasted six hours at the most. They could only hope that subsequent ones would end as quickly and as well.

CHAPTER NINE

Spring 1962

1.

Laden down with trinkets and tchotchkes, Barbra and Cis climbed the stairs to the little railroad flat above Oscar's Salt of the Sea restaurant at 1155 Third Avenue, just down from Sixty-seventh Street. The rank odor of greasy fried fish that filled up the narrow, windowless stairwell could turn back even strong men, but Barbra charged ahead with gusto, anxious to finish decorating the very first apartment she could call her own.

With *Wholesale* still enjoying good box office, Barbra's $150-a-week salary seemed stable. So Don Softness had finally said to her, "Barbra, you're the toast of Broadway. Isn't it time to move into a place of your own?" She agreed, and found the nineteenth-century tenement with four rooms, each about eight feet by five feet, one right after another in a line. Rent was sixty dollars a month. Given her salary, Barbra could have afforded more; she could have taken a larger — and less smelly — place. But she was being frugal; she'd been living hand-to-mouth not so long ago. *Wholesale* would eventually end, and who was to say she wouldn't find herself bereft again? Better to take a cheaper place where she could save a bit of what she made. Besides, the apartment was right around the block from the DuMont Tele-Centre and *PM East*, and more than luxury, Barbra liked convenience.

Her landlord, Oscar Karp, who ran the eponymous seafood restaurant beneath her, was a disagreeable man who dressed entirely in black and insulted his customers. His restaurant was popular, however, and there was often a long wait for tables. Lines regularly snaked out the door onto Third Avenue.

With Cis following behind, Barbra hurried into her apartment, anxious to arrange the latest adornments she'd purchased for the place. To be sure, it needed some help. An ancient claw-foot bathtub sat in the kitchen because there wasn't room in the bathroom. Barbra used the tub to both bathe and wash dishes, since there was no sink. A window looked out on a stark black brick wall, but at least it let in some air — though given the restaurant below, that wasn't always a good thing. At the far end of the flat was the tiny bedroom, where a broken dumbwaiter from the last century went absolutely nowhere.

Hardly the place one would imagine a Tony nominee calling home. That spring, all sorts of miraculous things were happening to her. When the Tony nominations were announced on April 3, there among them was the name Barbra Streisand — "the kid from nowhere who knew nobody," she called herself to a friend — nominated along with Elizabeth Allan for *The Gay Life*, Barbara Harris for *From the Second City*, and Phyllis Newman, for David Merrick's other show that season, *Subways Are for Sleeping*. The morning after the nominees were announced, a slightly dazed Barbra had risen well before dawn to appear on the *Today Show*, where she sang "Right as the Rain" and was quizzed by host John Chancellor about whether she was made of songs. No, she told him, wincing. "Flesh and bones."

It was certainly a busy period. With the rest of the *Wholesale* company, she'd trooped up to the Columbia Records studio on Seventh Avenue to record the cast album. Spotting Goddard Lieberson in the corridor, she'd called him by his first name. If some found her approach brazen, the record exec didn't seem disturbed by it. In fact, Lieberson had developed some affection for the nonconformist teenager since her last visit to the studio and was seen giving her some special coaching while she recorded "Miss Marmelstein." Not long after this, she ran into Lieberson again at the DuMont Tele-Centre, when they both appeared on *PM East*. Another guest that night was Sammy Cahn, composer of "Day by Day," one of the first songs Barbra ever sang in public — and the one she and Carl Esser had recorded in Barré's apartment seemingly a lifetime ago.

Barbra was soon back at Columbia cutting a second album, this one a twenty-five-year-anniversary tribute to another of Harold Rome's scores, *Pins and Needles*. Despite Rome's animosity toward Barbra, the composer had insisted she be a part of the project, no doubt because he knew the buzz surrounding her performance in *Wholesale* would guarantee some extra record sales. Barbra sang four numbers; the best, some reviewers thought, was "Doing the Reactionary." But the most image-building in terms of the way the public saw her was "Nobody Makes a Pass at Me," yet another homely-girl-looking-for-love lament that could have been the flipside of "Miss Marmelstein." For help in practicing it, Barbra had actually rung Barré, who'd changed the spelling of his name to the more prosaic "Barry" after one too many casting directors had expressed confusion over his gender while perusing his résumé. The practice session had gone well, and Barbra had thanked her ex warmly. Barry hoped they could see each other more often, and Barbra was open to the idea. The relationship with Elliott seemed to have finally healed that old wound.

With all that rehearsing and recording, it was no small wonder that Barbra was exhausted. That didn't mean she sat around being lazy, however. Far from it. With Cis, Barbra had embarked upon several buying sprees, scouring the thrift shops and antique stores along Third Avenue to finish transforming her new place into a home she could call her own. Watching Barbra defy the flat's limitations had left Cis amazed. Barbra's mother had visited and recoiled from the place, telling her daughter she should move back to Brooklyn immediately. But Cis, as always, stepped in when Diana disappointed. When Barbra hung an empty gilt picture frame on the wall and arranged old beaded bags around it, Cis declared the composition "beautiful." When Barbra discovered an antique desk and lugged it upstairs as a centerpiece for the living room, Cis marveled at her friend's unerring eye. "Who knew what antiques meant [at such a young age]?" Cis asked. Barbra's decorating skills left her in awe.

Barbra had managed to make the cramped, awkward apartment eminently livable, at least according to her standards. She hung screens, arranged lacquered chests, and filled a rusted old dentist's cabinet with antique shoe buckles. Those four tiny rooms proved Barry's influence still hovered: Tiffany lamps stood on tables; and feather boas, old fedoras, and movie posters adorned the walls. There was even what looked like a World War II oxygen mask, likely picked up at an Army Navy store.

What made the experience so satisfying for Barbra was that she had paid for all of it herself. No friend, no manager, no publicist had helped her out financially. Shopping with Cis, Barbra had eagerly snapped up "things [she] could never afford before," even if she could have afforded quite a bit more — more, at least, than trinkets and empty picture frames. But she'd quickly learned "the more money you make, the more money you spend," so she'd reeled in her impulse to buy up the store. Her frugality hadn't disappeared just because her paychecks had gotten larger. All that mattered was that her place had style, and that every last scrap, every single idea, had come from *her*. With deep contentment, Barbra flopped into a chair to survey her domain.

That was when Cis announced she was heading home. It had been a long day, and she was tired. It was time to unwind with Harvey and her family, maybe watch some television, or read a book, or have a glass of wine.

Barbra looked at her friend. The reality of how different their lives had become suddenly hit her. "What is this?" she thought. "There's something very strange here."

At the end of a long day, there was no rest for Barbra, no relaxed evening with family or friends, no glass of wine. Instead, she had to traipse across town to the theater, slather on all that makeup, wriggle into that outrageous costume, and play Miss Marmelstein for what was now going on the sixtieth time. Every night the same lines. Every night the same movements. And there was no end in sight. She often showed up at the theater at the very last possible moment, right before the curtain, infuriating the stage manager and her fellow players.

To those hordes of actors who would have severed a limb for a part in a successful Broadway show, Barbra's attitude must have seemed the height of ingratitude. But she'd discovered that with a certain measure of success comes a corresponding loss of more simple pleasures, like the leisure to sit around her new apartment with friends. Barbra would claim that what really made her happy wasn't the show, but enjoying a good malted or getting flowers from Elliott. Indeed, part of her did love such simple things just as much as she loved success and affirmation. And when the success that she had achieved wasn't quite what she had imagined it would be, the conflict became even more apparent.

It was her old repugnance for doing the same thing twice. To combat mental fatigue, she tried playing her part a little differently each night, which, of course, threw her fellow cast members off when she wasn't in her assigned position on stage or when she altered a line, even subtly. "What does it matter if I don't stand in exactly the same spot?" Barbra bellyached. Scolded for being undisciplined, she called such criticism nonsense. "It's just that I believe in being a person," she told one reporter, defending her oscillating style.

Consequently, some nights she was better than others, and she knew it—though her audiences never seemed to discern the difference. Every night, on cue, they erupted for Miss Marmelstein when she came rolling out on her casters. They'd been waiting for the moment; they'd been told by the critics that the kid playing the secretary was a big deal, and so no matter how Barbra performed, they screamed and applauded just the same. Walter Winchell, the doyen of Broadway columnists, had raved about Barbra's "jolly-dollying," calling her the "brightest femmtertainer in years."

That was all well and good, terrific publicity for the show, of course. But for Barbra, it was excellence that ultimately mattered, and if she was going to get applause, she wanted it to be because she really deserved it. And she was beginning to feel excellence was something she'd never really attain playing this stock character in a musical that really wasn't, despite Arthur Laurents's best efforts, all that great.

What irked her most, however, was the claim made by some reporters that she had "hit the big time." Yes, she had been nominated for a Tony, but as far as Barbra was concerned, Miss Marmelstein was miles away from the big time. Certainly she wanted to win the award — very much — but she was never going to be satisfied with "featured performer" status; she wanted the "best actress" prize, the possibility of which was still too far in the future for her liking. So when columnists claimed she had received "lots of offers" for more work, Barbra slammed the stories as "a big lie." True, her new agent at Associated Booking, Joe Sully, who also handled Louis Armstrong, had gotten her a new gig at the Bon Soir, and there was talk about appearing on some television shows. But those kinds of things didn't count. When someone asked her to play Medea, then they could talk about hitting the big time.

To one reporter, Barbra carefully explained that she wasn't yet a success because she wasn't really famous. Just the other day, she had gone shopping at Bergdorf Goodman and couldn't get anyone to wait on her. "If I was famous," she said, "they would have waited on me. But I looked too young, I guess, and too — I don't know, like I couldn't afford to shop there." Then she laid down the parameters for success as she saw it. "I'll be a success when I'm famous enough to get waited on at Bergdorf Goodman."

2.

At long last, Barbra was no longer a teenager. On April 24, Barbra's twentieth birthday, the producers of *PM East* presented her with a cake during the taping of the show, which was scheduled to air later that night. Diana and eleven-year-old Rosalind had come in from Brooklyn for a cute, on-air birthday celebration. Even Mike Wallace joined in as the cast and crew sang "Happy Birthday" to Barbra.

But there was more important business to attend to on this particular show, and Don Softness kept his fingers crossed that it would all work out. Marty had asked him to come up with a "gimmick" to get Barbra noticed by the producers — David Merrick included — who were planning the Fanny Brice musical. So Softness had rung his old pal George Q. Lewis, the legendary comedy writer and workshop teacher who'd helped Milton Berle, Henny Youngman, Jack Benny, and others polish their gags. Lewis had established a mostly phony organization called the National Association of Gag Writers that could be used for promotional purposes — which was just what Softness had in mind. He asked Lewis if the association would give Barbra their annual "Fanny Brice Award."

"But we don't have a Fanny Brice Award," Lewis replied.

"You do now," Softness told him.

So, on the air that night, Barbra was presented with more than a birthday cake. Out came a fancy framed certificate from the National Association of Gag Writers, signed by Lewis. Mike Wallace read from the statement prepared by Softness, telling the audience that the "annual award" was being presented to Miss Streisand because "the pathos of her comedy epitomizes the devotion to her art reminiscent of the late, great Fanny Brice." Barbra acted suitably surprised and impressed as she accepted the certificate. Everyone involved knew it was both the first and the last annual Fanny Brice Award.

In the meantime, Softness had reached out to another colleague, Richard Falk, a fast-talking, stunt-loving publicity man who'd started out as an assistant to Claude Greneker, the press agent for the Ziegfeld Follies in the 1930s. Falk was known as "the Mayor of Forty-second Street" for all his connections up and down the Great White Way, as well as for such PR gambits as checking a trained flea into the Waldorf-Astoria. If anyone could get Barbra noticed, Softness reasoned that it was Falk.

One of the first things Falk suggested was to ratchet up the kook business. If landing the part of Fanny Brice was the goal, kookiness was definitely the way to go, as Brice was known for her quirks and whims. Keep playing up the thrift shops and vintage clothes, Falk advised. Barbra had been making references to "Second Hand Rose," one of Brice's best-known songs, at least as far back as her Detroit days, so they were on the right track. Meanwhile, the new publicist began issuing regular bulletins to all the columnists, most of whom he knew personally. Within days, Leonard Lyons was reporting that showman Billy Rose, Brice's third husband, had been "reading all the casting reports on the musical about the late Fanny Brice," and "of all the comediennes he's seen, the one whose comic qualities most closely approach Miss Brice's is Barbra Streisand of *I Can Get It for You Wholesale.*" Rose, of course, was one of Falk's cronies. It was all part of the plan.

But the Brice show was just one of many possible targets. The best way to secure the parts Barbra wanted, Falk understood, was to get enough people interested in her and talking about her that offers would start flowing in. To that end, he arranged some appearances for her on the *Joe Franklin Show,* a morning New York television talk show on WABC, and set up some interviews for her with a handful of his reporter pals. The result was a flurry of syndicated articles that spring about "the twenty-year-old comedienne sensation." One was by Dick Kleiner, a popular Broadway writer whose profiles and reviews were syndicated through the Newspaper Enterprise Association, which meant he was read in hundreds of papers across the country. In Kleiner's piece, Barbra the Kook came through loud and clear. He called her a "character," and to illustrate that, he had her tell the story of dyeing her hair in school and wearing "strange color lipstick and eye-shadow."

More of the same followed. Some reporters clued in to the fact that Barbra wasn't playing entirely straight with them, that she had a mission, and that no matter what the journalist asked, she wasn't going to stray from the grand design that she and her publicists had laid out. "Instead of giving me an honest answer to my questions," Edward Robb Ellis, a reporter for the *New York World-Telegram*, recorded in his diary after meeting her, "she lied to me, toyed with me, tried to manipulate me." Since Barbra told him nothing authentic about herself, Ellis decided to focus his entire piece on the character of Miss Marmelstein. She was as real, it seemed, as the woman he'd just interviewed.

In a major coup, Barbra's publicity team secured a brief profile in *The New Yorker,* and more than anything else, this piece established the tone of the budding star's subsequent coverage. The unnamed "Talk of the Town" writer, clearly playing up Barbra's kooky reputation, chose to string everything she said closely together, as if she never paused for breath and spoke in one long stream of consciousness: "I used to baby-sit for a Chinese couple in Brooklyn; they had a restaurant and taught me to enjoy Chinese dishes. I often go to Chinatown to eat late at night. You get wonderful white hot breads with the center filled with shrimp at the little coffee shops there. Only ten cents! I love food. I look forward to it all day. My body responds to it. Everything else seems so nebulous."

Of course, Barbra did talk fast and furious, but this was way, way over the top. "I was bald until I was two," Barbra rambled on. "I think I'm some sort of Martian. I exist on my will power, being Taurus. I hate the name Barbara; I dropped the second 'a,' and I think I'll gradually cut the whole thing down to B. That will save exertion in handwriting. I sometimes call myself Angelina Scarangella, which won't." There was much more in a similar vein. At the close of the piece, Barbra said, "I like interviews — they're still a novelty — but by the time they appear they look funny to me, because my attitude changes from week to week." Which attitudes, she was asked. "Oh, toward smoked foods, say," she replied — a reference to *PM East,* where the whole kook image had been born. The *New Yorker* piece was a wonderfully entertaining article; no wonder the writer ended by saying he "rushed to the phone" to file his copy.

Another profile, this one for United Press International, revealed how Barbra wore nightgowns as dresses. By turning the nightgown backward, Barbra explained, she could achieve an Empire bust-line — "You know, like in Napoleon's time." No doubt she really did buy that nightgown, though whether she'd really worn it "the other day," as the piece claimed, no one was sure. Nor did anyone really care. Barbra had been told to "play up the kook" by her publicists, so she did — and not all journalists were as resistant to following her lead as Ellis. Most of them quickly learned this Streisand kid was very good copy. Marvelously creative pieces could be structured around her persona.

Richard Falk was continually surprised that Barbra understood his directions. When he spoke with her, it seemed as if she wasn't even listening, "not there at all . . . a little off-center." Softness, however, knew that Barbra heard everything that was said to her. She just processed it all very quickly, he said, then "moved on to the next thing." Barbra took to the merchandizing of her image like a duck to water.

Of course, if the product they were trying to sell wasn't any good, no one would have bought it, and people were definitely buying Barbra. The fact that she was extravagantly talented made her publicists' jobs a lot easier. The week before her Fanny Brice Award, Barbra had won the New York Drama Critics' Circle Award for her part in *Wholesale*. She'd been given the honor at a cocktail party at the Algonquin Hotel, hobnobbing with critics like Howard Taubman, Walter Kerr, and John Chapman, all of whom had sung her praises. (The rest of *Wholesale* was ignored, however; the choice for best musical was *How to Succeed in Business Without Really Trying*, with which Barbra's show had so often been unfavorably compared.) While Barbra's fortune might have been her voice, her fate was assured by the team that made sure that voice got heard.

And now, in large part because of their efforts, she really did have a shot at the big time. The Critics' Circle Award meant Barbra had the blessing of the city's most important star-makers. But she already knew that the critics loved her. What Barbra really wanted was the Tony — the affirmation of her peers.

3.

Stan Berman was a Brooklyn cabbie who called himself the "world's greatest gate-crasher." Earlier that month, he'd crashed the Academy Awards in Santa Monica, California, presenting host Bob Hope with a two-dollar replica of an Oscar. Now, on April 29, as Broadway's glitterati gathered at the Waldorf-Astoria for the sixteenth annual Tony Awards, Berman once again walked through the front door looking "very official" without anyone stopping him to ask for credentials. He was carrying orchids, which he hoped to present to the winners.

Another Brooklynite at the Waldorf that night might have been feeling a bit like a gate-crasher herself, as she sat among such people as Judith Anderson, Helen Hayes, Jason Robards, Olivia de Havilland, and Robert Goulet. But Barbra Streisand was getting used to being in the presence of celebrities. Three nights before, she'd been one of a select group of New Yorkers invited to watch Judy Garland record a new album at the Manhattan Center. Unpublicized, the concert had started at midnight, and a dazzling mix of celebrities, socialites, and other A-listers had filed into the hall. But as Barbra took her seat with a few others from the *Wholesale* company, she couldn't quite comprehend what all the excitement was about. Despite Garland's recent triumph at Carnegie Hall and her three decades in the limelight, Barbra insisted that she had "never heard of her." Some friends thought she was playing the diva, but maybe she really hadn't heard about Carnegie Hall, or seen *The Wizard of Oz,* or made the connection when she'd sung Garland's part in her duet with Mickey Rooney. Maybe she had forgotten the Garland records Barré had played for her. To friends, all of that seemed extremely unlikely, but then again, Barbra had never been one for idols.

When Garland came out on stage, without any introduction, just strolling in from behind the curtain in a simple dress and high heels, Barbra probably wasn't all that impressed. The thirty-nine-year-old singer had just gotten out of Columbia Presbyterian Medical Center, where she'd been hospitalized for exhaustion, and was in the midst of a bitter fight with her estranged husband, Sid Luft, over their children. The strain showed. She also had laryngitis, which left her croaking through her songs. Ultimately she was just too hoarse and had to end the concert early. If this was truly Barbra's first exposure to the woman many were already calling a legend, then she might have been forgiven for wondering what the fuss was all about.

No doubt there was a similar detachment at the Waldorf on Tony night. Barbra was there for one purpose only: to win the award. Stargazing had never held much interest for her. Stan Berman the Brooklyn cabbie might be hiding backstage, eager to snatch a glimpse of the winners, but Barbra the Brooklyn chanteuse hardly strayed from her table, too busy putting away her London broil and baked potato to do much mingling. The Tony dinner-dance, despite its star wattage, was a rather homey affair, far less showy than the Oscar gala. Although New Yorkers could watch the ceremony on their local NBC affiliate, the rest of the country barely knew it was taking place, as the Tonys weren't broadcast nationally like the Oscars were. Consequently, there was far less playing to the camera. Barbra's only chance to make an impression, then, would come when she strode up to the lectern to collect her award.

And everyone was certain she would win. None of the other nominees had generated as much publicity as Barbra had these last two months. Even David Merrick, who still didn't like her, predicted she'd take home the prize. He'd chosen to sit with the company from his other show, *Subways Are for Sleeping;* after all, *Subways* had racked up three nominations to *Wholesale*'s one. But when it came time for the Best Featured Actress Award, Merrick callously turned to Phyllis Newman, Barbra's competition, and told her, "Streisand's going to win. I voted for her." So confident of Barbra's victory was the egotistical producer that he wanted it known before the fact that he was on her side. Merrick could never allow himself to be associated with losers.

So when it was Phyllis Newman's name that was called out as the winner, Merrick switched allegiances in that very instant, jumping up and congratulating her as if he'd been rooting for her the whole time. It was a surprise win, but explainable. The critics might not have cared how often Barbra had been late to the theater, so long as the final performance was excellent. But word of her occasional lack of professionalism had gotten around, and her peers, apparently, didn't approve. Better to honor Newman, who'd been paying her dues on Broadway since 1953.

After she collected her Tony, Newman headed backstage, where Stan Berman bounded out from the shadows to present her with an orchid. Meanwhile, Barbra gathered her things and slipped out the back door. She'd finished her meal. There was no reason to stick around and watch other people win awards.

4.

On a piece of cardboard, Jerome Robbins scrawled the names of the actresses who had been mentioned as possibly playing the part of Fanny Brice in the play he was going to direct for David Merrick and Ray Stark. At the top was Chita Rivera (an interesting choice). Then came Tammy Grimes. Judy Holliday. Paula Prentiss. Susan Pleshette. (Robbins meant Suzanne.) Mimi Hines. Kaye Stevens. Eydie Gormé. And then a woman whom Robbins clearly had little knowledge of. "Barbara Streisman."

All the famed choreographer of *Gypsy, West Side Story,* and the New York City Ballet probably knew of the "Streisman" girl at that point was that she was appearing in another of Merrick's productions. If Robbins had seen *Wholesale,* he didn't mention it in correspondence with friends.

Instead, his passion was reserved for someone who wasn't even on that list. Anne Bancroft, who'd won the Tony for Best Actress for *The Miracle Worker* two years ago and for Best Featured Actress for *Two for the Seesaw* three years ago, was Robbins's first choice. Indeed, they'd been talking with Bancroft about the role for some time now. The chance to work with "Annie," as Robbins called her, was a large part of the reason he'd signed on to the project in the first place.

But Ray Stark, Merrick's coproducer and the one really in the driver's seat for this show, had his reservations about Bancroft. Stark was married to Fanny Brice's daughter, and he had a personal investment in the casting—literally: He'd had to make deals with his wife, his brother-in-law, and even his own children since they were all part of Brice's estate. He'd had to buy the rights to the story of his father-in-law, Nick Arnstein, Brice's second husband, who was still living. So with all that riding on the project, Stark was going to be very particular about their leading lady. Very quickly, he—or maybe it was Mrs. Stark, no one knew for sure—had soured on Bancroft. She didn't want to play Fanny Brice, Stark insisted; she wanted to play a "new character based on" the legendary comedienne. If they did it Bancroft's way, Stark wrote to Robbins and composer Jule Styne, they'd be left with nothing of Brice: "The personality of Anne Bancroft, not only through characterization but also through the style of singing and dancing, will be the only personality to emerge."

Still, Robbins preferred Bancroft over everyone else Stark kept suggesting as alternatives. Last fall, the producer had been set on Kaye Stevens, whom he called "the most exciting girl" and the "answer to our quest." Stevens was a bubbly singer and comedienne who, with her carrot-red hair and slender body, resembled "a Spanish exclamation point," as one scribe thought. Stevens was attractive enough, but no great beauty by any means. The real Fanny Brice had also been far from pretty and was known for her large nose. But there were some who thought Frances Stark only wanted an attractive, ladylike actress to play her mother. (Her original choice for the part had been Mary Martin.) Enthused by Kaye Stevens—perhaps hoping she'd be the perfect compromise between the reality of the part and his wife's unrealistic expectations—Stark had pleaded with Robbins to fly out to the Coast to meet her. But the director, busy fixing *A Funny Thing Happened on the Way to the Forum* for George Abbott and Hal Prince, had declined, which infuriated the producer.

They were very different personalities, Stark and Robbins. The former was soft-spoken and winsome—one account called him "pixieish" — where the latter could be surly, bombastic, and overwrought. Robbins's ferocious temper was legendary. It usually erupted during times of self-doubt, which for Robbins was pretty much all of the time. Even after so much success, he still struggled with a deep sense of not being good enough. After the triumphant premiere of his show *Fancy Free* in 1944, for example, his first thought had been that he now had enough money for analysis. Robbins's fears and self-doubts could be traced directly to deep-seated conflicts over both his Jewishness and his homosexuality: Most of the time, Robbins wished he were neither. When, in 1953, he named six of his colleagues as Communists to the U.S. House Committee on Un-American Activities, he sidestepped the blacklist, but gave himself yet another layer of shame to live under for the rest of his life.

Ray Stark, on the other hand, was utterly without shame. Soft-spoken and winsome he might be, but that pixieish grin was cover for a shrewd, often cutthroat mind. Like David Merrick, Stark thought nothing of playing collaborators against each other, rationalizing that if it was good for the project, the ends justified the means. Director John Huston thought Stark's penchant for starting rows among his company emerged from a belief "that out of the fires of dissension flows molten excellence." But Stark's devilry was always conducted with a smile. With Jerry Robbins, people tended to know where they stood: He was either screaming at them or lauding them with praise. But Stark left them guessing. He could tell an actor he was brilliant in the morning but fire him by lunchtime.

The kind of doubts and anxieties that plagued Robbins had no place in Stark's life. Self-reflection was a waste of time, and Ray Stark had no time to waste. Among his favorite expressions was one word: "Commit." From everyone he worked with Stark expected complete commitment because he himself gave two hundred percent. He was always on the lookout for what was next, whether it be the next film for his production company, Seven Arts, or a follow-up to his first stage success, *The World of Suzie Wong*. To all of them he brought the same level of unflagging commitment. No other producer, said Arthur Laurents, had "more infectious enthusiasm" than Ray Stark.

And nowhere was that enthusiasm more obvious, Laurents added, than when Stark was "casting young actresses." Ray's eye for the ladies was notorious. He was known to walk actresses he found attractive through his sculpture garden back in Beverly Hills and compare their buttocks to those on the nude statues. It was one final detail that set Stark apart from Robbins, and it suggests that it wasn't only Mrs. Stark who was rooting for a pretty candidate to play Fanny Brice.

Whatever the reasons, it seemed Stark and Robbins simply could not see eye to eye on who should play Fanny. In November, Stark was pushing the attractive Georgia Brown, known best for playing Nancy in the West End production of *Oliver!* But Robbins argued if they weren't going with Anne Bancroft, then they should go with Carol Burnett, the wacky sidekick from *The Garry Moore Show* who'd proven her Broadway power—and vocal chops—for more than a year in *Once Upon a Mattress*. Advance word on Burnett's television special with Julie Andrews, written by Mike Nichols and to be called *Julie and Carol at Carnegie Hall,* was outstanding. With her offbeat looks, comedic timing, star presence, and big Broadway voice, Burnett seemed to Robbins the perfect choice to play Fanny Brice. On the surface, Stark was open to Burnett, insisting he wanted "to see her in person because television doesn't necessarily do her justice." But at the same time, he was offering actress Paula Prentiss—who was far more conventionally attractive—as an alternative.

That was where they stood now. The list Robbins had scrawled on that piece of cardboard was a mix of his ideas and Stark's, though "Barbara Streisman" was probably neither's. She'd made the list, most likely, because—thanks to Richard Falk and the Softness brothers—people kept bringing up her name: columnists, stage managers, TV commentators. Whether Robbins had seen or heard a mention of "Barbara Streisman" is unknown. But clearly someone had, with the result that Barbra's name, however misspelled, was added to Jerry Robbins's list.

5.

When Bob, with Barry Dennen in tow, showed up at the Lichee Tree restaurant at 65 East Eighth Street, just before midnight on May 10, the place was mobbed with several hundred people. The night was a bit chilly, but partygoers were spilling out onto the sidewalk since the restaurant was packed to the walls inside. Photographers were snapping away as Mike Wallace, Abe Burrows, Phyllis Diller, and others arrived bearing gifts. The reason for all the fuss? The official celebration of Barbra's twentieth birthday.

Bob was carrying a framed drawing he'd done of Barbra. But once he and Barry worked their way inside, there seemed to be no place to leave it for her. Every available table was crowded with huge floral tributes from David Merrick, Leonard Bernstein, Richard Rodgers, and others. "Many more, sweetheart," Mike Nichols had written on a card attached to a bouquet. Another card read: "With love from Ethel Merman." Bob looked over at Barry and cracked, "Gee, what do you think the pope sent?"

"Matzo balls," Barry deadpanned.

Glancing around the crowded room, they couldn't see Barbra, but they could sure smell the feast that was being laid out. Sizzling Go Ba combined chunks of lobster and crab with snow peas, bamboo shoots, and mushrooms. Filet mignon was flavored with the sweet berries of the lichee tree and served on a bed of bean sprouts and rice noodles. Irene Yuan Kuo, who ran the restaurant with her husband, prepared the menus and planned the parties. She had taken a liking to Barbra, who was a frequent patron, and so when Don Softness approached her about hosting the party, she'd happily agreed. In China, Kuo told Softness, it was traditional to "welcome a girl into the realm of womanhood when she attains the age of twenty." The Kuos had agreed to foot the bill because they believed—or were convinced—that the publicity would be good for their two-year-old eatery. When Barry learned that salient little fact, he marveled over the "genius for self-promotion" his former girlfriend had developed since the days when they were putting up posters for her weekly appearances at the Lion.

Since she hadn't won the Tony, Barbra needed some other kind of exposure to keep her name in the news — and in the running for the Fanny Brice show. Howard Taubman had just included her in a list of the top ten newcomers on Broadway for a photo spread in the *New York Times,* even using her publicists' talking points: "a natural comedienne who has been likened to Fanny Brice." But more was still needed. Weaving in and out of the crowd at the Lichee Tree was Don Softness, working the room for his client. His focus was the gaggle of newspaper columnists who always showed up whenever free food was offered. Already he'd lassoed Leonard Lyons for their cause; now Earl Wilson was being wined and dined. The party was as much for the press, Softness admitted, as it was for Barbra's friends and coworkers.

The birthday girl herself finally emerged, wearing a long wool dress that she'd bought at Filene's Basement while the show had been in previews in Boston. Softness made sure to tell everyone that she'd paid $12.50 for it — marked down from $100. That was what the press had come to expect from Barbra's wardrobe. Thrifty. Quirky. Kooky.

Elliott was at her side. For her actual birthday he'd given her a rose, which had made her happy, though she'd told her mother that he'd given her cash. At least that's what she told the press that she'd told her mother. It was getting hard to know what Barbra really said versus what she said that she said — or what her publicists said that she said.

At her party, Barbra didn't approach anyone; people came to her. Marty ran interference, keeping all but a few from getting in too close. Terry Leong never even got a chance to say hello to his old friend, even though he was planning to move to Europe soon to study fashion. Barry, pleased and surprised to have received an invitation, nevertheless was kept at arm's length by Marty every time he tried to start a conversation with Barbra. Barry felt that the obstruction was "deliberate." He believed that Barbra had given instructions to Marty beforehand "to keep her old friends at a distance."

Bob, however, was more sympathetic as always. He pointed out that with such a large crowd, intimacy was impossible. If anything, Bob blamed Elliott for the distance they felt from Barbra. From the start, Elliott had been uncomfortable around Barbra's old friends, perhaps because they knew a part of her that he didn't. Largely because of the "vulnerability" he perceived in Elliott, Bob had withdrawn, no longer asking Barbra to join him at some of their favorite old haunts. Their long telephone conversations and late-night makeup sessions were now things of the past. Barbra hadn't shared much with Bob about her relationship with Elliott, but Bob thought he could figure it out. Elliott was very much in love with Barbra, which no doubt must have been exhilarating for her, given what she'd been through with Barry. And with Elliott "really lusting after Barbra," she had "total control over him," Bob observed. What more could Barbra want?

As they stood off to the side, catching glimpses of Barbra through the crowd, Bob and Barry both had a sense that their old friend had left them for good. "I always thought you would be the legend," Bob told Barry in a moment of reflection.

"I don't want to be a legend," Barry insisted. "I just want to be a working actor."

Behind them, flashcubes were popping and people were applauding. Barbra was slicing her birthday cake.

6.

Her hair done up in a bun, Barbra rode onto the stage in a motorized cart with Robert Goulet, the star of *Camelot,* at the wheel. The announcer introduced them, but they seemed not to hear very well, since Barbra waved to the audience when Goulet's name was mentioned and he waved when hers was. It was all part of a silly opening number on the May 29 episode of *The Garry Moore Show,* in which pairs of performers tramped across the stage in three-legged pants singing about teamwork. Barbra and Goulet were spared that indignity, though they struggled to sing along, mostly succumbing to giggles instead.

Sharing the stage was Barbra's rival for the Fanny Brice show, Carol Burnett, who most observers figured had better odds at landing the part since she was better known and already an Emmy-winning star comedienne. Perhaps for that reason the writers of the Moore show had given them no scenes together — a pity, because their humor might have worked well in tandem. Instead, Barbra was largely on her own. Moore introduced her after delivering his pitch for the show's sponsor, Winston cigarettes. "One of the biggest thrills for a guy who's been around this business as long as I have is the advent of a bright new young star." The teleprompter speech he was reading from had been prepared from materials submitted by Barbra's publicists, and they'd made sure to indicate exactly how to say Barbra's name. With clear, specific emphasis, Moore enunciated "Streisand" as if he'd been practicing it or if he were reading from a pronunciation guide. The mispronunciation of her name during introductions was one of Barbra's pet peeves, and she'd insisted to her publicists that it must not happen here.

Moore went on, using the line about *Wholesale* that Softness had practically patented by now ("she stopped the show cold") and then summed up with "I was delighted to learn during rehearsals this week that she is equally effective in straight numbers as she is when she's being zany." Moore was setting up a bit of business for later in the show, but Barbra usually seemed to find a way to have that point made in her television appearances.

The camera moved over to a set designed to look like a tenement balcony. Barbra opened the doors and came walking out, all slinky, nothing like the giggly child glimpsed in the opening act. Her hair was long and loose around her shoulders, and she wore a dark, form-fitting dress with straps that crossed over her chest. She sang "When the Sun Comes Out," never stepping from her spot as she used her arms to make a grand, sensual sweep, bouncing ever so slightly as the lyrics heated up: "And the rain stops beating on my windowpane . . ." It was a startlingly sexy performance. As the camera moved in for a close-up, Barbra looked gorgeous, full-figured and full of passion. In that moment, it was easy to understand why Elliott was so turned on by her.

Barbra was always at her sexiest and most attractive when she was feeling confident, and on the Moore show she was brimming over with belief in herself. When she finished the number and the host joined her onstage, their banter, though rehearsed, flowed easily, as if it were completely extemporaneous. "Barbra, I saw you in *I Can Get It for You Wholesale*," Moore said, "and while you do have a comedy role, I also suspect that you are a very fine dramatic actress."

"Yes, you're right, Garry," Barbra agreed, delivering the line exactly right, disguising the arrogance with humor, placing her hand on Moore's shoulder and hanging her head for an instant, laughing at herself as the audience laughed with her.

Moore asked if she could prove her claim of being a great actress, and Barbra replied that she had a speech prepared. "Ladies and gentlemen!" she suddenly shouted, gripping the balcony railing as if she were a South American dictator addressing her people. Laughing for a moment, she quickly recovered her mock serious tone. "I ask you . . . to stay with us!" Gesturing dramatically, her voice grew louder and more Shakespearean. "We! Shall return! Immediately! After a word from our sponsor!" Moore mimed wiping a tear from his eye as they cut to a commercial. Barbra had been absolutely endearing, confident enough to have a little fun with herself and her own ambition.

But it was in her next number that she proved transcendent. If anyone doubted that underneath her kooky, musical comedy exterior beat the heart of a woman who still wanted to play Juliet, all they had to do was watch her perform "Happy Days Are Here Again." It was part of a regular segment on the Moore show called "That Wonderful Year," in which the songs and events of various years were remembered. Tonight, the year was 1929. "Let's be honest, 1929 was not a wonderful year," Moore said, referring to the stock market crash. "On that Black Tuesday in October, there were many expensively dressed people without a penny to their name." Cue the piano introduction to "Happy Days" as the camera switched over to the set of a darkened bar with a waiter wiping down tables. In walked Barbra, swathed in mink, diamonds dripping from her ears.

One of the show's composers, Ken Welch, who'd helped with arrangements on *Julie and Carol at Carnegie Hall,* had come up with the idea to use the song as an ironic commentary instead of the usual upbeat rallying cry. Barbra had jumped at the opportunity to prove — all kidding aside — that she really could act. No doubt it was the rehearsals for "Happy Days" that Moore had alluded to when he'd said he'd learned that Barbra was "equally effective" in straight as well as zany numbers.

She was more than effective, actually. She was a revelation. In the three-and-a-half-minute number, Barbra created a fully realized, fully human characterization. Before she sat down at the table, she ran a finger along the seat of the chair, withering the waiter with a disapproving look because of the dust. It was clear that this was a woman used to the finer things in life. But, like most people in 1929, she was broke. "Will a four-carat earring buy a glass of champagne?" she sang, removing the bauble from her ear, in lyrics specially written for this little introduction. The waiter, played by Bob Harris, a former chorus member on *The Fred Waring Show,* nodded and took the earring, heading off to fetch some bubbly. In song, Barbra went on to muse that she needed to celebrate, since her last million dollars had just gone down the drain.

She was positively giddy in her denial of what awaited her. She was broke, she was poor, she was right back where she started from. The waiter brought the champagne and she downed the glass, immediately declaring she'd have another. The waiter pointed to her remaining earring. With a smile, she handed it over, then launched into the song. "Happy days are here again, the skies above are clear again . . ."

She sang louder and more boldly than most singers did on television, perhaps out of habit from singing every night on the Broadway stage. And though she kept a smile on her face, it was clear through the ironic words of the song that Barbra was feeling the pain and terror and desperation of her character. Snapping her fingers, she brought the waiter back for a third glass, this time giving him a ring in return. She seemed like a woman on the verge of tears — or madness. A bracelet was exchanged for a fourth glass of champagne, and when she sang about her cares and troubles being gone, the heartbreak was palpable. She ended the number shedding her mink and sensually caressing the champagne bottle. The applause went on for twenty seconds, longer than usual. Moore blew her a kiss and murmured under his breath, "Powerful."

The host was clearly impressed. So were the millions watching at home. Peter Daniels was in the wings, and in that moment he knew "Happy Days" had to go into Barbra's act. It had the potential to be a signature song, as quirky and as unexpected as "Who's Afraid of the Big Bad Wolf?" but far more profound and poetic. In such roughs as TV variety shows, Daniels realized, were the occasional diamonds found.

7.

It seemed as if Ray Stark was always in the air. He lived in Beverly Hills, but every ten days he flew to New York, where he had a suite at the Hotel Navarro on Central Park South, and once a month he continued on across the pond to Europe, usually to Paris or London, but sometimes other cities as well. Stark logged about half a million miles in the air a year.

But somehow this never slowed him down. For a man such as Stark, there was no time for jet lag. So, after his latest trip to Europe, he'd accepted Jule Styne's invitation to see David Merrick's *I Can Get It for You Wholesale* before he headed back to the Coast. There was a girl in the show, Styne told him, who'd make a perfect Fanny Brice. Since he was at an impasse with Robbins over the casting and eager to find someone to knock Anne Bancroft out of the running, Stark was very glad to consider any and all suggestions. The girl's name, Styne said, was Barbra Streisand.

After seeing the show, Stark had agreed that the Streisand kid was good. But her Miss Marmelstein was far from the vision he had for Fanny. The part needed pathos and intelligence and anger and sacrifice, not just broad comedy and a big voice. Styne agreed. That was why he insisted that Stark accompany him next to the Bon Soir. Barbra had started another run at the nightclub, and after seeing her once, Styne had been back every single night, so mesmerized had he become by her voice and personality. One regular patron thought that the composer seemed "smitten like a schoolboy."

And so, on a night in late May, Ray Stark carefully navigated his way down those dark, steep steps. Finding a table with Styne, he settled in to wait for Barbra Streisand. In that tiny room, on that tiny stage, she'd be so close he'd be able to see her sweat.

The fact that Styne was so enthusiastic about the kid carried considerable weight with Stark. Jule Styne, who'd composed the music for *High Button Shoes, Gentlemen Prefer Blondes, My Sister Eileen, Gypsy,* and other shows, as well as many popular songs — including the Oscar-winning "Three Coins in the Fountain" — was already a Broadway and Hollywood legend. That was precisely why Stark had hired him to compose the music for the Fanny Brice show: He wanted only the best for a show about his mother-in-law.

Stark had been trying to get the project off the ground for more than a decade. Shortly before her death in 1951, Brice had been writing a memoir, sitting down with a tape recorder and a good friend — none other than Goddard Lieberson. After Brice's death, Stark had taken these reminiscences and, with the help of a paid writer, assembled them into a book. But the final product so displeased the family that Stark had paid the publisher $50,000 to get the plates back, which kept the book from ever being published. Instead, Stark decided to turn Brice's tape-recorded notes into a film, commissioning first Ben

Hecht (*His Girl Friday, Notorious*) and later Isobel Lennart (*Anchors Aweigh, It Happened in Brooklyn*) to write the screenplay. When the film idea failed to attract interest, Stark turned his eyes to the stage, asking Lennart to adapt her screenplay into a book for a musical. Like Robbins, Lennart had saved her career during the inquisitions of the 1950s by naming names to the House Un-American Activities Committee. It was, perhaps, an unspoken bond between her and Robbins, as the two had grown extremely close.

Stark, however, wasn't as enamored of Lennart as his director was. She had assured him that she could easily adapt her screenplay even though she'd never written for the theater before. To the producer's mounting dismay, Lennart had yet to make good on her promise. Jule Styne and his partner, Bob Merrill (who'd come in when Stephen Sondheim bowed out), had written some extraordinary music. A ballad called "People" was especially good, and so was the rousing "Don't Rain on My Parade." But the book was still lacking — a fact that even so ardent a supporter of Lennart's as Robbins couldn't deny.

That night, as Stark waited in the dark for the show to begin at the Bon Soir, he was probably more worried about getting the book right than he was about finding the right actress to play Fanny. The book was the project's Achilles heel, and he knew it. If there was one thing Ray Stark had learned, right at the beginning of his career, it was the importance of story. He'd started out as a literary agent, representing Ben Hecht and Raymond Chandler, among others. He'd learned that "the story" was the "essential foundation" for any project. No amount of great directing, great music, or great acting could make up for the lack of good story.

Stark saw the Brice project not as "a literal biography," but as "an affectionate one," which meant the writer was free to take liberties in telling Brice's story. Neither Stark nor his wife cared much about the parts of Brice's life that the public most remembered — her zaniness, her crazy faces, her Baby Snooks radio character. Instead, they wanted to tell the tragic love story between Brice and her second husband, the gambler Nick Arnstein, and to do so, Brice needed to be elevated to a dignified, even aristocratic, status. In private life, the offbeat comedienne was noted for her style and class; in her later years, she worked as an interior decorator, hailed for her restrained, elegant taste. This was the Brice the Starks wanted to memorialize, not the nonsense-jabbering Snooks, even if it was a bit of a distortion. Kaye Ballard had recorded an album of Brice's songs with an eye toward playing the comedienne herself. But Fran Stark quickly nixed the idea. "Fran Stark had this fantasy that her mother was this beautiful, delicate creature," Ballard complained. "Fanny *was* beautiful," she said, "after you got to know her, but not beautiful in the way [the Starks] wanted to portray her."

To those who knew them, it wasn't surprising that the Starks wanted to portray Fanny Brice as cultured and refined. It was the image they had cultivated for themselves as well, hosting swanky parties at their Beverly Hills home, assembling an impressive collection of art, and sending their children to prestigious private schools. Ray Stark projected an air of affluence, as if he'd been to the manor born. But, like so many other power brokers in show business, he hadn't always been so prosperous; he'd done his share of hustling to get where he was.

Stark's grandfather had emigrated from Silesia, now part of Poland, and worked as a piano tuner, eking out a living for his family on Manhattan's Lower East Side at the turn of the century. His son, Max, had set his sights higher, working as a clerk in the office of the Manhattan borough president. He also married a young woman of some means, Sadie Vera Gotlieb, whose father was a florist and the owner of a large piece of property at 32 East Fifty-eighth Street, at Madison Avenue, worth about $50,000 in 1930. The florist shop was on the ground floor of the brownstone building; the family apartments were above. It was here that in 1915 Raymond Stark was born.

Although he shared with Barbra Streisand a third-generation Jewish immigrant identity, Ray Stark enjoyed a childhood far more comfortable than the one endured by the singer he was waiting to hear. For one thing, the Starks employed a live-in Irish maid, something Barbra would have found completely unimaginable. But she would have recognized Ray's drive. As a boy, he had helped out in his uncle's florist shop, but he made it clear that his ambition extended beyond roses and peonies. At fourteen — sometimes he'd add "and a half" — he was accepted into Rutgers University, though he was cagey about whether he ever actually graduated. Only rarely did Stark admit the truth: that he was thrown out of college, more than once, for "inattention to his studies."

The problem was that Stark's ambition seemed always to get ahead of itself. After working as a cub reporter on several New York papers, Stark turned his eyes west, driving across the country with a sixty-seven-year-old neighbor to share expenses. In Hollywood, he took a job making floral wreaths at Forest Lawn cemetery, grateful, at least temporarily, for his experience in his uncle's shop. But when he landed a position in the publicity department at Warner Bros., Stark found his life's passion. Showbiz. And that became even more apparent to him when, not long after, he met Frances Arnstein and her famous mother.

"There's something about having your girlfriend say, 'Come on, let's stop a minute and see Snooks,'" Stark remembered, "that keeps you from thinking in dignified terms like 'mother-in-law.'" When he visited Fran at home, Fanny could usually be found listening to the Tijuana races on the radio and "making book" with a visiting Katharine Hepburn or Orry-Kelly. Fanny didn't always remember Stark's name, calling him "Franny's boy," but he liked her anyway. When Ray and Fran married in 1940, Fanny threw a big gala at her house in Holmby Hills.

From Warners, Stark moved on to Fawcett Publications, where he was the West Coast entertainment editor for *Family Circle, Motion Picture, Screen Secrets,* and other magazines. During World War II, he served in the navy. Both his father and uncle died while Stark was in the service; his mother passed away soon after he returned home. The resulting sale of the family properties gave Stark a much-needed financial boost as he attempted to restart his career in Tinseltown. The literary agent job led to Charles Feldman's Famous Artists Agency, where Stark repped Lana Turner, Ava Gardner, William Holden, Kirk Douglas, and Ronald Reagan. But after a few years, he wanted out. As an agent, Stark made only ten percent on every deal he negotiated. He "decided to make a stab" for the remaining "ninety percent" and became a producer on his own.

With a partner, Eliot Hyman, Stark founded Seven Arts Productions in 1957, a company *Variety* quickly nicknamed "Hollywood's eighth major" after the seven top studios. Seven Arts had a string of successes producing films that were distributed by others: *Thunder in the Sun* for Paramount, *The Misfits* for United Artists, *Lolita* for MGM. Stark and Hyman tended to invest their own money in projects — a credo that violated the usual Hollywood production pattern — but that way they had the ability to make quick decisions. Stark and Hyman owned the largest block of stock in Seven Arts, and they wanted to keep it that way. Movies, theater, television — all fell under the Seven Arts banner. The company had purchased the rights to *The World of Suzie Wong*, a novel by Richard Mason, while the book was still in galleys, and raised the money for the successful Broadway production. A year later, they had a terrific hit with the film, which Stark personally produced. It was that same formula he had in mind for the Brice project.

But he needed two things first. One, a better script. *Suzie Wong* had had a tight-as-a-drum book by Paul Osborn. It had also had the charming France Nuyen in the lead, who turned out to be a sensation. That, of course, was the second thing Stark needed. Someone who'd make the critics take notice, who'd surprise them, intrigue them, dazzle them. So, as a spotlight suddenly appeared on the tiny stage at the Bon Soir, Stark sat back in his chair and kept his eyes peeled for Barbra Streisand.

8.

Backstage, Barbra was very aware of who was in the audience that night. Jule Styne, who'd showed up in her dressing room after a performance of *Wholesale* not long before and basically declared himself her servant for life, had informed her that he'd brought Ray Stark, Fanny Brice's son-in-law and David Merrick's coproducer. And in no uncertain terms, Styne advised her that for tonight she should dispense with the usual eccentric banter and concentrate on singing. Barbra agreed to take his advice.

The last time she'd played here, Barbra had been the warm-up act; now she was the headliner. The contract her new agent, Joe Sully, had banged out guaranteed her "100 percent sole star billing," and he'd also arranged for the club to pay Peter Daniels as Barbra's accompanist. Plus there was a car to whisk her from the theater to the Village every night. Quite the difference from the days when Barbra had first stumbled through the darkness, having no say in how things were done. Everything was different this time around. The club had a new owner, Nat Sackin, a handsome, somewhat mysterious character, and the flamboyant Jimmie Daniels had been replaced as emcee by Barbra's old friend and booster, Burke McHugh. At least one reviewer missed Daniels's "terse, mocking intros," especially given how "sincere, sentimental and very long" McHugh's monologues tended to be.

But the biggest difference between now and the last time Barbra had appeared at the Bon Soir was how much more they were paying her. A year ago, she'd collected $175 a week. Now, a Broadway show, a Tony nomination, and a Drama Critics' Circle Award later, she pulled in seven times that — $1,250. Once upon a time, it had been Barbra who hoped her association with the Bon Soir would raise her profile. Now it was the club that wanted her name to help sell itself as hip, timely, and relevant.

With Barbra backstage, as usual, was Elliott. Since the start of her run at the Bon Soir, he could usually be spotted "hanging around" the club somewhere, as noticed by Dick Gautier, the opening act. Elliott's ubiquitous presence meant that others were prevented from spending too much one-on-one time with Barbra. One regular Bon Soir patron thought that Elliott acted as a kind of shield for her. According to this patron, Barbra seemed to have grown "a little wary of mingling too much with her fan base," since she no longer came out and sat at the tables between shows. But it wasn't just she who had changed; her fan base had, too. Once a friendly group of Villagers, many of whom knew Barry or Bob or Terry, now it had grown into an authentic phenomenon, a pack of mostly gay men whom Barbra had never met and who showed up every night to see her.

Gautier had no illusions that the standing-room-only crowds every night had much to do with him. On opening night, when he looked out into the room and saw Helen Hayes and other Broadway bigwigs, he knew they hadn't come for his jokes, but to hear the girl who "stopped the show" every night over at the Shubert Theatre. But to Barbra's credit, she never engaged in any one-upmanship, even though she enjoyed, as per her contract, "100 percent sole star billing." She shared with Gautier, the original Conrad Birdie in the Broadway smash *Bye Bye Birdie,* a "mutual respect" that befitted two Tony-nominated Broadway performers.

Certainly Barbra was grateful that Gautier always handed over an upbeat audience to her. This night was no exception. The crowd was applauding in anticipation even before Burke McHugh had finished his introduction. Given his history with Barbra, and the very real credit McHugh could take for launching her career, his intro may have been one of the long and sentimental ones he was known for. But no matter what words he used or how long it took him to say them, the audience erupted into applause when the spotlight picked Barbra out, standing by Peter Daniels's piano on the dark stage.

"Twenty-year-old Barbra Streisand returns to Gotham's intime [intimate] nitery circuit with the assurance of a performer who knows that the road ahead is strictly upward," *Variety* had observed after opening night. "She knows what she's about and makes the tablers aware that there's something special happening on stage."

Reviews rarely came much better than that. Barbra's triumphant return to the Bon Soir meant that she was no fluke, no passing trend, and that she was so much more than Miss Marmelstein. One night, Alan and Marilyn Bergman, a songwriting couple who'd written the title track to Dean Martin's *Sleep Warm* album, came backstage and asked her, "Do you know how wonderful you are?" Barbra didn't answer, but the Bergmans thought she did know. "You can't be that wonderful and not know," they mused.

It was clear that Barbra did know she was pretty wonderful, though as *Variety* observed, she didn't come across "arrogant or smart-alecky." She was simply suffused with confidence. When she sang Leonard Bernstein's "My Name Is Barbara," from his *I Hate Music: A Cycle of Five Kids' Songs for Soprano and Piano,* she made it utterly her own, no matter its operatic style and that pesky extra "a." "Value," from *Harry Stoones,* once again proved a crowd-pleaser, as was Harold Arlen's "I Had Myself a True Love." But it was Barbra's daring cover of "Lover Man," so indelibly associated with Billie Holiday, that really impressed the crowd. Barbra might have been blissfully in love with a man who loved her back, but she was still able to put over the heartache of a lonely woman. As her voice trailed off on the last line — "Lover man, oh where can you be?" — the audience was jumping to its feet and banging the tables in appreciation.

This night, she obeyed Styne's decree to tone down the banter, but her personality no doubt still came through, if only in the way she smiled or shrugged. So ingrained into her act was Barbra's shtick by now that it had become impossible to completely eliminate. *Variety* had recognized that her "infectious juve [juvenile] giggle," her "grimace," her "wispy mood," and her "straightforward belt" were all "calculated for maximum impact." But such calculation didn't make her act any less "winning," the trade paper declared. "It works and that's what counts."

What remained to be seen was whether Ray Stark agreed with that assessment. When he came backstage to meet Barbra after the show, he said very little to her, although he did ask her to come in to his office the next week and give a reading from Lennart's script. That was promising, but what he actually thought of Barbra as a performer he did not reveal. Ray Stark was known to be a secretive man. In Hollywood, where everyone had "a masseur, an analyst and a wife" who could potentially blab details before a deal was inked, Stark had developed a real fetish for secrecy. He'd insist on absolute oaths of privacy when making a deal, ending his negotiations with "Swearsies?" The hard-driving dealmaker retained that childlike enjoyment of the high-stakes game he was so good at playing.

So when Stark left the club that night, Barbra — and Marty and Elliott and anyone else who had been watching his reactions carefully — would have had little clue as to what the producer was actually thinking. But Jule Styne surely knew. After the show, Stark told his collaborator what he had realized as he watched the kid perform. Barbra *was* Fanny Brice. And from that point on, Ray Stark could never think "of anyone else in the part."

CHAPTER TEN

Summer 1962

1.

Barbra strode into the room wearing a buttons-and-epaulets outfit that Jule Styne thought looked like a Russian Cossack uniform. He might have been her biggest fan, but he thought the outfit was horrible. Fortunately, it wasn't her clothes that were auditioning that day in early June. Instead, Barbra stood bravely in front of Styne, Ray Stark, Jerry Robbins, Bob Merrill, and David Merrick ready to show them that she could act. They knew she could sing; they'd all been to the Bon Soir by this point. Handing her Isobel Lennart's script for *The Funny Girl* — the name now attached to the project — they were willing to overlook the buttons and epaulets if she could convince them that she was Fanny Brice.

As usual, Marty Erlichman was at Barbra's side. Marty, they all understood, made things happen for her. Barbra had come that day at Stark's bidding, but it had been Marty who had made that invitation inevitable. Under Marty's direction, the Softness brothers had kept up their wooing of newspaper columnists, and as a result, Earl Wilson was currently suggesting in papers all across the country that Barbra should play Fanny Brice (with Jan Murray as Nick Arnstein).

Stark and his collaborators couldn't have missed it. Meanwhile, Marty had also wangled Barbra fancy new representation with the William Morris Agency, a major step up from the more provincial Associated Booking, although the latter continued to handle her nightclub appearances. If Barbra was going to play in the major leagues — and it didn't get much more major than the quintet sitting in front of her — she'd need major-league representation.

So the young woman who walked into the room that day was hardly some kid off the street, as the power brokers who sat watching her with keen, discerning eyes liked to call her in the press. "An unknown," Ray Stark described her. That was nonsense. Barbra might not have been an Anne Bancroft, or even a Carol Burnett, but an "unknown" wouldn't have generated the kind of buzz she was getting that summer. The two albums she'd participated in — the cast recording of *Wholesale* and the *Pins and Needles* tribute — had just been released, and Barbra dominated virtually every review. John S. Wilson in the *New York Times* put it plainly: *Wholesale* wouldn't be remembered for Harold Rome's score, but rather as Barbra Streisand's Broadway debut. "Miss Streisand has such a vivid and pungent style of delivery," Wilson declared, "that she rises out of the laboring ordinariness of her surroundings on this disk like a dazzling beacon." Reviews for *Pins and Needles* nearly always trumpeted Barbra as well.

The irony was that both disks had been released by Columbia Records. But even those two successful albums hadn't convinced Goddard Lieberson to offer Barbra a contract. Both Capitol and Atlantic had stepped forward with offers, but Marty insisted they hold out for Columbia. Barbra's tireless manager spent many evenings at the Ho-Ho, a Chinese restaurant-bar where the record execs gathered after work, buying rounds of drinks for everybody and regaling them all with updates on the auditions for *The Funny Girl*. Lieberson, after all, had been Fanny Brice's pal — though word was that he didn't feel Barbra was right for the part.

Thankfully, those in the room that day thought otherwise. Even David Merrick, so opposed to Barbra in the past, seemed to be coming around, or at least that's what they were hearing. Not long before, Bob had accompanied a friend to a swanky society party in Morristown, New Jersey, where, much to his surprise, he was introduced to the mercurial producer. Explaining that he was Barbra's friend, Bob bravely asked Merrick if it was true that he didn't want her for the Fanny Brice show. On the contrary, Merrick replied, he'd "*love* to work with her." In fact, Barbra "could even be a producing partner" if she so chose — though that much, at least, was probably the champagne talking.

Still, Merrick's change of heart appeared genuine. It had apparently come about after he'd seen her at the Bon Soir — which seemed to do the trick for any doubter. After the show, impressed with a new maturity in Barbra's performance, Merrick told Marty, "Tell Barbra I think she's aged." Not long afterward, upon the expiration of Barbra's current *Wholesale* contract, Merrick gave her an increase in salary, bringing her more in line with what Elliott and Lillian Roth were making.

So Barbra was a bona fide Broadway professional when she came in that day to read from Lennart's script. She might have been just twenty years old, a supporting player in a so-so play, but she was also a star in the world of nightclubs and a darling of the critics. She was also a television celebrity, a critical point in her favor everyone would have appreciated. Although *PM East* had recently been cancelled, it had made Barbra's name and face familiar to a wide swath of the public who had never been to a New York nightclub or a Broadway show.

Accepting the script for her read-through, Barbra looked into the faces of the five men who had the power to give her either the boost she craved or stop her cold in her tracks. But one face was missing from *The Funny Girl* team that day: the very author of the material Barbra held in her hand. Isobel Lennart might have tempered some of the testosterone-fueled pressure in the room, but she was three thousand miles away at her home in Malibu, frantically revising the first act. Even as Barbra read through her scenes, everyone knew the book remained deeply flawed. In her glass-enclosed "teahouse" overlooking the ocean, Lennart was trying to figure out how to balance the comedy of the first act with the tragedy of the second. "God knows she has it in her," Robbins, ever Lennart's champion, had written to Stark, "but she and I are well aware of the problem of translating this into a different medium" — screenplay to libretto.

Stark, however, wasn't as optimistic. He'd asked John Patrick, who'd written the screenplay for *The World of Suzie Wong*, if he could improve Lennart's book, but Patrick was doubtful that much could be done without starting over from scratch — which none of them wanted to do. There simply wasn't time. Merrick was talking about an opening date in October, which was just five months away, and Stark had sent around a memo stating it was his "desire and intention to proceed on this basis." That would mean, if Barbra was cast, that she'd have to bow out of *Wholesale*. Since Merrick held her contract, that wouldn't be a problem. But they had lost the luxury of time.

There was another important reason they needed to start right away. Jerry Robbins had indicated that if they didn't move forward soon, he was out of the project. Producer Cheryl Crawford was eager for him to direct a version of Bertolt Brecht's *Mother Courage and Her Children*. Robbins didn't want to lose this opportunity if *The Funny Girl* was delayed further.

So it was decision time. With Lennart trying to fix the book, casting was the next order of business. Not long before, Stark had circulated another list of possibilities for Fanny to his collaborators: Burnett, Streisand, Gwen Verdon, Mitzi Gaynor, Janis Paige, Betty Comden, Elaine May, Elaine Stritch, and (probably just to placate his wife) Mary Martin. They were "listed haphazardly," he insisted, "and not in order of preference." One name, however, was conspicuous by its absence. "For the record," Stark wrote, "I would like to say that I have a negative feeling regarding Anne Bancroft, predicated on the fact that she may have a completely different concept of the kind of play we all desire." If others wanted to keep Bancroft in the running, Stark wanted to be reassured that she was "capable of singing from a stage." Bottom line, Stark said, he felt "a lack of humor and warmth" from her, "which most certainly is the basis of our characterization."

Robbins begged to differ. "If she can sing," he wrote of Bancroft, "then I still feel she would be the best for it." He'd recently spoken with her, and Bancroft remained "interested," though she was waiting to see what Lennart came up with for the new first act. Yet while Robbins's support for Bancroft remained strong, there were growing doubts about the viability of her casting. She was insisting on an eighteen-month clause, which would allow her to escape from the show after just a year and a half. Stark argued that this would make a successful run "very difficult." But the bigger worry was her voice, which even Robbins seemed to acknowledge, given his caveat "if she can sing."

The composers had their own doubts as well. Months earlier, Styne and Merrill had run through the score for Bancroft. There was some history there: Merrill and Bancroft had dated, and the relationship had ended badly. Merrill suspected some of the hostility Bancroft displayed that day at the Beverly Hills Hotel, as she listened to them sing the score, grew out of old personal resentments. Despite the fact that Merrill had actually written "People" with Bancroft in mind, she'd been unimpressed when she'd heard it, stalking out of the hotel in a huff, claiming it was "unsingable."

Maybe, Stark had come to believe, *nothing* was singable for Bancroft, who, after all, was known more for her dramatic prowess than her singing voice. Robbins may have begun to agree with him on that point, since in the past few weeks he'd been advocating strongly for Carol Burnett as his second choice. Burnett wanted to do it, Robbins informed his collaborators just days before Barbra came in to do her reading. But he also acknowledged that he would need "to work with her a bit on the dramatic scenes to see whether she [was] capable of them." The concerns they had with Burnett were the exact opposite of the concerns they had with Bancroft.

What they were looking for on the day Barbra strolled in looking like a Cossack was someone who could both sing *and* act. Ray Stark and Jule Styne thought they'd found that someone, and Merrick seemed at least amenable to the idea. But there were two holdouts. Robbins had seen Barbra at the Bon Soir and agreed that she was terrific, but nonetheless she remained third on his list. Bob Merrill's doubts were bigger, which made for some awkwardness between him and Styne, his partner. But then again, their contrasts seemed to define them as a team. Styne was short and stout and loquacious; Merrill was tall and thin and taciturn. Styne was always upbeat, Merrill often dour. But together they had produced a score that everyone involved believed was destined to become a classic.

Merrill's objections to Barbra were fundamental. He, too, had seen her at the Bon Soir, but for once the magic hadn't happened. As a songwriter, Merrill didn't like how Barbra played fast and loose with words and tempos. He believed songs were written a certain way by their composers and such authorial choices should be respected. Barbra, Merrill felt, assumed far too much ownership of other people's work.

But there was more to his visceral dislike of her — or at least his wife, Suzanne, came to suspect as much. Merrill was a ladies' man. If he wrote a song for a woman, he wanted to be attracted to her; the dynamic inspired him creatively, even if no romance ever bloomed between them. And Barbra, to Merrill, was not "girlfriend material," his wife understood.

It wasn't as frivolous an objection as it might sound, and Merrill probably had some sympathy from Merrick at least, if not from the smitten Styne. Beauty was obviously in the eye of the beholder, but their Fanny Brice had to be attractive enough not to look completely incongruous playing opposite the actor cast as Nick — who, judging from the list then being circulated by Stark, was going to be a looker. Christopher Plummer, Tony Franciosa, Robert Goulet, Keith Michell, and Farley Granger were the top choices, though Merrick wanted to approach Rock Hudson as well. "People insist he wants to be in a

Broadway musical," Merrick's office had told Robbins. "Sounds un-likely, doesn't it?" Unlikely or not, the idea to cast the top box-office star in the country was intriguing — and surely had them all consid-ering how Barbra Streisand would look opposite the extravagantly handsome Hudson.

Barbra's audition changed no minds that day. Those who wanted her continued to want her; those who had doubts remained doubtful. Robbins would admit that Barbra had given "a marvelously sensitive reading," but he cautioned they needed "to face the problem of her youth." Could a twenty-year-old convincingly play the middle-aged Fanny of the second act? Robbins was skeptical and was soon back to sending notes of encouragement to Anne Bancroft. Merrick, mean-while, perhaps heeding Merrill's reservations, was suddenly "really anxious" to have Eydie Gormé come in and audition.

In a letter he wrote to Robbins not long after Barbra's reading, Stark said he appreciated everyone's varying opinions. With tremendous diplomacy, he recognized that all of the candidates had their advan-tages and that he was thankful to Robbins for considering them all. "You, of course, know my preference," he wrote at the end.

His preference remained Barbra. Yet what Stark failed to mention was his wife's preference or if he'd even broached Barbra's name with her at this point. And it would be Fran Stark, everyone knew, who would have the last word.

2.

Sitting in the audience that night at the Shubert Theatre was Lillian Gish, the exquisite and ethereal star of the silent screen, who, with pioneering director D. W. Griffith, had made some of the most im-portant early American films: *The Birth of a Nation, Way Down East, Broken Blossoms.* Backstage, Gish's presence caused some excitement among the company's cineastes, but Barbra seemed clueless. She was in a foul mood that night. She was tired of the show, tired of Miss

Marmelstein. She hoped fervently that come this fall she'd be play-ing Fanny Brice in *The Funny Girl,* not just for the artistic challenges the role offered but simply for the chance to get out of *Wholesale.* If this was the reality of Broadway — doing the same damn thing every night — Barbra told friends that maybe she really should start think-ing about movies. Not that she knew much about them — as evi-denced by her lack of recognition of Miss Gish.

Her boredom with the show was trying the patience of her fellow castmates and the stage manager, who attempted, without much ef-fect, to get firm with her. Barbra was still showing up late, repeating a pattern that had developed during rehearsals. Even an official repri-mand from Actors' Equity hadn't changed her behavior. Arthur Lau-rents's assistant, Ashley Feinstein, thought Barbra's unprofessionalism stood out all the more starkly because everyone else in the show was so professional. Even Elliott, who was never late, didn't seem to be able to get through to Barbra.

And everyone could tell when she was just "phoning it in," said a frequent member of the audience, one of the growing number of Streisand devotees who showed up several times a week to see the show. Yet still the applause came, which, as always, infuriated Barbra. She knew when she was good and when she wasn't, and she resented undeserved applause. But what she really resented was performing the part at all. She needed a change — and fast. She hoped that Stark and Robbins and the rest would make their decision soon.

That night, "she wasn't great," said the frequent audience member, "but she wasn't terrible either." Lillian Gish, however, thought Barbra was absolutely marvelous. Making her way backstage, Gish removed the earrings she'd been wearing and handed them over to Barbra as a token of her admiration. It was a tremendous gesture from a legend-ary figure, and Barbra accepted the earrings graciously — although only later did she fully discover who Gish was and why she mattered. Barry could have told her, or Bob or Terry. But they, of course, weren't around anymore.

3.

On the screen, a giant caterpillar made a meal of a few cars. Barbra and Elliott sat in the dark, cool theater, a relief from the ninety-degree temperatures outside, eyes fixed on *Mothra,* a badly dubbed Japanese monster flick. The lovers, sharing a bag of popcorn, were enjoying a rare break from *Wholesale* and all the other myriad obligations of their careers.

Actually, it was Barbra who had the myriad obligations. Elliott only had to show up every night at the Shubert. Barbra had to do that and make her way afterward to the Blue Angel (she'd finished her run at the Bon Soir only to start another engagement uptown). These days, she also was frequently meeting reporters for interviews or waking up early for one of her frequent appearances on Joe Franklin's show. There were also regular strategy sessions with Marty and Richard Falk and the Softness brothers on publicity, especially on ways to influence Goddard Lieberson into giving her a contract. Finding the time for a date with Elliott must have felt like a gift from heaven.

Not that they had trouble seeing each other. Elliott had moved in with her, sharing the railroad flat over Oscar's Salt of the Sea and settling into a rather blissful pattern of domesticity. Although they could have easily afforded a bigger one, they kept Barbra's twin bed, which, given Elliott's large frame and long limbs, must have made sleeping uncomfortable at times — but also very intimate. They insisted that a bigger bed wouldn't have fit; maybe that was true. But Barbra always seemed to find room for other pieces of furniture that caught her eye. Just recently she'd bought two "marvelous Victorian cabinets with glass shelves," she told a writer from *The New Yorker,* at a shop called Foyniture Limited on Eighty-third Street. She seemed to get a kick out of the spelling.

Elliott adored living with her. He found her style "just wild . . . genius, really." As a dining table, they used an old Singer sewing-machine stand. For meals, they ate Swanson's TV dinners and bricks of coffee ice cream for dessert. Like the kids they still were, they snacked on grapefruit, brownies, and pickled herring. When they saw a tail "about a yard long" flicking back and forth underneath their stove, they ran off in terror to a motel. But when the landlord refused to pay to exterminate, they moved back in and made peace with the rat, naming him Oscar after the cheapskate downstairs. They played Monopoly and checkers, and acted out scenes they hoped to someday play together, Barbra as Medea and Elliott as Jason. Calling each other Hansel and Gretel, they made a halfhearted attempt to learn Greek so they "could speak a secret language nobody else could understand." For the first time in their lives, Barbra and Elliott were deliriously happy being with another person. Elliott found it all "really romantic," likening Barbra and himself to "kids in a treehouse."

When *Mothra* was over, the oversized caterpillar having hatched into a giant imago and flown back to its island home, Barbra and Elliott walked hand in hand outside into Times Square. They enjoyed the fact that they could be stars on Broadway but still be largely anonymous on the streets of New York. That night, or one very much like it, they wandered the city, no one stopping them, no one telling them to look this way or sing that song. They played Pokerino in penny arcades. They bought glassware for the apartment. They ate vegetable fried rice in a greasy Chinese restaurant.

Such anonymity was important to Barbra. The fierce ambition the Softness brothers witnessed every time she barged into their offices, or the uncanny knack she had for drawing attention to herself, was not in the service of notoriety. It was part of her pursuit of excellence and achievement. But when she left the theater or the studio or the nightclub, Barbra wanted her life back. She wanted to wander through the streets of New York with her boyfriend unaccosted by people. So far, she still had that luxury. No matter how big a role she might someday land, she hoped that this much would never change.

Yet a future of anonymity seemed unlikely. Earl Wilson had just revealed the "hot romance backstage" between Barbra and Elliott, and was readying another column in which he would report the belief among cast members that the couple had secretly married. Such gossip was an inevitable byproduct of courting the columnists for other, more sought-after kinds of publicity, such as the items about the Brice show. Yet Barbra was unwilling to accept gossip about her personal life as an unavoidable component of her fame, and she had started speaking out against the practice. "They print such rotten things," she complained to one interviewer. "Like they wrote that I was smooching at the Harwyn Club." But then, impishly, she added, "It was 21" — showing that while she might detest such intrusive publicity, she knew how to make the best of it.

Barry was right: Barbra had indeed become very good at merchandizing herself. She told the press that it was she, with little to no help from Arthur Laurents, who had made Miss Marmelstein what she was. Barbra explained that she'd needed to "talk back to the director" in order to "work into the character" her own way. And if Laurents had persisted in obstructing her, she said, she would have walked out. "I just didn't care what happened," Barbra claimed. "I could go out and work in a nightclub again." Laurents scoffed at the contention that Barbra would have willingly walked away from a part in a Broadway show to return to singing in nightclubs.

But in selling Barbra Streisand to the public, it was important that the product be marketed as uniquely self-made. The narrative that Marty had been building over the last year — Barbra as the once-in-a-generation talent discovered like a glittering pearl in the brackish oyster beds of Brooklyn — could not accommodate stories of "helpers" or "boosters." She had to be given to the world fully formed, with no whiff of public-relations chicanery. If the contributions of a maestro such as Arthur Laurents had to be airbrushed out of her biography, then those less well-known people who had helped shape the creature being marketed as Barbra Streisand could certainly never expect to receive any kind of public acknowledgment.

It was, perhaps, easier to sell this rewritten history because so many associates from Barbra's early days were no longer around. Terry Leong had headed for Europe without ever getting the chance to reconnect with the old friend whose style he had heavily influenced.

Bob, too, had just sailed for Paris for an indefinite stay. And while there'd been a rapprochement with Barry, there'd been no attempt to stay in touch; in fact, he continued to feel that he was being deliberately kept away. Given how he'd broken her heart, it was easy for some friends to sympathize with Barbra on that point. But keeping Barry at a distance also meant that the enormous contributions he'd made to her career — from suggesting she enter the contest at the Lion in the first place to teaching her so much about music and performance — would be given no public forum.

Some old friends, such as Elaine Sobel, resented being held at arm's length. Now waiting tables at the Russian Tea Room, Elaine felt she'd been "brushed out" of Barbra's life just as her former roommate hit the big time on Broadway. Barbra, Elaine said, had taken advantage of her at a time when she, Barbra, needed help, but hadn't offered any reciprocation now that she was in a position to give it. That, perhaps, was key to understanding who survived in Barbra's orbit and who didn't. Those who could still help her — such as Marty, Peter Daniels, and Don Softness — remained. Those who might want something from her now that she'd achieved a degree of fame and clout — such as Terry, Elaine, Barry, and possibly even Bob — did not. It was a common experience for many celebrities, and while unfortunate, not really all that difficult to understand.

And then there was Cis, who wanted absolutely nothing from Barbra except friendship. Cis remained Barbra's rock, the one person with whom she could be herself completely, without any pretense, performance, or marketing. By the summer of 1962, Barbra's three closest — and likely *only* — intimates were Cis, Marty, and Elliott.

But for a young woman in love, it was probably enough. Walking through the city with Elliott, her hand in his, her head resting occasionally on his shoulder, Barbra was content. Elliott understood her. They'd both grown up with mother issues; they'd both felt cheated out of real childhoods. Barbra could vent all her frustrations to Elliott, and he never pushed her away. He was "the stable one" in the relationship, she thought. When they'd occasionally argue, Barbra sometimes felt like stalking off, but Elliott always stopped her and got her to talk about what was really bothering her. She appreciated his "very clear mind." Elliott, Barbra said, "knows what he wants." And what was so thrilling, so wonderful, was that he wanted her.

4.

A pall hung over the crowd at the Blue Angel. People were still grieving Marilyn Monroe, who'd been found dead a week earlier at her home in Brentwood, either from an accidental overdose or suicide. One man who frequented the cabaret thought a sense of finality thrummed in the air that week, an awareness of an era coming to a close. Elizabeth Taylor still generated headlines, but few, if any, of the new generation of stars seemed to inspire the fascination and devotion that their predecessors did. That kind of stardom, many thought, was hopelessly moribund.

And yet, there was an undercurrent of excitement in the air as well. The young woman who was performing at the Angel for one final night seemed to trigger something in people. Grown men would sometimes act like teenaged girls when she sang. The young man who frequented the cabaret did so not because he particularly liked the Blue Angel's upholstered interior — he didn't — but because Barbra Streisand, the headliner, made him cry every time she sang. And laugh, and smile, and "feel all the things a really great singer can make a person feel," he said.

David Kapralik, a young executive at Columbia, could no doubt relate. He was there that night at the Blue Angel, just as he had been there the night before and the night before that. It was Barbra's last performance; he wouldn't have missed it. His admiration for her had started when he'd heard her sing "Happy Days" on *The Garry Moore Show*. He had realized that she was the kid Marty Erlichman had been pushing Columbia so hard about. Impressed with her voice, Kapralik had made it a point to see Barbra at the Angel. In no time at all, he had morphed, in his own words, into a "groupie."

Kapralik was just one of the growing number of young men and women Dorothy Kilgallen observed "packing into the clubs to see Barbra Streisand and her magnetic nonsense." If she and other pundits had taken a closer look at the phenomenon, they would have been disabused of any fears that old-time stardom, the kind manifested by Marilyn, was on its way out. Barbra's "groupies" adored her with all the same fervor that an earlier generation had brought to Frank Sinatra or Judy Garland. They were artsy, bohemian types who bucked trends: at the moment, the trend was toward folk singers like Peter, Paul, and Mary, though the rock-pop of Neil Sedaka and Dion still dominated the charts. Barbra didn't fit either category, which her fans seemed to appreciate. And, like all true devotees, they recruited others into the faith. This night, Kapralik had brought his boss, Goddard Lieberson, nattily dressed as always.

Marty, of course, was thrilled that Lieberson had finally shown up. Marty believed that only by hearing Barbra sing in front of an audience, especially *her* audience, could the record exec really comprehend the effect she had on people. Lieberson had been softening. No doubt it was more than just Kapralik's enthusiasm that had finally moved him to come hear Barbra sing. The glowing reviews she'd gotten for the *Wholesale* and *Pins and Needles* disks couldn't have escaped his notice. Even God may have begun to doubt himself, to wonder whether he'd been wrong not to sign her.

Like her Bon Soir homecoming, Barbra's return to the Blue Angel had been marked by a welcome change in status. Last time she'd played second fiddle to Pat Harrington; now she was front and center, heading a bill that also included comic Bob Lewis and the Phoenix Singers, a folk trio who often sang with Harry Belafonte. A few weeks earlier, Max Gordon had bought out Herbert Jacoby's share in the club; Barbra was the first headliner under his solo management. She joked to Earl Wilson that she'd "hit the big time" since she was finally being paid as much as Peter Daniels, her accompanist. Obviously Gordon had as much faith in Barbra as she had in herself.

No doubt Lieberson had also seen the reviews for the show, which was wrapping up after five sold-out weeks. "Miss Streisand is a delightful and mercurial sprite," *Variety* had observed, keying in on the unpredictability that so enchanted her fans. "She is amply appreciated," the review concluded — an understatement.

And yet, at the Angel, sometimes appreciation was hard to discern. Performers had to "crack through the reserve," Dick Gautier found. At the posh club — peopled with blue bloods and celebrities who were often as famous, or more so, than those on the stage — it was "gauche to laugh too much, or applaud too much," Gautier said.

So it was saying a great deal that the applause following Barbra's "oddball" (*Variety*'s word) rendition of "Much More" from *The Fantasticks* was loud and enthusiastic. On that little stage she stood, looking out into that long, narrow, coffinlike room suffused with the subtle fragrance of gladiolas, singing her heart out, knowing that Lieberson sat only a few feet away from her. It was not unlike the way she'd "auditioned" for Ray Stark at the Bon Soir. In both cases, she was hoping to provide for herself an escape hatch, a jailbreak from the stultifying routine of *Wholesale*. Not long before, she'd done what had once been unthinkable to her: She'd turned over the part of Miss Marmelstein to Louise Lasser, her understudy, for several days and taken a much-needed holiday.

Not that she'd rested. There never seemed to be time for that. The weekend of July 14 she, Elliott, Marty, Diana, and little Rosalind had driven up to Bill Hahn's Hotel in Westbrook, Connecticut, on Long Island Sound, about two and a half hours from New York. The big, gregarious proprietor was hosting a birthday party for his swanky hotel with proceeds going to the American Cancer Society. He'd roped in Art Carney, who lived nearby, for the top of the bill, backed up by Barbra, Henny Youngman, jazz singer Johnny Hartman, and pop singer Tommy Sands, who introduced his wife, Nancy Sinatra, from the audience. The party was "strictly private for hotel guests," who tended to be affluent New York Jews. The thing Barbra probably enjoyed best was Hahn's giant birthday cake, which was sliced up and passed around during intermission, though the pay — likely approaching four figures — was nice, too. But simply spending a few nights in the sea air, far away from *Wholesale,* would alone have made it all worthwhile.

Her publicists, in fact, had started a rumor that she might be ditching Broadway for good. Several columns that summer carried stories that Barbra was applying to Dartmouth College, which was discussing opening its doors to women for the first time. According to these reports, Barbra wanted to major in economics and languages: Italian, Japanese, and Greek. That was the giveaway that it was all just hype, a way to keep Barbra's name in the papers: Greek was the language she and Elliott imagined speaking among themselves, and Barbra's nightclub act often had her pretending to speak in various tongues. No doubt Don Softness or Richard Falk had read about Dartmouth going co-ed and thought of an angle for Barbra, who was of college age and known as a bit of a rebel. It might also have served as a nudge to Stark and Merrick — they'd better hurry up and sign her before she went off to school.

But higher education was hardly Barbra's goal. Out there in the audience, Lieberson was close to making up his mind. He'd said no so many times before, but he'd come to hear her tonight. That was a very good sign. Making an album might not have been Barbra's big dream, but it could help ease her out of *Wholesale* — not to mention make her a good deal of money. So she put everything she had into her time on the Blue Angel stage. This night, there was no phoning it in.

"Right as the Rain" was solid ground for her; she knew it like she knew her own name, and once again Barbra nailed it. But she was also singing a newer, riskier addition to her repertoire. Peter had reworked "Happy Days Are Here Again" for her, slowing it down even more than was done for *The Garry Moore Show,* making it almost unbearably poignant. As Barbra launched into the song, a hush came over the club. It was, as the frequent Blue Angel patron put it, "truly an electric moment between Barbra and her audience." The emotion, he said, "quite literally crackled between her and us." The hairs on his arm stood up. Without even knowing it, he began to cry.

"So let's sing a song of cheer again," Barbra was keening, "happy days are here again."

With "Happy Days," Barbra smashed through the Angel's legendary reserve. People were on their feet, and even the club's upholstered walls couldn't muffle the sounds of whistles and cheers. Goddard Lieberson stood with the crowd. It seemed Barbra's performance had allowed him finally to glimpse her star potential. Marilyn Monroe might have been dead, and with her an entire era. But a whole new kind of star was about to explode.

5.

Jerry Robbins read the latest revisions Isobel Lennart had sent to him from Malibu and nearly wept. The man who had directed *The Pajama Game, Bells Are Ringing, West Side Story,* and *Gypsy,* and doctored a dozen more ailing shows that needed his help, knew what a good libretto read like, and this script for *The Funny Girl,* no matter how much he adored Isobel, fell far short of the mark.

Surely Ray Stark, with his understanding of story, knew it, too. But what frustrated Robbins was the producer's absolute insistence that they move forward nonetheless. Stark was planning to return to New York from Beverly Hills now that Lennart had completed her revisions, and he felt it was "urgent [that an] immediate decision be made on casting." He hadn't changed his mind about his preferred candidate either. "I hope you will have settled on Barbra," Stark wrote to Robbins, and he urged the director to begin working with her on the show's second act.

The last time he'd been in New York, Stark had had a session with Carol Burnett, during which she'd read for the part and sung a few numbers. "A tremendous talent and a lovely gal," Stark concluded, but he didn't think she'd "turn out to be right for Fanny." Robbins had apparently come to the same conclusion. After a short talk with the director outside an elevator after Burnett's audition, Stark had realized there was no need to send the second act to Burnett. Robbins, it seemed, was staying just as firm on his first choice as Stark was. He still wanted Anne Bancroft for the role.

"Dear Annie," Robbins had written when he sent her a copy of the script. "It's a rough with much over-written and too-explained-away moments. Isobel is already at work taking out all things that tend to weaken or sentimentalize. She will 'shorten, tighten, and toughen.'" He implored her to take the part even though the script wasn't ready, telling her they'd been playing "a waiting game" with all the other candidates until they heard from her. "I know it's going to be a wonderful play and you can fire it way up into the skies if you become part of it." He promised she'd have a "hard-working, tough-fighting ally" in him and "truly creative and cooperative collaborators" in Lennart, Styne, and Merrill. He didn't mention Stark.

That was because the producer was firing off his own communication to his own preferred candidate. "Dear Barbara," he wrote, misspelling her name, which surely didn't please her. "Jerry Robbins will probably be calling you within the next few days." He enclosed Lennart's revisions for her to study. Before he'd left town, he'd made it a point to see her at the Blue Angel, and he told her again what "a lovely evening" it had been. If not as effusive as Robbins's letter to Bancroft, it still gave Barbra reason to hope that the part might be hers — even if she was going to have to give Stark a lesson in spelling.

Yet other names continued to be considered for Fanny, mostly funneled in from Merrick's casting agent, Michael Shurtleff. Eydie Gormé still seemed to excite Merrick, as did Judy Holliday, both of whom were attractive enough, and Jewish to boot. Stark, of course, had given up the idea of a conventionally pretty leading lady the moment he'd settled on Barbra, but his producing partner was, despite his decreased hostility, still concerned about appearances. And what remained a big unknown for everyone involved was what Fran Stark would say when she finally got a look at the candidate they all agreed upon so it was smart to keep Gormé and Holliday in reserve.

As he read through Lennart's revisions, however, Robbins seemed to harden in his resolve that only Bancroft could save them. Lennart might have shortened, but she hadn't tightened or toughened. By now, Robbins felt he had done as much as he could, "pushing the script until certain solutions were found." Much of what worked had, in fact, come from him. Lennart would "surely agree," Robbins believed, "that each scene as she wrote it" had been sent to him and that they had gone over each of them "with a fine-tooth comb." The same was also true for the music and lyrics. Styne and Merrill had run songs and arrangements by Robbins, and he'd had his say about them. While he didn't "point to any one line of dialogue or particular lyric" as being authored by himself, Robbins did claim credit for the way all the "scenes, relationships, songs, musical conceptions, characters, settings, [and] musical ideas" came together.

Nowhere was this more obvious than in the very first scene in the show — where Fanny gets fired by theater owner Max Spiegel for being too outlandish. Robbins had considered the arguments made by stage manager Dave to keep Fanny because she's special as "a small microcosm of the play." That had been Robbins's vision, setting up the entire story in that one scene. Robbins's fingerprints continued in a similar way all through the libretto. It was his idea to make Ziegfeld just a voice coming from above during his first meeting with Fanny, and to cut directly from Fanny's line "Anything Ziegfeld wants me to do, I'll do" to her declaration: "I'm not going to wear this costume!" In Lennart's original script, a whole scene had separated the two lines. Robbins had cut the scene for the contrast it would offer — and the laugh it would get.

He'd also shaped the musical numbers. On "I'm the Greatest Star," the original idea had been for Fanny to sing it "out and out," as if she really meant it. But Robbins asked that it be changed so that she starts out kidding, mocking herself. During the course of the song, however, when she sees people like Dave who really believe in her, she evolves and "the guts come out and the tempo changes and she lets loose, free and wild, with her own feelings," as Robbins described it. Written by its composers with a time signature of 2/4 all the way through, it was

Robbins's idea "to make it 2/4 only at the end." As such, it was a brilliant bit of characterization layered into a musical number.

Robbins also had been working with Styne and Merrill to open up the "People" number by including Dave and Nick. Fanny singing the song alone, he felt, was just "too strong a come-on." Likewise, he'd moved "Don't Rain on My Parade" to the end of the first act. Originally, it had come near the beginning of the show, sung by Fanny to her mother's friends who were discouraging her from a career. Robbins, astutely, saw the song as a way to showcase Fanny's determination to win Nick's love and knew it would make a great send-off before intermission and possibly be reprised at the very end of the show.

But perhaps most significant, it had been Robbins who'd homed in right away on one of the chief flaws in the story: the characterization of Nick Arnstein, Fanny's great love. Nick was a gambler, a con man, and a bit of rogue in real life, but Lennart had written him as upstanding and noble, a victim of circumstances. He was, after all, Fran Stark's father. Robbins pushed Lennart to make him more of the "reckless, shadowy promoter" that he really was. In the "Will I Talk?" number, it was Robbins's idea to have Nick sing it in "an evil, sardonic way," and then have Fanny reprise it in a more "positive" way. That helped the story get off to a better start, but the book still bogged down during the second act, precisely because it was hard to sympathize with Nick because he was a crook or Fanny because she was blindsided by a crook. And so far, for all his tremendous input, Robbins hadn't figured out a way to solve that problem.

And Stark and Merrick wanted to open in October!

Robbins had had enough. Increasingly, he was feeling manipulated by Stark. When Robbins had come on board to direct the Brice musical, Stark had agreed to invest $125,000 in *Mother Courage*, the project Robbins was planning with Cheryl Crawford, and for which he had far more passion than he did for this current show. Stark's investment had been a bit of a quid pro quo: He'd put up the money if Crawford delayed the production and allowed Robbins to direct *The Funny*

Girl first. Now, with the script so lacking, Robbins felt stuck between a rock and a hard place: Should he go forward with production the way Stark and Merrick were insisting and risk a terrible critical and commercial flop, or should he insist on still more rewrites and push *Mother Courage* even farther into the future?

Stark wasn't helping matters by doing everything he could to prevent the casting of Anne Bancroft and impose Barbra Streisand on the show. "If you don't hear today or tomorrow from Anne," he'd written just the other day to Robbins, "we should tie up Barbara [*sic*] before we lose her" — as if that were a real danger.

It wasn't that Robbins disliked Barbra. She was "extraordinarily talented," he thought. But with the book so deficient, it needed the skills of an experienced actress such as Bancroft. Robbins felt his reputation was on the line, and he didn't feel safe entrusting it to such a novice as Barbra.

By now, he'd largely given up on any hopes that he and Stark would ever agree on much about the show. Conceding that the book wasn't right, the producer was arguing they should use more from Brice's actual life, as the original screenplay had done. They should also change the title to *My Man,* after Brice's best-known torch song. "A more honest or exploitable title" he couldn't imagine, Stark wrote to Robbins, even though they'd all previously decided the score should be entirely new, with nothing from Brice's actual repertoire. Robbins made no reply to Stark's latest suggestions. He knew Anne Bancroft was never going to sing "My Man"; after all, she'd originally wanted to change the name of the character and make her only "based on" Fanny Brice.

For Robbins, it was decision time. If he stayed on and Bancroft wasn't cast, could he work with Barbra Streisand? Knowing his dilemma, Isobel Lennart, who'd yet to see Barbra herself, had asked a friend, Doris Vidor, to check the young singer out at the Blue Angel and make an honest report to Robbins. Vidor was Hollywood royalty: the daughter of Harry Warner, a founder of Warner Bros.; widow of director Charles Vidor; and ex-wife of director Mervyn LeRoy. Vidor also worked for United Artists as a sort of "broker between script and stars." Not long before, she'd arranged a deal that brought Gary Cooper to the studio for three pictures. So Doris Vidor knew a little something about star quality.

And what she observed at the Blue Angel impressed her very much. "I have rarely seen anyone so talented," Vidor wrote to Robbins. "But it was the personality and what she stirred in me that impressed me so. There is a sadness and a deep, emotional impact that this girl projects to the audience that is very unique. It seemed to me that she was the young Fanny Brice as you want her to appear."

Robbins didn't dispute that. But Barbra had to be more than the *young* Fanny Brice. She had to be the *older* Fanny, too, and he was just not convinced she'd be believable as that. When there was a flurry of interest among the collaborators about the fifty-three-year-old English actor Michael Rennie playing Nick, Robbins pointed out that if they went with Barbra as Fanny, "the relationship really becomes like that in *A Star Is Born*." That "worried him," as well it should have. There was no more talk of Rennie.

There was, however, talk of Rip Torn, Brian Bedford, Harry Guardino, Peter Falk, Stuart Damon, Pernell Roberts, George Maharis, and George Chakiris. And word had reached them that Peter Lawford was "very interested" in playing Nick, though everyone agreed that Lawford didn't possess "a big enough voice."

That was not a problem with Barbra, of course. So Robbins had brought her back in for yet another reading, probably at the Imperial Theatre, on Forty-fifth Street, where Merrick's *Carnival!* was still running at night. In a few days, he'd be heading back to the Imperial to watch George Segal and Larry Hagman (Mary Martin's son) audition for the part of Dave. There were also auditions slated for the parts of Nora, Fanny's beautiful chorus-girl best friend, and Mrs. Brice — and, significantly, for Fanny herself. On the call sheet for two thirty on the afternoon of August 30 was Lee Becker, who'd played Anybodys in *West Side Story* and whom Robbins had once asked to marry him. Becker's audition suggested that no matter how hard Stark was pushing, and no matter all the superlatives from Doris Vidor and others, the director was still not quite ready to accept Barbra Streisand as the star of his production.

As the summer drew to a close, the principals behind *The Funny Girl* seemed headed for a face-off. No one could predict what that would mean for the show.

6.

The legendary Groucho Marx wasn't one to tangle with. He was the master of the one-liner, the ad-lib, the put-down, the comeback, the double entendre. Sitting at the desk of *The Tonight Show* on the night of August 21, he puffed on his ubiquitous cigar and wiggled his thick, lascivious eyebrows as he spoke with Lillian Roth about *I Can Get It for You Wholesale,* now in its sixth month on Broadway. Since Jack Paar's departure earlier that year, Groucho had proved to be one of *Tonight's* more frequent and popular guest hosts, keeping the chair warm for the incoming Johnny Carson, who still had several more weeks to go on his contract with rival network ABC.

After the break, the announcer, Hugh Downs, introduced Groucho's next guest. It was Barbra Streisand. Except he pronounced it "Stree-sand."

Barbra was furious. Downs should have known better! She'd been on this show twice before, and he hadn't messed up her name then. She was seething as she strode out onto the stage.

Groucho greeted her warmly. "You're a big success — "

But Barbra cut him off — actually cut off Groucho Marx! "How could I be such a big success," she asked, "if he calls me Stree-sand? My name is Barbra Streisand!"

Groucho tried to make a joke, but Barbra was having none of it. If it wasn't somebody placing that damned extra "a" in her first name, it was somebody else mangling her last name. When was she going to be famous enough that people got her name right?

Yet her crankiness was at least partly an act. In fact, that night with

Groucho, Barbra was probably in a very good mood indeed. At long last, Goddard Lieberson had agreed to give her a recording contract. Terms were still being negotiated, but she was in. Marty had done it. He hadn't failed her yet.

Not only that, but Ray Stark was being very solicitous of her. Even if she still wasn't entirely sure Merrick was on her side, Barbra certainly had to feel that Stark was rooting for her. Big things, she must have felt, were right around the corner.

Indeed, Groucho thought so, too. "Now, Barbra Streisand," he said, making sure he enunciated her name precisely, "you are a big success. I hear about you on the Coast . . ."

"No kiddin'," she replied, perfectly in character. "Nothin' you can prove, though, right?"

"Yes," Groucho said, a little thrown off course, not used to playing the straight man. "Jule Styne, for example. I had dinner with him on the Coast last week, and he said you'd be just great for that show he's doing. What's the name of it, uh . . . ?"

Barbra helped him out. "The Fanny Brice story?"

"Yes, the Fanny Brice story. He said, 'It's between her and the girl who works for Garry Moore.'"

"Carol Burnett?"

Obviously Groucho's conversation with Styne had taken place before Robbins and Stark mutually decided against proceeding further with Burnett. But Groucho also knew about Anne Bancroft — Styne didn't share Stark's penchant for secrecy — and he mentioned her as being in the running, too. "That's pretty big-league company," Groucho told Barbra. "If they are considering you against those two, I would say you have arrived."

Barbra never liked such compliments. Being compared to other people, even to say she was in the same league as greats, never felt like flattery to her. She wasn't out to be as good as anyone else, or to be the next whoever. She wanted to be the best that ever was, in her own way, under her own name — spelled and pronounced correctly. So the humble thank-you that someone else might have offered in reply to such a statement wasn't forthcoming from her. Instead, she just kept up the shtick.

"It's been very good, I guess," she said. "I mean, I go to department stores and they still don't wait on me."

It was the Bergdorf Goodman line she'd used in other interviews and, as she intended, it got a big laugh.

But not everyone was laughing. An interesting phenomenon was occurring as Barbra became more successful. She was not only accumulating fans, but also a smaller, though increasingly vocal, group of detractors — critics and reviewers who stood defiantly outside her circle of applause. These opposing voices insisted that Barbra was "inauthentic" and "overhyped," even as they begrudgingly admitted the voice was "worthy of praise" — though some sniped that she really should be singing more true "standards" instead of crazy concoctions like "Who's Afraid of the Big Bad Wolf?" which seemed to them more attention-getting than anything else. One Chicago writer dismissed Barbra as simply a "publicist's creation."

But everyone had a shtick; that was a fact of showbiz. Yet for some reason, there were those who really seemed to resent Barbra's. Dorothy Kilgallen had called Barbra's act "magnetic nonsense," and while it had seemed a sort of compliment, nonsense was still nonsense no matter how magnetic it was, and that was Kilgallen's point.

One of Barbra's earliest boosters, Kilgallen had turned on her by the summer of 1962. She started by chiding the "strong-minded Barbra" for putting her hairdresser "in a swivet" on a recent television appearance (probably *The Garry Moore Show*) by insisting that she appear on camera with her hair "mussed." That was bad enough, Kilgallen thought, but as word continued to reach her about Barbra's demanding style and her recurrent lateness for *Wholesale,* the columnist began sharpening her claws. After observing Barbra's pique on *The Tonight Show* with Groucho, Kilgallen had this to say in her next column: "Friends of the sensationally talented Barbra Streisand wish she'd shed that 'angry woman' attitude. She's successful enough now to be relaxed and pleasant."

It wasn't entirely clear why Kilgallen had soured on her, or why Barbra seemed to elicit such hostility from certain quarters. Part of it, no doubt, could be explained by the fact that she didn't play by the rules: the refusal to observe the political niceties that had so irked Harold Rome, for example. Had she, knowingly or not, snubbed Kilgallen in some way? But there was more to it. One entertainer who sometimes competed with Barbra for gigs and talk-show slots observed "a great deal of resentment building against her," and she attributed it to a feeling that "Barbra didn't deserve everything she was getting because she hadn't paid all of her dues." Worse than that, the entertainer said, was the sense that Barbra "wasn't even grateful for all she was being given."

Dues paid or not, Barbra had just won a recording contract, plus it seemed very likely that she'd be starring on Broadway the following season. "Barbra Streisand is the front-runner for the Fanny Brice show," Dorothy Kilgallen revealed that summer, "and she'd be great in the part." But these days Kilgallen rarely offered any praise for Barbra unqualified by criticism. "One important member of the executive cast," the columnist continued, "is cool to the idea because Barbra made such trouble for the producers of *I Can Get It for You Wholesale*." Kilgallen could only have meant Merrick, so perhaps the producer's enthusiasm for Eydie Gormé had caused him to reconsider his reconsideration of Barbra. Kilgallen added that the show would not include "My Man," or Brice as her Baby Snooks character, or a re-creation of the Ziegfeld Follies. "So what's left?" she asked. "Good question." Barbra, of course, would be left, if she was chosen to be the star — but for Kilgallen, apparently, that fact wasn't significant. The columnist had succeeded in her apparent goal: saying something nice about Barbra for a change to demonstrate her objectivity, but then slipping in a potshot and throwing cold water on the whole idea of the show.

Two camps were indeed forming as Barbra became more prominent, but her detractors, no matter how vocal their resentment, remained far outnumbered by her admirers. Even as Kilgallen was preparing her censorious commentary, another figure, much more esteemed, was drafting a very different take on the rising star. Harold Clurman, in a long piece for the *New York Times* on the importance of musical theater, extolled the Mermans and Bolgers and Martins of the past, but he also looked toward the future. Perhaps, Clurman mused, Tammy Grimes, Robert Morse, and Barbra Streisand would be the greats of tomorrow.

Not a bad place to be for a young woman who, just a year ago, had been hounding a pair of novice producers to cast her in their off-Broadway show, but had to first convince them that she could hold her own against such "big" names as Diana Sands and Dom DeLuise. Since that time, Barbra had ridden a rocket, though she would be the first to point out that it hadn't quite taken her all the way to the top. And the top, of course, was the only place she intended to go.

CHAPTER ELEVEN

Fall 1962

1.

From the stove wafted the mouthwatering aroma of chicken soup, vanquishing, at least for the moment, the pungency of fried fish. With a gentle nudge and a kiss on the forehead, Elliott woke Barbra, telling her breakfast was ready. He'd made the soup for her, filling the role her mother had long performed. With Diana keeping her distance now that her daughter was, as friends put it, "shacking up with" a man, Elliott had gladly stepped in to play Barbra's chief cook and bottle washer.

He was blissfully happy. In their little tree house, Hansel and Gretel had only themselves. No managers, no publicists, no agents, no columnists, no audiences. When all the stress of their careers got to be too much, they retreated here and unburdened the frustrations of the day. Elliott was aware how "very dependent on each other" he and Barbra had become, but certainly that could only be a good thing for two people in love. After all, they were "so right for each other," he believed—especially in terms of "ambition and business and identity and power." They were both going to be big, big stars, they believed—important, serious actors. They would become rich and powerful, too, and they would chart their careers according to their terms and nobody else's.

Such were the dreams, anyway, of a twenty-four-year-old kid and his twenty-year-old girlfriend. On this much, they saw eye to eye.

Finally getting out of bed, Barbra made her way to the sewing-machine stand where a steaming bowl of soup awaited. Elliott had learned how to make it just the way she liked it — which meant just the way her mother had always done. In learning how to make Barbra happy, Elliott had been an eager student. His was a personality that aimed to please. He'd grown up obeying without question the directions of his parents — especially his mother. It was no surprise that Elliott should prove to be the perfect boyfriend for Barbra, who rarely aimed to please anyone other than herself and for whom questioning directions was standard operating procedure. Elliott was correct in believing they were right for each other — but their compatibility was due as much to the fact that they were opposites as it was to the fact that they were in sync about their careers.

It boiled down to a simple dynamic. Barbra decided; Elliott agreed with her decisions. When Barbra was tired after a performance at the Bon Soir or Blue Angel, Elliott knew they would head immediately home, and that was fine with him. When she wanted to stay awhile and talk with people, they stayed and talked, and Elliott was never seen protesting. When Barbra wanted a new piece of furniture to cram into their already crowded flat, Elliott always seemed to concur that it was actually needed. By now, her tastes had completely rubbed off on him. Like Barbra, Elliott loved "old things and bizarre things and funny things"; he could be spotted buying his own antique Coca-Cola trays or painted toy soldiers to hang on the walls or stand on the tables. And when at one point Barbra didn't like a painting he'd bought, he declared that "on second thought it wasn't really right" and tossed it out with the trash, as one *Wholesale* company member observed.

But any differences between them seemed only to inspire Elliott to love Barbra more. While he was very aware of current events, Barbra didn't "listen to the radio" or "know what was going on in the world," Elliott said — unless, of course, it was nuclear testing, and even that she hadn't been following closely these last few months. While Elliott loved music, Barbra had "never heard the Temptations sing." Of course not. She rarely saw further than her own sphere of existence, her own plans and pursuits. But still, Elliott thought she was "remarkable."

That was because Barbra wasn't always so imperious as she seemed at first glance. She could, in fact, be very tender with Elliott. For his birthday just a week or so earlier, she'd presented him with a gold cup representing "the first annual Alexander the Great Award," a takeoff on her "first annual Fanny Brice Award." In the quiet of their little flat, with taxicabs bleating from the street below and Oscar the rat scuttling under the stove, they made a vow to never be apart on each other's birthdays.

In giving Elliott an award to balance hers, Barbra was being particularly sensitive to the man she loved. On stage at the Shubert Theatre, Elliott was the star; she was just a supporting player. But as soon as they stepped out beyond the footlights, their positions leapfrogged. Not since *Wholesale* opened had there been any major media attention on Elliott. When he was mentioned at all in the press, it was as Barbra's boyfriend.

Barbra said that she "didn't want Elliott to be hurt . . . by [her] success." So she trod very carefully, preserving two things that she wanted very much: professional success and personal fulfillment. Elliott's love for her — and *lust* — had wrought an extraordinary transformation. The young woman who'd once believed herself too ugly for ribbons now saw herself as desirable. The theater student once too embarrassed to act out a scene from *The Rose Tattoo* now viewed sex as a thrilling enterprise. When asked what she liked best in a man, Barbra unambiguously replied, "Animalism . . . a certain animal quality." She liked hair on a man, she said; hair was "important." And Elliott had "great hair." She admitted she was turned on by a man's calves.

Barbra's newfound sexual power extended past the confines of her little railroad flat. She enjoyed the authority it gave her, and she was becoming skilled at knowing exactly when "to turn it on," one friend thought. At the theater, she'd flirt and smile and laugh with producers, musicians, or engineers who were "playful and sweet with her" and "who treated her like a woman." Being treated that way was still something new and exciting for her. But at twenty, with the acne of her teen years gone, Barbra suddenly felt like a desirable woman — no matter how many critics still made snide mention of her nose. When she walked into a room, all eyes would immediately turn to her, and people seemed to fixate on her. Jule Styne was a good example of this phenomenon. And as the experience with Styne had demonstrated, Barbra was becoming an expert at exploiting her new powers.

For that, she could thank Elliott. Bob had made her see herself as beautiful and had given form and shape to the vision she'd had of herself as a little girl. But Bob had never desired her, at least not the way Elliott did. Sitting across from her, watching Barbra sip her soup, her hair still mussed from sleeping and her breasts peeking out from her nightgown, Elliott may well have decided that breakfast could wait. He may have stood, taken her by the hand, and led her back to bed. If it didn't happen that day, it happened on plenty of others, and even the scavenging of Oscar the rat wouldn't have been a distraction.

2.

It was the first time Barbra had ever seen palm trees, even if it was difficult for her to see through her tears.

Bob Banner, the producer for Garry Moore, had flown her out to Los Angeles to appear on *The Dinah Shore Show,* which he also produced. Ray Stark saw it as an opportunity to introduce Barbra to Isobel Lennart and, even more critical, to his wife. It was clear they were getting close to offering her the part; they'd even begun talking salary. Stark's continuing enthusiasm for her must have encouraged Barbra, but even that couldn't brighten her spirits as she was driven through the streets of L.A., nor did the chance to play hooky from *Wholesale* for a whole week. What had brought on the tears was her first pro-longed separation from Elliott, which made her first visit to the Coast feel like, in her own word, "hell."

But it was an important trip. Barbra's limo brought her to a boxy, warehouselike building at the corner of Alameda and Olive in Burbank. Near the top, the letters NBC glowed green. This was NBC's Color City, the first television studio in the world equipped exclusively for color broadcasting. Whereas the other networks occasionally broadcast specials in color, NBC was leading a revolution, with the goal of achieving 100 percent color programming within a few years. While the soundstages of Color City were hardly the ornate theaters of Broadway, or even the grand, classical architecture that housed the recording and television studios of New York, they did represent the future.

Making her way into the capacious structure, Barbra knew that her performance on the Shore show was to be, yet again, an audition of sorts. In the studio audience that night would be Fran Stark, whose opinion, as it turned out, mattered as much as her husband's. Barbra had met Mrs. Stark soon after her arrival in Los Angeles, at the Starks' palatial home. The encounter between Brooklyn Barbra and Beverly Hills Fran was watched by everyone involved with eager eyes. The two women were cordial to each other, even if their contrasts were glaring to those present. Fran was elegant, poised, and reserved; Barbra was avant-garde, awkward, and earnest. Ray did his best to facilitate an affable occasion. Styne was there, too, no doubt also doing his best to keep everything flowing smoothly. Columnist Louella Parsons reported that Styne had come to L.A. on "some special business"; no doubt it involved Barbra and Fran.

Fran Stark was one generation removed from the tenements and hardscrabble streets of her mother's — and Barbra's — youth. She'd been educated at the prestigious Dalton School on Manhattan's Upper East Side. Every summer, young Frances had accompanied her mother to Europe, where they lived at the Hotel Carlton in Cannes, or at the Majestic Hotel, where Fanny took over an entire floor and gambled to her heart's content. Meanwhile, Fran, who her mother had decided would be raised as a proper lady, was being taught French by a French mademoiselle.

In her teens, Fran became an accomplished horsewoman, winning awards at the National Horse Show. When her mother moved to Hollywood, Fran was introduced around as one of the more eligible young ladies in town, but her heart was won by the up-and-coming Ray Stark. Their marriage was one of the social events of the season for the movie colony. The newlyweds filled their home on South Peck Drive with modern art, starting with a single Chagall, then adding a Rouault, which they placed over the mantel. Now Fran was one of the great ladies of Hollywood, a perennial on best-dressed lists, ranking alongside Jackie Kennedy and Babe Paley.

It was, no doubt, with a raised eyebrow or two that she regarded Barbra's more bohemian wardrobe. Both of the Starks could be snobbish. They were particular about their images and their hard-won place in society. Their children were Peter, eighteen when Barbra met him, and Wendy, sixteen. Even their names suggested the magical world to which their parents aspired. Peter and Wendy grew up among the other offspring of the rich and famous. Wendy played with Candice Bergen, went to school with Liza Minnelli, and shopped Rodeo Drive with Yasmin Khan. In that elite Hollywood social circle, parents competed against one another to throw the most spectacular birthday parties for their children. The Starks often won. On one birthday, Wendy was startled when her father shouted "Surprise!" and pulled back the curtain to reveal two elephants, one big and one small, grazing in her backyard.

The Starks threw some of the biggest, most elaborate parties in Los Angeles, with large tents and usually a theme. It took Fran at least a month to plan her gatherings. There had to be two bands: one for traditional dancing music during the dinner, and then a dance band for afterward — to play the bossa nova or the twist. A Stark soiree two years ago was still being called "the outstanding Hollywood party of the season." A tent had been erected in the backyard large enough to accommodate a small circus. Under this big top sat 280 guests at twenty-eight tables. Thrown for investors in the film version of *The World of Suzie Wong,* the goal of the bash was to "launch" (Hollywood jargon for "introduce") Nancy Kwan, who was taking over the lead in the film. The usual mix of Los Angeles society—Rosalind Russell and Freddie Brisson, Nancy and Ronald Reagan, Betsy and Alfred Bloomingdale, William Haines and Jimmie Shields—had sipped champagne and air-kissed each other. At the end of the night, Fran was just pleased that no one "had fallen into the swimming pool"—it had happened before—and that all of the jewelry that had been lost had been reclaimed. Except for one topaz ring. "I suppose," Fran confided to a reporter, "since it is not a diamond no one will admit wearing it."

No such extravaganza, however, was thrown in Barbra's honor; she wasn't, after all, signed yet. The first meeting between Barbra and Fran Stark most likely was just a small affair, cocktails or maybe a light dinner. Yet no doubt it was enough for Barbra to get a glimpse of a very alien world. From Barry and Bob, she had heard a little about life among Southern California's upper class, but seeing it firsthand—the swimming pools and housekeepers and long winding driveways and Aston Martins and Bentleys—was something else entirely. Although Barbra told one friend she found Fran Stark "pretentious," she was also intrigued by the world in which she and Ray lived. When Fran shook Barbra's hand for the first time, her wrists sparkled with platinum-and-emerald bracelets and her ears dripped with diamonds. Upstairs there was a treasure chest of gems worth hundreds of thousands of dollars. Standing under the chandelier in the Starks' home, surrounded by Picassos and Calders, Barbra had entered a world far, far away from her mother's apartment in Brooklyn, where everything reeked of kale, and where tattered cookbooks and cracked china were piled on the dining-room table.

Heading into the studio to tape the Shore show, Barbra knew that Fran Stark sat out in the audience waiting to judge her. Rehearsals, sans audience, had gone well, and there was every reason to think that this final taping would proceed just as smoothly. But given Barbra's tendency for first-night jitters, there was, almost certainly, more than a little anxiety as she slipped into her dress for the evening. A thumbs-down from Fran could kill the whole deal, no matter how much Ray and Jule might plead her case. To lose *The Funny Girl* now was unthinkable. Barbra had sought out her old teacher Allan Miller for some private coaching so she'd get better and better at each reading. But none of that would matter if the elegantly dressed woman sitting out in the audience tonight didn't like what she saw and heard.

So it was with considerable determination that Barbra steadied her nerves and headed out in front of the cameras.

Dinah Shore was a television mainstay, having hosted various shows for a decade. This current series aired once a month, in color, on Sunday nights after *Bonanza*—a terrific ratings lead-in. Tonight's episode, which would be taped for a later airdate, was to be pitched as "a group of vocal performers" who, in Shore's opinion, would be the "important entertainers of tomorrow." In addition to Barbra, the guests were Georgia Brown, who'd briefly also been in the running to play Fanny Brice; pop singer Sam Fletcher; and the Chad Mitchell Trio, who were folk singers.

Shore, the daughter of Jewish immigrants, had grown up in Tennessee; with her lilting accent, she cultivated the image of a Southern belle. She swept out onto the stage this night in a long gown and glittering top, her earrings sparkling as the orchestra played a soulful introduction. She read from a script prepared by the show's writers, with input from Marty, that was intended to keep the momentum going for Barbra. But right off the bat, Shore got it wrong.

"Barbra Streisand," she said, placing the accent only on the first syllable of "Streisand" and practically swallowing the second. To Barbra, such pronunciation was like fingernails on a blackboard. Someone, evidently, had failed to school Shore the way they'd schooled Garry Moore. Shore, unaware, went on in her flowery drawl. She called her next guest "a girl barely out of her teens," who was "wistful, funny, appealing, and enormously talented." Then came the obligatory key point, made every time Barbra appeared on television but which to-night was especially important since Fran Stark was sitting in the au-dience. "She's basically a comedienne," Shore said of Barbra, "but she's a fine dramatic actress, too, as you'll see when she sings her torch song."

The giant TK-41 color television camera then dollied across the stark, expressionist set to find Barbra standing at the foot of an open staircase. She seemed somewhat ill at ease. The added pressure of the night couldn't have helped, but Barbra's nerves could also have sprung from the proximity of that monstrous mechanical beast. The cam-era had to be rolled in practically to her toes whenever a close shot was needed, as it contained no zoom lens. Yet Barbra looked fabu-lous, taking full advantage of the color broadcast by wearing a bright orange, floor-length, Grecian-style dress secured by a brooch at the waist — a perfect representation of Bob's "white goddess."

But when she opened her mouth to sing, a rather strange thing occurred. Usually this was the moment when people described the hair standing up on the backs of their necks, or tingles suddenly vi-brating down their spines, or some other physical manifestation of their reaction to Barbra's voice. But something was off tonight. To at least one reviewer, who saw the show when it was broadcast, Bar-bra seemed "anxious." Whether it was Fran Stark, the metal leviathan at her shoulder, or Shore mispronouncing her name, Barbra was off her game. She launched into a shrill, stylized rendition of "Cry Me a River," a song that usually blew people away in nightclubs, but which here seemed overdone, overwrought, almost a parody of a "serious actress" trying to express herself in a song. Barbra's eyes seemed to keep crossing as she snapped out the lyrics, staccato-style, and at times she was all mouth, summoning very little of the pathos she'd brought to the song in the days when the pain of losing Barry had been so recent.

Then, after the audience's applause, she dramatically flung her filmy tangerine cape over her shoulder and ascended the stairs to emerge into another modernistic set, where she sang "Happy Days Are Here

Again." The song had become Barbra's signature very quickly during her nightclub appearances. For some loyal fans, however, who'd heard Barbra sing it dozens of times at the Bon Soir or the Blue Angel, it was impossible not to think she was performing it this night as if she were Fanny Brice keening "My Man." She seemed to be summoning the same heartache that Brice had brought to her own signature song, the same defiant strength in the face of adversity. But did it feel real? That much her fans were divided on. Once again, she was all mouth and teeth as she threw back her head. "Happy days are . . . here . . . a . . . gain!"

Later in the show, there was a little more lightheartedness, as Barbra joined Shore and the rest of the cast for an upbeat rendition of "Brotherhood of Man," from *Wholesale*'s chief Broadway rival, *How to Succeed in Business Without Really Trying*. Perhaps it might have been smarter to pair "Happy Days" with something more rousing like this, because Barbra's two solo numbers hadn't allowed for any of her quirky humor. Styne, of course, had previously advised her to play that down, and she seemed to be heeding his words again this night. Whether that was a mistake was unknown, as the critics wouldn't get a crack at the show until it was aired a few months down the road.

But one critic had already seen all she needed to see. Whether it was the lack of humor and warmth, the stylized singing, the odd facial expressions, or something else entirely, Fran Stark had not been won over by Barbra's performance. Privately, she would declare that if it were up to her, Barbra Streisand would never play her mother.

3.

Sitting at a desk, wearing a dark dress and a long strand of pearls, Barbra raised her eyes to the photographer who was recording the moment for posterity — and for distribution in Columbia press kits. Standing beside her was Goddard Lieberson, smartly dressed in a well-cut suit and a French-cuffed, tab-collared shirt. As Barbra looked on beaming, God leaned down and signed the contract that had been placed in front of her on the desk. That day, October 1, Barbra officially became a Columbia recording artist.

Soon after her return from Los Angeles, she'd learned from Marty that, after weeks of negotiations, her contract was ready to be signed. Dorothy Kilgallen had reported, without hiding her scorn, that Marty had been seeking $100,000 as an advance for his client — which, Kilgallen sniped, was "a lot of loot for a new name, especially a singer who hasn't hit it big by herself in the record market." At such a figure Columbia had indeed balked, but Marty had just moved on to what he had really wanted for Barbra all along: complete "creative control, no coupling, and the right to choose her own material." (Coupling meant being paired with another artist.) This was granted. After all, David Kapralik reasoned, Barbra had built a successful nightclub career on her own. Why mess with a proven formula? Plus, Marty had secured a clause that allowed her, should she get cast in another Broadway show after *Wholesale,* to participate in a show-tune album with another record label. As always, Marty thought ahead.

The rest of the contract was pretty standard. A small advance — twenty grand — with a five percent royalty against ninety-eight percent of records sold. The deal between them was for five years — which actually meant one year, after which Columbia had the option for the next four years to keep Barbra or let her go. But these ordinary clauses weren't what most observers noticed. Instead, they saw a twenty-year-old kid waltzing into Columbia and demanding — and getting — full creative control from a man as legendarily omnipotent as Lieberson. It left some industry stalwarts flabbergasted. And what was more, the $100,000 figure floated by Kilgallen was never retracted. Whether that was an oversight or whether Marty deliberately chose not to correct the columnist is unknown. But it would certainly fit his strategy of positioning Barbra as an extraordinary artist being extended extraordinary privileges by the powers that be.

For many people, that was precisely the image they came away with, and their beliefs seemed to be confirmed by Kilgallen's follow-up column. "After months of negotiations," she reported, "Barbra Streisand is signing with Columbia Records this week, and will cut her first solo discs for the company within a few days. They'll go all out to promote her, of course — at those staggering rates." For Kilgallen's readers, who included nearly everybody in showbiz, the impression was that Barbra had actually gotten that hundred grand. It wasn't surprising that many of them felt angry or jealous.

In the fall of 1962, the ranks of that small but vocal minority of Streisand detractors were beginning to swell. Not only was Barbra catching breaks that other performers believed were being denied to them, but she remained, to their view, ungrateful for all that she was getting. On a recent radio program, Barbra had been asked by interviewer Lee Jordan how her success felt. "It doesn't feel like anything," she'd replied cavalierly. She went on to reiterate her resentment at not being able to do what she wanted at night because she had to be at the theater. "Already she's complaining," Jordan commented, and many listeners shared the surprise and disdain that was apparent in his voice.

It was the Columbia contract that really seemed to tip the scales for a lot of people. "What I would have given for a contract like that, guaranteeing me complete creative control," groused one singer, who'd been around a lot longer than Barbra. Grasping around for an explanation, some of them latched on to the idea of a network of "Jewish helping hands," an informal but deliberate collusion among Jewish power brokers to promote one of their own. "They wanted to have their say about what was beautiful, what was talented," said another performer, who was not Jewish. "For so long they had been self-conscious about being Jewish themselves, always having to promote these pretty blonde Gentile girls with perky little noses, and then along came Barbra and they suddenly had a chance to build up a real obvious Jewish girl."

Was there some merit to the theory? As far back as Eddie Blum, there had been men in positions of power, Jewish men, who had taken more kindly to Barbra because of her ethnicity. More recently, Arthur Laurents had gone to bat for her with Goddard Lieberson, urging the record producer to help out this talented *kalleh moid*. Indeed, most of those who had opened doors for Barbra — hiring her for shows or clubs, extending her runs, writing material for her, promoting her to the press, giving her contracts — had been Jewish. In addition to Laurents and Lieberson, there had been Jerome Weidman, Harold Rome, David Kapralik, Max Gordon, and, although reluctantly, David Merrick. Currently, Ray Stark and Jule Styne were attempting to open yet more doors for her. Barbra was also benefiting from the support of an important new fan and booster, the composer Harold Arlen, who was known to rave at influential cocktail parties about how wonderfully she sang his songs — "A Sleepin' Bee," "Right as the Rain," "When the Sun Comes Out," among others. And it was perhaps noteworthy that the one least enthusiastic about her — Merrick — was also the one most uncomfortable with his own Jewishness. Merrick, according to witnesses, would "bristle" when he heard Barbra speaking in her pronounced Jewish Brooklynese. Was Merrick the exception among Barbra's Jewish godfathers who proved the rule?

But not all the helping hands had been Jewish. The very first people to give Barbra a leg up the ladder had been Gentiles: Burke McHugh, Ernie Sgroi, Sam and Les Gruber. And Barbra's Jewishness had been as much a handicap at times as it had been an asset: How many of the snide reviews, especially those commenting on her looks, had been stoked by anti-Semitism? The truth was, for all the belief in some great Jewish conspiracy to elevate Barbra Streisand, if there had not been two Broadway shows — *Wholesale* and now *The Funny Girl* — that required eccentric Jewish characters, none of Barbra's benefactors, even if they'd wanted to, could have helped her much beyond nightclubs and records. As it was, Barbra had come along at just the right moment for both these shows — and, consequently, for her own success.

There was also a change in the air, a "democratization" as Bob called it, inspired by the Kennedys in the White House and the civil rights movement taking place across the country, a sense that "fashion and beauty and talent were for everybody," not just those who looked like Audrey Hepburn and Marilyn Monroe. That year, Diahann Carroll had won the Tony as Best Actress for Richard Rodgers's *No Strings* — a first for an African American and a feat unthinkable even a few years earlier. Johnny Mathis was selling records and making teenaged girls swoon in the way Pat Boone and other white singers had done before him. Nightclubs and theaters were filling up with faces and voices that unambiguously reflected the experience of ethnicities rarely encountered by white-bread America until now: Woody Allen, Lenny Bruce, Dick Gregory, Dustin Hoffman, Joan Rivers, Chita Rivera, Bill Cosby, and Totie Fields, to name just a few. Even Barbra realized the shift that was taking place. People, she said, "were ready" for her.

It was clear that Columbia Records was ready for her. Shaking hands with Lieberson and posing for the last of the publicity photos, Barbra was done with pleasantries — which she never tolerated for too long — and eager to get busy. Mike Berniker, a young up-and-comer from A&R (the artists and repertoire division), was assigned as her producer. Berniker had just produced a Tammy Grimes album and sent it over to Barbra so she could get a sense of his work. After having a listen, Barbra called him and said, "Yeah, let's go." They set the date of October 16 for Barbra to record her first disks. But, as Berniker and everyone else at Columbia would discover, Barbra would turn out to be a very different artist from Tammy Grimes — from everyone else, in fact, on their label.

4.

Barbra and her castmates were practicing their new marks, entrances, and exits now that *Wholesale* had moved over to the Broadway Theatre, on Broadway near Fifty-third Street. Changing theaters midrun was never easy for a company that had been doing the same exact things, in the same exact places, for seven months. Alone among them, Barbra was probably glad for the change in scenery; any shake-up to her *Wholesale* routine was welcome to her. But the move to a new theater was hardly consolation for losing *The Funny Girl*.

She hadn't quite lost it yet, but things didn't look good. Just a couple of weeks ago, the part of Fanny Brice had seemed within her grasp. Earl Wilson had reported, "David Merrick may hold up his Fanny Brice musical while it's tailored to young Barbra Streisand." Louella Parsons had confirmed the report, sourcing Jule Styne and announcing that Anne Bancroft was now "completely out of the Fanny Brice story." In no uncertain terms, Styne had told Parsons, "When we make it, Barbra Streisand . . . will play Fanny." It would require "a whole rewrite job," Styne explained, as the "story had been written with Anne Bancroft in mind." Barbra, it seemed, had the job.

Then, out of the blue, the entire Brice project stalled. No one was returning Marty's calls. How much Barbra knew about Fran Stark's opposition to her is unknown, but in fact it was much more than just that putting on the brakes. Surely Barbra had heard rumors by now of what was afoot and what had really caused all the preparations for *The Funny Girl* to come to a grinding halt.

In late September, Jerry Robbins had quit. "Although Jerry has been working on the Fanny Brice musical for many months," his lawyer had written to Stark's lawyer, "it is now obvious to everyone that it is not ready for rehearsals. If it is rewritten and becomes ready for production (a hope he cherishes) he will be glad to consider directing and choreographing it." But for now, he was through.

Robbins's letter of resignation had come after a series of "ghastly sessions" (so called by Isobel Lennart) with Ray Stark. The long-simmering tensions between director and producer had finally boiled over. Robbins had bluntly told Stark the book was "not ready yet, despite everyone's work and creative contributions." Moreover, he resented being coerced into moving ahead on the project, especially because it meant postponing *Mother Courage*, which was ready to go.

What really ticked Robbins off, however, was a letter Stark then wrote to his attorneys, pointing out that he, Stark, was an investor in *Mother Courage* and so had some say over Robbins's decisions. "I think there can be no question of the fact," Stark wrote, "that never has a director received so many benefits as Jerry is now receiving." Enraged and offended, Robbins called Stark's assertions "slanderous," and then added pointedly, "As for delivering stage successes on Broadway, I'm a veteran compared to you, this being your first time up at bat."

From there, it could only go downhill. In his resignation letter, Robbins stressed that if he did not do the play, he would "not want any of his ideas or material used." It was that clause, even more than Robbins's departure, that had halted the project. Robbins's contributions were woven all through the book, and no one knew this better than Lennart. She'd have to scrap everything and start over, writing an entirely new script, while Stark and Merrick began searching around for a new director. This was the real reason the book needed to be rewritten; it wasn't to accommodate Barbra, as Styne had told Parsons, but rather to accommodate Jerry Robbins.

But, in public, Barbra was being used as the reason for the show's delay — even though she hadn't even been signed yet and, given Fran Stark's opposition, might never be. If the producers had really been delaying the show so they could "tailor" it to Barbra, they would have already signed her. But as it was, there was no show to sign her for, and if there ever was again, they might still go with someone else. Given how smart both Barbra and Marty were, they surely knew exactly how they were being used by Stark and Merrick. It couldn't have been a pleasant predicament. They couldn't complain or object too loudly, as Barbra was still being touted as the "leading" candidate. But they also had no bargaining power in this game of wait and see.

It didn't take Marty long to realize that they might have a way to influence the situation after all. Soon he was making a few calls to the columnists on his own, and within days Earl Wilson was reporting, "Barbra Streisand, who's been practically set for the delayed Fanny Brice musical (but never signed for it), is reading for the new show *The Student Gypsy*." This was a musical written by Rick Besoyan, the author of the long-running off-Broadway satire *Little Mary Sunshine*. The message to Stark and Merrick was plain: If they wanted Barbra, they'd better act fast in putting their show back together.

But the producers were stuck. Without a script, without a director, they could go no further. Lennart had already been floundering; how could she possibly write an entirely new book devoid of Robbins's contributions? Would they need to hire another librettist? In such chaos, *The Funny Girl* might easily wither away, as so many failed concepts had done before it. And with it, so too would wither away Barbra's best chance to reach the top. When would another musical come along that needed a funny Jewish girl with a big nose as its star?

So, with undoubtedly a heavy heart, Barbra resumed learning her new marks for *Wholesale.* She also went back on *The Tonight Show,* where the new host, Johnny Carson, mispronounced her last name just like everybody else did. And she signed a contract for yet another gig at the Bon Soir. Same as it ever was.

5.

Peter Daniels looked through his thick glasses at the young woman perusing the sheet music in front of him. Usually it was just the two of them, or the two of them plus a trio. But now thirty or more musicians surrounded Barbra and Peter, all tuning their instruments, a cacophony of notes sounding in that magnificent space, with its hundred-foot ceilings matched by a hundred feet of floor space. Above them dangled mikes and long copper wires leading to the recording equipment. From the small glass booth on the second floor, a gaggle of solemn men in suits looked down at everything they did. Peter took his seat at the piano, playing a few keys to familiarize himself. Barbra continued looking over the music, psyching herself up to record her first disks under her contract.

Early this morning, Tuesday, October 16, a warm, overcast day, Peter had trekked down to Columbia's Studio C at 207 East Thirtieth with Barbra and Marty. It was an old Presbyterian Church, and it offered some of the best acoustics of any recording studio in the city. Miles Davis would record nowhere else. When Barbra looked down from the control room at all the musicians, Mike Berniker thought she was trembling. He took her by the hand and led her to the floor.

At the moment, unbeknownst to anyone, the Kennedy administration was facing down the Soviet Union in what came to be called the Cuban Missile Crisis. Although tension was everywhere, Barbra had no idea just how close the country was to nuclear war as she tested the mikes in the studio that morning.

Peter found he could work well with the orchestra, conducted by George Williams, a true master, who'd arranged for Glenn Miller, Tommy Dorsey, and Lionel Hampton. Together they had reworked "Happy Days" yet again, finding a synthesis of the various renditions Barbra had performed so far. With the goal of producing two records that day, with two sides each, Peter had also rearranged "Right as the Rain," "When the Sun Comes Out," and "Lover, Come Back to Me." He'd been with Barbra long enough now to know exactly what worked, what didn't, what they'd tried before, and what they still might play around with.

Barbra had come a long way since Peter had first laid eyes on the pimply-faced kid with enormous chutzpah auditioning for *The Sound of Music*. He'd been there for the first Bon Soir show, for the Blue Angel gigs, and for so many other performances. Many times Barbra had slept on the floor of Peter's studio after a long practice session. In the last several months, Peter had been spending far more time with Barbra than he had with his wife, Anita, causing not a few problems at home. But Peter, a brilliant, offbeat, march-to-his-own-drummer kind of guy, had left England at a young age and come to America with a single goal in mind: to become a famous musician. Peter wanted to be a star — to be recognized — almost as much as Barbra did, and he knew attaching himself to her would pay off. In fact, it already had. His steady gigs at both the Bon Soir and the Blue Angel were in part because of his connection to her. While this time he might have been at Columbia to make Barbra's first records, next time, he hoped, he could be making his.

Nearly all of the songs Barbra had used to establish herself had been arranged by Peter; his influence could be heard every time she opened her mouth to sing. It was Peter who had thought to have her hold the notes as long as she did in "Right as the Rain"; it was he who'd had the idea to sex up "When the Sun Comes Out." Occasionally he'd suggest something that didn't work, but usually Barbra was able to accomplish whatever Peter had in mind, continually surprising him with her ability to take one of his ideas and elaborate on it. Theirs was an easy partnership, though not without quarrels. Barbra was demanding, and while Peter could usually roll with her tetchiness, sometimes he had to get up off his stool and take a walk around the block.

Of the songs Barbra was to record that day, "Lover, Come Back to Me" dated back the furthest, all the way to her first Bon Soir appearance more than two years ago. It had been Barry who'd helped her arrange that song, playing the record over and over for her in his apartment. Back then, Barbra had had trouble with one line, never seeming to get through it without tripping over the words, but now the song flowed easily and smoothly, like the old friend it was. Peter had kept the fast, almost freight-train tempo that Barry had devised, but he had given the song an extra bounciness that brought out its soul. Barbra might have been singing about missing a lover, but she did so gaily, almost giddily. Hearing her sing the song, there was no question that her lover was coming back.

But nowhere was Peter's talent expressed better than in the new arrangement he'd come up with, in partnership with George Williams, for "Happy Days Are Here Again." As Barbra sang that signature number into the microphone hanging in front of her, there was a sense in the room of something wonderful coming together. For this rendition, Barbra was able to perfectly balance the song's original jubilation with the sense of melancholy she'd brought to it. What they brought forth that day was a haunting, complex number, celebratory and cautionary at the same time, a call of joy as well as a cry of sadness. It was, in the end, whatever the listener believed it to be, which, of course, is the mark of transcendence. Barbra's voice, a gorgeous instrument on its own, never sounded better than here, surrounded by that thirty-piece orchestra in that exquisitely acoustic room. When they were finished, and Williams lowered his conductor's baton, Peter knew in his heart they had just wrought a masterpiece.

6.

Hoping to change his wife's mind about Barbra, Ray Stark had brought Fran to the Bon Soir. Seeing Barbra in the more relaxed setting of a nightclub, he anticipated, might soften Fran's vehement opposition. The show was tentatively back on track, now being called *The Luckiest People,* after a line in the Styne-Merrill song "People." They would tiptoe their way around the legal issues with Robbins the best they could. But recent press reports were stating that Kaye Ballard was now being considered for the lead. On *The Perry Como Show,* where she was a regular, Ballard was doing some superb impressions of Brice. The *New York Times*'s Sam Zolotow, who knew about such things, had called Ballard a contender for the part. But that was hype. Ray Stark hadn't lost his faith in Barbra.

Fran, however, was another story. That was why Barbra, waiting in that cramped little dressing room that had become something of a second home, had to go out on the stage one more time to try to win her over. It seemed she was forever auditioning.

She should have been riding high, especially with the release earlier that month of the "Happy Days" single. Yet despite its brilliance, the disk had gone precisely nowhere. That was because, as Marty discovered, the head of the sales department, a conservative fellow by the name of Bill Gallagher, had doubted the commercial viability of "Happy Days." Just to be safe, he'd pressed only five hundred disks and distributed them only in New York. Enraged, Marty had demanded that Columbia release the second single as soon as possible and get one hundred percent behind promoting it this time.

In response, Lieberson had suggested a live album. Indeed, an album was what Marty had been angling for all along. So, just a few days before the Starks' appearance at the Bon Soir, Columbia had sent in a team to the club to record Barbra live. Lieberson had introduced Barbra to the audience himself, calling her "a singular artist" who couldn't be categorized. With beauty and grace she rendered "My Name Is Barbara" and the crowd was on their feet applauding. But then a microphone fuse blew. "You're kidding me!" Barbra wailed. That was just the beginning. When she restarted her set, the Columbia photographer, hoping for a jacket cover, kept snapping pictures and distracting her. Finally Barbra had to ask him to stop. These were hardly the conditions under which she wanted to record an album. She needed the kind of control she'd had at the Thirtieth Street studio, without worries of extraneous noise or echoes. If this was what making albums was like, then she wanted no part of it.

Faced with the vacuum left by the collapse of the Brice musical, Barbra had taken Marty's advice and signed with new publicists. Richard Falk had already left her, reportedly because Marty "was doing everything" himself. But it was Barbra who'd made the break with the Softness brothers. Quite simply, she felt she had outgrown them. She'd offered Don Softness, with whom she had the closer relationship, a chance to stay on, providing he got rid of all of his other clients to focus only on her. The offer was "tempting," Softness said, but ultimately he turned Barbra down. He "had a company to run," he said, and besides, a future of "being the tail that wagged the dog" was not something he looked forward to. Barbra may have been hurt, since rejection of any kind was never easy for her, which might explain why she had no further contact with Softness, not even to pay the last of the expenses he'd incurred in promoting her.

Her new publicist, Lee Solters, had far more connections than the Softness Group. And, like Marty, he was willing to come on board without any binding contract, assured only by an absolute belief in Barbra's greatness and ultimate destiny. At least, that was the word that Solters let get around once he was in the job; it certainly fit the narrative Marty had already established. Solters, born Nathan Cohen in Brooklyn and always called "Nussy," was a bald-headed, raspy-voiced character who'd been working as a press agent for David Merrick for more than a decade. It was Solters who'd been the architect of the ingenious "Mr. Clutterbuck" ploy. Grabbing publicity came naturally to him, one observer said, "like putting on a pair of shoes."

While promoting *Wholesale*, Solters had encountered Barbra and quickly became impressed with her moxie and determination to get her name out there. It became clear to Barbra that Solters, far more than Softness or even Falk, had the clout to make her a household name. In addition to Merrick's shows, Solters had also flacked for *Guys and Dolls, Gypsy, My Fair Lady, The King and I*, and *Camelot*. Just recently, he'd picked up none other than Frank Sinatra as a client. Solters knew everybody.

And while he hoped to raise Barbra's publicity to new heights, Solters chose to continue, even intensify, the meme originated by Softness of Barbra as "kook." Not only was it ideal positioning for the Fanny Brice musical, but even if that show never came to fruition, Barbra's "kookiness" ensured that the press kept coming back for more. Who wouldn't want great copy like Earl Wilson had been getting, or the fabulous stream of consciousness that had made the *New Yorker* piece required reading among the theater crowd? Barbra's kookiness had certainly entranced Johnny Carson when she'd appeared with him on *The Tonight Show*. When the host had asked her if she thought of herself as a kook, Barbra had replied, "I don't understand it really. I'll tell you this, it's very interesting because when I decided, well, not decided, I always knew I wanted to be in the theater, but I never made rounds or anything like that, it was very depressing. But I did for two days. It was during the winter. It was very cold and I wore a big coat and a big hat because I can't stand the cold. So I walked into offices and they really thought I was nuts. Like one woman said to me, 'When you go make rounds and you meet people, you should wear stockings and high heels' and so forth. I said, 'It's freezing out, lady. It's so cold, what difference does it make if I'm an actress, if I am talented or not talented, what difference does it make if I wear tights or not?' So kooky people said I was kooky."

Of course, that was classic Barbra — she meant every word of it, even if she was likely conflating episodes (was the hat and coat a reference to her *Wholesale* audition?) and ignoring actual chronology, as was her custom. All that mattered was that she told an entertaining story in an entertaining way. That had been Softness's instruction, and now it was Solters's as well. Barbra shouldn't hold back, her publicists told her; she should say whatever came into her head — and the quirkier the better. So, after telling Carson she didn't understand being called a kook, she gave evidence to demonstrate that she was, in fact, exactly what they called her. Carson, his amiable expressions showing an earnest, if exaggerated, attempt to follow her logic, clearly enjoyed her. As she had on *PM East,* Barbra could pull viewers in with her far-out style. Since that first appearance, Carson, looking to boost his ratings, had already had her back on the show once — a gig for which Marty also managed to get the Clancy Brothers included — and had slated her for still another appearance in early January.

That fall, Barbra stood over Solters's shoulder, as Arthur Laurents understood, admonishing him to "get her something new." Accordingly, Solters was busy preparing a multimedia promotional campaign for her: print, television, radio. He succeeded in getting Ed Sullivan, the king of variety television, to come down to the Bon Soir to catch Barbra's performance. Sullivan hired her on the spot for his television show and, having enjoyed the evening so much, also hired Barbra's warm-up act, comedian Sammy Shore, to appear with her. The date was set for early in December.

For Barbra, finally landing a spot on the top variety show was no doubt satisfying, though, in its own way, probably a little unsettling as well. Everything she did seemed to be an audition for something else, for something bigger.

Just as it was tonight with Fran Stark.

Taking one last look in the mirror, Barbra headed out onto the stage. If she was hoping for a decision, some sign that she'd cinched the deal, she was disappointed. Everyone was cordial at the end of the night, but whether she'd changed Fran's mind, Barbra had no idea. Mrs. Stark was playing it all very cool.

7.

The news had come with just a couple of days' notice. A letter from Merrick posted backstage thanked them all for their work and dedication, then dropped the bomb: *Wholesale* would be closing on Saturday, December 8. After a strong start, the show had faltered in recent months, and even various special half-price ticket deals that were promoted to boost attendance hadn't made a difference. The great hope that the show's low production budget, coupled with strong early box office, would mean profits for everyone hadn't materialized; by the start of December, *Wholesale* was $140,000 in the hole and sinking further. Even all the publicity about the girl who "stopped the show cold" every night had failed to keep up the momentum.

There were tears all around, but not from Barbra. Now, on the show's last night, when the final curtain dropped, she bounded backstage chortling, "I'm free! I'm free!" Wiping off her makeup and discarding Miss Marmelstein's frumpy dress for the last time, Barbra, with Elliott at her side, practically danced out into the cold dark night, the air swirling with snow flurries. They might have, as so many theater people did on finding themselves suddenly out of work, enjoyed a bit of a holiday, gotten away from showbiz for a while, taken a much-needed breather. But Barbra had no time for such luxuries. She had to get the tracks laid down for her album, which Columbia had agreed to produce in the studio next month after the results of their live recording effort at the Bon Soir had proven unsatisfactory to everyone. She also had to rehearse for the Sullivan show, which was coming up in just a few days. No, there was no time for any holiday.

Elliott, on the other hand, had all the time in the world. On Monday, as Barbra headed over to Peter Daniels's studio to practice, Elliott slunk down to the labor offices on Fifty-eighth Street and applied for fifty dollars a week in unemployment benefits.

CHAPTER TWELVE

Winter 1963

1.

Barbra had had it. All during rehearsals Ed Sullivan had been saying, "Now let's hear it from the Columbia recording star Barbra Streisland." No matter how many times she tried to correct him, he still got her name wrong, and few things irritated her more. Now, during the live broadcast, furious with fear that he'd do it again, Barbra positioned herself right behind the curtain, waiting to pounce as soon as the commercial break was over and it was her turn to be introduced.

The light on the camera flashed, indicating they were about to go live. "Streisand!" Barbra hissed through the curtain. "Streisand! Like sand on the beach!"

Sullivan started to laugh, then realized he was on camera. "She's breaking me up over here," he said as way of explanation. Then, composing himself, he announced: "Here's a young Columbia star, a very great talent, here's Barbra Streisand" — he said it perfectly — "so let's have a nice welcome."

Clearly relieved, Barbra did a little jig as she hurried out onto stage. She wore a short white dress and her hair was flipped out at the ends, with a big bun on top. She sang two songs for Sullivan. Her rendition of "Lover, Come Back to Me" turned out to be very hubba-hubba, conjuring up red-hot-mama Sophie Tucker. "Lover" was the flipside of Barbra's second single, which had just been released. As promised, Columbia had put more effort into this one, pressing twenty thousand copies and mailing demos to DJs all across the country. The front side of the single was the John Kander–Fred Ebb composition "My Coloring Book," recorded just a few days before, and Barbra also performed it that night on the Sullivan show. Kander and Ebb had written the song for Kaye Ballard, but when she'd wanted to perform it on *The Perry Como Show,* she was denied permission, because it was too serious and she was the show's comedienne. Enter Barbra, who recorded the song and made it her own, much to Ballard's exasperation.

"My Coloring Book" was Barbra doing what she did best, bringing an almost unbearable poignancy to a simple song about heartbreak. Marty immediately sent a copy to Ray Stark in California, and the producer, reportedly, was "bowled over." Whether his wife shared his opinion, no one was quite sure. Fran Stark had fallen utterly silent on the matter of Barbra Streisand. There were reports that she'd left the Bon Soir after Barbra's performance still adamantly opposed to her; others said Barbra's performance had won her over. What seems to have been the case is that, no matter her own personal feelings, Fran was simply deferring to her husband's judgment. But her silence fostered stories that Mrs. Stark was waging a fierce, one-woman, behind-the-scenes campaign against Barbra.

It was hard, however, to imagine such a position in the wake of the release of "My Coloring Book." The song might have been schmaltz, but Barbra's heartbreak was beautifully convincing. If anyone had doubted her ability to convey the range of emotions needed to play Fanny Brice, all they needed to do was listen to this record.

The richness of the emotion apparent in Barbra's voice may have arisen from a new, and unexpected, understanding of the lyrics. She sang of watching the man she loved drift away: "Color him gone." As 1962 turned into 1963, Barbra and Elliott had suddenly found life in their little tree house was no longer quite so harmonious. Their hectic, yet sustaining, routine had been shattered by the closing of *Wholesale*. Barbra was still rushing hither and yon, but Elliott, never good at being idle, just moped around the apartment. He was developing "terrible anxieties" waiting in the unemployment line. He felt, he admitted, like "such a failure collecting that $50."

For all his insistence that both men and women needed to "break tradition" in their relationships with each other, Elliott found himself hopelessly stuck in an earlier view: He was the man and he was out of work, dependent on the income of a woman, so, ergo, he must be a failure. The fact that Barbra's success kept steamrolling along even after *Wholesale* closed — even if she herself was dissatisfied with its progress — was very difficult for Elliott. He had been the star — but Barbra had ended up making as much as he had in *Wholesale*, and now, while she got calls for nightclubs and television shows, he was schlepping down to the labor office.

One acquaintance thought it was "a bit of a self-pity party Elliott was throwing for himself." Since, in fact, those unemployment checks were just temporary. Elliott had very quickly landed himself another job after *Wholesale* closed. Although he wouldn't start until the following spring, Elliott had won the lead in the London revival of *On the Town*, to be staged at the Prince of Wales Theatre. But where the job should have made him feel more secure, it caused a whole new set of problems. Elliott wanted Barbra to go with him to London; if she didn't, who knew how long they'd be apart and what would happen to their relationship then. The uncertainty of all that frightened Barbra, too, so she may have genuinely considered director Joe Layton's offer of a part in the show. He proposed that she play Hildy, the man-hungry taxi driver who'd been brought to life on the Broadway stage by Nancy Walker — in a show, by the way, conceived and choreographed by Jerome Robbins. Taking a supporting role in another musical that starred Elliott would keep them together. It would also re-create the dynamic of the past half year.

But Barbra knew it would be a career misstep. Playing Hildy would have typed her as a character actress and conceivably prevented her from ever being considered for a leading role. Agreeing to *On the Town* would not only have meant losing out on Fanny Brice if that show made it to the stage, but also forfeiting, according to her agents, $100,000 worth of other offers — a year or more of television, nightclubs, and records — an estimate that Lee Solters made sure to supply Earl Wilson, who ran it in his column to explain why Barbra had turned the part down. The implication was clear: She had become too important to play a secondary part in Elliott's show.

The reality of that fractured their home life. One photographer who came to take photos of Barbra for some interview was witness to a noisy argument between the couple, with some "pretty heavy shouting," though the photographer couldn't tell "what they were shouting about." One day, Diana made a rare visit — every once in a while she still felt obliged to stop by with some soup — and found the atmosphere in her daughter's apartment to be "so thick with tension it could be cut with a pair of scissors," said a friend who was with her. Barbra was sulking in one corner and Elliott was in another, neither speaking to the other, which made things rather difficult, given how small the flat was.

One acquaintance thought their squabbling reflected more than just a case of clashing egos or a contest over who was more successful. Their rancor grew even more, their acquaintance said, from a sense of "fear — a deep-rooted fear that everything was changing, and that without the glue of *Wholesale,* their relationship was coming apart."

For Barbra, it was a core dilemma. She wanted success and acclaim, everyone knew that; but she also wanted love. The decisions she'd be asked to make in the next few months would force her to make some hard choices between those two competing desires.

2.

In just twelve hours, the temperature in New York had plunged thirty-three degrees, bottoming out at five above zero. Snow blew into Barbra's face as she stepped out of the car, wrapped, almost certainly, in her caracul coat and wool hat. At least there was no one telling her that she should be wearing stockings and high heels.

Hurrying into the Columbia Records headquarters on Seventh Avenue, Barbra shook the snow from her coat and headed into the elevator. It was January 24, the second day of recording her album. This time it was Studio A, at the top of the building, where she was working her magic. Yesterday, she'd recorded "A Taste of Honey," "I'll Tell the Man in the Street," and "Soon It's Gonna Rain," but today the agenda was more ambitious, with "My Honey's Lovin' Arms," "Keepin' Out of Mischief Now," "Come to the Supermarket in Old Peking," and "Who's Afraid of the Big Bad Wolf?" all on the roster. And if they had time, she'd record even more, as "Bewitched, Bothered, and Bewildered," "Cry Me a River," "A Sleepin' Bee," "Much More," and, of course, "Happy Days Are Here Again" were set to be included on the album as well.

If Barbra was tired — she was, after all, back at the Blue Angel every night, her name above the club's in newspaper advertisements — she didn't sound it. On these tracks, her voice was absolutely exquisite. Part of the reason why she sounded so good was the man she greeted as she slipped off her snowy coat: Peter Matz, the arranger and conductor Harold Arlen had recommended she work with on the album. Right from the start, Barbra had adored the bespectacled, goateed thirty-four-year-old Matz, trusting his artistic instincts completely. He'd arranged for Marlene Dietrich and Noël Coward, and just this past year had been nominated for a Tony for his musical direction of *No Strings*. Coward had called Matz "vital and imaginative," and thought the young arranger knew "more about the range of various instruments and the potentialities of different combinations than anyone . . . very exciting and stimulating."

Matz also had a sense of humor so dry that Coward's secretary called it "dehydrated." Delivering his droll observations with a straight face, Matz could make Barbra laugh, which wasn't easy, and which always went a very long way with her.

They'd worked out most of the songs ahead of time in Matz's West End Avenue apartment, just the two of them at the piano, while Matz's wife and two young sons listened from the other room. Matz took Peter Daniels's arrangements and expanded them for the orchestra, which Daniels considered "a big compliment." Although Matz had taken over as accompanist, Daniels still felt part of the collaboration and was set to go on tour with Barbra the following month to promote the album after its release.

In a remarkably short time, Barbra had developed a working relationship with this new Peter that was nearly as smooth and fruitful as the one with Daniels. Janet Matz, sitting behind a glass partition the day of the recording, marveled at how fluidly her husband and Barbra worked together. She knew Pete could be a bit of a perfectionist, and sometimes two perfectionists clashed, but she saw "no conflict whatsoever" with Barbra. Pete "took cues from her," Janet observed. If he saw Barbra struggling with a note, for example, he might say, "Let's keep the strings out here," knowing intuitively how to solve the problem. All Barbra needed to do was lift an eyebrow and Matz would understand he ought to consider slowing down the tempo or changing the color of the piece. In the control booth, engineer Frank Laico thought some of Barbra's vocals were "very harsh at times," but with Matz's "colors she sounded so great."

The collaboration with Matz worked so well, his wife believed, because he had "a strong personality" that matched Barbra's own. "Pete wasn't afraid of telling anyone off" if necessary, and so there were times when he bluntly told Barbra to just trust him and stop bellyaching. But neither was Matz someone who needed to have his way all the time. "Other people's ideas didn't threaten him," his wife said — the way Barbra had seemed to suspect Laurents or Weidman or Rome had felt threatened when she'd suggested changing something in *Wholesale*. To her delight, Matz was open to hearing what she thought, and sometimes he actually used her ideas. He discovered that two and a half years of nightclubs and Broadway had taught this young woman with no formal training an awful lot. Barbra's musical abilities, Matz concluded, were "monumental."

Yet still the Columbia brass wasn't sure of her. Mike Berniker was "walking a tightrope," Matz observed, "between the upstairs guys" and those in the recording studio. The execs were still telling Berniker, "Look, we can't spend a lot of money on this, we don't know if this woman is going to sell records." So the orchestra was doled out to Matz in small combinations in different sessions, rather than as one big band as he would have preferred. One session would have a small string section; another one, a rhythm section and four trombones. All because the guys in the suits still weren't sure this eccentric kid with the big voice would make them any money.

Undeterred by their lack of faith in her, Barbra took her place beside the microphone. Outside, the wind and snow were raging, but Barbra stayed supremely focused on the task at hand. She put everything out of her mind — the winter storm, the moneymen's doubts, the fear and anxiety she felt at home — and began to sing. Listening to her, the man conducting the orchestra was filled with far more faith in her potential than the record executives possessed. Before the year was out, Peter Matz believed, Barbra Streisand "would be a very big star."

3.

Lee Solters had his work cut out for him. Just as he was about to inaugurate a major publicity blitz for Barbra, all seven New York newspapers, plus two Long Island dailies, went on strike. That had happened on December 8; the strike was now approaching its second month. That meant no New York reviews for Barbra's album, set to be released in a few weeks, nor any for her Blue Angel engagement. In fact, to get the word out that she was even at the club, Max Gordon had advertised in the *Wall Street Journal,* which wasn't affected by the strike. But most significantly, the strike meant no New York coverage of Barbra herself — no profiles, no interviews — a critical loss at a very critical time. For, as Arthur Laurents had heard, Barbra was continually haranguing her publicists and agents, "Get me out there! Get me something new!"

Solters picked up the phone and started dialing. In his raspy Brooklyn accent, he pitched stories about this twenty-year-old sensation who'd stopped the show cold and was kooky as all get-out and possessed the voice of an angel — the standard talking points when pitching Barbra. With the strike on, Solters knew he'd have to rely on the syndicated columnists, even if most of the people who did the important hiring wouldn't see items run in the *Idaho Falls Post Reporter* or the *Corpus Christi Times*.

Some columnists, however, such as Earl Wilson and Dorothy Kilgallen, had their columns clipped and mailed regularly to Broadway producers and managers, and Wilson, at least, could be counted on to give Barbra good press. He'd just declared her the "hottest young comedienne in the country." Solters secured a number of such syndicated pieces during the strike and made sure to clip and mail them himself if necessary to get them into the hands of the city's movers and shakers.

And if the articles Solters arranged lacked New York visibility, they made up for it in their enthusiasm toward Barbra. Robert Ruark, whose thrice-weekly column for the Scripps-Howard newspapers was further distributed through the United Features Syndicate, wrote about everything that made him "glad, sad or mad." And Barbra Streisand made him glad. "She packs more personal dynamic power than anybody I can recall since Libby Holman or Helen Morgan," Ruark wrote after seeing Barbra at the Blue Angel. "She is the hottest thing to hit the entertainment field since Lena Horne erupted, and she will be around fifty years from now if good songs are still written to be sung by good singers."

Yet while the piece was a paean to Barbra's talent, style, and personality — "the next musical she makes will see her name over the title," Ruark wrote, which certainly went right into Barbra's press kit, highlighted for any prospective employers to see — it also spent a considerable amount of ink on her appearance. In 1963, Barbra Streisand's difference — her "otherness" — was so striking that people couldn't help but comment on it. "Her nose is more evocative of moose than muse," Ruark wrote, suggesting only the Blue Angel could have "established a girl with a bumpy nose and the unwieldy name of Streisand as a candidate for immortality." As the night went on, Ruark concluded, Barbra became "beautiful in your ears."

While Ruark's point was that appearances shouldn't matter, Solters decided a little counteroffensive was necessary when it came to Barbra's looks. He seems to have gotten an early look at Ruark's column, for nearly simultaneously, Earl Wilson's column carried what seemed like a rebuttal: "A bump on a girl's nose doesn't make any difference," Wilson quoted Barbra as saying. "After all, what is sex appeal but the bumps not only on a girl's nose but elsewhere?"

This became the new meme. Rather than just sit back and wait for the next snide comment about Barbra's "anteater nose," Solters now presented her as the girl who would "never get her nose fixed." She was defiant, proud of herself just as she was. No one need ever know she'd once considered a little reconstructive surgery.

Another piece orchestrated by Solters at this time was written by Mel Heimer, a Yonkers-based columnist for the King Features Syndicate, whose "My New York" column was a perfect venue for Barbra, especially during the strike. This one pushed that other recurring meme — Barbra the kook — and firmly established the term as being synonymous with the performer. "There is a full-blown, top-drawer kook in town," Heimer reported. "Miss Streisand has a good part of New York in the air, wondering if she's for real. Miss S. is a slim, slightly round-shouldered sort who, even when being interviewed, seems to have her eyes and ears fixed on the sight and sound of far-away flutes." (Rarely has an interviewer described Barbra's ambition better.) "She will do anything to arouse attention, the first requirement of a good kook." (As examples, Heimer gave the "born in Madagascar" line and the bit about the nightgown being worn as a dress.) "These nights she's doubling into places like the Bon Soir and Blue Angel to sing, and all I can only hope is that meeting normal people won't standardize her." (Barbra's kookiness, then, was something to love.)

The most unusual publicity Solters was able to wrangle for his client that strike-hobbled winter was inclusion in a "Singing Valentines" spread in the February issue of *Show* magazine. Various celebrities were photographed in amusing situations accompanied by a Valentine's verse. Barbra was shot from above hooked up to a cardiogram machine — how much kookier could one get? — while curled in a fetal position, her hair loose and her eyes closed. "Roses are red, cardiograms are blue," her verse went. "I'm Barbra Streisand . . . so *nu*?" An asterisk led to a definition of *nu* as a "central European" word to describe a mix of assertion, *weltschmerz* (world weariness), and wonder. "Miss Streisand," the magazine assured its readers, "uses it here to mean Happy Valentine's Day."

Finally, there was more of that old publicity trick of strategically placing questions in syndicated "TV Mailbag" columns. "I think Barbara Streisand is a very exciting performer," wrote one correspondent, who, of course, was really Solters, misspelling her name purposely and making sure to mention her single "My Coloring Book," which had just been released. "What else has she done?" he wanted to know. The answer, also written by Solters, pointed out the correct spelling was "Barbra," and revealed that she was "packing them in every night at the Blue Angel" — a nice bit of publicity for that show since the local papers weren't able to report on it.

This was extraordinary coverage for a young woman who no longer had a regular television or Broadway show to make her newsworthy. The flurry of publicity that Solters managed to rake up for Barbra during the winter of 1962–63 proved how valuable he could be to her. Not only was he attempting to drum up business for her at the Blue Angel, but he was also keeping her long-range goals in mind as well. To Mike Connolly, the gossip columnist for the *Hollywood Reporter,* Solters seems to have passed on a few juicy, if unsubstantiated, tidbits. Connolly had just announced that Barbra was set to fly out to the Coast to do an episode of the television show *Stoney Burke,* a Western series starring Jack Lord. "From there," Connolly continued, it would "be just a step for Barbra to star in *The Fanny Brice Story.*" If there was ever talk about Barbra appearing on *Stoney Burke,* it was just that — talk — and certainly any announcement about starring in the Brice story was still just wishful thinking. But that hardly got in the way of a good press agent like Solters. Besides, he knew the *Hollywood Reporter* was read every day by Ray Stark, and of all the people he didn't want forgetting Barbra during this interval, Stark was on the top of his list.

4.

Backstage at the Shubert Theatre, where Barbra had dressed every night for *Wholesale* not so long ago, Barry Dennen was practicing the lead role for the national touring company of the Broadway smash, David Merrick's *Stop the World — I Want to Get Off.* He wasn't practicing the lead because he had the lead — that had gone to Joel Grey — but because he was the lead's understudy. Still, after so much summer stock and off-Broadway, Barry was exultant that he was "in a Broadway theater at last." It was his "first real, important job." The company planned to open in Milwaukee, but for now they were rehearsing at the Shubert, where the Broadway version was still running. In the process they'd gotten to know some of the Broadway cast, including the director-star Anthony Newley. On this afternoon, Newley popped his head out of his dressing room and invited Barry and a few others to come in and hear a new album of a "really fabulous performer . . . [a] wonderful singer."

For some reason, Barry felt uneasy. Inside the dressing room, he discovered the reason for his dread when Newley held up the album for them to see. On the cover was a photograph of Barbra, emerging from the shadows, standing in front of a microphone in a herringbone vest, her red lips pursed in song. Her eyes were heavy with the mascara and false eyelashes Barry had seen Bob give her dozens of times in his apartment. *The Barbra Streisand Album* was the simple yet effective title.

Newley dropped the disk onto the record player. "Cry Me a River" was the first track, a song Barry had never heard Barbra sing, but which, in its earliest renditions, had been all about him. Other tracks were more familiar. Barry had been the one to teach Barbra "A Sleepin' Bee" and "Keepin' Out of Mischief Now." Barbra had never heard these songs until Barry had played them for her. Now they were on her album. But the hardest of all to hear was "Who's Afraid of the Big Bad Wolf?" Barry still remembered the day they'd dreamed it up, almost as a joke.

Looking around at his fellow actors as they enjoyed the album, Barry wondered how he might explain to them his "part in Barbra's story." He realized it would be impossible. He'd probably sound bitter, or jealous, or regretful for not treating her better — or, worse still, as if he were trying to name-drop. It was hard to believe that saying he knew Barbra Streisand — the skinny kid with the shopping bags — might now be considered name-dropping. Overcome with emotion, Barry slipped out of Newley's dressing room, making his way out to the empty theater. There, slumping down into a seat, he buried his face in his hands.

5.

Standing in front of a distracted crowd at the Café Pompeii at the Eden Roc Hotel in Miami Beach, Barbra might have been forgiven for thinking that the more things changed, the more they stayed the same. Here she was, back on a nightclub tour, singing to rooms that were sometimes half empty and almost always noisy. But she was on tour to promote her album, which needed all the help it could get. Released on February 25, *The Barbra Streisand Album* — a title she'd settled on after Columbia had suggested *Sweet and Saucy Streisand,* which had made her nauseous — had gotten off to a lackluster start, despite a decent (albeit somewhat late) review from *Billboard,* which predicted it "should draw an enormous amount of play from the good radio stations."

So far that hadn't happened. Barbra's album was overshadowed by blockbusters from, among others, Joan Baez, who'd released a live concert album, and Peter, Paul, and Mary, who were riding the wave of their number one hit, "Puff, the Magic Dragon." Barbra, however, was doing her best to drive up sales. Her tour had been arranged by Marty and Joe Glaser, the president and founder of Associated Booking who had taken over as her nightclub agent, which showed how high Barbra had risen in the agency's esteem. She'd kicked off things at the beginning of February at the Revere Frolic, a seaside theater outside Boston, where she performed two shows nightly. Although *Billboard* thought Barbra was "getting the kind of reception [at the Frolic] accorded artists on their way up," the *Boston Globe* advertised her as "Miss Marmel Steisand," clearly having no idea who she was.

The indignities only continued. From Boston it was on to Cleveland, where she cohosted *The Mike Douglas Show* for a week starting February 11. With the genial host, Barbra had spoofed Jeanette MacDonald–Nelson Eddy movies, played tiddlywinks on the floor, and participated in some calisthenics taught by a visiting exercise instructor — though not with much enthusiasm. By the end of the set, Barbra — never much of a "joiner" — had retreated to the back where she stood watching the rest of the cast bend and squat, a somewhat condescending smile fixed on her face. There were, apparently, some limits to what she would put herself through.

But the Douglas show also gave her the chance to sing every song from the upcoming album — fantastic publicity as far as it went, which actually wasn't very far at all. The syndicated show, a Westinghouse production like *PM East*, reached only Midwest audiences; the New York, Boston, Baltimore, Philadelphia, and West Coast markets had no idea as yet who Mike Douglas was. Going into the gig, Barbra and Marty would have understood that any boost the Douglas show might bring to her album sales would be confined to the Midwest. No doubt that was why they'd asked for a concurrent nightclub act, to maximize their time and effort. Douglas got them booked at the Chateau, located in Lakewood, a west-side suburb of Cleveland. Barbra was paid $2,500 for the week—decent money, but it turned out to be a dismal experience. A cold snap inhibited turnout, and Barbra played to half-empty houses for most of her run. Peter Daniels, who'd come along as her accompanist, could see that she was "a little depressed."

A little depression turned into a whole lot by the time she faced the indifferent audiences at the Eden Roc in Miami. Soldiering on with her nightclub appearances, Barbra had been distressed to realize that for all her effort, the tour hadn't seemed to help the album much at all. A few weeks after its release, *The Barbra Streisand Album* remained mired at the bottom of the charts.

Yet whenever she'd fret, Marty assured her that he believed the album would take off. She had, after all, the backing of some pretty important people in the world of music. Jule Styne was still out there rooting for her. Stephen Sondheim, once unsure of her, was now considering her for a musical he was writing, *Anyone Can Whistle*. Leonard Bernstein, impressed with how she sang "My Name Is Barbara," was talking her up to colleagues. Sammy Cahn thought she was absolutely adorable after she'd told him that he looked like her dentist, so he gave her a little box inscribed TO THE SINGER FROM THE DENTIST and told everyone within earshot that he thought she was the best.

And, in the most public expression of support of all, Harold Arlen had written her album's back-cover liner notes. "Did you ever hear Helen Morgan sing?" Arlen asked, with the album designer cleverly positioning a thumbnail photo of Morgan next to the question. "Or were you ever at the theatre when Fanny Brice clowned in her classic comedic way—or Beatrice Lillie deliciously poked fun at all sham and pomp?" (Thumbnails of Brice and Lillie accompanied the text.) "Have you heard our top vocalists 'belt,' 'whisper,' or sing with that steady and urgent beat behind them? Have you ever seen a painting by Modigliani?" (A little sketch of an odd-looking woman followed.) "If you have, do not think the above has been ballooned out of proportion. I advise you to watch Barbra Streisand's career. This young lady (a mere twenty) has a stunning future."

The old-guard musical-theater elite had lined up in solid support behind the enterprise of Barbra Streisand. Word up and down Broadway was that the album was a must; it was no surprise that a musical-theater type such as Anthony Newley had it in his hands soon after it was released. But what was missing from Barbra's publicity was any sense of youth. Comparing her to Helen Morgan and Beatrice Lillie was hardly going to attract those who were buying the albums of Joan Baez and Peter, Paul, and Mary. Still, the biggest-selling album at the moment was the soundtrack to *West Side Story,* so Broadway music was still profitable. The trouble was that *The Barbra Streisand Album,* for all Barbra's Broadway provenance, wasn't a show-tunes record. Just what it was remained something of mystery.

And that was a problem. Goddard Lieberson had said that Barbra couldn't be categorized — and while he'd used that as a compliment when he'd introduced her at the Bon Soir, he had also worried about that fact right from the start. The question remained how to position Barbra and her album, which contained a mix of up- and down-tempo songs, offbeat standards, and performance pieces such as "Come to the Supermarket" and "Big Bad Wolf." For the predominately youthful record-buying market, these weren't draws, and no amount of accolades from Harold Arlen was going to persuade a young fan of Elvis Presley or Lesley Gore to give Barbra's album a shot.

By the middle part of March, while Barbra was languishing in Miami, there was a terrible feeling among everyone involved that the album was sinking like a rock. It had now been out for a month, and it still hadn't caught fire. Maybe Lieberson had been right: Barbra was simply too special for records. The lack of enthusiasm at the Chateau and the Eden Roc seemed to prove that her audience of gay men, urban hipsters, and theater aficionados was just too small for major commercial success. After all the trouble of the contract and the tour, it would be a terrible admission for Barbra and Marty to have to make.

As Barbra walked offstage and headed back to her room, the depression she was feeling was as much personal as it was professional. Elliott had been with her for the start of the tour in Boston and Cleveland. But during a brief interim in New York before she'd flown to Florida, Barbra had bid her boyfriend farewell as he headed off to London to start rehearsals for *On the Town*. Earl Wilson reported that Barbra had been "talked out of going to London" with Elliott by her managers, who "feared she would stop her career right when it [was] starting." In return for Barbra's agreement to stay in the U.S., Wilson revealed, her managers promised to get her three television shows in England "so she could visit three times" in the course of the next year.

Still, it was hard for some to believe that she ever truly considered going to London without a job just so she could cling to Elliott's side. Barbra was hardly "the backstage kind of girlfriend," Bob said. Besides, with the possibility of the Brice show still out there — or *The Student Gypsy*, or *Anyone Can Whistle*, or David Merrick's musical revival of *The Rainmaker*, for which her name had also been mentioned — Barbra wasn't likely to go anywhere that made it difficult for her to get in to audition.

And maybe a bit of a break from Elliott wasn't all that terrible to contemplate. Barbra was still in love with him and still committed to making the relationship work. No one doubted that. In fact, as friends had heard, there had even been a brief consideration of marriage before he left, to seal the deal between them and provide a veneer of protection while they were apart. But Elliott had a dim view of the institution of marriage. He thought it imposed "something technical on an otherwise viable relationship," and he worried it could change things "dramatically." That Barbra didn't push it suggested that she, too, wasn't quite ready, and that maybe she saw some benefit in having a bit of a breather. They had been arguing more than ever after all, and Barbra had found herself increasingly impatient with Elliott's career insecurities, especially as she was going through her own anxieties.

So she retreated alone to her room at the Eden Roc. After this, it

As Barbra and Chaplin pose for their *Playbill* photo, their body language provides evidence that their affair, once passionate, was over. © *Bettmann/CORBIS*

A rare glimpse of the *Funny Girl* company before their Boston preview, December 1963. Danny Meehan, Allyn Ann McLerie, Sydney Chaplin, and Barbra listen to director Garson Kanin. Within the month, Meehan's part would be marginalized and McLerie's would be cut entirely. Kanin would be fired after the show premiered in Boston. *Photofest*

Barbra with the men who wrote the songs that would provide the soundtrack to her legend: Jule Styne (at piano) and Bob Merrill. Styne was infatuated with her; Merrill was more wary.

© *Bettmann/CORBIS*

The famous pregnant bride scene from *Funny Girl.* Barbra had proven that she was as much a "kook" as Fanny Brice ever was; by now, the two had been conflated into one image. *Photofest*

Fran Stark—Ray's wife and Fanny Brice's daughter—had been less enthusiastic about Barbra's casting, but by the time of the premiere, she was all smiles. Here she is presenting the star to her brother, William Brice. *mptvimages.com*

With their marriage back on track (for the moment), Elliott kisses Barbra at the opening night party after the *Funny Girl* premiere. He knew how uncomfortable she was and wanted to protect her. © *Bettmann/CORBIS*

The man who'd guided Barbra's rise to the top, her manager, Marty Erlichman, continued to keep a close eye on his charge even as she tries to escape the theater in disguise. Barbra had come to fear the crush of fans every night outside the stage door. *Collection of Matt Howe*

For all her acclaim, Barbra still found it difficult to win praise from her mother, Diana Kind, who joined her backstage (top) with an uncle and aunt, and who insisted Barbra and Elliott be present for sister Rozzie's sweet-sixteen birthday party. The stress of performing every night was getting to Barbra, and if the photo (bottom) is any evidence, she had started smoking again. *Collection of Stuart Lippner*

In just five years, a redefinition of beauty, talent, and success.

© 1978 Bob Willoughby / mptvimages.com

was off to San Francisco to fulfill her long-ago contract with Enrico Banducci at the hungry i, then back to New York for a gig at Basin Street East at the Shelton Towers Hotel. There were more clubs after that if she could bear to look at the list. And after that — who knew? All Barbra could have known at that point was that the winter of 1963 looked an awful lot like the winter of 1961. Whatever had happened to going straight to the top?

6.

The crowds had returned to hear her, but now the problem was something else. Barbra couldn't sing. Or she didn't *think* she could sing.

With Marty at her side, she found the little studio opposite the Safeway grocery store on Oakland's busy College Avenue, about half an hour's walk from the Berkeley campus. This was where she'd been told she could find the woman who might help her. Anxious and frightened, Barbra made her way inside a small room with all the curtains drawn to keep out the light.

A few nights earlier, she'd opened at the hungry i across the bay in San Francisco. Banducci had done a good job of talking her up: "This town will go crazy for her," he quoted himself on the posters announcing her opening night. To the press, he also told the story of their first meeting back in New York, reframing it with the buzzwords of Barbra's current publicity: "She was easily the kookiest, most arresting-looking kid I'd ever seen." In building up her offbeat appeal, Banducci had Barbra calling him a "moron" and an "idiot" in Irvin Arthur's office, and instead of being offended, he said he'd replied, "Sign that girl for me right away." Certainly Barbra had been calculatingly direct in that first meeting, but she wasn't the type to call someone names, especially someone she'd just met. But the theatrical Banducci knew how to plant the seeds of a legend.

Meanwhile, Columbia, responding to Marty's calls to do more to promote the album, had sent out invitations to some of San Francisco's better-known critics to a special preshow concert at six PM.

That meant Barbra had to go on stage *three* times that first evening, since she performed two shows a night, at eight and eleven. (The two shows were distinct from each other, and some people from the first show stayed for the second.) But the preshow event proved to be a smart move because it created a real buzz about her, and the tough-to-please critics, feeling catered to, had responded enthusiastically, ensuring sizeable crowds every night since.

"Barbra Streisand is unquestionably one of the most successful performers ever to appear at the hungry i," Ralph J. Gleason wrote in the *San Francisco Chronicle*. "People went away talking about her and three hours later, I heard two couples on Broadway singing one of the songs she did. Barbra Streisand has that kind of impact." The *Chronicle* ran photos of Barbra making all sorts of faces as she sang—pouting, serious, comical—next to the headline: A SPECIAL KIND OF MAGIC.

But all that singing was getting to her. Barbra was finding that she was having trouble holding her notes. When she had arrived in San Francisco, her voice had been somewhat hoarse. Certainly all the leapfrogging from climate to climate couldn't have helped: mid-twenties in Cleveland; teens and icy rain in New York; eighties in Miami; forties and rainy when she'd made a quick flight back to New York to make another appearance on *The Ed Sullivan Show;* then the low fifties, cloudy and damp, when she'd arrived in San Francisco. After all that, who wouldn't catch a cold? But clearly Barbra worried that her voice troubles were the result of more than just a passing bug. That's why Marty had asked Banducci if he might recommend a vocal coach with whom Barbra could do some work. The club owner had known exactly the woman to send them to. And so they made their way to this dark little studio on College Avenue.

Judy Davis called herself "a vocal plumber." What she did was simple: "I fix pipes," she said. She was a brassy, grandiloquent lady who dressed in colorful clothes and reminded at least one student of Auntie Mame. "Well, my dear," she'd say, after listening to a prospective student sing and examining his or her throat and diaphragm, "I must tell you, this is exactly what you're doing wrong. We're going to have to rearrange some of these things, break this habit." Singers had many bad habits, Davis believed, like improper breathing or insufficient projection. "Singers are not known to be bright," she'd tell a pupil who didn't regularly perform the exercises she'd prescribed, "but don't prove it to the world."

For all her expertise, Davis herself couldn't sing a note. When she was nineteen, her vocal chords had been injured during a tonsillectomy, leaving her with a raspy voice that prevented a singing career of her own. To understand what had happened to her on the operating table, Davis turned to *Gray's Anatomy,* thoroughly familiarizing herself with the physiology of the human voice. After earning bachelor's and master's degrees in music from the University of California at Berkeley, she headed to Los Angeles, where she taught movie actors how to lip-synch soundtracks. Now married to professional tennis player Frank Kovacs, Davis attracted a stellar clientele to her voice studio in Oakland. Frank Sinatra had been known to fly her to Las Vegas to help him practice before a show. Much of the talent that came through the hungry i or its sister club across the street, the Purple Onion, had spent time in Davis's studio. She had pretty much taught the Kingston Trio how to sing. When people asked her to describe her methods, which they often did, Davis found she was unable to do so. She just knew when people were "obstructing the performance of their vocal chords," she explained, and through exercises and breathing techniques, she could show them "how not to do that."

The fear that had brought Barbra to Judy Davis was as much psychological as physical. It was, after all, an extremely low period for her. She felt Elliott's absence keenly. That may have been why she'd allowed a story to spread that they had gotten married. Earl Wilson was reporting, "Funny singer Barbra Streisand wanted to keep it a secret that she married actor Elliott Gould just before he left for London, but forgot herself and wore her wedding ring to *The Ed Sullivan Show.*" Whatever ring Barbra had been wearing when she'd made that flying trip from Miami to New York hadn't been a wedding band, but apparently she was okay with giving that impression. She knew that admitting she'd been living with a man outside of matrimony would have been completely unacceptable to a large swath of the public; surely Lee Solters had pointed out that the bluenoses still hadn't forgiven Elizabeth Taylor for shacking up with Richard Burton. Unmarried cohabitation simply wasn't tolerated in the public eye. Even couples clearly not ready to tie the knot, such as Sandra Dee and Bobby Darin, had been forced to do so anyway to ward off impressions that they might be sleeping together.

Yet for Barbra, some friends believed, the lie about being married to Elliott went even deeper than that. She was lonely, feeling untethered to the man she loved. So Barbra may have liked imagining that something was holding her and Elliott together.

For the moment, all she had to sustain her was her voice. If her voice went, she had nothing. And suddenly, in the midst of her depression, she began questioning herself: How *did* she hold her notes so long? How *was* she able to sing without ever having been trained in voice?

In the past, Barbra had just shrugged off such questions. If she willed herself, she believed, she could do anything. But now her self-confidence had plummeted. One night she suspected she wasn't holding her notes quite as long, and when she tried deliberately to hold them, she found she couldn't. Her "consciousness of an unconscious thing," she realized, had made her "impotent."

Sitting there in Davis's dimly lit studio, Barbra felt like, in her own words, "a person who was paralyzed in her legs having to relearn to walk." She was being dramatic; it was hardly as bad as all that. She was performing two shows every night at the hungry i, and the applause was certainly greater there than it had been in Cleveland or Miami. But what mattered was how Barbra *felt* — and she felt she wasn't at her best. No doubt she remembered off nights during *Wholesale* when she knew she was less than perfect and the way people had still applauded for her. She felt they'd been conditioned to do so; and she probably felt that way now. She didn't deserve the applause, she believed, and Barbra could never enjoy acclaim that she hadn't earned.

And this particular gig was crucial. In some ways, San Francisco was as important as New York to a singer's career. The city by the bay was a cultural mecca of its own, fiercely independent, producing and nurturing talent like nowhere else — and the hungry i, at 599 Jackson Street in the North Beach neighborhood, was its chief breeding ground. Mort Sahl, the sharp-tongued political comedian, had gotten his start there; so had the Kingston Trio. Both Phyllis Diller and Orson Bean had played the club, and Bill Cosby, folk singer Glenn Yarbrough, jazzman Vince Guaraldi, comedian Shelley Berman, and musical satirist Tom Lehrer had all received career boosts from the i. For the first few nights of Barbra's run, her opening act had been fellow game changer and rule breaker, comedian Woody Allen.

It was with justification that Howard Taubman of the *New York Times* called the i "the most influential nightclub west of the Mississippi." If Barbra could make it there, winning over San Francisco sophisticates, then she'd prove she wasn't just a New York phenomenon. She needed to generate the kind of buzz on the West Coast that she already enjoyed on the East if her career was ever going to go national.

So there was a great deal riding on the slender shoulders of the scared twenty-year-old who sat looking up at Judy Davis and asking for her help. Davis's heart went out to the kid. She recognized that Barbra was "being catapulted into a position" most performers took many years to reach, "almost as if she were shot out of a cannon," Davis thought. What this "sensitive girl" craved, Davis realized, was "a hand to hold and a pat on the back and somebody to tell her everything was all right." Certainly that had never been the norm in Barbra's life; it was precisely what she had given up expecting so many years ago from her mother. But when Davis offered her a hand to hold, Barbra took it eagerly. That day, in the forty-four-year-old nurturing Davis, Barbra found another mother substitute, a parental figure to fill that hole in the middle of herself.

Immediately the two of them got down to work. The little studio was a safe haven for Barbra; its simple piano and soft, diffused light — and the frolicking of Davis's black poodle Poupette — made Barbra feel at home. Davis was under no illusions that she needed to teach Barbra to sing, even if that was what her client suddenly believed she needed to learn. "No singing teacher can teach anyone to sing," she explained. A singer was born a singer, she said, and all she could do was teach "what tones are right and what techniques are best." She found Barbra to be "a curious, searching girl" who wanted to understand how "this instrument of hers" worked. Davis produced photographs and diagrams of the lungs, esophagus, and diaphragm, explaining to Barbra the physical process of singing. That alone seemed to ease some of Barbra's fears.

Yet no doubt what she responded to most were the tender, yet firm, ministrations of an empathetic older woman she respected. There was a similar patronage taking place at the hungry i, where Barbra flourished under the careful, compassionate care of Banducci. Three thousand miles from home, Barbra had found, even if just temporarily, the parents she never had. Banducci was as erudite and sophisticated — if a bit more florid and flamboyant — as she imagined her father would have been. Like Barbra, he had discarded an inadequate first name — Harry — for something more distinctive, taking "Enrico" as a tribute to Enrico Caruso. At the age of thirteen he'd left his provincial hometown of Bakersfield, California, for exciting San Francisco, where he'd studied under the concertmaster of the San Francisco Symphony. As proprietor of the hungry i — it meant "hungry intellectual" — since 1950, Banducci had been one of the first, along with Jay Landesman, another of Barbra's patrons, to popularize the beatnik movement. To one reporter, Banducci "modestly disclaimed having everything to do with the beatnik craze that . . . spread across the country," but he was also "careful to imply that it did not happen without his good offices." Nowadays the heavy-set, pencil-mustachioed Banducci was never seen without his brown beret, white sneakers, tan chinos, and "the most expansive white and figured sweater ever to encumber a man's neck, chest, waist, and arms."

It didn't take long for Barbra to regain her footing in this supportive environment. Although she had struggled with distracted audiences elsewhere on this tour, she didn't need to worry about that at the i, thanks to Banducci. The three-hundred-person audience was seated in a semicircle around the stage. And while their canvas chairs had wide, flat arms ideal for setting down their drinks — which were served by a solicitous corps of Japanese waiters — once the lights dimmed, all drinking and eating in the auditorium ceased. Banducci insisted on a "quietude in the audience" when the performer stepped out onto the stage. All alone, lit by a battery of spotlights in front of a stark brick wall, the performer could command the attention of the audience without any competition. For this, especially so soon after the Eden Roc fiasco, Barbra was no doubt very grateful to her host.

She'd also become close with the club's announcer. Alvah Bessie had been a novelist, journalist, and Hollywood screenwriter, nominated for an Academy Award for *Objective Burma* in 1945. He'd also been a member of the Hollywood Ten, imprisoned for ten months and blacklisted by the film industry for refusing to testify in front of the House Un-American Activities Committee. The blacklisting had destroyed his career. Now he was running the lights and sound board at the hungry i and introducing the entertainers. Bessie's story was the complete inverse of those of Jerry Robbins and Isobel Lennart, two others of Barbra's acquaintance who had histories with HUAC. Barbra likely took notice of how very different Bessie's life was — hunched down anonymously in the shadows, positioning the spotlight on other people — from the lives of informers such as Robbins and Lennart — making movies and Broadway shows and being publicly acclaimed for it. For someone as perceptive as Barbra, the injustice must have resonated.

Her interval in San Francisco was a turning point for her. As she had in Detroit, she found a home away from home, a place where new friends and new challenges provided her with just the balm she needed. Certainly no place she'd ever been had *looked* quite as magical as San Francisco: the hills and the steep, winding streets, the delicate Queen Anne houses and Spanish mission churches, the Golden Gate Bridge shining in the distance, the clanging of the cable cars, and everywhere breathtaking vistas of land, sea, and sky. For Barbra, the city was a place of healing and tranquility.

7.

On a night well into her four-week run at the hungry i, after numerous sessions with Judy Davis had restored a measure of her self-confidence, Barbra waited backstage for Alvah Bessie to announce her. She was ready for her comeback. She was, as local critic Ralph Gleason described her, "a tawny, feline, long-haired girl with a mouth like a character from Oz" who was "a practiced performer . . . expert and effective." Her ease onstage had returned, showing up in everything she did: the way she stood or sat, "her approach to the microphone, the tilt of her head, the spreading of her arms, the tossing of her hair, the raising of her eyebrows."

Tonight the show would be recorded by a young engineer named Reese Hamel, who kept his equipment in the back of his Volkswagen bus and dragged his cables through the club's back door. A little less sophisticated than Columbia's elaborate recording session at the Bon Soir in the fall, but it would prove far more successful. Hamel had suggested to Barbra that she might someday want to add a live recording to her Columbia catalog. When she'd agreed, he'd hauled in his cables. Obviously Barbra felt that her voice was better if she consented to be recorded.

"Now ladies and gentlemen," Bessie announced over the loudspeaker, "the hungry i takes great pride in presenting Miss Barbra Streisand." No doubt he had been instructed carefully by the lady herself on how to pronounce her name correctly, and he did.

As the packed house gave her a warm welcome, Barbra sailed into

"Any Place I Hang My Hat Is Home." As if to demonstrate that she was back in top form, she held the last note of the song for nine and a half seconds, an extraordinarily long time. If it seemed a bit show-offy, she didn't care. All that mattered was that she could still do it. Next up was "Cry Me a River." This night, Barbra's rendition of the song was far superior to the manic howl she'd displayed on *The Dinah Shore Show* (though that program still hadn't aired). She eschewed the theatrics that had so repelled Fran Stark and concentrated once again on the raw heartache of the song — which maybe, just maybe, reflected her own *via dolorosa* these past few months regarding Elliott. When she was finished, she clearly appreciated the applause. "*Grazie, grazie,*" she murmured.

She then launched into the kind of monologue that had been part of her act almost from the very start, but which in recent months had gained a more structured format. "I don't like to sing all the time," she said, and that much was certainly true. "I mean, one song right after another." What she was doing was setting up a segment of her show that she'd rehearsed nearly as vigorously as the songs. "Let's see," she mused, "what should I talk about?" When someone shouted for her to talk about "Who's Afraid of the Big Bad Wolf?" she responded, "I *sing* that. I can't talk about that."

Of course, she needed no suggestions; she knew exactly what she was going to talk about. She commenced the story of a girl — "an African girl," Barbra explained — whose sister had run off with her lover. Thinking this was the lead-in to a sad ballad, the audience sat in rapt, respectful silence. "She decided to kill herself," Barbra said of the girl. "And she figured the best way to do this was to drown herself in the river." Still the audience sat mute, hanging on every word. Could this be some old tribal morality tale? "So it was this one day," Barbra went on, "and she was strolling down to the river to drown, and she tripped and scraped her knees." A beat. "And also broke her glasses."

Finally the audience tittered, starting to suspect that this all might be a joke. "Just at this moment," Barbra continued, "the lover and the sister drove by in a taxi — they have them in Africa — and they started laughing at her." By now the audience was laughing, too. The story went on from there — a long, ridiculous, rambling tale that ultimately ended with a feeble punch line that made little sense. But it didn't matter that the story wasn't really very funny or witty. By breaking out of the serious singer-by-the-piano mode, Barbra had shaken up tradition and thereby set herself apart — precisely what the "kooky" reputation was intended to do, whether in print or on television or on the stage. And the audience adored her for it.

She was, in fact, selling her personality as much as her voice. This came through again a short time later as she introduced the band. Slipping into her old Mae West impersonation, she gestured to drummer Benny Barth and cooed, "On the left side heah, weighin' in at one-hundred-'n'-eighty-three in black trunks . . . is Benny." There was another beat. "And he doesn't." Barbra waited for the audience to get her pun. When a handful of people started to laugh, she giggled. "Benny" was slang for Benzedrine tablets, which many in the night-club scene took illegally as stimulants.

Barth and the rest of the band — which also included a bass and guitar — were hungry i employees. But the pianist, of course, was Peter Daniels, Barbra's faithful companion on the road. She introduced him a little more intimately than she did the others, though she characteristically resisted sentimentality by affecting the air of a snooty society lady. "And now, for your pleasure, on the piano — he's not on the piano, he's sitting there in front of the piano — a very fine musician. He's more than a pianist. He's more than an arranger. He's more than a friend. He's — Petah!" She said his name as if she were Bette Davis, and this brought hoots from the audience right away. "Petah Daniels!"

The rest of the concert was more straightforward, though she did have some fun with the "Wolf" song, as she called it. "I'm going to do a standard," she announced, playing on the old criticism that she rarely sang the kind of standards that encouraged people to "sing along, swing along, snap [their] fingers," as Barbra put it. So, she announced, she would "compromise." What she gave them, of course, was "Who's Afraid of the Big Bad Wolf?" Some people did indeed sing along. Wrapping up the show was "Happy Days Are Here Again," which Barbra put over gorgeously, and which earned sustained applause. "You'd be so nice to come home to," she purred in gratitude to the audience.

Of course, at the moment, she had no one to come home to. She remained despondent without Elliott. But despondent did not mean desperate. What Hamel's recording had documented for posterity was that, by the end of her run at the hungry i, Barbra had found herself again. Thanks to the solicitude of Judy Davis, the guardianship of Enrico Banducci, and the nightly outpouring of affection from San Franciscans, Barbra would leave that city on a wave of acclaim. She might not have a play, or a best-selling album, but the young woman on Hamel's tape recording believed in herself again, and that was enough for now.

CHAPTER THIRTEEN

Spring 1963

1.

After almost a year, Barbra and Bob were enjoying a happy reunion. This afternoon they were hunched down in a movie theater, popping handfuls of Raisinets, watching Dolores Hart jet around the world as a stewardess in *Come Fly with Me*. As Frankie Avalon crooned the title tune, panoramic shots of London, Paris, and the Mediterranean filled the screen, and Barbra let out a sigh. "Wouldn't it be great to go there someday?" she mused.

"But, Barbra," Bob said, "we're already here."

That was the odd thing. They were in Oxford, England, watching the film, not New York. A couple of weeks earlier, Bob, whose extended Paris vacation had turned into a residency when he started contributing to magazines there, had gotten a wire from Barbra. She was flying to London to see Elliott. But since Elliott had rehearsals during the day, could Bob pop over from Paris to keep her company? Barbra's old pal had happily obliged, but now that he was there, he could barely get her out of her hotel room. Barbra preferred staying put, "steaming her clothes, folding and organizing them, then folding and organizing them again," Bob observed. The movie theater was the farthest she'd strayed so far.

But Barbra hadn't come to England for sightseeing. She'd come with one purpose and one purpose only: to reconnect with Elliott. The separation had been weighing heavily on her. If she hadn't come now, she wouldn't have had another chance to see him until maybe next fall, since she was booked solid through the summer. At the moment, she had a bit of a break before her next obligation, a two-week engagement at the New York nightclub Basin Street East that started on May 13. And besides, hadn't she and Elliott made a vow to always be together on their birthdays? So, very soon after leaving San Francisco, Barbra, her new passport in hand, had boarded a flight for her first transcontinental trip. On April 24, she had turned twenty-one in England, Elliott at her side. Which was the way it was supposed to be.

Not that it had been all honey pie and happiness between them. Barbra found that Elliott had been gambling quite a bit, and he seemed to want to believe that she'd been cheating on him in New York or San Francisco. He was also consumed with rehearsals most of the time, which were being held at a small theater in the town of Oxford. The cast was lodged at a local hotel, where Barbra had settled in as well. As much as Oxford might be, in the words of the poet Matthew Arnold, the "sweet city with her dreaming spires," and home to a magnificent medieval university, it was hardly swinging London. Barbra quickly grew bored with Elliott gone all day and often into the evenings. She'd been thrilled when Bob had showed up — though she still wouldn't risk venturing too far afield with him just in case Elliott got out of rehearsals early.

Wandering the streets of Oxford with Bob, daffodils growing everywhere, Barbra wore a heavy fur coat, bell-bottomed jeans, and tennis shoes. In the United States, thanks to all her TV appearances, she was beginning to be recognized as she strolled through New York or other cities. But here she was still anonymous. She and Bob often ate at a Chinese restaurant near the hotel, where Barbra enjoyed paying with the colorful British money. In her head, however, she was always converting pounds into dollars, keeping track of how much she was spending on this trip.

Despite her frugality, money was no longer really an issue for her. Not only were there the increased revenues from nightclubs, but at last report, Barbra's album was finally on the move. On April 18, the disk had made it on to *Billboard*'s chart of the Top 150 Albums (at number 118). This reflected sales from the week before, and Barbra could thank San Francisco record buyers for much of her surge, as well as her March 24 appearance on *Ed Sullivan,* on which she'd sung "Cry Me a River." The following week the album had raced up the chart to number 83 and won *Billboard*'s coveted red star that indicated an album markedly on the rise. By the following week, April 27, *The Barbra Streisand Album* had reached number 41. The momentum was clear.

Barbra's impressive rise on the charts was also fueled by a sudden explosion of reviews, which Solters had finally managed to secure a month and a half after the album's release. No doubt he'd been working the phones and calling in as many favors as he could. Record critic Dick Van Patten admitted that he'd overlooked the album the previous month, rectifying the situation by calling Barbra "a potentially great new stylist [who] sounds like a veteran already." Dick Kleiner, who'd already been an advocate for Barbra, now listed her ahead of Judy Garland in his syndicated roundup of the best new albums for the Newspaper Enterprise Association, saying that with this disk, Barbra "shows herself to be one of the greatest." Walter Winchell also weighed in, raving about the album and especially the way Barbra put "the silk in 'Happy Days Are Here Again.'" The columnist added that she reminded him of "Judy, Lena, and Peggy."

After they left the movie theater, or on a night very similar, Barbra brought Bob to dinner with Elliott and Elspeth March, who was playing Madam Dilly, the music teacher, in *On the Town.* March, once married to the movie actor Stewart Granger, had made a number of films in the past year — *Playboy of the Western World* and *Dr. Crippen,* among others — and was about to go into production on *The Three Lives of Thomasina,* in which she would provide the voice of the cat. Barbra peppered the older actress with questions about moviemaking. She seemed to like how March had been able to play so many different characters in the course of a year.

To the distinguished British actress, Barbra must have seemed like a wide-eyed young novice. Not to March was Barbra anything noteworthy. She didn't know about the nightclub appearances, or the kooky guest spots with Carson and Sullivan, or the album that was climbing the charts. Elliott may have tried telling his castmates about Barbra, but since they were so far away from it all, none of it would have really sunk in. Here, in Oxford, Barbra was just the girlfriend of the star of the show. For the moment, the situation between her and Elliott had reverted to what it had been back in the very beginning. He was the star; she was his girlfriend. But they both must have known, deep down, that the moment was fleeting. Elliott, raising his pint of ale in a toast to the success of *On the Town,* made sure to enjoy it while he could.

2.

That spring, Ray Stark was a busy man. He'd had to fly to Dublin, where problems had arisen on the set of Seven Arts's remake of *Of Human Bondage.* Kim Novak was having trouble with the part of the Cockney waitress, Mildred, and the situation wasn't helped when kidnap threats were made against her and costar Laurence Harvey. After dealing with all of that, Stark had needed to swoop down to Puerto Vallarta, Mexico, to scout locations for Seven Arts's upcoming production of *The Night of the Iguana.* Then it was back across the Atlantic to London, where he'd courted Elizabeth Taylor as a possible replacement for Novak in *Bondage.*

Now Stark was back in California, but his social calendar for May was already very full. All of this left precious little opportunity for him to get anything done on *Funny Girl* — which is what they were now calling the musical about his mother-in-law — but for a worka-holic such as Stark, there was always time to be found. He was still burned up over Jerry Robbins and the monkey wrench he'd thrown into the project, but he was determined to get things moving again. And he'd found the ideal man to make that happen: Bob Fosse, the young, celebrated choreographer of *The Pajama Game* and *How to Succeed in Business Without Really Trying* who'd recently started directing as well (*Redhead* and *Little Me*). Sam Zolotow in the *New York Times* said *Funny Girl* was "almost definite" on Fosse's agenda.

That still left them with the problem of the book, however. Stark had sent Fosse a copy of the last finished script and urged him to consider how they might strip it of Robbins's imprint without losing the whole storyline.

It was, to say the least, a daunting task — made even more daunting by an ailing Broadway economy. This past season had been the worst in memory. Investors had lost more than five million dollars, according to an official study conducted by the *New York Times;* other estimates placed the losses at closer to seven million. The reasons were many: a slump on Wall Street the previous spring; the newspaper strike; the increasing popularity of art-house films taking people away from the theater; and an ill-timed increase in ticket prices. This was hardly a good time to try to get a show off the ground.

The only way to do it, Stark understood, was to hire a surefire crowd-pleaser. Kaye Ballard was knocking them dead at the Persian Room in the Plaza Hotel with her uncanny impersonations of Brice. Kaye Stevens was drawing raves after adding "My Man" to her act. But Stark had no doubt noticed that *The Barbra Streisand Album* had just passed Eydie Gormé's *Blame It on the Bossa Nova* on *Billboard*'s chart. The music industry's trade journal probably sat right beside Stark's copies of *Variety* and the *Hollywood Reporter* on his poolside table. The producer would surely have taken note of the red star next to Barbra's name, indicating that she was on a fast ride to the top. Stark had been right all along about her potential. None of the others had red stars next to their names.

Barbra was the one with the momentum. Columnists were regularly linking her name with the show anyway; some presumed she'd already been cast. When Barbra had performed in San Francisco, the local press reported she'd "been signed for the role." Whether that was a journalist's error or a strategic exaggeration on the part of Lee Solters, neither Barbra's camp nor Ray Stark had seen the need to correct the claim.

The producer did act to fix something else, however. No doubt at her husband's request, Fran Stark had diplomatically withdrawn from any public comment on Barbra. But there was still a lingering perception out there that she disapproved. So Stark placed a call to Mike Connolly at the *Hollywood Reporter.* A conversation with Ray Stark was the only explanation for the interesting little item that Connolly subsequently ran, quoting a reader asking what had happened to the Fanny Brice musical. "They've been having a tough time finding the right girl for this great part," Connolly replied. "But ever since Mrs. Ray Stark, Fanny's daughter, saw Barbra Streisand in *I Can Get It for You Wholesale* she's been insisting on Barbra for it."

That, of course, was a bit of Orwellian revision, but the spin was necessary if they were going to tamp down the stories of Fran's disapproval. A few weeks later, Connolly was reporting even more definitively on the matter: "That funny Barbra Streisand is all set to star in the Broadway-bound *Funny Girl,* formerly *The Fanny Brice Story.*"

That's what Stark had been communicating privately to Marty Erlichman as well. Now all he needed was Bob Fosse to come through, and they'd have a show.

3.

Barbra sat in what she considered "an ordinary beauty shop" in London, getting her hair cut, "shorter in back than on the sides," as she described it. The look was catching on among the swinging chicks in the capital, an asymmetrical bob popularized by celebrity hairstylist Vidal Sassoon that relied on the natural shine and shape of the hair for its effect. That meant no more curlers or hairpieces or lacquers or endless fussing in front of a mirror. With her hair cut this way, Barbra could just wash it, shake it, and *voilà!* She was done. That made her very happy indeed.

What was more, she now looked like a very contemporary, hip young woman, a more grown-up version of the cosmopolite look Bob had styled a couple of years back. Having finally made it out of her hotel room in Oxford to London, Barbra seemed to come alive amid the city's cultural renaissance. It was an optimistic period that celebrated the new and the modern in fashion, art, and personal expression. Girls sashayed down the street in oversized sunglasses and knee-high vinyl boots; their boyfriends sported double-breasted blazers and patent-leather ankle shoes with zippers. And everywhere Barbra went, she would have heard the music of the Beatles — an exciting new rock-and-roll band consisting of four young men from Liverpool — soaring from radios and record players. The Beatles' songs "Love Me Do" and "From Me to You," as well as others from their debut album, *Please Please Me,* provided an exuberant soundtrack to life in London during the spring of 1963. They might not have been songs she'd sing, but Barbra was enchanted. She absolutely loved the city.

The move to London had come as rehearsals for *On the Town* were transferred to the show's eventual venue, the Prince of Wales Theatre, on the corner of Coventry and Oxendon Street. The theater's white artificial stone was a landmark on the walk from Piccadilly to Leicester Square. To Barbra, the West End seemed every bit as exciting as Broadway. With Bob, she'd seen *Half a Sixpence* at the Cambridge Theatre, a few blocks away from the Prince of Wales on the corner of Earlham and Mercer streets. The show starred Tommy Steele, one of Britain's most popular teen idols.

During the day, Barbra wandered the city with Bob, who'd taken off time from his job to be with her, taking in antique shops and outdoor markets. Elliott sometimes accompanied them as well when he wasn't rehearsing. But when Elliott was with them, there was always a bit of tension. Barbra's boyfriend rarely spoke directly to her old friend, avoiding eye contact at all times. Such behavior grew out of Elliott's self-described "insecurities with everyone," but Bob thought it also had to do with the fact that Elliott was still "uncomfortable with anyone who knew Barbra from the old days."

After Bob returned to Paris, however, Elliott livened up. Strolling through London with Barbra on his arm wasn't so different from the days when they used to wander New York in complete anonymity. They'd poke through the shops along Carnaby Street, trying on clothes, eating fish and chips or Indian food, and buying tchotchkes that caught their eyes. Any suspicions or fears that had festered between them during their separation dissolved as they rediscovered the simple joys of being together. Barbra realized, "to her great relief," one friend noticed, that she was "still in love with Elliott and he with her." The trip to London had been worth it.

Sometimes on their tours of the city they were also joined by the director of *On the Town*, Joe Layton, a tall, dark man with sharp features, and his wife, the actress Evelyn Russell. Both Laytons possessed keen senses of humor that Barbra enjoyed. Like Peter Matz, Joe Layton had been boosted in his career by Noël Coward, who called him "the most sought-after and up-and-coming young choreographer on the scene." Layton had choreographed Coward's *Sail Away*, for which Matz had done the music arrangements. Now he turned his attentions to *On the Town*, and he had great hopes for the production. Leonard Bernstein had thrown his support behind the revival, and planned to be there on opening night, which was now just a few weeks away. Elliott, as ever, was bedeviled by self-doubt, fearful he wouldn't be able to hold his own playing a part that had been immortalized by Gene Kelly in the film version. He didn't voice such fears. But if one looked closely, the terror could be discerned in the way Elliott's eyes darted from place to place whenever someone asked him about the show.

Meanwhile, Barbra was all confidence. Sitting at a Covent Garden café sipping Earl Grey tea with her fellow New Yorkers, Barbra told them that *Funny Girl* was finally moving again. By the time she got back to the States, Marty expected to have a contract waiting for her to sign.

Such an outcome would mean, of course, that she'd be starring on Broadway while Elliott was headlining in the West End, separated by more than three thousand miles of ocean for who knew how long. But this trip, for all its difficulties, had reestablished the connection between them. They'd find a way to make things work.

4.

On a cool evening in the middle part of May, Kaye Ballard arrived at Basin Street East with composer Arthur Siegel. They were there to see Barbra Streisand's new show. The "little girl with the big voice," as Ballard called her, had just become the top solo female recording artist in America. *The Barbra Streisand Album* had reached number 15 on the *Billboard* chart, passing Joan Baez, who'd fallen to number 19.

Ballard was set to headline at Basin Street East when Barbra's run ended, and Siegel had known the young star for years, supplying her with sheet music at a time when she was too poor to afford it. Both assumed Barbra would be pleased if they popped backstage before the show to congratulate her on her recent successes. With the assent of the house manager, they knocked on Barbra's dressing room.

The door opened slightly. The face of a "flack," as Ballard described him, peered out at them. They asked if they might see Barbra. No, they were told sharply. Miss Streisand wasn't seeing anyone. She was "much too busy." The flack closed the door in their faces.

It was standard practice for other "names" to stop by the dressing rooms of performers either before or after a show. To snub someone in this way was a major breach of protocol. Barbra, however, as always, didn't make time for niceties, least of all when she was getting ready to go on stage. She was more concerned with quieting her own nerves than bruising other people's feelings. She may also have felt awkward having a conversation with Ballard, since the older actress was still being mentioned occasionally for *Funny Girl* — and Barbra now knew the show was almost hers.

Any nerves about that evening's performance were understandable, however, since her gig at Basin Street East was her highest-profile one yet. The club itself wasn't all that special: a red-plush room on the ground floor of the Shelton Towers Hotel at Forty-eighth Street and Lexington Avenue. But it had showcased some impressive performers over the years: Louis Armstrong, Count Basie, Sarah Vaughan, and Ella Fitzgerald. Originally called La Vie en Rose, the club had introduced Eartha Kitt to the world. More recently, it was one of Peggy Lee's most frequent engagements.

Four hundred and fifty people could be seated for a show — the biggest room Barbra had ever played — and since the start of her run on May 13, she'd been selling out the house. On opening night, she'd actually had an overflow audience, filled with celebrities and "the town's top agents, bookers, record people and scribes." Up near the front had sat Truman Capote, Cecil Beaton, the singer Connie Francis, the producer George Abbott, and Georgia Brown, Barbra's erstwhile rival for Fanny Brice. One of the songs Barbra sang that night was "Who Will Buy?" from Brown's show *Oliver!* — and Brown led the cheers. Backstage, Barbra received congratulatory telegrams from Cary Grant and Audrey Hepburn.

Opening night had been a triumph. Columnist Louis Sobol, also in that first-night crowd, had noted how Capote and Beaton kept "shouting their enthusiasm" every time Barbra finished a number. "She's fabulous," Capote gushed in his high-pitched voice to the columnist after the show. George Abbott had made a beeline backstage — Barbra didn't turn *him* away — and told her she'd be perfect for his upcoming show *Love Is Just Around the Corner.* That little tidbit made its way to both Earl Wilson and Dorothy Kilgallen, courtesy of Lee Solters, who hoped Ray Stark would read it.

Most important, the critics had loved her. "A potent belter with a load of style," *Variety* had declared. *Billboard* opined that few entertainers had come along in the past decade "with the talent and ability of Barbra Streisand," and echoed Solters's talking point of comparing her comedy style to Beatrice Lillie. "Barbra," the obviously smitten reviewer had concluded, "you're quite a girl and all performer."

This was what the audience had been coming back for every night. As Ballard and Siegel took their seats — miffed but not so much that they'd miss the show — there was a definite energy in the air, an expectation of big things. With the newspaper strike over, New Yorkers were once again reading about Barbra in their local papers, and they had turned out in droves to Basin Street East.

As Barbra stepped out on stage, there was a huge roar of applause. Barbra looked terrific in the new do she'd gotten in London. One reviewer called it a "Kenneth coif," assuming that she, like so many fashion-conscious celebrities, had made a visit to Kenneth Battelle, Jacqueline Kennedy's hairstylist, who was bestowing a similar, Sassoon-inspired look on his clients. But Barbra was a trendsetter, never a follower. She had made her dress herself out of pink-and-white checked gingham: V-necked, sleeveless, Empire-waisted, and darted at the bust. Around the bottom she'd sewn some frill. She was terribly proud that she'd designed the dress herself, even if the same reviewer who'd approved of her new hairdo thought that her penchant for Empire waists didn't "suit her frame."

Still, her look set her apart. In a widely syndicated article for the UPI, writer Rick DuBrow had called Barbra "a different kind of mama" — and some commentators were still resistant to that difference. Harriet Van Horne, for example, writing for the Scripps-Howard news service, wished Barbra would "attempt one of the great old show tunes," something by Rodgers and Hart. But such old-guard lamentations were mostly drowned out by the groundswell of enthusiasm for this different kind of mama. The night Kaye Ballard was in the audience, the crowd at Basin Street East shouted themselves hoarse each time Barbra finished a number.

Not everyone had come to hear Barbra, however. The actual headliner was legendary jazzman Benny Goodman. In Barbra's contract, it was plainly stated that her billing would be only seventy-five percent of Goodman's. The contract had been signed in March before her album had taken off; if it had been signed now, Barbra's agents probably could have gotten equal billing and more than her $2,500 salary for the three-week run. With Barbra's sudden elevation to the big leagues, there was some assumption that she and Goodman were "costars," which is the way a few newspapers billed them even if it wasn't true.

There was a bit of resentment between the two camps, especially when some of Barbra's audiences left after she was finished. Barbra had to be careful because she was using Goodman's sextet as her backup musicians. At one point, she "playfully mocked" upstaging the jazzman with his own band, which Goodman trombonist Tyree Glenn did not find amusing in the slightest.

This pairing of Benny Goodman and Barbra Streisand was bound to produce a clash of generations. The "juxtaposition of the music/record biz's old . . . and the new" might be "a happy event for the Basin Street buffs," as *Variety* claimed, guaranteeing "plenty of action at the ropes." But comparisons were still going to be drawn, even if they were between apples and oranges. Barbra "was an exciting young performer" whose "showbiz potential in all media" was "immense," while Goodman, *Billboard* complained, was "turning himself into a period piece" with a repertoire that seemed "to date from the 1930s." And while Barbra also had some old-time numbers in her act, she had shaken them up and brought a very modern sensibility to her interpretations.

Her set ran about thirty-five minutes. With the exception of "Big Bad Wolf," she gave the Basin Street audience mostly ballads. There was also another long "involved story," a variant of her African folktale, this one set up as a lead-in to an old Estonian folk song "which she never sang," according to *Billboard*. It was a shtick that people seemed to like but that Barbra seemed to like even more, since she insisted there be one such monologue for every half hour of singing. (In other shows it might be "an Armenian folk song about an ill-starred butcher named Arnie.") Clearly, Barbra still didn't like singing one song after another.

After the monologue, Peter Daniels played the first few bars of "Cry Me a River," and the audience, recognizing what had become another of their heroine's signature songs, erupted into applause. Kaye Ballard might have been feeling hurt by Barbra's snub earlier in the evening, but she couldn't deny how gorgeously Barbra put the number across. Thankfully, it was toned down from the version she'd given on Dinah Shore's show — which had finally aired just a few nights earlier. Now, in direct contrast to the elegant way she sang it at the Basin Street East, the entire country had gotten to see Barbra's over-the-top television rendition.

And Fran Stark wasn't the only one who'd recoiled from it. "The last act of *Tosca* couldn't impose more strain on artist and audience than Miss S crying us a river," Harriet Van Horne wrote after seeing the Shore show. "In truth, the number would be more effective were Miss S to cry us a mere gushing rill." Columnist Alan Gill was even harsher, calling Barbra "a Flatbush gamine with the tonsils of a fish peddler." He thought that maybe her left foot had been "caught in a badger trap." But in the eyes of the diehards, Barbra could do no wrong. For Rick DuBrow, Barbra's "Cry Me a River" on *Dinah Shore* was a cathartic experience. He felt like "crawling under a table for fear that she would hiss forth a forked and poisonous tongue at two-timing men everywhere." (He meant this as a compliment.) DuBrow went on to hit every public-relations bullet point as if Lee Solters himself wrote the review. Barbra was "quickly becoming known as a torch singer who acts within her songs more extraordinarily since Lena Horne came up." She was "a little bit of Fanny Brice and Alice Ghostley and Carol Burnett, with a dash of Mort Sahl."

Even if Barbra's performance had polarized viewers, the Shore show kept them talking about her — and buying her album. Television, Marty understood, was key to his client's success, so he continued booking her on various programs to keep the exposure going.

Barbra had just taped an appearance on the summer-replacement show for Garry Moore, a variety hour hosted by Keefe Brasselle, a frenetic song-and-dance man best known for playing the title role in *The Eddie Cantor Story*. There was also another *Ed Sullivan* to look forward to, and when the new season began in the fall, Marty expected there to be other shows as well.

But the biggest news was that Barbra was going to sing for the president. Marty had gotten a call from Murray Schwartz, Merv Griffin's agent, after Griffin had been selected by Kennedy to host that year's White House press correspondents dinner. As host, Griffin was also responsible for lining up the entertainment. Would Barbra join them in Washington on May 23? It didn't take long for Marty to answer yes.

As the crowd at Basin Street East rose to its feet, cheering Barbra's final number, they were saluting a star whose time had arrived, in what seemed like the blink of an eye. Kaye Ballard left Basin Street East that night in a state of astonishment. "This little girl," she said, "who seemed to come from nowhere, who seemed to know no one, suddenly had the world at her fingertips."

5.

Barbra bid the last of her entourage good night and headed home. It had been a good show. She couldn't help but be pleased with the way things were going. But after all the words of praise were over, Barbra returned to that little railroad flat over Oscar's Salt of the Sea all alone.

Even with so much acclaim, Barbra still lived in that airless apartment. She could have afforded better. Friends and associates were urging her to find a place that suited her increasing stature. But she didn't want to move quite yet. She didn't want to "live in-between," she explained to one interviewer, in some way station between poverty and wealth. She declared that she would "live in this rat hole" until she "could afford a duplex penthouse."

Besides, this was the home she shared with Elliott. How could she abandon it when he wasn't there? This apartment was the only tangible connection she had at the moment to the man she loved. His clothes, his things, his tchotchkes were here. This was their tree house, after all, where they'd cooked and played and made love. No, she couldn't just box everything up and move someplace else.

On the Town was set to open on May 30, a little more than a week away. The show could be a big hit, keeping Elliott in London for months, maybe even a year.

Or it could flop.

Elliott would either be gone for a very long time, or he would soon be right back here with her.

Either way, for the time being, Barbra, the toast of the town, was alone as she slipped into her little twin bed and turned off the light — except for maybe Oscar the rat scuttling under the kitchen stove.

6.

As a kid, Barbra had dreamed of seeing places beyond the grimy tenements of Brooklyn. In the last couple of years, she had fulfilled that dream. In the last few months alone, she had been to Miami, San Francisco, and London. Now it was Washington, D.C., the nation's capital. On a brief drive through the city, she and Peter Daniels gazed out at the gleaming white marble of the Washington Monument and the shining dome of the Capitol.

Their destination, however, was a bit removed from downtown. They were heading to the fir-and-oak-shaded Woodley Park neighborhood in the northwest part of the city, where the stately Sheraton Park Hotel rose above the trees. Here was where Barbra would sing for the president of the United States.

Before she'd left New York, she'd called her mother to tell her where she was going. These days, such calls were rare. Diana told friends that she didn't often hear from her daughter because she was "very busy with her singing career." She no longer pestered Barbra about getting out of showbiz and finding a steady job. But Barbra knew better than to ask her mother's opinion on any performances. To her friends, Diana might express a degree of pride, however reserved ("she didn't want to appear to be bragging," said one), but she still seemed to hold firm to that old belief that too much praise would go to Barbra's head. Her mother's lack of enthusiasm was never going to change, Barbra knew. So they kept a certain, safe distance. It was better for everyone that way.

But when she was invited to sing for the president, Barbra couldn't hold back. She'd picked up the phone and called her mother. She knew how much Diana loved the young, handsome, energetic president. To Barbra's great surprise, her mother had, for the first time, bubbled over with excitement about something Barbra was involved in. Of course, there were no "congratulations," no "you deserve this, Barbra." That would be too much to hope for. But the enthusiasm was there nonetheless, and Barbra was happy for that.

Stepping out of the car, she headed into the horseshoe-shaped hotel. After rehearsals, Barbra hurried upstairs to change into her dress — short-sleeved white satin, scoop-necked, with buttons down the front — then grabbed her boa and made her way to the ballroom. There she took her seat with the other entertainers. Edie Adams had flown in from Los Angeles, and cabaret impresario Julius Monk had winged in from Chicago. Basin Street East had agreed to give Barbra the night off, but only if she dug "down in her own purse to pay for her one-night replacement." Shrewd enough not to replace herself with another singer, Barbra had chosen comedian Jack E. Leonard instead.

The president, in a well-fitting tuxedo, sat at the head table. Barbra could hardly take her eyes off him. Celebrities didn't impress her, but John F. Kennedy did. Merriman Smith, president of the White House Correspondents' Association, presented the commander in chief with an electric bread slicer, a wry comment on the fact that Kennedy had recently shown up at a press conference with a bandaged finger, a wound he blamed on slicing bread. Then master of ceremonies Merv Griffin took the podium. Speaking about the new home being built by President and Mrs. Kennedy near Rattlesnake Mountain, Virginia, a place that would be leased out for the summer, Griffin said, "I wouldn't want the president of the United States to be my landlord. I'd be a little reluctant in the middle of the night to call the White House to complain that there's no hot water."

Laughter followed each speaker's remarks, but when Barbra came on stage, she played it mostly straight. Peter Daniels took his seat at the piano as Barbra stood at the mike. If she was nervous — and with her history of opening-night jitters, she probably was — it wasn't detectable. She sang five numbers, but it was the last one that carried the most relevance. "Happy Days Are Here Again" had been used in Franklin Roosevelt's successful 1932 presidential campaign, and since then it had become an unofficial anthem of the Democratic Party. Singing the song for Kennedy wasn't just entertainment; it was Barbra's way of saying she was on board with his leadership of America. When she was done, Kennedy applauded heartily. Barbra dropped a curtsy, exposing a flash of cleavage.

Afterward, the entertainers stood in line waiting to meet the president. The protocol had been explained to them: Kennedy was not to be detained. He'd shake hands and exchange a few pleasantries, but that was all. Barbra, of course, never cared much for protocol, so when the president reached her, she told him that her mother was a great fan of his and asked him to sign her program. He smiled and complied.

"How long have you been singing?" he asked her.

"Just as long as you've been president," she said. When he handed her the program, she said, "You're a doll."

She had just called the president of the United States a "doll."

Meanwhile, a battery of newspaper photographers was snapping away. Merv Griffin, observing the moment, knew whose photo would make the papers the next day: the girl who'd dared to ask the president for his autograph. "Smart girl, that one," Griffin thought. He was right on that score.

7.

The woman just wouldn't stop talking. Barbra was at the point in her act when she introduced her band, and this woman, seated near the front of the audience and quite possibly drunk, kept interrupting her, trying to make jokes of her own. So when Barbra introduced Peter Daniels, she mentioned that he was English and then turned to the obnoxious heckler. "He knows you well, madam," Barbra said. "He's an ex–cabinet minister."

The audience broke up in laughter. After being effectively called a prostitute — Barbra was referencing the Profumo Affair, which was currently dominating British politics — the woman shut up for the rest of the show.

This month — June — it was Chicago's turn to meet Barbra Streisand, and her chance to get to know the Windy City. She was performing a three-week run at Mister Kelly's, a popular jazz-and-comedy club in the city's North Rush Street café belt. Its name was spelled outside in giant neon letters. She'd been doing bang-up business. The reviewer for *Chicago's American* thought that, based on the size of the crowds that had packed the club on her first few nights, Barbra's "three-week showing [would be] a hefty winner." Of course, television was critical. She'd arrived in Chicago after another *Ed Sullivan Show,* in which she'd sung "When the Sun Comes Out" wearing a raincoat and pearls. Then, a few days after her gig at Mister Kelly's started, she'd appeared on *The Irv Kupcinet Show,* the Chicago-based program of the popular local columnist. Now the marquee out front under her name carried the tagline: "FANTASTIC" — KUP. A recommendation from Kup was all it took for many Chicagoans to take in a show.

After the bigness of Basin Street East, Mister Kelly's offered Barbra a return to the intimate feel of her earlier clubs. About four tables deep and twenty tables wide, the club was like playing in "somebody's living room," thought the comedian Bob Newhart. Named after its first manager, Pat Kelly, the venue was run by the brothers Oscar and

George Marienthal, who'd practically cornered the market on Chicago entertainment. In addition to Mister Kelly's, they also ran the London House, a jazz joint on North Michigan, and the Happy Medium, a showplace at Rush and Delaware. But it was Mister Kelly's that was, according to one observer, "the place to see and be seen on Chicago's hippest strip."

The one being seen now was Barbra — and Chicagoans seemed to like what they saw. "A cross between a sweet-voiced canary and a whooping crane, but she's sparkling and fresh," columnist Sam Lesner quipped in the *Chicago Daily News*. Before Barbra had arrived, Will Leonard in the *Chicago Tribune* had been leery of the advance praise from the likes of Truman Capote and David Merrick in her publicity material: "That's almost enough to unsell a man who likes to wait and see," Leonard wrote. But in the end, he agreed they were right. Charlie Dawn in *Chicago's American* answered all of Barbra's critics by saying her unorthodox versions of songs like "Happy Days" and "Cry Me a River" had made them "alive and thrilling all over again." Plus — and this was a milestone — he'd actually called her "comely." It wasn't a typo for "homely." A major critic had just called Barbra "comely" — as in attractive. Pretty, even.

Silencing that heckler showed that Barbra was in top form. She was confident, even a little cocky. Good news kept flowing in every week regarding her album. She'd held on to the title of best-selling female solo artist for three weeks. *The Barbra Streisand Album* had reached number 14 on *Billboard*'s chart on June 1. When, the following week, the album's sales suddenly plummeted to number 31, allowing Joan Baez to retake the title, Columbia had responded by taking out a full-page ad in *Billboard* with a photo of Barbra's album and the tagline: A FANTASTIC FIRST! They needn't have worried. Barbra's appearance on *The Ed Sullivan Show* had ensured that her drop would be no free fall, and by June 15, she was back to number 17 on the chart. As icing on the cake, the stereo version of her album, which had just been released, quickly made *Billboard*'s "breakout" column.

To a record company once dubious of her widespread commercial appeal, Barbra had proven herself. She'd done so by trekking around the country, by showing up on practically every television show and singing her heart out. So successfully had she proven herself that Columbia had given the green light for a second album to be released later that year. Before she'd left New York, Barbra had recorded more than a dozen tracks, including, for the first time, a new song written just for her by Peter Matz, "Gotta Move." He'd composed the jazzy number with her speech patterns — and some autobiography — in mind: "Gotta move! Gotta get out! Gotta leave this place! Gotta find some place . . . where each face I see won't be staring back at me, telling me what to be and how to be it." It was the most modern song Barbra had sung yet.

Also recorded were some other favorites from the nightclub act that hadn't made the first cut: "Any Place I Hang My Hat Is Home," "Right as the Rain," "I Stayed Too Long at the Fair." This time, barging into Studio A, Barbra had been much more aggressive, sticking her fingers into every aspect of the session. Having soaked up the process the first time, she now acted as if she were an expert, suggesting that engineer Frank Laico "do this [and] do that." It was her record, after all.

Surprised by her change in manner, Laico had leveled with her: "You didn't know anything with that first album, and look how successful it's become . . . I have the same ears. I'm not going to let you down." But Barbra couldn't be put off her ideas. Not only had she decided what to sing, but she would decide how to sing it, where to sing it, and how to record it. Laico and the others thought her ego had gotten puffed up by her success, but Barbra didn't buy that argument. "If I have ideas about sets and the orchestrations and production, is that ego?" she asked. No, it was the pursuit of excellence. Barbra insisted that the "range of [her] talent" extended into all areas of record production. "To have ego means to believe in your own strengths," she insisted.

But that didn't make it any easier on the engineers. At one point, both Barbra and Marty latched on to Laico in the control booth, one talking into his left ear, the other into his right. The engineer threatened to quit, though he stuck around, and somehow — no doubt because of the calm precision and artistry of Peter Matz, again serving as arranger — the album got finished.

The success of Barbra's first disk had empowered her to behave in such a way. Once reluctant to sign her, now Columbia was desperate not to lose her. When Laico had taken his complaints about Barbra's controlling behavior to Mike Berniker, the album producer had told him to be careful. "We don't want to upset them," he said, meaning Barbra and Marty. There were other record labels that would be very happy to sign Barbra if she tried backing out of her contract, and Columbia knew this.

The success of *The Barbra Streisand Album* was a turning point in Barbra's career. Marty felt it had given her "a national reputation." It was a turning point for Marty as well. In the spring of 1963, it was clear that Barbra really *was* going to be as big as his publicity about her had always predicted. So that meant some changes were in order. Whether Barbra had given him an ultimatum like the one she'd given Ted Rozar or whether Marty had reached the decision on his own, he dropped the Clancy Brothers as clients so he could focus all his attention on Barbra. He broke the news to the brothers as they were riding in a car on the Pennsylvania Turnpike. The story making the rounds had the Clancys pulling over, telling Marty to get out of the car, and then leaving him stranded somewhere outside Pittsburgh.

If the story was true, the hike home was undoubtedly worth it. Marty could see the future. The strategy for building Barbra up had worked like a charm so far. There was every reason to think it would continue working, all the way to the very top — wherever and whatever that might be.

So that spring the media machine kicked into high gear. Lee Solters had been handed a PR bonanza with Barbra's singing for the president. Suddenly Earl Wilson, bombarded with memos from the publicist, was writing that Kennedy had "demanded" a copy of "Happy Days Are Here Again" after Barbra had sung it to him. Another baloney story being spread by Wilson had Barbra — as ever in these tales, the unpredictable kook — taking one look at Kennedy when he started in "with the Bostonese" and saying, "Come on now, you can talk natural with me." Column inch by column inch, a legend was taking shape.

Yet if she had asked to see something at the sales counter at Bergdorf Goodman — her acid test for fame — would the clerk have known who she was? Barbra had reason to doubt it. Just a few weeks before, when she'd shown up for *The Ed Sullivan Show,* the security guard at the Studio 50 theater hadn't recognized her. He'd refused to let her in until he checked with his bosses. Barbra was no doubt abashed.

The only answer was to get a show of her own. Notices in gossip columns, appearances on variety shows, even record albums could only do so much. More than ever, she needed *Funny Girl.* Barbra had started taking ballet lessons to learn poise and coordination in anticipation of the dancing she would need to do as the star of a show. She was so close to grabbing it she could practically smell the greasepaint, but the part remained just out of reach. Jule Styne told *Billboard* that he was still working on the Fanny Brice story — "which may star Barbra Streisand." *May* star. *May* wasn't good enough. Barbra wanted an answer.

And she wanted it even more now given that Elliott's success seemed assured. *On the Town* had opened on May 30 to an "ovation," according to the headline in the *New York Times.* Although reviews were mixed, even the negative ones were predicting long-lasting box-office success. The *Daily Telegraph* declared that the show's "mad speed, noise and violence" would keep patrons coming back "for months and months." Even though it would prolong the separation between them, Barbra wanted a show for herself with at least as much success as Elliott's.

8.

The sun was just beginning to rise over the eastern shore of Lake Michigan, sending ripples of pink and gold across the calm surface of the water. Barbra came skipping barefoot through the sand of Oak Street Beach, the morning sun reflecting off the majestic skyscrapers of downtown Chicago. She'd been up all night, having finished her last show at Mister Kelly's in the wee hours of the morning and then kicked back at an all-night eatery with some pals, including the one she was with now, the photographer Don Bronstein, who had his camera in tow.

They'd come to the beach to take photos — maybe for Barbra's album, maybe for something else. Bronstein just wanted to photograph her, which was quite the compliment. After all, he'd been the first staff photographer for *Playboy* magazine, and had snapped some of the world's most beautiful women for covers and centerfolds over the last decade. Bronstein didn't expect that Barbra would disrobe the way those models had done, but he did plan on getting some shots that revealed a very different side of the singer. He had a way of getting women to relax and open up to the camera — a prerequisite for photographing models who took off their clothes. But as Bronstein encouraged Barbra to scamper out into the surf, it was clear he could elicit a similar au naturel quality from his subjects even when they kept their clothes on.

Barbra was glowing. Marty had at last received confirmation from Stark that she would star in *Funny Girl*. True, it wasn't absolutely official — no announcement had yet been made by Stark or Merrick — but Earl Wilson reported she was "practically at the contract-signing stage," and he would have definitely confirmed that kind of information before going to the printer with it. Mike Connolly also seemed to know the inside scoop. He was a bit premature in saying that Barbra had already been signed, but he was clearly writing with Stark's approval. Clearly, sometime in early June, a final decision had been made, and Barbra learned of it shortly thereafter. She would play Fanny Brice. She would get that show of her own.

Running through the surf and sand, Barbra smiled and tossed her hair while Bronstein kept snapping away with his camera. As the sun rose higher in the sky, Barbra tied the ends of her red-and-white-checked shirt together, exposing a hint of skin. She was as free and natural with the camera as if she'd been modeling all her life — and in some ways, she had been, starting back in the days when she'd try out different poses in the photo booths of the penny arcades of Brooklyn. Now she turned and faced Bronstein's camera, her arms behind her head. She showed off her shapely legs in tight Capri pants. She turned and faced away from the camera, looking at the water. At one point she slipped a muumuu over herself and lifted her right leg behind her.

She was flirting with the camera, flirting with Bronstein. If he had a way with women, Barbra also had a way with men. At Mister Kelly's, one fan thought she was "a saucy little coquette" after her shows, batting her eyelashes at the men, young and old, who came up to her. Now prancing across the sand, she threw her head back and placed a hand on her hip, pouting sexily. She was clearly having a ball.

Part of her good mood may also have come from some other recent news. On the phone with Elliott, she had learned that *On the Town* wasn't doing as well as that piece in the *Times* had led many Americans to believe. They were playing to whole sections of empty seats every night. That didn't bode well for a long run. So maybe Elliott would be coming home soon. Barbra probably didn't suggest such a thing, since Elliott was clearly upset about the show's prospects. But maybe things were working out just as she'd hoped. She'd gotten the show. Maybe now she'd get her boyfriend back, too.

It seemed like a good time to start looking for that penthouse.

CHAPTER FOURTEEN

Summer 1963

1.

Liberace — that flashy, flamboyant pianist, the idol of millions of blue-haired old ladies and the highest paid entertainer in the world — stood on the stage in his red-sequined tuxedo with a smile as wide as the silver candelabrum on his grand piano. He was getting ready to introduce Barbra, as he'd done nearly every night since they'd started their run together at the Riviera Hotel in Las Vegas. He thought Barbra was marvelous, and he intended for his audiences to think so, too. Barbra might be his opening act, but Liberace wanted his fans to know he considered her far more special than that.

The glitzy musician had been an admirer of Barbra's since seeing her at the Bon Soir; more recently, he'd appeared with her on *Ed Sullivan*. He'd been ecstatic to sign her for his Vegas show, but very quickly he discovered that his fans weren't necessarily hers. The first couple of nights, the audience of ladies with too much costume jewelry and reluctant husbands sitting beside them hadn't applauded Barbra quite as loudly as she was used to. Nor had they seemed to get her jokes. Barbra's long, rambling African or Estonian or Armenian folktales probably fell horrendously flat in Vegas; even sophisticated hipsters in New York and San Francisco didn't always know what to make of them. Peter Daniels, cringing at the piano, thought those first two nights were "disastrous." So Liberace had decided to come out at the top of the show and do a bit of an opening number, then introduce Barbra as his "discovery." He'd give it, he promised, "the old schmaltz."

Opening his glittering arms as if to embrace the crowd packed into the gaudy Versailles Room, Liberace told them they were in for a real treat. This young lady, Barbra Streisand, had wowed them in New York and had a huge career ahead of her. With such a benediction from the master, Barbra could have then come out and read from *Robert's Rules of Order* and Liberace's audience would still have loved her. The pianist's sway over his following was tremendous. He claimed more than two hundred official fan clubs with a combined membership of a quarter of a million. At the Riviera, he was a king, making a triumphant return after a five-year absence. The hotel promoted its headliners by printing thirty thousand souvenir postcards to sell in their gift shops. For Debbie Reynolds and Vince Edwards, that was plenty to last throughout their runs. But for Liberace, thirty thousand disappeared in three days.

Barbra was very grateful to "Lee," as his friends knew the pianist. His introduction of her was extraordinarily generous. Not many performers would get all made up, coiffed, and costumed — and for Liberace that took no small amount of time — only to give up the stage after a few minutes. Yet because of the showman's graciousness, things had completely turned around for Barbra. Now she took the stage to warm, welcoming applause.

Vegas was, in fact, abuzz about her. "By far the hottest singer on the circuit today," one local columnist called her. Another Sin City reviewer declared that while Liberace might have "the edge in experience and publicity on his costar," his readers should "watch the 21-year-old catch on like the doughnut." *Variety* thought that those who were tired of "assembly-line singers will be quite happy with Miss Streisand."

No doubt Charles Kahn, the Riviera's vice president, was quite happy by the turnaround in Barbra's reception at the hotel. After all, he was paying her $7,500 a week. For Barbra's publicists, that figure was a selling point. All that summer she was being heralded as the "girl who went from $150 to $7,500," though the comparison could have been made even more dramatic by using a starting figure of $108, which was what the Bon Soir had paid her at the very beginning.

Yet for all her success on the Strip, Barbra didn't particularly like Las Vegas. Despite the opulence of the Riviera — the hotel was called "a city in a tower of luxury," since under its roof were contained "swank shops," a sidewalk café, a swimming pool, fountains, slot machines, blackjack tables, and a gourmet restaurant — Barbra thought it was all just too noisy. The constant jangling of the slot machines no doubt irritated her tinnitus. She was also becoming enough of a world traveler by now to compare and contrast the cities she'd visited, and Vegas just couldn't compare in terms of culture to San Francisco or London or Chicago.

She was pleased, however, that friends had come to visit. In the audience were Joe and Evelyn Layton, back from London now that *On the Town* was running on its own — or running out of steam, no one was quite sure. But what was abundantly clear was that Elliott's director was now one of Barbra's biggest boosters. His wife shared his view. They'd come to Vegas specifically to see Barbra, and Evelyn was telling her friends they should see her, too. "If you haven't heard Barbra sing," she wrote to one pal, "run this minute and get her record. Greatest woman talent of this century — and she's only twenty-one. I could crack her right in the mush."

Lots of people were running to get Barbra's record. All that touring and constant exposure had paid off. The week Barbra had opened in Vegas, *The Barbra Streisand Album* broke into the Top Ten on *Billboard*'s chart. Barbra's reign as the top-selling woman in pop music continued. Her name was now enough of a draw that CBS had decided to use her appearance on *The Keefe Brasselle Show* as the premiere episode, bumping the original premiere, featuring Carol

Channing, to the second week. Critics savaged the show except for the moments Barbra took center stage, when it "burst to astonishing life." Rick DuBrow, who'd already made clear his love for Barbra in previous articles, called her "a one-woman recovery operation" and declared that she was "so far the superior of any of her competitors that there is really no one even in her league." With reviews such as that, it was no surprise that some commentators, no doubt egged on by Lee Solters, had started calling 1963 "the year of Barbra Streisand."

Tonight the audience in the Versailles Room seemed to agree. Barbra made a joke about the Mother Hubbard gown she was wearing, made entirely of gingham. The columnist Mike Connolly called it an "enigma of a gown," and Barbra seemed to recognize, even relish, its eccentricity. She told the audience that the three novices who'd woven the gown in Brussels had been blind. Another time, sitting on a stool and smoothing out the gown over her knees, Barbra quipped, "I don't want to wrinkle my tablecloth." These sorts of lines, as she expected, drew big laughs.

After the show, Barbra and the Laytons caught up. She shared with them the news that she had found a new place to live, a gorgeous duplex on Central Park West. They might not have admitted it, but they all suspected that Elliott would be home soon. And Central Park West was a rather upmarket address for an unemployed actor.

2.

When Elliott gambled, he was always ready with a story. In London, he'd run up some pretty significant debts, and rarely had he been able to pay them. So he'd done "some of the best acting" of his career in order to make a quick escape. "Great inventive tales" were concocted on the spot as to why he was "temporarily without funds." Usually this enabled him to get off the hook without getting too far in the hole.

Now he was back in New York, and his pockets were still empty. *On the Town* had closed on July 13. It had run just over a month, just over fifty performances. No way could that be spun as a success. The lukewarm review of the show in the *Times* hadn't even mentioned him, while singling out Elspeth March and others. Elliott was humiliated. So back across the Atlantic he'd slunk, back to that smelly old apartment. Once he got there, he had orders from Barbra. Start packing.

They were taking everything they had to the new place. Not that their few pieces of furniture could fill the huge duplex on Central Park West. But Barbra was sentimentally attached to everything in the old apartment, all the antiques she'd found at shops and consignment stores, so she wanted to bring them all.

She was also, it would seem, sentimentally attached to Elliott, since she was letting him tag along even though he had very little money to chip in to the venture. To the world, of course, they were married. "Streisand's husband comes home," Earl Wilson wrote, heralding Elliott's return to New York. And the public expected husbands and wives to live together.

As he stuffed books and boas and shoes into boxes, Elliott was, in his own words, "very depressed." It was back to the unemployment line, and this time there were no job offers on the horizon. He paced a lot, constantly popping sunflower seeds in his mouth and smoking a ridiculous amount of pot. Marijuana was his salvation, Elliott believed; it allowed him to "switch into certain inner places" and escape all outer worries and frustrations. He saw no problem with smoking as much as he did. Grass, as he called it, didn't make him do anything he "wouldn't be capable of doing otherwise," and besides, it was "far more pleasant than drinking . . . less messy and more private." He didn't have "the patience to sit in a bar and drink." So he sat at home and got stoned.

Meanwhile, out there in the world, Barbra had just officially been announced as the star of *Funny Girl.* Dorothy Kilgallen, of all people, had broken the story on July 22: "After reading a zillion Broadway-bound scripts, Barbra Streisand has agreed to do *Funny Girl* for David Merrick. She's a very hot property these days." Kilgallen, perhaps trying to make amends for her recent cattiness, went on to suggest that Barbra's album would soon be number 1. It had already reached number 8 on *Billboard's* chart.

As Barbra soared, Elliott knew he had some decisions to make. Did he bolt? Did he expose their "marriage" as a sham and scramble out of her spotlight before the bluenoses started tossing bricks at her for living out of wedlock? Or did he stick around and let her carry him until he could find another job?

What made it worse was that people were talking about their situation. A very curious item had recently turned up in Walter Winchell's column. Barbra was supposedly consoling a girlfriend, whose husband bought her everything she desired, but he had ceased being much of a conversationalist. "What do you want," Barbra had reportedly asked, "a master of ceremonies or a meal ticket?" It was a line that could have, and maybe did, come directly from her act. But the irony was that, in her own case, it was Barbra who was the meal ticket for her "husband."

3.

Ray Stark looked again at the magazine he held in his hands. It was the venerable *Saturday Evening Post,* and on the cover was a reverential drawing of the new pope, Paul VI. But it was the piece inside, decidedly less reverential, if still in its own way hagiographic, that interested him. GOODBYE BROOKLYN HELLO FAME was the headline. The subhead read: "A refugee from Flatbush with a wacky manner and steamy voice, Barbra Streisand is streaking to stardom."

The article was written by Pete Hamill, a rising star in the world of journalism, but it had been engineered by Lee Solters, as well as by Stark himself. It was Solters — or possibly his partner, Harvey Sabinson — who, some weeks earlier, had pitched the idea to the *Saturday Evening Post,* and it was Stark who had called the editor to confirm that Barbra was indeed about to be named the star of *Funny Girl.* That made the piece timely, gave it a hook. And so the story was assigned

to Hamill, a former reporter for the *New York Post* who had started
writing for the magazine during the newspaper strike.

The two met, and Barbra, in that inimitable way she had with reporters, provided the bare bones of her life embellished with all the
idiosyncrasies of her public persona. There was kookiness: "I like
food, sleep, and clothes," she said. "Food is a tangible thing, and so
is sleep. When you're tired, it's so great." And there was bold ambition mixed with hubris: "They tell me I'll win everything eventually.
The Emmy for TV, the Grammy for records, the Tony on Broadway,
and the Oscar for the movies. It would be beautiful to win all those
awards, to be rich, to have my name on marquees all over the world.
And I guess a lot of those things will happen to me. I kind of feel they
will."

On the emerging Streisand mythos, Hamill left his own imprint.
"To many observers," he wrote, "her overnight success is bewildering.
Show business, after all, is largely a bazaar for that tinselly commodity, glamour. To achieve stardom, unendowed young girls customarily
acquire bobbed noses, capped teeth and cantilevered underwear. Not
Barbra Streisand. 'I'm me,' she says with a disarming shrug. 'And that's
all there is.'"

Of course, that was far from all there was, but that disarming shrug
went a very long way toward establishing some radical new rules for
that tinselly commodity. Maybe glamour in 1963 didn't require bobbed
noses. Maybe a bit of genuineness was just as attractive, maybe even
more so. "She's telling you the story of her life every time she gets up
there," Hamill quoted one friend of Barbra's. "And the facts of that
life have made her very sensitive." The Barbra who emerged from
Hamill's piece was a genuine, real-life kid, a Cinderella who'd escaped
"that bosky dell known as Flatbush" and a high school "gluey with
fraternities and sororities" that was indifferent to the "honor student"
with the "modest looks." Most readers could relate. Even if Barbra
was more ambitious than most, she was an everywoman — and why
shouldn't an everywoman win awards? Why did it always have to be
the beautiful blond girls?

The Hamill piece was the ultimate documentation of the Streisand legend in the public's mind, the culmination of a three-year process that had begun with Don Softness's mimeograph machine. Yet while the article may have been just what Barbra needed at the time, just what her team had been hoping for, there were some points that were now settling into the collective consciousness that Barbra felt went too far. Hamill had quoted a "friend" of hers as saying that, to Barbra, Brooklyn "meant baseball, boredom, and bad breath." It was true that she'd wanted out, and it was true that she'd felt Manhattan was "where people really lived." But Barbra had never gone so far as to denigrate her hometown, and the line deeply troubled her. Yet these were the risks of opening the Pandora's box of publicity: Journalists were going to dig up their own quotes and draw their own conclusions. The narrative could only be controlled so far.

From Ray Stark's perspective, however, the article was the best possible propaganda for his show. The "angular young girl with the nose of an eagle, slightly out-of-focus eyes and a mouth engaged in a battle with a wad of gum" could just as easily have been Fanny Brice as Barbra Streisand. Stark was aware that by conflating the two — using Barbra's established persona and biographical narrative to create and sell *Funny Girl* — he was, in some ways, eliminating his mother-in-law from the show. A year earlier, he'd been adamantly opposed to a similar suggestion from Anne Bancroft that she remake the character in her own image. "The personality of Anne Bancroft," Stark had complained to Robbins and Styne, "will be the only personality to emerge." Yet this was exactly what he was now allowing to occur with Barbra.

The difference was that Jerry Robbins was no longer with the show. By building on Barbra's own mythos, Stark and his collaborators could claim they were basing nothing on Robbins's contributions. That was going to be key, because as soon as Bob Fosse was announced, Robbins's lawyer had written to Stark insisting that none of his client's "suggestions, ideas, and material" be used "in any manner." Aware of the bind that could put the show in, Stark had replied through his own attorney that he knew of "no creative contribution by Jerry" since he hadn't been "privileged to attend the creative meetings." And while Robbins hadn't parried that wily legal maneuver so far, Stark knew they'd have to proceed with caution.

But Barbra's background gave them the freedom they needed. If they had to start over, Stark reasoned, why not jump on a bandwagon that had already proven its marketability? Barbra's quirky personality was already familiar to many people; Robbins's contributions could be papered over with Barbra's own well-known persona — the plucky wallflower who cracks jokes to cover up her longing for true love. Streisand was already "Second Hand Rose" (the title of one of Brice's songs) in the public's mind. If Robbins complained, Stark could simply counter that they weren't using the Fanny Brice he'd created; they were using the Barbra Streisand created by Streisand herself.

So when Fanny got up to sing, "I'm the greatest star, I am by far, but no one knows it," the line would resonate for anyone who'd read Hamill's piece or any of the others like it. In the face of Robbins's intractability, Stark saw Barbra as their way forward. Wherever possible, the producer encouraged Fosse to accentuate similarities between the lives of Barbra and Fanny. As Arthur Laurents understood it, "They needed to become the same thing, at least for promotional purposes."

On one of his early scripts, Fosse penciled the remark "Make it like B." next to Fanny's confrontation with a theater owner. In working with his new leading lady, the director instructed her not to study Fanny Brice, because she'd "become a caricature." Rather, Fosse told her, Barbra should just be herself. "I'm not approaching it as a life story of anybody," Barbra told reporters. "I'm doing it as an actress doing another character." Now that she was finally the star, Barbra wasn't about to share top billing with anyone, not even with the woman she was playing.

Making everything circular, the persona Stark and Fosse were so happy to claim as a stand-in for Fanny's own had been designed by Barbra and her team precisely to secure the role of Fanny Brice. So

Barbra had been imitating Fanny to get *Funny Girl* and now *Funny Girl* was imitating Barbra imitating Fanny. Barbra told the press that she'd been chosen for the "certain natural characteristics" she shared with Fanny, and those were obvious: the prominent nose, the mother who worried she wouldn't make it in showbiz, the childhood in Brooklyn where no one believed in her, the self-confidence that made success seem inevitable. But there were aspects of Barbra's public persona that were less authentic and more calculated, such as all the kooky talk and behavior that had been invented specifically to draw comparisons with Brice. In fact, the two women weren't as much alike as the *Funny Girl* team tried to insist. Fanny Brice had never longed to play Juliet, and her aspirations to be accepted by the ruling classes would have been anathema to Barbra. Most significantly, Fanny had let men run her career, and occasionally ruin it, which was about as far from Barbra as one could get.

Yet none of that mattered to Stark. What was relevant to this show was that both Barbra and Fanny were different-looking, different-sounding, different-acting ladies of great personal charisma who redefined what it meant to be glamorous.

Stark knew that he was giving the twenty-one-year-old an enormous gift. It wasn't often that entire Broadway shows were built around actors with as little experience as Barbra. But Barbra's story was the answer to his problems with both Robbins and the show. The book could now practically write itself — or at least he hoped it could. So up to Vegas he trekked with Fran to pose for photographs with Barbra showing how pleased they all were with her casting. Jule Styne and Bob Merrill also made the trip, running through the entire score for Barbra in her hotel room, tweaking lyrics where necessary. Everything was done now with Barbra in mind.

4.

Elliott paced anxiously at the corner of Ninety-second Street and Central Park West, smoking a cigarette. A friend of his, another out-of-work actor, spotted him and tried to engage him in conversation, but Elliott seemed distant and preoccupied. He kept looking over his shoulder as if he were waiting for someone. At last his friend saw a young woman come bounding around the block. He didn't recognize her at first. She was wearing oversized sunglasses and black boots and a knee-length gingham dress. When Elliott kissed her, his friend realized this was his girlfriend, Barbra Streisand, whom everybody seemed to be talking about these days. The young man knew Barbra and Elliott weren't married, and wondered why they kept up the pretense to the press that they were. They seemed to be very much in love. Barbra kept patting Elliott's hand and kissing his scruffy cheek. Finally Elliott muttered a good-bye to his friend — Barbra hadn't even said hello — and they hurried off.

But not far. Elliott's friend was surprised to see the pair enter the exclusive apartment building behind them. What he didn't know was that this was Barbra and Elliott's new home. When he learned that fact later, the out-of-work actor was mightily impressed, especially since he remembered the railroad flat over Oscar's Salt of the Sea. He also presumed the reason for the couple's continuing marital ruse was the fact that they were now very publicly living together.

Indeed, it would have been difficult to keep private their move into the Ardsley at 320 Central Park West, one of Manhattan's most impressive Art Deco structures. With Barbra freshly back from Vegas, many columnists gushed over her sudden ascension to the heights, which was evidenced by her stately new address. Built in 1931, the Ardsley had been designed by Emery Roth, the famed architect of so many of the city's definitive hotels and apartment towers. Barbra's new home was a stunning composition of black brick and bold geometric patterns; above the fifteenth floor, cantilevered balconies alternated with a series of setbacks to produce what one architecture critic called "an animated yet balanced profile." Most of the Ardsley's 198 apartments were small, the exceptions being the lavish duplex penthouses, one of which, at the very top, was now occupied by Barbra Streisand and Elliott Gould.

The couple had considerable work ahead of them to furnish and decorate this place. Fifteen-foot-high ceilings buttressed by elegant crown moldings meant a lot of wall space for art. There were six rooms downstairs, with a grand circular staircase leading up to three more in the tower, where the master bedroom opened on to a roof-top terrace. The lower floor was also ringed with terraces from which Barbra could look down on the passing traffic on Central Park West or across the street into the bright summer green of the park itself. Rent for this palazzo in the sky was over $1,000 a week — an astronomical jump from $60. And the only smell here was the fragrance of freshly polished wood.

Barbra and Elliott quickly became aware that while the place stood mostly empty at the moment, it was nonetheless jumping with ghosts. Lights suddenly came on without switches being flipped; the ring of the telephone sometimes caused the television set to turn on. The building had, as they were discovering, a rather storied history. For most of its three decades, the Ardsley had been home to wealthy industrial barons, doctors, and city officials.

But it was in Barbra's own apartment where the most famous ghosts still danced. In 1939, lyricist Lorenz Hart had rented these very same rooms, installing his mother downstairs and himself up in the tower. That was the year Hart and his songwriting partner Richard Rodgers had *I Married an Angel, The Boys from Syracuse,* and *Too Many Girls* all running on Broadway. Over the next half decade, in the same rooms Barbra and Elliott now occupied, Hart had written the words to such songs as "It Never Entered My Mind" for *Higher and Higher* and "Bewitched, Bothered, and Bewildered" for *Pal Joey,* which was now one of Barbra's staples. Here, under these same chandeliers, Hart had entertained George Abbott, Ethel Merman, Gene Kelly, George Balanchine, Vera Zorina, Jimmy Durante, Ray Bolger, Josh Logan, June Havoc, and so many other Broadway luminaries of the period. Most likely David Merrick had been inside Barbra's apartment years before she stepped across the threshold. And then there had been Hart's more private parties, where the hard-drinking lyricist, known for his revelries, had entertained what one writer called "the homosexual elite": Cole Porter and George Cukor visiting from Hollywood, or Noël Coward and John Gielgud from London, with all the attendant handsome young men who traveled with them.

In those few days she had in New York before flying off again, Barbra was anxious to start decorating her new place. She'd had most of her old furniture brought uptown — the dentist's cabinet and the Victorian piece with the glass shelves — but there were so many more antiques yet to be found. The one piece of furniture she had managed to acquire so far was an Elizabethan four-poster canopy bed, three hundred years old and set up on a tiered marble platform so that it took two steps to get into bed — rather like ascending a dais, some friends joked, or a throne. Gone was that little single bed that had barely provided enough space for Barbra and Elliott to turn over. This new one offered them far more room, if perhaps a little less of the old intimacy.

But shopping sprees and decorating sessions would have to wait. Barbra's tour wasn't quite over yet. She'd closed out Vegas with a flourish. Liberace had left a night early, turning over the stage — and the starring position — to Barbra for her last show on August 4. The comedians Dan Rowan and Dick Martin had been her opening act. During her run at the Riviera, Barbra had gotten a fifty percent raise from Charles Kahn, and she'd reciprocated with a parting gift to him of a leather jewel box inscribed TO FLO FROM FANNY — appropriate since she'd been announced for *Funny Girl* while on Kahn's stage. But Barbra's real guardian angel during her time in Vegas had been Liberace. The showman had been so good to her that Barbra had agreed to perform with him again the following month at Harrah's in Lake Tahoe.

From Vegas, Barbra had flown back East and immediately headed out to Long Island to perform for one night at the Lido Club on Long Beach. The next day it was up to Kiamesha Lake in the Catskills for a show at the Concord Hotel. What her tour had done was prove to the doubters — and to Barbra herself — that she could play the big rooms.

At the Concord, she'd sung for close to a thousand people in the hotel's enormous auditorium, and she'd "torn the place apart," said one man who was there.

Now there was a bit of a breather, but there still wasn't much time to shop. Instead, Barbra occupied herself with designing the outfit she would wear at her next engagement. It was a white satin blouse with black piping in the style of a midshipman's shirt, with a black collar that snapped into the low V-neck. Barbra seemed indifferent to the brickbats that were frequently tossed her way from critics who loved her voice but remained unimpressed with her couturiere skills. In fact, sniping about her clothes had largely replaced slandering her looks. In Vegas, Barney Glazer had recoiled from that infamous Mother Hubbard gingham gown. "My mind reverted to those historic days in Salem, Mass.," the columnist wrote, "when the public played a game called Heap the Wood High, Strike the Matches Hard, Oh, No, You Didn't Forget the Kerosene Again?"

Yet being compared to a witch didn't seem to faze Barbra because here she was, designing another unique look to wear on stage. No doubt she expected her next destination would be a little looser, a little more sophisticated, a little more willing to try new things. On August 21, she was opening at the legendary Cocoanut Grove at the Ambassador Hotel in Los Angeles.

It was time for Barbra Streisand to meet Hollywood.

5.

As Barbra prepared to fly to Los Angeles, rehearsing daily with Peter Daniels and making last-minute adjustments to her satin sailor's blouse with the seamstress, Elliott was undertaking a mission of his own. In a quiet little office somewhere in the city, he sat down opposite a Freudian psychoanalyst, seeking professional help for his rapidly worsening depression.

Elliott's state of mind seemed to ratchet lower with every new success enjoyed by his girlfriend-cum-wife. When, in a recent column,

Earl Wilson had declared Barbra "suddenly one of the hottest stars in the country," he'd mentioned the fact that she'd just moved into a duplex penthouse with "her husband, Elliott Gould." But he hadn't included anything about Elliott's current projects. That was because there weren't any.

Elliott listened closely as his analyst asked him a question, and he gave it considerable thought before attempting an answer. He was taking his analysis very seriously. He was, he said, determined to restore some harmony in his life. "Without flats," he'd come to realize, "the sharp notes stick out." Using another metaphor, he said that he felt as if he were stuck in a leaky boat, constantly bailing to stay afloat. But with analysis, he was temporarily beaching his boat so he could find out where the holes were and then patch them. Elliott knew that taking their boat off the water was scary for some people; they feared they would never get it back out again. But Elliott had no choice. His boat was going down.

Was Barbra among the "some people" Elliott thought were too afraid to take their boats off the water? Quite possibly—for Barbra had tried analysis herself not long before, very likely at Elliott's urging. Perhaps she'd even accompanied him to one of his sessions. In any event, she hadn't liked it. The analyst kept winking at her. She wasn't sure if he was putting her on or making a pass. So she'd walked out on him. "Maybe he was crazy," she said—which seemed to be her verdict on the entire mental-health profession. Going to an analyst or a psychiatrist, Barbra said, was a "cop-out, [a] self-indulgence." And while she indulged herself plenty when it came to her career, sitting around moaning about her problems had never been her style. She believed in getting out there and making things happen; if she griped about something, it was to someone who could do something about it, not to someone who would just sit there and nod his head.

When Pete Hamill had asked about her career, how she'd gotten to where she was, Barbra had demurred, saying she couldn't "verbalize about it." If she did, she feared, she'd "analyze it all out the window." Clearly, to her, analysis was a fruitless and pointless exercise. "You're paying to talk about yourself," she said. "It's really pampering yourself." Besides, it "cost too much money."

Was she footing the bill for Elliott's analysis? Or was she resentful that his money was going toward such endeavors when she was paying most of the household bills? If Elliott's analysis caused tension between them, neither of them said so. But certainly Elliott held a very different view of the process than Barbra did. Analysis wasn't easy, he believed, but it was worth it. It was opening him up to "self-discovery," he insisted. Barbra might be on a journey that took her ever farther out into the world, but Elliott hoped to go just as far inward.

6.

Barbra's plane touched down at Los Angeles Airport. In the center stood the newly constructed Theme Building, designed to resemble a flying saucer landing on four spindly legs. New York's airports sure didn't look like this.

Stepping out of the plane, Barbra glanced down at the tarmac and spotted four waiting limousines. Another surprise. They were all for her.

The limos had been sent by David Begelman and Freddie Fields, two young, hotshot Hollywood agents who'd recently formed a company called Creative Management Associates. Begelman and Fields had been the reason Judy Garland had secured a weekly television program; at the moment, CMA was putting the finishing touches on a deal to bring Phil Silvers back to TV. Not so very long before, Begelman and Fields had turned Barbra down as a client. Now that she'd "hit it big," as Marty observed with no small amount of satisfaction, they'd "changed their minds." Begelman and Fields were calling him "two, three times a day" to win her over. The limousines were just the latest salvo in their campaign to woo her.

Making her way down the steps, Barbra watched as the chauffeur of the lead limo hopped out to open the door for her. Lined up behind, the other limos carried a menagerie of CMA agents, managers, and publicists, "each ready and eager to help her career," noted columnist Bill Slocum. "Sammy Glicks don't run anymore," Slocum added wryly, referencing the ambitious Hollywood con man from *What Makes Sammy Run?* "They use air-conditioned Cadillacs."

Barbra settled into the Cadillac's leather seat as Marty took one of the limos behind her. A third limo may have been for Barbra's new business manager — another Marty, this one named Bregman — who'd been hired because Barbra was suddenly making more money than the first Marty could manage on his own. Once everyone was settled into their respective limos, the sleek vehicles started their engines and rolled out across the tarmac. As they pulled onto the street, they resembled a presidential motorcade.

Quite a ride for a girl who'd grown up taking the subway. On her second trip to Los Angeles, Barbra was treated like visiting royalty, installed in a luxurious suite on the fifth floor of the Ambassador Hotel, located at 3400 Wilshire Boulevard. But she had little time to luxuriate. She had a show to do in a few days, and ahead of that, a good deal of promotion. And so, very soon after her arrival — maybe that afternoon or possibly the next day — she sat down with a public-relations man named Marv Schwartz, who had a few questions he wanted to ask her.

This was how things worked in the business of public relations: Barbra's publicists, Solters and Sabinson, arranged for Schwartz, whose own agency, Kaufman Schwartz and Associates, had close connections to Hollywood columnists such as Sidney Skolsky, to interview their client upon her arrival in L.A. Schwartz would then have the interview transcribed, cut, pasted, and rearranged into a form suitable to send out to columnists — in this case, Skolsky, whose "Tintypes" were widely read in Tinseltown. A "Tintype" would be prepared on Barbra that was ready for publication; all Skolsky would have to do is add his byline. This process eliminated the possibility of an independent reporter probing too far or straying off that day's message.

It also meant that, in the course of the interview, Barbra could ramble along, stream-of-consciousness style, the way she tended to do, without her publicists feeling the need to constrain her. They'd filter and finesse her comments long before they reached the public. Yet the tape recorder was running as Barbra sat there talking with Schwartz, preserving exactly how she was thinking and feeling on that warm, sunny day of August 14, 1963, a point when it seemed she had just rounded the last hill on her climb to stardom and caught a glimpse of the summit up ahead.

"What do you really enjoy doing when you're not singing?" Schwartz asked.

"I hate to sing," Barbra replied, "so what do you mean, what do I like doing away from singing?"

"You hate to sing?"

"Yeah."

Schwartz was clearly incredulous. After all, this was the top female recording star in America. "Why do you hate to sing?" he asked.

"Well, it's a big . . ." Barbra's voice trailed off. "It's just all that worry that goes into it, you know. You get on stage and they don't applaud enough, you're a nervous wreck, you know, and all that stuff."

So, Schwartz wondered, would she give up singing for straight dramatic roles? No, Barbra replied, she wouldn't give up singing entirely. "Why should I?" she asked. But singing remained "too hard . . . to enjoy."

She didn't mean nightclub singing necessarily. A nightclub no longer seemed such an anathema to her. Now that she was heading back to Broadway, Barbra suddenly seemed nostalgic for the world of clubs and cabarets. Despite all the time she'd spent feeling like a "floozy," she seemed sad that her nightclub career might be ending. After all, "every night was different" in a club, she explained. To lure the audience's attention away from "the influence of food and liquor," she had to be spontaneous, varying her act to respond to circumstances. She told Schwartz that performing for people who just sat there "watching you" was "no fun" — a very peculiar sentiment coming from an actress about to open a Broadway show.

She was tired, she said, of all the "kooky" business. But she realized her public persona had taken on a life of its own. When Johnny Carson had asked her on *The Tonight Show* if she thought she was kooky, Barbra had heard what the audience was telling her through their laughter and applause. She felt they were saying, "Give us a yes!" — and it made her angry. The public didn't know her "real" self, she believed, and didn't "want to know." That was fine; she wanted her privacy; if she had her druthers, she'd "rather shut up and let 'em guess" anyway. Barbra had come to understand that "the public creates stars" and "they don't want the illusion to be broken."

Still, she wanted to move past the kook. The thrift-shop angle was "a gimmick," she admitted, that had run its course. She was tired of wearing all those old-time fashions; it was no longer the image she wanted to project. Instead, Barbra wanted to be contemporary. That's why she'd gotten the new hairstyle — updated and maintained by celebrity stylist Fred Glaser — and why she'd started designing her own clothes. Her favorite fabric was gingham. It cost just sixty-nine cents a yard and was "more elegant" in its own way, she said, than all the shiny fabric and beads other singers wore.

Schwartz asked her about acting, and without much prompting, Barbra launched into a rather defensive spiel about actors who took themselves too seriously. Was she maybe feeling just a trifle self-conscious about heading into what some might consider a lightweight musical? Certainly the Actors Studio — and its exclusive environment of serious study — remained a sore subject for her, though she brought it up on her own to Schwartz. Barbra made it seem as if *she* had turned Lee Strasberg down, not the other way around. She insisted that she'd told Strasberg, "I'm not here to study with you. I have a teacher I'm perfectly happy with" — even though her great desire had been to study with Strasberg. But to Schwartz, Barbra implied that she'd just been a curious outsider sitting in on one of Strasberg's classes. In her telling, there was no audition, no campaign to become one of Strasberg's disciples. Not to Schwartz did she mention the Actors Studio acceptance letter that she kept as a "prized possession."

Barbra seemed to feel the need to dismiss the culture that had so cavalierly dismissed her. "People like that kind of school," she told Schwartz, "have no sense of what reality is . . . Their life is showing Strasberg they're good. To me that's stupid . . . Acting is so simple, you know, it's really a pity to see people have to study it." She told Schwartz she found it "a bore watching everybody work and going through these terrible agonies." Eventually she was "fed up" with the Actors Studio pretension, she said, so she had walked out.

Even as she stood on the cusp of potentially enormous fame, Barbra remained bitter about having been rejected all those years ago. Her exclusion from the world of serious actors still stung enough that she was attempting to rewrite history in order to erase the hurt and humiliation. But as Schwartz continued to question her about the Actors Studio, the awestruck teenager she'd once been slowly reawakened. Barbra wondered now that she was "sort of" famous, if Strasberg would finally let her into one of his classes. "I wonder if he remembers me," she mused. When Schwartz suggested she call Strasberg, Barbra admitted she was "afraid" to do so. Despite the fact that she'd just dismissed his whole school, she declared, "He's the master, you know." (She would go so far, in another setting, to call him "like a Zen master.") And that was why she wanted "to be friends with him," she said. Barbra told Schwartz that she and Strasberg had a great deal in common, "a certain sensitivity that's on the same level." She saw herself as Strasberg's equal; if only he would see her that way as well!

It wasn't all that surprising, then, that when Schwartz asked her if success was what she thought it would be, Barbra said no. She was particularly unprepared for the envy that surrounded her. "People who don't have success hate success," she observed. "They hate famous people really." Who was she talking about? Critics who needled her? Former friends who complained she wasn't doing enough to help them? Colleagues jealous of her quick rise to the top? Whoever they were, Barbra felt there were lots of people out there waiting for "any opportunity" to take her down, watching for her "to make a mistake." It was "a very scary position to be in," she said.

But the fear she felt as she became more successful also arose from trying to navigate a terrain that remained very alien to her. When people asked for her autograph, Barbra told Schwartz, she often thought they were putting her on, making a joke. When she read stories about herself or saw her name on a club's marquee, she felt strangely disconnected to it all. Barbra Streisand was "this kid" she remembered "from a long time ago." So when people said to her that she was going to be "one of the greatest stars . . . in the history of the entertainment business," even though that had been her life's goal, she had a hard time reconciling the two visions of herself: ugly, unwanted kid and glamorous, acclaimed star.

What Barbra was revealing to Schwartz was the defining dichotomy of her life. To another reporter, she admitted that sometimes, when she saw herself on television, she'd think, "What am I doing here? I don't look good; I don't sound good. What is it that they flip over?" True, Barbra had gotten as far as she had because of the enormous belief she had in herself, which, in turn, had inspired others to believe in her as well. But deep down, the little girl who'd once crawled on her belly so she wouldn't disturb her stepfather was still there, seeking approval, craving acclaim, and convinced that if she ever got it, it would be quickly snatched away. So when Barbra saw her name on the marquee, she thought, "It's this kid from Brooklyn. It's not me."

But that kid from Brooklyn had glimpsed the future, and she liked what she saw. "I'm really very young," she reminded Schwartz, and there was still so much more to do and get and experience. "I want homes all over the world," Barbra said. "I'd like to live different places different parts of the year, in Europe, Mexico maybe . . ." Plus, she was going to be great. "I want to do everything," she said. She wanted to make records "and be the greatest and sell the most." She wanted to be on television and "get all the reviews." She wanted to be in the theater and "be magnificent." Despite the nagging, deep-down doubts, Barbra recognized she'd already done pretty damn well for herself. "So far," she said, "it seems I've been pretty lucky about doing whatever I want to do."

Finally, Schwartz asked what she would be doing if she wasn't in show business. Barbra didn't wait long to reply. She said, very simply, "I don't think I'd be alive."

7.

There were movie stars waiting for her downstairs.

Big movie stars. Some of the biggest ever. Henry Fonda, who'd liked Barbra so much back in Philadelphia. Edward G. Robinson and Ray Milland. Natalie Wood with her date, Arthur Loew, Jr., son of the president of MGM and grandson of two of Hollywood's founders, Marcus Loew and Adolph Zukor. Wood's ex-husband Robert Wagner, with his new wife, Marion. Kirk and Anne Douglas, with Kirk glad-handing all around the room. Jack and Mary Benny. Gracie Allen. Roddy McDowall with Tammy Grimes. Director John Huston, whose face lit up when he met the young and pretty Sue Lyon, who'd just scored in *Lolita.*

And then there were the songwriters. Jimmy McHugh, Sammy Cahn, and, of course, Jule Styne, who'd flown out from New York with his wife, Maggie, to be there for Barbra's Hollywood debut. Afterward, Styne and Cahn were hosting a soiree in her honor. Singer Tony Bennett was there, too, checking out the young woman he was sometimes compared with, and with whom he was currently sharing the charts.

In all, there were fifteen hundred people at the Grove that night, a record. There were even more outside, where fans mobbed the entrance, eager for a night of stargazing. As each celebrity arrived, cheers exploded from the crowd. Paparazzi cameras flashed. Long accustomed to the glare of the spotlight, Fonda, Douglas, and Wood smiled and waved graciously as they made their way inside.

Upstairs in her fifth-floor hideout, however, Barbra was definitely not accustomed to all the hoopla. From the street below, she could hear the cheers from the crowd, and she grew more anxious by the moment. Proving herself to Hollywood was an enormous challenge. If she ever wanted to make movies — and more and more she talked about that — then these were the people who would make that happen, or not. She'd already received the benediction of the influential columnist Sheilah Graham, who'd written in her column that Fanny Brice "would have approved" of Barbra. That carried weight, because Graham had known Brice. But then again, so did an awful lot of the people who were waiting downstairs to see Barbra — including those two old warhorses Hedda Hopper and Louella Parsons, seated on opposite sides of the room from each other. Hopper was at Sammy Cahn's table; Parsons was with Harriet and Armand Deutsch, Los Angeles society mainstays. Both columnists were waiting, eagle-eyed, to report on this young New York songstress who was going to play "their" Fanny Brice.

But of all the audience members down there waiting for her, it was probably Fran Stark whom Barbra was most eager to impress. Ray and Fran, of course, were seated at one of the head tables. Barbra was their find; they were her benefactors. Barbra knew as many eyes would be on them as on her.

Slipping into her black skirt and white midshipman's blouse, Barbra may well have ruminated over who was *not* there as much as who was. She'd "wanted her mother to come to Los Angeles very much, to be there to see all those movie stars," one friend of Diana's understood. Maybe then, Barbra seemed to hope, Diana might grasp just how important her daughter had become. With all of Barbra's travels, she hadn't seen her mother in a while; Barbra had yet to give her the president's autograph. Trying to remedy that, she'd offered to fly Diana out to Los Angeles, but her mother had turned her down flat. Diana was "much too afraid to fly," her friend knew. To Barbra, however, it may have felt like yet another brush-off, one more example of her mother's indifference toward her. But to her friends, Diana was bragging that "her Barbra" was singing where "Marlene Dietrich used to sing."

As Barbra dried her hair with a newfangled, handheld dryer, a knock at the door of her suite drew her attention. It was Sammy Cahn, wishing her well. David Begelman and Freddie Fields also came by, accompanied by Fields's wife, actress Polly Bergen, who looked as "gay as a bird in a smart summer-flowered dress," Hedda Hopper thought. Begelman and Fields were still eager to win Barbra as a client. A few days earlier, they had helped book her on *The Jack Barry Show,* a comeback program for the television host caught up in the quiz-show scandals of the 1950s. Now Barry hosted a variety-format program on KTLA Channel 5 for celebrities promoting local appearances.

But what Marty really wanted from Begelman and Fields was a guest spot for Barbra on *The Judy Garland Show,* which was set to premiere that fall. Since Garland was a client of theirs, the agents promised to see what they could do.

Barbra was finally ready to head downstairs. She took one final glance in the mirror. She'd put on some weight. Where she'd once been a spindly 110, she was now a more curvy 125. All that ice cream and calorie-rich Chinese food she'd consumed on the road had packed on the pounds. But the extra weight made her look better than ever. She was sexier, more mature, more substantial. Those few extra pounds seemed to imbue her with greater authority and gravitas.

The Cocoanut Grove lounge, on the first floor of the hotel, dated back to the very beginnings of Hollywood. In the Roaring Twenties, Joan Crawford had danced the Charleston on tabletops there; Clara Bow, Gloria Swanson, and Rudolph Valentino had raised glasses spiked with bootleg liquor to their lips. Under the Grove's three-story-high ceiling, painted to resemble a dark blue night sky studded with stars, Academy Awards and Golden Globes had been handed out over the years to Mary Pickford, Vivien Leigh, Hattie McDaniel, and Jennifer Jones. In the grove of giant potted palms, Frank Sinatra had sung; Martin and Lewis had traded barbs; and Dizzy Gillespie had fired up the house with his hot jazz.

Barbra made her entrance through the back, the spotlight following her dramatically through the dark as the crowd gave her a rousing welcome. She had kept them waiting just long enough to settle her own nerves and to build a sense of anticipation in the audience.

Roddy McDowall thought her entrance was perfectly timed — "just late enough to get people's attention" but before anyone "started complaining."

Taking the stage, Barbra basked for a moment in the applause. "I'm the kind of nut who reads movie magazines," she told the crowd, "and here you all are alive." Then she delivered the evening's best line: "If I'd known the place was going to be so crowded, I'd have had my nose fixed." The audience roared in laughter. She'd broken the ice. With that one wisecrack, Barbra had won Hollywood over. By confronting head-on the supposedly insurmountable barrier to her potential movie stardom — her looks — Barbra, through her wit and personality, had rendered that argument obsolete.

Of course, her voice helped, too. She warmed them up with "Any Place I Hang My Hat Is Home," made them wistful with "I Stayed Too Long at the Fair," and seduced them with "Lover, Come Back to Me." Every song received sustained applause.

Sitting there spellbound, Hedda Hopper thought Barbra used "her extraordinary voice range beautifully." Hopper's only problem was her tablemate, Sammy Cahn, who, having heard it all before, had hooked up a transistor radio to his ears so he could listen to the Los Angeles Dodgers play the St. Louis Cardinals. In the middle of Barbra's rendering of "Bewitched, Bothered, and Bewildered," Cahn whispered to the table, "Dodgers won — sixteenth inning — 2 to 1." Hopper considered Cahn's susurration "a bit disturbing," but it didn't spoil her enjoyment of the song. She was likely already composing in her head what she would write about Barbra the next day: "As relaxed as a cat on a hearth rug, she makes old songs sound new."

Her rival, Louella Parsons, went a step further in her support. Barbra, she wrote, would "be great as our beloved Fanny." That seemed to be the consensus as the stellar crowd rose to its feet to cheer Barbra at the end of the night. Polly Bergen whispered to Freddie Fields, "I gave up singing just in time" — a line that her husband made sure to get out to the press. Although *Los Angeles Times* critic Margaret Harford overheard a couple of ladies in the powder room sniffing that they "didn't care for her," Barbra had won a host of other admirers that night. "She has high standards, direct methods and a voice that may still be shattering glass in Fresno," Harford wrote in the *Times*. "I hope she never changes at the behest of press agents and powder room critics. Some of the sexy, no-talent babes who call themselves 'vocalists' should hear Miss Streisand. They would, I'm sure, go home and cut their pretty, pipsqueak throats." Lee Solters himself couldn't have written a more ringing endorsement of Barbra's new kind of stardom.

Outside, the fans were still cheering as the stars filed out of the Grove at one o'clock in the morning. Hurrying back upstairs, Barbra changed into a red-gingham dress with white puffy sleeves — also her own creation — and then made her way to the reception in her honor. Marty, as always, was right by her side. Passing through a battalion of photographers, Barbra lifted her hands to shield her face from the blinding flashes of the cameras.

But things were more genteel at the party. Overcoming her old feelings of shyness when surrounded by so many people, Barbra allowed the Starks to lead her around, introducing her to all their Hollywood friends. Celebrities shouldered their way through the crowd to pay her homage. Tony Bennett congratulated her. Robert Wagner — the actor Elliott had always wished he looked like — posed for a photograph with her. Natalie Wood — one of the most beautiful women in Hollywood — told her that she was gorgeous. But mostly Barbra stuck close to Fran Stark's side, their great big smiles telling the world that Fanny Brice's daughter, no matter what anyone might have heard, thought the kid from Brooklyn was just swell.

8.

Elliott arrived in Los Angeles just in time for his birthday, August 29. Sitting in the Ambassador Hotel restaurant on a clear, warm, gorgeous day, Barbra ordered a slice of cake and asked the waitress to stick a candle in it. When the cake was set down on the table between them, Barbra told Elliott to make a wish.

"I hope the Dodgers win the pennant," he said, and blew out the candle.

It was only natural for Elliott to be rooting for the Los Angeles Dodgers since they'd once been the Brooklyn Dodgers, the team he'd followed as a boy. That night the team was playing the San Francisco Giants, hoping to solidify their lead in the National League. But clearly baseball wasn't all that was on Elliott's mind that day.

"Let's get married," he suddenly blurted.

"Too late," Barbra replied. "Candle's out."

She was playing with him. She knew they had to get married. They were in a precarious situation. Everyone assumed they were already husband and wife. They were very publicly living together. The *Saturday Evening Post* piece had made their marriage a major focal point, quoting some friend — Barbra wasn't sure who — who'd said "the marriage to Elliott" had been more important to her than even her fame. "Here was a girl . . . who never had the guys chasing her, never went steady and who really felt ugly inside," this "friend" opined. "And then the leading man, a big, handsome, virile guy, falls in love and marries her."

Barbra's friends all knew she wasn't really married; anyone who was pontificating on the significance of her "marriage" would have had an ulterior motive for doing so. And since Pete Hamill would admit that at least one of his sources was Harvey Sabinson, this quote, too, may well have sprung from Barbra's publicists. Indeed, it went to the heart of one of the fundamental components of her public persona: the wallflower who felt "ugly inside." But now this pathetic image could be updated and transcended by the validation that came with the love of a good man. Even the descriptions of Elliott — "handsome" and "virile" — sounded as if they came from a press agent's talking points. Barbra's "marriage," therefore, was good for the image.

Eventually, however, someone would catch on that they weren't really hitched. Although Barbra had deliberately called Elliott her husband when she'd sat down with Marv Schwartz — "Some nights I sleep in my husband's pajamas," she said — she also declared him off-limits to the discussion: "I can't talk about him," she replied when Schwartz asked her a question about Elliott. Barbra and Elliott were clearly going to have to be very careful in any interviews they gave.

And, at least for Barbra, that would take considerable effort, since suddenly she was everywhere. In nearly every major entertainment column, Barbra had become a regular boldface name. She'd recently sat down with Lloyd Shearer of *Parade* for a major piece to be run in the popular Sunday newspaper supplement. She'd also just taped the season premiere of Bob Hope's show, which was a surefire ratings winner. Barbra had sung "Any Place I Hang My Hat Is Home" and "Gotta Move." She'd also participated in a comedy skit, playing Bessie Mae, the distaff side of a hillbilly band called the Hog Chitlins and the Goat Grabber Three. Slung over her shoulders were two washboards that she played as instruments: "I'm in stereo," she punned. They sang a version of "Blue Tail Fly," but Barbra's hillbilly accent didn't work, and the jokes were painfully unfunny. And she seemed to know it.

Far more accolades came for her continuing show at the Cocoanut Grove, where the box office sold out every night. Barbra had become "the new pet of the movie crowd," in the words of one journalist. One night, Rosalind Russell hosted a table of ten, and Barbra was cued by Marty to introduce both her and Norma Shearer from the stage. Also at the table were Kate Paley, the teenaged daughter of the CBS founder, and her escort, Carter Burden, a young socialite and Vander-bilt cousin. Danny Thomas had been back to see Barbra at the Grove a couple of times, eager to sign her for an appearance on his show. Jack Paar was also asking, apparently no longer making cracks about Barbra's looks.

But Marty turned them both down, at least for the moment. He'd gotten a better offer — indeed, the one he'd been aiming for. Begel-man and Fields had come through: Barbra was booked to appear on *The Judy Garland Show* that fall. And so the pair from CMA officially became Barbra's new agents. They knew how to make things happen, and that's what Barbra needed. For Garland, they'd refocused and revitalized her career. "You two are the luckiest thing that ever happened to me," Garland had exulted. The pair, according to one observer, were "young, smart and, beneath their well-tailored suits, ferocious." Just the kind of people Barbra wanted handling her affairs. Begelman and Fields promised her the world, even movies — though, in an attempt to not rattle Ray Stark too much, Barbra fibbed through her teeth when reporters asked if she was interested in making films. No, she told them: "I've got a job."

But her new agents knew better. Surely it was Begelman and Fields who lined up the tour Barbra took of Metro-Goldwyn-Mayer. She was driven onto that legendary lot past the tall Corinthian columns into a fantasy world replete with New York brownstones, Tarzan's jungle, Chinese temples, and Andy Hardy's middle-American neighborhood. Afterward, Barbra toured the soundstages, where director George Sidney was filming a number with Ann-Margret for the upcoming *Viva Las Vegas*. After the sexy redhead purred through her song, the two singers were introduced. Enterprising press agents embroidered a bit of fluff from that meeting, claiming Barbra had asked Ann-Margret, "Where did you get the crazy spelling of your name?" To which the Swedish bombshell had supposedly replied, "I was just going to ask you the same question."

For all its monkeyshines and hoopla, Barbra loved Hollywood. The weather, the fragrance of citrus trees, the dream-factory atmosphere. "If you want to get away from everything," Barbra's friend Evelyn Layton said about Hollywood, "this place is perfect — so unreal it's like being on another planet." Heart-shaped swimming pools, shiny convertible cars, beach houses made out of glass. The place was magical. And that wasn't even counting Disneyland, where Barbra got to spend a day, even if the lines had been too long for her to get on many of the rides.

Besides, in Hollywood she was surrounded by people who kept telling her she was soon to be the biggest star in the world. NBC was reported to be "going to great pains to line up an exclusive contract" with her. She may have been discussing all her many options the night that Louis Sobol spotted her at La Scala, the swank Beverly Hills eatery, with Freddie Fields. In his column a few days later, Sobol wrote up a description of Barbra's table, mentioning that Fields was accompanied by his wife, Polly Bergen, and that Phil Silvers, who was also present, had his wife with him as well.

Yet if Barbra's "spouse" was there, too — as Elliott almost certainly was — Sobol failed to include his name. After all, the columnist was only interested in names he could boldface, and the tall, gangly man with bushy hair who sat beside Barbra could have been anybody, or nobody. Such a description seemed to sum up Elliott's position pretty well — just a guy in the background as Barbra took the movie colony by storm.

9.

Bob Fosse, by his own admission, was beginning to feel a little bit paranoid.

The director of *Funny Girl* was doing his best to get the book in order so they could start rehearsals sometime that fall. The script was spread out in front of him, and his penciled comments were scrawled across every page. But the more he worked with Ray Stark, the less Fosse trusted him. When all the principals were present — Fosse, Stark, Barbra, Styne, Merrill, Lennart, and production designer Bob Randolph — everything seemed fine. The relationships among the collaborators seemed "good and productive." Fosse found himself particularly "excited about Barbra."

But when he was alone with Stark, or with Stark and just one or two others, Fosse noticed the producer's penchant for talking behind people's backs. This was classic Stark, keeping people on edge by playing them against each other. But it was nonetheless unnerving for Fosse to hear the producer "threatening to replace everyone." If Stark was saying this about his authors or his designer, Fosse feared, he was likely saying it about his director as well.

That fear touched a nerve. Fosse hadn't sought out this project; Stark had begged him to take it on when Robbins departed. Fosse had agreed only if Stark and Merrick were "willing to go all the way with him" — which meant he wanted a guarantee that he wouldn't be fired out of town, something he'd seen happen all too often before. Fosse was concerned that "the inexperienced Stark" would "panic and make rash and often destructive decisions." So he asked that everyone involved "think twice" and "not just grab [him] because the project was limping." To make sure he was the right fit, Fosse even offered to work on spec "until everyone concerned had made up their minds."

Stark had dismissed his concerns and assured him of their commitment. In good faith, Fosse had started work, picking up where Robbins had left off. It wasn't easy. He had to eliminate anything that his predecessor might claim was his invention. For example, Fosse ditched the direct cut from Fanny's line that she'd do anything that Ziegfeld asked her to the scene where she balks: "I'm not going to wear this costume!" He surely knew he'd lose the laugh, but there was little else he could do; Robbins had made clear the bit was his. Still, there were places Fosse could bring his own imprint. He brought on Carol Haney, the actress he'd helped nurture into a choreographer on *The Pajama Game,* to help with the musical numbers.

But his paranoia was growing by the week. In July he'd flown to Los Angeles, where he was overseeing the staging of *How to Succeed in Business Without Really Trying* at the Philharmonic Auditorium. While Fosse was away, Stark had approached Cy Feuer and Ernest Martin, the producers of *How to Succeed,* and reportedly asked them if they honestly thought the man who'd staged the musical numbers for their gigantic hit was "capable" as a director. When the pair pointed out that it was "a little late for that kind of question," the wily producer of *Funny Girl* had replied, "No, we haven't signed him yet."

That was true. The contract still sat on Fosse's lawyer's desk. Why the director had so far withheld his signature was unclear. Stark had agreed to the language Fosse had requested, promising not to interfere with his direction "or hire anyone else to do his job." If the agreement was violated, the producers of *Funny Girl* would still have to pay Fosse the rest of what he was owed (he was being paid $7,500, for which he'd receive $2,500 on signing, the rest in weekly intervals, plus three and a quarter percent of the box office gross per week). The contract seemed ironclad in its protections of Fosse, but although it was dated August 1, by the end of the month he still had not signed.

Part of the reason was his pique at Stark for his comments to Feuer and Martin, who had lost no time in repeating them back to Fosse. The director described himself as "stunned," though he felt the news simply "affirmed [his] previous suspicions." At first, he wondered if it was only Stark who was against him. Confiding his concerns to Barbra and Lennart, Fosse eventually came to the conclusion that "Stark had acted on his own." So, as the summer ended and the start of rehearsals approached, he was left unsure of whether he really wanted to sign on with a man he could not fundamentally trust.

Still, Fosse plowed on. Looking at the script in front of him, he read the new opening that Lennart had come up with. Previous versions had opened in a theater with Fanny messing up a line of chorus girls. But in this new scene, Lennart had Fanny walking in, crossing the stage, then turning to look at herself in a mirror. "Hello, gorgeous," she deadpans sarcastically. Then she picks up a stick of greasepaint and draws a line across her cheek, the first step in making herself up as an Indian for a comedy skit.

The scene was terrific. Fosse agreed it should open the show. But he crossed out the greasepaint, letting the bit end on "Hello, gorgeous." It seemed more powerful that way. What a terrific star entrance for Barbra Streisand.

10.

Usually Lake Tahoe sparkled in the sunlight as it stretched off to the snowcapped mountains on the horizon. But this morning, September 13, as the rental car headed north on Route 50, snaking along the lake's eastern edge, the sky was gray. Periodic sprinkles kept the windshield wipers moving across the glass. Thunderstorms threatened, and temperatures edged into the nineties. Despite the mugginess, Barbra,

Elliott, and the two Martys — Erlichman and Bregman — were on a mission that morning, heading out of the bustling town of South Lake Tahoe, California, and crossing the border into Nevada. There, in the capital, Carson City, Barbra and Elliott planned to get married.

That previous weekend, the *Parade* magazine profile had appeared, turning up on the kitchen tables of tens of millions of Americans. Lloyd Shearer had reported that Barbra and "her husband" had married the previous March and since then had moved into a New York penthouse together. It had been Elliott's love, Shearer surmised, that had "erased some of the insecurity of [Barbra's] former years" and "calmed down some of her earlier 'kookiness.'" Since a more serious, less kooky Barbra Streisand was something they all wanted the public to embrace, they were glad to promote the angle of "Elliott's love" if that's what it took.

But the lie was starting to rub just a little too close. They couldn't keep saying Barbra and Elliott were married when they weren't. Sooner or later, one of them would mess up in an interview, or some enterprising reporter would dig a little too deep. So they needed to get hitched and fast. And what better place than Nevada, which required no blood tests and had no community property laws? It might have been Friday the thirteenth, but it was also Marty Erlichman's birthday, so it seemed as good a day as any to tie the knot.

For Elliott, the decision to get married had seemed almost like a business arrangement. It was as if they "shook on it," he said. In some ways, given the publicity that increasingly made their marriage necessary, it *was* a business arrangement. From this point forward, Elliott understood he could not speak of Carson City. He couldn't give the date of September 13. He'd have to backdate the ceremony to the previous winter, and he'd have to lie that he'd flown not to the West Coast but to Florida, where they would make believe he and Barbra had married just before he'd set off for London. Of course, Elliott knew — they all must have known — that the ruse was only as tenable as the privacy laws governing Florida's public records.

Yet as the foursome drove up Route 50 in the rain, a white haze hanging over the lake to their left, they probably spoke about many other things besides the wedding. After all, the *Parade* piece had been Barbra's best publicity yet. If not as long or as detailed as the *Saturday Evening Post* profile, it had reached many more people. Shearer had called Barbra "the hottest canary in the country." His subject, however, wasn't happy with the piece, feeling that it didn't spend enough time on her acting ambitions, and she probably spent at least part of the ride grumbling about it. Marty, no doubt, felt that *Parade* was great advertising for the albums, but Barbra didn't like to read anything written about herself. No matter how glowing a piece might ultimately be, there was always some point, large or small, that she believed the writer hadn't understood or that should have been presented differently.

Even the *Saturday Evening Post* article was unsatisfactory. "Most newcomers would be thrilled by a story in the *Saturday Evening Post*," observed the columnist Barney Glazer, but not Barbra. She claimed that Hamill had "stretched the facts to make the copy more interesting." She vowed that from then on, she wouldn't give any more interviews unless she saw "the advance copy." Lee Solters obviously knew that wasn't always going to be possible, but he probably hadn't challenged her on her demand; that was never smart strategy with Barbra. Besides, she was getting famous enough that maybe someday she really could make such a demand and get away with it.

The *Parade* article had also reported that Barbra's earnings for 1964 would be "somewhere between four and six hundred thousand dollars." At Harrah's Lake Tahoe, where she was currently appearing, once again alongside Liberace, Barbra was making ten thousand dollars a week. And her second album had just debuted on the *Billboard* chart. Everyone expected it would perform at least as well as the first.

Or maybe even better. Where *The Barbra Streisand Album* had languished for months before getting its first write-ups, critics were waiting on tenterhooks for *The Second Barbra Streisand Album*. "A fine new voice with an unusual quality and with tremendous acting ability," one reviewer wrote. Another opined, "The results are best described as thrilling." *Billboard* thought the disk had "precise phrasing, clarity of tone, and dramatic impact," and that Barbra took her listeners "on a fine vocal-coaster ride." These were "great tracks tailored for spins and sails," the trade journal concluded. Columbia was sparing no effort this time, taking out full-page ads featuring the covers of both albums and the tagline: NOW THERE ARE TWO.

The album deserved the praise it was getting. It was that rare sophomore attempt that surpassed a superlative original. The raw sexuality of "Any Place I Hang My Hat Is Home" seemed to jump off the vinyl; "Who Will Buy?" and "I Stayed Too Long at the Fair" startled listeners with their ageless poignancy, especially given Barbra's youth; and the passionate "Gotta Move" exposed all of her ambition and willpower. Clearly Peter Matz was to Barbra what Nelson Riddle had been to Sinatra: an arranger who perfectly and intuitively understood her — "when to emphasize the brass for her 'belt' voice and when to float the vocal on a cushion of strings," as one writer observed. The many reviews that pointed out Barbra's dramatic acting efforts on the disk weren't just following Lee Solters's bullet points: these tracks really *were* miniature plays, and Barbra brilliantly interpreted every one of them. The excellence of the disk seemed to justify the control she'd seized in the studio and wielded over the defiant technicians. In her mind, she'd needed to take charge if she was to move from good to excellent. And now she had what she considered irrefutable proof that her way had been the right way. She wouldn't let Columbia forget it.

For her soon-to-be husband, life with a woman who believed her way was, ipso facto, the right way was never going to be easy. No doubt Elliott still had his doubts about the advantages of marriage, fearful of the "technical" impositions it might bring to "an otherwise viable relationship." But was their relationship still viable? That was the question. In London, Bob had witnessed the insecurities that bubbled beneath the surface. Other friends had seen — and heard — the arguments, "the boots being thrown across the room and the cascade of tears afterward."

But one intimate insisted that in the midst of "all the exciting things that were happening to her," Barbra still believed that "no one else was going to love her like Elliott did." And Elliott, like the little boy he'd once been who'd looked to his mother to solve all his problems, remained "fixed on Barbra," who was, to him, "like the sun, rising and setting." Elliott himself admitted that, despite all their difficulties and distance, he hadn't fallen out of love with Barbra. He was still besotted with her. Indeed, Arthur Laurents thought "something real . . . held them together," even if it was fragile.

At the Ormsby County Courthouse, they brought the car to a stop. Stepping out and stretching their legs, they looked around and breathed in the slightly cooler air of the high desert. Carson City still resembled the frontier town it once had been. The streets were wide, the buildings were set far apart from each other, and many city and county officials wore different hats — not uncommon in a city of less than fifteen thousand inhabitants. The justice of the peace, who they'd come to see, was also the municipal court judge, the city recorder, and the coroner. As they headed up the steps of the courthouse, a neoclassical structure with four Tuscan columns out front, they would have discovered that the offices of the justice of the peace were on the first floor, while the second floor housed the sheriff and the jail cells.

Since marriages were only performed by appointment, Justice Pete Supera was waiting for them. A friendly, bespectacled man, Supera was in his third term as justice, having been elected twice without opposition. He'd told his wife that Barbra Streisand, the singer, was coming up from Lake Tahoe that morning to get married, and she'd hoped Pete might bring the couple to their home for the ceremony. But Barbra and Elliott didn't have much time; the courthouse would have to suffice. They said their vows and signed their names; Barbra, just to make sure everything was legal, gave the spelling as "Barbara" for the marriage certificate. The two Martys affixed their own signatures as witnesses. With a final nod and a handshake, Supera pronounced Elliott and Barbra man and wife.

Barbra was now a married lady. One of the songs Styne and Merrill had written for *Funny Girl* was called "Sadie, Sadie, Married Lady," in which Fanny Brice gushed over finally landing a man, swearing she'd do her "wifely job" and "sit at home, become a slob." But where Barbra might have shared some of Fanny's thrill that the man she loved had slipped a ring on her finger, she no doubt also saw the irony in the rest of the song's lyrics. It wasn't Barbra who'd be sitting around doing her nails, as Fanny imagined for herself, while her husband supported her in style. It would be, in fact, the very opposite. It would be Elliott for whom "all day the records play." And despite the kisses, hugs, and congratulations they all surely bestowed on each other, that little fact was almost certainly on their minds as they returned to that hot, sweaty car and headed back to Tahoe so Barbra could make her eight o'clock curtain.

CHAPTER FIFTEEN

Fall 1963

1.

The aroma of chlorine on her skin and in her hair, Barbra leaped onto Elliott's back, producing a great splash of water. Around them enormous palm trees shot up against a startlingly blue sky, ringing the sun-dappled swimming pool nestled inside the pink walls of the Beverly Hills Hotel. Barbra, in a bikini, her hair tied up on top of her head, was clinging to Elliott's torso as he hoisted her onto his right shoulder. They were standing in the shallow end of the pool.

On the deck, photographer Bob Willoughby was focusing his camera. Willoughby had made a name for himself photographing Judy Garland, and Begelman and Fields had arranged a shoot for him with their newest client. At some point, Willoughby suggested that Barbra climb up on Elliott's shoulders. But once she was up there, surely it was her idea to do what she did next.

Just as Willoughby snapped the picture, Barbra reached her left hand around to cover Elliott's face. The resulting photo revealed a small Mona Lisa smile on Barbra's face.

It was all in jest, of course. They were having fun. Lots of photos were taken that day. Lots of splashing went on in the pool, lots of lounging was enjoyed poolside. At least for now, it was the closest to a honeymoon that Barbra and Elliott were going to get. They told reporters they hoped to escape to Italy before Barbra started rehearsals for *Funny Girl* — but at the moment the big question was if those rehearsals would happen at all. Yet again, there had been a major setback for the show, and *Funny Girl* faced the possibility of being postponed once more. As everyone knew, whenever a show was postponed, there was a chance it would never start up again.

Bob Fosse had resigned from the show. The press called it an "unexpected change," but Barbra likely saw it coming since Fosse had confided in her his continuing distrust of Stark. When Feuer and Martin, his producers on *How to Succeed,* asked him to direct their forthcoming musical, *I Picked a Daisy,* with a score by Burton Lane and Alan Jay Lerner, Fosse bolted. Stark, in Puerto Vallarta, Mexico, supervising the start of filming on *The Night of the Iguana,* was furious. "Cannot believe that [a] professional like you would attempt to quit show at this late date," he wired Fosse, demanding that the director fulfill his agreement or face an injunction. Stark warned of "losses running into the thousands of dollars" for which he insisted Fosse would be held liable.

The erstwhile director was not intimidated. Writing to Barbra, Lennart, Styne, and Merrill, Fosse expressed his desire to "just withdraw and leave to you any and all ideas" he had contributed so far. But the threatened lawsuit from Stark, he explained, precluded him from being "so generous at the moment." That left them exactly where they'd been when Robbins left: potentially starting over from scratch.

The restrictions placed on the script by Robbins had exacerbated Fosse's problems at the helm of *Funny Girl.* Shortly before he resigned, an itemized list of contributions made by his predecessor had been received from Robbins's lawyer, who was finally parrying Stark's legal maneuvers. Since Stark hadn't attended creative meetings, Robbins's lawyer had insisted, not only could he not say what Robbins's creative contributions were, he could also not say for sure that he "didn't make contributions." An "upset and angry" Robbins had tape-recorded an hour-long recitation of every single scene, line of dialogue, song change, and character suggestion he'd ever made during his time with the project. The "only practical resolution," Robbins's lawyer said, would be to pay his client royalties if even one word or one idea of his was used in the show.

With such an exhaustive catalog of contributions, it was clear that nearly every page of the script owed something to Robbins — an idea Isobel Lennart couldn't honestly challenge. Fosse may have felt the show was doomed, since the book was now in such drastic need of overhaul, though he couldn't admit that as a reason for wanting out. It was more strategic to pin the blame on Stark's backstabbing. "Mr. Stark imposed an atmosphere of distrust that I found too difficult to overcome," Fosse wrote to Barbra and his other collaborators, never mentioning that the contract he left unsigned contained precisely the kind of language he'd insisted upon as self-protection.

The show was once again without a director, and for all intents and purposes, given Robbins's threats, without a book. Just how rehearsals could begin in a matter of months was anybody's guess.

Barbra knew that her contract with David Merrick meant they'd have to pay her a pretty penny if they postponed the show. Not for nothing did Barbra's camp keep reminding the columnists — and through them, Stark and Merrick — that she was forfeiting a hundred grand in club dates by signing on for *Funny Girl*. But as much as she enjoyed having it, money was secondary to Barbra; it was the possibility of seeing this — her best and quite possibly only chance to star in a Broadway show — slip through her fingers that no doubt truly distressed her. Finishing her Lake Tahoe gig, Barbra likely found the few days of lounging around the pool at the Beverly Hills Hotel very welcome indeed.

She still planned to head back to New York, however; no one had yet called off rehearsals. In fact, Carol Haney was still on the job as choreographer, already auditioning dancers. The deal that Fosse eventually struck with Stark had allowed them to use his ideas and contributions if the threat of a lawsuit was dropped and if they kept Haney on board. So, at least to the outside world, the show was proceeding apace. The columns continued to buzz over who might be Barbra's costar. Hedda Hopper reported that Hugh O'Brian was "ready to sign," then reversed herself and said Tony Martin was in as Nick. Mike Connolly claimed Efrem Zimbalist, Jr., was in the running; Walter Winchell declared Nick was going to be played by Richard Kiley.

The one name no one ever mentioned was Elliott. He was clearly not viewed as a big enough name. But Elliott wasn't likely all that eager to play second fiddle to his wife, either. Indeed, he'd recognized that he needed to establish himself independent of Barbra, and so he had decided to stick around on the West Coast even after Barbra went back East, staying "long enough to make one serious Hollywood bid," he told columnist Barney Glazer. It would mean another separation from Barbra, but Elliott had to find a way to start bringing in some money to their household. Besides, Barbra wasn't leaving California for a while: she had the Garland show to do in a couple of weeks, plus the concert at the Hollywood Bowl. Hansel and Gretel could frolic in the pool a while longer — even if Gretel did tend to cover Hansel's face in photographs.

Meanwhile, Diana had sent them a wedding gift. She'd been saving for this day, a little bit from her paycheck over the years whenever she could afford it. She'd managed to accumulate $750. To Diana, that was a substantial sum with which to start married life. If her own mother had given her that much money when she married Emanuel, she would have been overjoyed and overwhelmed. Barbra expressed her thanks, of course, but her mother's gift hardly registered among the multiple savings and investment accounts now being managed by Marty Bregman. The truth was, Barbra didn't need any money from Diana. What she needed from her mother was something else entirely, but she had long ago stopped hoping to get it.

2.

As she'd been doing for the last few weeks, Judy Garland was playing *The Barbra Streisand Album,* becoming familiar with the young singer — twenty years her junior — who'd be appearing on her show. It was the first day of rehearsals, and Barbra would be arriving at the CBS Television City studios at Fairfax and Beverly within moments, if she wasn't already there. When musical director Mel Tormé walked into Garland's dressing room, he found the star singing along to "Happy Days Are Here Again" — except that she was singing her own song "Get Happy" from the movie *Summer Stock.* Tormé thought the combination sounded "electrifying" and decided on the spot that Judy and Barbra should sing the two songs in counterpoint on the show. Garland smiled. That had been her plan all along. She had just wanted it to be somebody else's idea, in case Barbra didn't like it.

At forty-one, Garland looked a decade older. Pills, alcohol, heartache, illness, roller coaster dieting — and the recent ongoing battles with her husband over their children — had all taken their toll. This television show, for which she'd now taped eight episodes, was supposed to make her rich. That was what Begelman and Fields had promised. Garland was always broke, due to bad financial management and overspending. She envied male contemporaries such as Bing Crosby and Bob Hope who were rolling in the dough, much of it earned in television. This show, she hoped, would change all that. Her agents had never been wrong before.

But problems had arisen almost from the start. Garland's first producer was fired after six weeks, and another crew was brought in. The format of the show went through several changes before it made it on the air. CBS President James T. Aubrey, Jr. — known as "the Smiling Cobra" — never liked the program. The network was spending a great deal of money on Garland: $100,000 to refurbish the stage alone. In addition, Garland's dressing room was an elaborate one-hundred-ten-foot-long trailer decorated to resemble the star's Brentwood home, and the hallway leading from the dressing room to the stage was a replica of the Yellow Brick Road from *The Wizard of Oz*. Only if the show turned out to be a huge ratings hit would Aubrey feel the expense had been worth it.

The first episode had just aired on September 29. Although the official ratings weren't in, overnight projections had showed Garland coming in second to NBC's western drama, *Bonanza*. Still, supporters pointed out that in certain markets, such as Philadelphia, Garland had been number one, and nearly everywhere she'd left all other rivals in the dust, including the crime drama *Arrest and Trial* on ABC. That wasn't a bad start at all. The reviews, however, had been decidedly mixed. Most seemed to feel Garland herself was "in fine fettle," but no one seemed to like her comic foil, Jerry Van Dyke. The writing and pacing of the show came under fire.

Perhaps there were those at Television City who recalled the reviews for *The Keefe Brasselle Show* that had described Barbra as "a one-woman recovery operation." Certainly Barbra had always been a standout guest on all her previous television spots. So it was with tremendous enthusiasm that Tormé and Norman Jewison, Garland's producer, welcomed Barbra to the show. With the possible exception of Lena Horne, with whom they'd taped an episode in July, Barbra was the most exciting, most talked-about guest they'd had on their brandnew revolving stage since they'd started production. Everyone was hoping Barbra could bring a little of the razzle-dazzle she'd bestowed upon Brasselle and Garry Moore and Dinah Shore—and the ratings and the reviews as well.

In her trailer at the end of the mock Yellow Brick Road, Garland wasn't unaware of the excitement being generated by the arrival of this Streisand kid. She was "nervous and anxious and jealous," one friend, Tucker Fleming, observed. Looking at her face in the mirror, Garland ran her fingers down the wrinkles and creases she saw there, clearly aware of the youthful features of the singer she would soon be rehearsing with. It was one thing to perform alongside her own seventeen-year-old daughter, Liza Minnelli, as Garland had done on a previous show, taped and waiting to be broadcast. But the only other female guests she'd had on the show so far had been Horne and June Allyson. Garland was "very aware of how she looked" as compared to the twenty-one-year-old Streisand, and "it made her very insecure and anxious," Fleming said.

To Garland, Barbra wasn't ugly or funny-looking. She was young, fresh-faced, her eyes undamaged by the battle between insomnia and sleeping pills. David Begelman had introduced his two clients in Lake Tahoe, where he'd brought Garland to see Barbra perform at Harrah's. So the old pro had witnessed firsthand the confident, youthful energy Barbra exuded onstage. No wonder she was insecure. While Garland still conjured an exquisite alchemy in front of an audience, youth and confidence were two attributes she definitely did not possess.

Barbra also had a voice that everyone was raving about, in ways Garland "could only remember people raving about her," said Fleming. That was why she'd come up with the idea of singing in counterpoint. Her "competitive nature had been fired up," Fleming observed; she wasn't going to just passively hand the show over to this young whippersnapper. She'd arrived on the set sharp and sober and ready to roll, her makeup done perfectly, her hair coiffed expertly, even if her hands did tremble as she lifted Barbra's album from the turntable, pleased that Tormé had taken her hint.

The truth was that the unanimous chorus of voices that were shouting *brava!* for the Streisand kid was "daunting" to Judy, as Fleming could plainly see. Harold Arlen, Sammy Cahn, and Jule Styne adored Garland, but even in all her years of glory, never had such a group of heavyweights ever coalesced behind her to deliberately boost her career in the way they were doing now for Barbra. There were "plenty of times when Judy could have used" such support, observed Fleming, "but she didn't always have the backing of the musical-theater 'establishment,' so to speak, the way Streisand did." Garland held no personal animosity toward the youngster. She was just anxious to prove she could hold her own against her.

By the fall of 1963, the patronage Barbra enjoyed from that "musical-theater establishment" made her a force to be reckoned with. Where she'd once been a popular, even best-selling recording artist and nightclub chanteuse, her casting in *Funny Girl* had turned her into a powerhouse. Wags had started referring to the "cult of Barbra Streisand," which referenced the cabal of influential tastemakers who had decided that Barbra was "it" and who were determined to use their leverage to carry her to the top. Columnist Jack Gaver may have been the first to use the term: "A sort of Streisand cult," he wrote, "has been mushrooming to the point where non-cultists soon might find themselves in danger of being picketed by the pros." Then had come Lloyd Shearer's article in *Parade,* which had bannered THE CULT OF BARBRA STREISAND in big black letters on its first page. That was what millions of Americans had seen on their Sunday kitchen tables, right beside their cups of coffee and bacon and eggs.

"In today's show business world," Shearer wrote, "thousands of girl singers are offered at eight cents a dozen. In the face of such tremendous imbalance, what is the magic ingredient that jets one girl to the top while others fall by the wayside?" Although he'd credited Barbra's talent — "born of nature and practically no training" — Shearer had ascribed the lion's share of her success to the influence of "a growing army of followers who insist that Barbra is in the great tradition of Helen Morgan, Judy Garland, Lena Horne." *Pageant* magazine had gone a step further, naming names in that army: Arlen, of course, and Truman Capote and George Abbott. This kind of talk was what made some of Barbra's contemporaries so envious.

No wonder Judy Garland's hands were shaking as she headed down the Yellow Brick Road to meet Barbra Streisand, who was waiting for her on the soundstage.

3.

By rights, it should have been the other way around.

It should have been the twenty-one-year-old kid, the neophyte singer who'd been performing for barely three years, who was trembling to meet Judy Garland. But Barbra's nerves were steady, her manner calm, as the cameras began rolling on Friday, October 4, for the final taping of the show. They'd had two days of run-throughs, plus a final dress rehearsal from five thirty to seven o'clock; now, at nine, Barbra felt confident she knew all her marks and dialogue. If the presence in the audience that night of the Smiling Cobra and other CBS brass unsettled Garland, it seemed to have no discernible effect on her young guest star.

Garland emerged to the applause of the audience wearing a light-colored, sparkly gown. "We have a very exciting show for" — her voice caught, and for a split second she lost her way, but she made a quick recovery — "planned for you tonight. We've got marvelous people." This was part of her standard opening segment, called "Be My Guest," in which Garland talked-sang the introductions. Her voice lifting uneasily, her nerves impossible to fully disguise, she trilled, "We've got Barbra Streisand — I think she's nice and she has such poise and she's got such elegance — It's a joy to have her on my show — Darling!" As Garland beamed and reached out her arm, Barbra joined her on the stage. They kissed as the audience applauded.

The two made a striking contrast. Barbra stood a head taller than her hostess, and her dark velvet suit offset Garland's lighter hues. As they'd practiced, they kept up the musical introduction sketch, Judy frequently reaching over to grab Barbra's arm, as if to steady herself.

"Judy," Barbra trilled, "it's great to be with you . . ."

"Be my guest, be my guest . . ."

"You know I've been a fan of yours since I was two," Barbra continued. It was a dig Garland's writers had thrown in to exploit the age difference. But the bigger irony was the fact that Barbra hadn't been a fan since she was two. She'd barely been a fan for a year, and even then, "fan" might have been pushing it since Barbra wasn't a fan of many people, no matter how good they were, and she'd claimed not to have even *heard* of Garland not so long ago. Still, she understood that it was politic to give the impression that she'd been one of the millions who'd loved Judy all these years.

Yet if she had once been indifferent toward the lady, the last couple of days had changed Barbra's take on Judy Garland. She had walked onto that soundstage feeling very "secure," she admitted, unafraid "of failure or anything." And then she met her hostess. The veteran star kept taking Barbra's hands, touching her, putting her arm around her. She was trembling. Barbra was flabbergasted. Garland was older, successful, venerated. Why should she be shaking when meeting a girl who was just starting out? Barbra didn't get it.

Her heart went out to Garland. An "instant soul connection" was how Barbra described her encounter with the older woman. She probably didn't know the full story of what was going on behind the scenes, or the sense of trepidation that Garland lived with nearly every moment on the show. If the fragile star made one false step, she feared that they'd give her the ax. Aubrey was pursuing a strategy of "deglamorizing" Garland, bringing her down to the level of mortals. He thought it was the only way for the show to succeed. So the show's writers were always poking fun at Judy. Digs about her weight issues, her tardiness, her nerves, her age — all were fair game according to CBS. So scripting a line for Barbra to say in that opening number — "Can I replace you?" — was par for the course, and no doubt it sent shivers down Judy's spine.

But Judy didn't give them the satisfaction of any oversized mugging. Whether it was her choice to do so or the advice of director Bill Hobin, Garland deflected the jab and moved without comment to introduce her next guests, the Smothers Brothers. Barbra smiled as her one-time lover walked out onto the stage, looking spiffy in a tuxedo. If the banter with Barbra had been banal, the lines between Judy and Tommy and Dick were even worse. The writers were scraping the barrel.

Then Garland turned back to Barbra and asked her what she wanted to do on the show that night. Barbra launched into their rehearsed skit. "I tawt I'd like ta do a lil numbah, ya know whud I mean?" she said in a bad imitation of old James Cagney gangster movies. Garland replied in kind, then Barbra switched to a slightly more successful English accent, saying she'd like "veddy much to do the 'Song of India.'" Here the script called for a bit of business with Barbra insisting on having the actual Taj Mahal used for her number, but either the dialogue was scratched at the last minute or Garland got confused, because she turned back at that point to the Smothers Brothers. Certainly her halting manner suggested that she might have been confused or nervous or both. At times Barbra looked over at Garland in the midst of their scripted dialogue, and the sympathy in her eyes was impossible to miss.

As they were taping, Roddy McDowall, child star turned character actor and photographer to the stars, was running around the set, snapping pictures. A huge fan and friend of Garland's, McDowall had become an ardent admirer of Barbra's as well after seeing her at the Cocoanut Grove. McDowall had been snapping away throughout the dress rehearsal, documenting what he felt certain was someday going to be considered a "historic meeting of two great icons." He was also aware of the special surprise the show had planned for the audience later on, and he'd be on hand to capture that moment as well.

Barbra sang two solo numbers that night. On "Bewitched, Bothered, and Bewildered," having changed into her white satin sailor's blouse from the Grove, she was sublime. Shot in medium close-up, she looked absolutely stunning, and her confident, assured articulation of the lyrics displayed an exquisite rhythm and pacing of the song that was all her own (and Peter Matz's). When she held the notes, the sheer power of her voice inspired shivers, her lower lip quivering every now and again with the intensity of her performance. It was a beautifully measured interpretation.

Barbra was just as good on "Down with Love," but in a whole different way. Striding toward the camera, her shapely leg making an appearance from her black slit skirt, she was sexy and aggressive and like nothing that had ever appeared on a television variety show before. She turned the tune into a jazzy, stylized repudiation of romance: "Down with eyes, romantic and stupid, down with sighs and down with Cupid — Brother, let's stuff that dove, down with love!" She was completely and utterly in control, especially when the pace picked up and she sang faster and faster, every word perfectly articulated as it rolled off her lips, every note hit expertly.

Yet as good as her solo numbers were, it was the duets with Garland that everyone was waiting for. Once Barbra had finished "Down with Love," she walked over to join the hostess, who was clapping enthusiastically for her. "We've got all your albums at home," Judy gushed, whereupon they were forced to endure more of the hackneyed banter the writers kept imposing on them, some nonsense about who hated the other more for being so talented. "Don't stop hatin' me," Barbra said. "I need the confidence" — probably the most ironic line of the night for those who knew the real dynamics backstage. Giving each other a little air kiss, they sat down to sing.

The familiar piano introduction for "Happy Days" began. "Happy days are here again," Barbra sang, as Judy matched her with "Forget your troubles, come on, get happy." The older woman seemed to be holding on to the younger one for dear life; Barbra felt, once again, the trembling of Garland's body. During rehearsals, the two had developed a tender chemistry that emerged now in front of the cameras, real and vivid and palpable. It may have been borne of sympathy on Barbra's part and competition on Judy's, but it was genuine, and it made for fascinating television. Masterfully arranged, the counterpoint of "Happy Days" and "Get Happy" riveted the audience, including those hard-to-please network execs.

But in some ways, as transcendent as the counterpoint had been, it was their next duet that showed them to best advantage. The "Howdy, Neighbor" production number kicked off in silliness, offering another chance for some inside commentary on the state of affairs at the Garland show. Judy came out singing with a bunch of dancers, only to be thwarted by Jerry Van Dyke, who rushed out and shooed the dancers offstage, complaining of costs. As the props were taken away, Van Dyke placed two stools on the stage and barked, "There's your set!" Garland then brought Barbra out to sing with her. As they took their seats, Garland declared, "There's one thing they can't cut out of the budget and that's our voices." Barbra laughed in agreement.

What followed was pure magic. Dressed in matching red-checkered shirts and white slacks, the two singers ran through a medley of various songs including "How About You?," "After You've Gone," "Hooray for Love," and "Lover, Come Back to Me." Garland started out a bit slow, her voice a little crackly with air pockets. But then she got it together, turned on the sass, and showed the kid she still had what it took. On "How About You?," she started to sing the line, "I love a Gershwin tune," but then switched midway to "an Arlen tune" — a tribute to one of Barbra's biggest boosters and the composer of Judy's signature song, "Over the Rainbow." By now any feelings of fear, pity, or rivalry seemed to have dissipated: Barbra and Judy were just two pros at the very top of their games, singing their hearts out. "We have found when we're singing together," they trilled, "the state of the weather turns from gray to blue." They demonstrated the sheer mastery of their craft at the very end of the number, when each took the medley in completely different places, cross-singing and hitting incongruous notes, but without ever losing the elegance of the duet or their connection with each other. With astonishing precision, they ended triumphantly, then fell into each other's arms, smiling and laughing.

At the top half of the second half hour, there had been another bit with Barbra, a regular feature of the show called "Tea Time," in which Garland supposedly enjoyed some informal chitchat with her guest in front of a tea table. Thankfully, what could have been another badly scripted tête-à-tête — or an opportunity for Barbra to ramble on like a kook the way she did on talk shows — was planned as something very different. Barbra was now dressed in a burgundy version of the midshipman's blouse, and Garland was asking her how long she'd been singing. They were clearly waiting for something to happen. And happen it did. All at once their conversation was interrupted by a voice from the audience singing a couple of lines from "You're Just in Love." And not just any voice: It was the voice of Ethel Merman, who'd originated the song in *Call Me Madam*. "You don't need ana-lyzin'," Merman sang. "It's not so surprisin'."

The premise was that Merman had been down the hall in an-other studio shooting *The Red Skelton Show* when she'd heard all the "beltin'" coming from the Garland stage, and naturally she just had to see what all the fuss was about. The awkwardness of the premise meant that the ladies were awkward presenting it as well; at one point, Garland almost tripped backward over the set, prompting Merman to bellow, "Watch the tea!" Barbra, wisely, remained quiet through most of the ad-libbed dialogue. "Isn't this great?" Merman said, looking at the youngster. "The new belter." She was delighted to hear that Jule Styne and David Merrick were the composer and producer of *Funny Girl* (as if she didn't know). "You're in good hands," she told Barbra.

She sure was. Barbra had been a national celebrity for less than a year, and here she was, on the same stage with Judy Garland and Ethel Merman. The message to the world was clear: She was in their league. Barbra, however, seemed to take it all in stride. She gave the impres-sion of finding it all just a trifle silly, which it was. When Garland asked Merman if she'd "belt" with them, the Merm countered that she wasn't "beltin'" unless the two of them belted with her. So they all burst out with "There's No Business like Show Business," Merman drowning out the others by sucking all the oxygen out of the room. Looking uncomfortable in their three-woman conga line, Barbra made crazy eyes. She had to do something if no one could hear her voice.

The entire experience left her more bemused than impressed. Gar-land noticed Barbra's rather entitled attitude, telling friends, "The kid felt it was her due." Not that she begrudged Barbra's confidence. The younger woman remained amiable enough that Garland — and Mer-man, too — seemed absolutely delighted to give her this initiation.

Once the cameras had stopped rolling, and the cast was all hugging one another good-bye, the Smiling Cobra made a beeline over to Bill

Hobin. Aubrey told the director that the show he'd just seen was so good that it should replace the one they had in the can waiting for the next broadcast. Aubrey decreed that the show should be edited over the weekend and gotten on the air by Monday night.

Barbra Streisand had just scored some points in Judy Garland's favor with the network brass.

4.

On a crisp early November day, Barbra spent the morning buying furniture for her new home, paying cash for an antique captain's desk and a set of Portuguese chairs. It was good to be back in New York, even if Elliott had remained in Los Angeles to try to find a job. It was even better to be able to buy things without worrying about what they cost — except that, after she bought them, Barbra did worry. To one friend she wondered if she'd "ever get used to having money" or ever stop fearing she'd "be poor again."

Barbra had left the Coast on October 5, right after her concert at the Hollywood Bowl. That night had seemed to be a pinnacle for her, a benchmark of her success. Sharing the bill with Sammy Davis, Jr., and the Dave Brubeck Quartet, she'd looked out at the *eighteen thousand* people filling the amphitheater. Brubeck had observed her "trembling like a leaf" before she went on. In front of the television cameras, it had been Judy Garland who had trembled while Barbra had remained cool and collected. But at the Bowl Barbra's sense of calm had evaporated, at least temporarily. She'd had first-night jitters before, but this was different. So many people were out there, more than ever before, and all of them expected her to be as great as Harold Arlen and Sammy Cahn said she was. Swallowing her nerves, Barbra had taken the stage and "killed that crowd," Brubeck noted with awe. She sang eleven songs, all the usual suspects, ending with "Bewitched" and "Happy Days." "Dynamic, sensitive," the *Los Angeles Times* had judged her performance, "transcending the category of a mere vocalist." No doubt gratifying words to read, but the experience had left Barbra unsure if her stage fright had been merely an aberration.

The next day, the Garland show had aired to great acclaim. Barbra's old adversary Dorothy Kilgallen was now squarely in her corner: "Barbra Streisand came on like gangbusters," the columnist wrote. There was more good news as well. At the beginning of October, Barbra's second album had overtaken the first and was now at number 2 on the *Billboard* chart. In fact, both albums were in the Top Ten at the moment, with Barbra holding steady as the nation's top female recording artist. "The hottest of the past year's newcomers," one record reviewer declared, "and fast solidifying herself in the top bracket of entertainers." Yet while Barbra might be the queen of the charts, she really wanted that number one position. Just one little burst of sales could nudge *The Second Barbra Streisand Album* into the top spot. It seemed there was always something more to strive for.

Since returning to New York, she'd given one small concert at the private Harmonie Club on East Sixtieth Street, at a tribute to Leonard Goldenson, president of the ABC television network and the Paramount theater chain, and she still had a few big playdates — including a return to Washington to sing at the White House at the president's invitation — scheduled for the rest of the fall. But Barbra was increasingly turning her attention to *Funny Girl*.

No matter the game of musical chairs being played by his directors, Ray Stark wasn't going to let anything stand in his way of realizing his long-held dream. With Fosse allowing the use of his working scripts in exchange for not being sued, Stark grudgingly accepted the idea of paying Robbins royalties, if necessary, and so the show was back on track. As *Funny Girl*'s third director in a year, Garson Kanin had come on board in early October. "Gar," as he was known, was a successful playwright (*Born Yesterday*) and director (he'd helmed *The Diary of Anne Frank* on Broadway, which Barbra had seen as a teenager). But he was probably best known as the screenwriter of the Katharine

Hepburn–Spencer Tracy films *Adam's Rib* and *Pat and Mike,* credits he shared with his wife, the actress Ruth Gordon.

With a director in place, *Funny Girl* could at last set an opening date of February 27, 1964, at the Winter Garden Theatre, with previews (in Boston and Philadelphia) starting on January 13. Since this was practically around the corner, the rest of the company was quickly assembled. Song-and-dance man Danny Meehan was chosen as the love-struck stage manager who enables Fanny's first break, called "Dave" in early scripts but now renamed Eddie Ryan. Kay Medford, the original "Mama" in *Bye Bye Birdie,* would play Fanny's mother. For the small part of Vera, a showgirl, Stark had cast the voluptuous Lainie Kazan, who, as Lainie Levine, had graduated from Erasmus Hall High School just a few years before Barbra, though their paths never crossed.

Finally there was Allyn Ann McLerie for the part of Nora, the glamorous showgirl who's particularly close to Ziegfeld. In the production notes, Nora was described as "quite beautiful [with] the quality of a lady," to make her the opposite of Fanny. McLerie's contract guaranteed billing as the first featured performer just below Barbra and her leading man. It was a showy part. Nora got to call Fanny out on her narcissism at the end of Act One and again in Act Two, the second time while drunk. McLerie was ideal for Nora. A classy, consummate theater professional, she'd danced for Agnes de Mille, taken direction from Moss Hart, sung the music of Irving Berlin, and won the Theatre World Award for *Where's Charley?* in 1948, later re-creating her part in the film version. When her career started to fade, McLerie managed a brilliant comeback as Anita in the 1960 revival of *West Side Story.* She might have been as "Latin as Yorkshire pudding," one critic wrote, but she proved "stunning" in the part, her "mop of red hair like an oil burner being turned on." At thirty-six years old, McLerie still cut a trim and sexy figure. She would make an exquisite Ziegfeld Girl and, according to Garson Kanin, brought a certain balance to the book, which was otherwise dominated by the character of Fanny.

Indeed, Fanny — Barbra — was now set to sing *nine* solos. "That doesn't happen very often on the Main Stem," Kilgallen wrote, "until a girl is in the Merman-Mary Martin class." Plus there were at least three more numbers where Barbra would sing with other members of the cast. Clearly everyone was now depending on the sheer force of Barbra's voice and personality to make up for the defects of the book. The conflation of Barbra and Fanny had continued. After reading Isobel Lennart's latest script, Barbra had told one reporter approvingly, "Everything seems like me." That was, she said, "except the second act." Unlike Fanny, Barbra didn't have two children. Apparently a few concessions to historical reality were necessary.

But on nearly every other score, there was a deliberate attempt that fall to meld the two women — and not just in the script. A major new publicity blitz showed this stratagem quite clearly. During this November, three magazines had hit the stands with profiles of Barbra: the digest-sized *Pageant,* the men's magazine (and *Playboy* competitor) *Rogue,* and the travel journal *Holiday.* And while in other interviews Barbra was trying to tamp down the kookiness, in these pieces she came across full of Fanny-like eccentricities. The *Pageant* reporter described Barbra at one hotel, declaring she needed to go on a diet. So she phoned room service to ask them about their "physical fitness special" meal. "Uh-huh, uh-huh," she said, listening over the phone, mugging for the reporter's benefit. "Well, send me instead a stack of pancakes, half a dozen strips of crisp bacon, and lots of butter, syrup and milk." It was a line that could have easily been slipped into the script for *Funny Girl.* For that matter, so could Barbra's plucky defense of her looks in the *Pageant* article: "I know I'm not beautiful, but many people in the art world think I have marvelous features." It was easy to imagine Fanny Brice saying the same thing.

Over at *Rogue,* the writer went a step further. In rehashing the tale of Barbra confronting Enrico Banducci about hiring her for the hungry i, he was drawing a direct parallel with Fanny's own experiences. Barbra was quoted as telling Banducci: "You're going to be down on your scabby knees begging me for a contract before the year is out!"

That was awfully close to an early scene in the book for *Funny Girl,* where Fanny confronts theater manager Spiegel for refusing her a job. When the stage manager says he's sorry, Fanny replies: "So am I. And so's Spiegel going to be. Any minute now . . . it'll be my turn!"

In some ways it was chickens and eggs: Which came first? The Banducci anecdote had clearly happened; the club owner had spoken of it himself during Barbra's appearance in San Francisco. And the Fanny-Spiegel scene had existed in the script, in various permutations, even before Barbra had been cast. But the fact that Banducci was brought up again now suggested that life and art were influencing each other. Was the *Rogue* writer responding to publicity given to him by Barbra's team — a press release that may have included the Banducci anecdote? Or did the reporter dig up the story on his own, having read about Banducci in a San Francisco paper, and in so doing, provide one more gem for the writer and producer of *Funny Girl* to use in furthering their goal of turning Barbra into Fanny and vice versa?

Jerry Weidman, who unlike his partner, Harold Rome, had retained some affection for Barbra, authored the third big magazine piece that November. For *Holiday,* Weidman wrote about Barbra's audition for her first Broadway show in such a way that it was impossible not to think of Fanny in her early audition scenes. Even if Weidman hadn't seen a copy of Lennart's book, he knew the general story. A piece like the one he wrote for *Holiday* would have been received as a great big present by Merrick and Stark — at a time, not incidentally, when Weidman was between projects and currying favor with Broadway power brokers was a smart thing to do. In fact, might Merrick or one of the show's publicists specifically have asked Weidman to write something about Barbra and send it out?

In his piece, Weidman wrote about an unattractive, misfit girl who talked back to, even insulted, the director and producers — something Arthur Laurents would never have tolerated and insisted never happened. But it sure fit the character of Fanny Brice. Part of Weidman's Barbra was authentic — the self-confidence and determination — but the impertinence, though certainly part of Barbra's DNA, was mostly invention, the work of a talented playwright to make the piece as entertaining as possible. And, almost certainly, to promote Barbra as Fanny and Fanny as Barbra.

With such an oversized star, it was vitally important that Barbra's leading man have enough charisma and stage presence to hold his own. That month, a decision was finally made. After some prolonged consideration of Tommy Leonetti, the American pop singer who'd made it big in Australia, Stark and Merrick had settled on Sydney Chaplin, the flamboyantly handsome actor who'd won a Tony for *Bells Are Ringing* and starred in Merrick's *Subways Are for Sleeping*.

Clearly the producers had gone with charisma — so important to staying visible beside a performer like Barbra — over acting ability. "Sydney was a man of inordinate charm," said his best friend, Orson Bean, "and very limited abilities as an actor. He was so funny at parties that directors would always say that if they could only bring out those qualities on stage, he could be a great star." But they never seemed to make that happen. Bean believed that Sydney's Tony had come because his leading lady, Judy Holliday, had been such a fine actress that, by looking at Sydney "with such great love in her eyes," she had convinced everybody he was brilliant. All of Sydney's leading ladies, Bean said, fell head over heels in love with him.

In some ways, he was perfect casting for the charming, lady-killing con man Nick Arnstein. Right from the start, Barbra adored him. Any man who could make her laugh won points right away. And she sensed some vulnerability in Sydney as well, which was just as important. She knew that, despite his Broadway success, Sydney still lived in the shadow of his father, Charlie Chaplin. Rare was the interview that the younger Chaplin wasn't asked about the elder. The pressure to prove himself sometimes made Sydney anxious: At his audition for *Bells Are Ringing,* he liked to joke that he had "sounded like Minnie Mouse" when he attempted to sing "On the Street Where You Live." Such stories had a way of connecting with Barbra, who, though she adored "maleness," also preferred a little vulnerability in men, a more "sensitive, feminine side." Sydney Chaplin seemed to fit the bill on all counts.

And he seemed as drawn to Barbra as she was to him. Chaplin's first meetings with his leading lady had left him convinced that she "didn't find herself attractive and was compensating with this enormous drive to succeed." Sitting beside her as they read through the script, listening to her impassioned ideas, Chaplin found "those qualities . . . rather attractive." One friend saw the way Sydney looked at Barbra, as if she were this "rare exotic flower" — and Sydney, his friend knew, "loved collecting exotic things."

Sydney was married to the ballerina Noelle Adam, and they had a three-year-old son, Stephan. But marriage hadn't necessarily tamed his roving eye in the past. Dorothy Kilgallen had reported that during *Subways,* David Merrick had been forced to write a letter to Actors' Equity protesting his star's "misbehaving," although Equity claimed no knowledge of it. Sydney's friend suspected the misbehavior may have had something to do with "chasing women and not concentrating on his role." Yet whatever the issue may have been, Merrick hadn't been opposed to hiring Sydney again.

At the moment, Sydney's wife and child were in New York. But soon they'd be returning to Paris, which they called home and where Sydney owned a restaurant, Chez Moustache, the fashionable place to be seen when in the French capital. Now that he was cast in *Funny Girl,* however, Sydney expected to be away from his business for long stretches of time — and away from his wife, too. Once Noelle and his little boy headed back across the pond, Sydney realized that both he and Barbra would find themselves spouseless just as rehearsals got underway.

5.

Under blue skies and palm trees, Elliott drove his rental car along Sunset Boulevard, hurrying to yet another meeting with some Hollywood honcho. By now, he knew how it would go. There would be backslapping and bear hugs, and lots of promises would be made. But so far, nothing had come from any of his meetings. Four months after the closing of *On the Town,* Elliott still had no job offers.

Except one, if Walter Winchell was to be believed.

Elliott was considering taking a "bit role" in *Funny Girl.*

Whether Winchell's legmen were wrong on that one or whether Barbra had prevailed upon Ray Stark to offer her husband a role in the show no one was quite sure. Whether the role was offered and Elliott refused, or whether he offered and they refused — no one was sure about that either. And if it was just a rumor, no one knew how hearing it must have made Elliott feel, as he drove along those wide boulevards of the movie capital, looking up at billboards for the latest films about to be released and wondering if his name would ever be up there.

In fact, no one knew much about what was going on that fall for Elliott Gould. "Everybody knows Barbra Streisand, star of stage, nightclubs and concerts," wrote columnist Barney Glazer, "but few have heard about her husband, Elliott Gould. At one time, the reverse was true. Gould was the singing-dancing-acting star of the Broadway musical *I Can Get It for You Wholesale.* Barbra was his supporting comedienne." Not a few gossips began comparing Elliott's story to that of Norman Maine in *A Star Is Born,* the actor who is eclipsed in fame by his wife.

Elliott insisted it was "no big thing" for him that "reporters were constantly around, asking [Barbra] questions." What were they going to ask him — how he did in his "three-man basketball games"? He didn't *want* to be asked anything about himself, he said. The problem arose when he and Barbra were out in public together, which, thankfully, was "seldom." But when Elliott did accompany Barbra to shows or restaurants, it was "devastating" for him. Reporters, cameramen, and fans paid no attention to him. And yet Elliott felt an obligation to attend with his wife — "no matter who the fuck people thought I was, Prince Philip or Mr. Streisand or whatever." It was the "consistent discouragement" that put him in the doldrums, he said, and consequently, there was more pot and more gambling. He was trying his "damnedest not to take seriously" the fact that Barbra had become "an enormous celebrity" and he had not. But the depression only got worse, increasing his dependence on analysis — and marijuana.

That fall, a rumor had sprung up that Barbra was pregnant, or "babying," as Walter Winchell put it. Few knew how unlikely that was given how little time she and Elliott had spent together. It was theoretically possible — there'd been the interval at the Beverly Hills Hotel, after all — so Barbra had called Winchell to put a stop to the story. "I get worried about such false reports," she said, in typical Streisand fashion. "Maybe they know something I don't."

Barney Glazer tried to put a positive spin on the Goulds' marital situation. "The public throws brickbats at celebrities when they change mates frequently on their mad merry-go-round," he wrote in his column. "Barbra and Elliott present another side of the picture and deserve praise for staying together while apart. Two traveling careers in one family never was the proper mixture to cement a marital foundation."

That was true. No surprise, then, that after his latest Hollywood meeting went nowhere, Elliott decided to throw in the towel and return to New York. Maybe there was still time to take that Italian honeymoon before Barbra got too wrapped up in rehearsals and started spending all her time with the *Funny Girl* company — a company that now included, as Elliott was surely aware, the very handsome, very debonair Sydney Chaplin.

6.

Barbra was taking advantage of the sunny, unseasonably warm November afternoon, with temperatures in the mid-sixties, to indulge herself a bit, wandering among the city's antique shops. She still had an apartment to furnish, and in just a matter of days she'd be off on the road again. It was her final tour before settling into *Funny Girl*. And, as she'd admit to friends, it was a tour that she felt vaguely anxious about. These were all big-venue gigs, she explained, designed to establish her as a concert artist in league with Sinatra. Yet the sheer size of the audiences she was to face left Barbra nervous as she remembered her unexpected stage fright at the Hollywood Bowl.

That evening, she was planning to meet Peter Daniels at the St. Regis Hotel on Fifty-fifth Street to rehearse some of the material they'd be performing at the Arie Crown Theater in Chicago, the first stop on the tour. But for now, Barbra had a little time, and she spent it doing what she loved to do, inspecting vintage scarves and boots and knick-knacks, even if these days she had to wear oversized sunglasses to keep from being recognized when she did so.

She was getting used to this part of fame, but that didn't mean she liked it. When people came up to her and asked her for an autograph, she felt frightened. Who could feel easy about a stranger coming up and demanding something from you, even if the stranger was telling you he loved you? That in itself could be a little unnerving.

The increased notoriety was a byproduct of the publicity machine, which continued to grind on Barbra's behalf that fall. Her wardrobe, once dismissed as kooky, was now being sold as "fashion," and given the number of fans who showed up at concerts dressed in their own thrift-shop wear or in self-designed, iconoclastic outfits, Barbra's style was indeed having an impact. Gay Pauley, women's editor for United Press International, met Barbra at a benefit showing of fashions by Pauline Trigère and Maurice Rentner at the Hilton Hotel, and commented that her style was the same as "the younger-looking buyers." Pauley particularly homed in on Barbra's brown crocodile boots that reached to just below the knee, as well as her fur coat and hat. When Pauley asked what kind of fur it was, Barbra replied, "Why should I tell you when everyone thinks it's sable?" Whatever it was, Pauley liked it, and she ended up pronouncing, "Boots are in. Curly hair is out. The fur hat is in" — which described Barbra's look that day to a T. Pauley's widely syndicated piece was a far cry from previous coverage that had used Barbra's fashion choices as punch lines.

That came as a great relief to Barbra, who was growing seriously weary of the kook narrative. "A kook is a person who puts on things that aren't real," she insisted to an Associated Press reporter, who went on to headline his piece YOUNG SINGER CONFIDENT OF ABILITIES BUT MAINTAINS SHE IS NOT A KOOK. Whenever a factual inaccuracy popped up in her press, making her appear "too out there" in her words, Barbra took great umbrage — no matter all those stories about Madagascar in her program bios. But what she mostly objected to were stories that claimed she was an "overnight success." How could anyone consider "overnight" three years of traipsing around the continent singing in nightclubs and resorts, often to obnoxious drunks? Those who'd been traipsing for considerably longer than three years, that was who.

Still it had taken a lot of time and effort to get where she was, and Barbra insisted on telling her origin story the way she wanted it told. For all her annoyance at reporters who got facts wrong, she herself was invariably free and loose with details. "Anyway, here I was in an old long black dress," she said in one interview, describing her Bon Soir debut. "I decided the first song I'd do was one I'd never done before. It was 'Keepin' Out of Mischief Now,' by Fats Waller, and the club pianist had never even played it before. When we were getting ready to begin, I'd keep saying, 'What's the first note? Where do I come in?' Things like that. They loved me, I don't know why."

Of course, that wasn't the way it happened at all. She and Barry had worked the song out in painstaking detail weeks ahead of time, and then she'd rehearsed it with Peter Daniels — the very club pianist she claimed had never played it before. A similar misremembering of facts occurred when she related the origins of "Happy Days Are Here Again." Barbra had come to feel that *she'd* been the one to slow it down. She said she could hear "the changes of the chords" and thought "maybe it would sound nice slow." Of course, the idea had been Ken Welch's, and Peter Daniels had been the one to suggest it as a regular number in her act.

At least for "Big Bad Wolf," Barbra did give credit where it was due. That song was "Barry's suggestion," she told *Rogue,* describing

"Barry" as one of her "arrangers." To *Pageant,* she provided a little more background: "I knew a guy who had a big collection of old 78 rpm records." Of course, there was so much more behind the words "I knew a guy," but Barbra, understandably, wasn't about to get into all of that.

If Barbra was casually rewriting her origins, Marty, always there behind the scenes, was much more conscious of carving her stone tablets. To *Pageant,* Barbra's indefatigable manager articulated the position he had been advancing since day one. "Barbra's stardom was not artificially created," he told the magazine, "but had to happen." He spoke of "well-meaning advisers" who were constantly advising her to change her nose or her act. "But Barbra and I merely stood our ground and waited for her talent to speak for itself."

Her talent had, of course, spoken for itself loudly and successfully—but Marty's statement left out the considerable backstory that had been orchestrated so brilliantly by himself and others: the first annual "Fanny Brice Award," the marketing of the kook, the birthday party at the Lichee Tree, the well-placed items in Earl Wilson's columns, the well-timed letters about Barbra in TV Mailbags. His goal was to render invisible all the backstage deals, all the negotiations with club managers, all the schmoozing of Columbia execs at the Ho-Ho lounge, all the hundreds of press releases that flew out of mimeograph machines every time Barbra appeared on television. But that, of course, was what a good manager should do.

And now Barbra was so famous she had to wear sunglasses as she browsed through antique shops and so rich she could afford anything she liked.

It was a brooch that caught her eye this day. She carried it to the front desk. As she finished paying for it, the radio behind the counter crackled with a breaking news story. Barbra wasn't sure she heard it correctly.

She listened again.

President Kennedy had been assassinated in Dallas.

"A hoax," Barbra thought, remembering Orson Welles's 1938 radio broadcast of a Martian invasion. She staggered outside and told her driver to take her home. Heading back uptown, Barbra spotted Elliott inside a taxi on his way to a singing lesson. They both jumped out into the street and embraced each other in the middle of traffic. How could the president be dead? She was supposed to sing for him again in just a couple of weeks!

That night, rehearsing with Peter Daniels, Barbra broke down when she tried to sing "Happy Days Are Here Again," the song Kennedy had loved so much.

Living in the public eye just got more precarious, more dangerous, and more untenable.

7.

"Controlled hysteria." That was how Ralph Gleason, the columnist for the *San Francisco Chronicle,* described backstage at the San Jose Civic Auditorium on the night of December 4, as Barbra and her musicians and engineers prepared for her concert that night. Wisecracking stage manager Jerry Frank was rehearsing the lighting crew, who stood in a semicircle around him. "At the end of 'Quiet Time,'" Frank said, "she holds the note longer than the Bank of America." He told the guys to hold the spot on Barbra until she was finished. Then it was "Cue orchestra, then out!" Looking down the list of songs, the stage manager added, "At 'Down with Love,' you go up, hold it a minute, then out!" Their instructions in place, the crew scurried off to their places.

Outside, the fans were lining up, waiting for the three-thousand-seat arena to open its doors. Gleason stood in the shadows watching it all, taking notes as he spoke with Marty Erlichman. "It takes her a year to work into a song," Marty told the reporter. "That song, 'Quiet Time,' is the first time she's done it in public. She's had it for a year and taped it and listened to it and changed it around. That's why there's no arrangement. She has to work it out like that until she's satisfied. Then there'll be an arrangement."

"Spotlight out, out!" Frank yelled into his phone.

"She got 'Happy Days' from *The Garry Moore Show,*" Marty continued, as Gleason scribbled copious notes. "She was supposed to go on and do a quick bit . . . and when the piano player started it, ta ta ta, da da do do, she said, 'I don't sing songs like that, can we try it as a ballad?' Everybody thought it wouldn't work, but she sang it as a ballad and Joe Hamilton, the director, ran up and said, 'Keep it in, keep it in!'"

Gleason took down the legend just as Erlichman described it, even if it wasn't the way it had happened at all.

Conductor Jerry Gray passed them, heading out into the audience to check on how the music sounded from far away. Peter Daniels was up on the stage, warming up the orchestra for him.

Suddenly Gleason realized that Barbra had inched up behind Marty in her white midshipman's outfit. "How many people outside?" she whispered.

That was the worry they all had. Leaving behind the intimate niteries, as *Variety* called nightclubs, Barbra was embarking on a whole new phase of her career. She'd passed the test with flying colors a few nights earlier in Chicago, where she'd performed for two nights at the five-thousand-seat Arie Crown Theater. *Billboard* called it her first "one-girl concert." The second show had been added when the first sold out. "It would be laboring a cliché to say that Barbra Streisand's first Chicago concert . . . was a smash success," *Billboard* reviewed, "but in all honesty, what else is there to say?"

From there, it was on to Indianapolis for a concert at Clowes Memorial Hall, which seated 2,200, and then here, to San Jose, where advance ticket sales hadn't quite kept up with the other venues. An unusually chilly night added to the jitters in the box office. That was why Barbra had ventured out of her dressing room to check with Marty. That was also why Marty was taking the time to speak with Ralph Gleason. Next up after this was a concert at the Masonic Auditorium in San Francisco, and Marty was taking no chances. He hoped that a good write-up from Gleason would ensure a rush on tickets.

There hadn't been a lot of publicity for this tour, none of the usual television spots that had helped so much in the past. There simply hadn't been time. All they had to rely on to get her name out there were her albums: "There is only one Barbra Streisand," the ads in newspapers read, almost daily, "but now there are two Barbra Streisand Columbia albums!" It was a symbiotic thing, since the tour was designed to sell the albums as well. And yet, *The Second Barbra Streisand Album* had remained stuck at number 2 all month, unable to dislodge, of all rivals, *The Singing Nun* — Jeanine Deckers, or Sister Smile — who now claimed Barbra's crown as top female recording star in the country. Some observers thought Deckers's soft, spiritual sound would never have climbed so high on the charts if it hadn't been for John Kennedy's assassination. There was still time to hit number 1, Marty assured Barbra, and everyone hoped this tour would help the album do just that.

"She does it herself," Marty continued telling Gleason, as final preparations were made to open the doors and let in the crowd. "She listens to people. Peter Daniels, her accompanist, will make a suggestion. Harold Arlen. She adores Harold Arlen. But it's her." Gleason took it all down. That was the bottom-line message of all the publicity about Barbra: *It was her.*

Finally the stagehands and the lighting crew were ready. The doors were opened. As it turned out, the house wasn't full. The audience was small but "highly enthusiastic," braving "the cold night air to hear her." If she was disappointed by the turnout, Barbra didn't show it. She gave them an hour of her songs and patter — "a lot for your money," Gleason wrote, "from a girl whose stage confidence belies her twenty-one years."

8.

With Lainie Kazan on one side of her and Allyn Ann McLerie on the other, Barbra had at last begun rehearsing the role of Fanny Brice. Garson Kanin was putting them through their paces as they worked out the details of a scene. On the unusually wide stage of the Winter

Garden Theatre, under its lower-than-average proscenium arch, Barbra was treading where Mistinguett had once sung, where Josephine Baker, Gypsy Rose Lee, Gaby Deslys, and Marilyn Miller had all performed. But among these ghosts none was quite as welcome as that of Fanny Brice herself, whose last performance in the Ziegfeld Follies had taken place on that very same stage in 1936.

Although Barbra, Kazan, and McLerie might have been dressed in street clothes and flat shoes this day, they were pretending to be outfitted in elaborate Ziegfeldian costumes — hats, boas, bustles, the works. They were imagining themselves in a backstage corridor of a Baltimore theater, where, as Fanny listened, her two beautiful show-girl companions — Kazan as Vera, McLerie as Nora — lamented that someday their looks would be gone.

"Not me," Barbra as Fanny interjected. "For *my* public, I can stop being gorgeous whenever I want." A beat. "I could even *start* being gorgeous if I weren't always standing next to one of you."

Suddenly she threw down the script. "I don't like this scene," Barbra declared. "We need to work on this."

Lainie Kazan watched in wonder. Ever since rehearsals had started on December 10, Barbra had been running the show, and producer Stark and director Kanin, to everyone's amazement, had been letting her. Kazan, who'd played small parts in *The Happiest Girl in the World,* with Cyril Ritchard and Janice Rule, and *Bravo Giovanni,* with Michele Lee, had never seen anything like this before. Barbra looked out into the audience where Ray Stark was sitting, his leg in a cast propped up in the aisle. He'd fractured it skiing, but that didn't stop him from hobbling on his crutches and following Barbra to her dressing room when she stalked off the stage, Isobel Lennart close behind. Garson Kanin, however, remained seated where he was, fifth row center in the empty auditorium, whispering urgently with his wife, Ruth Gordon, who was present at every rehearsal.

Lainie Kazan presumed this was "the modus operandi of all musical stars," until she realized that Janice Rule and Michele Lee had never behaved this way. Kazan could only assume that once a star got to Barbra's rank, they "had that kind of power to stop rehearsals and throw off schedules, that they could be difficult and that was okay." But then it hit her that *Funny Girl* was Barbra's first starring role. Kazan was left awestruck by Barbra's "moxie" — for want of a better word.

When she'd first heard that a show was being staged about Fanny Brice, Kazan had wanted the lead herself. She'd been making a name for herself as a lusty, busty torch singer at such clubs as the Living Room and the Colonial Tavern, and she'd studied dancing with Carol Haney. Like her fellow Erasmus Hall graduate, Kazan "wanted to make it big, be really successful." But that was where her similarities with Barbra ended. Kazan had been voted most popular girl in her class. She'd also been a star of the glee club, incredibly outgoing and social, and, in the biggest difference from Barbra, pretty. All the boys liked Lainie. "A totally different ball of wax," Kazan said, comparing her high school experience with Barbra's.

Was that why Barbra refused to warm to her? Kazan had tried joking with her, the way she'd done with the leading ladies on other shows, but Barbra would have none of it. She was "too intent on what she was doing," Kazan observed, and uninterested in becoming "part of the team." Kazan suspected that the different routes each had taken to get to this point colored their approaches to the show. Barbra had come from nightclubs, where the spotlight had centered solely on her. Kazan had been in the chorus of several shows, and in the chorus "everyone learned to work together, to be good to each other, to help each other." That kind of camaraderie Barbra had never known in any part of her life.

Her distance from the company reflected her own anxieties about not fitting in, which, of course, ran very deep. Barbra was also painfully aware that success or failure largely rested on her own slim shoulders, and as she'd done on her second album, she was willing to take control if she deemed it necessary — and she'd quickly decided it was. As rehearsals had gotten underway, Barbra found a company lacking the kind of military precision she remembered under Arthur

Laurents. Everyone seemed to like Garson Kanin, but not one person was afraid of him — which was no way to run a show.

Meanwhile, adding yet more confusion in another of those upheavals that had so far characterized *Funny Girl,* David Merrick quit, leaving Stark as sole producer. No wonder Barbra cracked to Earl Wilson soon after the first rehearsal, "This is worse than opening night." She'd had more fun, she said, when she was "sharing the bill and could take the play away from the star." Not exactly the most politic admission, since that same star was now her husband, but at least it was honest.

Merrick's departure had left everyone uneasy. The clash between the mercurial Merrick and the manipulative Stark had been inevitable, especially as their business entanglements multiplied. Merrick was currently in partnership with Seven Arts on the production of *One Flew Over the Cuckoo's Nest,* and was also in talks to coproduce a dramatization of Rumer Godden's novel *A Candle for St. Jude.* Stark had been frustrated by Merrick's greater attention to his other shows, primarily *Hello, Dolly!,* while Merrick had become increasingly leery of Stark's gerrymandering of movie-rights deals, since all of their productions were destined for big-screen development. Saying "life is too short to deal with Ray Stark," Merrick withdrew as producer of *Funny Girl,* selling his shares to his former partner for a sum reported to be in excess of $100,000.

While Stark had produced *The World of Suzie Wong,* he'd done so in conjunction with Seven Arts. Now, for the first time, he was the sole pilot steering a major Broadway show. Everyone knew that Stark was an expert at making movies. But could he bring those same skills to the theater?

Making matters more complicated, Barbra's contract had been with Merrick; at the time of signing, Stark hadn't possessed an Actors' Equity agreement. That was why having Merrick as a partner had been so advantageous. But now that Barbra's contract was suddenly moot, *Funny Girl,* in effect, no longer had a star. From Barbra's point of view, she was starting rehearsals without a contract.

A new agreement was needed with Stark, and Barbra drew up a

list of demands. It was only right, her agents argued. Since signing with Merrick last summer, Barbra had become the most successful woman in the recording industry, regularly selling out huge arena-sized venues. No longer was she just Liberace's warm-up act, as she'd been when she'd signed with Merrick. So Barbra told Begelman and Fields that she wanted a raise from $3,500 to $7,500 a week. She could make that much in club dates, as the columnists were pointing out. In addition to asking for a raise, Barbra wanted a private hairstylist, free meals every day, and a chauffeured limousine to take her between her apartment and the theater. Finally, she was hoping, her long-ago dream of being driven around the city might come true.

Watching as Barbra huffed off to her dressing room, the rest of the company was aware that their leading lady was demanding a great deal. Kazan wondered if Stark, shouting after her on his crutches, would give in. He hadn't yet acceded to all of Barbra's demands for a new contract, but everyone — Barbra included — understood that she was in the driver's seat. There was no show without her. That was why Stark had hobbled after her so solicitously. Kazan thought that Barbra had him right where she wanted him. And if there was anyone in the cast with insights into Ray Stark, it was Lainie Kazan.

After Barbra had won the part of Fanny, Kazan had put the show out of her mind until the night Carol Haney had brought Stark to the Living Room to hear her sing. After the show, a very enthusiastic Stark had come up to Kazan and asked her to audition for the part of Vera. Kazan didn't think she wanted it — she could make more money, $350 a week, singing in clubs — but Stark wouldn't take no for an answer. He pestered her for days until she finally agreed to a meeting with him. He told her he'd send a car right over to pick her up. No one was surprised that Stark would pursue Kazan so aggressively. At twenty-three, she was absolutely gorgeous — she'd turned down a stint at the Playboy Club — and everyone knew Stark's eye for the ladies.

At the scheduled time, Kazan looked out the window of her room at the Whitby, a theatrical boarding house on Forty-fifth Street between Eighth and Ninth avenues, and saw a Bentley waiting. A uniformed chauffeur was there to open the door for her. She wasn't being taken to the theater, Kazan discovered, but to Stark's private suite at the Hotel Navarro. Ushered into his room, she found the producer lying in bed, his left leg suspended in traction. He'd fractured it, Stark explained, in a skiing accident in Sun Valley, Idaho. Underneath his specially tailored trousers was a white plaster cast, autographed by famous people.

Stark encouraged Kazan to sit on the side of the bed as they spoke. "You are fabulous, terrific," he told her. He wanted to sign her not just for the show, he told her, but also to a seven-year movie contract. Kazan was smart enough to know that he was "coming on" to her. She was also smart enough to take advantage of it. Stark arranged for a contract promising "vocal and dramatic coaching and instruction for the purpose of enhancing [her] talent as a singer and actress in the various fields of entertainment." In addition to her *Funny Girl* salary, Kazan would also collect a weekly paycheck of $300 as a Seven Arts employee, with a promise of increases up to $2,000 a week if she remained in exclusive contract with the production company. The one part of the deal she wasn't sure about was the offer to be Barbra's understudy. But when Stark promised to pay her $50 more a week to do so, the struggling young actress agreed.

How much Barbra knew about this private meeting with Stark, Kazan wasn't sure. But secrets were hard to keep backstage. Was that one more reason Barbra cold-shouldered her? On a show where she was finally the star — where, at long last, Barbra was supposed to be the center of attention — one of the pretty, popular girls — and from Erasmus Hall yet! — had waltzed in and stolen the producer's eye away from her.

No wonder she was demanding her own package of favors from Stark. Whether Barbra knew the exact details of Kazan's contract or not, she probably knew that her understudy was getting a pretty sweet deal from Stark. Which, of course, only made her more determined to secure a deal that was even sweeter.

In her dressing room, complaining about the script to Stark and Lennart, Barbra was demanding a great deal. This wasn't ego: This was survival. Garson Kanin, she complained, was far too easygoing in his direction. He "said very little, and his directions were always very laid back," said another member of the company. Kanin pretty much stayed in his fifth row center seat, listening to the cast read through their parts and "nodding a lot." Most of his time was spent conferring privately with his wife. For Barbra, the fact that Kanin was "reportedly getting the biggest percentage ever given to a director" was no doubt galling, given how ineffectual he was proving to be. Without a strong director, Barbra had decided to fill the power vacuum herself.

In her dressing room, she went over the script, circling scenes that needed to be worked on and crossing out scenes she felt should be cut. If people called her controlling, then so be it. It was the only way she could work. It wasn't about having control, she told one interviewer, explaining her tendency to seize authority on a project. It was about assuming "artistic responsibility." She was the star of the show, after all; she was the one people were coming to see. So she'd rather have her "taste on the line," Barbra argued, than anyone else's.

To Marv Schwartz, she had admitted she was "affected by things." If she didn't like "the color of the rug," for example, she'd become "affected," and so the color had to be changed. She couldn't help that; she was "a sensory kind of person." And she truly believed that what affected her also affected her ability to work, and that, in turn, affected the show. If she seemed demanding, it was only in the interest of the project at hand. "I'm the easiest person to work with and the hardest to work with," she said. She never demanded retakes when appearing on television, for example. Since she believed there was "no such thing as making a mistake," she accepted it when she sang a little differently than she intended. It wasn't wrong; it was just different. She insisted that she would never walk off in the middle of a performance, as she'd seen some pretty big names do. Instead, she'd stick around and figure out what the problem was and then correct it. "So if the musicians are lousy," she said, "I've got to . . . work harder."

That was what she was doing with *Funny Girl.* The director, in her opinion, was lousy. The script wasn't all that terrific either. So Barbra was working harder. Sometimes it was hard to explain her reasons, but she knew, in her gut, that she was right. That made things difficult sometimes. "It's hard to argue with me," she conceded.

Heading back out onto the stage with Stark and Lennart and a revised script, Barbra was very pleased with the authority she'd been given. If she was honest with herself, which she could sometimes be, she'd admit that occasionally simply winning an argument was as important as achieving the desired change in the script, or the costume, or the music. Just a few months ago, Marv Schwartz had asked her if she demanded certain things because she really believed in them or because she just wanted to have her own way. It hadn't taken long for Barbra to answer. "Both," she had said.

9.

The one person who didn't think Barbra knew better than everyone else was Bob Merrill. Sitting with her at the piano, he was ready to tell her, quite frankly, to go to hell, but he let the more diplomatic Jule Styne take the lead, as he usually did in these matters.

What had them up in arms was a note they'd received from Marty Erlichman telling them that, upon consideration, Barbra "didn't think she wanted to sing" either "People" or "Don't Rain on My Parade."

Styne had immediately gotten her on the phone. "Barbra," he told her, "you don't sing 'People,' you don't sing my score."

For Styne to have been so firm with her was unusual and emphasized the passion he felt about the issue. Right from the start, those two songs had defined the score. Merrill's notebooks documented how much time he had spent composing the lyrics, especially on "Don't Rain on My Parade." He'd experimented with various couplets — "Don't tell me not to fly, I've started soarin', The stars are flyin' by, The wind is roarin'" — before crossing them out and settling on the final lyrics. He and Styne had spent two years on these songs, and now Barbra didn't want to sing them.

Styne was devastated; Merrill was furious. Why she suddenly, inexplicably, wanted the two songs excised — or "given to someone else," as Merrill understood — they didn't know. Perhaps Barbra, like others, thought "People," as lovely as it was, made little sense in the show, or at least where it was placed in the show. Fanny, at that early stage, isn't thinking about needing other people: She just wants to be famous. Or perhaps Barbra didn't like how difficult the songs were to sing, each in their own way, as Merrill's wife, Suzanne, wondered. Whatever Barbra's reasons, the composers weren't backing down. With great patience, Styne had explained to their leading lady that those two songs were "going to be the ones everyone remembered." Maybe that would make a difference to her, he told Merrill.

And it seemed it had. Standing beside the piano, Barbra blithely told the composers that she'd come around and now shared their viewpoint. Both Styne and Merrill breathed long sighs of relief. A serious crisis had been averted. Yet Barbra's easy capitulation raised the question of how serious she had been. Merrill wondered if she had been playing them.

He still hadn't entirely warmed to her. He still felt Barbra was "a know-it-all." And it seemed as soon as one issue was resolved, another one arose. Now it was Barbra's first song in the show, "If a Girl Isn't Pretty." She was to sing a reprise of it after it was introduced by Mrs. Brice and her friend, Mrs. Strakosh. Barbra hated it. Talk about autobiography. The song was all about people telling an ugly duckling she can never be a swan. "Is a nose with deviation such a crime against the nation?" went one line. Maybe, instead of ditching the other two, she could ditch this one?

That was a question for Kanin, the composers told her. They'd written these songs with certain characters in mind, but shuffling numbers among the cast was par for the course in musicals. The problem that really hung Merrill up was the liberties Barbra took in interpreting the words he'd written. He believed it was "very important to a lyricist to have the singer pronounce the words the way he intended them." Inflections, accents, emphasis could all change meanings, throw off rhymes. As Barbra sang the sad ballad "Who Are You Now?" — one of the last numbers in the show — Merrill jumped up and complained that she held the word "someone" too long in the line "Are you some-one better?" It changed his intent, he argued. "This is my song," he said, "and I want you to do it this way." Barbra was equally adamant she knew how to sing a lyric.

Merrill didn't view it as an artistic interpretation. He saw it as "fiddling" with his composition. In some ways, he was an awful lot like Barbra. Merrill felt he knew the best way to sing something, and he didn't want anyone telling him otherwise. His wife thought "Don't Rain on My Parade" could have been Merrill's theme song: "Don't bug me, get out of my way" was exactly the message he sent to those around him.

As always, it was Styne who played the good cop to his partner's bad cop. "Everyone loved Jule," Merrill's wife observed. "Not everyone loved Bob." It would be Styne who approached Barbra to ask her tactfully if she might try to sing a song differently; failing that, he might try adjusting the music to appease them both. The "teeny tiny" Styne would get up out of his seat and bustle from person to person, Lainie Kazan observed, always followed by two assistants who matched him in diminutive size. Kazan couldn't help but smile when she saw "these three little people moving across the room in unison," putting out fires, carrying ideas, trying new arrangements, and trying to keep the peace. Styne was always talking, Kazan noted — always chirping away giddily, anxiously, expressively. Merrill sat there silently.

Perhaps some of Styne's energy came from his belief, as he put it, that he was "in a desperate race with the calendar." Despite all his great movie compositions, he felt his career hadn't really gotten moving until 1952, when he'd coproduced a revival of *Pal Joey* with Richard Rodgers. It was Broadway where Styne's heart resided, and at the age of fifty-seven, even with *Gypsy* and other shows under his belt, there was still "so much [he wanted] to say musically." He longed to be a singular artist, to have his work easily identifiable as being his. "Don't be a minor Cole Porter," Rodgers had told him. "Be yourself and the critics will gradually have respect for you." This was Styne's greatest hope.

And so it was a good thing that Barbra was singing "People" and "Don't Rain on My Parade." *Funny Girl,* Styne sensed, might be a very important part of his legacy.

10.

The Christmas season arrived in New York that year in sheets of snow and gloom. Still in mourning for their slain president, most Americans headed into the holiday celebrations more muted than usual, trying to come to grips with the murder and its grisly aftermath, in which the president's assassin, Lee Harvey Oswald, had himself been murdered, giving rise to all sorts of conspiracy theories. Frigid temperatures had gripped the northeast in a stranglehold, plunging New York into a kind of perpetual shudder. That year, few smiles cracked the cold, red faces of those who shopped along Fifth Avenue.

Heading to rehearsals in a cab, Barbra wasn't smiling either. Stark hadn't met her terms. He'd offered $5,000 instead of $7,500 and had nixed the other perks, including the chauffeured limousine. Barbra felt the producer was being stingy; Stark felt she had tried to take advantage of Merrick's departure by setting her high-powered agents on him. What had been a largely cordial relationship suddenly turned antagonistic. Fosse's complaints about Stark's devious nature may suddenly have resonated with Barbra. Stark had called her bluff. He knew she wasn't any more willing to walk away from the show than he was to lose her.

The aggravation over contract negotiations couldn't have helped the mood at rehearsals, which every day was becoming bleaker. As Barbra arrived at the Winter Garden on a frosty morning in mid-December, she knew that something had to change. Garson Kanin just sat there, giving her hardly any feedback, while the scenes went "on and on with no sense of cohesion," one member of the company observed. The show was too long, Barbra believed.

Any cuts couldn't affect the main storyline, however, which concerned Fanny's rise to the top while falling in love with, and then losing, Nick. So while there were some bits with Fanny that could be deleted — a roller-skating scene Barbra had been practicing for weeks, for example — the majority of cuts would affect the supporting characters. Eddie Ryan had a solo, "Take Something for Nothing," that seemed destined for the chopping block, even though it fleshed out his character by showing his love for Fanny. The chorus girls, all compellingly individual in early scripts, would have to be blended together.

But it was the part of the beautiful Nora that Barbra objected to most. She seemed "uncomfortable with how significant that part was," one company member thought, watching the number of changes in the scenes between Fanny and Nora. From Stark and the show's composers, Lainie Kazan observed a growing sense that "the entire focus of *Funny Girl* needed to be Fanny." As a consequence, she said, "everyone else became incidental." When Nora came into a scene, for example, she "took away from Fanny," and that was a problem that needed to be addressed.

McLerie had a solo number, "Baltimore Sun," that she sung toward the end of Act One, at the point where she and Vera lament their fading looks. "Enter the star, wearing pearls to save insurance and brown paper bags to save tips," Nora was scripted to say as Fanny made her entrance. That led to the line where Fanny declared she didn't worry about losing her looks. To which Nora was to reply, in one of the several astute confrontations the script gave her: "But you *like* standing next to us. And proving that what you have is so much better. That there isn't a man you couldn't get away from any one of us — if you really wanted to."

That was one of the underlying themes of *Funny Girl*: Fanny's desirability wasn't dependent on looks. But what Nora was doing was actually pointing out Fanny's narcissism, a fact that was made even clearer later on when, drunk and depressed, Nora laments that she won't be in next year's Follies. Fanny tells her to fight back. Nora replies, "Don't you ever look at the people you care about? Don't you ever see them?" Fanny tells her that she cares about people. Nora waits a beat before answering. "Very depressing, how big you are," she says at last. "Makes smaller people feel — too small."

Her message was plain: Not everyone — not Nora, not Nick — was as strong as Fanny. Fanny was superhuman in her strength, and those high standards — that perfectionism — kept her separated from those who might be a little less mighty, but perhaps more human, than she was. Fanny, according to Ray Stark, "very probably made it difficult for the man she married to live up to her, or with her." The autobiography was perhaps getting a little too close for Barbra. Whispers had already begun that Elliott, another gambler living in the shadow of a famous wife, was not so different from Nick. How long would the scene stay in the show? That was the question some were asking.

But autobiography was what *Funny Girl* had become. It had, in fact, become a selling point. "This play is really about me," Barbra told the Associated Press. "It simply happened to happen before to Fanny Brice."

There was one moment that carried particular resonance. In an early scene, before Fanny has become famous, she makes the case that she ought to be given a chance. "Look," she says. "Suppose all you ever had for breakfast was onion rolls. All of a sudden one morning in walks a bagel. You'd say, 'Ugh! What's that?' Until you tried it. That's my problem. I'm a bagel on a plateful of onion rolls!" That about summed up what Barbra had been dealing with ever since she'd started out on her quest for fame.

To another reporter, Barbra mused on how long it had taken Stark to get this show produced. "Ten years ago they started on this idea," she said, "when I was only eleven years old." When the reporter asked why it had taken so long, Barbra replied, "I wasn't old enough then. They were waiting for me." She was only half joking. While she and

Fanny had become in many ways interchangeable, Barbra insisted that she was not Fanny, even if Fanny had become her. "I don't want to imitate anybody," Barbra admitted to one reporter. "My ego's too big."

Without that healthy ego, Barbra would never have made it to the stage of the Winter Garden Theatre — but for some people, that superhuman confidence was as grating as it was to Nora in the script. Sheilah Graham, who'd been so complimentary ahead of Barbra's performance at the Cocoanut Grove, had subsequently been turned off by the young singer-actress's boast that she'd win every award there was. "Little girl," Graham wrote now. "This is too much, too soon."

But that little girl was the show's best chance for success. Her voice and personality and yes, her ego, were intended to carry *Funny Girl* despite the substandard script. That was why Ray Stark was letting Barbra take the director's reins away from Kanin. Most of the company agreed that their director wasn't up to fixing the problems inherent in the book, and they looked to Barbra to make things right. She seemed "to know exactly what she was doing," said one company member, "to instinctively know what was best for the show." So everyone put their faith in their twenty-one-year-old leading lady.

Including the leading man.

11.

"We hate each other," Barbra teased, looking across the table at Sydney Chaplin at the Italian restaurant where they were having supper together.

But the reporter interviewing them knew that was just an "inverted way of expressing mutual admiration." Barbra and Sydney, he observed, were "two of a kind."

In fact, they were more like complementary opposites. Sydney was the perfect follower to Barbra's leader. Barbra had heard stories of Sydney's temper, but to her he had never been less than flattering or accommodating. Playing love scenes with Sydney proved to be very pleasant indeed. Once Barbra had asked why a girl like her couldn't play love scenes. Now she was in the hero's arms, and the company noticed just how much she seemed to enjoy being kissed by Sydney in front of everyone. "She glowed," said dancer Sharon Vaughn. "She loved it," said a member of the chorus. Wardrobe lady Ceil Mack detected sparks flying between the show's two leads. Kanin, too, became aware of how "very chummy" Barbra and Sydney had suddenly become.

But while much of their chemistry was personal, there was also a professional reason for it. Sydney shared Barbra's belief that *Funny Girl* "needed to be their story" and proved to be a powerful ally in her determination to streamline the production. At the moment, the show ran more than four hours. There was no question that it needed to be cut.

Consequently, over Kanin's objections, a decision was made to fire Allyn Ann McLerie. Kanin argued that Nora had brought "a note to the show which it needed" — a note of balance, since otherwise it was all Fanny, all the time. But clearly Kanin was overruled on the matter. The only people with enough clout to do that would have been Stark and Barbra. The official reason given for McLerie's ouster, and it was partly true, was "the length of the musical." *Funny Girl* was indeed too long. But without her, the script tipped precariously close to becoming a one-woman show.

The bigger problem, at least according to Barbra, was Kanin himself. The director was never going to be someone she held in high regard. The thin, gray-haired Kanin affected a certain simplicity, wearing wool shirts and knitted ties, but he could be very showy in other ways. He had a reedy little voice that he used to pontificate on various subjects, whether it be socialism or Hollywood art direction. He covered his wife in so much jewelry that Cecil Beaton thought she resembled "a little Burmese idol." Kanin's marriage to the much-older Gordon had not only produced an extremely successful professional partnership, but had also provided cover for his deeply conflicted and circumspect homosexuality. "Gar" could be warm and friendly, but also sly and manipulative, and he invariably chose passive aggression over direct action. In that way, Kanin resembled Ray Stark, and Barbra already had one Stark to deal with.

It was Kanin's reticence to take a stand on what she was doing with the role that really unsettled her. He just sat there, with his ubiquitous wife, watching her. Once, during a run-through of "People," Barbra had done everything opposite from the way they'd originally rehearsed it, and Kanin had remained immobile, never saying a word. Jule Styne, meanwhile, had thought Barbra was "on fire" and told the musical director to let her go and have the orchestra follow her lead. Styne thought Barbra's interpretation had been brilliant, far better than what Kanin had tried to set up. But Kanin said not a word, either in protest or in praise. His method of directing Barbra, he said, "was to attempt to get her to realize all those important facets of her own personality." It was his job as director, he said, to simply "create an atmosphere in which her personality could flower." In other words, it was all up to her.

While it was very true that Barbra didn't like being told what to do, she also resented the supposed top guy just sitting there and letting her do all the work. Arthur Laurents hadn't abdicated his authority in this way; neither had Barbra when she walked into the studio to make her second album. She was willing to do the same here. But unlike her album, where she'd been through the process before, this was her first time starring in a Broadway show. A little help, a little direction, was going to be necessary.

A director, in her opinion, couldn't be neutral. "The actor has to have some feedback, some mirror, some opinion, even if it's wrong," she said. She was going to have her own ideas, that was a given — but she needed to bounce them off someone she respected. A director needed "to talk to the actors, give them a sense of their own importance." She also needed to feel that her director "loved [her] . . . wanted to make [her] beautiful." Laurents had done both. Kanin seemed to do neither.

Just a few days earlier, she had asked him a question, and Kanin had replied by asking what *she* thought. "Fuck you," Barbra had said to him, and walked away, leaving Lainie Kazan and others in the company with mouths agape.

"I have a problem with tact," Barbra admitted. "I only know how to be direct." She didn't know how to *shmeykhl* somebody, she said, how to beat around the bush, to get something she wanted — especially not with a director who was supposed to be ensuring her show would be a hit.

Sitting with Sydney in that Italian restaurant, Barbra didn't raise such concerns, not with a reporter from the *Boston Globe* present. But she knew Sydney shared her worries. In her quarrels with Kanin, he had supported her one hundred percent. Sydney had even started looking to Barbra for advice on how he should play the part of Nick. He agreed that the show wasn't in anywhere near the shape it should be this close to their first previews. They were working from a deeply flawed book, and both of them knew it. The trick was not letting anyone outside the show know they knew it. "Whatever happens to the show," Barbra told the reporter, putting the best face on things, "it will have been fun."

When word came that they were needed back at rehearsals, the two costars stood to leave. Sydney, silent for so much of the interview, turned to the reporter. "It'll be a hit," he said. No doubt he believed that, too, as he followed his fiery, determined, tactless leading lady back into the theater.

12.

The Gotham Hotel was one of New York's great old luxury lodgings. On the southwest corner of Fifth Avenue and Fifty-fifth Street, the granite Beaux Arts structure shot up twenty-four stories. Barbra had arrived at the hotel on the cold and snowy evening of December 27 to accept the Entertainer of the Year Award from *Cue* magazine, an honor that had previously gone to Diahann Carroll and Zero Mostel. Not only was she getting the award, but her face also graced the cover of *Cue,* "the entertainment guide to New York and suburbs," with a circulation of more than 200,000 for its five different editions. As she walked into the jam-packed Grand Ballroom, filled with hundreds of showmen, pressmen, and performers, all of them applauding for her, Barbra was on the threshold of achieving everything she'd once dreamed about, of claiming the future she'd often been unable to visualize as a kid back in Brooklyn.

At the moment, an Associated Press story about her, running in hundreds of papers all across the country, was calling her the "world's hottest young star." She'd just finished recording the tracks for her third album, which Columbia wanted out early next year before *Funny Girl* opened. *Mademoiselle* magazine had recently presented her with one of their ten annual Merit Awards given to young women of achievement, honoring her alongside Russian cosmonaut Valentina Tereshkova, fashion designer Deanna Littell, French-Indian actress Leela Naidu, and writer Susan Sontag. More heady company came in Louis Sobol's column featuring the most exciting New Yorkers of 1963. Here Barbra was included with British transplant Albert Finney, Senator Jacob Javits, and playwright Edward Albee. Not bad for a kid from the corner of Newkirk and Nostrand.

Outside of showbiz, though, things were a little different. Barbra no longer had any real friends except for Cis and Harvey Corman, the only people she spent time with when she wasn't working. Rarely did Barbra accept social invitations from professional colleagues; she almost never asked people to her home. She could have, of course: the duplex was gradually coming together, with antique spool cabinets and beautifully mismatched china sets and glowing theater exit signs over the doors. The place was built for entertaining. Around the enormous bar, Larry Hart had once played host to hundreds. But since Barbra had moved in, the bar remained unadorned and unused.

Instead, the heart of the house for Barbra had become the kitchen, where she'd covered the walls with red patent leather and added antique stools. She might not cook big dinners for friends, but here Elliott whipped up her chicken soup, waiting for her to come home from the theater. In the mornings he called Barbra on the intercom to come down and eat. Most nights, it was just the two of them.

In some ways, as one journalist put it, Barbra and Elliott were "encamped there like a pair of gypsies in a half-wrecked enchanted castle, leading a grandiose, accelerated version of the same raggle-taggle life they led over the fish restaurant." Beside their bed in the tower suite they'd installed a refrigerator so they wouldn't have to trudge all the way downstairs if they wanted a dish of Breyer's coffee or cherry-vanilla ice cream late at night. Elliott liked to believe he and Barbra remained very simple people. One of their "conjugal delights," he said, was still a Nathan's hot dog.

But their seclusion from the social whirl of New York also grew out of Barbra's shyness, her fear of discovering that among these sophisticated socialites, she wouldn't fit in. A part of her scorned them for their pretenses. Deep down, Barbra knew that even her move to the apartment at the Ardsley had been a concession to a pretentious, affected way of thinking: "I am now a mature, successful woman," she said to one writer, explaining the move. "Hah! So I should move out of my tiny third-floor walk-up. And I did, into a large duplex, because the more successful you get, the less secure you get. It's the nature of the business."

If there was one thing Barbra understood after her extraordinary year, it was the nature of the business she was in. Image mattered. Not for nothing did Barbra donate five hundred dollars' worth of her old clothes to a local thrift shop and allow her publicists to leak word of it to the columnists. Metaphorically, she was shedding the old, kooky, thrift-shop Barbra. She was now a self-proclaimed couturiere, designing her own clothes and being written up in fashion columns. Earl Wilson pointed out that Barbra had once shopped in thrift stores because that was all she could afford; now she was handing over her surplus to them. "And that's what one year can do for you in show business," Wilson wrote.

As people stepped aside to let her pass, Barbra took the stage at the Gotham, accepting the award from *Cue* publisher Edward Loeb.

If she had looked out into the crowd, she would have seen her face everywhere, as copies of the current issue were held in nearly every hand. Inside, a piece by editor Emory Lewis explained why they had chosen this twenty-one-year-old over so many others. "Streisand is an original," Lewis wrote, "and originals are rare in our industrial, homogenized society." But how far could an original go? Barbra might be the entertainer of the year, but what about next year? What happened if *Funny Girl* flopped, doomed by its deficient book and ineffectual director? How long could an original like Barbra last?

CHAPTER SIXTEEN

Winter 1964

1.

All over the city of Boston on the night of January 8, residents double locked their doors, still on edge. The latest victim of the infamous Strangler had been found in an apartment on Charles Street. There was no moon this night, and temperatures hovered just above freezing. And in the quiet, carpeted corridors of a luxurious Back Bay hotel, Sydney Chaplin, convinced that most everyone was sound asleep, decided it was time to make his move.

They'd all arrived that afternoon for two days of rehearsals at the Shubert Theatre on Tremont Street. Ray Stark, still on crutches, conducted a series of meet and greets with the local press, sharing his optimism about the show, especially the music. Despite his earlier arguments to the contrary, Stark now insisted he was glad that none of "the old things" that Fanny Brice used to sing, such as "My Man," were in the show because they "wouldn't stand up to the Styne-Merrill score." Stark seemed to truly believe that all the show's problems had been solved, or maybe he'd simply instructed everyone to give that impression ahead of *Funny Girl*'s first preview, a benefit for the Boston Lying-in Hospital on January 11. Indeed, when columnist

Marjorie Mills spotted Garson Kanin, he was "trying his best not to look jubilant."

In the still of the night, Sydney rapped lightly on Barbra's door.

She was twenty-one years old. He was thirty-seven. She was a kid from Brooklyn; he was Hollywood royalty. She was always being reminded of her unconventional looks; he was equally celebrated for being matinee-idol handsome. She was the leading lady; he was her leading man. Barbra would have needed to be made of stone not to let him in.

Whether their affair began that night, as Sydney's friends believed, or on a night not long before or after, it began nonetheless. Back in New York, Elliott was helping the vivacious Italian actress Anna Maria Alberghetti stage a new nightclub act with song-and-dance man John W. Bubbles. Alberghetti was beautiful and single, and Elliott worked with her late into the night. There was talk, as of course there would be. Barbra may have heard the talk, which may have been one more reason why she opened the door when Sydney knocked.

Barbra's trysts with Sydney were conducted in the privacy of hotel rooms, always in secret. The company couldn't know; the press certainly couldn't know. Unlike the exuberant couple of *Wholesale,* whose affair had started the same way and who hadn't minded if the occupants of adjoining rooms could hear them, Barbra and Sydney were both married to other people. So this had to be discreet. But there was no question that it also had to be.

The attraction had been impossible to resist. Barbra had become a young woman who unapologetically liked sex, even if the sex was often about "playing games with men — that image game," as she explained in her own words. Here she and Sydney were, astride their world, the queen and her king. In theatrical companies, said Sydney's friend Orson Bean, "the leading man and the leading lady often fell in love," finding only in each other a worthy companion.

It was true, too, that Sydney filled a need that Elliott hadn't satisfied in some time. Barbra was attracted to confident, successful men. Sydney was a Tony winner; Elliott was still unemployed. Sydney seemed to know exactly who he was; Elliott, Barbra believed, "really didn't have a sense of himself." Barbra had tried telling him he was a brilliant comedian, a fine actor, and a smart businessman. But Elliott never seemed to listen.

He was also gambling again. Elliott admitted there was something within himself that was "very self-destructive." He gambled in large part because "winning or losing a bet seemed to represent a hard-edged reality" that offset the artificiality of show business. He really was not so different from the Nick Arnstein of the play, whose gambling destroys his marriage to Fanny. And like Arnstein, Elliott gambled out of a deep lack of self-worth. He'd had more respect for himself, Elliott said, when he was a teenager "operating the night elevator in the Park Royal Hotel." Certainly it had offered steadier work; certainly he'd felt more needed. By now, Elliott was deeper than ever into analysis. "I'm just finding myself," he explained — a laudable goal, but to Barbra, he might have been speaking a foreign language.

In his quest for greater self-awareness, Elliott was also still smoking a lot of grass and experimenting with other drugs. Some of the "trips" he'd been on had given him an "inner understanding" of himself that he might not have achieved otherwise. Barbra, of course, was far too single-minded, far too self-controlled to participate in such trips. And so the experiences of husband and wife grew even more separate.

Meanwhile, there was Sydney, waiting for her every day at rehearsals. He had begun whispering in her ear, "Kid, you're gorgeous" or "Baby, you're brilliant." Sydney couldn't flatter her enough. Bean thought that such flattery, at least in part, stemmed from Sydney's worries that Barbra's self-confidence might flag as they approached the opening, and he knew that without the force of her strong personality, the show would sink. But he was also, his friend said, as dazzled with her as she was with him.

Alone in their Boston hotel room, their spouses far away, a debonair Sydney was winning over a tough, driven Barbra in much the same way their characters were doing on the stage. Elliott wasn't the only one who resembled Nick Arnstein; Sydney was as much the smooth operator as the man he played on stage. If she felt any guilt, Barbra kept it as private as she kept the affair. "Sydney was giving Barbra the confidence to be great," Bean said. Such encouragement, so necessary at that point, could never have come from her depressed husband. It could only come from Barbra's very own real-life Nicky Arnstein.

2.

The snow started falling early on the morning of January 13. By noon, there were already several inches on the ground, and weather forecasters were telling the city to batten down the hatches for an "old fashioned nor'easter." By late in the afternoon, the winds were hitting sixty miles per hour, the temperature had dropped to zero, and the beaches were flooded. Trains and buses were thrown off schedule. Logan Airport was closed. A citywide parking ban was instituted. By the time it was all over, forecasters warned, Beantown would be covered in a foot of snow.

Inside the Shubert Theatre, the decision was made that the show would go on.

They couldn't cancel their first official preview. The house was sold out. To try to refund and reschedule now would produce a disaster worse than the blizzard. And so the company proceeded to makeup and then to wardrobe. The lighting men and engineers climbed into the booth. Everyone hoped for the best.

Their unofficial preview, two nights earlier, had gone well. The Shubert had been packed with a fashionable audience dressed in glittering gowns and tuxedos. To support the Lying-in Hospital, the crème of Boston society had turned out: the Harborne Stuarts, the John Marshalls, the Bayard Henrys, and so many others, weighted down with jewelry and social connections. They were all there to see Barbra Streisand, a young woman who'd grown up rather far away from Beacon Hill and Harvard Square. And even though the show had run until after midnight, all the socialites were still in their seats cheering when the curtain finally came down. As agreed, none of the press in attendance published a word about the show itself, leaving that for the official preview, though one writer from the *Globe* couldn't resist commenting on "the handsome Irene Sharaff costumes" and how the legendary designer herself watched the show from a box.

Now, as the snow piled up outside and the wind whistled through the eaves of the fifty-year-old theater, Sharaff made last-minute in-spections of the show's seven glamorous showgirls as they stepped into and zipped up their extraordinary Ziegfeldian costumes. Lainie Kazan's hat needed to come down a little more over her eyes. Boas were fluffed, hems were straightened, and bustiers tightened to push up more cleavage. Sharaff had won a Tony for *The King and I,* Oscars for *West Side Story* and *Cleopatra.* She had dressed Gertrude Law-rence, Judy Garland, Elizabeth Taylor, and Ingrid Bergman. Now she added Barbra Streisand to that list.

From outside, they could probably hear the plows, busy removing snow from the streets, a thankless job since half an hour later they had to do it again. The heavy winds created drifts that were higher than a man's head. The storm was forecast to continue straight through to morning without letting up. All Boston-area schools were closed until further notice. Shubert house manager M. D. "Doc" Howe told Ray Stark to expect quite a few unfilled seats at tonight's performance.

What was it about this show that brought a new crisis every few months? Now, at the moment when it was finally ready to present to the world, when they could finally brace themselves for critical reac-tion, they were being stalled yet again. And right at the point where everything finally seemed set. Kanin had acquiesced to many of the changes Barbra had insisted on, and Lennart had dashed out yet an-other script in time for the Boston premiere. With the part of Nora eliminated, the plot seemed to flow more seamlessly. What was left of Nora's dialogue was given to the character of Mimsey, played by Sharon Vaughn, a recent addition to the cast. A number of songs were also sliced out, disappointing chorus girls like Diana Lee Nielsen, who now had no songs of their own. Nielsen was told "The songs were un-important to the story" — Fanny's story.

Now it was the critics' turn to tell them what else, if anything, needed to be changed. This was the cast's chance to get much-needed outside feedback before they froze the show for Broadway. It was a vital part of the process. Richard Rodgers said he "wouldn't open a can of sardines without taking it first to Boston."

Stark kept an eye out front. A few hardy souls, shaking the snow from their boots in the lobby, had arrived. Stark was a wreck. The show needed a good response in Boston if they were going to roll into New York with the kind of word of mouth that would win over Broadway. Of course, if the critics hated the show, maybe it would be better if there wasn't much of an audience to confirm their opinions. But a good house could also fire up the actors; empty houses were dispiriting.

Then, from backstage, came word that one of the dancers had just broken her foot. Would the curse never end?

But in the end, their worries were for naught. As the eight o'clock showtime neared, all but two of the auditorium's 1,600 seats were filled. William Sarmento, reviewer for the nearby *Lowell Sun,* quipped that "every Barbra Streisand fan in existence showed up via dogsled, skis and snowshoes." Indeed, as columnist Herb Michelson, not al-ways such a fan himself, pointed out, Barbra was "pre-sold" to the audience, "a personality the crowds love before even seeing her."

Whether Barbra felt that love backstage is unknown. She was, however, getting some from Sydney, who whispered in her ear that she was wonderful. The overture was playing. Barbra waited for her cue, and when it came, she walked out onto the stage to generous ap-plause.

"Hello, gorgeous," she said into the onstage mirror, her Brooklyn twang echoing through the old Boston theater. The line received the titter of laughter it was supposed to generate. Maybe, despite all the worry, things would go okay after all.

3.

They didn't.

Nearly three weeks after the premiere, Garson Kanin was still trying to fix all the things the critics had said were wrong. With much of the cast assembled on the Shubert stage, the director was running them through scene after scene, while his wife sat fifth row center, flipping through the script. Whenever she'd call, "Oh, Gar . . . ," Kanin would stop whatever he was doing and hurry over to hear her thoughts.

Those first-night reviews still hung heavy over all of them. "What begins with bright, cheeky promise ends, I'm afraid, close to the edge of disaster," Kevin Kelly had written in the *Boston Globe*. During the first act, the show had seemed "like a winner," Kelly wrote, but then "a downpour of dullness" — a pun on the "Don't Rain on My Parade" number — had overcome the second act. It was a common refrain, and none of the criticism could have come as much of a surprise: the problem, as always, boiled down to the script. "The music almost has enough force to make the book unimportant," Kelly wrote, "but not quite." Cameron DeWar in *Billboard* thought Lennart had written "more of a movie scenario than a stage piece," and that the second act was "tedious and inept." All the reviews said a variant of the same thing.

They had something else in common as well: They all thought Barbra was fantastic. As with *Wholesale*, the critics were largely sour on the show but sweet on her: Was it even possible for Barbra to get a bad review? Kelly thought she was "very nearly perfect." DeWar said she "scored a bull's eye." William Sarmento in the *Lowell Sun* suggested the producers of *Funny Girl* might have been better off "to sell the costumes and scenery, disband the supporting players, and give the audience a three-hour concert of Miss Streisand." Elinor Hughes in the *Boston Herald* thought Barbra had "a quality that makes you want her on the stage every minute and leaves you thinking about her when she is in the wings."

That was the problem with the second act: Barbra wasn't front and center enough. "The second act becomes Nick's act more than it becomes Fanny's," Hughes wrote in a second review of the show a few nights later, "and though Sydney Chaplin is personable and charming, the figure that he creates isn't really alive and interesting, and what happens to him doesn't matter, except that we see less of Barbra-Fanny." Hughes was actually kind in her assessment of Sydney. Elliot Norton, in the *Boston Evening American,* declared Sydney made "the weakness of the libretto glaringly apparent." Kelly, in the *Globe,* thought Sydney played Nick Arnstein in "a heavy, oracular style" and "sung in a voice resonant with nothing whatever musical." He placed the blame clearly: "Arnstein botches the show."

For Sydney, it was a tremendous blow to his ego, especially as his ladylove was being lauded to the skies. He wasn't just embarrassed; he was angry. When Dorothy Kilgallen read the *Evening American* review, she thought Norton was "auditioning for a punch in the nose from the terrible-tempered Sydney." Chaplin didn't think his performance was the problem; the problem was Lennart's book, he believed, which gave him so little to work with. Barbra was sympathetic. But she also started giving Sydney tips about how he might improve his performance, much to his chagrin. It was all terribly similar to what had happened during *Wholesale.*

Loud, boisterous, often chaotic rehearsals followed, with everyone — Stark, Styne, Merrill, Lennart, and certainly Barbra — offering their ideas to Kanin about how the show could be fixed. Much of the revisions did, indeed, center around Sydney. Tireless choreographer Carol Haney had despaired of ever teaching him to dance. With her pixie face, shaggy hair, and throaty voice, Haney had proven to be a regular dynamo during rehearsals. Every other day, it seemed, she'd had to conceive and orchestrate a new dance number to go along with the new songs being added, which were just as frequently taken out. Buzz Miller, like many of the dancers in the show, had a long history with Haney; they'd danced together in the famous "Steam Heat" number in *Pajama Game,* the role that had made Haney an overnight sensation. In the last few weeks, as he'd watched Haney work, Miller had worried that "she was driving herself to death." But nothing seemed to slow her down — until Sydney Chaplin. Haney, who struggled to keep a drinking problem under control, was sorely tested in working with Sydney. His soft-shoe number, "Temporary Arrangement," was switched with another, "Come Along with Me," in which he didn't have to move, just sing.

As changes such as these were made, new scripts were prepared and handed out to the cast, who sometimes had less than a day to learn new lines, new steps, and new entrances. The critics, of course, came back to see how they were doing, and the prognosis was not good. "I regret to report *Funny Girl* is little better than it was the first time," Sarmento reported, questioning the wisdom of giving another number to Sydney, "who makes every note sound like he needed to gargle." Elinor Hughes still wasn't happy with the second act; she still found it too depressing. She thought Fanny Brice would be advising them: "Leave 'em laughing!" The *Globe*'s "Stage Today" column ran a daily capsule review of the show that pretty much said it all — and no doubt left Sydney steaming: "The first half is a delight, the second is a drag, but Barbra Streisand is magnetic. The cast also includes Sydney Chaplin, who's not very good."

What made it worse were the national columnists, who were getting wind of the situation. Kilgallen told her readers that "they still haven't decided whether it's supposed to be a funny musical or a dramatic 'plot' musical." Walter Winchell gushed about Barbra: "She excels . . . in every dept. . . . her second year in showbiz!" He added, "Three years ago she lived in a Brooklyn cold-water flat" (not so, it was in Manhattan and she had hot water) and "her entire wardrobe was draped over a chair" (it was more like crammed into a shopping bag). Hedda Hopper reported that Barbra was "a sensation . . . but the book will be overhauled before the New York opening" because "the writers devoted too much attention to Fanny's husband."

Of course, at the same time, they were still selling out nearly every night in Boston, so the reviews hadn't hurt them very much. Barbra was a powerful drawing card. As William Sarmento had pointed out in the *Lowell Sun,* Barbra, like Judy Garland, brought in "a cult of worshippers" to everything she did, who cheered and whistled at her every move." Because of Barbra, *Funny Girl* was still the show to be seen and to be seen at. Promoting her film *Strait-Jacket* at local theaters, Joan Crawford made sure to attend a performance, being welcomed with a standing ovation from the audience when she was spotted and recognized. So there was no danger of them going under. As Elinor Hughes had pointed out, "If a musical comedy with only the public's advance confidence can open to a sold-out and enthusiastic house on the night of Boston's worst snow storm in some time, then its future should be a prosperous one."

But they couldn't roll into New York with good notices for only their leading lady. "The hard fact," Kevin Kelly had written in the *Globe,* "is that *Funny Girl* is meant to be more than the exploitation of a single talent."

Barbra could have coasted; the reviews hadn't blamed her. She could have sat around pointing fingers. But she didn't. She was at every rehearsal, every meeting, wolfing down greasy take-out Chinese food with everyone else — eating so much, in fact, that her costumes were getting tight. Barbra was there to try out new numbers and observe the ones (very few) that she was not in. She worked just as hard as everyone else in trying to make the show better.

And maybe even a little harder. Few knew that the "cousin" who'd dropped by to watch Barbra during rehearsals was actually Allan Miller. Barbra had come a long way since her days at the Theatre Studio, much further than Miller had ever expected, even if Fanny Brice was hardly the Medea he'd guided her through in acting class. As a starry-eyed teenager, Barbra had thought no one was smarter or understood theater better than Miller, who was now teaching at the Circle in the Square Theatre School. It was natural that she would turn to him now, absent a director she trusted. Miller had first come around while they'd been rehearsing in New York, watching Barbra and giving her pointers at night. Barbra had insisted to Stark that she needed Miller's continued assistance, so Stark had hired him as her coach, provided that Kanin never find out. Now, with the show in trouble, Barbra had summoned Miller to Boston, where she hoped he might offer some advice on what they could do to save it.

But Kanin grew suspicious of the eagle-eyed "cousin" watching them rehearse. When he ascertained Miller's true identity, he threw a fit and, uncharacteristically aggressive, ordered him out of the theater. "Biggest screaming scene of the season," Walter Winchell reported. "When director Garson Kanin discovered star Barbra Streisand's drama coach in the balcony during a run-through, everything stopt [*sic*] until he was escorted out by the elbows with both feet four inches off terra firma." Whether it was really that dramatic or not, Miller was no longer permitted to come around, though Barbra still sought his advice on her own.

Kanin had his own ideas about how to fix the show. With his cast assembled on stage, his wife finally silent behind him, he was running through a new comedy number for Act Two. If the critics had thought the second act was too depressing, then he'd give them something to laugh at. It was February 1, the last night of their Boston run. From here it was on to Philadelphia. Kanin hoped that this new number, written by Styne and Merrill, would allow them to go out with a bang.

The song was called "Something About Me." Lainie Kazan and half a dozen others were dressed as babies, wearing swaddling clothes and seated in cribs. Barbra came on stage, singing about the ways to tell little boy babies from little girl babies. It was a strange number, and they might have all been more inclined to laugh about it had there not been so much backstage drama of late.

Kazan was at the center of the conflict. She had started dating Peter Daniels, who was working, thanks to Barbra, as an assistant conductor in the orchestra. When Garson Kanin suggested Kazan practice her numbers with Daniels, the spark between the two had been lit. Peter had insisted they keep their romance secret from Barbra, though Kazan couldn't understand why. But such secrets, as Barbra and Sydney were also discovering, were very hard to keep in such close proximity.

When word of the Daniels-Kazan affair leaked, Barbra was furious. Peter, in response, got angry right back, allowing some long-simmering tensions to finally boil over. It had been Peter's arrangements that had made Barbra famous, after all, dating all the way back to the Bon Soir, and he felt that she had given him very little recognition. A wound was opened between the two old friends that never healed. Kazan came to realize that Barbra "didn't like to share," whether it be a role or a longtime arranger. Probably the fact that it was Kazan — Ray Stark's protégée and fellow Erasmus Hall alumna — made her anger even worse.

Yet everyone was professional enough not to crack the eggshells on which they walked, and so they got through rehearsals. On that last night in Boston, they headed out onto the stage to give the show one more try. All of them remained committed to making this show a hit.

So was their producer, sitting out in the audience. While Barbra had gone around the director and placed a call for help to Allan Miller, Ray Stark had made his own surreptitious appeal, and to a very unlikely person. He sat with this potential savior now, watching the "Something About Me" number, with the cast all dressed as babies. Even as she performed it, Lainie Kazan knew the number was terrible, and if they weren't literally "booed off the stage," that would be how she'd remember the audience's unenthusiastic reaction to the number.

No doubt, watching his cast make fools of themselves on the stage, Ray Stark was very glad to be sitting next to Jerome Robbins. The show's original director had come up to Boston, and he was going on with them to Philadelphia. He was the only man on earth, Stark had come to realize, who could save *Funny Girl*.

4.

What made it particularly awkward for Jerry Robbins was that he and Garson Kanin were staying at the same hotel in Philadelphia. Barbra and Sydney were over at the Warwick, while Robbins, Kanin, Ray Stark, Isobel Lennart, and Jule Styne were all at the Barclay, running into one another on the elevators, in the cozy Chinese Chippendale corner bar, or at the ornate Victorian filigreed front desk. Except not for much longer. After the little meeting Ray Stark had just called between the principals, no one expected Kanin to still be around in the morning.

That was why Robbins was writing to him tonight. "Dear Gar," he penned. "I want you to know that I consider *Funny Girl* your show. I was hoping to work on it with you but Ray, in deciding to take advantage of the little time left out of town, felt it could only proceed this way. I am very sorry indeed, believe me. I just hope I fulfill the very wonderful job you've already left here."

He called a bellhop to deliver the note to Kanin's room. Then he began planning how to undo much of Kanin's "wonderful job."

Robbins and Stark had indeed hoped to work with Kanin, and with Carol Hancy. Robbins had tentatively agreed not to take a credit. He'd come, he told everyone, only to advise. And they had plenty of time to rehearse now; Stark had managed to get the New York premiere pushed back from February 27 to March 17, which gave them almost seven weeks to work. But then the show had opened at the Forrest Theatre on Walnut Street, and the first reviews had come in, and they weren't that much different from those in Boston. "The first triumph belongs to Barbra Streisand," wrote Henry T. Murdock in the *Philadelphia Inquirer*. That much was no doubt expected. But Murdock also saw scenes that went on past their logical conclusions, and songs whose potential would only be realized "as the run progresses." In his second review of the show, Murdock concluded succinctly: "The funny girl should be funnier."

Robbins's attempts to make that happen had been thwarted at every turn by objections from a deeply affronted Kanin, or from his equally aggrieved wife. It became clear that Robbins needed a free hand to whip the show into shape. Their seven weeks were now down to four. That meant Kanin had to go. Haney, too, as Robbins needed complete control over the choreography as well.

Clearly Barbra was pushing for Robbins to take over; the director was exchanging notes with her about her performance almost daily, and it was common knowledge that she had lost faith in Kanin. But some wondered why Robbins had come back to a project that had given him so much aggravation in the past — and to a producer he frankly couldn't stand and didn't respect. No doubt Stark had concluded that if he was going to be paying Robbins royalties anyway for the use of his material, he might as well have him back on the job. Asking Robbins to return, however, must have been very difficult for the proud Stark. Humbling himself before a man he'd tried to outmaneuver legally less than a year before showed the desperation the producer was feeling — as well as his determination not to give up. For Robbins, it may have been the satisfaction of being told that he had been right all along that brought him back — that and a hefty financial agreement, the details of which were still being worked out. There may also have been a personal consideration: Buzz Miller, one of the lead dancers, was Robbins's former lover and someone who still held a piece of his heart.

And so, the next day, Kanin and his wife were gone. There were no good-byes made to the company. "He just kind of disappeared," Sharon Vaughn said of their director. Kanin would keep his credit on the show, but soon everyone in Broadway circles knew he had been fired. As consolation, Stark sent him a set of antique china.

Lainie Kazan felt sorry about Kanin's departure, but she felt far worse for Carol Haney, who many in the company believed had been treated cavalierly. She had worked so hard and was willing to keep working hard, but Robbins wanted complete control. Haney, too, would keep her credit, even if the new director-choreographer was already reworking her steps and routines as he saw fit. Soon the company was hearing reports that Haney, stunned and depressed by her dismissal, was drinking again.

5.

Had Barbra switched on the television set in her room at the Warwick on the night of February 9, she would have seen that group of four Liverpool lads she'd heard while in London perform live on *The Ed Sullivan Show.* Almost from out of nowhere, the Beatles had exploded onto the American scene that winter, enjoying a meteoric ride to the top that made even Barbra's ascent seem like a long time coming. They sang four songs on the Sullivan show, all of which were nearly drowned out by screaming teenaged fans in the audience, especially the last, "I Want to Hold Your Hand." Sullivan declared, "This city has never witnessed the excitement stirred by these youngsters."

As they headed out on their first stateside tour, the Beatles were suddenly everywhere. "The British group, something like Presley quadruplets, have taken over the American record market," one columnist observed. Cynthia Lowry of the Associated Press complained it was "impossible to get a radio weather bulletin or time signal without running into 'I Want to Hold Your Hand.'" Meanwhile, the Beatles' first album had skyrocketed up the charts and managed to accomplish what Barbra hadn't: knock the Singing Nun from the top spot. Along the way, the quartet had also passed Barbra's second and first albums, now at numbers 9 and 14 respectively.

The change at the top couldn't have been more dramatic. Sister Smile's simple, soothing sounds had been replaced by the Beatles' vivacious, rule-breaking rock and roll — a sign that Americans, at least young Americans, were ready to start living again after the horrors of the fall. If Barbra, cloistered at the Forrest Theatre, hadn't been paying much attention to what was happening in the music world, she would soon have to, for she had a new album on the way — and a new single as well.

Arriving backstage a few hours before curtain time, one member of the company was still singing along to the Beatles tune she'd been playing in her hotel room. "She loves you, yeah, yeah, yeah," she warbled as she headed up the stairs to the dressing rooms. That was when she heard Barbra singing, too — only she quickly realized it wasn't Barbra singing live, but on a record, and she was singing a song from the show, "You Are Woman," the humorous love song she shared with Nick. But it sounded different somehow. Listening closely, the company member realized that Barbra was singing it solo, and the words had been changed to "I Am Woman." When she got into the dressing room she shared with the other girls, she saw Marty Erlichman. He had just brought the single over and was playing it for them. The record had just been released to radio stations all across the country. The company member looked down at the disk spinning on the turntable and thought, "This sure ain't the Beatles."

Indeed, it was suddenly a very different market. Although "I Am Woman" — with its flipside, "People" — earned some positive reviews and inclusion in Dick Kleiner's top picks in his syndicated record column, it didn't really stand a chance on a Top Ten list now dominated by Beatles hits (that week it was "I Want to Hold Your Hand" and "She Loves You") and other rock-pop singers such as Lesley Gore and the Four Seasons. Probably no one expected "I Am Woman" to chart very high. Recorded before Barbra left New York, the single was intended mostly as radio promotion for the show. But getting airplay was going to be very tough in this new market.

That didn't mean Barbra wasn't making news on other fronts. Her weight gain hadn't gone unnoticed, and that prompted rumors that she was pregnant. No surprise that Dorothy Kilgallen was the one to start the ball rolling. "*Funny Girl* must agree with Barbra Streisand, despite all the strenuous out-of-town performances and rehearsals," the columnist insinuated. "She's actually put on weight and some of her costumes have had to be altered." That was enough to set tongues wagging, as Kilgallen surely intended. It led to someone — Stark? Marty? Solters? Barbra herself? — calling the ever-reliable Earl Wilson to set the record straight. "Tisn't so, comes the word, loud and clear, from Philadelphia," Wilson dutifully wrote.

What made the rumors especially awkward was the affair going on between Barbra and Sydney. For those in the company who suspected some hanky-panky between their leading man and lady, talk of pregnancy led to all sorts of questions. The same company member who had heard Barbra's record playing also heard stories of her romance with Sydney. At one point, she worked up the nerve to ask Jule Styne if, therefore, the pregnancy stories might be true. He told her "never to utter anything that crazy ever again." So she didn't.

For his part, Sydney was hoping that Robbins could fix things for him along with the rest of the show. Indeed, there were indications that he might no longer be the albatross that the Boston reviews had made him out to be. Critics in the City of Brotherly Love had been much kinder to Sydney: Henry Murdock had found him "graceful, nimble, handsome, and most vocally able." No doubt this pleased Barbra and likely kept the relationship between the two of them humming along even as chaos reigned in rehearsals. Now that Carol Haney had departed, Barbra and Sydney were the only ones among the principals to be lodged at the Warwick. That gave them a certain amount of privacy, just in case they wanted to spend any time together late at night after the curtain had been rung down.

6.

Jerry Robbins called them all together under the Erlanger Theatre's glittery crystal chandelier and told them point-blank that they were running out of time.

Ray Stark had just pulled off the impossible and gotten them yet another reprieve. Their Broadway opening night had been moved from March 17 to March 24. That meant they had exactly twenty-five days to get this thing right.

First order of the day, Robbins announced, as the company scrambled up onto the stage, many of them in socks or ballet shoes, was to rehearse the new "Sadie, Sadie" number. Originally part of an earlier script, the song was being brought back into the show to replace "Home" and "Who Are You Now?" at the top of the second act. "Home" would be scrapped; "Who Are You Now?" would be moved toward the end of the show. To kick off Act Two, they'd tried using the "Rat-Tat-Tat-Tat" number, the Ziegfeld Follies tribute to World War I doughboys that served no real plot purpose except to pep things up during the dreary second hour. But a transition was needed after the intermission to show that Fanny was now married, and Robbins didn't want another duet with Sydney. So out came "Sadie." He told the orchestra to hit it.

"I'm Sadie, Sadie, married lady," Barbra sang, as the company followed her across the stage in steps originally worked out by Haney and now finessed by Robbins to contain the number to three minutes.

"She's Sadie, Sadie, married lady," the company echoed.

"To tell the truth," trilled Barbra, "it hurt my pride, the groom was prettier than the bride!"

Yet another reference to her looks, but Barbra went along with it, no complaint, because Robbins liked the song. And at that point, she would have done almost anything Robbins suggested. Star and director were "getting along famously," Lainie Kazan observed, even if the rest of the cast, used to the easygoing Kanin, wasn't too happy about the "ferocious taskmaster" who'd showed up one day out of the blue and started making their lives more difficult.

Barbra, however, was having a ball. The more Robbins changed the scenes, the more she liked it. The more she had different songs to try out, the more she loved it. "Forty-one different last scenes!" she exclaimed, indicating the various versions of the script they were working from. Her castmates wilted under the pressure to keep all the different versions distinct, but Barbra found it "exciting, stimulating." Anything to keep away the boredom she'd known during *Wholesale*.

Working with Robbins was like putting a different show on every day — which, in a sense, they were. Theatergoers who saw the show on a Wednesday would see a slightly different — or possibly even a radically different — show if they came back on a Friday. Lines were changed, songs were moved around. Not only that, but the production had actually switched theaters, vacating the Forrest for the Erlanger, on the northwest corner of Market and Twenty-first streets.

The change had been made necessary by their extended tryout: *Anyone Can Whistle* was scheduled to open at the Forrest, and even though Stark had offered producer Kermit Bloomgarden ten thousand dollars to switch theaters, he couldn't make a deal. So that meant packing everything up — props, costumes, equipment — and relearning the layout and sight lines of a brand-new venue. Barbra accepted it as one more adventure.

Settling into a seat in the empty auditorium to watch her cavort on the stage, Robbins marveled at this fascinating creature he'd inherited from Fosse and Kanin. Barbra hadn't been his first choice for Fanny, of course. But now he couldn't see anyone else in the part, not even his beloved Anne Bancroft. Barbra's talent had impressed him, but it was her fierce dedication to the role that had finally won him over. Robbins found Barbra "jet-fueled with the robust, all-daring energy" of a novice, but "tempered by the taste, instinct and delicacy" of a veteran. She often arrived late to rehearsals, "haphazardly dressed," but accepted the "twelve pages of new material" Robbins handed her without protest, "schnorring" part of his sandwich and "someone else's Coke" as she read them. During rehearsals, "in her untidy exploratory meteoric fashion," Barbra was "never afraid . . . to try anything," Robbins observed. And as soon as she had figured out how to play a scene, she seemed "a sorceress sailing through every change without hesitation, leaving wallowing fellow players in her wake."

And she hadn't even turned twenty-two.

That was what was so uncanny, because the work they had been doing over the last few weeks — and the work they needed to keep doing for the next twenty-five days — might have sapped the creativity of even the most experienced old theater pro. Barbra was like no performer Robbins had ever worked with before. No matter the line in "Sadie," the director thought she was exquisite. Musing about his leading lady, Robbins wrote, "Her beauty astounds, composed of impossibly unconventional features." Her movements were both "wildly bizarre and completely elegant," and her "El Greco hands" seemed to have "studied Siamese dancing and observed the antennae of insects."

It was Barbra's contradictions he admired most: "Her cool is as strong as her passion. The child is also the woman. The first you want to protect, the second keep. She comes on with defiant independence — yet communicates an urgent need for both admiration and approval. She laughs at sexiness. She is sexy. She tests you with childish stubbornness, impetuosity and conceit, concedes you are right without admission, and balances all with her generous artistry and grace."

Yet for all his fascination with the show's leading lady, Robbins never really considered *Funny Girl* his own after he came back. There was a certain detachment, members of the company felt. Too many people had been involved by now for Robbins to ever feel very proprietary about the product. Still, if the show was a hit, he stood to make out pretty well. He'd just signed his contract with Stark, guaranteeing him five thousand dollars for his services plus two-and-a-half percent of the gross weekly box office, both during previews and after the Broadway opening, and including all performances of any subsequent road tour. He also was paid ten thousand dollars for the movie rights to his material; if the film was not made within seven years, Stark would need to come back to him for another agreement. The contract was a clear recognition of Robbins's authorship, as well as the fact that previous directors' imprints were minimal. Indeed, the show was now practically unrecognizable from the one that had premiered in Boston, and would be different still by the time they opened on Broadway.

No matter all the fixing going on, Robbins knew what he was doing was simply patching the holes in the book, not rebuilding a great play. Isobel Lennart admitted her work had fallen far short of the mark. "After twenty years of working in a field [screenwriting] where I know what am I doing and can do my job very well," she told a reporter, "I have had the humbling experience of trying to do something I quickly discovered I knew nothing about." In the little time they had left, Robbins was trying to salvage what he could. One of the first things he'd jettisoned was "Something About Me," Kanin's disastrous babies-in-the-cribs number, despite the loss of some ten thousand dollars in discarded costumes and props. He also sliced out "I'd Be Good for Her" and "Eddie's Fifth Encore," completely eliminating Eddie Ryan's subplot. Robbins and Stark might not have agreed on much, but both understood that for *Funny Girl* to have any shot at success, it had to be all about Barbra.

Other changes Robbins wrought were less dramatic, but just as significant. Sitting in the back of the theater every night, he scribbled notes on Barclay Hotel stationery to present to the cast the next day. After the performance on the twenty-fourth, he'd thought Barbra was "working too hard" during "I'm the Greatest Star," and she needed to be careful not to break up the lyrics so much during "Who Are You Now?" After the performance on the twenty-fifth, Robbins had switched "Cornet Man" and "Rat-Tat-Tat-Tat," and told Barbra not to show her face after she sat down in the "You Are Woman" number and for once let Nick take center stage.

He'd also declared, interestingly, that there was entirely "too much kissing" in the show, which, knowing what was going on after hours between Barbra and Sydney, might have had a little more resonance than Robbins indicated in his notes.

Every day, there was something else to be changed. On the twenty-sixth, Robbins had requested new watercolors be done for the sets and an entire redesign of the Henry Street bar where Fanny's mother held court. On the twenty-seventh, he had submitted a list to Lennart of various cuts and changes. The speeches of Emma, Fanny's maid, were too long, and Nick's dialogue with Fanny had to emphasize his intention "to be head of the house."

There was just so much, so very much, to do between now and opening night. Jule Styne was frequently sending over lists of changes he thought should be made, such as when inner curtains ought to be raised during songs and which lights should be used during different numbers. He'd also come up with an idea to close the show with a line from Fanny, "Hey, gorgeous, here we go again." But although Robbins penciled "ok" next to the suggestion, he never used it. Clearly the director thought ending on a reprise of "Don't Rain on My Parade" was the better way to close.

Not everything he tried worked. At one point, Robbins had brought in a pair of wolfhounds to lead Fanny out onto the stage when she made her first entrance. Nothing says "star" more than a couple of hounds on a diamond-studded leash. But the dogs wouldn't stop center stage as they were supposed to, so they were sent back to their trainer. Robbins had canned the song "A Helluva Group," sung by the Henry Street saloon regulars as a lead-in to "People," and replaced it with "Block Party," and then "Downtown Rag," but he still wasn't happy. He had Styne and Merrill working up something else.

He'd also tried firing Lainie Kazan. His reasons were unclear. Had she been too close to Kanin? Was it a request from Barbra? Did he disapprove of the deal with Stark? From the moment Robbins arrived, Kazan felt he had ignored her. Through the grapevine she heard he was saying she was "too attractive to understudy Fanny Brice." But when she got her notice to vacate, Kazan decided she wouldn't go easily. She called Robbins and asked for ten minutes. "I'm going to sing for you and do a scene for you, and if you really don't like me, you can fire me," she said. The director agreed, and Kazan sang "I'm the Greatest Star." In response, Robbins said nothing, which left the anxious actress hanging. But the next day Kazan got a new script at her hotel room, which meant she could stay on. Probably Ray Stark, who had Kazan under contract, had had as much influence as her rendition of "I'm the Greatest Star."

It was also true that Robbins had difficulty finding anyone else who could understudy Barbra. On the twenty-sixth, he had interviewed several potential understudies, including Louise Lasser, who had the experience, and Carol Arthur, who'd played with Elliott in *On the Town*. But none had seemed to catch fire with him. Robbins also had the idea of publicizing "standbys" for Barbra — celebrities who might step in and do the part when Barbra wanted a night off. He had in mind Eydie Gormé, Edie Adams, and Gisele MacKenzie, among others. But Gormé turned Robbins down quite publicly. Her manager issued a statement saying the job was "not in keeping with the image of a star of Eydie's stature." Apparently, since she'd been up for the part, Gormé wanted to play Fanny Brice full time or not at all.

Of all the changes Robbins brought to the show, nothing was more crucial than the insights he gave to the actors about the characters they were playing, something Kanin, apparently, hadn't done. This was what Barbra had been craving. "Everything we know of [Fanny] must be shown," Robbins told her, in words that could have come straight from her Theatre Studio classes, "not analyzed in talk and thus 'forgiven' or 'understood.'" The trick wasn't to find a plot device to explain Fanny's foolishness in choosing (and staying with) Nick, but to make her real enough that the audience sympathized with her without needing any of that. "It must be put into action," Robbins told Barbra. "Go, move, need, fight, want, fear, love, hate. We love [Fanny] not for her understanding, but from ours of her. Don't beg off!"

These sessions with Barbra showed just how completely the two personas, Barbra's and Fanny's, had merged. Robbins explained to her that Nick needed Fanny so he could "feel needed and strong," while Fanny needed Nick "to feel worthy and feminine." One couldn't get much closer to a description of Barbra and Elliott, but there was still more to come. Robbins put together a list of Fanny's beliefs about herself: "I'm a dog. I get reaction through making people react to me. I can make them laugh or cry. I *get even* this way [Robbins's emphasis]. I *win* their love. I must feel wanted. There is a large sensitive hole that needs filling up." That last one, in particular, must have resonated with Barbra, echoing the line from Medea that she'd carried around with her for so long.

Whether Robbins knew how closely he was delineating Barbra's own life isn't clear. But the best directors, and that would certainly describe Robbins, always knew their actors inside and out. With so much focus over the last six months on conflating star and subject, Robbins must have been aware that he was asking Barbra not so much to create a character but to play herself—or at least to play the self that had seeped into the public consciousness by now. Yet Robbins's descriptions went to the core of who Barbra was, to parts of herself that she kept hidden from her public and even from her friends. "Fanny has made out well with all the boys," Robbins told Barbra, after believing for so long that she could never accomplish such a feat. She has even won "the best-looking" of them. But "then, having had them, finding she could get them, she threw them over with contempt because she thought them fools for wanting her."

Was that what Barbra was doing with Elliott? Was it what Robbins *thought* she was doing with him? Certainly the dynamic was there in the show, layered into the character of Fanny, and it didn't take long to find other comparisons. Nick, like Elliott, had "the seeds of self-destruction in him." His attraction to Fanny "will either cure him or kill him." At its core, Robbins argued, this was the "story of a strong woman who, to feel like a woman, picks an elegant, loving but weak man — and her own strength corrupts and kills his love and manliness." That seemed to be precisely what was happening with Elliott. And with Sydney, too, as his selfish, masculine pride was wounded by the greater acclaim given to Barbra.

That dynamic between the lovers wasn't helped by what Robbins did next. Despite the decent reviews Sydney had gotten in Philadelphia, it was clear that Lennart had never solved the essential problem of Nick's character. Was he a good guy or a bad guy? Was he noble or weak? He may have been all of those, but there simply wasn't enough material in the book to show him in any complexity. Since it was too late to rewrite very much, the answer was simply to cut. Sydney had a major number in the second act, "Sleep Now, Baby Bunting," in which he sang a lullaby to his newborn daughter, bitterly calling himself "Mr. Fanny Brice." The number was key to his character, explaining his resentment at being married to a woman who was more successful than he was. But Robbins cut it. His decision may have saved Elliott from squirming in his seat when he saw the show, but it also left Sydney with just two songs, both of which were duets with Barbra. He was not pleased.

But Ray Stark was. Back in New York, at a cost of ten thousand dollars, he'd erected an enormous, block-long sign announcing *Funny Girl* over the Winter Garden Theatre, giving it "several extra coats of paint," Dorothy Kilgallen reported, "because he's confident of a long, long run." He was telling Robbins he was a genius and that "for the first time since the show started, he was able to have two dinners and go to the movies over the weekend." He couldn't believe what Robbins had done "for the morale of the company." Stark had to put all of this in letters to Robbins's secretary and ask that it be conveyed to him, however, because Robbins made it a point to spend as little time with Stark as possible.

But the combative producer could afford to be generous in his praise for his old adversary. Advance ticket sales for *Funny Girl* were averaging twenty thousand dollars a day. That was a very good thing, too, as the newspapers pointed out: given how much Stark had had to pay Merrick, plus "the top figure deal with the high-priced Jerome Robbins," plus whatever deal had been worked out with Kanin, plus all the delays, *Funny Girl* was likely to arrive on Broadway as "the highest budgeted musical on record." Some were estimating Stark's costs to be in excess of half a million dollars.

And to think it all depended on one small, now slightly chubby, twenty-one-year-old kid.

7.

In her dressing room at the Erlanger, Barbra took the call from Earl Wilson herself. No, she told him firmly, denying yet again the story that she was pregnant. This was getting tedious. Wilson promised he'd print her denial.

Barbra's new album had just been released, but all these newspapermen wanted to talk about was whether or not she was expecting a baby. Even the record columns weren't giving her much ink, at least not compared to the last time she'd released a record. Maybe that was because her third album was fated to go head-to-head with the Beatles, which were all anybody seemed to want to talk about. But Barbra knew the album was good, maybe her best yet. Among the tracks she'd chosen this time were more traditional standards, giving in to those who complained her "standards" were usually too offbeat. So she sang "My Melancholy Baby," "As Time Goes By," "It Had to Be You," and, of course, "Bewitched, Bothered, and Bewildered." She worked with Peter Matz again, and her voice was pristine and supremely confident. It was the work of an artist who had found her groove and enjoyed an easy, smooth mastery over her many gifts. The songs together took the listener on a journey from longing to joy, from grief to hope. The gift for conveying a depth of emotion far greater than her years, displayed early on in Barbra's career, had clearly never left her and, in fact, had deepened.

She called it, naturally, *The Third Album*. Kilgallen had reported that someone from Barbra's team, maybe Solters or Marty, had told her they were planning on calling it *The Fourth Barbra Streisand Album*. That way, the fans would be "dashing into the record stores asking for the third Barbra Streisand album, which doesn't exist," Kilgallen said, calling it a "great gimmick." But if anyone ever really considered such an idea, sanity prevailed. It was a class act all the way. Barbra even gave Peter Daniels credit on "Bewitched." Roddy McDowall's adorable shot of Barbra in her midshipman's blouse from the Garland show was used as the cover. Sammy Cahn, following in the tradition of Arlen and Styne, wrote the liner notes.

Once again, Barbra had insisted on complete control of the production, getting her fingers into everything from "the arrangements, the cover, the copy, the editing." This time, there were fewer complaints about her involvement. The early reviews, once again, seemed to justify all her efforts. "Every moment in the album is an exciting musical experience," *Billboard* wrote. Syndicated record reviewer Al Price, in his "Platter Chatter" column, thought it possessed a "spellbinding effect . . . that is hard to describe." *The Third Album* had landed on the charts at number 110, but by the next week, it was at 53. Maybe not Beatles-style velocity, but it was still quite respectable.

Barbra knew she had a good product, especially when she compared it to her first album, which now embarrassed her, she said. For all its freshness and youthful vitality, the first album was not as polished or as emotionally deep as her second and third outings. Barbra cringed remembering how she'd ended "Happy Days" on that first disk, wailing "oooooo, aaaaaay," and her voice cracking. She'd been "yearning for just so much" back then, she said, that she could hear it in her voice, "very young, very high, very thin, like a bird."

Of course, she'd never felt much a part of the music industry and that was even more the case now, competing with the likes of the Beatles, and Joan Baez, and even fourteen-year-old Stevie Wonder, who all wrote their own music or played their own instruments. Barbra admitted to feeling a little bit "inadequate [about] singing other people's songs." There was also the generational conflict. The teenagers who were buying millions of copies of *Meet the Beatles!* weren't also buying *The Third Album*. That was left up to a rather eclectic group of housewives, gay men, theater aficionados, and artistic types, of which only a small percentage were likely teenagers. And yet Barbra was the same age as Paul McCartney, and two years *younger* than John Lennon and Ringo Starr. She might indeed be "a mixture of old and new," as she called herself in one interview, but her newness didn't seem to have the same impact on the youth market as Baez or the Beatles did.

That was significant because the success of those acts had demonstrated there was a huge, untapped slice of the market out there. Teenagers had always been a subset of the record-buying audience, driving the sales of Elvis Presley and other rock-and-rollers. But they had not been the major force of sales. Now, as the "baby boomers" — those born in the decade after the end of World War II — reached their teens, it was becoming increasingly clear that the future of the music industry lay with young people. Barbra's age and her iconoclasm should have made her a natural favorite for this group. But her music — chosen for her by her theater and nightclub handlers — was their parents' music.

A poll taken of teenagers at the end of the previous year — before the Beatles' breakout — showed that their favorite female singers were Connie Francis, Joan Baez, Brenda Lee, Connie Stevens, and Lesley Gore. Only Lee and Gore were younger than Barbra. And only when teenagers were asked about stars of the future did Barbra turn up at all: the kids predicted Gore, Peggy March, and Barbra, in that order. Folk music was their favorite genre, beating out rock and pop. If taken in March 1964, the poll likely would have showed a different result, given the unprecedented success of the Beatles. But the point remained: Barbra was no folk singer, and she was even less a rock-and-roller. Exactly where and how could she compete in an industry dominated by teenagers? As her third album made its way up the charts, only time would tell.

Such speculation, however, was better left to her managers and publicists. For Barbra, one goal predominated: getting *Funny Girl* to Broadway in one piece. As she headed out of her dressing room, she may have run into Sydney, as she often did, on her way to the stage. He still liked to tell her that she was brilliant and gorgeous. He may have whispered it again in her ear. But the truth was, with all the glowing reviews, she didn't really need to hear it anymore. Her confidence didn't need that extra boost. And Sydney realized that. It made him feel "less necessary, less important," Orson Bean understood. It was a feeling Elliott Gould could have empathized with.

To Bean, Sydney would share his suspicions on why his amorous relationship with Barbra had suddenly cooled in those last few days in Philadelphia. "Once his numbers were cut and the show didn't need him as much," Bean said, "Sydney felt Barbra wasn't in love with him anymore."

He may have been right. Besides, they were going back to New York. And Barbra had a husband waiting for her there.

8.

The block-long sign announcing *Funny Girl* above the Winter Garden on Broadway had been weathering in the rain, snow, sun, and city soot for the past several weeks as the premiere was delayed yet again, from March 24 to March 26. The show still wasn't ready. At least the company was now back in New York under the Winter Garden's roof, and curious theatergoers were flocking to the previews in order to get a peek at the show in development before Jerry Robbins froze it on opening night.

Backstage, Barbra greeted the well-wishers who thronged the hallway and pushed their way into her dressing room, many bearing flowers. No one seemed to be waiting for the official premiere. Already there was buzz that Barbra was a hit. Word was spreading about the elaborate way she took her curtain calls, "like rituals performed in a Buddhist temple," Dorothy Kilgallen said. Most of the columnists had come to see the show; it seemed there wasn't anyone of any standing or influence in the theatrical community who hadn't been by. "The craze to get in ahead of time" made fashion columnist Eugenia Sheppard nostalgic for "the old days when any kind of opening was a big thrill." Now, she said, the official opening night was "for squares."

Of course, no newspaper would publish a review quite yet, but they did send reporters to check things out. On this night, Joanne Stang of the *New York Times* observed the procession of people trooping into Barbra's dressing room to tell her how magnificent she'd been out on the stage. Shouldering his way through them came Jule Styne, who told Barbra he was concerned that the show still ran too long. In his opinion, they "should cut at least twenty-eight minutes." While all this was going on, Barbra was being fussed over by "a press agent, a personal manager, a photographer, a maid, a dressmaker, and two costume assistants waving swatches of fabrics." Each one received her attention in turn, and she dealt with each issue they raised in a quiet manner. Then the new script for the next day was delivered to her, with requests from Robbins and Lennart that she "go over the new changes right away."

As the crowd dispersed from the room, Stang watched as Barbra stretched out on an army cot covered in pink sheets in the corner of the room. She began flipping through the script. "We had three new scenes in the second act tonight," she told Stang, "so I'm a little tired." But she was loving it. She loved getting new scripts with different things to say and do and sing every night. Robbins was still scribbling notes during each and every performance and going over them with the cast and crew the next day. Sometimes the changes were big — a whole new scene — and sometimes they were small — a rewrite of a line. But Barbra loved the challenge of something new every night.

There had been new lyrics to "I'm the Greatest Star" that had come and gone. There had been a new version of "Cornet Man" that had stuck. "Downtown Rag" had been replaced with an entirely new number, "Henry Street." Robbins had even asked Carol Haney to come in and fix the ending of "Rat-Tat-Tat-Tat" and put a finish on "Find Yourself a Man," Mrs. Brice's humorous number in the second act, yet another attempt to liven up the show's last hour, though whether Haney came is unclear.

And every morning Robbins arrived at Barbra's dressing room with a handful of notes just for her. He had reversed his earlier objections and come to the conclusion that Barbra should sing "People" alone. No longer, apparently, did he find it "too strong a come-on." After the performance on March 2, Robbins had also cautioned his leading lady against seeming "too desperate" at the ending of "Greatest Star." After the performance on the fifth, Robbins had asked Barbra for more concentration in the mirror before she said, "Hello, gorgeous." A few days later, he was telling her to wait longer for the laugh after Nick's line, "I'm minding them for a friend." And sometimes, Robbins said, there was just "too much Mae West" in her Fanny Brice.

After they had started the New York previews on the tenth, Robbins's criticism had gotten sharper. He told Barbra to stand up straight during "Rat-Tat-Tat-Tat," and to let the curtain hit the floor before she exited. She needed to be less harsh on the line "Whatever he tells me to do, I'll do," and at the end of the bride blackout, where Fanny shocks the audience by showing up pregnant in a wedding dress, Robbins wanted Barbra to hold her pose longer. She should shrug before the line "I would have ordered roast beef and potatoes" and laugh after the line "I'm not bossy," because she knew she was. Lines such as "Oy, what a day I had" the director wanted to be more Jewish, and Barbra "should be more elegant, like a showgirl" during "Sadie." And after watching Barbra play Fanny's farewell scene with Eddie, an exhausted Robbins handed her a note with just one short bit of feedback: "Barbra — class!"

But the biggest problem in Barbra's performance, it seemed, was how she related to Sydney. "What are you playing while Sydney sings 'You Are Woman'?" Robbins asked her with some befuddlement. The scene just didn't work; Ray Stark even sent Robbins a memo complaining that it was no longer "getting the laughs it used to," that the "small laughs" were "killing the big laughs." The chemistry between the two players seemed suddenly off. A week later, Robbins was still asking the same question: "What are you playing?" Taking both his leads aside, Robbins rehearsed them extra hard, just the three of them in the room. The problems weren't confined to "You Are Woman." The railroad scene, where Fanny and Nick part and the audience is supposed to feel their heartache, wasn't working either. Robbins encouraged Barbra and Sydney to rehearse all their scenes together on their own. No longer was he complaining about too much kissing. Now he wanted more passion, a quality that had seemed to evaporate in the past couple of weeks.

Very possibly, what the director was picking up on was the cooling of the affair between his two leads. Barbra had begun to distance herself from Sydney, and he was both hurt and angry. No doubt, too, he was frustrated by the fact that Robbins kept singling him out for criticism. The essential problem of Nick as a character had never been solved. Robbins was still trying to figure out "how to make Nick a wheeler-dealer and still make him sympathetic." One idea was to make him funnier with the addition of some new dialogue on the twentieth: "Whose oil well?" Fanny asks. "Our oil well," Nick replies. "When does our oil well start producing?" Fanny wants to know. "As soon as we dig it," Nick tells her. Robbins worried what the critics would say about Sydney after the official opening night.

Barbra, however, didn't need to wait that long to know what her reviews would be. The audience's reaction at every preview told her all she needed to know. Joanne Stang of the *Times* had been struck at how some people had stood on their seats to applaud Barbra at the end. Indeed, starting on the seventeenth, the notes Robbins sent to Barbra were more compliments than critiques. Even Bob Merrill had come around. The lyricist had been impressed with Barbra's progress in the show, "astounded by the way she had refined all the rough edges," his wife said. Merrill believed Barbra had "metamorphosed from an angry, rebellious kid to an elegant, polished, powerful performer with the ability to transmit great emotion — maybe even more than he and Jule had written," his wife thought.

Outside the theater, however, things weren't quite so sanguine. The five delays *Funny Girl* had endured had left ticket agents and theatergoers unhappy. Stark couldn't deny they faced "the wrath of the public." Notifying customers of changed dates meant considerable extra costs and clerical work; so far, the show's delays were estimated to have added close to one hundred thousand dollars to its costs, bringing total production expenses to more than six hundred thousand. They were still in the black, since about nine hundred thousand dollars in advance sales had already been made. But it was a very small cushion of comfort.

No doubt the numbers made Ray Stark anxious. That could explain the night he made a beeline for Barbra's dressing room after one preview — he had gotten surprisingly fast on those crutches — and began shouting at her in a "shrill and high-pitched" voice, as one company member overheard. On the twentieth, he had complained to Robbins about a lack of depth in Barbra's performance of certain scenes; maybe he was frustrated that he hadn't seen an improvement. Whatever his reasons, he was unhappy, and let Barbra know it in no uncertain terms.

Barbra had her own grievances with the producer. While she was pleased that Stark and Seven Arts had decided that she should play

Fanny in the inevitable movie version of *Funny Girl,* she wasn't happy about the terms of the deal, and neither were Begelman and Fields. True, it was reportedly "one of the biggest deals ever given an actress for her first film role" — one million dollars was the figure being bandied about — but it came with a catch: Barbra would be, in effect, Stark's personal property for the next eight years. Most actresses just starting out in pictures would have been thrilled by the job security; but Barbra, of course, was not most actresses. She knew that the four pictures she'd be required to make for Stark would be, "in essence," his choices; Barbra would only get to make films that Stark green-lighted, and she'd already discovered how often they failed to see eye to eye on things.

Just as he had with the contract for the show, Stark had played hardball. If Barbra didn't want to sign the long-term contract, then she wouldn't play Fanny Brice in the movie version of *Funny Girl.* There was precedent. When *Gentlemen Prefer Blondes* had been made into a film, Howard Hawks hadn't used Carol Channing, who'd been a smash as Lorelei Lee on Broadway. Instead, he'd hired Marilyn Monroe. When, just this past year, George Cukor had cast *My Fair Lady,* he hadn't gone with Julie Andrews, even though she'd been such a hit in the part on the stage. He'd hired Audrey Hepburn. There were plenty of big Hollywood names who would jump at playing Fanny Brice in the movie version — Anne Bancroft, perhaps? — and Barbra knew it.

She resented being backed into a corner like that. It was one of the things she disliked most about show business. Ray Stark had become both benefactor and bête noire. To Barbra, he was "a real character, an original." Without his early championship, she would not have been sitting in that dressing room at the Winter Garden Theatre. But ever since the contract battles of the previous fall, the relationship between producer and leading lady had turned into what she called a "love-hate" tug-of-war. Stark could be a bully, Barbra admitted. For all his charm, for all his patrician good manners, there were those who remembered how he'd shoved and kicked a photographer at Idlewild Airport who'd tried to take his and Fran's photograph. For all his graciousness, there were those who thought he behaved terribly to his own son, Peter, a dreamy, artistic boy whom Stark was always trying to toughen up by browbeating him in public. No doubt that Ray Stark could be a bully, and Barbra felt she was being bullied over the movie contract.

She appealed to Fields for help. "Look, if you're prepared to lose it," her agent told her, "then we can say sorry, we'll sign only one picture at a time." But Barbra was "not prepared to lose it." She knew the risks. She didn't want to be Carol Channing or Julie Andrews. So she signed the four-picture deal with Stark and had been resentful about it ever since.

That could explain why, when Stark started shouting at her in her dressing room, Barbra had a simple reply: "Fuck you." She'd cursed similarly at Kanin, but directing the words at Stark was a much bigger deal.

"You can't say that to me," the producer sputtered.

"This is my dressing room," Barbra said, "and I'm saying it to you."

Later, she'd express amazement with herself for her words, but she didn't have to worry about any real repercussions. She was untouchable, at least until the show premiered.

9.

At last, Elliott had a job. He would play the Jester in Carol Burnett's television adaptation of her hit Broadway show *Once Upon a Mattress*. Joe Layton was set to direct, which was probably how Elliott had gotten the part. It might be just a supporting role, but it was a job. With a paycheck.

Three months ago, a job for Elliott would have been cause for joyous celebration between Barbra and him, and maybe they did celebrate now. But there was a good deal of other emotion weighing them down at the moment that may have kept the corks from popping.

Elliott had heard the stories about Barbra's affair with Sydney. There had been some blind items in the columns that could only have meant the two of them. And when Elliott had confronted Barbra with the rumors, she hadn't denied them.

On March 17, Mike Connolly wrote, "The stories about the domestic status of Barbra Streisand and Elliott Gould are sad," but just what those sad stories were, he didn't elaborate. Whatever his feelings about the affair, Elliott obviously didn't think it warranted the end of the marriage. In public, no matter their "sad domestic status," the Goulds put on happy faces. Elliott was frequently present at the Winter Garden, especially as opening night drew closer, posing for pictures with Barbra. It was from observing Elliott during this difficult period that Jerry Robbins formed some lasting impressions of Barbra's husband. "He handles it all very, very well," Robbins said. "Elliott is a gentleman."

10.

On March 26, *Funny Girl* finally opened on Broadway.

Tenacious radio reporter Fred Robbins kept thrusting his mike in Barbra's face as she prepared to go on stage. "So how do you feel?" he asked her.

"Nervous," she replied, pronouncing it in heavy Brooklynese — "noivous." Already she was in character.

"Just nervous?" Robbins pressed.

"Yeah, not much more. We've had many openings already."

For Barbra, it was all rather anticlimactic. In some ways she felt that the show had "been open about two years." The only real difference tonight was all the press swarming around the place, and the knowledge that there would be no more rewrites, no new scenes to rehearse. They'd frozen the show into place last night.

"You've been projected to the highest echelon of performers," Fred Robbins was saying. "How have you been able to adjust to it?"

"I haven't thought about it," Barbra replied. "I mean, I'm the same person. Things don't change me. I'm not impressed by things. With added success comes added problems."

"In your wildest dreams did you think this would happen?"

The look Barbra must have shot him was undoubtedly classic. "Of course," she said, and went off to do the show.

In her dressing room sat telegrams from the famous. "Dear Barbra," Natalie Wood had cabled. "All the best tonight because you are." Ed Sullivan had wired, "Barb, I brought you up to Fifty-third Street, now you've slipped back to Fiftieth Street, so we are not making progress. Every wonderful wish." The place was filled with flowers from Jack Benny, Harold Arlen, Ethel Merman, and so many others that the vases were lined out into the hall. Barbra could never keep them all. She'd have to give some away to the stagehands.

Out in the theater, the audience was filling up, and despite the presence of some high-profile celebrities — Merman, Lauren Bacall, Jason Robards, Lee Radziwill, Jacob Javits, diplomat and civil rights activist Ralph Bunche — Eugenia Sheppard thought that "fashion wise," the opening was a "flop . . . compared with the glamorous previews that had gone before." But this was the show that really counted, and the house was packed with those who wanted to witness Barbra's big night. Such crowds would be the norm for the foreseeable future: the Winter Garden was back to making between fifteen and eighteen thousand dollars a day in advance ticketing.

As people took their seats, they were handed their *Playbill*s, Barbra and Sydney on the cover, as themselves, not in character, in a serene pose, Barbra wearing pearls. She looked quite pretty and extraordinarily young. Yet inside, her biography reflected her new maturity. There were no mentions of Madagascar or Turkey, though she did claim to play field hockey and string crystal beads for sale in a Vermont general store. "For more personal information," the reader was told, "write to her mother."

The program also reflected the compromise that had been reached between Stark, Robbins, Kanin, and Haney. The show was still "directed by" Kanin and "musical staging" was still by Haney, but the special billing — "production supervised by Jerome Robbins," in the same point size as the other credits — told Broadway insiders all they needed to know.

Backstage, Robbins had left a note for the cast. "You can be my bagel on a plateful of onion rolls anytime! Love, luck, and many thanks, Jerry."

The overture was playing. Barbra had done this first scene many times now, in rehearsals, in Boston, in Philadelphia, in New York previews. But tonight there were people out there with little pencils writing in critics' notebooks.

Sitting in the audience was Ray Kennedy, a thirty-year-old writer for *Time* magazine. "Barbra Streisand crosses the stage," he wrote, "stopping in the center to gaze out over the audience, her look preoccupied. She gives a shrug and goes off. In the moment's pause before she disappears as quickly as she came, she leaves an image in the eye — of a carelessly stacked girl with a long nose and bones awry, wearing a lumpy brown leopard-trimmed coat and looking like the star of nothing. But there is something in her clear, elliptical gaze that is beyond resistance. It invites too much sympathy to be as aggressive as it seems. People watching it can almost hear the last few ticks before Barbra Streisand explodes."

Sympathy and aggression — perhaps the two elemental components of Barbra's success. And explode, of course, was exactly what she was about to do.

"Hello, gorgeous," Barbra said into the mirror when she returned to the stage.

The show was underway.

Even from just a night or two before, it was different. The last half hour of the show Barbra would carry almost entirely on her own. She had three solo numbers in a row, right up to the last reprise of "Don't Rain on My Parade," just before the curtain. With the exception of Kay Medford, who still had a song about her character ("Find Yourself a Man"), all the other parts and musical numbers now existed solely in service to Fanny's character. The show would hit or miss because of Barbra and Barbra alone.

It hit. The laughs came in all the right places, the songs reached every note perfectly. Kennedy thought Barbra turned "the air around her into a cloud of tired ions." As she sang the last lines of the night — "Nobody, no, nobody is gonna rain on my parade!" — the audience seemed unable to restrain themselves, applauding even before she was done, jumping to their feet, shouting and yelling as the curtain came down. This time Barbra made sure to wait until it touched the floor before she moved from the spot.

Then, suddenly, chaos. It was impossible to move backstage. Barbra's dressing room swarmed with press and well-wishers. Ethel Merman bounded in to pose for a photo with the new star. But Barbra had to get over to the big extravaganza Ray Stark was hosting at the Rainbow Room, at the top of the RCA Building, sixty-five floors high above Rockefeller Center. Already Lainie Kazan and Sharon Vaughn had made their way there, greeted by an army of photographers, flashbulbs popping, people shouting. Hundreds of invited guests were being treated to dinner and dancing with a live orchestra, all on Stark's dime.

Fred Robbins was weaving in and out of the crowd with his microphone, corraling the famous, drinks in hand, to comment for his radio show about what they had seen and heard that night.

"She has everything that I will call a star," declared Sophie Tucker. "From now on, nothing will stop Barbra Streisand."

Jason Robards was "stunned" by her performance. "I felt, you know, what am I doing? This twenty-one-year-old girl has all this talent and class."

Robards's wife, Lauren Bacall, agreed. "I saw the best thing I ever saw in my life in that girl. She can act, she can sing, she has an electric personality, which is what makes a star."

The principals were arriving, and the radio interviewer hurried over to them. "We've written some songs," Jule Styne said as he came in with Bob Merrill, "and we heard them really sung tonight by Barbra Streisand. She's one of the greatest singers of my time, and I've heard them all."

Merrill added, "She's going to be in the theater for a long, long time. The theater needs Barbra Streisand and she needs the theater."

Then came Stark, walking with a cane. "The show seems to have gone very, very well," he said, in that soft-spoken, measured voice of his. "I think Barbra was brilliant."

Someone pointed out to Robbins a small woman looking a bit lost. "Well, Mama Streisand," the radioman asked, approaching Diana with his microphone, "what do you think of this whole thing?"

"Well, I'm terribly elated," she replied.

"Where does the spark come from?"

"Actually," Diana said, holding nothing back, "her singing would come from her mother and her acting ability would also come from her mother. Her intelligence, however" — she laughed — "stems from her dear father, who was a PhD who helped many pupils on the road to gain self-respect."

Robbins commented that if only Barbra's father had lived to see this night.

Diana seemed uncomfortable with the sentiment. "Oh, he . . . ," she said. "Well, he's just with us right now."

Earl Wilson also grabbed the star's mother, whom he described as "overlooking the lights of the city her twenty-one-year-old daughter had just captured." He asked her if she'd taken the "a" out of Barbra's name. Diana seemed to bristle at the question. "She left it out, I didn't. She's a riot. Always was. She had a ninety-three average in school but always seemed to do the wrong things." She paused. "Till now."

A commotion at the entrance signaled the star had arrived. Barbra came into the room on Elliott's arm, "her face stiff, her backbone stiffer," one reporter thought. When she spotted someone she knew in the crowd, Barbra's features "contorted with relief for a moment." But then she was led away by Elliott into the crush of television lights and cameras. Some assistants ran on ahead, clearing a path so she could walk, while others surged in behind her. Barbra no longer seemed to be moving on her own accord. Rather, she seemed "swept and lifted into the ballroom."

"You tired, honey?" Fred Robbins asked her, his microphone back in her face.

"Yeah, I'm exhausted." Her voice sounded it. "I hate opening nights. Just horrible."

What she hated was the judging, she told Robbins, and the fact that the pressures of opening night "cut off" people's "emotional reaction" to the show. That was what she wanted — emotional reaction — not a microphone in her face. Elliott saw his wife's discomfort, saw the way "people were pawing her, sticking mikes down her bosom, telling her things she couldn't believe." This — all the cameras and the lights and the crush of people — hadn't been part of the dream. The show, yes, and the creation of the character and the applause and the good reviews and the declarations that she was great, very much yes. But not this. "All those cameras and lights" scared her, she said. The Rainbow Room's guest of honor just wanted to go home.

Then Barbra spotted her mother and rushed up to her. "Mama!" she said. "You didn't bring chicken soup."

"To the Rockefellers' nice building?" Diana replied.

They embraced. For all Barbra's problems with her mother, Diana was at least familiar to her. She was at least real.

CHAPTER SEVENTEEN

Spring 1964

1.

Barbra came gliding down the winding staircase from her tower bed-room wearing a padded lemon-silk robe, "looking as stylized and el-egant as a Japanese empress," her visitor thought, "the mannered ef-fect jarred by a kitchen spoon of tomato-dripping stew in her slender hand."

An interior decorator thrust a handful of swatches at her. "Which flocking for the foyer?" he asked.

Barbra glanced over at the swatches and pointed out the ones she liked, all while compiling a shopping list in her head. "Mayonnaise, garbage bags," she itemized to herself. Barbra hadn't gotten as far in her career as she had without knowing how to accomplish more than one thing at a time.

Her visitor that day was Shana Alexander, a writer for *Life* maga-zine and, not incidentally, the daughter of Milton Ager, the man who'd written "Happy Days Are Here Again." Alexander had arrived at Bar-bra's duplex to write a cover story on the young woman who'd taken Broadway by storm, and she had walked into the middle of a major decoration project. After nine months in the place, Barbra had decided it was high time to get the apartment furnished and decorated.

"Didja see the bed yet?" Barbra asked Alexander. "Upstairs. It's the first thing that we bought."

But the bed, for all its Elizabethan grandness, was nearly bare. Upholsterers were busy fluttering around it, considering ideas. Barbra told them she wanted the entire bed "draped and skirted with olive-gold damask," and the top should be folded so that it made "a crown, with sort of tassels hanging down." And she wanted "a red fur bedspread," and damask curtains surrounding the bed that could either be pulled to enclose her or looped back to the bedposts to expose the lace curtains inside.

"Lace!" the decorator shrieked.

It wasn't surprising that Barbra wanted the bed of a queen. Just days earlier, she'd sat for her portrait, like some sixteenth-century monarch. *Life* wasn't the only magazine doing a cover story on her. So was *Time,* and the publisher there, Bernhard Auer, had sent over Henry Koerner, who had painted President Kennedy, to get Barbra's likeness. She had sat for him in three sittings, staring straight ahead, her chin held still, her eyes painted with the signature Egyptian look Bob had designed for her so long ago. Astors and Vanderbilts got their portraits painted. Now Streisands did, too.

It had been a regal few weeks for Barbra. When, in the wee hours of the morning, the *Funny Girl* reviews had come rolling into the Rainbow Room, they'd all been predictably superlative. "Everybody knew that Barbra Streisand would be a star, and so she is," Walter Kerr proclaimed in the *Herald Tribune.* "Hail to thee, Barbra Streisand!" exulted Norman Nadel in the *World-Telegram.* Barbra "proves . . . she can sing and clown in a way to live up to her immodest advance billing," Richard P. Cooke judged in the *Wall Street Journal.* John Chapman in the *Daily News* thought the show was a "remarkable demonstration of skill and endurance on the part of Barbra Streisand."

She'd run away with all the personal reviews, though a few critics had also offered kind words about Kay Medford, Danny Meehan, and even Sydney, who Chapman thought gave a "poised and likeable performance." But Barbra dominated, and the magnitude of her performance was so blinding that critics truly didn't care that the book remained fundamentally unsound. Kerr acknowledged that the second act was "thinner than it should be," but declared that this wasn't enough of a letdown to make him reconsider the entire play. Nadel said the show was "just this side of great," but its defects paled beside the "big-voiced, belting singer and brass gong of a personality" that was Barbra.

Yet the most important reviews, for Barbra at least, were those that actually considered her acting as much as her voice and personality. Howard Taubman in the *New York Times* thought there was some "honest emotion underneath the clowning," and Kerr had pointed to a moment near the end where he thought Barbra justified her stardom with some brilliant acting. It was the moment when Fanny is willing to take Nick back, but then realizes that he has come to ask for a divorce, so she covers up her true feelings. Kerr observed that in that brief scene, Barbra momentarily dropped "the maturity [Fanny] has been struggling toward through the entire second act" and reverted to the innocent, love-struck girl of the beginning. And she did so, the critic stressed, in a "half-sentence." Kerr felt Barbra showed Fanny to be "an oak with the spine of a willow inside," which, of course, could describe Barbra as well.

Trailed by Shana Alexander and her reporter's notebook, Barbra gathered her entourage and hurried from the bedroom down to the street, where she hailed a fleet of taxis. It was time, she announced, to do some shopping. Elliott came along, too. At one antique shop, he grumbled about how much money Barbra was spending on an old, ornate piano that didn't play. Barbra was certain it could be fixed, and besides, as everyone knew, it was her money, and she could spend it as she pleased.

Perhaps that was what irked Elliott. He wouldn't let the matter of the piano drop, even though there was a reporter present. Or maybe, in some perverse way, Alexander's presence actually spurred him on. The squabbling seemed to begin in jest, a "mock-fight, an actors' fight," Alexander thought. But suddenly the carefully crafted façade of a happy marriage cracked. Before the startled eyes of the reporter from *Life*, the Goulds were suddenly in the midst of "a screaming, four-letter fight in the street, hopping in and out of taxis, over curbs, past startled pedestrians, oblivious of decorator, friends, passersby." It was big and theatrical and very unlike Barbra, for whom, most of the time, nothing seemed more important than control.

But the fault lines had become too unstable; as Barbra soared and Elliott stumbled, it was impossible to keep the tension between them hidden any longer. Alexander knew the conflict wasn't really about the piano. It was about who was "in charge." The next day, Barbra would make sure the reporter knew about the cactus plant adorned with a single rose that Elliott sent to her dressing room as a peace offering. But the damage was done. If they couldn't pretend to the public that their marriage was secure and happy, how could they go on pretending to themselves?

2.

They'd vowed to always be together on their birthdays, but on April 24, the day Barbra turned twenty-two, Elliott wasn't there.

Ray Stark had sent around champagne and chocolate cake for everybody, which meant the stagehands had sticky fingers as they worked the curtains that night. After the show, Marty was hosting a supper party in Barbra's honor. But none of it took the place of Elliott. Not long before, Barbra's husband had flown to Jamaica, where he was shooting *The Confession,* an independent film starring Ginger Rogers and Ray Milland. The island's Blue Mountain Inn was doubling as a northern Italian bordello presided over by Rogers as a black-wigged madam. The director was one of the old Hollywood greats, William Dieterle, whose credits stretched back to the silent era. Elliott was playing a deaf-mute who suddenly finds his voice after a shock. There was every reason, he had told Barbra, to expect big things.

Barbra was pleased that Elliott had work, but she missed him. No matter their squabbles, this would be the first birthday they weren't together, and her husband's absence was painfully significant. He'd been powerless to change location shooting dates, especially when the location was in the middle of the Caribbean Sea.

So Elliott made sure the gifts he sent Barbra were memorable. If he couldn't be there with her on her special day, he provided her with some company: a rabbit, a canary, and a goldfish. Her publicists made sure to get the story to Earl Wilson, but if there was any particular significance to the animals, it wasn't revealed. When Bob heard the story, he wondered if the gifts were Elliott's codes for "sex, singing, and their life in a goldfish bowl."

Putting aside any feelings of loneliness, Barbra prepared to go on stage. It had now been a month since opening night, and the boredom had set in just as it had on *Wholesale*. Barbra felt as if she were "locked up in prison" doing the same thing in exactly the same way every night, and her two-year sentence had only just begun. Walter Kerr, in his review of the show, had predicted it might happen. So much of *Funny Girl* was all about Fanny that he suspected it would only be a matter of time before "inspiration wanes and craft must make do in its place." Kerr probably hadn't expected it to happen this quickly, but he'd identified the problem clearly: "One feels the management is trying to cram an entire career into one show."

It wasn't just boredom Barbra was feeling. There was a growing antagonism with Sydney, whose ego had never recovered from being dumped and whose supporting role to the woman who had dumped him was beginning to chafe. The antagonism was only exacerbated by Barbra's requests that Sydney change certain things that disturbed the "flow of her performance," as she put it in notes left for him in his dressing room. Clearly Barbra hadn't learned from doing a similar thing with Elliott. Instead of honoring her requests, Sydney tossed Barbra's notes aside and began whispering to her as she came off the stage, "You really fucked that number up" or "You really ought to start writing some notes to yourself." It was exactly the opposite of the little whispers of encouragement he'd once given her.

Yet there was even more to turn the young star into a nervous wreck backstage. Copies of *Time* with Barbra's face on the cover were strewn everywhere. "She is the sort that comes along once in a generation," the magazine had proclaimed. All those grandiose statements on opening night from people such as Lauren Bacall ("best thing I ever saw") and Jule Styne ("greatest singer of my time") might have been exactly what Barbra had been waiting to hear all her life. But they also had the power to overwhelm and terrify her. In the end, to everyone's great surprise, including her own, the kid was only human.

"Now that I'm supposed to be a success," Barbra told Joanne Stang, "I'm worried about the responsibility. People will no longer be coming to see a new talent they've heard about. I now have to live up to their concept of a great success. I'm not the underdog, the homely kid from Brooklyn they can root for anymore. I'm fair game." Her stomach began to twist up at the most inconvenient times. Before a show she often felt nauseous or wracked with the worst heartburn. The doctors had prescribed Donnatal to control her intestinal cramping.

That night, Barbra took her curtain calls to the usual rapturous applause. She'd been wonderful as always; no one would have known that she felt sick to her stomach, pressured and claustrophobic, bullied by her costar, and lonely for her husband. But they did know something else. Suddenly, someone from a box seat called out, "Happy birthday!" Another box holder from across the way took up the cry, and then another, and then people in the balconies were shouting it. Soon the orchestra was striking up "Happy Birthday" and the whole theater was singing to her. Barbra, touched but also embarrassed, began tossing the roses she was given every night back over the footlights to the audience.

All those people out there whom she didn't know — people she couldn't see, people she'd probably never encounter again — loved her. They didn't know her — they knew only the image she had given them — but they really seemed to love her.

It was something Barbra struggled to understand.

3.

Stuart Lippner was a young man of sixteen who'd been to see *Funny Girl* multiple times. He'd first become aware of Barbra on *PM East*, when his mother had called him in from the other room to see some "nut on TV." From that moment on, Stuart had been fascinated. "Here she was," he said, "a nothing, telling important people they were schizy and all that." He liked her "because she wasn't afraid of people bigger than she was." Yet for the longest time he wasn't even sure of her name. She was just "the nut from TV."

But Stuart sure knew Barbra's name now, as did all the "Winter Garden Kids," as they called themselves, who were gathered around the stage door. They were there for every performance, waiting for their heroine to arrive. Many of them were school dropouts, so that meant they could be there all the time for every show. "Their lives were just wrapped around Barbra," Stuart explained. Some of them saved their money and followed her on tour. They owned all her records. If they couldn't afford to buy the disks themselves, they shared them with one another.

Stuart was still in school, and he worked in the evenings, so he was on the periphery of the Winter Garden Kids. But he knew them all from being there on weekends, and he shared their devotion. These kids dressed like Barbra, with thrift-shop hats and scarves, and talked like her, too, even the ones who didn't hail from Brooklyn. Stuart was a fellow Brooklynite, however, and expressed gratitude to Barbra for "doing a lot" for the accent. "A lot of kids aren't ashamed of it anymore," he told a reporter.

Out on the street, one of the boys was posted as a lookout, to let the rest of them know when Barbra arrived. Usually she never made it to the theater until half an hour before showtime. Other teenagers might idolize the Beatles, but these kids were different from the rest. They were "misfits," Stuart said. Boys and girls who weren't the sports heroes or the cheerleaders, who weren't the pretty ones who got all the dates. Many of them were gay, Stuart realized, like himself, even if few admitted it. A number of them had "fucked-up home lives." To them, Barbra was an inspiration. One boy named David admired how "everything she did was premeditated." Barbra had wanted "to look weird" to get attention, David told a reporter who had come to interview the Winter Garden Kids, which made her not so different from himself or the other kids at the stage door, with their bushy sideburns and pointy shoes and black eye makeup. One girl named Barbara — spelled with three a's, at least for now — thought that because their heroine "couldn't look common and couldn't look beautiful . . . she chose to look different." And what, she asked, was wrong with that?

"Nothing," Stuart replied. "She made it work. I give her credit for it."

Stuart might not have been an official member of the Winter Garden Kids, but they sure envied him. That was because he'd actually made contact with their heroine, if a little indirectly. After reading in Barbra's program bio that anyone who wanted "more personal information" should write to her mother, Stuart had thought, "Why not?"

Except he hadn't written, he'd called. As it turned out, Mrs. Louis Kind was listed in the Brooklyn phonebook. When a young female voice answered, Stuart assumed it was Barbra, but contained his excitement and asked for Mrs. Kind. When Diana came to the phone, Stuart explained the reason he was calling, mentioning the program bio. Barbra's mother seemed amused. Stuart asked if that had been Barbra who'd answered.

"No, that was Barbra's younger sister, Rosalind," Diana said. She paused. "How old are you?" she asked. Stuart told her sixteen. "Are you Jewish?" Mrs. Kind asked next. When he told her that he was,

Barbra's mother said, "Well, Rosalind is fifteen. Would you like to come over?"

Stuart jumped at the chance. Of course, he was aware that Mrs. Kind was attempting to "set him up with Rozzie," but that didn't stop him. Romance might not have been in the cards, but Stuart and Rozzie quickly became fast friends. Barbra's little sister now weighed close to two hundred pounds, standing barely five-two. Far shyer than her older sister had ever been, Rozzie was so dowdy that some people mistook her for Barbra's aunt. The young, impressionable girl envied her hotshot sister and longed to be a star just like she was, but the poor kid often froze up when speaking with Barbra. She didn't know "how to approach a big sister who had gotten so famous," Diana observed.

But with Stuart she found a soul mate. Despite Barbra's discomfort with a fan getting so close with her family, Diana invited the young man back often to spend time with her younger daughter. Sometimes Stuart stayed for dinner. Afterward Rozzie would play the *Funny Girl* album, and the two of them would sing along, knowing all the words and imitating Barbra together.

One night, Stuart took Rozzie to meet the Winter Garden Kids, and Barbra's younger sister had been much friendlier to them than the star herself. That was the strange paradox of it all: Here were these kids with so much affection for her, and Barbra seemed not to want it from them.

The lookout shouted that Barbra had arrived. The kids quickly arranged themselves so she would have to pass through them. "Hi, Barbra!" they shouted. "We love you, Barbra!" "Can we come up with you to your dressing room? Please, Barbra?"

From Barbra's vantage point, the kids seemed like a gang of hoodlums waiting to jump her. She felt "threatened and frightened" as she hurried past them. Dressed in her usual attire, a pair of white wool pants and a knee-length cabled sweater — a look a number of the girls and even some of the boys were copying — Barbra did her best not to make eye contact with any of them. These kids hadn't been part of the picture when she'd dreamed of being famous, nor were the fans who chased after her on the street shouting for an autograph. Barbra often felt as if she were being followed around. Presents were left for her outside her apartment building. One time some kid had jumped in front of her out of nowhere as she was getting into a cab to pay her fare for her. "It's insane," she told a reporter.

As her fan mail swelled, Marty started going through it to take out "the real screwy ones," as Barbra called them, before they could frighten her further. That didn't mean there weren't some "nice, great letters" that made her feel good, letters that began "I've never written a fan letter before." The sincerity of these letters moved Barbra. These people were responding to her work — to her art — not to her personality, she felt. And, to her relief, they were usually safely removed from her, in places like Albuquerque or Ottawa. They weren't kids dressing up to look like her and running after her in the street.

As the Winter Garden Kids shouted they loved her, Barbra covered her face and rushed past them into the theater. Barbra felt they loved "the symbol" of what she was, not "the flesh and blood," because they didn't know the flesh and blood. The fans who had sung to her in the theater might have known it was her birthday, but that was all they knew. It frustrated her that fans and journalists could speak and write as if they knew her — her private self, not the public creature from television talk shows and nightclub acts. She was determined to keep a dividing line between the two. Barbra wished fervently she could just "be admired on the stage and then left alone in life." But she was coming to realize that was impossible.

Back outside the stage door, her snub hadn't discouraged the Winter Garden Kids. They were used to it. They remained steadfast in their devotion. "She reminds me of Shaw's Cleopatra," Stuart told a reporter. "She has the same ability to charm people without beauty. She has ambition and will. Personally, I think her success will be greater than Cleopatra's."

"Let's hope she doesn't end the same way," said the Barbara with three a's.

4.

When word reached her backstage that she'd been nominated for an Emmy, Barbra was both thrilled and a little embarrassed. On the one hand, almost as if by a miracle, she was proving her prediction that she'd win all four major showbiz awards. The Grammy nominations had been expected: *The Barbra Streisand Album* was up for Best Album, Barbra herself was up for Best Female Vocal Performance, and "Happy Days Are Here Again" — which Columbia had paid so little attention to on its release — was up for Record of the Year. But no one had really dared to hope that Barbra would get an Emmy nod as well. The television academy had seen fit to give her one anyhow, for Outstanding Performance in a Variety or Musical Program or Series. The problem was that Barbra was nominated for her appearance on *The Judy Garland Show,* and so was Garland in the very same category. Thus, Barbra's one-shot was competing against Judy's entire season. That was the reason for the embarrassment.

Some in the company thought Barbra seemed "a little too cocky" after the nominations came out; others, such as recently hired swing boy Bob Avian, felt nothing but pride in their leading lady. But there was no denying that Barbra called the shots now; with Robbins off to work on *Fiddler on the Roof* and Stark mostly in Los Angeles, it was Barbra who decided how the show would go each night.

So it wasn't surprising on this evening for Sharon Vaughn to overhear Barbra telling Richard Evans, *Funny Girl*'s young, bearded production manager, that she would make her own script for the show. It had become common practice. During the period when they'd all been recording the cast album, Barbra had suggested a few tucks and trims to the script so the tired and overworked cast could get out of the theater ten or fifteen minutes earlier each night. But even after the album was finished, Barbra had continued to switch things around. She might ask the orchestra to end "Don't Rain on My Parade" a little early, for example, or decide that "Cornet Man" should go on without its introduction.

It was a way of stirring things up, of tackling the boredom Barbra experienced doing the exact same thing every night. She was careful, however, never to alter the basic framework, Bob Avian said, understanding "the frame was just as important as she was." Any cuts Barbra asked for were never going to hurt the show, Avian insisted. Someone who'd been to see *Funny Girl* before might not even notice such small changes.

But this night, unbeknownst to Barbra or the cast, Ray Stark had slipped into the audience. Either he had decided to make a rare, surprise visit from the Coast or someone had clued him in to what was going on. Not everyone was as complacent with Barbra's tinkering, after all. Sydney Chaplin, who would certainly have had a motive for cluing Stark in, thought Barbra's tinkering was "completely and utterly unprofessional," one company member understood.

Backstage, Vaughn watched as Barbra went over the night's changes with Evans. A few song introductions were moved around; a few scenes were shortened, eliminating the need for a couple of costumes. The production manager nodded in assent.

At the end of the show, there was great, tumultuous applause, just as there always was. But then, as the curtain dropped for the last time and the lights came up, the company heard the shouting.

Vaughn stopped cold in her tracks. Stark was limping backstage, shouting at the top of his lungs. "You will never change my show again! You will not change your costumes as you did! You will not change your songs! Do you understand me?"

Barbra understood all too well. She had hoped she was through with Stark's outbursts, but it was clear that she was bound to him in all the ways she had feared. This was what the next eight years would look like: a series of high-decibel clashes between two people who abhorred the art of compromise. For now, Barbra held her tongue. There were ways to work around Ray Stark, she'd come to learn. She knew that soon he'd be consumed with getting *The Night of the Iguana* ready for release, and she could go back to tweaking the show. She really had no other choice. It was the only way she could keep herself from going stir-crazy.

5.

Under the Jamaican sun, Elliott was sweltering. Temperatures spiked into the nineties, but it was the humidity that really wore people out. The Jamaican government was financing *The Confession* as part of an initiative to bring in foreign filmmakers. The film's producer was the cowboy-booted William Marshall, whose only qualification for the job was that he was Ginger Rogers's husband. But William Dieterle was an old hand at moviemaking; he kept the shoot progressing, even if conditions were difficult. Most of the bit parts were being filled by Jamaican locals, who proved rather stiff in front of the cameras. "Now look," the German-born Dieterle directed them. "Vy you look so sad? You are entering a brothel! You are about to have a voman! You must look happy!"

As Elliott waited to be called for his scenes, he knew that his own woman, some fifteen hundred miles northeast of him, was, if possible, having an even more difficult time of things. The pressures of carrying *Funny Girl* were intense, and that wasn't even considering all the demands Barbra faced from the media, the public, and the fans. More and more, Elliott felt he needed to get back to New York in order to "protect her." It may have been rather chauvinistic of him: "She was my woman," he said as an explanation for his feelings, and Barbra needed protection from "those fucking fan-magazine photographers" who stalked her every time she headed out on the street. Elliott was no doubt pleased that Dieterle thought they'd be wrapping up the shoot in the next week or so. For all his conflicts with his wife over the last few months, Elliott wasn't ready to give up on their marriage quite yet.

Still, he wanted to believe the separation had been worth it. People were saying he was giving "a remarkable performance" in this film. He would need good reviews from *The Confession* to take his career to the next level because, as usual, there wasn't anything else on the horizon, except the television play with Carol Burnett. There'd been talk that he might be cast in *Fiddler on the Roof,* but that had come to nothing.

So he sweated through the shoot and endured the sunburn. Three days of shooting in the oven of a roofless, ruined church without windows had turned the cast into baked goods. Maybe Elliott's analyst had been right when he'd called him a "masochist." But suffering through heat and humidity was the least of it. The real masochism, Elliott surely knew, would start again when he was back in New York. As much as he wanted to be by Barbra's side, he also knew that once he returned, he'd fall right back into the old pattern, trying to keep up with his wife's soaring success. The "perversity of fame," as he so astutely called it, would prove far more debilitating than the Jamaican sun.

6.

On the stage of the Grand Ballroom at the Waldorf-Astoria, singer Jack Jones suddenly froze, forgetting the lyrics to the song he was singing, "The Good Life," one of the nominees for Song of the Year. Tony Bennett came bounding up from his seat and relieved Jones of the microphone, finishing the number with aplomb. But except for that little kerfuffle, the ninth annual Grammy Awards banquet had been pretty boring.

Barbra sat at a table with, among others, Mike Berniker. The two of them had come a long way in the last year and a half. Berniker had taken Barbra on when she'd been an unproven commodity that no one else at Columbia was eager to produce. Back then, Barbra had said to Berniker, "Let's go," and go they certainly had. Currently, *The Third Album* was holding steady at number 8 on the charts, and even all these months later, the first and second albums were at 24 and 23, respectively. Barbra had ended up making an extraordinary amount of money for Columbia.

Now they hoped that she'd win them a Grammy, or two or three. But Barbra had known disappointment in this room before. It was here at the Waldorf that she hadn't won the Tony Award for *Wholesale*. Still, in the last few days, it had seemed as if her audacious prediction was on the fast track to coming true: first the three Grammy nominations, then the unexpected Emmy nomination, and finally, on May 4, the Tony nomination for *Funny Girl*. Only the Oscar would have to wait.

But for every premium her success paid, Barbra seemed also to be reminded of the costs of fame. On the morning after the Tony nominations had been announced, Carol Haney had been found unconscious in the Bowery. Their erstwhile choreographer had been nominated for her work in the show — work that had been significantly restructured by Jerry Robbins, as Haney well knew. She'd been drinking heavily; she was also a diabetic and had been without insulin for a dangerously long time. Rushed to Valley Hospital in Ridgewood, New Jersey, she was diagnosed with bronchial pneumonia, but that was only the surface of her problems. Haney was later transferred to New York Hospital, where, two days ago, she had died.

Some people thought Haney's dismissal from *Funny Girl* had played a part in her death. "It not only destroyed her career," Lainie Kazan said, "but her life." When, twenty minutes before showtime, word reached the Winter Garden that Haney had passed away, a pall had fallen over the company. A suggestion that her death be announced to the audience was nixed, however. "There's nothing we can do for her except to do her steps," Richard Evans said. "We have got to do her work tonight, no matter how hard it is for us." Upstairs, in her dressing room, Barbra received word of Haney's death from a reporter. She was solemn as she ran her fingers through her hair. "God," she said. "She was so talented and so gentle."

But gentle didn't often survive in a world of wolves. Barbra had understood that right from the start.

Sitting at the table at the Waldorf, Barbra heard her name called as the winner for Best Female Vocal Performance. She'd just been named the "best" by her peers, which mattered a great deal to her. Who would have thought such a thing possible the day she'd sung "Day by Day" in Barry's apartment? Now, more than four years later, Barbra had just been adjudged better than any of her fellow nominees — Eydie Gormé, Miriam Makeba, Peggy Lee — *Peggy Lee!* — and, in an occurrence that no doubt made Barbra smile, the Singing Nun. She wasn't just the most commercially successful; she was also the *best*.

She was disappointed when Henry Mancini's "Days of Wine and Roses" beat out "Happy Days Are Here Again" as Record of the Year. But the big prize was still ahead. At the end of the evening, the nominees were announced for Album of the Year. Barbra was up against the Singing Nun, Mancini, Al Hirt, and the Swingle Singers, who used their voices to interpret Bach's great compositions. When the envelope was opened, *The Barbra Streisand Album* was named the winner.

Better than even Bach, it seemed.

Technically, this was Berniker's award as producer. As the room filled with applause, however, he leaned over to Barbra. "Thank you," he said quietly.

She looked at him. "That's my line," she said, "because you did it." Then she added, "I love you."

It was a thoughtful, if slightly uncharacteristic, moment. Barbra didn't always recognize the efforts of other people who had roles in bringing her to the top. But she wasn't all drive and self-absorbed ambition.

She could also sometimes be gentle.

7.

In Paris, Bob was eager for news of home.

He'd asked a friend who was visiting the United States to bring him back some newspapers and magazines. Bob had been in Europe for almost two years now, and he felt out of touch. So it was with considerable excitement that he received the publications his friend had brought back. But when he got a look at the covers of *Time* and *Life*, he stopped short.

Barbra was on both of them.

His friend Barbra. The girl he'd put up on a stool to experiment with hairdos and makeup. The same Barbra who'd once talked with him for hours on the phone about her dreams and her ambitions and her favorite flavors of ice cream.

Bob was aware that Barbra had been doing well. He knew she'd cut several albums. She'd sent him copies, in fact, asking him to get them out to "influential people" in Paris. He'd given the albums to the *disquaire* affiliated with Chez Castel, the popular Parisian discotheque. And the last time he'd seen her, in London, Barbra was hoping to get the part in *Funny Girl*. Bob had heard she'd gotten it, and he was aware she'd opened on Broadway a couple of months ago, so he knew things were going great for her.

But these covers . . .

Bob hadn't been around to see the gradual climb, the Ed Sullivan and Judy Garland shows, the Cocoanut Grove, the Hollywood Bowl, the first, second, and then third albums prominently displayed in record stores. Even though he knew Barbra was doing very well for herself, Bob still had a picture of her in his mind as a little girl in pink nylons and scarlet satin shoes wandering around Greenwich Village with a shopping bag full of boas. Once that little girl had pointed up to the marquees of Broadway and told Bob she wanted her name up there someday.

Bob looked again at the face of his friend on the magazine covers.

She was wearing the distinctive eye makeup he'd designed for her, that she had made her own through her inability to glue false eyelashes by herself.

He knew Barbra had become a success.

But, in fact, he'd had no idea.

8.

Stuart Lippner was flushed with excitement. Mrs. Kind was taking him to the holiest of holies: Barbra's dressing room.

The Winter Garden Kids burned green with envy as Stuart walked past them into the theater behind Barbra's mother, carrying a large Tupperware container of chicken soup. The young man had been spending a great deal of time at the Kinds' apartment. Diana often included him in meals or on outings she'd take with Rozzie. Stuart liked Mrs. Kind. She wasn't a "come here, bubby, let me give you a hug" type, but she was very maternal in her own way, he thought, always cooking up a storm and enjoying being able to dole it out to her family. Sheldon and his wife and daughter were often there for dinner, and Stuart would take his place at the table beside Rozzie. But so far, Barbra and Elliott had never shown up, even though Mrs. Kind insisted she'd asked them.

So Diana brought the soup to Barbra instead of Barbra coming to the soup. She also brought fruit. Peaches, apples, cantaloupes. Barbra needed fruit for the vitamins they provided. She had a tendency to be anemic — her mother had not forgotten.

Watching the two of them in Barbra's dressing room, Stuart, an outsider, saw their relationship in a way they could not. Mother and daughter seemed stuck somehow, incapable of telling each other what they really wanted to say. That there was great love there, Stuart had no doubt. He'd seen all the photographs of Barbra in Diana's apartment. Not so many childhood photos that he could see, but eight-by-ten glossies from Columbia Records, or images carefully clipped out of magazines. Diana's apartment was crammed with stuff — it looked as if she never threw anything away — but all Stuart had had to do was move one stack of papers to realize that most of it was all about Barbra.

Stuart would often walk in and find Diana singing along to Barbra's albums in "a beautiful, clear soprano voice." Rozzie had told Stuart that her mother's father, the cantor, hadn't let her sing at the Met. Stuart thought maybe Diana was jealous of her daughter, sometimes unconsciously and sometimes not.

It wasn't so much that Diana had wanted to be a star, her brief dreams of the opera notwithstanding. It was that Barbra had been able to see beyond the concrete tenement walls that had penned them in and kept them back, something Diana had never been able to do. With frightening audacity, Barbra had declared that she would go through those walls and see what the world looked like on the other side. Diana had declared it an impossible dream. And when Barbra had shown that one could indeed break free, her mother had worried that she'd end up disappointed and frustrated, pushed back into her place by a world that put no stock in homely Jewish girls from Brooklyn tenements.

How could she have known how wrong she'd be?

And Diana couldn't admit to being wrong. People who'd had to scrape and struggle all their lives were never going to find it easy to admit that the world might not be as limiting as they'd always imagined it to be.

Barbra was standing there now in her dressing room, in costume and makeup, a posse of photographers around her while an assistant did her nails. Thanking her mother for the chicken soup, she said she didn't have time to talk. She had a show to do.

It was just like her mother to show up just before the curtain. In truth, Diana embarrassed Barbra. Her mother was "simple [and] nonintellectual," she told the press. To observers, the two women seemed to be completely different creatures, Barbra in her duplex on Central Park West, Diana in her Brooklyn tenement. So far Diana had resisted Barbra's offers to move her into a more fashionable apartment in Manhattan. But she *had* accepted a fur coat, the fulfillment of a long-ago pledge Barbra had made to herself.

Yet her mother's gratitude seemed minimal. Diana might call and tell Barbra that "so-and-so in the office . . . read something nice" about her in some article. But it never seemed "to mean anything to her personally," Barbra felt. That was what still stuck in her craw even after all these years.

Maybe that was why Barbra still pushed herself so hard, or at least part of the reason. And why rejection still stung. Certainly there'd been a run of rejection of late. She hadn't won the Tony. After everyone had been telling Barbra that she was a shoo-in, Carol Channing had taken the award for *Hello, Dolly!* — the show for which David Merrick had dumped *Funny Girl*. How Ray Stark had seethed when Merrick had won Best Musical as well. No one from *Funny Girl* had won a damn thing — not Sydney, not Styne and Merrill, not Kay Medford, not Danny Meehan, not poor Carol Haney, even though they'd all been nominated. *Hello, Dolly!* pretty much crushed everybody else.

And, on top of that, Barbra hadn't won the Emmy either. Danny Kaye had taken the award, winning over both Barbra and Judy Garland, whose show had finally been cancelled even after she'd submitted to such humiliation from network executives. It was one more lesson in the vagaries of fame, and the dangers of not being tough enough.

Barbra had come to realize that in some very real way her mother was responsible for her fighting spirit. Diana's limited view of the world and their place in it hadn't discouraged Barbra: It had challenged her. When all she'd heard growing up was "No, no, can't be done," Barbra grew determined to prove that yes, yes, it could. To one interviewer, she declared she was actually "thankful" to her mother. By not believing there was a way through to the other side of the wall, Diana had forced her obstinate, strong-willed, defiant daughter to keep chipping away, bit by bit, until she'd broken through. And so Barbra, as she bid her mother good-bye and headed out on stage to a groundswell of applause, was very pleased for all Diana had and hadn't done.

Somewhere deep down, the teenaged Diana Rosen, the one who'd been accepted to sing with the Metropolitan Opera Chorus, was probably pleased as well.

9.

On a warm, balmy night in June, Barbra sauntered into fashion designer Rudi Gernreich's fashion show at the Gotham Hotel wearing a white linen suit, a white straw hat encircled by a black patent leather band, a black pullover, a rope of pearls, and silvery iridescent polish on her long nails. For a moment, everyone turned away from Gernreich's infamous topless bathing suit to get a look at the glamorous Broadway star.

The fashionistas loved her. Not long before, Barbra had turned up for Cosmo Sirchio's collection, amid talk she might make him her personal designer. Now Gernreich spoke of dressing Barbra for a fashion layout, maybe for *Vogue* or another magazine. Barbra had predicted this would happen. "I am high fashion!" she had exclaimed just last winter. "Pretty soon women will copy what I wear."

Now they were doing just that, and it wasn't only the Winter Garden Kids. Barbra had become a regular boldface name in Eugenia Sheppard's fashion column. No matter that she'd also been named to the worst-dressed list by that stuffy Mr. Blackwell — below Zsa Zsa Gabor and Elizabeth Taylor but above Bette Davis and Elliott's co-star, Ginger Rogers — Barbra had become a fashion icon. If anyone doubted that fact, all they needed to do was watch the fashion writers gush over her purchase of Gernreich's black chiffon, above-the-knee baby dress, to be worn over black tights. They knew Barbra could set the style. What they didn't know was that, less than five years earlier, Barbra had known nothing about fashion. Terry Leong had had to explain to her the differences between Alberto Fabiani and Pauline Trigère.

Now Barbra wore all the latest designers. Money, of course, was no object, even if she still instinctively peeked at the price tags. She knew she wasn't supposed to "ask how much things cost," given that people were aware of how much money she made. Still, there were times when Barbra felt she *needed* to ask: Life could become "mushy if you don't evaluate things sometimes," she said. Her accountant gave her a weekly allowance of $25 for pocket money, but Barbra never spent it. She saved it, out of habit, as if she were back at the switchboard at Ben Sackheim and earmarking part of her pay for rent, part for food, and part to splurge on taxis.

To one interviewer, she tried describing how she had gotten from there to here. She'd never had a room of her own as a kid, she said. And when you don't have a room of your own, she explained, "All you think about is 'How can I *get* a room of my own?' You just get to the point where you *have* to make good."

She'd made good all right. That black designer dress, the duplex apartment, the mink coat Earl Wilson said cost twelve thousand dollars were all evidence of that. True, people still sometimes misspelled or mispronounced her name, but the instances were far fewer now. And when Barbra shopped at Bergdorf Goodman, the clerks all knew who she was.

10.

Sitting, literally, on top of the world in her penthouse apartment, as decorators trundled expensive antique furniture through the door, Barbra looked out her windows over the treetops of Central Park. Beyond them rose the East Side peaks, and beyond those lay Brooklyn. Barbra couldn't see it, but she knew it was there.

That morning, the *Times* had broken some rather big news about the star of *Funny Girl*. Barbra had been signed to a million-dollar television contract by CBS. Marty was crowing that he'd just negotiated the biggest deal ever made in television and offered to pay one-hundredth of that sum to anyone who could prove otherwise. Barbra's contract allowed her to star in one one-hour special per year for the next decade, and she was guaranteed $100,000 annually. The specials could be of her choosing: comedy, variety, or musical drama. Outraged over this newcomer's unprecedented terms, old pros like Danny Kaye and Lucille Ball unleashed their agents on the network. "The screaming," one columnist reported, "could be heard up and down Madison Avenue."

Three years earlier, Marty had promised to take Barbra to the top, and he had delivered. This latest coup was being hailed in the press as "nothing less than phenomenal" and garnered a rare public acknowledgment of Barbra's "brilliant young manager." Those who weren't expressing envy of Barbra were asking to work with her. Carol Burnett proposed a joint special, like the one she'd done with Julie Andrews, but Barbra preferred to go it solo. She hadn't worked this hard to share top billing.

If screaming was raging along Madison Avenue, a quiet contemplation had settled over Central Park West this morning. Sitting there looking out of her window, waiting for the clock to demand that she head downtown to play Fanny Brice for the hundred and fiftieth or hundred and sixtieth time, Barbra had begun to wonder just how long she could be happy living here. Despite all her antiques and redecoration, when she looked out over the city, all she could see was the "traffic going by." Suddenly she was painfully aware that she "never really saw the sky."

By the late spring of 1964, Barbra's success, for all the envy and admiration it engendered in others, was not what she'd dreamed it would be. Despite the Donnatal, her anxieties before every performance had only worsened, and she found herself admitting that the stage fright that had been creeping up on her ever since the Hollywood Bowl was not going away. Some nights were worse than others; for one show, she bounded out in front of the audience with all her old confidence, but for another she'd be a wreck backstage. There seemed to be no rhyme or reason for her fears, except that she knew interaction with people was becoming more difficult. It was seeing the faces of those watching her, judging her, and following her that left her rattled. More than ever Barbra missed her old anonymity. Critics called her arrogant, and claimed that success had gone to her head for refusing interviews or not shaking hands with fans. Only Cis, her cherished Cis, seemed to understand: "Stardom is a part of [Barbra's] life that has always been difficult for her," Cis tried to explain to one reporter.

What was more, Barbra hadn't counted on her heart getting in the way of her enjoying her success. She and Elliott had settled into a sort of fun-house existence, where nothing was quite what it seemed. True, they had reconciled after their terrible winter; they were making a determined go of things. "To end the rash of rumors," columnist Alex Freeman reported, "Barbra Streisand is neither pregnant nor unhappily married to actor Elliott Gould. The Goulds weathered their first big marital crisis recently and everything is swinging."

Swinging. Was that the word? Despite all the hope and hype of the last few months, Elliott was still struggling to make himself known. He'd been cute in *Once Upon a Mattress* and witty on an episode of the topical television series *That Was the Week That Was*. But *The Confession* had been confiscated by its Jamaican financial backers; producer William Marshall was now suing to get the rights. There was no idea when, if ever, the film would be released. Trying to boost her husband, Barbra told reporters that Elliott was "going to be a big movie star," that he was "the American Jean-Paul Belmondo." But all the American Belmondo had on tap was a summer-stock tour of *The Fantasticks* with Judy Garland's eighteen-year-old daughter, Liza Minnelli. Elliott fell deeper into analysis and found himself depending more and more on pot. His marriage to Barbra, he said in his own eccentric style, was like taking "a bath in lava."

So when people envied her, Barbra thought, "Oh, God, don't envy me. I have my own pains. Money doesn't wipe that out."

What she wanted, she said, was to see the sky.

Sitting there at her window looking down on the bleating, congested traffic of Central Park West, Barbra held in her mind an idyllic image of California's blue skies and palm trees. Sure, sometimes the sky in Los Angeles was smoggy, but there one could live in a gated estate surrounded by trees and beautiful gardens. In Los Angeles, one traveled in limousines. There was always a protective barrier between a star and those fans who would accost her if they had a chance, unlike New York, where they could wait for her in the street, or right outside her door, or gather at the theater, jumping her every time she went in or came out.

And in Los Angeles, they made movies.

Barbra's name was finally up on a Broadway marquee — the final destination on the roadmap to success that she'd charted for herself some five years earlier. But she'd only been able to see so far. With the brass ring now in her hand, Barbra was faced with a set of questions that had never occurred to her before. Where did she go from here? Finding herself on the summit she'd always dreamed of reaching, she looked off into the distance and spotted yet another peak waiting to be scaled. And along its craggy hills rambled one word: HOLLYWOOD.

"Being a star is being a movie star," Barbra now declared. Movie stars didn't have to do the same thing exactly the same way every night for two years. She had a contract to make four pictures, and she was prepared to fight Ray Stark with all of her considerable strength if necessary to make the films she wanted to make. After *Funny Girl,* she insisted, she was through with musicals. Didn't people know she was an actress? That was what had set her on this path: she had wanted a chance to play Juliet. And if she couldn't play Juliet on the stage, then maybe she could play her on the screen.

Elliott, if Barbra had asked him, might have responded that her discontent was classic, at least in psychoanalytic terms: The more one achieves, the more one wants. Someone who grew up feeling dissatisfied wasn't going to suddenly become satisfied by the simple accumulation of things or achievements. Barbra might even have agreed with that assessment. She was "a practical person," or at least she liked to call herself one, and she could be unsparingly honest about her own needs and motivations at times. "The dream," she mused. "You never achieve it and that's what's depressing. The excitement of life lies in the hope, in the stirring for something rather than the attainment." She lamented that she "couldn't hold success in her hand like a hard-boiled egg."

But how could it be otherwise, especially for her? Barbra had grown up feeling as if something were always missing. Not knowing her father had started Barbra "off on the track of always feeling resentful," she admitted; it would leave her "always missing something" in her life. The crisis of faith she experienced once *Funny Girl* was on the stage led to something she couldn't have predicted a year before. Like Elliott, Barbra surrendered to analysis, where it seemed certain that her father would be a prime topic of conversation. When she finally worked up the courage to confront her mother about why she never mentioned Emanuel's name — why Barbra's father had always been one of the great unspoken tensions between them — Diana replied, "I didn't want you to miss him." As if not speaking about him could have prevented that.

And so Barbra had no choice but to keep on climbing.

Along the way, she'd lose some of those who'd started the climb with her. The intimates dwindled to a very few. Cis, as always, was steadfast. Marty remained her chief lieutenant. But when Terry Leong tried to connect with Barbra backstage at *Funny Girl*, he was told she was too busy to see him. When Barry Dennen refused to hand over the tapes he'd made of her, claiming they belonged to him, Barbra threatened legal action, though she never followed through. With Peter Daniels, tensions continued to escalate, especially after Lainie Kazan went on in Barbra's place one night during *Funny Girl*'s first year and alerted the press to come see her. Soon afterward, Kazan was out of the show, and Daniels wasn't far behind. Only decades later would Barbra acknowledge her longtime accompanist's influence and help, dedicating a concert to him. Even Bob Schulenberg fell out of Barbra's orbit when he returned from Europe, finding he shared little in common with his old pal turned superstar.

Sitting there at her window overlooking Central Park, watching the traffic and longing for the sky, Barbra described feeling "alone with

[her] thoughts" and dreading "the hour of showtime." That first year of *Funny Girl* proved to be excruciating. Sydney Chaplin's hostility only got worse, to the point where he was cursing at Barbra onstage and trying to deliberately throw her off track. In early 1965, she filed harassment charges against him with Actors' Equity. Although the sympathetic "old boys' club," as Orson Bean called them, let Chaplin off after interviewing him, Barbra's ex-lover departed the show soon after that, much to her relief, replaced by Johnny Desmond.

Later that same year, Diana finally consented to her daughter's insistence that she move into an upscale, all-expenses-paid apartment in Manhattan. Little Rosalind would drop the weight and change her name to Roslyn and, before the decade was out, launch a career of her own as a singer, headlining at nightclubs and enduring comparisons with her more famous sister. Diana told friends she felt Rozzie was by far the more talented of the two.

Arguments and separations continued to mark the marriage of Barbra and Elliott, but they strove to stay together, even having a baby, Jason, in December 1966. But after a couple more years, they finally called it quits and were divorced in 1971. Only after splitting with Barbra did Elliott's career take off again. He became a top box-office movie star with *Bob & Carol & Ted & Alice* and *M*A*S*H,* among others. Still, as successful as he became, Elliott never considered himself "larger than life" in the way he saw Barbra. Looking back on all he and his former wife had been through, Elliott had to wonder why anyone would want to "make themselves into something that wasn't real."

What Barbra had made herself into was a movie star. After two long, tedious years on the stage in *Funny Girl,* both on Broadway and in London, Barbra turned her back on the theater and went to Hollywood, where she starred in the film version of *Funny Girl* and won an Oscar for doing so. Within a few years, she was the biggest female movie star in the world, and by now, no one was surprised. She did relent and make more musical films — people were always clamoring for her to sing — but she also got to play the kinds of parts she'd always wanted, glamorous women and complex characters, even if, to date, she still has never played Juliet or Medea. But she did get to play Dolly Levi, and Daisy Gamble, and Esther Hoffman, and Katie in *The Way We Were*. And with all those profits she fashioned herself a palace overlooking the Pacific Ocean that provided her with plentiful views of the sky.

Working with Ray Stark, as Barbra anticipated, wasn't easy, and the battles with her mercurial producer continued. When, in 1974, she had finally fulfilled her four-picture contract with him (*Funny Girl, The Owl and the Pussycat, The Way We Were,* and *Funny Lady,* once more putting on Fanny Brice's cloche hats), Barbra presented Stark with an antique mirror on which she had scrawled in lipstick PAID IN FULL. Yet for all the frustrations and bitterness she carried, she still recognized that without Stark's early championship she might not have come as far as she had, or at least she would have needed to have taken a very different route.

Of course, it wasn't enough to simply remain a successful actress, so Barbra became a director, starting in 1983 with *Yentl,* and won accolades for her work. She kept on recording, too, staying relevant by making a successful transition to rock-pop with the *Stoney End* album in 1971. She ended up with more Top Ten albums than any other female artist in history — fifty-one of them gold, thirty platinum, and thirteen multiplatinum. And then it wasn't enough to just *sing* her songs, but she had to *write* them, too. Barbra won another Oscar for her composition of "Evergreen" for *A Star Is Born*. With a special Tony for theatrical excellence, Barbra had made good on her goal to win all four major showbiz awards. From that old doubter, Sheilah Graham, nothing was heard.

And, at last, after many ups and downs, there seemed to be some personal fulfillment, too. In 1996 Barbra met James Brolin and married him two years later. They are still together.

All of her childhood dreams had come true, and on her own terms. But as the years went on, the older Streisand seemed less genuine, less spontaneous, and more guarded than the girl of that first half decade.

Barbra's fear of not being as good as people claimed she was — or not being as good as she was on her last record or in her last film — only magnified as she aged. She found herself holding back more, no longer giving her all when she sang. "You must only give three-quarters," she explained. "Five eighths." Giving one's all, Barbra believed, exposed a desperate need to be loved by the public, and she wasn't desperate for that, not if that meant letting the public in too close. After all, giving one's all was what Judy Garland had done, and Judy was dead, burned out, at the age of forty-seven. So increasingly Barbra withheld parts of herself, leaving her audiences always wanting more. That wasn't necessarily a bad thing, emotionally or strategically, since it kept people coming back. But it did make some people nostalgic for that young singer who'd so fearlessly exposed the empty place in the middle of her heart every time she got up to sing.

Of course, Streisand had always been made of stronger stuff than Garland. From the time she was very young, Barbra had seen and heard things beyond the range of mere mortals; she had understood her own specialness. "I have visions in my head," she said, looking back and trying to explain the unexplainable — the drive that had always propelled her forward. "I hear music. I dream."

She had needed to be great — great enough to transcend the boring, the quotidian, the desultory Brooklyn afternoons. That was why she had started to climb and what would keep her scaling the heights. In her striving, there was a message, and it said, "Keep on." If Garland was the goddess of self-destruction and vulnerability, Streisand was the diva of self-confidence and strength — as well as of a certain kind of magic, one that can elevate the everyday and transform even an ordinary kid into a star.

"Her performances astound, arouse, fulfill," Jerry Robbins had declared. Watching Barbra move across the stage in *Funny Girl,* he had glimpsed potential still untapped. "She is still forming. There is more to come, things will change, something will happen. The next is not going to be like the last."

Sitting there in her duplex penthouse, with showtime looming,

Barbra cast one last glance over the treetops of Central Park and pulled herself away from the window.

Down on the street, a car waited to take her to the theater. Stony-faced, Barbra rushed past the fans who waited, as always, along the curb. Suddenly one young man shouted, "Keep on daring to dream, Barbra!"

For once Barbra stopped. Somehow the words had penetrated the invisible armor she always wore in public. For the first time that her fans could recall, their heroine turned to look at them. They were surprised to see a little smile blooming on her face. "You can count on that," Barbra said.

Then she got into the car and sped away.

Acknowledgments

Although I had enjoyed the work of Barbra Streisand in the past, I certainly didn't consider myself a fan when my editor suggested her as the subject of my next book. To be honest, I didn't really understand Streisand's massive appeal — why she was such a big deal to so many. What I knew about her at that point consisted mostly of *The Way We Were* and *Yentl* — which, as it turned out, would be far beyond the scope of my study.

So, being a Streisand novice, I embarked on a quest to discover everything I could about her first years in showbiz: her nightclub performances, her television appearances, her singles, her albums. Fortunately, I didn't have to re-create the wheel. There have been dozens of Streisand biographies, several of them excellent, and my use of them is cited in the notes. Even when some of their fundamental assumptions were wrong — Ray Stark being opposed to Streisand's casting in *Funny Girl,* for example — I was grateful that previous authors had snared interviews with key figures who have since passed on. I was also very lucky to have the help and advice of several Streisand veterans who were far more knowledgeable of the lady's career than I was at the time. My gratitude especially goes to Christopher Nickens.

Still, the kind of crash course I needed to take in Streisandiana wasn't going to be easy. Fortunately, most of Streisand's early television spots are now online. Even the audio of some of her nightclub performances — at the hungry i, for example — is available. What's truly remarkable is the fact that much of this critical primary material has been gathered under one umbrella, the exceptional Barbra-Archives.com, run by the exacting Matt Howe. On day one, I bookmarked Matt's site; rarely did a period of time go by that I didn't visit once, twice, or more times a day. At the height of writing the book, I just left the site open on my desktop because I was constantly checking something. I could not have written this book without the Barbra Archives. My thanks to Matt not only for his phenomenal work online, but also for answering the many questions I lobbed his way. Also helpful were other excellent Streisand websites, including but not limited to the All About Barbra fanzine site, Barbra Timeless, Barbra News, and Streisand's own website.

I was also aided by a bootleg copy of the DVD *Just for the Record,* which had been intended to supplement Streisand's CD of the same name but was never actually released. So much early material is included on this DVD that I could easily contrast, for example, the way Streisand sang "Cry Me a River" on *The Dinah Shore Show* with the way she sang it on *Ed Sullivan,* or see how she responded to Groucho Marx as compared to Johnny Carson. (A special thank-you to the source who provided me with a copy, who asked to remain nameless.)

The digitization of newspapers also gave my research the kind of authority I could only have dreamed about when I first started writing biographies in the mid-1990s. There's no need anymore to make vague statements about what the columnists were saying at any particular time. Now I've got virtually every single column written by Earl Wilson, Dorothy Kilgallen, Walter Winchell, Hedda Hopper, and hundreds of others. With this technology in place for the Streisand project, I could pinpoint when contracts were signed, when singles were released, when albums started climbing the charts, when rumors started, and when publicity changed course.

But, as always, the most important sources were the collections of personal papers of some of my subject's most important collaborators. At the top of the list, of course, is the Jerome Robbins Collection in the Jerome Robbins Dance Division of the New York Public Library, but nearly as important are the Bob Fosse Collection and the Robert Merrill Collection at the Library of Congress. Also, the collections of David Merrick (Library of Congress); Herbert Ross and Roddy McDowall (Howard Gotlieb Archival Research Center); Sidney Skolsky, Jane Ardmore, Jack Hirshberg, Hedda Hopper (Margaret Herrick Library); Lainie Kazan, Jo Mielziner, Thomas Higgins (for Joe and Evelyn Layton), Leland Hayward, Richard Lewine, and Abe Burrows (New York Public Library for the Performing Arts) were also helpful. All collections are fully cited in the notes.

I'd also like to single out a few archivists who provided special assistance: Mark Horowitz at the Music Division of the Library of Congress; Barbara Hall at the Margaret Herrick Library of the Academy of Motion Picture Arts and Sciences; Jeremy Megraw at the New York Public Library for the Performing Arts; and J. C. Johnson at the Howard Gotlieb Archival Research Center at Boston University.

I must also note the extraordinary collection of Lou Papalas, whose careful preservation of so much Streisand memorabilia — from magazines to costumes to photographs to scripts — has truly been a labor of love. I am especially grateful to Lou for allowing me to see many of Streisand's original contracts.

Personal interviews with those who were actually *there* — friends, lovers, colleagues, publicists, managers, fans — provide the human perspective in this book. I am grateful to everyone who shared their stories, insights, and memorabilia, not just on Streisand but also on the times of the early 1960s: Bob Schulenberg, who is truly blessed with the gift of total recall; Barry Dennen; Don Softness; Phyllis Diller; Orson Bean; Ted Rozar; Kaye Ballard; Lainie Kazan; Suzanne Merrill; Janet Matz; Dick Gautier; Sammy Shore; Paul Dooley; Carole Gister; Bob Avian; Linda Gerard; Stuart Lippner; Adam Pollock, partner of

Terry Leong; and several others — friends, family, and colleagues of Streisand, Elliott Gould, Diana Kind, Marty Erlichman, Ray Stark, and others — who asked that their identities be kept anonymous. There were more of these people than usual on this book, given my subject's well-known dislike of biographies. All are extremely reliable sources.

I was particularly fortunate to have interviewed Arthur Laurents on a couple of previous occasions, although his passing meant I was not able to ask a handful of follow-up questions. Still, what he'd shared earlier about his work with Streisand proved invaluable to this book. I was also blessed to be good friends with the late Tucker Fleming and the late Charles Williamson who, as intimates of Judy Garland, had shared with me Garland's impressions of working with Streisand.

Also paramount to my study were the dozens of men and women I spoke with who were there to see Streisand perform in New York, Detroit, San Francisco, and elsewhere, or who were friends of her associates, or who worked with journalists who interviewed her, or who bought the albums when they first came out, or who were in New York gay bars watching her when she appeared on *PM East* back in 1962. Given the structure of this book, I have not always used their names in the actual narrative, though many can be found in the notes. To these lifelong fans, I am deeply grateful for helping me to understand the passion that has followed Streisand ever since she first appeared on the scene and that has lifted her to the lofty heights she enjoys today.

Thanks also to my friends and colleagues who provided connections, advice, information, and other help or material: Clark Bason, Tom Judson, Steven Brinberg, Mitch Villari, Jeremy Kinser, Wayne Lawson, Tim Teeman, and Michael Childers.

My original editor, George Hodgman, was the true Streisand fan behind this project right from the start; his imprint remains on every page. My current editor, Andrea Schulz, provided keen insight and a much-needed steadying hand. Johnathan Wilber was a help at every turn and made things happen. Michaela Sullivan designed a beautiful cover. David Hough, once again, brought his sharp eye and keen ear to the manuscript. My agent, Malaga Baldi, was, as always, indomitable. And my first and best critic will always be my husband, Dr. Tim Huber. My gratitude to all.

Finally, thanks to Barbra Joan Streisand, for not throwing up any roadblocks and for making me finally understand why she really was, and remains, such a big deal.

Notes

Abbreviations

AMPAS = Margaret Herrick Library for the Performing Arts, Academy of Motion Picture Arts and Sciences

BFC = Bob Fosse/Gwen Verdon Collection

JRC = Jerome Robbins Collection

LAT = *Los Angeles Times*

LoC = Library of Congress

NYPL = New York Public Library for the Performing Arts

NYT = *New York Times*

Where not cited, quotes are taken from personal interviews with the author. On occasion, quotes from printed sources have had grammar adjusted and/or ellipses discarded, but only if the original intent, meaning, or accuracy of the quote was not altered by doing so.

Why Streisand Now

2 "one of the natural wonders": *High Fidelity,* May 19/6.

3 "to be a star having": Interview with publicist Jack Hirshberg, July 9, 1968, Hirshberg Collection, AMPAS. Hirshberg conducted in-depth interviews with clients, then polished them up and released portions to newspaper columnists and reporters. This is taken from the unedited transcript of his interview with Streisand.
"It was right to the top": *Time,* April 10, 1964.

4 "for her talent to speak": *Pageant,* November 1963.

5 "carried her own": *Time,* April 10, 1964.
"I don't think so": *The Rosie O'Donnell Show,* November 21, 1997.
"That goes so deep": *O, The Oprah Magazine,* October 2006.
"Barbra Streisand doesn't sound": Kaufman Schwartz and Associates interview with Streisand, August 15, 1963, submitted to Sidney Skolsky, Skolsky Collection, AMPAS.

6 "negative implications": *Playboy,* October 1977.
"each ear is," "I really don't": *O, The Oprah Magazine,* October 2006.
"What is so offensive": *Playboy,* October 1977.

1. Winter 1960

9 For sixty-five cents: Sue Anderson, a friend of Carl Esser's, related a story Esser told her about being with Streisand on her father's birthday eating fish at a diner on Broadway south of Times Square. Anderson said he used the phrase: "ninety-three cents and some pocket lint."

10 called her "*farbrent*": *Vanity Fair,* September 1991.
"what life should be": *Vanity Fair,* September 1991.
"a need to be great," "preacher": *Family Weekly,* February 2, 1964.
"where people really": *Look,* April 5, 1966.

11 never seen Duse act: Later Streisand would see Duse in an Italian film from 1916 and call it "extraordinary." James Spada, *Streisand: Her Life* (New York: Random House Value Publishing, 1997).

13 "duty to squelch": These were Streisand's exact words when she confronted Susskind a few years later on *PM East.*
"a coat of some immense": *Ladies' Home Journal,* August 1966.
Jules Feiffer cartoon: LAT, September 10, 1963.
"I never hear": *Playboy,* October 1977; *TV Guide,* January 22–29, 2000.
a hundred such institutions: Background on the Theatre Studio and other acting schools in New York of the period was found in an article in the *New York World-Telegram,* February 21, 1959.
weekly radio program: *Theatre Studio on the Air* was broadcast on Wednesday evenings. Whether Streisand ever participated is not known; all students were eligible, but no one was promised participation. Among the productions aired while she was at the school were Sophocles' *Antigone* on October 11, 1959; Sean O'Casey's *Pictures in the Hallway*

with the original Broadway cast on November 4, 1959; Chekhov's *Swan Song* on February 24, 1960; and Shakespeare's sonnets on August 17, 1960.

The school offered: Theatre Studio pamphlet, 1960, Curt Conway file, NYPL.

14 some of the greats: Advertisements for the Theatre Studio, *Village Voice,* September 30, 1959; NYT, October 14, 1959, and January 9, 1961. The Theatre Studio should not be confused with its competitor, Stella Adler's Theatre Studio, which operated at 150 East Thirty-ninth Street. To avoid confusion, the Theatre Studio was sometimes advertised as "Curt Conway's Theatre Studio."

with enough "appetite": Allan Miller, *A Passion for Acting: Exploring the Creative Process* (Sherman Oaks, CA: Dynamic Productions, 1995).

a nice review in the local newspaper: "As the homely sister, Barbara Streisand is transformed from a tomboy to a pretty girl, aware of her powers, in a wholly believable transition." *Berkshire Eagle,* August 31, 1957.

"like someone who": Spada, *Streisand: Her Life.*

$180 for a fifteen-week course: Theatre Studio pamphlet, 1960, Curt Conway file, NYPL.

named Dustin Hoffman: Streisand spoke about Hoffman being the "janitor" at the Theatre Studio on *Friday Night with Jonathan Ross,* BBC, October 2, 2009. Hoffman was quoted about being at the Theatre Studio with Streisand in the *National Enquirer,* January 2, 2005.

15 Socrates, Euripides: Kaufman Schwartz and Associates transcript of interview, August 15, 1963, Sidney Skolsky Collection, AMPAS. In this interview, Streisand said she "never read any of our American authors."

"Can you imagine": *Playboy,* October 1977.

"ever did in high school": Unsourced magazine clipping, circa 1970, NYPL.

"Acting is the only art": Theatre Studio pamphlet, 1960, Curt Conway file, NYPL.

"very awkward, emotionally": Randall Riese, *Her Name Is Barbra* (New York: St. Martin's Press, 1994).

"the political niceties": Riese, *Her Name Is Barbra.*

16 "real ugly kid": *Ladies' Home Journal,* August 1966.

"couldn't bear to look": *Life,* March 18, 1966.

"very pretty and attractive": Spada, *Streisand: Her Life.*

17 "You'll get a disease": *Playboy,* October 1977.

"the sexiest scene": Riese, *Her Name Is Barbra.* Streisand also described performing the scene in *Playboy,* October 1977.

18 "a big deal": Streisand's attitude toward Vasek Simek comes from an interview with Barry Dennen.

What exactly did she "vibrate": *Playboy,* October 1977.

"supersonic hearing": *Playboy,* October 1977.

19 "right to the top": *Time,* April 10, 1964.

"Where did you *ever*": I have based my description of Barbara's shopping expedition with Terry Leong on interviews with Adam Pollock, Barry Dennen, and another friend of Terry's who asked to be kept anonymous. I have also used newspaper descriptions of Third Avenue during the period and of the various boutiques that operated along it. Terry's friend recalled he shopped at Stuart's.

"delicately attenuated": Barry Dennen, *My Life with Barbra* (Amherst, NY: Prometheus Books, 1997).

21 Terry sat her down: That Terry Leong taught Streisand a great deal about fashion and

style was insisted upon by Adam Pollock: "Knowing her background, she'd have had no idea who those designers were. I'm sure he had a hand in her education whether she wants to admit it or not."

"secrets, and codes": Dennen, *My Life with Barbra.*

22 "about love and life and sex": *Playboy,* October 1977.

She accepted the news: Interview with Adam Pollock.

"You know, once": *Players Magazine,* Spring 1965.

"double-dealing, marauding": *New York World-Telegram,* June 4, 1948.

23 "remotely adolescent": *Redbook,* January 1968.

After Barbara played: *Vanity Fair,* September 1991.

The Cormans were now: The description is culled from various interviews Barbra and Cis gave over the years, as well as from the recollections of a friend of one of the Corman children, who remembered seeing the young Streisand at the house in the early morning, watching the goings-on without saying a word.

grandparents' living room: *O, The Oprah Magazine,* October 2006.

"an amazing thing": *Vanity Fair,* November 1994.

24 one friend out of her atheism: *Playboy,* October 1977.

"I am deeply Jewish": *Playboy,* October 1977.

"Christmas, Christmas, Christmas": *New York,* September 9, 1968.

"I don't remember": *Rogue Magazine,* November 1963.

25 "last chance of freedom": Streisand made this statement when she appeared as a guest on *What's My Line?* on April 12, 1964.

ninety-four average: *Pageant,* November 1963.

"Why isn't this kid": *O, The Oprah Magazine,* October 2006.

"further experience": Streisand's mother's note to her teachers is quoted in Spada, *Streisand: Her Life.*

"actual beatniks": *Pageant,* November 1963.

"You'll get paid": *O, The Oprah Magazine,* October 2006.

26 "You're smart, you're pretty": *60 Minutes,* November 24, 1991.

"Don't go out in the rain": *Playboy,* October 1977.

left her at the same time: *60 Minutes,* November 24, 1991.

Her paternal grandmother: Interview with Stuart Lippner.

"rubber tummy": *New York,* September 9, 1968.

27 taught her mother how to smoke: *O, The Oprah Magazine,* October 2006.

"allergic to kids": *Playboy,* October 1977.

"I tried to imagine": *Ladies' Home Journal,* August 1966.

28 "kind of a wild": *O, The Oprah Magazine,* October 2006.

"you weren't supposed to do": *Inside the Actors Studio,* March 24, 2004.

29 The first thing: I have based my description of Diana Kind's apartment, her life, and her attitudes toward her daughters on interviews with Stuart Lippner, Mo Fisher, and two others who knew her well. I have also referenced an interview Diana gave to the *Daily Mail,* April 23, 1994.

30 Barbara at the age of one: *Inside the Actors Studio,* March 24, 2004.

31 "No pay": Spada, *Streisand: Her Life.*

32 "scandalously flaunting": Divorce papers of Diana and Louis Kind, May 2, 1957, Clerk's Office, Kings County Supreme Court.

33 "had failed to do": *Daily Mail,* April 23, 1994.

34   the students were busy preparing: It's not clear what kind of performance Streisand invited her mother to watch. It was likely one of the special workshops the Theatre Studio held for its more advanced students, which used both "experimental work on new plays and classical material." Theatre Studio pamphlet, 1960, Curt Conway file, NYPL. My description of the night comes from Sue Anderson and several friends of Terry Leong's.
"white slavery": Spada, *Streisand: Her Life.*
"missed as a child": *Life,* March 18, 1966.
"a lot of time and money": *Time,* April 10, 1964.
"Is it crazy": *Pageant,* November 1963.
"bring so many": *Cosmopolitan,* May 1965.
"I have this hole": *Vanity Fair,* September 1991.

35   "I can do that": *Today Show* interview, 2009.
the Actors Studio was her own personal mecca: There have been various stories, differing in detail, about Streisand's experience with the Actors Studio. She herself has always been vague about the experience. One account has Streisand being asked to return for an audition but never following up, which seems highly unlikely given how much she wanted to be a part of the school. Appearing on *Inside the Actors Studio,* Streisand described crying through her rendition of *The Young and Fair,* calling it an "audition." But in 1963, when her memory was presumably clearer, she described the experience as a "three-month course." (Kaufman Schwartz and Associates interview transcript, August 14, 1963, Sidney Skolsky Collection, AMPAS.) It is from this interview that I have taken the quotes about her fellow students. The "prized possession" quote comes from *Inside the Actors Studio,* March 24, 2004.

36   everyone applauded: I have based my description of this night on an interview with a friend of Terry Leong's, as well as the account provided by Marilyn Fried in Spada, *Streisand: Her Life.*

2. Spring 1960

37   "Did you never": Dennen, *My Life with Barbra.* The description of Barbara and Barré rehearsing *The Insect Comedy* is also derived from personal interviews with Dennen, Bob Schulenberg, Carole Gister, and Sue Anderson. Whenever my description differs slightly from Dennen's book, it is because it was told to me that way in interviews, sometimes by Dennen himself, during which I endeavored to make timelines and descriptions as accurate as possible.

41   "Stop humming": Spada, *Streisand: Her Life;* Anne Edwards, *Streisand: A Biography* (Boston: Little, Brown, 1997).
The Sound of Music was preparing: Auditions were taking place in the spring of 1960, which corroborates Barry Dennen's account that Barbara tried out for Liesl soon after *The Insect Comedy* closed. Henderson was named in several columns that spring as being a likely Maria von Trapp; she was officially signed in October. Plans for the road company were postponed by a labor dispute on June 8, but auditions would likely have proceeded.
Florence Henderson: various newspaper reports, *Sound of Music* file, NYPL.
When she was a kid: "I could sing, so people liked me. If I didn't have talent, they didn't have to like me." *TV Guide,* January 22–28, 2000.
Eddie Blum and Peter Daniels: Details of Streisand's audition with Blum, which was also

her first meeting with Daniels, come from interviews with Lainie Kazan and Jim Moore, a friend of Daniels's.

43 Streisand tapes "Day by Day": My account is based on interviews with Barry Dennen as well as his book *My Life with Barbra,* with my best efforts to reconcile both into the most accurate timeline. A conversation with Sue Anderson, a friend of Carl Esser's, was also helpful.

45 Cokes, and ice-cream cones. *Look,* April 5, 1966.
chantilly lace: Unsourced clip, April 13, 1965, profile by Hal Boyle, see Barbra Archives.

46 "unconventional," "like them straight away": Interview with Jack Hirshberg, July 9, 1968, Hirshberg Collection, AMPAS.

47 "Ya know," she said. "I'm going": *Vanity Fair,* September 1991.

48 The King Arthur Room: In *My Life with Barbra,* Dennen wrote that he took Streisand to see Mabel Mercer at the RSVP Room, which was located on East Fifty-fifth Street across from the Blue Angel. However, Mercer had left the RSVP by the end of 1959 and by January 1960 was ensconced at the King Arthur Room. See Danton Walker's syndicated Broadway column, January 7, 1960. Mercer was still at the King Arthur Room in October of that year. Dennen may have remembered seeing Mercer at the RSVP earlier, but by the time he took Streisand, Mercer was definitely at the King Arthur.
The talent shows: Flyer for the Lion, 1959–1960 season, NYPL. Various accounts have placed them on Mondays, or on weekends, but the flyer provides documentation.

49 Dawn Hampton: NYT, April 26, 1960; September 29, 1960; June 11, 1982. Dawn Hampton was *not* the niece of Lionel Hampton, as some biographies have claimed.
"sang like there was": Riese, *Her Name Is Barbra.*

50 "learn from a record": *Rogue,* November 1963.
Mabel Mercer was an old crust: For a detailed consideration of Mercer as a café singer, see James Gavin, *Intimate Nights: The Golden Age of New York Cabaret* (New York: Back Stage Books, 2006).

51 "what not to do": *Rogue,* November 1963.

52 watching Barré lather his face: Dennen, *My Life with Barbra* as well as interviews with him, with my best efforts to order the timeline into the most accurate narrative.
"You don't screw anybody": *Playboy,* October 1977.
Mae West double entendres: Dennen wrote in *My Life with Barbra* that they stayed up late to watch Mae West in a film in which she performs with Duke Ellington's orchestra. That describes *Belle of the Nineties,* but *Belle of the Nineties* did not air on New York television stations during the year that Streisand and Dennen were close. After an exhaustive search of television listings, the only film of West's that aired in the period in question was *My Little Chickadee,* which was shown on Saturday, June 18, 1960, which fits the time Dennen was describing.
"What's the matter with your animal?": This line comes from West's autobiography. Dennen wrote about it in *My Life with Barbra,* and Bob Schulenberg also remembered the catchphrase.

53 Burke McHugh ran the Lion: Riese, *Her Name Is Barbra;* publicity flyers from the Lion, NYPL.

54 "Talented in a way": Interview with Tom Hall, a friend of Burke McHugh's.
With his classic: Background on Burke McHugh comes from an interview with his friend Tom Hall, as well as NYT, May 7, 1957; April 26, 1960; May 20, 1994; and the *New York World-Telegram,* September 28, 1960.

other performers to the Lion: From an interview with Paul Dooley. Many performers did come to see Streisand perform at the Lion. Yet despite stories that claim Noël Coward was one of them, Coward's diaries reveal that he was not in New York during the dates Streisand was singing there.

55 "terribly nervous": Clemons was quoted in Charles Kaiser, *The Gay Metropolis* (Boston: Houghton Mifflin, 1997). Although he played piano for Mercer early on, he was most famous as a writer. His collection of stories, *The Poison Tree*, was published in 1959. In the cab on the way: Interview with Adam Pollock.

56 "because that was too false": *CBS Sunday Morning*, September 27, 2009.
"hated" the name Barbara: *Rogue,* November 1963.
"losing touch with reality": *Family Weekly,* February 2, 1964.
strode over to Burke McHugh: Riese, *Her Name Is Barbra;* interview with Tom Hall.
"the only Barbra in the world": AP wire story, as in *The Derrick* (Oil City, Pennsylvania), October 11, 1963. Note that in his memoir *My Life with Barbra,* Dennen wrote that he changed the spelling of his name to Barry around the time Barbara became Barbra, and most accounts of her life have used the latter spelling for his name after this point. But newspaper notices of Dennen's appearances in theatrical productions reveal that he was still spelling his name with an "é" instead of a "y" as late as September 1961.

3. Summer 1960

58 "as funny as Shakespeare": NYT, June 30, 1960.

59 "promised participation": Theatre Studio pamphlet, 1960, Curt Conway file, NYPL. Although it was established works such as *The Boy Friend* and *Look Homeward, Angel* that paid the bills, the Cecilwood served primarily to try out new work. That summer Conway was presenting *Cry of the Raindrop,* written by his Theatre Studio partner Lonny Chapman, as well as the Studs Terkel drama *Amazing Grace,* featuring Peter Fonda in one of his first roles.
He desperately wanted: I've taken my account of Streisand's late arrival at *Henry V* from personal interviews with Dennen and Schulenberg, as well as Dennen's *My Life with Barbra,* attempting, as ever, to establish the most accurate narrative.

61 "to keep one hand": *Look,* April 5, 1966.

63 Not long after: Interviews with Barry Dennen, Bob Schulenberg, and Dennen's *My Life with Barbra.*

64 "change the tilt": *Playboy,* October 1977. In a personal interview, Barry Dennen also reported having essentially the same conversation with Streisand in the summer of 1960.
"loved her bump": *Playboy,* October 1977. Streisand also told Oprah Winfrey she'd always liked her bump. *O, The Oprah Magazine,* October 2006.
her father's nose: *Pageant,* November 1963.

65 "They're not ripped": *Time,* April 10, 1964.
Ben Sackheim, Inc.: Information on the company comes from the NYT, August 28, 1941; July 12, 1951; August 18, 1959; October 20, 1959; April 18, 1960; November 16, 1960; July 26, 1965; and January 3, 1966, as well as the online magazine *Postscripts,* October 31, 2009.

66 "acting alive": *Friday Night with Jonathan Ross,* BBC, October 2, 2009.
"made-up foreign languages": *Time,* April 10, 1964.

67 "Greenwich Village version": *Variety,* February 27, 1952.

"one of the lead funspots": *New York World-Telegram,* November 11, 1959.

"wanted to do something": *Rogue,* November 1963.

68   "Kid, you are going": *All About Barbra,* undated clipping, Barbra Streisand file, AMPAS.

$108 a week: This is the figure reported in a profile of her career in the *Saturday Evening Post,* July 27–August 3, 1963. In *Streisand: Her Life,* James Spada gives the figure as $125 a week.

"It just seems": syndicated UPI article, as in the *Press-Courier* (Oxnard, California), July 26, 1962, and elsewhere.

69   "chauffeured around": *This Week,* February 5, 1966.

Since returning to Manhattan: In *My Life with Barbra,* Dennen described Streisand as moving in with him earlier than this point. Although there were likely overnight stays, Bob Schulenberg, whose memory is uncannily accurate, insisted that it was not until right before her appearance at the Bon Soir that Streisand moved in with Dennen.

70   "French from the moon": Spada, *Streisand: Her Life.*

Barré's apartment: Dennen, *My Life with Barbra,* as well as interviews with Dennen and Schulenberg.

73   "If I can identify": *CBS Sunday Morning* interview, September 27, 2009.

75   "once again throbbing": NYT, October 20, 1960.

"Box offices are busy": Dorothy Kilgallen's syndicated column, as in the *Daytona Beach Morning Journal,* September 30, 1960.

"tucked behind a façade": NYT, October 13, 1960.

76   "Customers who jam": NYT, October 13, 1960.

77   "far-out females": *Variety,* January 4, 1962.

"all the gay guys": Quotes and observations from Kaye Ballard come from a personal interview as well as her memoir, *How I Lost 10 Pounds in 53 Years* (New York: Back Stage Books, 2006).

"the funniest woman": Dorothy Kilgallen's syndicated column, as in the *Daytona Beach Morning Journal,* September 30, 1960.

78   the size of a peapod: Quotes and observations from Diller come from a personal interview as well as her memoir, *Like a Lampshade in a Whorehouse* (New York: Penguin, 2005).

Around eleven, the place started: Various sources report that the Three Flames began playing around ten PM, but a contemporary account of evenings at the Bon Soir in the NYT, November 10, 1960, when Streisand was on the bill, reported that the place didn't begin to fill up until eleven thirty and that Tony and Eddie went on at midnight. I've calculated that the band probably started the evening's entertainment closer to eleven than to ten. The Three Flames played a half-hour set.

79   "a-twinkle with glow worms": NYT, November 10, 1960.

"Keepin' Out of Mischief Now": Anne Edwards in *Streisand: A Biography* wrote that her first number was "A Sleepin' Bee," calling it "a brave opening," since most cabaret acts began with "a spirited number to catch the audience's attention." According to Barry Dennen, who has tapes and notes from that performance, her first song was "Keepin' Out of Mischief Now," exactly the sort of spirited number that could, and did, grab the audience's attention. Edwards also reported that she sang "When the Sun Comes Out," but Dennen refutes that. In *Streisand: Her Life,* Spada reports that among the numbers she sang that first night was "Who Can I Turn to Now?" but Dennen also denies that. That song was added, however, to the repertoire before the Bon Soir run ended.

81 "triumphant roar": *Pageant,* November 1963.

4. Fall 1960

83 "one of the biggest": NYT, September 13, 1960.
"the find of the year": *New York World-Telegram,* September 16, 1960.
"The pros are talking: *New York Journal-American,* September 15, 1960.

84 "a dynamic passion": *Rogue,* November 1963.
"too trapped by her": Judge wrote about seeing Streisand at the Bon Soir in the *New York Journal-American,* April 25, 1965.

86 Diana bragged: This description comes from several friends of Diana's, including Stuart Lippner, and is bolstered by Streisand's own comment on *Inside the Actors Studio:* "My mother was the type of woman who praised me to other people but not to my face. She used to say, 'I don't want you to get a swelled head.'"
"a series of manic ups": Barry Dennen, *My Life with Barbra.* This chapter is also supplemented by a personal interview with Dennen.

88 "feminine wiles": *Vanity Fair,* September 1991.

90 "just in time for the World Series": NYT, October 3, 1960. The sale ran from the end of September through October 25.

91 "too dear": "My Life with Barbra," unpublished manuscript by Donald G. Softness, courtesy Softness.
"original designs created": NYT, October 16, 1960.

94 "A startlingly young": NYT, November 10, 1960. This was not a specific review of a particular Streisand performance, but came within a larger profile of the nightclub scene.

96 "the whitest white man": Dennen, *My Life with Barbra.* My description of that first meeting is also supplemented by personal interviews with Dennen and Ted Rozar, which did not always jibe when considered together, but I have done my best to square their memories with the available facts.
"you can take me to dinner": During my interview with Rozar, he told me, "Barbra still owes me that dinner she promised."

97 "ninety percent of jazz's": *The Daily Reporter,* November 18, 1959.
somewhere deep in the fir forests: Neither Rozar nor Dennen could remember exactly where the hotel was, and Streisand has never talked about it. An exhaustive search through clippings and digitized newspaper databases also did not turn up the location or the exact date. I hope that some dogged Streisand fan will someday turn up the details.

98 Carl Esser had just opened: program bio, *Whisper to Me,* November 21, 1960, NYPL; *Bridgeport Post,* July 17, 1960.
Roy Scott, was currently in rehearsals: NYT, January 9, 1961; *Montserrat* program, NYPL.

101 Outside, it was snowing: NYT, December 20–24, 1960.

102 And Barbra was having her revenge: I've based my description on the strife between the two of them on personal interviews with Dennen and Schulenberg, as well as Dennen, *My Life with Barbra.*

103   a club called the Townhouse: Spada, *Streisand: Her Life.*

She walked in to find: My description of this fateful New Year's Eve is based on Dennen's *My Life with Barbra* as well as, more important, a personal interview, in which he described Streisand, years later, confronting him about that night. Dennen said he had "blocked out" the details of the incident, claiming he did not recall having sex with a light-skinned black man, but he did not dispute Streisand's account of it. "I don't want to remember it, but it's perfectly possible it happened," he admitted. According to Dennen, Streisand told him there were "moments in life one never forgets," and for her, catching him with a man that New Year's Eve was one of them.

"A lot, yeah": *Playboy,* October 1977. Asked if it was anything like she expected it to be, she replied: "Yes and no."

5. Winter–Spring 1961

106   "all the cold-shouldering": Personal interview with Barry Dennen.

London Chop House: In 1961, chef and food critic James Beard named the Chopper as one of the ten best restaurants nationwide, the same year it won a Dartnell Survey award as one of America's Favorites. Various newspapers, digitized collections.

107   Les Gruber had looked at: *Detroit News,* August 26, 2000.

"weird" was the only way: *Detroit Magazine,* March 27, 1966.

"a hippie": *Detroit News,* August 26, 2000.

"a big stack of dog-eared music": *Detroit Magazine,* March 27, 1966.

"I'm a fast learner": *Detroit Magazine,* March 27, 1966. The legend that Streisand learned ten songs that very first night, in just the few hours before her first show, originates here, with Chapman's rather fanciful account, told when Streisand was a big star. Those who had worked with her in Detroit were looking back from the vantage point of 1966 with romantic nostalgia. Streisand was indeed a fast learner, but working out all that new material in such a short time defies credibility. In fact, much later, a less starry-eyed Matt Michaels told an interviewer that on her first night, Barbra sang the five (not four) songs she already knew. (*Detroit News,* August 26, 2000.) This shouldn't detract from Streisand's achievement, however. In a week's time she was singing at least four new numbers and being hailed for them. That's impressive enough without needing to embellish.

108   "All she needed": *Detroit Magazine,* March 27, 1966.

"tough lady": *Detroit News,* August 26, 2000.

"shut up," " to be a star," "in front of a mirror," "belligerence": *Detroit Magazine,* March 27, 1966.

109   "could do a squib": *Detroit Magazine,* March 27, 1966.

"came from Brooklyn": Streisand made this statement on *PM East* on July 12, 1961.

110   By day Fred Tew: *Wall Street Journal,* January 3, 1968; *Detroit Magazine,* March 27, 1966; archives of *Detroit Free Press,* for which Tew wrote for many years before moving to Chrysler; interview with Mike Walter, *Detroit News,* August 26, 2000.

Her little press junket: *Detroit News,* March 4, 1961; *Windsor Star,* March 6, 1961.

111   "I'm comin' in to play": Spada, *Streisand: Her Life.*

112   "striking rather than beautiful": *Variety,* March 8, 1961.

113   "sociable downtown gang": *Detroit News,* August 26, 2000.

"bachelors about town": *Detroit News,* October 18, 2000.

"critiques," "Do you know": *Detroit News,* August 26, 2000.

114 "You're great": *Detroit Magazine,* March 27, 1966.

Barbra a new contract: Agreement between London Chop House and "Barbara Striechsand," dated March 1, 1961. www.barbra-archives.com.

"turn off people": *Playboy,* October 1977.

115 It had all happened rather suddenly: Anne Edwards, in *Streisand: A Biography,* quotes Bob Shanks, talent coordinator for the Paar show, as saying Streisand herself kept calling to try to book herself on the show. "I said no to Barbra Streisand," Shanks told Edwards. This, however, was simply not how booking was done. Both Orson Bean and Ted Rozar were clear that they got Streisand the gig together. The story Shanks told of Streisand asking for his advice may have happened later, but not before she had been a guest. The image of a completely unknown Streisand calling and cajoling the Paar show on her own, making up outlandish stories to get a job, seems part of the later legend that insisted she was single-handedly responsible for her own fame.

116 Madame Daunou's salon: NYT, February 17, 1950; April 16, 1950; April 4, 1966. Also a detailed interview with Bob Schulenberg.

117 "Barbara Strysand": *Hartford Courant,* others, April 5, 1961; NYT, April 5, 1961. As to whether Dennen watched the show, he said he did not recall.

118 "This girl was a young girl": Fortunately many of Streisand's early television appearances have been uploaded to YouTube. This first Paar show is included on the DVD *Just for the Record,* planned as a companion to the CD set of Streisand's music in 1991 but never released. Thankfully, a bootleg version has circulated among fans for years, and it has allowed me to be precise in describing Streisand's radio and television appearances.

122 "could be accused": *Variety,* December 27, 2004.

"hep audience": *Variety,* August 2, 1961.

"as relaxed as an old shoe": *Variety,* May 3, 1961.

"to showcase rising new talent": *St. Louis Post-Dispatch,* April 14, 1961.

123 "a zippy revue": *St. Louis Post-Dispatch,* April 21, 1961.

"their sort of patter": Spada, *Streisand: Her Life.* Bob Schulenberg also shared stories of how the humorous patter in between Streisand's songs originated.

124 "inimitable, sultry way": *Variety,* May 3, 1961.

less than forty-eight hours: It's often been stated that Streisand ended her run in St. Louis on May 8 and started up at the Bon Soir the very next night. But notices and advertisements in the *St. Louis Post-Dispatch* reveal that her last show at the Crystal Palace was on Saturday, May 6. Her contract with the Bon Soir indicates she began there on Tuesday, May 9. So most likely she would have flown out of St. Louis on Sunday, May 7.

125 salary raised to $175: Contract dated April 17, 1961, reproduced on Barbra Archives, www.barbra-archives.com.

"wrong," "a floozy job": Interview on *Late Night Line-Up,* BBC2, 1966. This attitude was also confirmed by Bob Schulenberg and Don Softness.

magnanimous of her to lend: Both Randall Riese and James Spada report versions of this story in their respective biographies. According to Pim Allen, a regular patron of the Bon Soir who was there for much of Streisand's run, this occurred only on opening night.

"only intermittent nutritional value": *Variety,* May 17, 1961.

126 "bastardizing her art": *Late Night Line-Up,* BBC2, 1966.

127 "chills through all of them": *Vanity Fair,* September 1991.

"industry people," "a lot to learn": Spada, *Streisand: Her Life.* It is not recorded what five songs Streisand sang at this second engagement at the Bon Soir. It's possible that the ballad she opened with was "A Sleepin' Bee," but that's just speculation.

born in Brooklyn: Most accounts say Erlichman was born in the Bronx, but the 1930 census shows him, at age seven months, living with his parents on Quentin Road in Brooklyn.

128 "Jazz on the Hudson": NYT, May 24, 1959.

Marty certainly wouldn't have pegged Barbra: Erlichman, of course, insisted he knew right away that she was going to be huge, that he saw Oscar and Emmy and Grammy in her future, and wanted to be her manager even if she didn't pay him right away. This sounds much like the same way Ted Rozar described his own first experience with Streisand and is, in fact, typical hyperbole from a personal manager. At the time, *Variety* was saying of Streisand's second Bon Soir engagement that she had not "developed much box office" (May 17, 1961). Various observers from the period, such as Bob Schulenberg, Don Softness, Phyllis Diller, and others believed Erlichman's later insistence that he knew right from the start that Barbra would be a giant superstar was simply a personal manager saying the right thing about a client.

"what Chaplin had": *Saturday Evening Post,* September 27, 1963.

Without any niceties: My description of the first meeting between Streisand and Erlichman comes after critical reconsideration of what both have said about it and how others remember it. As noted earlier, Erlichman described their initial encounter with all sorts of hyperbole, as a shrewd manager should. He reported telling Streisand that very first night that she'd win all the awards and that she would be "the biggest movie star of them all." This he told to the press long after Streisand had actually become a big movie star, and it suited the legend they had shaped: that she was a born star and those with keen eyes had seen the truth of that from the start. Bob Schulenberg, however, remembered the first meeting between Streisand and Erlichman much less dramatically. It was brief and pleasant. Each left an impression, but neither was making grandiose predictions about the other. However, it does seem likely that Erlichman *did* tell Streisand, as he's always claimed, that she shouldn't change a thing about herself. Schulenberg remembered asking Streisand soon after she met Erlichman if he wanted her to change her nose or her name, and she replied that he did not.

131 Diana Kind was hopping mad: I have based my account of Diana's reaction to Paar's insult of her daughter on anecdotes shared with me by three of her friends, two of whom asked for anonymity. The third was Stuart Lippner, who heard the story from both Diana and Roslyn Kind.

Barbra on the Paar show: This appearance is not always listed among Streisand's credits, but television listings reveal she appeared on the Paar show for a second time on May 22, 1961, again billed as "Barbara Strysand." As she wasn't using "Strysand" in her concurrent appearances at the Bon Soir, I suspect this was an error on the press release sent out by NBC to the newspapers, which seems to have been using the same spelling Streisand had given them a month earlier.

132 did Barbra ever know: It's possible she did find out later, or that there was a similar

incident when Diana defended her daughter to a critic. In the May 1965 issue of *Cosmopolitan,* Streisand told an anecdote about her mother writing a letter objecting to some reporter who'd said the young singer had "Fu Manchu nails." According to Streisand, Diana signed the letter "Barbra's mother."

6. Summer 1961

133 the studio technicians to stop: Interview with Don Softness.

135 A week or so before Barbra: The Clancy Brothers appeared on the June 22 show; Streisand first appeared on July 12.

its debut on June 12: Background on *PM East* comes from various newspaper coverage, particularly the NYT, June 3, June 11, June 13, and June 22, 1961.

Parading into the studio: I have based my description of Streisand's first appearance on *PM East* on interviews with Don Softness, Bob Schulenberg, and Ted Rozar, as well as Mike Wallace's memoir, *Between You and Me* (New York: Hyperion, 2005).

Mike Wallace was aggressive: For background on Wallace, see *Between You and Me.*

136 "self-absorption": Wallace admitted during his 1991 *60 Minutes* interview with Streisand that he "really didn't like her" during their time on *PM East* and that he found her "totally self-absorbed."

"the demeanor of a diva": Wallace, *Between You and Me.*

"New York is just full of unusual": *Just for the Record* DVD.

"more like the studio mail girl": *Hartford Courant,* June 24, 1962.

137 old friend from acting school: Rick Edelstein was interviewed on WNYC radio, September 30, 2009, and recounted the story of sneaking Barbra into the Vanguard and serving her a ginger ale because she didn't drink.

138 "an eye for promising": Gavin, *Intimate Nights: The Golden Age of New York Cabaret.*

When Edelstein suggested. The story of Streisand's tryout at the Village Vanguard has been extremely difficult to pin down. Much misinformation has been written about it, turning the tryout into the stuff of myth and legend, especially in light of Streisand's much-heralded "return" to the club in 2009. Max Gordon, in his memoir, *Live at the Village Vanguard,* remembered that she sang three numbers at the club during a Sunday matinee that Miles Davis headlined. Gordon's wife, Lorraine, in her own memoir, *Alive at the Village Vanguard,* recalled that when Streisand tried out there she had been "singing off and on" at the Bon Soir. This dates Streisand's appearance at the Vanguard to 1961. That year, Davis performed at the club in February, July, September, and December. In February, Streisand was in Detroit, and by September she had already gotten the job at Gordon's other club, the Blue Angel, which had been an indirect result of her tryout at the Vanguard. So that dates her one-time appearance at the Village Vanguard to July 1961, and almost certainly to July 2, since she was in Winnipeg from July 3 to July 15. (By the time she got back to New York, Davis was gone from the Vanguard.) Along with the Gordons' recollections, I have used Edelstein's interview on WNYC to reconstruct this rather mythic performance. Bob Schulenberg also contributed to my understanding of the experience.

His name was Stanley Beck: My account of the Stanley Beck romance comes from Spada, *Streisand: Her Life,* as well as from the recollections of various friends.

140 "You are fantastic": Rick Edelstein interview, WNYC, September 30, 2009.

"Beautiful," "very posh": Streisand made this statement on *The Tonight Show with Johnny Carson*, October 4, 1962.

141 taken her out horseback riding: Kaufman Schwartz and Associates interview transcript, August 14, 1963, Sidney Skolsky Collection, AMPAS.

both dull and noisy: Elaine Sobel told James Spada for *Streisand: Her Life* that Streisand found the audiences at the Town 'n' Country "emotionless and dull," and several accounts attest to their noisiness.

"Miss Streisand is the type": *Winnipeg Free Press*, July 4, 1961.

142 she went on the next night: It is a myth that Streisand was fired from her gig at the Town 'n' Country in Winnipeg. Newspaper advertisements from July 1961 show that Streisand played out her entire two-week engagement. "Last time tonite Barbara [*sic*] Streisand," reads the Town 'n' Country ad in the *Winnipeg Free Press* from July 15. This was supported by Helen Chandler, a waitress at the club, who told Winnipeg columnist Morley Walker in 2006 that Streisand "played out her whole two weeks" (*Winnipeg Free Press*, November 11, 2006). While agreeing that the firing was merely a legend, Walker suggested that Streisand may have left early to take "a big gig in the U.S.," and that singer Mary Nelson replaced her at the Town 'n' Country. This is not true, either. Again looking at contemporary newspaper ads, Mary Nelson played the Town 'n' Country in February, not July. Final proof, if any is needed given the irrefutable evidence of the July 15 newspaper ad, comes from an interview Streisand gave to Johnny Carson a year later, when she spoke about appearing in Winnipeg. She wouldn't have been so fond in her recollections if she had been fired.

"What's she doing?": Streisand made this statement to Johnny Carson on the *Tonight Show*, October 4, 1962.

"I've seen her act": Hoffman recalled watching Streisand on *PM East* in the *National Enquirer*, January 2, 2005.

"beauties of New York": *The Daily Review*, July 12, 1961.

143 "Let us get this straight": *Vanity Fair*, September 1991.

Yet Marty's shrewdness: I am indebted to several people for sharing with me insights into Erlichman's brilliant management of Streisand's career. These include Don Softness, Ted Rozar, Phyllis Diller, and Orson Bean. Others, very close to the people involved, have asked for anonymity. Letters from and references to Erlichman in the collections of William Wyler, Herbert Ross, Jerome Robbins, Smith and Dale, and Richard Lewine also reveal his management skills.

146 "buy him off": Spada, *Streisand: Her Life*. The rest of my description of the scene with Rozar comes from a personal interview with Rozar.

"one of his cyclical": *San Francisco Chronicle*, March 24, 1963.

the question was "a bit": *Rogue*, November 1963.

147 His mother kept mispronouncing: Background on *Another Evening with Harry Stoones* comes from an undated, unsourced article, authored by Jeff Harris, found in the clippings collection for the show at the NYPL.

148 "people who hate revues": Publicity for *Another Evening with Harry Stoones*, September 3, 1961, NYPL.

"epidemic": Undated press release for *Another Evening with Harry Stoones*, NYPL.

managed to raise $15,000: Press release, "Sunday Drama," August 27, 1961, NYPL.

149 "hot, clearly talented": Spada, *Streisand: Her Life*.

150 Susan Belink: She later changed her name to Susan Belling and became a successful soprano at the Metropolitan Opera and elsewhere.

151 he thought she'd fit in: "I put her into the Blue Angel later," Gordon wrote of Streisand in *Live at the Village Vanguard.*

into Goddard Lieberson's office: I have based my account of this meeting on interviews with Columbia employee Lynnie Johnson, as well as two anonymous sources. In addition, various newspaper articles on Lieberson, and Shaun Considine, *Barbra Streisand: The Woman, the Myth, the Music* (New York: Delacorte, 1985), and Spada, *Streisand: Her Life.*

"own fiefdom": Walter Yetnikoff, *Howling at the Moon: The Odyssey of a Monstrous Music Mogul in an Age of Excess* (New York: Broadway Books, 2004).

153 "Listen to her when the phones": Considine, *Barbra Streisand: The Woman, the Myth, the Music.*

7. Fall 1961

154 "so enthusiastic": Wallace, *Between You and Me.*

marveled at the way the kid: Don Softness's observations and recollections of working with Streisand on *PM East* come from a personal interview with him, as well as his unpublished manuscript, "My Life with Barbra," used here courtesy Softness.

155 Tony Franciosa might star: Hedda Hopper syndicated column, as in the *Hartford Courant,* August 9, 1961.

Arthur Laurents would direct: NYT, October 5, 1961.

156 the Softness Group: *Miami News,* December 8, 1963; NYT, July 23, 1973; September 21, 1974; March 5, 1979; March 29, 1987; April 29, 1987.

her picture in the *New York Times:* NYT, October 15, 1961.

159 Jerome Weidman's mood: Weidman's perspective on Streisand's audition comes from a first-person piece he penned for *Holiday,* November 1963.

Laurents was already at the theater: Laurents's perspective on Streisand's audition comes from a personal interview as well as his memoir, *Original Story By: A Memoir of Broadway and Hollywood* (New York: Hal Leonard/Applause Books, 2009). Quotes not cited in the notes come from the personal interview.

"must have been turned down": Laurents, *Original Story By.*

"flawed," "unmarked for success": Laurents, *Mainly on Directing: Gypsy, West Side Story, and Other Musicals* (New York: Knopf/Borzoi Books, 2009).

161 "calculated spontaneity": Laurents, *Original Story By.*

She was nervous: Streisand remembered: "At my audition, I was asked to sit in a chair because I was nervous and because I thought it was an interesting concept." (*TV Guide,* January 22–28, 2000.) Laurents said it was she who asked for the chair. Her statement that she thought sitting in it was an "interesting concept" was more telling, Laurents believed. "She knew exactly what she was doing," he said.

162 this "fantastic freak": *Life,* May 22, 1964.

"the weirdo of all times": *Time,* April 10, 1964.

"None too stimulating": NYT, October 23, 1964.

"quick, flippant": *New Yorker,* November 4, 1961.

"gleeful," "riotous": *Women's Wear Daily,* November 5, 1961.

"quite strong enough": *Village Voice,* October 30, 1961.

163 "excellent flair for dropping": *Variety,* October 28, 1961.

Barbra briskly replied: Weidman wrote a highly romanticized account in *Holiday* of Streisand's audition, with whole pages of fabricated dialogue. He had Barbra saying things such as "Can I sing? If I couldn't sing, would I have the nerve to come out here in a thing like this coat?" and when asked if she could come back to sing for David Merrick, "Gee, I don't know. Marty, what time's my hair appointment?" When he read this dialogue, Arthur Laurents replied: "Legend!" Although Streisand was eccentric and even a little cocky in her audition, just as she was on *PM East,* she would never have been so blunt or so rude when auditioning for a major Broadway show. "She would have killed her chances right there," Laurents said, if she'd hesitated about returning to sing for Merrick or mouthed off the way some accounts portray. Weidman's account, published in November 1963, was written after Streisand had become well-known. It remarkably resembled a scene in her upcoming musical, *Funny Girl* — almost certainly an intentional connection. Similarly, the description of the audition from Merrick's casting director, Michael Shurtleff, given to Anne Edwards for *Streisand: A Biography,* seems equally fanciful, part of a post-1964 phenomenon that turned every account of Streisand's life into a mirror of Fanny Brice in *Funny Girl.* This phenomenon, both unconscious and deliberate, found its way into many sources, including Howard Kissel's *David Merrick: The Abominable Showman* (New York: Hal Leonard/Applause Books, 2000) and most Streisand biographies.

164 they might call her back: Although most accounts say Streisand came back that same day, Laurents said that wasn't the case. "Not how it worked," he said. She would have been called in for a second audition at a later date. Besides, it wasn't "very realistic," he said, to believe she came back later that same afternoon when she had her opening at the Blue Angel to prepare for. But again, "that's how myths are made," he said. "And a lot of myths were made about Barbra Streisand."

"You said you wanted": *Life,* May 22, 1964. Streisand also told the story in *Playboy,* October 1977.

There'd been no real feeling: On the *Let's Talk to Lucy* radio show that aired October 7, 1964, host Lucille Ball asked Streisand if she'd fallen for Gould the first time she saw him. "No" was the plain and simple answer. Ball then tried to get Streisand to say something romantic about their first meeting, or at least to say that she'd found Gould attractive right from the start. But Streisand seemed to reject the whole line of questioning and changed the subject.

165 Lorraine had also involved Barbra: Lorraine Gordon, *Alive at the Village Vanguard.*

The team from *What's in It for Me?*: According to an article in the *Saturday Evening Post,* July 27, 1963, David Merrick "strolled in" one night to hear Streisand before signing her for *Wholesale.* Laurents, however, said Merrick never went to see her and based his judgments of her solely on her auditions.

166 "undisciplined," "another disappointment": *Variety,* November 22, 1961.

167 "had to be in the show": Laurents, *Original Story By.*

"the X quality": *Holiday,* November 1963.

169 David Merrick was one of those: I have based my description of Merrick on an interview with Arthur Laurents, as well as Kissel, *David Merrick: The Abominable Showman* and Merrick's NYT obituary by Frank Rich, April 27, 2000.

173 "didn't sing unless she was paid": I have based my account of Streisand's impromptu

performance of "Moon River," her eviction from her apartment, and Don Softness's influence on her public persona on a personal interview with Softness, as well as his unpublished manuscript, "My Life with Barbra," used courtesy Softness. Quotes used in this section come from both sources.

"You can't see them": *Hartford Courant,* June 24, 1962.

176   "The uphill grind": This was printed in various newspaper television listings, including the *Elyria* (Ohio) *Chronicle-Telegram,* December 21, 1961.

"as a young performer aspiring": www.barbra-archives.com.

8. Winter 1962

177   stepped into the Fifty-fourth Street Theatre: Rehearsals were held here according to Whitney Bolton's syndicated column, as in the *Cumberland Evening Times,* February 14, 1962. Other descriptions of the rehearsal come from an undated, unsourced newspaper article, circa 1965, David Merrick file, NYPL.

"a young Fagin," "funny looking": *Life,* May 22, 1964.

179   "A limited amount": Laurents, *Mainly on Directing.*

180   "I hear you're gonna": Riese, *Her Name Is Barbra.*

181   "very bad neighborhoods": *PM East,* October 1961, as recorded on the DVD *Just for the Record.*

"a loner": *Time,* April 10, 1964.

"like a little kid": *Life,* May 22, 1964.

she didn't inhale: Streisand said she didn't inhale on *Let's Talk to Lucy,* October 7, 1964.

Barbra was also scheduled: In *Alive at the Village Vanguard,* Gordon implied she was responsible for Streisand's getting hired for *PM East,* stating that it was her suggestion to Wallace, at the time of the January 2 show, that he bring "this young singer" on the show that secured Streisand a running gig. But Streisand had already been appearing on *PM East* for several months by the time Gordon appeared on the show.

183   "You're involved in this": The anecdote comes from Gordon, *Alive at the Village Vanguard.*

184   "just another piece of furniture": *Holiday,* November 1963.

"Too many twitches": Laurents, *Original Story By.*

185   "she was different": Laurents, *Original Story By.*

"on blueprinting exactly how": Unsourced article, July 26, 1962, www.barbra-archives.com.

But when she argued: Accounts that portray Streisand as openly defiant or contemptuous of the director, writers, or producers of *Wholesale* are inaccurate, Laurents insisted. She did not ignore direction. She had "her own mind," but she was not belligerent. Such tales come from a later image of Streisand being projected back to her early days and are quite simply wrong.

"low threshold": Laurents, *Original Story By.*

186   "ungrateful," "arrogant": Interview with Arthur Laurents.

"got something out of it": www.barbra-archives.com.

"too special for records": Laurents, *Original Story By.*

"I want to be a straight": *Hartford Courant,* June 24, 1962.

It took choreographer Herbert Ross: Streisand has insisted that it was her idea to sing the song in the chair all along. "They wouldn't let me do it," she said in an interview with *TV Guide,* January 22–29, 2000. "But the number wasn't working, so before opening night they finally said — the director said — 'do it in your goddamn chair.'" Arthur Laurents said it was true that she had auditioned that way, but there had been no suggestion, from her or from him, to do the number similarly until Herbert Ross conceived of it as a way "to give the song some structure."

187 "fascinated," "to be protected": *Time,* April 10, 1964.

a full-scale snowball fight: Gould described the snowball fight in *Time,* April 10, 1964. Streisand also described the snowball fight in *Life,* May 22, 1964. She conflated this event with another date she had with Gould, when they saw the film *Mothra,* describing both events as occurring on the same night. But *Mothra* did not show in New York until that summer.

Barbra was a combination of . . . "most innocent thing": *Life,* May 22, 1964.

188 "a throwback" to Louis Kind: *Vanity Fair,* November 1994.

Barbra's "weirdness," he realized: Gould said, "She always thought of herself as an ugly duckling, and made herself up to be weird as a defense." *Time,* April 10, 1964.

"Like out of a movie": *Time,* April 10, 1964.

189 "Just thirty years": *Philadelphia Inquirer,* February 12, 1962.

190 "from Brooklyn and brought up": *The Rosie O'Donnell Show* interview.

191 tastes tended more toward musicals: *Philadelphia Weekly Press,* August 26, 2009.

"range and versatility": *Philadelphia Inquirer,* February 13, 1962.

192 "brings down the house": *Philadelphia Inquirer,* February 13, 1962. Arthur Laurents, in the September 1991 issue of *Vanity Fair,* contended that out-of-town audiences didn't "get" Streisand as Miss Marmelstein. This review, as well as other contemporary accounts, would seem to dispute that view. Although some accounts have said that Merrick persisted in wanting to fire her all the way to New York, this seems highly unlikely given that she was often the only cast member singled out for such unqualified praise.

"She stops the show": *Philadelphia Inquirer,* February 18, 1962.

"registered considerable enthusiasm": Dorothy Kilgallen's syndicated column, as in *The News Tribune* (Fort Pierce, Florida), February 21, 1962.

"as large and melancholy": *Playboy,* November 1970.

193 "Godfathering the romance": Laurents, *Original Story By.*

"most of [his] life": *San Francisco Chronicle,* October 26, 1987.

"psychic power": *Playgirl,* May 1975.

"trip on anything": *Time,* September 7, 1970.

"communicate in a world": Interview with Elliott Gould at www.aish.com.

"get beneath the roots": *New York Post,* August 11, 2009.

194 "too much pride," "Four home runs": *Playboy,* November 1970.

Lucille was the offspring: 1920 and 1930 U.S. Census.

"didn't understand one another": NYT, March 4, 1973.

"Be careful, don't trust": *Playboy,* November 1970.

195 "in terror of conflict": *San Francisco Chronicle,* October 26, 1987.

"Mr. and Mrs. Captain Marvel": *Playboy,* November 1970.

"You won't ever have": *Esquire,* September 22, 2009.

"done out of love": *Time,* September 7, 1970.

"fat ass": *Playboy,* November 1970.

"creations of Hollywood": *Life,* December 12, 1969.

196 "looking to buy a kid": *Playboy,* November 1970.

"very withdrawn": Interview with Elliott Gould at www.aish.com.

"parenthesis-shaped legs": *New York* magazine, December 31, 1979.

"Fix up his diction," "Whoever got any": *Time,* September 7, 1970.

"Mary had a little lamb": *Playboy,* November 1970.

197 "has-been": *Time,* September 7, 1970.

198 "got sick on the bus": *Playboy,* November 1970.

"Telegram for Bill Callahan!": *Playboy,* November 1970.

high-waisted dancer's pants: *Playboy,* November 1970.

199 "From the Deli Lama": *Esquire,* September 22, 2009.

200 "ferocity," "scared of women": *Village Voice,* September 8, 1987. Although in various interviews, Gould sometimes implied he had lost his virginity earlier, in a proposal for an autobiography that made the rounds of New York publishers, he claimed he had "surrendered" his virginity to Streisand in Philadelphia. See Spada, *Streisand: Her Life.*

"terribly green": *Playboy,* November 1970.

201 "I bat from just one": NYT, March 4, 1973.

"trying to become a man": Spada, *Streisand: Her Life.*

the man didn't "necessarily": *Playboy,* October 1977.

202 the first commandment: Laurents, *Original Story By.*

"sweeten" and "explain": Stephen Sondheim to Roddy McDowall, March 5, 1962, McDowall Collection, Boston University.

"approach New York with": *Philadelphia Inquirer,* February 18, 1962.

203 "persevered . . . despite the usual": *Bedford Gazette,* February 16, 1962.

"were sprayed with sweat": Laurents, *Original Story By.*

204 "stage newcomer": *Boston Globe,* February 18, 1962.

"assertive young woman": Riese, *Her Name Is Barbra.*

205 "generally entertaining": *Boston Herald,* February 28, 1962.

"What, indeed, are they doing": *Boston Globe,* February 28, 1962.

"the piece of blubber": Laurents, *Original Story By.*

206 "Barbra is striking": "My Life with Barbra," unpublished manuscript by Donald G. Softness, courtesy Softness.

"by the name of Barbara": *Pittsburgh Press, Radio-TV Editor* supplement, January 8, 1962.

207 "Who does that girl": Kissel, *David Merrick: The Abominable Showman.*

Sam Zolotow had announced: NYT, December 4, 1961.

208 "a likeable newcomer": NYT, March 23, 1962.

"give affection or admiration": *New York Daily News,* March 23, 1962.

"How to Almost Succeed": *New York Journal-American,* March 23, 1962.

209 "something of a find": *Wall Street Journal,* March 26, 1962.

211 "like a little orphan": *Life,* May 22, 1964.

9. Spring 1962

212 Rent was sixty dollars: In other accounts, the rent has sometimes been reported to be somewhat more than sixty dollars, but according to a letter from Evelyn Layton, who was trying to arrange for a friend to sublet the place, the rent was sixty dollars even. Evelyn Layton to Tom Higgins, July 8, 1963, Higgins Family Collection, NYPL.

213 a disagreeable man: Softness, "My Life with Barbra." According to various online sites, Oscar Karp was also the inspiration for Oscar the Grouch on *Sesame Street.*

215 declared the composition "beautiful": *Redbook,* January 1968.
"things [she] could never afford": *Us* magazine, October 9, 2000.
"the more money you make": Kaufman Schwartz and Associates interview with Streisand, August 15, 1963, submitted to Sidney Skolsky, Skolsky Collection, AMPAS.
"What is this?": *Us* magazine, October 9, 2000.

216 what really made her happy: syndicated article that ran in various papers in late May through the middle part of June, as in the *Danville* (Virginia) *Register,* May 31, 1962, hereafter syndicated, May 31, 1962.
"What does it matter": syndicated, May 31, 1962.
"jolly-dollying": Walter Winchell's syndicated column, as in *Daily Times-News* (Burlington, North Carolina), April 7, 1962, and elsewhere.

218 "the Mayor of Forty-second Street": NYT, January 30, 1994.

219 "reading all the casting reports": Leonard Lyons's syndicated column, as in the *San Mateo Times,* April 23, 1962.
"strange color lipstick": syndicated, May 31, 1962.

220 "Instead of giving me": Edward Robb Ellis, *A Diary of the Century* (New York: Kodansha, 1996).
"I used to baby-sit for a": *The New Yorker,* May 19, 1962.

221 "You know, like in": syndicated UPI article, as in the *Press-Courier* (Oxnard, California), July 26, 1962, and elsewhere.
"not there at all": Riese, *Her Name Is Barbra.*

222 "world's greatest gate-crasher": *Bridgeport Post,* April 30, 1962.
"never heard of her": Scott Schechter, *Judy Garland: The Day-by-Day Chronicle of a Legend* (Boulder, CO: Cooper Square Press, 2002).

223 "Streisand's going to win": Kissel, *David Merrick: The Abominable Showman.*

224 "Barbara Streisman": Undated list in the Jerome Robbins Collection, Jerome Robbins Dance Division (hereafter JRC), NYPL.

225 had soured on Bancroft: Many accounts of Streisand's life have stated that Stark wanted Bancroft, but after at least late 1961, he was arguing against her, according to the Jerome Robbins Collection.
"new character based on": Ray Stark to Jerome Robbins and Jule Styne, October 25, 1961, JRC, NYPL.
"the most exciting girl": Ray Stark to Jerome Robbins, October 24, 1961, JRC, NYPL.
"a Spanish exclamation point": Jim Bishop's syndicated column, as in the *Newark* (Ohio) *Advocate,* May 5, 1963.

226 bombastic and overwrought: I have based my descriptions of Robbins on a thorough review of his papers at the NYPL, as well as on Greg Lawrence, *Dance With Demons: The Life of Jerome Robbins* (New York: Penguin, 2002); Deborah Jowitt, *Jerome Robbins: His Life, His Theater, His Dance* (New York: Simon and Schuster, 2004); and Amanda Vaill, *Somewhere: The Life of Jerome Robbins* (New York: Random House, 2008).
"that out of the fires": John Huston, *An Open Book* (Boston: Da Capo Press, 1994).
"Commit": LAT, August 27, 1967.

227 had "more infectious enthusiasm": Laurents, *Original Story By.*
"to see her in person": Ray Stark to Jerome Robbins, November 24, 1961, JRC, NYPL.

229 "a natural comedienne who has been": NYT, May 6, 1962.

    she'd told her mother: *Life,* May 22, 1964.

233 Bob Harris: He was also the father of actor Ed Harris.

234 he'd accepted Jule Styne's invitation: Most accounts of Streisand's life have stated, or implied, that Stark first saw her perform at the Bon Soir in November of 1962. But it is clear from correspondence in the Jerome Robbins Collection that he had seen her by the spring of that year. Stark said, "Barbra was an unknown when she was first brought to my attention in *I Can Get It for You Wholesale* and at the Bon Soir in New York." (LAT, August 27, 1967.) Since the Robbins correspondence shows Stark was sold on Streisand as the best choice to play Fanny Brice by the early summer of 1962, he must have seen her in these two places before that time. We know that Styne first saw Streisand at the Bon Soir in the spring, and we know that he brought Stark to see her, so it seems safe to conclude that it was sometime in the spring that Stark first saw her. He was back in Los Angeles by early June, when Hedda Hopper wrote in her column that he attended a party thrown by David Merrick at Chasen's, having just returned from Europe (*Hartford Courant,* June 18, 1962). So it seems likely he would have seen Streisand in *Wholesale* and at the Bon Soir in late May. I am also grateful to Suzanne Merrill, widow of Bob Merrill, for her insights on the chronology.

236 "a literal biography": NYT, September 15, 1968.

237 Stark's grandfather had emigrated: The Stark family history comes from the U.S. Census, New York, New York, 1880–1930, as well as military and immigration records. Also see the NYT, April 18, 1925; February 25, 1996.

238 "inattention to his studies": Hal Boyle's syndicated column for the Associated Press, as in the *Long Island Star Journal,* March 25, 1965.

    "There's something about having": NYT, September 15, 1968.

239 "decided to make a stab": Hal Boyle syndicated column for the Associated Press, as in the *Long Island Star Journal,* March 25, 1965.

240 "100 percent sole star billing": Associated Booking contract, www.barbra-archives.com.

    "terse, mocking intros": *New York World-Telegram,* January 4, 1962.

241 "Twenty-year-old Barbra": *Variety,* May 30, 1962.

242 "Do you know how wonderful": "A Love Song for Barbra," posted August 3, 2011, on the *Huffington Post.* Although the Bergmans wrote that this occurred when Streisand was eighteen, at her first Bon Soir appearance, she did not sing "My Name Is Barbara" until May 1962.

    "a masseur, an analyst and a wife": NYT, September 29, 1960.

243 "of anyone else in the part": LAT, August 27, 1967. It has become part of Streisand lore that Stark opposed her in *Funny Girl* right from the start, and only after much effort was he finally persuaded to cast her. But the Jerome Robbins Collection reveals that this was not the case at all. Although it seems to have taken Fran Stark longer to come around, Ray Stark was strongly in Streisand's corner by the late spring of 1962.

10. Summer 1962

244 thought the outfit was horrible: Spada, *Streisand: Her Life.*

    Earl Wilson was currently suggesting: Earl Wilson's syndicated column, as in the *Galveston* (Texas) *Daily News,* June 28, 1962.

245 William Morris Agency: Contract dated July 6, 1962, www.barbra-archives.com. Because Streisand was not yet twenty-one, her mother had to cosign with her. Diana chose to omit the "Kind" from her signature, using just "Streisand."

"An unknown": LAT, August 27, 1967.

"Miss Streisand has such": NYT, June 10, 1962.

Reviews for *Pins and Needles:* For example, *San Antonio Light,* August 5, 1962.

246 "Tell Barbra I think": Spada, *Streisand: Her Life.*

In her glass-enclosed "teahouse": *Boston Herald,* January 5, 1964.

247 "God knows she has": Jerome Robbins to Ray Stark, June 11, 1962, JRC, NYPL.

"desire and intention to": Ray Stark to Jerome Robbins, Isobel Lennart, Bob Merrill, and Jule Styne, May 17, 1962, JRC, NYPL.

"listed haphazardly": Ray Stark to Robbins, Lennart, Styne, and Merrill, May 17, 1962, JRC, NYPL.

248 "If she can sing": Jerome Robbins to Ray Stark, June 11, 1962.

Merrill and Bancroft had dated: Interview with Suzanne Merrill. I am grateful for her background not only on the relationship between Merrill and Streisand, but also Styne and Streisand.

"to work with her a bit": Jerome Robbins to Ray Stark, June 11, 1962.

249 "People insist he wants": David Merrick office memo to Jerome Robbins, June 12, 1962.

250 Barbra's audition changed no minds: Stories of Streisand's declaring she couldn't act with such terrible lines as the script provided seem to be so much mythmaking. There is absolutely no evidence of anything like that in the Robbins papers. There may have been such conflict later on, but Streisand's first reading was described as "marvelously sensitive" by Robbins, hardly likely if she had been argumentative or defensive.

"a marvelously sensitive reading": Jerome Robbins to Ray Stark, June 11, 1962, JRC, NYPL.

"really anxious": David Merrick's office to Jerome Robbins, June 29, 1962, JRC, NYPL.

"You, of course, know": Ray Stark to Jerome Robbins, June 20, 1962, JRC, NYPL.

Barbra seemed clueless: This anecdote was told to me by a longtime Streisand fan who was frequently in the audience, and occasionally backstage, during *Wholesale.* I confirmed that Lillian Gish was indeed in attendance one night, according to Earl Wilson's syndicated column, as in the *Delaware County Daily Times,* June 27, 1962.

251 Barbra's unprofessionalism: Riese, *Her Name Is Barbra.*

252 Barbra and Elliott sat in the dark: In an interview published in *Life,* May 22, 1964, Streisand recalled seeing a movie that could only be *Mothra* (the giant caterpillar eating cars) but conflated the experience with an earlier outing, which took place in the winter. *Mothra* opened in Manhattan on July 11.

"marvelous Victorian cabinets": *The New Yorker,* May 1962.

"just wild . . . genius": *Life,* May 22, 1964.

253 "hot romance backstage": Earl Wilson's syndicated column, as in the *Idaho Falls Post-Register,* July 20, 1962.

couple had secretly married: Earl Wilson's syndicated column, as in the *Uniontown* (Pennsylvania) *Evening Standard,* August 1, 1962.

254 "They print such rotten": syndicated article, May 31, 1962.

"talk back to the director": syndicated UPI article, as in the *Press-Courier* (Oxnard, California), July 26, 1962, and elsewhere.

255 "brushed out": Riese, *Her Name Is Barbra.*

"the stable one": *Let's Talk to Lucy,* October 7, 1964.

256 His admiration for her: Considine, *Barbra Streisand: The Woman, the Myth, the Music.*

257 "packing into the clubs": Dorothy Kilgallen's syndicated column, as in the *Montreal Gazette,* July 28, 1962.

"hit the big time": Earl Wilson's syndicated column, as in the *Reno* (Nevada) *Evening Gazette,* July 27, 1962.

258 "Miss Streisand is a delightful": *Variety,* July 25, 1962.

"strictly private for hotel guests": *Hartford Courant,* July 17, 1962. Also, the *Middletown Press,* July 16, 1962.

259 Barbra was applying to Dartmouth: See, for example, Lawrence Witte's syndicated column, as in the *Masillon* (Ohio) *Evening Independent,* August 1, 1962.

260 "urgent [that an] immediate": Ray Stark to Jerome Robbins, telegram, August 6, 1962, JRC, NYPL.

"I hope you will have": Ray Stark to Jerome Robbins, letter, August 6, 1962, JRC, NYPL.

"A tremendous talent": Ray Stark to Jerome Robbins, letter, August 6, 1962, JRC, NYPL.

261 "Dear Annie": Jerome Robbins to Anne Bancroft, July 30, 1962, JRC, NYPL.

"Dear Barbara": Ray Stark to Barbra Streisand, August 6, 1962, JRC, NYPL.

262 "pushing the script until certain": Jerome Robbins, "Statement of Contribution to *Funny Girl,*" sound recording, JRC, NYPL. All of my descriptions of Robbins's statements on the work he did on the script up to the fall of 1962 come from this source.

264 "If you don't hear": Ray Stark to Jerome Robbins, August 6, 1962, JRC, NYPL.

"A more honest or exploitable": Ray Stark to Jerome Robbins, August 21, 1962, JRC, NYPL.

265 "broker between script and stars": NYT, May 10, 1960.

"I have rarely seen anyone": Doris Vidor to Jerome Robbins, August 1, 1962, JRC, NYPL. Doris Vidor would later marry, and quickly divorce, Fanny Brice's third husband, Billy Rose.

"the relationship really becomes": Jerome Robbins to Ray Stark, August 10, 1962.

Peter Lawford was "very interested": Ray Stark to Jerome Robbins, August 22, 1962.

On the call sheet for two thirty: Audition sheet, August 30, 1962, JRC, NYPL.

268 "inauthentic" and "overhyped": Unsourced articles, dated June 4, 1962, and September 1, 1962, the latter a look-ahead at the coming nightclub season that predicted Streisand would be back at the Blue Angel, Barbra Streisand file, NYPL.

"strong-minded Barbra": Dorothy Kilgallen's syndicated column, as in the *Salt Lake Tribune,* June 1, 1962.

"Friends of the sensationally": Dorothy Kilgallen's syndicated column, as in the *Daytona Beach Morning Journal,* August 29, 1962.

269 "Barbra Streisand is the front-runner": Dorothy Kilgallen's syndicated column, as in the *Lowell Sun,* August 31, 1962.

270 Harold Clurman, in a long piece: NYT, September 23, 1962.

11. Fall 1962

271 "very dependent on each other": *Playboy,* November 1970.

"so right for each other": *Esquire,* September 22, 2009.

272 "old things and bizarre things": *Life,* December 12, 1969.

273 "listen to the radio": NYT, March 4, 1973.

"the first annual Alexander": *Life,* May 22, 1964.

"didn't want Elliott": *Playboy,* October 1977.

"Animalism . . . a certain animal quality": Kaufman Schwartz and Associates transcript of interview, August 15, 1963, Sidney Skolsky Collection, AMPAS.

274 begun talking salary: Earl Wilson reported that Streisand hadn't yet signed for the part because she was still "discussing salary." (Earl Wilson's syndicated column, as in the *Reno Evening Gazette,* September 17, 1962.) Not surprisingly, Dorothy Kilgallen put it in more negative terms: Streisand was "still dickering over salary." (Dorothy Kilgallen's syndicated column, as in the *Salt Lake Tribune,* September 18, 1962.)

275 in her own word, "hell": *Life,* May 22, 1964.

"some special business": Louella Parsons's syndicated column, as in the *Cedar Rapids Gazette,* October 4, 1962.

Barbra and Fran: A syndicated Hollywood column with no byline published in the *Hartford Courant,* September 30, 1962, stated: "While Barbra Streisand . . . was taping a Dinah Shore show, Fanny Brice's daughter, Fran (Mrs. Ray) Stark, showed up to ogle her for the title role in the coming musical based on Fanny's life."

276 Peter and Wendy grew up: *Interview,* September 1985.

"the outstanding Hollywood party": NYT, September 29, 1960.

277 a treasure chest of gems: In June 1953, the Starks, staying at the Sherry-Netherland Hotel in New York on their way to Paris, had their room broken into; $40,000 worth of jewelry was taken. The thief overlooked other jewelry worth $13,700 sitting atop a dresser in the bedroom. The jewels were only "partly insured." Stolen was a platinum-and-gold ring with two eight-carat diamonds as well as a platinum bracelet holding a six-carat diamond and three emeralds, each valued at $20,000. Left behind on the dresser were two pearl rings, a pearl necklace, platinum earrings, and a diamond-and-platinum wedding band. Associated Press newswire, as in the *Lima* (Ohio) *News,* June 28, 1953.

278 "a group of vocal performers": *Hartford Courant,* May 12, 1963.

279 Barbra seemed "anxious": syndicated Scripps-Howard article, as in the *Albuquerque Tribune,* May 13, 1963.

280 Barbra Streisand would never play: A quote from Fran Stark, "That woman will never play my mother" or some variant thereof, has shown up in virtually every account of Streisand's life. John Patrick told Anne Edwards for *Streisand: A Biography* that Fran Stark spoke the line directly to him. Given that the quote has usually been accompanied by the erroneous assertion that Ray Stark, as well as his wife, opposed Streisand's casting, I was tempted to doubt its authenticity. However, Jule Styne, who was very much on the scene during the period in question, was quoted in several accounts confirming Fran's opposition; Kaye Ballard, who by this time was in the running for the part, and Suzanne Merrill also remembered it. In Spada's *Streisand: Her Life,* however, Styne was quoted as saying it was *Ray* Stark who said Streisand would never play his mother-in-law, which the Robbins papers clearly disprove.

281 "a lot of loot": Dorothy Kilgallen's syndicated column, as in the *Lowell Sun,* September 29, 1962.

"creative control, no coupling": Considine, *Barbra Streisand: The Woman, the Myth, the Music.*

Marty had secured a clause: *Billboard,* August 3, 1963.

"After months of negotiations": Dorothy Kilgallen's syndicated column, as in the *Dunkirk* (New York) *Evening Observer,* October 8, 1962.

282 "It doesn't feel like": *Backstage with Lee Jordan,* WXYZ radio, September 1962, included on the *Just for the Record* DVD.

283 Merrick would "bristle": Kissel, *David Merrick: The Abominable Showman.*

284 "Yeah, let's go": Considine, *Barbra Streisand: The Woman, the Myth, the Music.*

285 "David Merrick may hold": LAT, September 29, 1962.

"completely out of": Louella Parsons's syndicated column, as in the *Cedar Rapids Gazette,* October 4, 1962.

"Although Jerry has been": Floria Lasky to Albert da Silva, September 20, 1962, JRC, NYPL.

"ghastly sessions": Isobel Lennart to Jerome Robbins, [nd, September 1962], JRC, NYPL.

"not ready yet": Jerome Robbins to Ray Stark, [nd, September 1962], JRC, NYPL.

"I think there can be": Ray Stark to Albert da Silva, August 31, 1962, JRC, NYPL.

286 "As for delivering": Jerome Robbins to Ray Stark, [nd, September 1962], JRC, NYPL.

"not want any": Floria Lasky to Albert da Silva, September 20, 1962, JRC, NYPL.

"Barbra Streisand, who's been practically": Earl Wilson's syndicated column, as in the *Wisconsin State Journal,* October 5, 1962.

288 Peter found he could work: For background and insight into Peter Daniels, I am grateful to Lainie Kazan.

290 press reports were stating that Kaye Ballard: NYT, October 10, 1962.

291 "was doing everything": Riese, *Her Name Is Barbra.*

292 "like putting on": NYT, May 21, 2009.

294 *Wholesale* was $140,000: Kissel, *David Merrick: The Abominable Showman.*

"I'm free! I'm free!": Spada, *Streisand: Her Life.*

12. Winter 1963

295 "Now let's hear it from": Liner notes from Streisand's *Just for the Record* CD album, 1991.

"She's breaking me up": *Just for the Record* DVD. Streisand appeared on the Sullivan show on December 16. She had been advertised in some TV listings to appear on December 9, but perhaps that date was changed since *Wholesale* had just ended the day before, and it was decided not to let that cloud Streisand's appearance.

296 There were reports: John Patrick told Anne Edwards for *Streisand: A Biography* that after the Bon Soir, Fran Stark had said that Barbra would never play Fanny Brice. But a reliable source told me that she "softened" on Barbra after the Bon Soir and from then on kept her views very private so as not to interfere with her husband's work.

297 "terrible anxieties": *Playboy,* November 1970.

director Joe Layton's offer of a part: Earl Wilson's syndicated column, as in the *Idaho Falls Post Reporter,* December 3, 1962.

298 forfeiting $100,000 worth: Earl Wilson's syndicated column, as in the *Delaware County Times,* January 14, 1963.

"pretty heavy shouting": Riese, *Her Name Is Barbra.*

In just twelve hours: NYT, January 25, 1963.

299 "vital and imaginative": Graham Payn and Sheridan Morley, eds., *The Noël Coward Diaries* (Boston: Da Capo Press, 2000).

"dehydrated": Cole Lesley, *The Life of Noël Coward* (New York: Penguin, 1988).

300 "a big compliment," "very harsh at times": Considine, *Barbra Streisand: The Woman, the Myth, the Music.*

301 "walking a tightrope": Spada, *Streisand: Her Life.*

302 had their columns clipped: Interview with Don Softness.

"hottest young comedienne": Earl Wilson's syndicated column, as in the *Delaware County Times,* January 14, 1963.

"glad, sad or mad": NYT, July 1, 1965.

"She packs more personal": Robert Ruark's syndicated column, as in the *El Paso Herald-Post,* January 18, 1963.

303 "A bump on a girl's": Earl Wilson's syndicated column, as in the *Delaware County Times,* January 14, 1963.

"There is a full-blown": Mel Heimer's syndicated column, as in the *Massillon* (Ohio) *Evening Independent,* December 29, 1962.

304 "I think Barbara Streisand is": *Bridgeport Post,* January 25, 1963.

Barbra was set to fly out: *Hollywood Reporter,* February 1, 1963.

305 "in a Broadway theater at last": Dennen, *My Life with Barbra.* My account is also supplemented by a personal interview with Dennen.

307 "should draw an enormous amount": *Billboard,* March 23, 1963.

"getting the kind of reception": *Billboard,* March 2, 1963.

"Miss Marmel Steisand": *Boston Globe,* February 1, 1963.

had retreated to the back: See the series of photographs at www.barbra-archives.com.

reached only Midwest audiences: As an advertisement in the NYT on July 31, 1963, makes clear, Group W was planning to bring *The Mike Douglas Show* into the New York and other markets soon, but had not yet done so. "A big success in Cleveland," the advertisement calls the show.

308 "To the singer from": Kaufman Schwartz and Associates transcript of interview, August 15, 1963, Sidney Skolsky Collection, AMPAS.

310 "talked out of going": Earl Wilson's syndicated column, as in the *Manitowoc* (Wisconsin) *Herald Times,* February 28, 1963.

"something technical on": *Playboy,* November 1970.

311 "She was easily the kookiest": *San Francisco Chronicle,* March 24, 1963.

312 "Barbra Streisand is unquestionably": *San Francisco Chronicle,* April 1, 1963.

"a vocal plumber": *San Francisco Chronicle,* March 5, 1995.

"Well, my dear": *San Francisco Chronicle,* January 31, 2001. The quote comes from Country Joe McDonald, who was also the one to liken Davis to Auntie Mame.

313 "Singers are not known": *People,* July 6, 1981.

"obstructing the performance": *San Francisco Chronicle,* March 5, 1995.

"Funny singer Barbra Streisand": *Galveston* (Texas) *Daily News,* March 28, 1963.

314 "consciousness of an unconscious": *People,* July 6, 1981.

315 comedian Woody Allen: Allen closed at the hungry i on March 30, so he and Streisand overlapped by four days. *San Francisco Chronicle,* March 30, 1963.

"the most influential nightclub": NYT, May 13, 1961.

"being catapulted into": *Oakland Tribune,* April 13, 1964.

316 "modestly disclaimed having": NYT, May 13, 1961.

318 "a tawny, feline, long-haired": *San Francisco Chronicle,* April 1, 1963.

a young engineer named Reese Hamel: See *All About Barbra* fanzine, number 37, as well as www.barbra-archives.com. The recording of that night is available online.

13. Spring 1963

324 "a potentially great new stylist": *Syracuse Post Standard,* April 14, 1963.

"shows herself to be one": *Altoona* (Pennsylvania) *Mirror,* April 8, 1963.

"the silk in 'Happy Days'": Walter Winchell's syndicated column, as in the *San Antonio Light,* April 13, 1963.

326 "almost definite": NYT, April 26, 1963.

Investors had lost: NYT, May 4, 1963.

327 "been signed for the role": *Oakland Tribune,* March 23, 1963. The *San Francisco Chronicle* also reported she'd been signed on March 26. Both publications, however, referred to the Brice project as a film.

"They've been having a tough": Mike Connolly's syndicated column, as in the *Pasadena Independent,* April 18, 1963.

"That funny Barbra Streisand": Mike Connolly's syndicated column, as in the *Pasadena Star News,* May 7, 1963.

"an ordinary beauty shop": *Cosmopolitan,* May 1965.

329 "the most sought-after": Payn and Morley, eds., *The Noël Coward Diaries.*

330 *The Barbra Streisand Album* had reached: *Billboard,* May 18, 1963. Mary Travers, of Peter, Paul, and Mary, was higher than Streisand on the chart, but only as part of her group.

"much too busy": This anecdote is recounted in Ballard's memoir, *How I Lost 10 Pounds in 53 Years,* and was also told in more detail in a personal interview.

331 Originally called La Vie en Rose: NYT, October 25, 1967.

"the town's top agents": *Billboard,* May 25, 1963.

Cary Grant and Audrey Hepburn: Grant's telegram was reported in Earl Wilson's syndicated column, as in the *Uniontown* (Maryland) *Morning Herald,* May 16, 1963. For Hepburn, see Riese, *Her Name Is Barbra.*

"shouting their enthusiasm": Louis Sobol's syndicated column, as in the *Cedar Rapids Gazette,* May 19, 1963.

for his upcoming show: Earl Wilson's syndicated column, as in the *Lowell* (Massachusetts) *Sun,* May 17, 1963, and Dorothy Kilgallen's syndicated column, as also in the *Lowell Sun,* May 19, 1963.

"A potent belter": *Variety,* May 22, 1963.

332 "with the talent and ability": *Billboard,* May 25, 1963.

"Kenneth coif": *Variety,* May 22, 1963.

"a different kind of mama": syndicated UPI article, as in the *Columbus* (Nebraska) *Daily Telegram,* May 13, 1963.

"attempt one of the great": syndicated Scripps-Howard article, as in the *Albuquerque Tribune,* May 13, 1963.

333 "playfully mocked": *Sir!* magazine, October 1963.

"juxtaposition of the music": *Variety,* May 22, 1963.

"turning himself into a period piece": *Billboard,* May 25, 1963.

334 "an Armenian folk song": *Saturday Evening Post,* July 27, 1963.

"The last act of *Tosca*": syndicated Scripps-Howard article, as in the *Albuquerque Tribune,* May 13, 1963.

"a Flatbush gamine": Alan Gill's syndicated column, as in the *Cedar Rapids Gazette,* May 16, 1963.

"crawling under a table": syndicated UPI article, as in the *Columbus* (Nebraska) *Daily Telegram,* May 13, 1963.

335 hosted by Keefe Brasselle: According to the *Hartford Courant,* May 28, 1963, Brasselle had four summer shows taped and "in the can"; according to Alan Gill's column, as in the *Cedar Rapids Gazette,* May 30, 1963, one of those shows was the one with Streisand.

"live in-between": Unedited transcript of a Kaufman Schwartz and Associates public-relations interview with Streisand, August 15, 1963, submitted to Sidney Skolsky, Skolsky Collection, AMPAS. An extraordinary unexpurgated account straight from Streisand's lips. Hereafter, Kaufman Schwartz interview.

337 "down in her own purse": Merriman Smith, president of the White House Correspondents' Association, wrote about the gala in a UPI report, as in the *Cedar Rapids Gazette,* May 26, 1963.

comedian Jack E. Leonard: Earl Wilson's column, as in the *Idaho Falls Post Register,* May 24, 1963.

an electric bread slicer: My account of the dinner and gala comes from the NYT, May 25, 1963, and various wire reports.

338 "Just as long as you've been": This iconic meeting of Kennedy and Streisand has taken on much mythology over the years. Peter Daniels, who was there, gave his eyewitness account to Shaun Considine for *Barbra Streisand: The Woman, the Myth, the Music,* so I have based much of my account on his. However, Daniels told Considine that Kennedy used his back to sign Streisand's program. But a photograph of the moment shows the president signing it in his hand as Daniels and Streisand look on. Merv Griffin, in his memoir, *Merv: An Autobiography,* wrote that he asked Streisand the next day why she'd broken protocol, but he did not seem angry that she had done so, despite what subsequent accounts have implied. In addition, Griffin said that when he asked Streisand what Kennedy had written, she replied, "Fuck you. The president." This was clearly a joke, a good example of Streisand's sense of humor. Kennedy wrote no such thing. But several accounts have presented the story as if it were true.

"Smart girl": Merv Griffin with Peter Barsocchini, *Merv: An Autobiography* (New York: Pocket Books, 1981).

339 "He knows you well": Walter Winchell's syndicated column, as in the *Lebanon* (Pennsylvania) *Daily News,* June 24, 1963.

"three-week showing": *Chicago's American,* June 13, 1963.

"somebody's living room": *Chicago Sun-Times,* August 21, 2005.

340 "A cross between a sweet-voiced": *Chicago Daily News,* June 15, 1963.

"That's almost enough": *Chicago Tribune,* June 16, 1963.

"alive and thrilling": *Chicago's American,* June 13, 1963.

"A fantastic first!": *Billboard,* June 29, 1963.

341 "do this [and] do that": Considine, *Barbra Streisand: The Woman, the Myth, the Music.*

"If I have ideas about sets": *Playboy,* October 1977.

342 "We don't want to upset": Spada, *Streisand: Her Life.*

"a national reputation": *Pageant,* November 1963.

"demanded" a copy: Earl Wilson's syndicated column, as in the *Galveston Daily News,* May 31, 1963.

343 "with the Bostonese": Earl Wilson's syndicated column, as in the *Idaho Falls Post-Reporter,* June 3, 1963.

the security guard at the Studio 50: *Saturday Evening Post,* July 27, 1963.

"which may star Barbra": *Billboard,* June 1, 1963.

to an "ovation": NYT, May 31, 1963.

344 "practically at the contract-signing": Earl Wilson's syndicated column, as in the *Idaho Falls Post-Reporter,* June 13, 1963.

Barbra had already been: Mike Connolly's syndicated column, as in the *Pasadena Independent,* June 6, 1963.

14. Summer 1963

346 Liberace wanted his fans: My account of Liberace introducing Streisand, and their time together in Vegas, comes from Bob Thomas, *Liberace: The True Story* (New York: St. Martin's Press, 1989), as well as memories of several Streisand friends. Many of the stories of Streisand being hostilely received at the Riviera in previous accounts seem exaggerated since, with the exception of one snide *Hollywood Reporter* review, contemporary coverage of her time in Vegas was glowing. Still, friends recalled that Liberace did help prepare his audience for Streisand. My account attempts to reconstruct that experience as accurately as possible.

347 two nights were "disastrous": Considine, *Barbra Streisand: The Woman, the Myth, the Music.*

thirty thousand souvenir postcards: *Oakland Tribune,* July 26, 1963.

"By far the hottest singer": *Oakland Tribune,* July 26, 1963.

"the edge in experience": *Van Nuys News,* July 5, 1963.

"assembly-line singers": *Variety,* July 8, 1963.

348 "If you haven't heard": Evelyn Russell Layton to Tom Higgins, July 8, 1963, Higgins Family Collection, Billy Rose Theatre Collection, NYPL.

349 "burst to astonishing life": LAT, June 28, 1963.

"a one-woman recovery": *Oxnard* (California) *Press-Courier,* June 26, 1963.

"the year of Barbra": Undated, unsourced AP wire story, clipping in Streisand file, NYPL.

"enigma of a gown": Mike Connolly's syndicated column, as in the *Pasadena Independent,* August 20, 1963.

"I don't want to wrinkle": AP wire story, as in *The Derrick* (Oil City, Pennsylvania), October 11, 1963.

she had found a new place: Some reports have said that Gould found the place on Central Park West. But he was in London through the second week of July, and it's clear from the Kaufman Schwartz interview that Streisand had the apartment by then. Perhaps Gould made the final arrangements once he returned home.

"some of the best acting": *Playboy,* November 1970.

350 The lukewarm review: *The Times,* May 31, 1963.

"switch into certain inner": *Playboy,* November 1970.

"After reading a zillion": Dorothy Kilgallen's syndicated column, as in the *Salt Lake Tribune,* July 22, 1963.

351 "What do you want": Walter Winchell's syndicated column, as in the *Eureka* (California) *Standard,* July 4, 1963.

"A refugee from Flatbush": *Saturday Evening Post,* July 27, 1963.

his partner, Harvey Sabinson: The reason I've suggested that it might have been Sabinson is that Hamill later admitted to Streisand that he had spoken to Sabinson for the piece and that Sabinson may have been the source of a quote she objected to. Streisand revealed this in a "Truth Alert" on her own official website.

353 "where people really lived": *Look,* April 5, 1966.

"The personality of Anne": Ray Stark to Jerome Robbins and Jule Styne, October 25, 1961, JRC, NYPL.

"suggestions, ideas, and material": Floria V. Lasky to Ray Stark, May 1, 1963, JRC, NYPL.

354 "no creative contribution": Albert da Silva to Floria V. Lasky, May 17, 1963, JRC, NYPL.

"Make it like B.": Script for *Funny Girl* dated June 19, 1963, BFC, LoC.

"become a caricature": NYT, July 26, 1963.

"I'm not approaching it": Kaufman Schwartz interview.

355 "certain natural characteristics": NYT, July 26, 1963.

356 They seemed to be very much: NYT, July 26, 1963.

"an animated yet balanced": Steven Ruttenbaum, *Mansions in the Clouds: The Skyscraper Palazzi of Emery Roth* (New York: Balsam Press, 1986).

357 a rather storied history: My account of the Ardsley's history was drawn from a digitized search of the *New York Times.*

Lorenz Hart had rented: Notice of Hart's rental was published in the NYT, August 5, 1939.

358 "the homosexual elite": NYT, May 28, 1999.

In those few days: Streisand closed in Las Vegas on August 4. She then appeared on Long Island on August 9 and in the Catskills on August 10. She gave the interview to Marv Schwartz on August 14 in Los Angeles. At the most, she would have had six nights free in New York to deal with her move, and maybe less, depending on when she returned from Las Vegas and when she left for Los Angeles.

Liberace had left a night early: *Van Nuys News,* August 2, 1963.

a fifty percent raise: Earl Wilson's syndicated column, as in the *Uniontown* (Pennsylvania) *Evening Standard,* August 9, 1963.

TO FLO FROM FANNY: *Van Nuys News,* August 9, 1963.

359 "torn the place apart": Robert Towers quoted in Myrna Katz Frommer and Harvey Frommer, *It Happened in the Catskills: An Oral History in the Words of Busboys, Bellhops, Guests, Proprietors, Comedians, Agents, and Others Who Lived It* (Albany, NY: State University of New York Press, 2009).

"My mind reverted": *Van Nuys News,* August 16, 1963.

360 "Without flats": *Playgirl,* May 1975.

a leaky boat: *Playboy,* November 1970.

"Maybe he was crazy": Kaufman Schwartz interview.

"verbalize about it": *Saturday Evening Post,* July 27, 1963.

361 "You're paying to talk": Kaufman Schwartz interview.

"self-discovery": *Playboy,* November 1970.

"hit it big": Considine, *Barbra Streisand: The Woman, the Myth, the Music.*

362 "each ready and eager": Slocum was filling in for Walter Winchell on his syndicated column, as in the *Lebanon* (Pennsylvania) *Daily News,* August 24, 1963.

363 "What do you really enjoy": Kaufman Schwartz interview.

365 "like a Zen master": *Playboy,* October 1977.

"to be friends with him": Kaufman Schwartz interview.

366 "What am I doing here?": *Family Weekly,* February 2, 1964.

"It's this kid from Brooklyn": Kaufman Schwartz interview.

367 There were movie stars: My description of the Cocoanut Grove audience comes from the syndicated columns of Hedda Hopper and Louella Parsons, who both provided first-hand detailed accounts of the evening. Hopper, as in the *Altoona* (Pennsylvania) *Mirror,* August 27, 1963, and Parsons, as in the *Anderson* (Indiana) *Daily Bulletin,* August 28, 1963.

368 "would have approved": Sheilah Graham's syndicated column, as in the *San Antonio Express and News,* August 17, 1963.

the president's autograph: Streisand never gave her mother the autograph; she reportedly lost it. See Considine, *Barbra Streisand: The Woman, the Myth, the Music.*

369 "gay as a bird": Hedda Hopper's syndicated column, as in the *Anderson* (Indiana) *Daily Bulletin,* August 28, 1963.

370 "just late enough to get": Notes for McDowall's book, *Double Exposure,* Roddy McDowall Collection, Howard Gotlieb Archival Research Center, Boston University. Accounts that have depicted the audience as hostile and resentful over Streisand's lateness are mythmaking. There is no contemporary mention of any displeasure over the starting time of the show.

"I'm the kind of nut": Associated Press syndicated article, as in the *Florence* (South Carolina) *Morning News,* September 1, 1963.

"If I'd known the place": LAT, August 24, 1963. The line has also been reported as "If I had known you were going to be on two sides of me, I would have had my nose fixed."

"Dodgers won — sixteenth inning": Hedda Hopper's syndicated column, as in the LAT, August 24, 1963. Randall Riese, in *Her Name Is Barbra,* apparently working from the same source, wrote that Cahn was disruptive and disrespectful. Yet Hopper did not give that impression at all.

"be great as our beloved": Louella Parsons's syndicated column, as in *Anderson* (Indiana) *Daily Bulletin,* August 28, 1963.

"I gave up singing": syndicated NEA article, as in the *Logansport* (Indiana) *Press,* September 7, 1963.

371 "didn't care for her": LAT, September 6, 1963.

372 "I hope the Dodgers": *Playboy,* November 1970.

"the marriage to Elliott": *Saturday Evening Post,* July 27, 1963.

373 Bob Hope's show: It is clear that Streisand taped *The Bob Hope Show* sometime in late August, since the *High Point* (North Carolina) *Enterprise* carried a photograph of the two of them together, in their hillbilly makeup, on September 1, 1963. Various articles reported that Hope had signed "red-hot" Barbra Streisand for the show on August 13, so it would seem that the taping was somewhere between those two dates.

"the new pet of the movie crowd": AP wire story, as in the *Appleton* (Wisconsin) *Post-Crescent,* October 6, 1963.

Rosalind Russell hosted: Louella Parsons's syndicated column, as in the *San Antonio Light,* September 9, 1963.

Danny Thomas had been: Louella Parsons's syndicated column, as in the *Anderson* (Indiana) *Daily Bulletin,* September 11, 1963.

"You two are the luckiest": Gerald Clarke, *Get Happy: The Life of Judy Garland* (New York: Random House, 2000).

374 "I've got a job": AP wire story, as in the *Appleton* (Wisconsin) *Post-Crescent,* October 6, 1963.

"Where did you get": LAT, October 6, 1963.

"If you want to get away": Evelyn Russell Layton to Tom Higgins, December 11, 1965, Higgins Family Papers, NYPL.

Disneyland, where Barbra got to spend: LAT, September 10, 1963.

"going to great pains": *Salt Lake Tribune,* August 31, 1963.

375 Sobol wrote up a description: Louis Sobol's syndicated column, as in the *Cedar Rapids Gazette,* September 2, 1963.

Bob Fosse, by his own admission: I have based my description of Fosse's problems with Stark on a draft of his resignation letter, written in his own hand, dated September 1963, BFC, LoC.

376 Fosse ditched the direct cut: I have compared the various scripts in Fosse's collection, including ones dated June 19, 1963, and September 6, 1963, BFC, LoC.

How to Succeed in Business: The show opened on July 29 and ran through August. LAT, July 27, and August 18, 1963.

"a little late for that kind": Draft of resignation letter, September 1963, BFC, LoC.

377 "Hello, gorgeous": *Funny Girl* script with Fosse's annotations, dated June 19, 1963, BFC, LoC.

378 "erased some of the insecurity": *Parade,* September 8, 1963.

"shook on it": *Life,* May 22, 1964. Gould did indeed honor his agreement to fabricate the date and place of the marriage. In the *Life* article, he said that two days after the wedding, he was pushed onto the plane to London.

379 "the hottest canary": *Parade,* September 8, 1963.

"Most newcomers would be": Barney Glazer's syndicated column, as in the *Van Nuys News,* November 19, 1963.

"A fine new voice": *Bakersfield Californian,* August 24, 1963.

"The results are best": *Brookfield* (Illinois) *Citizen,* September 9, 1963.

380 "precise phrasing, clarity": *Billboard,* September 14, 1963.

NOW THERE ARE: *Billboard,* August 31, 1963.

"when to emphasize": Tom Santopietro, *The Importance of Being Barbra: The Brilliant, Tumultuous Career of Barbra Streisand* (New York: Macmillan, 2006).

"an otherwise viable": *Playboy,* November 1970.

381 Justice Pete Supera: Background on Supera and Carson City comes from various digitized searches of the *Nevada State Journal* and the *Reno Evening Gazette.*

15. Fall 1963

384 to escape to Italy: Earl Wilson wrote of their intention to take a belated honeymoon in Italy in his syndicated column, as in the *Reno Evening Gazette,* November 20, 1963.

"an unexpected change": NYT, September 23, 1963.

I Picked a Daisy: As it turned out, Fosse did not work on the show, nor did Feuer and Martin produce it. Retitled *On a Clear Day You Can See Forever,* it opened in October 1965, produced by Alan Jay Lerner, directed by Robert Lewis, and choreographed by Herbert Ross. Barbra Streisand would star in the 1970 film version.

"Cannot believe that [a] professional": Ray Stark to Bob Fosse, September 17, 1963, BFC, LoC.

"just withdraw and leave to you": Bob Fosse to Streisand, et al., [nd] September 1963, BFC, LoC.

385 "didn't make contributions": Floria V. Lasky to Albert da Silva, September 3, 1963.
"upset and angry": Jerome Robbins to Floria V. Lasky, September 5, 1963, JRC, NYPL.
tape-recorded an hour-long recitation: This tape recording still exists, a fascinating arti-
fact. To listen to Robbins in his own voice describe everything he contributed to *Funny
Girl* up to that point was an extraordinary experience. "Statement of Contribution to
Funny Girl," JRC, NYPL.

386 Hugh O'Brian was "ready to sign": Hedda Hopper's syndicated column, as in the *Lima*
(Ohio) *News*, August 29, 1963.
Tony Martin was in as Nick: Hedda Hopper's syndicated column, as in the *Hartford
Courant*, September 16, 1963.
Efrem Zimbalist, Jr., was in the running: Mike Connolly's syndicated column, as in the
Pasadena Independent Star-News, September 15, 1963.
played by Richard Kiley: Walter Winchell's syndicated column, *Eureka* (California)
Humboldt Standard, October 2, 1963.
"long enough to make": Barney Glazer's column, *Van Nuys News*, November 19, 1963.
She'd been saving: Riese, *Her Name Is Barbra*.

387 Tormé thought the combination: Anne Edwards interviewed Tormé for *Judy Garland: A
Biography*. Tucker Fleming confirmed for me that the counterpoint had been Garland's
idea.

388 in certain markets: *Lowell Sun*, October 9, 1963.
"in fine fettle": *Variety*, October 1, 1963.

389 David Begelman had introduced his two: In Scott Schechter's *Judy Garland: A Day-to-
Day Chronicle of a Legend*, a photograph of Garland and Begelman is identified as being
taken on September 13, the "closing night" of Streisand's run at the Cocoanut Grove. On
September 13, however, Streisand was already performing at Harrah's in Lake Tahoe.
Numerous press items at the time reported that Garland had seen Streisand perform in
"Vegas"; this was recalled also by Garland's friend Tucker Fleming, who is the source of
the quotes here. But Streisand was not yet a client of Begelman's, nor had she signed for
the Garland show, during her run in Las Vegas. It would make more sense for Begelman
to take Garland to see Streisand after these two events had occurred. I am concluding
that Lake Tahoe was misreported and misremembered as "Vegas."

390 "A sort of Streisand cult": *Bakersfield Californian*, July 30, 1963.
"In today's show business": *Parade*, September 8, 1963.
Pageant magazine had gone a step: *Pageant*, November 1963.

392 feeling very "secure": *Primetime* interview with Diane Sawyer, September 22, 2005. Streisand spoke of her perplexity about Garland's nerves on this show. She also mentioned
Garland on the liner notes for *Just for the Record* (1991).

393 the script called for: Matt Howe has reproduced a page of the script at www.barbra-
archives.com, but the actual televised show does not follow it after a point.
"historic meeting of two": Notes to *Double Exposure*, Roddy McDowall Collection,
Howard Gotlieb Archival Research Center, Boston University.

395 Garland started out a bit: The DVD of *The Judy Garland Show* allowed me to see first-
hand what that magical night was like, but I am especially grateful to Seth Rudetsky's
brilliant deconstruction of their medley, available on YouTube, for helping me to grasp
what made their pairing so remarkable.

397 Aubrey decreed that: *San Antonio Express*, October 7, 1963.

"Dynamic, sensitive": LAT, October 8, 1963.

398 "Barbra Streisand came on": Dorothy Kilgallen's syndicated column, as in the *Coshocton* (Ohio) *Tribune,* October 14, 1963.

both albums were in the Top Ten: *Billboard,* November 9, 1963.

"The hottest of the past year's": *Tucson Daily Citizen,* October 12, 1963.

Kanin had come on board in early October: Kanin gave an interview to Anne Edwards for her *Streisand: A Biography* in which he stated he'd been hired much earlier, even before Streisand. But that was untrue. Fosse was director until mid-September, and Streisand was hired probably in late June, certainly by early July. Kanin, who told elaborate stories to Edwards about how he'd helped engineer Streisand's hiring, was clearly endeavoring to spin his own myth, which he was very good at doing. The NYT reported Kanin was hired as director of *Funny Girl* on October 14, 1963.

399 Allyn Ann McLerie for the part: *The New York Herald-Tribune* reported on McLerie's casting on November 14, 1963.

"quite beautiful": Michael Shurtleff, on David Merrick stationery, to Jerome Robbins, August 6, 1962, JRC, NYPL.

"Latin as Yorkshire pudding": Whitney Bolton, the *New York Morning Telegraph,* May 16, 1960.

400 "That doesn't happen": Dorothy Kilgallen's syndicated column, as in the *Coshocton* (Ohio) *Tribune,* November 12, 1963.

"Everything seems like me": *Boston Globe,* December 29, 1963.

"physical fitness special": *Pageant,* November 1963.

402 consideration of Tommy Leonetti: Dorothy Kilgallen's syndicated column, as in the *Mansfield* (Ohio) *News Journal,* October 16, 1963.

"sounded like Minnie Mouse": *People,* March 20, 1989.

403 "maleness," "sensitive, feminine side": *Vanity Fair,* September 1991.

his star's "misbehaving": Dorothy Kilgallen's syndicated column, as in the *Daytona Beach Morning Journal,* July 13, 1962.

fashionable place to be seen: NYT, November 12, 1963.

404 "bit role" in *Funny Girl:* Walter Winchell's syndicated column, as in the *Logansport* (Indiana) *Pharos-Tribune,* November 20, 1963.

"Everybody knows Barbra Streisand": *Van Nuys News,* November 19, 1963.

"no big thing": *Playboy,* November 1970.

"consistent discouragement": *Playgirl,* May 1975.

405 "damnedest not to take seriously": *Playboy,* November 1970.

"I get worried about such": Walter Winchell's syndicated column, as in the *Sarasota Journal,* October 2, 1963.

"The public throws": *Van Nuys News,* November 19, 1963.

406 "the younger-looking buyers": UPI syndicated article, as in the *Redlands* (California) *Daily Facts,* November 13, 1963. The benefit fashion show was announced on November 8 in the NYT.

407 "A kook is a person": Associated Press syndicated article, as in *The Derrick* (Oil City, Pennsylvania), October 11, 1963.

"Anyway, here I was": *Pageant,* November 1963.

408 "A hoax," Barbra thought: My description of Streisand's reaction to Kennedy's death comes from Spada, *Streisand: Her Life;* Considine, *Barbra Streisand: The Woman, the*

Myth, the Music; and an undated newspaper clipping, "Barbra and JFK," in the Streisand file, NYPL.

409 "Controlled hysteria": *San Francisco Chronicle,* December 6, 1963.

410 "one-girl concert": *Billboard,* November 30, 1963.

There hadn't been a lot of publicity: Streisand had been scheduled to appear on *The Jack Paar Program* on November 29, apparently hoping to tape it right before heading out to Chicago. Her name was included in hundreds of TV listings for that date. Liberace was also scheduled to be a guest. It's not clear if Streisand appeared, however; no video has surfaced, and the Internet Movie Database does not list her as a guest for that date, although it does list Liberace. Perhaps Streisand cancelled at the last minute in order to get to Chicago on time.

412 "Not me": Script for *Funny Girl,* dated December 1963, Bob Merrill Collection, LoC.

414 "This is worse than opening night": Earl Wilson's syndicated column, as in the *Reno Evening Gazette,* December 16, 1963.

"life is too short to deal": Kissel, *David Merrick: The Abominable Showman.*

in excess of $100,000: Louis Sobol's syndicated column, as in the *Cedar Rapids Gazette,* March 1, 1964.

415 she wanted a raise to $7,500: Some reports have said that Streisand was originally signed for $1,500; however, Mike Connolly reported in his column that she was being paid $3,500, ten times what Merrick had paid her for *Wholesale.* As in the *Pasadena Star News,* October 29, 1963.

$350 a week, singing in clubs: Contracts between Lainie Kazan and the Colonial Tavern and Huddle's Embers, May 21, 1963, and September 27, 1963, respectively, Lainie Kazan Collection, NYPL.

416 specially tailored trousers: UPI syndicated article, as in the *Wisconsin State Journal,* January 19, 1964.

"vocal and dramatic coaching": Contract between Seven Arts and Lainie Kazan, 1964, Lainie Kazan Collection, NYPL.

417 "said very little": Personal interview with Sharon Vaughn.

"reportedly getting the biggest": Dorothy Kilgallen's syndicated column, as in the *Coshocton* (Ohio) *Tribune,* January 29, 1964.

"artistic responsibility": *Playboy,* October 1977.

"affected by things": Kaufman Schwartz interview.

418 "didn't think she wanted": *Vanity Fair,* September 1991. Suzanne Merrill also provided additional information and confirmation of this episode.

"Don't tell me not to fly": Bob Merrill notebooks, Bob Merrill Collection, LoC.

420 "in a desperate race": NYT, May 24, 1964.

423 "very probably made it difficult": *Boston Herald,* January 9, 1964.

"This play is really about": Associated Press story, as in the *Hartford Courant,* January 26, 1964.

"Ten years ago they started": *Oakland Tribune,* December 13, 1963.

424 "I don't want to imitate": Associated Press story, as in the *Hartford Courant,* January 26, 1964.

"Little girl": Sheilah Graham's syndicated column, as in the *San Antonio Express,* December 2, 1963.

"We hate each other": *Boston Globe,* December 29, 1963. I am also grateful to Orson

Bean, a close friend of Chaplin's, for background on the relationship between Streisand and Chaplin.

425 "very chummy": Spada, *Streisand: Her Life.*

"a note to the show": The Garson Kanin papers at the Library of Congress do not contain any material on *Funny Girl.* Apparently Kanin or his widow, Marian Seldes, withheld these when the donation was made, for the material does exist, or at least, it *did* exist when Kanin shared the letter he wrote to McLerie, dated February 28, 1964, with Anne Edwards for her *Streisand: A Biography.* Kanin also supplied McLerie's reply, which shows her to have been very gracious, calling her firing part of "the hazards of the trade." McLerie had, perhaps, reason to be gracious: she'd been signed to a one-year contract, so unless a settlement was arranged, she'd still be paid her full year's salary.

"the length of the musical": NYT, December 30, 1963.

"a little Burmese idol": Cecil Beaton, *Photobiography* (Garden City, NY: Doubleday & Company, 1951).

426 Barbra was "on fire": Theodore Taylor, *Jule: The Story of Composer Jule Styne* (New York: Random House, 1979).

"was to attempt to get her": *Players Magazine,* Spring 1965.

"The actor has to have some": *Playboy,* October 1977.

"loved [her] . . . wanted to make": *New West,* November 22, 1976.

427 "Whatever happens to the show": *Boston Globe,* December 29, 1963.

428 Louis Sobol's column featuring: Louis Sobol's syndicated column, as in the *Cedar Rapids Gazette,* November 15, 1963.

no longer had any real friends: *Vanity Fair,* November 1994. In this piece, Streisand talked about the Cormans being her only friends, not accepting invitations, and not having people at her place.

429 "encamped there like a pair": *Time,* April 10, 1964.

remained very simple: *Playboy,* November 1970.

"I am now a mature": *Pageant,* November 1963.

"And that's what one year": Earl Wilson's syndicated column, as in the *Reno Evening Gazette,* January 10, 1964.

430 "Streisand is an original": *Cue,* December 28, 1963.

16. Winter 1964

431 to make his move: I have based my account of the beginning of Streisand's affair with Chaplin on accounts provided by Orson Bean and another friend of Chaplin's, who said the affair began on the first night of their stay in Boston when Chaplin went to her room.

"the old things": *Boston Herald,* January 9, 1964.

432 "trying his best": *Boston Herald,* January 10, 1964.

unapologetically liked sex: Consider her response to the question of her favorite sound on *Inside the Actors Studio.* It was "the sound of orgasms."

"playing games with men": *Playboy,* October 1977.

433 "really didn't have": *Playboy,* October 1977.

"very self-destructive": *Playboy,* November 1970.

"I'm just finding myself": *Life,* December 12, 1969.

"trips," "inner understanding": *Playboy,* November 1970.

"Kid, you're gorgeous": Interview with Orson Bean, also referenced in many other accounts.

434 the Harborne Stuarts: *Boston Globe,* January 13, 1964.

436 "the songs were unimportant": *Oakland Tribune,* February 2, 1964.

"wouldn't open a can of sardines": NYT, February 12, 1964.

all but two of the auditorium's: *Boston Herald,* January 14, 1964.

"every Barbra Streisand fan": *Lowell Sun,* January 14, 1964.

"a personality the crowds": *Oakland Tribune,* February 2, 1964.

437 "What begins with bright": *Boston Globe,* January 14, 1964.

"more of a movie scenario": *Billboard,* January 25, 1964.

"to sell the costumes and scenery": *Lowell Sun,* January 14, 1964.

"a quality that makes you want": *Boston Herald,* January 14, 1964.

438 "The second act becomes": *Boston Herald,* January 19, 1964.

"the weakness of the libretto": *Boston Evening American,* January 14, 1964.

"a heavy, oracular style": *Boston Globe,* January 14, 1964.

"auditioning for a punch": Dorothy Kilgallen's syndicated column, as in the *Salt Lake Tribune,* February 1, 1964.

439 "she was driving herself": NYT, May 12, 1964.

"who makes every note sound": *Lowell Sun,* February 3, 1964.

"Leave 'em laughing!": *Boston Herald,* January 19, 1964.

"The first half is a delight": *Boston Globe,* January 26, 1964, and other dates.

"they still haven't decided": Dorothy Kilgallen's syndicated column, as in the *Coshocton* (Ohio) *Tribune,* January 29, 1964.

"She excels . . . in every dept.": Walter Winchell's syndicated column, as in the *Eureka* (California) *Humboldt Standard,* January 27, 1964.

"Three years ago she lived": Walter Winchell's syndicated column, as in the *Nevada State Journal,* January 29, 1964.

"a sensation . . . but the book": Hedda Hopper's syndicated column, as in the *Lima* (Ohio) *News,* January 23, 1964.

440 "a cult of worshippers": *Lowell Sun,* January 14, 1964.

Joan Crawford made sure: Hedda Hopper's syndicated column, as in the *Lima* (Ohio) *News,* January 23, 1964.

"If a musical comedy with": *Boston Herald,* January 14, 1964.

441 "Biggest screaming scene": Walter Winchell's syndicated column, as in the *Eureka* (California) *Humboldt Standard,* January 31, 1964.

last night of their Boston run: Lainie Kazan said "Something About Me" was performed on their last night in Boston.

442 at the same hotel: Hotel assignments are given in a memo in the *Funny Girl* papers, JRC, NYPL.

443 "Dear Gar": Jerome Robbins to Garson Kanin, February 18, 1964, JRC, NYPL.

"The first triumph belongs": *Philadelphia Inquirer,* February 5, 1964.

"The funny girl should": *Philadelphia Inquirer,* February 9, 1964.

444 Buzz Miller, one of the lead: See Vaill, *Somewhere: The Life of Jerome Robbins.*

445 "The British group, something like": *Zanesville* (Ohio) *Times Recorder,* February 15, 1964.

"impossible to get a radio": Associated Press syndicated article, as in the *Portland Oregonian,* February 11, 1964.

446 Dick Kleiner's top picks: Dick Kleiner's syndicated column, as in the *Lowell Sun,* February 17, 1964.

"*Funny Girl* must agree": Dorothy Kilgallen's syndicated column, as in the *Lowell Sun,* February 12, 1964.

"Tisn't so, comes the word": Earl Wilson's syndicated column, as in the *Delaware County* (Pennsylvania) *Daily Times,* February 14, 1964.

447 "graceful, nimble, handsome": *Philadelphia Inquirer,* February 5, 1964.

rehearse the new "Sadie, Sadie": Robbins's schedule indicated on February 28 that the "new version of Sadie, Sadie" was to be rehearsed. JRC, NYPL. Earlier he had given a pep talk to the company.

448 "Forty-one different last": *Playboy,* October 1977.

449 offered producer Kermit Bloomgarden: NYT, February 7, 1964.

"jet-fueled with the robust": "Barbra: Some Notes," a manuscript written by Jerome Robbins and submitted to Roddy McDowall for possible inclusion in his book *Double Exposure,* Roddy McDowall Collection, Howard Gotlieb Archival Research Center.

450 He'd just signed his contract: Contract between Jerome Robbins and Ray Stark, February 19, 1964, JRC, NYPL.

"After twenty years of working": NYT, March 22, 1964.

451 notes on Barclay Hotel stationery: These are all preserved in Robbins's *Funny Girl* papers, dated February 19–February 29, 1964, JRC, NYPL.

"Hey, gorgeous, here we go": Jule Styne to Jerome Robbins, February 19, 1964, JRC, NYPL.

453 "not in keeping with the image": Earl Wilson's syndicated column, as in the *Lima* (Ohio) *News,* March 17, 1964.

"Everything we know of": Undated rehearsal notes by Jerome Robbins, 1964, JRC, NYPL.

455 "several extra coats of paint": Dorothy Kilgallen's syndicated column, as in the *Lowell Sun,* February 20, 1964.

"for the first time since": Edith (Stark's secretary) to Jerome Robbins, February 24, 1964, JRC, NYPL.

"the top figure deal with": Louis Sobol's syndicated column, as in the *Cedar Rapids Gazette,* March 1, 1964.

the call from Earl Wilson: Earl Wilson's syndicated column, as in the *Petersburg* (Virginia) *Progress-Index,* February 26, 1964.

456 "dashing into the record stores": Dorothy Kilgallen's syndicated column, as in the *Mansfield* (Ohio) *News Journal,* December 28, 1963.

"the arrangements, the cover": *Playboy,* October 1977.

"Every moment in the album": *Billboard,* February 29, 1964.

"spellbinding effect": *Bakersfield Californian,* February 22, 1964.

457 "oooooo, aaaaaay": *Playboy,* October 1977.

"inadequate [about] singing": *Playboy,* October 1977.

"a mixture of old and new": *Oakland Tribune,* July 26, 1963.

A poll taken of teenagers: *Lowell Sun,* February 6, 1964.

459 "like rituals performed": Dorothy Kilgallen's syndicated column, as in the *Oneonta* (New York) *Star,* March 10, 1964.

"The craze to get in ahead": NYT, April 26, 1964.

"should cut at least twenty-eight": NYT, April 5, 1964.

460 a handful of notes just for her: These are all preserved in Robbins's *Funny Girl* papers, dated between March 1 and March 20, 1964, JRC, NYPL.

461 "getting the laughs it used to": Ray Stark to Jerome Robbins, March 20, 1964, JRC, NYPL.

462 "the wrath of the public": NYT, March 19, 1964.

463 "one of the biggest deals": Dorothy Kilgallen's syndicated column, as in the *Dunkirk* (New York) *Evening Observer,* March 5, 1964.

"in essence," "a real character": *Playboy,* October 1977.

Stark could be a bully: My description of Streisand's relationship with Stark at this point is drawn from several interviews: Lainie Kazan, Anne Francis, and two very important anonymous sources. Also, Frank Pierson wrote in *New West* magazine, November 22, 1976, that Streisand told him on the set of *A Star Is Born:* "I can't stand for someone to tell me what to do. Ray Stark always used to bully me, the son of a bitch."

464 shoved and kicked a photographer: Associated Press newswire, as in the *Lima* (Ohio) *News,* June 28, 1953.

"Look, if you're prepared": *Playboy,* October 1977.

"Fuck you": Two company members, one of them Lainie Kazan, recalled Streisand saying "Fuck you" to Stark. The belief was that she said it very soon before opening night. Allan Miller recalled a similar moment for James Spada in *Streisand: Her Life,* although it is implied that the words were spoken at an earlier point in the previews, while Kanin was still director. The dialogue I have quoted here comes from Miller's account. It could be that Streisand said "Fuck you" to Stark more than once. No one would be surprised. Elliott had a job: On March 17, 1964, in his syndicated column, as in the *Pasadena Star News,* Mike Connolly reported that Gould had been cast in Burnett's forthcoming Broadway show, *The Idol of Millions,* later called *Fade Out — Fade In,* with music by Jule Styne. As Gould was not in this show, I suspect Connolly got the name of the project wrong, and it was *Once Upon a Mattress* he should have reported. The presence of Layton as director seems to confirm that. It's possible, however, that Gould was going to be in *Fade Out — Fade In* and pulled out to do the film *The Confession.*

465 some blind items in the columns: Anne Edwards in *Streisand: A Biography* wrote that Earl Wilson had reported in the *New York Post:* "What new musical comedy star and her leading man are a romantic duet offstage to the fury of the actor's beautiful wife?" Edwards did not provide a date for that notice, and a check of the *Post* from January to April of 1964 did not locate the quote. That doesn't mean it wasn't there; the *Post* is not digitized before the 1990s and searching has to be done on microfilm, so I may have missed it. But a digitized search of other newspapers that carried Wilson's column in 1964 also did not locate the quote.

"The stories about the domestic": Mike Connolly's syndicated column, as in the *Pasadena Star News,* March 17, 1964.

"He handles it all very": *Ladies' Home Journal,* August 1966.

"So how do you feel?": Interview on the *Robbins Nest* radio program, WNEW, broadcast March 28, 1964, included on the *Just for the Record* DVD.

"been open about two years": NYT, April 5, 1964.

466 "Barb, I brought you up to Fifty-third Street": *Just for the Record* DVD.

"fashion wise": NYT, April 26, 1964.

between fifteen and eighteen thousand dollars: Earl Wilson's syndicated column, as in the *Lima* (Ohio) *News,* March 19, 1964.

467 "You can be my bagel": A copy was preserved in JRC, NYPL.

"Barbra Streisand crosses the stage": *Time,* April 10, 1964.
468 "She has everything that": *Robbins Nest* radio program, *Just for the Record* DVD.
469 "overlooking the lights": Earl Wilson's syndicated column, as in the *Galveston Daily News,* April 1, 1964.
"her face stiff, her backbone stiffer": NYT, April 5, 1964.
470 "You tired, honey?": *Robbins Nest* radio program, *Just for the Record* DVD.
"people were pawing her": *Life,* May 22, 1964.
"All those cameras and lights": NYT, April 5, 1964.
"You didn't bring chicken soup": Earl Wilson's syndicated column, as in the *Galveston Daily News,* April 1, 1964.

17. Spring 1964

471 "looking as stylized and elegant": *Life,* May 22, 1964.
472 "Everybody knew that Barbra": *New York Herald Tribune,* March 27, 1964.
"Hail to thee, Barbra": *New York World-Telegram,* March 27, 1964.
"proves . . . she can sing": *Wall Street Journal,* March 30, 1964.
"remarkable demonstration of skill": *New York Daily News,* March 27, 1964.
473 "honest emotion underneath": NYT, March 27, 1964.
474 champagne and chocolate cake: *Life,* May 22, 1964.
the island's Blue Mountain Inn: *The Daily Gleaner* (Kingston, Jamaica), May 6, 1961.
475 a rabbit, a canary: Earl Wilson's syndicated column, as in the *Galveston Daily News,* May 25, 1964.
"locked up in prison": *Playboy,* October 1977.
"inspiration wanes and craft": *New York Herald-Tribune,* March 27, 1964.
476 "Now that I'm supposed": NYT, April 5, 1964.
"Happy Birthday": *Life,* May 22, 1964.
477 "nut on TV": NYT, July 4, 1965. I have drawn my account of the Winter Garden Kids from both this newspaper report, in which a teenaged Lippner was interviewed, as well as several personal contemporary interviews with Lippner.
479 "how to approach a big sister": Spada, *Streisand: Her Life.*
"threatened and frightened": *Playboy,* October 1977.
480 Presents were left: *Players,* Spring 1965.
"the real screwy ones": Kaufman Schwartz interview.
481 and a little embarrassed: This can possibly be deduced from Streisand's statement: "I should have been in a different category," in a wire-service story, as in the *Tucson Daily Citizen,* May 30, 1964.
483 Under the Jamaican sun: Much of my description of *The Confession* shoot comes from *The Daily Gleaner* (Kingston, Jamaica), May 6, 1964.
"protect her," "She was my woman": *Playboy,* November 1970. I have also used various other interviews as context for his thoughts at this time.
484 "a remarkable performance": *The Daily Gleaner* (Kingston, Jamaica), May 6, 1964.
called him a "masochist": *Time,* September 7, 1970.
Jack Jones suddenly froze: I have taken my description of the 1964 Grammy Awards from the NYT, May 13, 1964; the AP wire story, as in the *Hartford Courant,* May 13, 1964; and the UPI wire story, as in the *Oxnard Press-Courier,* May 13, 1964.
485 "There's nothing we can do": NYT, May 12, 1964.

486 "That's my line": Dorothy Kilgallen's syndicated column, as in the *New Castle* (Pennsylvania) *News,* May 20, 1964.

489 "simple [and] nonintellectual": *Family Weekly,* February 2, 1964.

490 "No, no, can't be done": *Family Weekly,* February 2, 1964.

491 Barbra sauntered into fashion designer: Eugenia Sheppard's syndicated column, as in the *Hartford Courant,* June 25, 1964.

for Cosmo Sirchio's collection: Eugenia Sheppard's syndicated column, as in the *Hartford Courant,* May 24, 1964.

"I am high fashion!": *Family Weekly,* February 2, 1964.

named to the worst-dressed list: Louella Parsons's syndicated column, as in the *San Antonio Light,* January 23, 1964.

492 "ask how much things cost": *Sunday Bulletin,* April 25, 1965.

pocket money: *This Week,* February 5, 1966.

"All you think about is": *Family Weekly,* February 2, 1964.

million-dollar television contract: NYT, June 23, 1964.

Marty was crowing: Alex Freeman's syndicated column, as in the *Hartford Courant,* September 1, 1964.

493 "The screaming could be heard": Alex Freeman's syndicated column, as in the *Hartford Courant,* July 23, 1964.

Carol Burnett proposed a joint: *Hartford Courant,* October 11, 1964.

"traffic going by": *O, The Oprah Magazine,* October 2006.

494 "Stardom is a part of": *Vanity Fair,* September 1991.

"To end the rash of rumors": Alex Freeman's syndicated column, as in the *Hartford Courant,* May 18, 1964.

"going to be a big movie star": Wire-service story, as in the *Uniontown* (Pennsylvania) *Morning Herald,* May 20, 1964.

"a bath in lava": *Time,* September 7, 1970.

"Oh, God, don't envy me": *Playboy,* October 1977.

495 "Being a star is being a movie star": Rough copy for a "Tintype" column, 1964, Sydney Skolsky Collection, AMPAS.

"a practical person": *This Week,* February 5, 1966.

496 "off on the track of always": *Playboy,* October 1977.

"I didn't want you": *O, The Oprah Magazine,* October 2006.

497 "alone with [her] thoughts": Unsourced clipping, perhaps Dorothy Kilgallen's column, circa summer 1964, NYPL.

"larger than life": Interview with Elliott Gould at www.aish.com.

499 "You must only give three-quarters": *Playboy,* October 1977.

"I have visions in my head": *Playboy,* October 1977.

"Her performances astound": "Barbra: Some Notes" by Jerome Robbins, Roddy McDowall Collection, Howard Gotlieb Archival Research Center.

Index

Note: Throughout the index, *I Can Get It for You Wholesale* is abbreviated as *Wholesale*.